ORIGINS OF POLITICAL EXTREMISM

Political extremism is one of the most pernicious, destructive, and nihilistic forms of human expression. During the twentieth century, in excess of 100 million people had their lives taken from them as the result of extremist violence. In this wide-ranging book Manus I. Midlarsky suggests that ephemeral gains, together with mortality salience, form basic explanations for the origins of political extremism and constitute a theoretical framework that also explains later mass violence. Midlarsky applies his framework to multiple forms of political extremism, including the rise of Italian, Hungarian and Romanian fascism, Nazism, radical Islamism, and Soviet, Chinese, and Cambodian communism. Other applications include a rampaging military (Japan, Pakistan, Indonesia) and extreme nationalism in Serbia, Croatia, the Ottoman Empire, and Rwanda. Polish anti-Semitism after World War II and the rise of separatist violence in Sri Lanka are also examined.

MANUS I. MIDLARSKY is the Moses and Annuta Back Professor of International Peace and Conflict Resolution at Rutgers University, New Brunswick. He is the author of *The Killing Trap: Genocide in the Twentieth Century* (Cambridge University Press, 2005).

ORIGINS OF POLITICAL EXTREMISM

Mass Violence in the Twentieth Century and Beyond

MANUS I. MIDLARSKY

CAMBRIDGE
UNIVERSITY PRESS

CAMBRIDGE UNIVERSITY PRESS
Cambridge, New York, Melbourne, Madrid, Cape Town,
Singapore, São Paulo, Delhi, Tokyo, Mexico City

Cambridge University Press
The Edinburgh Building, Cambridge CB2 8RU, UK

Published in the United States of America by Cambridge University Press, New York

www.cambridge.org
Information on this title: www.cambridge.org/9780521700719

First published 2011

Printed in the United Kingdom at the University Press, Cambridge

A catalogue record for this publication is available from the British Library

Library of Congress Cataloguing in Publication data
Midlarsky, Manus I.
Origins of political extremism : mass violence in the twentieth century and beyond /
Manus I. Midlarsky.
p.   cm.
ISBN 978-0-521-70071-9 (pbk.)
1. Radicalism.   2. Violence.   3. Political violence.   I. Title.
HN49.R33M53 2011
303.609′04–dc22   2010051862

ISBN 978-0-521-87708-4 Hardback
ISBN 978-0-521-70071-9 Paperback

For Liz, as ever, a source of knowledge, love, and great comfort.
And for Aryeh, may he flourish.

Have you not done tormenting me with your accursed time! It's abominable! When! When! One day, is that not enough for you, one day like any other day, one day he went dumb, one day I went blind, one day we'll go deaf, one day we were born, one day we shall die, the same day, the same second, is that not enough for you? They give birth astride of a grave, the light gleams an instant, and then it's night once more.

— Pozzo, in Samuel Beckett's *Waiting for Godot*

The ultimate evil in the world is not war itself, but aggression.

— Amos Oz, accepting the Goethe Prize, Frankfurt, 2005

CONTENTS

FIGURES AND TABLES

Figures

Tables

PREFACE

Doing the research for and writing this book has been an adventure. Never did I suspect that I would be exploring in detail the early years of Stalin in Georgia and elsewhere in the Caucasus. Nor that I would find similarities between the attitudes toward Islam of an old Abkhazian Muslim in Batum (then in Russia on the Turkish border) who sheltered the young Stalin and certain Indian Muslim thinkers. Nor that data on Nazi perpetrators of genocide, or Romanian electoral data during the interwar period would prove to be so helpful. Nor that the outcome of the Crimean War and the experience of Turkish officers in Adrianople (today's Edirne) at the end of the Second Balkan War would help explain later extremist behavior towards the Armenians. Little-understood (at least in the West) events can be crucial in predicting later vastly disproportional consequences. And in one instance at least, these events led me to veer from my early confident treatment of communism as a separate path of extremism, quite distinct from fascism, to a realization that, despite differences detailed in this book, there exists a common etiological core.

At a more personal level, I was surprised to have two anomalies clarified, one of a more general nature, the other quite specific. First, after doing the research and writing it became clear to me why the Bible, despite its antiquity and fabular nature, is still, to my knowledge, the best-selling book in the world. Although the ephemeral gain was initially theorized entirely from secular sources, the more recent discovery that it had a sacral biblical counterpart in the story of Adam and Eve (Chapter 15) was a revelation. This fable of kindergarten lore actually is a metaphor for basic elements of the human condition that the compilers of the Hebrew Bible saw with great clarity.

The second anomaly concerns my surprise at the behavior of an otherwise very well-liked professor of mine years ago. Ivo Duchacek was a parliamentary member of a centrist party in Czechoslovakia before the war, escaping to England just before the Nazi occupation in 1939. Upon returning to Czechoslovakia immediately after the war, he was tasked with the responsibility of fairly applying criteria for the selection of citizens born of intermarriage within the Sudeten German community who could remain in the country and those who would be forced to leave. I recall (perhaps imperfectly) that a Czech patronymic would allow a person from mixed heritage to stay, while a German one would yield expulsion. Ivo, whom I later befriended, described to the class his anguish at having to apply such a uniform standard to cases that often defied simple categorization.

At the time, I was nonplussed first that a Czech who had seen his country suffer greatly at the hands of the Germans could be so concerned about the fate of the betraying Sudeten Germans, and second that he, a Christian, could, not very long after the Holocaust, describe the difficulties of such a procedure to a likely hostile group of students, most of whom were Jewish. However, the finding in Chapter 13 that the Sudetens were the Germans *least* likely to perpetrate war crimes was fully in keeping with Ivo's reaction to his extraordinarily difficult task. Actually partaking in the process of selection must have yielded the gut feeling that, at bottom, the vast majority of these people were fundamentally decent, and did not deserve the painful expulsion that followed.

I am very grateful for the insightful comments of Sheri Berman, Margit Bussmann, Giovanni Capoccia, Claudio Cioffi-Revilla, Charles Doran, Daniel Geller, Ron Hassner, Patrick James, Jan Kubik, Yosef Lapid, Rose McDermott, Jens Meierhenrich, Cas Mudde, Irfan Nooruddin, Alexander Ochs, Robert Pape, Michael Rossi, Ionas Rus, and Ekkart Zimmermann.

As always, my editor at Cambridge University Press, John Haslam, has been a delight to work with. I am also grateful for the steadfast and extremely competent efforts over time of my secretaries, Shwetha Kashi, Sara Kasman, and Sara Tofighbakhsh. Needless to say, I am greatly indebted to the Back family for funding the Moses and Annuta Back Chair in international peace and conflict resolution at Rutgers, New Brunswick.

Introduction

In his acclaimed book *The Age of Extremes: A History of the World, 1914–1991*, Eric Hobsbawm writes of the date January 30, 1933 when Hitler became chancellor of Germany. Hobsbawm was a 15-year-old boy of Jewish origin in Berlin walking with his younger sister from school when he saw the newspaper headline that he still sees "as in a dream."[1] His overall period of concern begins at World War I and ends with the collapse of communism in Europe, the beginning and presumed end of political extremism, with the advent of Hitler as its apotheosis. The rise of communism, fascism (Nazism as an especially malign form), rampant Japanese, Pakistani, and Indonesian militarism, as well as varieties of extreme nationalism such as the Polish and Serbian, together constituted an "age of extremes." Indeed, these cases will form a substantial portion of this book's empirical inquiry.

Although unlike Francis Fukuyama, Hobsbawm did not predict anything like "an end to history," in his work there is a sense that humankind, at least that portion living in the West, had reached a watershed. The possibility existed that the twentieth century extremes were a thing of the past.

Yet just one year prior to the 1994 publication of Hobsbawm's book, the first World Trade Center bombing occurred, Osama bin Laden "declared war" on America in 1998, and a form of extremism not even listed in Hobsbawm's index – radical Islamism – emerged full force, especially after 9/11. The question is not whether radical Islamism exists in many (although certainly not all) Muslim societies, but the depth of that penetration.

Also in 1993, Aleksandr Solzhenitsyn, in response to the euphoria attending the end of the Cold War and the Soviet Union, in a rare public address warned that all was not well. Anticipating the persistence of the old Communist Party and KGB officers in Russia, Vladimir Putin among them, Solzhenitsyn declared: "We were recently entertained by a naïve fable of the happy arrival at the 'end of history,' of the overflowing triumph of an all-democratic bliss; the ultimate global arrangement had supposedly been attained. But we all see and sense that something very different is coming, something new, and perhaps

---

[1] Hobsbawm 1994, 4.

1

quite stern. No, tranquility does not promise to descend on our planet, and will not be granted us so easily."[2]

If radical Islamism and extreme Russian nationalism are unlike any other forms of extremism, then Hobsbawm's ending the short twentieth century in 1991 is appropriate. But if in their origins they demonstrate similarities with other extremist movements such as the fascist or communist, then the "age of extremes" has been extended, at least for the foreseeable future. This is the major issue at stake in this book: whether there exists a common etiology that allows us to understand the origins of a variety of ostensibly unique political behaviors. And if there exists such an etiology, are there specific pathways to extremist behavior from a common origin that nevertheless later develop in different ways?

The age of extremes is also called by Hobsbawm "the age of catastrophe," understandably given the cataclysmic effect on him and his family and indeed, his entire society. Another near-apocalyptical lexicon is found in the Turkish reference to the Greco-Turkish War of 1919–22 as the "War of National Salvation," as is the Greek reference to it as the "Asia Minor Disaster." Hitler's reference to the "calamity" of 1919 and the loss of the Great War is another case in point, as is bin Laden's frequent mention of the "humiliation" of 1924 and the dissolution of the Muslim Caliphate in that year.

Yet each of the concerned individuals took different paths. Hobsbawm emigrated to England and became a distinguished historian, indeed according to the *New Republic* "one of the few genuinely great historians of our century." His was a creative response to personal and societal fears; in many respects his career has been devoted to explaining these momentous events. An adopted country, and a new, richer vocabulary of expression (English has many more words than German) were used to ascend from the abyss.

Mustapha Kemal (later Atatürk), military leader of a victorious but devastated Turkey, and soon to be its political head, adopted policies that were to fitfully secularize and modernize the nascent Turkish state that had emerged from the ruins of the Ottoman Empire. Although subject to recurrent interventions of the military into politics, and human rights abuses (albeit on a scale that is massively dwarfed by those of Nazism and communism), the recent sustained economic development of Turkey and its relatively stable democracy have been impressive enough to warrant consideration for admission to the European Union (EU). The eventual outcome may be in doubt, but the successes thus far are not.

Despite suffering the major losses of the Greco-Turkish War that entailed abandonment of all of conquered Anatolia, Greece retreated within its territory governed prior to 1919. Most important, it did not succumb to the temptations of fascism that engulfed so many other European states during the interwar period.

---

[2] Quoted in Remnick 2008, 21.

At most, it was governed by a military dictatorship under General Mataxas after 1936 that took on certain trappings of fascism (as did so many other non-fascist states like pre-*Anschluss* Austria, Franco's Spain, or Salazar's Portugal), but at bottom was a right-wing military government that indeed maintained its strong alliance with Britain right up to and during World War II.

Hitler, of course, followed a very different path of revanche, conquest, and the brutality of a war yielding 20 million dead, most of them innocent civilians or prisoners of war. Despite Mussolini's relatively decent behavior towards Jews during the Holocaust prior to the invasions of Sicily and mainland Italy by Allied forces, Italian Fascism was responsible for the deaths of hundreds of thousands of native North and East Africans. Osama bin Laden also has chosen an extremist direction that justifies the murder of innocents. And communism, of course, was responsible for the deaths of many millions, especially after Stalin's brutal reign provided a template for the future to be adopted by Mao's China and Pol Pot's Cambodia.

Why these major differences between those who adopted a constructive path of personal development or nation building on the one hand, and those who chose extremist positions that included justifications for mass murder? This is one of the questions that frame this inquiry. At the same time, an answer will be provided to the frequently asked question: Why did European countries like Britain and France that also suffered so much from the World War I experience not have extremist governments during the interwar period, while Italy and especially Germany did?

History and theory

"Too much history!" I exclaimed to my wife as we drove from the Dalmatian coast of Croatia to Sarajevo, the capital of Bosnia-Herzegovina. It was in Sarajevo, of course, that the Serbian nationalist Gavrilo Princip assassinated Archduke Franz Ferdinand, heir apparent to the throne of the tottering Austro-Hungarian Empire, igniting the spark that led to World War I and the rise of extremisms of all types. And it was the loss of Fiume (today's Rijeka on the Dalmatian coast) that was to be the cause célèbre of extreme nationalists such as Gabriele D'Annunzio and ultimately Mussolini, the prototypical fascist leader of the interwar period. One of the most bloodthirsty fascist organizations of this period, the Croatian Ustaše, was to be led by the Bosnian-born ethnic Croat, Ante Pavelić.

Yet it is not "too much history" in the aggregate that yields political extremism, it is history of a certain type that we must examine in detail. This particular historical trajectory will be specified as the succeeding chapters unfold.

At times, it is equally, perhaps even more, effective to make one's claims by indirection in place of forthright assertion. And Jacques Barzun, the Columbia dean, historian, cultural critic, and genuine polymath, presents a marvelously lucid foil against which I can frame my theoretical intent. According to Barzun:

> History, like a vast river, propels logs, vegetation, rafts, and debris; it is full of live and dead things, some destined for resurrection; it mingles many waters and holds in solution invisible substances stolen from distant soils. Anything may become part of it; that is why it can be an image of the continuity of mankind. And it is also why some of its freight turns up again in the social sciences: they were constructed out of the contents of history in the same way as houses in medieval Rome were made out of stones taken from the Coliseum. But the [social] sciences based on sorted facts cannot be mistaken for rivers flowing in time and full of persons and events. They are systems fashioned with concepts, numbers, and abstract relations. *For history, the reward of eluding method is to escape abstraction.*[3]

I am not concerned here with the infinitely variegated events that so intrigue historians like Barzun. For him, the abstractions of the social sciences temper the propulsion of the "vast river" of history, damming it in places, and sorting through its myriad pathways in order to capture only those of theoretical interest to the analyst. And this is precisely what I intend to do in the most concrete sense: examine only those historical trajectories that are deemed to be theoretically important, discarding those that are not, but at the same time allowing for the discovery of instances where the expected national trajectory is *not* found, but extremism *is*, thereby remaining open to the possibility of theoretical disconfirmation or emendation. The presence of that trajectory, but absence of political extremism, also would suggest disconfirmation or a required emendation. As we shall see, elements of context dependency will generate new causal pathways not initially postulated, which arise from the theoretically mandated historical trajectory associated with extremism. The historical context of Greece, in particular, will prove to be fertile ground for theoretical expansion.

From the outset let me make clear my theoretical intent. I am concerned with how individual persons become extremists in their behavior, whether as leaders of political parties, the military, or in social movements. To this extent I am not interested in extremist group formation or socialization, ably described by scholars such as Marc Sageman.[4] My image of the individual is one born into a particular historical configuration having a past, present, and anticipated future. The interface between that individual and his/her national trajectory is the focus of study. Although this may appear to be an analytical leap from aggregate to individual behavior, I hope that the following analyses will support my argument. In any event, inferences drawn from combining data at different levels of analysis have been shown to be a fruitful area of inquiry as demonstrated, for example, by Gary King.[5] Of course, the validity of the theoretical arguments put

---

[3] Emphasis added; quoted in Krystal 2007, 103.   [4] 2004.   [5] 1997.

forward here will have to stand or fall on the evidentiary base. That base consists of a wide range of cases, with some unexpected findings, at least to this writer. The intersection of historical trajectory and personal biography, for example, will reveal unforeseen aspects of the lives of political extremists who, in seeking to establish or reinforce their political programs, were responsible for the deaths of millions. In differing contexts, Joseph Stalin and the Young Turk leaders of the Armenian genocide are cases in point, as are 1,581 Nazi war criminals.

The study of political extremism

Why study political extremism? Well, extremists typically kill people in large numbers, as will be denoted in the definition of political extremism. Clearly this should be a sufficient reason to justify the study of its origins. Yet, there are also some non-obvious reasons to study this phenomenon, not included in the definition. Extremists tend to be disruptive not only to states but also to international regions. Hitler and Stalin are but two illustrations of extremist leaders who not only massively destroyed elements of their national cultures and state infrastructures, but also wreaked havoc on their international surroundings. After World War II, enormous rebuilding and restructuring were required, which, of course, assumed different forms in both East and West. In a real sense, it may be said that these new domestic and international structures were built on the corpses of the nearly 50 million people who died in that war.

When viewed in their totality, political extremism, mass death, and physical destruction form a seamless whole. This is especially true when ideologies associated with modern extremism make universal claims, which clearly apply beyond their points of national origin. Fascism, communism, and radical Islamism share this property.

As we shall see, even when truth claims are not framed in universal language, the international effects can be severe. The chapter on the rampaging military demonstrates the international consequences of military extremism in East Asia, South Asia, and Southeast Asia, involving the deaths of millions of people and the restructuring of entire societies. Without the Japanese invasion of China and its associated atrocities, we cannot fully understand the hardening American stance against Japan and the consequent Japanese attack on Pearl Harbor. The Pakistani army's atrocities in East Pakistan triggered the Indian invasion of 1971 and consequent formation of the new state of Bangladesh. And the mass murders by the Indonesian military in 1965 became part of a complete reorientation of Indonesian foreign policy away from the communist world, and set the stage for the later massacres in East Timor and its emergence as an independent state.

Serbian extremism in Bosnia and Kosovo vastly increased the probability of international intervention by the European Union and United States diplomatically, and by NATO militarily. The Rwandan genocide resulting from Hutu extremism led to diplomatic intervention by African states, followed by the extraordinary violence in Zaire (today's Democratic Republic of the Congo) leading to the additional deaths of up to 5.4 million people.[6]

Underpinnings

This book is based largely on diachronic change – that history matters because inescapably it molds our current circumstances either materially or more crucially in our perceptions. Critical events in national history often are the touchstones against which our present and future actions are evaluated both in their planning and in their subsequent retelling. American policy deliberations before the 1991 Gulf War for example, in emphasizing the need for overwhelming force, were heavily influenced by the Vietnam debacle, as are current debates (at the time of this writing) about the wisdom of remaining in Afghanistan. At the same time, World War II has been seen as an exemplar of the "correct" conduct of a war.

Most important, the extremist impulse typically arises in opposition to existing state policy. Hence, that policy and preceding policies even stretching far back into national history become fuel for deliberation on the desirability of future courses of action. Frequently, early national exemplars are found to contrast with existing state policy, or even the current condition of the polity, typically deemed to be execrable by extremist opponents. Why are political extremists so thoroughly opposed to the existing state of affairs? Some major event such as defeat in war, and/or a perceived national humiliation has sparked a grievance-based movement that seeks to rectify matters, often in extreme fashion. Various manifestations of this effort will be analyzed in the coming chapters.

But the study of extremism has an additional advantage beyond the face validity of arguments in favor of that enterprise. It addresses a problem that has existed in the study of genocide and other forms of mass murder – that of incommensurate cases. In writing *The Killing Trap*,[7] this difficulty puzzled me, but I had no preferred solution at that time. Large-N cross-national studies using aggregate data yielded valuable findings that have greatly enriched our understanding of the sources of genocide.[8] Yet in studies of this type, genocides incurring millions of deaths are included along with the Bosnian mass murders (only Srebrenica with its 8,000 Muslim male deaths has been deemed a genocide by the United Nations) that in the most recent authoritative estimate have totaled approximately 55,000 predominantly Muslim civilian victims of war or massacre.[9] The case of Srebrenica meets the United Nations' criterion of the destruction of an ethnic group "in whole or in part," yet elides the whole issue of magnitude that does indeed distinguish among individual cases. Instead of country-level units

---

[6] McGreal 2008.   [7] Midlarsky 2005b.
[8] See, for example, Krain (1997, 2005).   [9] Tabeau and Bijak 2006, 235.

of analysis used by these studies, a focus on the interface between the individual and society, frequently occurring at lower levels of aggregation (as in Ottoman or German city/provincial birthplace) can yield additional explanatory power.

In one sense, however, we can compare the seemingly incommensurate, if the unit of analysis is changed to political extremism. This change of unit lays the foundation for understanding how political extremism arises, which then can be enacted in the form of mass murder. Here we shift the emphasis to the category of people most likely to commit the most egregious cases of mass murder. And for the most part, they are political extremists.

Political extremism is defined as the will to power by a social movement in the service of a political program typically at variance with that supported by existing state authorities, and for which individual liberties are to be curtailed in the name of collective goals, including the mass murder of those who would actually or potentially disagree with that program. Restrictions on individual freedom in the interests of the collectivity and the willingness to kill massively are central to this definition; these elements characterize all of the extremist groups considered here. This definition is consistent with others put forward by scholars of fascism, say, and are found in a succeeding chapter.

This change in the unit of analysis to political extremism seems to me to be potentially valuable, both analytically in its own right, and in resolving what appear to be anomalies in prior data sets such as those stemming from the State Failure Task Force (renamed the Political Instability Task Force) used by systematic studies. As we shall see, the historical trajectory of Serbia reveals ephemeral gains that distinguish it from other European states; at the same time, it is the only European country to have abetted genocide after 1945, the mass murder of Muslim males at Srebrenica in 1995. Bulgaria, also an Eastern Orthodox Balkan state and, like Serbia, a former Ottoman colony, did not follow the genocidal path, despite the opportunity to do so during World War II. Even during that war, when the majority of Nazi occupied or Nazi allied European countries were complicit in the Holocaust, Bulgaria stands out as one of the few that saved the vast majority of its Jewish citizens from annihilation. Why these vastly different trajectories?

An answer will be found in the sources of extremism in Serbia, the Chetniks (in both earlier and latter-day versions), and the extremist policies of the Milošević government. The twentieth-century histories of Serbia and Bulgaria differ dramatically, despite their apparent similarities of major battlefield losses in World War I, communist governance after World War II, and often shaky, even dismal economic performance both before and after the retreat of communism. Culturally, their Slavic ethnicity and language, and Eastern Orthodox faith, including the public use of the Cyrillic alphabet represent additional commonalities between the two societies. Political extremism never really took root in Bulgaria, while it was episodically manifest in Serbia, especially during the Milošević period. In other words, although both Serbia and Bulgaria emerged from one of the empires (Ottoman) in decline that is cited as a principal source of massive twentieth-century political violence,[10] and suffered from another of these sources – ethnic conflict – their tendencies toward extremism fundamentally differed. The theory of ephemeral gains will point to the fundamental differences in historical trajectories that can make extremist ideation and behavior common in one country, but not in another.

Political extremisms of all sorts share a propensity towards the mass murder of actual or potential opponents of their political programs. For this reason, among others, these political regimes have led to greater loss of life during the past century than almost any other social construction of human beings. A recent authoritative estimate of the number of people murdered by the Soviet Union between 1917 and 1987 is 61,911,000; that for the Chinese Communist government between 1923 and 1987 is 76,692,000.[11]

An important focus of this work is mass violence, which has two major components. The first is the mass murder of innocents that is a frequent consequence of political extremism. But the second is mass murder on the battlefield during major wars that, as a consequence of mortality salience (see Chapter 2), makes later political extremism more likely. Thus, mass violence in one form – mortality salience on the battlefield – serves as an independent or explanatory variable in understanding the later rise of political extremism, but in another form is the dependent variable, or that which is to be explained, the mass murder of civilians.

Fascist governments have fewer victims on their records than their communist counterparts. However, during their shorter existence they accounted for millions wantonly murdered, in addition to the battle deaths induced by their military aggressions. In its even briefer existence, radical Islamism also has demonstrated its propensity towards mass murder. These losses of human life, in addition to the intrinsic fascination of understanding why human beings are attracted to these noxious forms of political organization, make the proposed analyses imperative.

This volume examines the origins of political extremism in the twentieth and twenty-first centuries, concentrating on the four most commonly occurring forms: fascism, communism, radical Islamism, and extreme nationalism (with rampant militarism and genocide as especially sanguinary forms). All of these "isms" are at the same time "totalisms" in that they pursue a singular view of the human being that is total in its conception. (I am avoiding use of the term "totalitarian" because of its implication of coercion. Totalisms can be coercive, but under conditions of a steady peaceful socialization over a long period of time, do not have to be.) All aspects of the person: cognitions, beliefs, daily activities, and worldview are conditioned, even dictated by the total ideational

---

[10] Ferguson 2006, xli.   [11] Rudolph Rummel, personal communication.

system, whether secular in origin or derived from sacred scripture. Although extreme nationalists, including rampant militarists, typically do not dictate a worldview per se, in the matter of military supremacy they are total, brooking no opposition to their governance. Even *potential* enemies can be murdered, as in the mass murder of Chinese civilians (Japan), Hindu and Muslim Bengalis in East Pakistan (Pakistan), or Communists and those even dimly suspected of communism (Indonesia). Extreme nationalists subscribe to the totality of their governance, frequently employing ethnic cleansing or even genocide to achieve complete political control.

All of these "isms" – fascism, communism, radical Islamism, and extreme nationalism including rampant militarism as an especially virulent form – have at their core "an attempt to embody the Enlightenment ideal of a world without…conflict."[12] According to James C. Scott,[13] high modernism in authoritarian form lies at the root of these political programs. The core of these efforts is anti-liberal, for the vast reordering of society needed to effect the elimination of future conflict must necessarily deny many individuals their civil rights that lie at the heart of liberalism. Elsewhere, commenting on religion in the political philosophy of Leszek Koltakowski, the British philosopher John Gray,[14] examines ostensibly secular ideologies such as communism or even democratic capitalism (especially as seen by Fukuyama). "Presupposing as they do a teleological view of history that cannot be stated in empirical terms, all such theories are religious narratives translated into secular language." Although apparently based on religious doctrine, al-Qaeda is a terrorist organization that hopes to achieve permanent peace through the re-establishment of the Caliphate as a supreme supranational entity. The essentially secular goal of establishing a new (revived) political entity to more effectively counter and ultimately dominate the West has a religion-based teleology. Thus, whether political action is motivated principally by religion or by secular goals is an essentially meaningless question, because the two sources often are so intertwined as to be frequently indistinguishable. Indeed, as we shall see, "concrete images, metaphors, and narratives,"[15] common to both secular and religion-based movements are an important part of the experiential system of information processing. At the same time, however, because these elements are already found in ancient belief systems, not requiring their establishment anew, religion can be adapted as a vehicle for extremist behavior.

The contemporary use of terror of course finds earlier European antecedents in the writings and activities of Russian revolutionaries such as Sergei Nechayev and Mikhail Bakunin. When asked which Romanovs (tsarist dynasts) were to be marked for death, Nechayev replied, "All of them."[16] Bakunin the anarchist famously remarked that, "The passion for destruction is also a creative passion."[17] Or

[12] Gray 2003, 2.   [13] 1998.   [14] 2008.   [15] Epstein 1994, 711.
[16] Quoted in Gray 2003, 22.   [17] Quoted in Gray 2003, 21.

more recently, as the Hungarian communist György Lukács put it, "Communist ethics makes it the highest duty to act wickedly…This is the greatest sacrifice revolution asks from us."[18] Describing these efforts by communists and Nazis, Edmund Stillman and William Pfaff[19] averred:

> To destroy a city, a state, an empire even, is an essentially finite act; but to attempt the total annihilation – the liquidation – of so ubiquitous but so theoretically or ideologically defined an entity as a social class or racial abstraction is quite another, and one impossible even in conception to a mind not conditioned by Western habits of thought.

Referring to al-Qaeda, Gray[20] comments, "Self-evidently, the belief that terror can remake the world is not a result of any kind of scientific inquiry. It is faith, pure and simple. No less incontrovertibly, the faith is uniquely western [sic]."

The contraction of authority space

This book advances the basic idea that the origins of political extremism are to be found in the contraction of authority space. The concept of authority space is a companion to one coined by Juan Linz[21] – that of political space. Whereas fascist political parties, according to Linz, require the political space (generally found in democracies and moderate autocracies)[22] to recruit new adherents, an authority space is required for governments to continue to exercise legitimate influence over the populations they govern. Authority space is understood to be the proportion of society over which governmental influence legitimately extends.

Hence, authority space can refer to the intrastate societal sectors that recognize governmental influence as legitimate; alternatively, it can also mean territories incorporated within the polity, therefore subject to governmental influence. If for some reason, say loss in interstate war, territories are excluded from specific regime governance, then contraction of authority space has occurred. Most spectacular were the contractions of authority space occurring after World War I when the Austro-Hungarian Empire disintegrated, the Ottoman Empire was shorn of much of its territory, and imperial Germany was truncated. But important varieties of authority space exist in which societal groups have "captured" a particular governmental authority space, and based on long custom, expect to continue occupying an authoritative position within a governmental sector. As we shall see, the disproportionately large representation of Tamils within the

---

[18] Quoted in "Marx after Communism" 2002.   [19] Quoted in Gray 2003, 117–18.
[20] Gray 2003, 118.   [21] 1980.
[22] Historically, multiparty systems in new democracies have provided that political space, as in Weimar Germany. For an analysis of the stability of party systems, see Midlarsky 1984, while the insecurity of new democracies is treated in Midlarsky 1999 and 2002.

Ceylonese British civil service is a case in point, and its loss in independent Sri Lanka constituted a major contraction of that authority space.

Governmental authority over territory is a binary variable; either the territory is under the authority of a particular state government or it is not. Hence, it is easy to recognize and measure simply by examining the political status of a territory in question. Intrastate governmental authority tends to be more continuous in the sense that it can shade from thorough legitimacy for some people to complete illegitimacy for others. However, when virtually an entire societal sector regards the government as illegitimate – for example, Russian students/intelligentsia around the turn of the twentieth century – then the binary condition is approximated. Another approximation is to be found in the *potential* for authority expansion or contraction.

If constraints are imposed on a country as in the Japanese view of the Washington Naval Accords of 1922 and the London Treaty of 1930 limiting the construction of certain categories of Japanese warships, then these limits are to be interpreted as a contraction of a country's authority space. (The expansion of limits on Japanese construction of naval warships to include heavy cruisers in the 1930 London Treaty was viewed as especially onerous. The Japanese had perfected their heavy cruiser shipbuilding and tactics to substitute for the limits on battleship construction imposed in 1922, as evidenced by their utterly one-sided defeat of an Allied cruiser force in the Battle of the Java Sea in 1942. To have this additional limitation imposed was ultimately unacceptable to the Japanese naval leaders.)

A historical evolutionary approach is taken in understanding the rise of political extremism in the twentieth century and its continuation into the twenty-first. The Russian Revolutions of 1905 and 1917 are the first twentieth-century consequences of a decline in authority space of the tsarist government. According to one French scholar of the reign of Alexander III (1881–94), Pierre Pascal, this period represented "an accentuated divorce between authority, resting on an artificially consolidated nobility, and the country in full economic and social evolution." By 1903–04, in his lectures in the United States, even a moderate liberal academic like Pavel Miliukov, a founder of the Constitutional Democratic Party, a strong opponent of Bolshevism, and a future foreign minister of the moderate Provisional Government in 1917, could state:

> Political reform – this is now the general cry of all shades of political opinion in Russia… Russia is passing through a crisis; she is sick; and her sickness is so grave as to demand immediate and radical cure. Palliatives can be of no use; rather, they but increase the gravity of the situation. To pretend that all is right in Russia, except for a few "ill-intentioned" persons who are making all the fuss, is no longer ridiculous, it is criminal.[23]

---

[23] Quoted in Mazour 1962, 345.

And this contraction of authority space is manifested in the grossly inappropriate and excessive reaction of the tsarist troops to the January 1905 peaceful march by Father Gapon (whatever his own political motives) and his followers leading to Bloody Sunday and the start of the 1905 Revolution. Contraction of authority space and a consequent state insecurity lead to such excesses in response to peaceful challenges to the existing governmental authority. More secure states operating within a broader authority space conferred by greater legitimacy, like liberal democracies, generally do not respond to challenges with excessive force. Instead, only the most extreme and violent dissident behaviors are targeted for elimination.

In this slow prelude to the actual rise of organized extremist movements, communism experienced an etiology different from that of fascism and radical Islamism. Instead of a slow contraction over time of governmental authority space that occurred in late nineteenth-century Russia, a far more rapid territorially based contraction occurred in the latter two instances of political extremism. Interstate war leading to territorial loss was the midwife for the birth of fascism and radical Islamism, as in fact it was for right-wing Russian extremism that was ultimately defeated by the better organized Bolsheviks in the Russian Civil War. Large-scale intranational violence was not characteristic of the birth of fascism and radical Islamism (the war in Afghanistan having been initiated by the Soviet invasion).

Because war and territorial loss have significant emotional content, especially in the modern era permeated by nationalist feeling, a major component of the theoretical foundation of the book is to be found in the emotions. Even under conditions of relative normalcy, as in a US presidential election, emotions can dominate political thinking. When subjects are confronted with information that is inconsistent with their partisan leanings, recent findings using MRI scanners indicate that the "cold reasoning" regions of the cortex are relatively quiet.[24] Instead, emotions guide the subjects' reactions. Elements of emotion theory will be used to understand the deeply consequential aspects of declines in authority space, and especially territorial loss.

While the forms of extremism analyzed here have different ideational roots, they share a vision of society which is radically at variance with that existing at the time of their formulation. Communism is ostensibly future oriented, based on a template found in the writings of Karl Marx, Vladimir Lenin, Joseph Stalin, or Mao Tse-tung (or some combination thereof). Yet, Friedrich Engels used the ancient hunter-gatherer society as an example of primitive communism. But fascism and radical Islamism hark back directly to a vision of society that is presumed to have existed at an earlier time. Essentially, communism turned out to be an experimental program based on the broad guidelines of

---

[24] Westen 2007; Westen *et al.* 2006.

centralized governmental control provided in the template, while fascism and radical Islamism are oriented toward the restoration of that which had (or is presumed to have had) an earlier historical existence. Extreme nationalism, especially rampant militarism, seeks to exercise unfettered authority over the subject population.

Communism was born in revolutionary activity – strikes, riots, assassinations, and other acts of terror – designed to inaugurate a new political beginning. Fascism and radical Islamism were both born in war and bore the unmistakable stamp of that milieu. Almost all of the innocent fascist victims of their own governments died during wartime. But a majority of citizens murdered by communist governments, especially in the Soviet Union and China, were killed during peacetime. Yet as we shall see, the tsarist defeat in the Russo-Japanese war of 1904–05, World War I and the Russian Civil War period of 1917–20 in which millions died, and the subsequent defeat by the Poles vastly increased the probability of Stalin's wholesale repressions leading to the deaths of many additional millions of innocent persons.

While fascism did not *necessarily* entail identification of a state enemy (e.g., Italy prior to its war experience, although socialists nearly attained that status), communism clearly identified capitalists and so-called exploiters of labor as the enemy targeted either for "re-education" or annihilation. Intense warfare served as a unifier of soldiers of common ethnicity who later disproportionately joined fascist movements. In contrast, ideologies of class and worker/peasant repression served to unify citizens of future communist countries even before their war experience. The three forms of extremism – communism, fascism, and radical Islamism – are treated separately. Extreme nationalism, including rampant militarism, is treated as a form of extremism that presumably differs from the other three, yet as we shall see emerges from a similar etiology. Indeed, A. James Gregor[25] puts forward a "criterial definition that sees fascism to have been an intensely nationalistic, antidemocratic, totalitarian, single-party-dominant, developmental system, animated by a mass-mobilizing formal ideology, irredentist in character, and *essentially militaristic*."

Territorial loss

Territory provides a clear and recognizable venue for the exercise of authority, and territorial loss, an immediate contraction of authority space. Why is territorial loss so important? In addition to refugees fleeing into the truncated remainder of the country generating feelings of anger toward those who presumably ejected the refugees from the lost territory, territorial loss has added significance. Territory represents security for the state and its loss inspires feelings of state insecurity. If the nation is an imagined community,[26] then its borders

---

[25] Emphasis added; 2006.   [26] Anderson 2006.

constitute an imagined fortress, a contemporary analog of the medieval castle.[27] All that occurs in the form of community development, legal arrangements, and armed defense takes place within the national territorial "walls."

Lost territory represents a breach of those walls, and if, for the first time in modern memory, territorial loss is incurred after a period of gains, then that breach becomes more salient. Lost territory now could set the precedent for later additional losses. An even moderately paranoid leader might reach the conclusion that there are enemies both within the state and without who need to be fought mercilessly. Fascism (and proto-fascism) is one manifestation of this tendency: a call to action in the name of restoration. The intractability of territorial conflict has been emphasized in several studies that together indicated robust findings.[28]

A single territorial dispute is perhaps emblematic. Dokdo (or Takeshima to the Japanese) is currently under South Korean administration. These nearly uninhabited islets lying between Korea and Japan came under Japanese control in 1905, as the result of the Russo-Japanese War, and it is understood by the Koreans that this was the prelude to the colonization of Korea by Japan in 1910. Thus, according to Cho Whan-bok, secretary general of the Northeast Asian History Foundation, "When Japan claims Dokdo as its own territory, we Koreans feel as outraged as if someone pointed at our wife and claimed that she is his own."[29] And Choe Sang-hun comments, "Among the post-World War II generations of Koreans, a desire to surpass Japan – and fear that they could once again be subjugated by a larger neighbor – remains a powerful driving force."[30] The fear of reversion to an earlier subordinate condition can be a powerful impetus, especially when territory is at issue. Even small islets with no apparent economic or strategic value nevertheless can have a strong symbolic presence.

At the Versailles conference in 1919, the penultimate moment of territorial importance in the international politics of the early twentieth century, maps were salient. According to a conference participant, Charles Seymour,[31] "One of the most picturesque scenes of the Conference took place in Mr. Wilson's drawing room in Paris, with the President on all fours in front of a large map on the parquet floor, other plenipotentiaries in like posture, with Orlando crawling like a bear to get a better view, as Wilson delivered a succinct and accurate lecture on the economics and physiography of the Klagenfurt Basin. Maps were everywhere… The appeal to the map in every discussion was constant."

Guntram Herb[32] comments: "The real worth of maps in the context of Wilson's Fourteen Points and the Paris peace conference went beyond the mere savings in

---

[27] Herz 1957.

[28] Vasquez 1993, 2000; Vasquez and Henehan 2001; Huth 1996; Huth and Allee 2002; Goertz and Diehl 1992; Diehl 1999; Toft 2003; Lake and O'Mahony 2006; Gartzke 2006; Walter 2003; Kahler and Walter 2006.

[29] Quoted in Sang-hun 2008, 6.   [30] Sang-hun 2008, 16.

[31] Quoted in Herb 1997, 17.   [32] Herb 1997, 17.

voluminous documentation: maps became powerful political tools for territorial claims… Already in 1909, the Polish nationalist Roman Dmowski appended an ethnographic map to his book *La Question polonaise* to support his claims for an independent Polish state. And in September 1914, Serbian nationalists prepared a map of the future political organization of Europe on the basis of the national aspirations of the peoples of Austria-Hungary." All of these national movements will be examined in succeeding chapters, and: "The pervasiveness of composite ethnographic maps is illustrated by the fact that they were even used by the [liberal, less territorially centered] Weimar government."[33]

The emotions

In understanding the impact of territory, more specifically territorial loss, examining emotional responses will prove to be important. Why approach the origins of political extremism from the perspective of the emotions instead of a rational actor approach? Although the two theoretical frameworks certainly are not mutually exclusive,[34] nevertheless they have different emphases (see also the chapters in Redlawsk[35]). A body of literature has emerged that indicates the strength of rationality as a basis for understanding the most extreme sorts of political behavior, including suicide terrorism. Robert Pape,[36] for one, argues that the strategic logic of suicide bombing is confirmed by the achievement of substantial gains over militarily more powerful adversaries by those who employ suicide terrorism. More generally, instances like the slaughter of Ugandans by Idi Amin, the obliteration of the Syrian town of Hama by Hafez al-Assad or the mass murder of Ethiopians by Mengistu Haile Mariam can be attributed to rational political calculation.

Shaul Mishal and Avraham Sela[37] conclude that, despite its apocalyptical goal of eliminating Israel "from the river to the sea," Hamas has responded to changes in its political context. The most recent example is the long truce with Israel that ended in December 2008, and then resumed in January 2009. Lisa Anderson[38] suggests that Islamic extremist movements become more pragmatic as the prospects of sharing power improve. Instrumentality, a *sine qua non* of rational decision making, is present even in al-Qaeda's decision calculus. According to Michael Doran,[39] "Polarizing the Islamic world between the umma and the regimes allied with the United States would help achieve bin Laden's primary goal: furthering the cause of Islamic revolution within the Muslim world itself, in the Arab lands especially and in Saudi Arabia above all… War with the United States was not a goal in and of itself but rather an *instrument* designed to help his brand of extremist Islam survive and flourish among the believers."

---

[33] Herb 1997, 109.   [34] Marcus, Neuman, and MacKuen 2000; McDermott 2004.
[35] 2006.   [36] 2005.   [37] 2000.   [38] 1997.   [39] Emphasis added; 2002, 23.

Recent systematic efforts have also centered on domestic and rational choice sources of fascism. Spencer Wellhofer,[40] for example, finds that rational choice theory best explains voting for fascism in the 1921 election for the Italian national legislature, as did William Brustein.[41] Brustein[42] also argues for the "rational fascist" with special attention to Nazism. Thus, "supporters were no different from average citizens, who usually select a political party or candidate they believe will promote their interests."[43]

Although these studies generally are oriented to the achievement of goals established by movements or groups, one could even argue that individual preferences of extremists are rationally determined. If, for example, the suicide bomber believes that salvation on Judgment Day is best achieved by actions involving the immolation of self as well as the presumed enemies of Islam, then utility maximization has occurred at the moment of explosion. The likelihood of a magnificent afterlife has been maximized.[44]

Yet these perspectives do not help us understand the *origins* of the extremist groups themselves, especially why they chose violence in the service of apocalyptical goals, whatever the short-term dictates of realpolitik they reluctantly accommodate. Thus, one of the purposes of this book is to understand the origins of these groups at the moment of formation. The focus here is on the leaders who form the extremist groups, but the only cases analyzed will be those in which the ephemeral gain was robust enough to influence a large enough following to ensure capture of the government. As we shall see, establishing etiology will also help reveal the sources of these ultimate goals; precisely because they are frequently apocalyptical, or at least not easily attained by peaceful methods, violence is the chosen instrument. Instability of the cognitive frame induced by an unstable historical trajectory fuels the extremist response.

In this sense, this book concentrates on extremist behavior as a *means* to an end, however much the ends differ among the cases examined here. Emblematic here is the thinking of Vladimir Lenin, "It is surely a great paradox of *What Is to Be Done?* that Lenin takes a subject – promoting revolution – that is inseparable from popular anger, violence, and the determination of new political *ends* and transforms it into a discourse on technical specialization, hierarchy, and the efficient and predictable organization of *means*."[45] Thus, violent means are the key ingredients of extremist behavior, which are based on popular anger that is to be efficiently channeled into the construction of a new political world.

Modern theories of the emotions will form the basis of the etiology developed here. Emotional reactions are some of the key determinants of violence. Consider statements of Hasan al-Banna, founder of the Society of Muslim Brothers in Egypt in 1928 and spiritual father to Sayyid Qutb, philosophical mentor of Osama bin Laden. For example,

---

[40] 2003.   [41] 1991.   [42] 1996.   [43] Brustein 1996, xii.
[44] Wiktorowicz 2005, 209.   [45] Emphases in original; Scott 1998, 152.

A wave of dissolution which undermined all firm beliefs, was engulfing Egypt in the name of intellectual emancipation. This trend attacked the morals, deeds and virtues under the pretext of personal freedom. Nothing could stand against this powerful and tyrannical stream of disbelief and permissiveness that was sweeping our country... Mustafa Kamal [sic] had announced the abolition of the Caliphate and separated the state from religion in a country which was until recently the site of the Commander of the Faithful [*Amir al-Mu'minin*]. The Turkish government proceeded rashly and blindly in this direction of all spheres of life. [In Cairo] it was thought that the Egyptian University could never be a secular university unless it revolted against religion and waged war against all social traditions which derived from Islam. The University plunged headlong after the materialistic thought and culture entirely taken over from the West... I saw the *social life of the beloved Egyptian people, oscillating between her dear and precious Islam which she had inherited, defended, lived with during fourteen centuries, and this severe Western invasion which was armed and equipped with all destructive influences of money, wealth, prestige, ostentation, power and means of propaganda.*[46]

The contrasts invoked by al-Banna between faith and disbelief, secularism and Islam, and a glorious Islamic past and modern Western intrusion, are emblematic of the approach taken in this book. Indeed, stark contrasts in historical trajectories will be found to be a basis for the emergence of political extremism. Existential issues, not typically found in most political discourse, are here raised in bold relief.[47]

Scope of the inquiry

To fix ideas, extremist *behavior* is the focus of this inquiry, not extremist ideation. I do not minimize the importance of ideas (indeed they occupy large portions of Chapters 4–8), but within an ideational sphere there can be vast differences in the propensity to use violence. Islamists can seek to govern by the Shari'a, but eschew the use of violence in that effort, thinking that random murder is un-Islamic, a violation of Qur'anic principles. Germans can seek to establish a German national supremacy, but within a *Rechtsstaat*, a state governed by laws, not wanton murder. As will be seen in Chapter 13, Nazi war criminals demonstrated wide variations in their propensity to kill, depending in part on their birthplace, subject to vastly different historical trajectories. Ideas themselves do not kill people. Motivations for the murder often are exogenous to the ideation

---

[46] Emphasis added; quoted in Lia 1998, 28.
[47] For treatments of such issues see Kaufman 2001, 2006; Long and Brecke 2003; Crawford 2000; Ross 1993, 2001. These works can be seen as describing the emotional antecedents of the fear and insecurities found in ethnic conflict. See also Horowitz 2000; Petersen 2002; Lake and Rothchild 1998; Posen 1993; and Snyder and Jervis 1999.

itself. At the same time, without ideation serving as a buttress or legitimator, the murder might not have occurred, at least to the extent that it did.

Religion, for example, has been claimed to be a source of terrorism or other forms of extremism. Yet religion in its various guises and manifestations has been around for millennia, but it is only under certain historical conditions that religion (or indeed any other ideational base) yields extremist consequences. Accordingly, Mark Juergensmeyer[48] remarked: "Religion is not innocent. But it does not ordinarily lead to violence. That happens only with the coalescence of a peculiar set of circumstances – political, social, and ideological – when religion becomes fused with violent expressions of social aspirations, personal pride, and movements for political change." Ideas can be interpreted to justify the murder but only under certain historical conditions, as will be seen throughout this book.

In addition to delineating the content of the book, it is imperative to indicate that which will *not* be included. Forms of extremism existing in the pre-modern period, such as the eleventh to thirteenth-century Middle Eastern Assassins, or the seventeenth to nineteenth-century Indian Thugs are excluded. Not only are these cases outside the nineteenth to twenty-first-century time period of analysis, but they were not especially political in orientation. This is particularly true of the Thugs who were mainly thieves as well as terrorist killers. Only *political* extremism in the sense of groups or governments having specific political goals is included. Thus, explicitly psychological forms of extremism emphasizing interiority of the individual without a political referent are excluded.

Also excluded are forms of extremism that are explicitly anti-democratic, but do not envision the use of violence to attain political goals. Much of the contemporary literature on extremism and democracy is concerned with anti-democratic political parties, especially in Europe. The Austrian Freedom Party is a case in point.[49] Historically, one of the best examples is the German National People's Party (DNVP) during the Weimar Republic, which was explicitly anti-democratic and anti-Semitic, but on the whole envisioned a *Rechtsstaat*, a state governed by laws. Mass murder certainly was not proposed; as will be seen in Chapter 16. Although detained briefly by the British army in 1945, Alfred Hugenberg, the founder of the party, never was charged with war crimes.

To be clear, I make no claims that the following analysis will be able to distinguish between *individuals* who are likely to commit extremist acts (such as suicide terrorism) and those who are not. Even explicitly psychological studies frequently cannot make such claims. Because this study is situated at the interface between the individual and his/her national environment, one can make *aggregate* predictions based on the national or social environment. Thus,

---

[48] 2000, 10. For accounts of various religions and their relationships (or non-relationships) with violence, see Almond, Appleby, and Sivan 2003; Appleby 2000; and Esposito 2003.
[49] Art 2006; Bale 2007; Capoccia 2005; Diamond and Gunther 2001; Mudde 2007.

as we shall see, exposure to national territorial loss within the ephemeral gain will make inhabitants of that country or region more likely to commit extremist acts than those of another country or region that did not experience such loss. In addition, a sudden awareness of mortality, or human loss, by ethnic kin in another country can trigger some people to engage in terroristic acts. This setting is far more likely to yield extremism than another in which mortality is absent.

Additionally, for the sake of clarity, a purpose of this book is to explain *extremist-induced* mass murder, not *all* mass murder. Although the numbers of persons murdered by extremists is a very large proportion – even a majority – of the victims of mass murder during the long twentieth century, there are other sources of these atrocities. As will be seen, the modeling of a Stalinist template of policy-driven mass murder can account for much of the Chinese and Cambodian mass murder, just as the mayhem in the Democratic Republic of the Congo stemmed initially from the spillover of Hutu extremists into that country after the 1994 genocide in Rwanda, with the Rwandese Patriotic Front in hot pursuit. Another kind of spillover, also not accounted for by the present framework, will be found in the case of late twentieth-century Guatemala, to be discussed briefly, as will Afghanistan at the time of the Soviet invasion. The adoption of ideologically cognate templates of mass murder in similar circumstances, as well as regional spillovers of mass murder are not addressed at length here, although some mention will be made of the preceding cases.

The analysis also initially will be confined to European cases, because here we find the principal locus of interstate wars that yielded communism, fascism, and other modern forms of political extremism. In the case of radical Islamism, of course, the analysis will be extended to the Middle East or other locations of Islamic concentration. Extreme nationalism is explored in Poland and the Balkans, cases that exhibited the most extreme behavior of this genre. In Poland, even after World War II, Jews were victims of mass murder. Serbia was the only European country that abetted genocide after World War II. Croatia was the only Nazi ally, which after the defeat of Yugoslavia in 1941 and without German help, engaged in genocidal behavior towards two sizable populations, Serbs and Jews. Rampant militarism is examined in Japan, Pakistan, and Indonesia as the cases that led to the greatest loss of innocent life during the twentieth century, after communism and fascism. Variations in individual extremist behavior within twentieth-century genocides, exemplified by those of the Armenians (of course not independent of rampant Turkish militarism), European Jews, and Tutsis in Rwanda are examined through the lens of this framework. The basis for the systematic selection of these cases is found in Chapter 3.

Interestingly, the late Berkeley historian Martin Malia, author of the article predicting the end of the Soviet Union[50] also singles out the humiliation of

---

[50] Malia 1990.

defeat in World War I (Germany), or of the terms of the Versailles Treaty (Italy) as a prime cause of the rise of fascism. As he put it, "In Germany the republic bore the onus of its birth out of national defeat, and in Italy the still recent adaptation of constitutional government to universal suffrage (in 1912) was compromised by national humiliation at Versailles."[51] In addition, Malia also asserts that

> Fascism and Nazism were much more than political authoritarianisms created in response to economic crisis: they were total movements for revolutionary regeneration in the wake of national failure in war. Their basic program was rejection of the restraints of constitutional democracy to achieve national mobilization for a return international engagement. Their revolutionary creed hence was summarized as the struggle of "the spirit of 1914 against the spirit of 1789."[52]

Thus, national unity, quintessentially demonstrated by European populations in 1914, was required for the reprise of World War I in the return engagement.

Yet his prescience as a historian somehow did not lead to an emphasis on territorial loss as a core variable resulting in the rise of fascism. Consequently, although he correctly identified Charles Maurras' *Action française* as at least a proto-fascist movement (without using that term) achieving its long-desired goals with the formation of the Vichy government in 1940 after the French defeat and resulting territorial losses, he altogether omitted Romania with its fascist Iron Guard government assuming power after the enormous territorial cessions of 1940. Nor is the rise of the Hungarian Arrow Cross party mentioned, notwithstanding its strong electoral success (proportionately better than the Nazis in Germany at the height of their electoral prowess) upon the massive Hungarian territorial losses after World War I. In other words, neglect of the territory variable leads to serious omissions among otherwise astute analyses such as that by Malia.

In its entirety, the book is based on the premise that extremists of virtually all persuasions believe in a societal "natural order." This order can be based on race (Nazism), class (communism), religion (radical Islamism), cultural/ ethnic superiority (Japanese and Pakistani military), or long tradition (Poland and Serbia). If these convictions are held strongly, and the political and social conditions to be detailed in the succeeding chapters hold, then extremist behavior follows. It is the task of this book to detail these conditions. At the same time, it must be emphasized that this book is principally about the *origins* of political extremism, including specific pathways to that end, not its spread or elaboration in social movements *after* the moment of genesis. These topics will be examined here, but nowhere nearly to the same extent as in the loci of origins.

---

[51] Malia 1999, 320.   [52] Malia 1999, 320.

Ephemeral gains and organization of the book

In two important ways – theoretical and empirical – this book is a major extension of *The Killing Trap*.[53] The theory of loss put forward in that book has now been extended back in time to encompass the idea of the ephemeral gain: that the losses in war or other political violence so consequential for the occurrence of genocide, as detailed in that earlier volume, were in fact preceded by a period of ascendancy, which in turn was preceded by subordination. A time of glory in the distant past prior to subordination is also relevant, for it is frequently invoked by extremists to justify their violent actions. Of course, the subject of concern is now political extremism in general that has the consequence of mass violence not typically resulting in genocide, although extremism certainly can have that apocalyptical outcome.

Thus, the empirical content is now far more extensive than in the earlier work. For not only do a larger variety of political behaviors become subject to analysis, but the Holocaust as the most extensive genocide occurring in approximately twenty European countries was necessarily emphasized in *The Killing Trap*, but not here. And the ephemeral gain, not necessarily entailing mortality, combined with the mortality inherent in war and other political violence yielding victory followed by defeat – the ephemeral victory – is an essential component of the present analysis. After the introductory material developed here, in Part I theories of the emotions and evidence in support of their validity are offered to buttress the salience of the ephemeral gain. Chapter 1 details this theoretical development, including several pathways from the ephemeral gain: (1) threat and fear of reversion to a former subordinate condition, (2) perceptions of injustice, anger, and blame, and (3) humiliation-shame. The threat and fear of reversion effectively is a coincidence of the shadow of the past and that of the future. When the future begins to look more like the past and its subordinate condition, extremism can occur.

Chapter 2 focuses on another contributor to extremism (but nowhere near sufficient as an explanation), mortality salience. Intimations of the politically finite in the ephemeral gain and the corporeally finite in mortality salience combine in the overall theory. Chapter 3 details the evidentiary base of the book, especially its mode of case selection.

In Part II, the major ostensibly secular "isms," fascism and communism, are treated respectively in Chapters 4 and 5. Part III analyzes radical Islam as a purportedly sacred "ism"; its origins are developed in Chapter 6. The carnage that can be inflicted by such extremism as in Beslan (Chapter 7) conforming to the ephemeral gain is contrasted with the virtual absence of radical Islam of the al-Qaeda variety among Indian Muslims, in the absence of any ephemeral gain (Chapter 8).

---

[53] Midlarsky 2005b.

In further contrast, Part IV, examining extreme nationalism, begins with the mostly Hindu extremist Liberation Tigers of Tamil Eelam (LTTE) that indeed also conform to the ephemeral gain in their origins (Chapter 9).

Poland (Chapter 10) presents the anomaly of a victimized population, the Poles, murdering large numbers of a far more thoroughly victimized group, the Jews, immediately after the defeat of their common enemy, Nazi Germany. The ephemeral gain goes far to explain this homicidal pattern, centering on one of its principal consequences, the threat and fear of reversion to an earlier subordinate condition. Extremism in the Balkans (Chapter 11) also reflects this threat and fear. In Chapter 12, the rampaging military is represented here by the most sanguinary cases of the twentieth century, Japan (1937–45), Pakistan (1971), and Indonesia (1965). By way of contrast, the shadow of the present, not a component of the basic theory, is used to understand other instances of mass murder by the military, as in the Democratic Republic of the Congo, Guatemala, and Afghanistan.

The last chapter in Part IV examines variations in extremist behavior among individuals involved in genocide, based on the ephemeral gains of their places of birth. Here, the local sources of extreme nationalism are on display. Late nineteenth-century Ottoman perpetrators of atrocity, leaders of the Ottoman Empire in World War I, Nazi war criminals and Hutu *génocidaires* are analyzed in this fashion. Pre-war Romanian electoral statistics also evoke the ephemeral gain.

The Conclusion begins with a review of the findings and differential applicability of the three suggested theoretical pathways from the ephemeral gain to the occurrence of extremism. Examination of the varying impacts of the threatened fear of reversion, humiliation-shame, and perceptions of injustice leads to the division between on the one hand, universal extremist movements – those whose ideations make virtually unlimited claims – and on the other, particularist groups whose claims are circumscribed, typified by unadorned nationalism. How these pertain to the recent rise of Russian willingness to use force in Georgia, even mass violence in Chechnya, is discussed, suggesting certain nuances and adaptations of the theory (Chapter 14).

Although unanticipated at the outset of this research program, the ephemeral gain finds resonance with ancient writings on the fall from grace. This consanguinity will be developed more fully in Chapter 15 on ethics and morality. Belief systems incorporating faith-based constraints on the human potential for unbridled violence can be understood as responses, in part, to the ephemeral gain found within human existence. How the ethical and moral restraints, both sacred and secular, which might have prevented such enormities, are obviated is examined in this chapter. The final chapter (16) suggests possible future trajectories of political extremism – the conditions under which extremism will spread or will experience a significant decline. Limitations of democracy are also explored through the lens of the ephemeral gain applied to current United States domestic and international politics.

PART I

Theory and Empirics

1

The Ephemeral Gain: Intimations of the Politically Finite

Two theoretical foci guide this inquiry. The first, that of the ephemeral gain, emerges from elements of the social psychology literature and an analysis of historical trajectories that are most likely to lead to political extremism. Three pathways are suggested to follow from the ephemeral gain: (1) the threat and fear of reversion to an earlier state of subordination, (2) perceptions of injustice leading to anger and blame, including a possible stereotyping of innocents, and (3) humiliation-shame. All three, separately or in some combination, can lead to extremist behavior. As we shall see, whereas Stalin's extremist behavior is best explained by the fear of reversion along with the humiliation and shame at earlier defeats, the rise of Nazism centers more on the sequence stemming from perceptions of injustice leading to anger, blame, and stereotyping behavior. Humiliation and shame at the German defeat ending World War I, of course, was also relevant. Illustrations of the three pathways and, where available, scientific evidence on their applicability are provided.

The second general source of extremism, mortality salience, treated in the following chapter, has received increasing prominence and arises directly from the social psychological literature. Separately, neither principal component of the theory has the explanatory power that both the ephemeral gain and mortality salience provide when taken together.

Finally, although not theoretically central because it does not explain the *sui generis* origins of political extremism as does the ephemeral gain combined with mortality salience, nevertheless the diffusion of extremist behaviors across national boundaries deserves mention. This process requires at least (1) a common ideation among the national leaders experiencing the diffusion of extremism, and (2) a common set of threatening conditions originating from within the state and/or from without. As we shall see, China and Cambodia fulfill these conditions in their respective employ of Stalinist and Maoist templates.

Ephemeral gains

An ephemeral gain occurs when a severe loss (territory, population) or threats of its imminent occurrence, typically perceived as a catastrophe, is preceded by a period of societal gain, which in turn is preceded by a period of subordination.

Ephemeral gains are reinforced when they occur in successive time periods. According to the cognitive neuroscientist, Daniel Schacter,[1] "Reminders
of difficult experiences can slow the normal fading of painful emotions over
time," and negative events are remembered in greater detail than positive ones.
Further, "Everyday experience and laboratory studies reveal that emotionally
charged incidents are better remembered than nonemotional events."[2] The term
"ephemeral gain" is used throughout to suggest control and then loss of political
authority within a given territory. In almost all cases, however, this control (and
its loss) stems from victory (and defeat) in war; hence the term "ephemeral victory" is sometimes used as a virtual synonym.

While most of the analysis is grounded in events occurring in the recent past,
frequently taking the form of transitory military ascendancies that occur after
a period of political subordination, there is a still earlier historical component.
This is the period prior to the subordination in which there existed a real or imagined empire of substantial proportions. Hitler's invocation of the Holy Roman
Empire occupying most of Central Europe (the first Reich) is a case in point, as
are his references to historic German rule in the East. Indeed, in the Deutsches
Historisches Museum in Berlin, the term *Roman Empire of the German Nation*
is used to describe this Ottonian political configuration. Equally, if not more
important, was the German folkloric yearning for a strong leader who would
restore the old order, as expressed in the famous lines of Stefan George:

> He shatters fetters, sweeps the rubble heaps
> Back into order, scourges stragglers home
> Back to eternal justice where grandeur once more is grand,
> Lord once more lord. Rule once more rule. He pins
> The true insigne to the race's banner.
> Through the storms of dreadful trumpet blasts
> Of reddening dawn he leads his band of liegemen
> To daylight's work of founding the New Reich.[3]

Or in his "Exhortation to Liberate Italy from the Barbarians [French, Spaniards,
Germans]," the last chapter of *The Prince*, Machiavelli ends with a quote from
Petrarch:

> Valor against fell wrath
> Will take up arms; and be the combat quickly sped!
> For, sure, the ancient worth,
> That in Italians stirs the heart, is not yet dead.

Mussolini's continued reference to ancient Rome as the model for Fascist Italy
(his use of fasces and the Roman salute reinforced this tendency), and Hungarian

---

[1] 2001, 165.   [2] Schacter 2001, 163; see also Ochsner and Schacter 2003.
[3] Quoted in Fest 1974, 102.

as well as Croatian extremist use of imagery derived from their earlier periods of independent existence prior to incorporation within the Austrian Empire are also cases in point. In the instance of Romania without much of a history of earlier independence, extremists in the Iron Guard found an appropriate religio-historical symbol in the Archangel Michael. Its intimate connection with Eastern Orthodoxy stemming from the Byzantine Empire resonated strongly with the Romanian faithful.

Even a country like Greece, which did not have a history replete with extremism, nevertheless had nationalist supporters who invoked its ancient glories. In an address to a Parisian audience in 1803, Adamantios Koraes exclaimed: "For the first time the nation surveys the hideous spectacle of its ignorance and trembles in measuring with the eye the distance separating it from its ancestors' glory. This painful *discovery*, however, does not precipitate the Greeks into despair: We are the descendants of Greeks, they implicitly told themselves, we must either try to become again worthy of this name, or we must not bear it."[4] Perhaps it was the absence of a unified Hellenic empire as a historical focus – only the Hellenistic under Macedonian leadership included substantial territory – which, with other influences, ultimately yielded a democratic European cultural orientation in Greece.

Although mostly forward looking in seeking to establish an earthly utopia, communism too found its ideal world in the distant past of the pre-agricultural period. According to Friedrich Engels in his formulation of Historical Materialism, one that Marx himself accepted, the first stage of economic production was that of the hunter-gatherers, of whom alone it could be said "to each according to his needs" – the Marxist characterization of the communist utopia. And Osama bin Laden, following his ideological mentors, Sayyid Qutb, and Abdallah Azzam, has vociferously proclaimed the necessity to resurrect the centuries-old Caliphate, the seat of political Islam. Military extremists also have a political vision of either a Greater East Asia Co-Prosperity Sphere shorn of any (recently arrived) European presence, with Japan reigning unchallenged at its head, an East Pakistan free of its Hindu and dissenting Muslim populations and restored to its "rightful" position subordinate to West Pakistan, or an Indonesia no longer threatened with the newly arrived specter of communist rule, both internal and in Chinese Communist garb.

Figure 1.1 presents the basic theory of an ephemeral gain in authority space, signified by the temporary peak in authority. This ephemeral period sometimes occurs after a much earlier grand or imperial period, which though only occasionally mentioned as significant for the contemporary polity, is salient to extremists. But because this triumphal period often is mythic in origin or is exaggerated by extremists, it appears in the figure in dotted lines. For this reason, the empirics of the following analysis do not investigate this earliest

---

[4] Emphasis in original; quoted in Anderson 2006, 72.

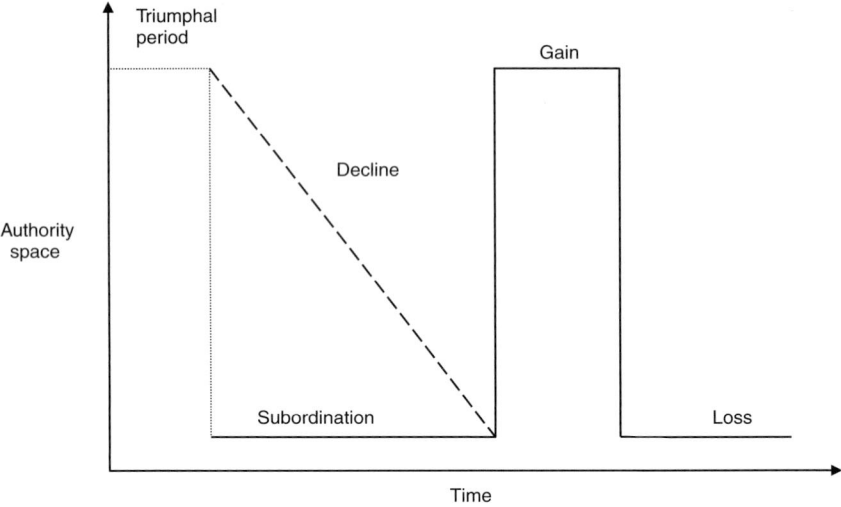

Figure 1.1:   Trajectory yielding the onset of extremism

period; only the ephemeral gain itself, beginning with subordination and ending with loss, will be examined empirically. This portion of the figure is emphasized.

Note that the figure here is not a smooth one, in order to signify that the increases or decreases in authority space take place abruptly at a war's end or some other discrete change, and not as the result of a continuous process of change.[5] The figure also does not show small changes in authority space that indeed can occur, but are dwarfed by the changes in authority space resulting from expansions or contractions of territorial domains or other losses. The dashed line signifies a slow contraction of authority space that can have the same consequence as a long period of subordination.

Surprise, vividness, and urgency

Surprise at the sudden loss has an important consequence in the form of vividness.[6] Both emotional pain and satisfaction can be multiplied substantially by the experience of surprise.[7] Or, as George Loewenstein and Jennifer Lerner[8] suggest, "people respond with greater emotional intensity to outcomes that are surprising – that is, unexpected."

---

[5] Theories that suggest reversals of fortune in the trajectories of state power are those of Doran (1980) and Thompson (1986), but the pathways tend to be smoother than the abrupt contractions in authority space considered here.
[6] Loewenstein 1996.   [7] Elster 2004, 160.   [8] 2003, 624.

The emotional intensity associated with surprise therefore can lead to vivid information – that which is most likely to be acted upon rapidly.[9] Because of the emotional intensity and consequent vividness, a sense of urgency is imparted, or as Nico Frijda[10] puts it, "Urgency is the irreflexive counterpart of felt emotional intensity." Urgency is demanded without the contemplation and introspection associated with reflexivity.[11] Anger can also independently lead to a sense of urgency.[12]

In the case of a previous loss prior to the existing one, an individual can explain the current defeat by referring to the earlier one: perhaps a syndrome of defeat stemming from battle against overwhelming odds. Effectively, nothing different had really happened in the second instance that requires explanation. But in the case of an earlier gain prior to the current loss, especially if substantial, then the present loss becomes puzzling, even frightening and then angering, for there must be a special reason for the current defeat. Often the simplest and most readily available explanation, even if erroneous, is seized upon, as in the increased presence of liberals, Jews, or Americans, depending on the particular case in question. Urgent action is then required against the putative offender to redress the loss, or at least to prevent further loss. Emotional distress increases the tendency to indulge immediate impulses. Long-term deliberations on the desirability of policy goals are minimized in this process.[13]

Finally, an important addendum emerges from prospect theory. This theory tells us that losses are more highly valued than gains, or put another way, that the lost entity is psychologically more valued than an entirely identical entity that is gained.[14] Experimental evidence has consistently demonstrated the asymmetry between losses and gains, even to the extent that, in contrast to gains, losses can generate extreme responses. Losses as the result of a shrinking spatial environment, therefore, may have a magnified role in the public consciousness, out of all proportion to their real-world consequences. When we add this asymmetry between gains and losses originating in prospect theory alone to the surprise, vividness, and emotional intensity stemming from the contrast between earlier gains and later losses, then these losses can be deeply consequential. Losses are also associated with risky behavior, and often with extremist movements.

The salience of bad events

The asymmetry between gains and losses indicated by prospect theory is part of a more general psychological uniformity: Bad is stronger than good. According to the social psychologist Roy Baumeister and his colleagues,[15] good is understood

---

[9] Mele 2003, 165.   [10] 1986, 206.   [11] Frijda 1986, 186–7.
[12] Elster 2004, 154.   [13] Tice, Bratslavsky, and Baumeister 2001.
[14] Kahneman and Tversky 1979, 2000; Levy 2000.   [15] 2001, 324–5.

to mean "desirable, beneficial, or pleasant outcomes including states or consequences. Bad is opposite: undesirable, harmful, or unpleasant. Strength refers to
the causal impact. To say that bad is stronger than good is thus to say that bad
things will produce larger, more consistent, more multifaceted, or more lasting
effects than good things."

Approximately three decades ago, even before the first reported findings of
prospect theory, the consequences of gain and loss were compared with each
other and with a control group. Lottery winners (gainers) did not report greater
happiness within a relatively short time period after the lottery win and its
momentary euphoria, while accident victims (losers) reported being less happy
over relatively long time periods after their accidents. Control group participants remained at about the same happiness level in the absence of life-changing
events.[16] Child-abuse victims and especially victims of trauma demonstrated
far more lasting effects of these profoundly negative experiences in comparison
with any good ones they enjoyed.[17] Sexual dysfunction was found to be far more
consequential for marriage (and its likely dissolution) than good sexual functioning.[18] Again, bad was stronger than good.

At the level of neurological functioning, fear-inducing events leave longer-
lasting traces than do other stimuli,[19] and fear takes precedence over other
emotional reactions.[20] The brain apparently also is hard-wired to correct self-
generated mistakes that, in turn, can result in bad outcome.[21] There exists a
specific neural marker for error detection.[22] Additionally, consistent with the
understanding that bad is stronger than good, children from poor families
exposed to a debilitating environment could have their IQs raised by consistent
educational effort, while those from wealthier families having positive environ-
ments could not. In other words, a good environment is relatively inconsequen-
tial when coupled with genetic heritability of intelligence, but a bad environment
can do much serious damage.[23] Many more examples of the greater impact of
bad relative to good are found in Baumeister *et al.*[24]

What are the reasons for this asymmetry between bad and good? Probably
the most widely cited explanations are found in evolutionary psychology.
"Survival requires urgent attention to possible bad outcomes, but it is less urgent
with regard to good ones. Hence, it would be adaptive to be psychologically
designed to respond to bad more strongly than good."[25] Or as Jonathan Haidt[26]
avers: "Responses to threats and unpleasantness are faster, stronger, and harder

---

[16] Brickman, Coates, and Janoff-Bulman 1978.   [17] Baumeister *et al.* 2001, 326–8.
[18] McCarthy 1999.   [19] LeDoux, Romanski, and Xagoraris 1989.
[20] Fox, Griggs, and Mouchlianitis 2007.   [21] Rabbit 1966.
[22] Miltner, Braun, and Coles 1997; Luu, Collins, and Tucker 2000.
[23] Rowe, Jacobson, and Van den Oord 1999.
[24] 2001.   [25] Baumeister *et al.* 2001, 325.   [26] 2006, 29.

to inhibit than responses to opportunities and pleasures." Unacknowledged dangers can lead to exceedingly bad outcomes such as maiming or death, while positive events rarely have such life-threatening implications. Therefore, we frequently acknowledge the former, even spending considerable amounts of time thinking about such dangers, while the pleasant moments tend to pass us by without much cognition. Not only do the bad or threatening events demand more of our thinking, but unexpected events, i.e., surprise, *independently* produce more cognition.[27] Hence, loss *combined* with surprise is more demanding of our attention than loss alone.

Bad events require problem solving,[28] good events do not. Consistent with this view is that of Kelly Kellerman,[29] who finds that bad information is more informative because it typically is further from the average or norm of expected events. And if societal loss stands in contrast to earlier good things (as opposed to neutral) such as societal gains, then the bad event is even more informative, attention demanding, and requiring action.

Although the argument here is principally diachronic in its emphasis on earlier historical periods for each nation, there exists a cross-sectional component as well. In his *Imagined Communities*, Benedict Anderson does not make much of the size of the community in question, merely that in the modern nation-state it is vastly larger than earlier pre-national communities in which almost everyone knew the other members of the community. But in the last stage of the ephemeral gain, in which territory typically is lost, the imagined community is necessarily smaller than during the ascendant period. How *much* smaller can vary considerably depending on how political leaders emphasize the loss. Irredentist sentiment can depend heavily on the reported size of the lost community (for it is now a community situated within the boundaries of another country). Hyper-nationalist media can portray each and every member of that community as a victim, thereby magnifying the numbers lost beyond the concern typically manifested for those remaining within the new borders of a new nation-state. Germans in the East who now found themselves within a newly independent Poland after World War I, although small in number relative to the total population of the German state, had their significance augmented significantly by the Hugenberg-dominated nationalist press during the interwar period.[30] These media treatments, of course, became fodder for the successful propaganda campaigns of the Nazi Party, especially as Polish-German diplomatic relations deteriorated during the late 1930s.[31]

---

[27] Abele 1985. [28] Taylor 1991. [29] 1984. [30] Snyder and Ballentine 1996.

[31] Yet, as Bates, Figueiredo, and Weingast (1998, 246) indicate in their game-theoretic analysis, the endless repetition of slogans from a monopolized medium is not sufficient to yield extremist outcomes, but requires external validation, suggested here to take the form of the ephemeral gain and its consequent pathways to extremism.

Shadow of the past, shadow of the future

The present theory should be compared with others which, at first glance, bear some resemblance to it. I refer specifically to future-oriented theories such as Marxism and especially the Davies J-curve.[32] While the latter incorporates the Marxist concept of emiseration occurring after a period of steady increase, it is fundamentally future oriented. By that I mean the Davies J-curve embodies a vision of the future that is very much a replication of the recent past, but even better. Marx emphasized a future that was to be fundamentally different from the emiserated past, to be achieved by revolution (early Marx), or through parliamentary methods (later Marx), at least in the democratic West. According to James C. Davies, the better future is achieved incrementally, until some downturn violates these expectations for the future. A revolution then occurs.

Although the onset of revolution can be understood through J-curve type mechanisms, this is not the purpose here. (Indeed, the onset of the French Revolution can perhaps be better understood through the influence of aristocratic French veterans of the American Revolution, leading the charge for equality in the French Assembly. The Marquis de Lafayette and the Vicomte de Noailles are cases in point;[33] particular, but important instances of R. R. Palmer's thesis in his classic, *The Age of the Democratic Revolution*.[34])

The purpose here instead is to understand the rise of extremism and its associated mass murder, whether or not incorporated within revolutions. In other words, where it has occurred, it is not the onset of revolution itself that is of interest here, but the extremist behavior that occurs *after* the revolution's onset. In one sense, this implies a narrower focus of explanation *within* the revolutionary process, but at the same time, a broader scope of explaining extremism in non-revolutionary settings. Certainly, Stalin's murderous behavior was associated with a major social revolution, as was Robespierre's. But fascist "revolutions" were almost never social-structural. Even Nazism respected most German societal traditions, of course for those of "Aryan" extraction, and there exists a host of extreme nationalisms or rampaging militarisms that have no connection with revolution, especially not the social-structural form, but emerge from different sources. Sri Lanka (the LTTE), Japan, Pakistan, Indonesia, and Serbia/Yugoslavia are cases in point that will be examined in this volume.

Beyond these differences between the present theory and seemingly related types, there are others that are even more critical. Instead of a future orientation as in Davies and Marx, the recent past here is decisive. When the shadow of the future looks more like that of the past, both periods substantially worse than the *recent* past, then political extremism and mass murder are more likely to occur.

---

[32] Davies 1962. See also Mason 2004.   [33] Doyle 2009.   [34] 1959–64.

In war, recognizing the possibility of defeat can begin the coincidence of the shadows of the past and of the future.

Further, Marx's principal concern with the economy and Davies' with need satisfaction are materially based. For Marx (the "withering away of the state" upon the advent of communism), even for Davies, the material condition of the population is paramount. If its needs are satisfied, the revolution and its attendant mass violence are unnecessary. In contrast, the present theory is *politically* centered, emphasizing territoriality or hierarchical control that in themselves do not imply need satisfaction. The lost territories of Germany, or those promised to Italy during World War I but not delivered were not central to either economy. Instead, it is the emotional component that is so salient when issues of territory or hierarchy are raised. Finally, mortality was not considered by Marx or Davies, but is central here especially in the impact of losses in war.

Because neither Davies nor Marx incorporated the shadow of the politically subordinate past into their theoretical cores, the idea of ephemerality is absent. Ephemerality itself and individual mortality have much in common. When the individual identifies with the state, and the state appears to be sufficiently vulnerable that it too could be ephemeral, then the awareness of mortality is intensified. Territorial loss combined with severe loss of life in war can establish that sense of national vulnerability, especially if the state was only recently constituted.

We now turn to an examination of the three principal pathways to extremism engendered by the ephemeral gain, beginning with the threat and fear of reversion. Again, it must be emphasized that, despite the existence of cases where a single pathway may dominate in its impact on extremism (Indonesia in 1965 is a case in point, as we shall see), many will combine at least two of the pathways.

The potential for reversion

Telling in its ultimate impact is the period *prior* to the increase in authority space. This period is not frequently considered, but is nevertheless important. If the period before the increase consists of a long decline or remains at a consistently small or nonexistent national authority space, then reversion to that condition may be a major fear. The subsequent ascendant portion of the trajectory can then be seen to be an exceptional blip in national history, if it is in turn followed by the downturn.

At the same time, fear can easily be generated by loss. Following Kim Witte,[35] fear is understood as "a negatively-valenced emotion, accompanied by a high level of arousal, and is elicited by a threat that is perceived to be significant and personally relevant." When the loss and consequent fear entail a likely or actual reversion to an earlier period of subordination, then they can be even more consequential.

---

[35] 1992, 331.

Political theorists and politicians frequently have hailed the liberating event as one that will give rise to the providential future virtually for all time. Karl Marx, of course, is famous for his utopian thinking in this regard. Once the workers have burst the capitalist bonds holding them in submission, the unraveling of the state will yield a future free of social deviance, especially state oppression. Infamous was Hitler's prediction of the 1,000 year Reich attendant upon his accession to power in 1933. Freed from the limitations of "race pollution" and Jewish financial dominance, the Nazi Aryan utopia could now persist through time immemorial.

More benign in their views were lesser known thinkers such as the sixteenth-century French writer Étienne de la Boétie. In his *The Discourse of Voluntary Servitude*, la Boétie wrote about masses of people tyrannized by a single individual, held in his grasp only by their tacit consent. Accordingly:

> To see an endless multitude of people not merely obeying, but driven to servility? Not ruled, but tyrannized over? These wretches have no wealth, no kin, nor wife nor children, not even life itself that they can call their own. They suffer plundering, wantonness, cruelty, not from an army, not from a barbarian horde, on account of whom they must shed their blood and sacrifice their lives, but from a single man; not from a Hercules nor from a Samson, but from a single little man.[36]

All that is required to change matters radically is to cease agreeing to his rule. "Resolve to serve no more, and you are at once freed. I do not ask that you place hands upon the tyrant to topple him over, but simply that you support him no longer; then you will behold him, like a great Colossus whose pedestal has been pulled away, fall of his own weight and break in pieces."[37] Now that consent has been withdrawn, the future is ever-bright for the once downtrodden population.

Recently, nations freed from colonial rule during the post-World War II era were often governed by politicians who entertained such glorious expectations. The early public statements of Sukarno in Indonesia, Bourguiba in Tunisia, Nkruma in Ghana, or Nehru in India (not to mention Mao in China) were replete with views containing unbridled optimism. Yet, as we know, these quantum historical leaps did not persist for very long. Communism in the Soviet Union and elsewhere failed, and Hitler's 1,000 year Reich lasted precisely 12 years. A recent horrific example of the failure of post-colonial rule is Mugabe's despotic government in Zimbabwe, especially when compared with his early lofty pronouncements.

All of this is to say that we simply cannot abandon our study of a society at the moment of "liberation" of whatever sort, but must look for the possibility of future reversion to subordination, and if it has not already occurred, the fear of its occurrence. Samuel Huntington[38] studied the phenomenon of political decay

---

[36] de la Boétie and Bonnefon [1553] 2007, 113.
[37] Quoted in de la Boétie and Bonnefon [1553] 2007, 67.   [38] 1968.

in the post-colonial period. I propose to concentrate on the potential consequences of a renewed subordination (or the fear generated by its possibility),
after the transition to a new, very optimistic stage of governance had earlier
taken place.

At this point, because of the paucity, indeed virtual absence, of research on the
fear of reversion as a pathway to extremism, a detailed illustration is useful to fix
ideas. Chinese Communism will later be used to illustrate humiliation-shame
as such a pathway; the rise of the Nazi Party and other genocidal groups will be
seen to stem partly from perceived injustice, anger, and consequent stereotyping and blame, the third possible pathway to extremism. Later, the succeeding
chapter will close with an example drawn from a very different time and place,
and will demonstrate the applicability of another key element of this theoretical
framework, mortality salience.

Robespierre

The fear of reversion and its consequences for extremism can be found in its
earliest modern incarnation – the French Revolution – especially its arch-
exponent of terror, Maximilien Robespierre. He exemplifies the extremist tendency to a degree that is congruent with some, but certainly not all, of Stalin's
excesses. In his analysis of evil, the philosopher John Kekes[39] used the horrific
acts of Robespierre, Franz Stangl, commandant of the Treblinka extermination
camp during World War II, and Charles Manson of "helter skelter" fame in the
US as illustrations. Because Robespierre was so emblematic of the extremist
leader confronted with the threat of reversion to an earlier subordinate condition, his experience is now detailed at some length.

Robespierre's extremist trajectory, along with other Jacobins such as
Georges Danton and Antoine Saint-Just may be dated from the first recognition that the Revolution was in danger from abroad as well as at home. As
Robespierre declared: "Let us recognize that there is a conspiracy against public liberty... It derives its strength from a criminal coalition...[that] aims at
the obstruction of the *patriotes* and the *patrie*. What is the remedy? To punish
the traitors."[40] Elsewhere he stated: "There are only two parties in France: the
people and its enemies. We must exterminate those miserable villains who are
eternally conspiring against the rights of man...we must exterminate all our
enemies."[41]

Individually, Robespierre was violence averse (as was Heinrich Himmler) to
the point that he collapsed in Arras after his legal duties required him to sentence a man to death (cf. Himmler's near collapse in Minsk upon observing the
executions of 200 Jews[42]).

---

[39] 2005. [40] Hampson 1974, 294; quoted in Kekes 2005, 33.
[41] Hampson 1974, 146; quoted in Kekes 2005, 33. [42] Höhne 1970, 366.

At first, Robespierre was resolutely anti-war, but as the European opposition to the Revolution burgeoned, he was transformed into a proponent of the war, and ultimately the mass murderer of suspected internal enemies. According to John Croker,[43] after Robespierre secured near dictatorial power over the Revolutionary Tribunal, within a 5-month period until his own execution, 2,217 people were guillotined in Paris. In contrast, during the preceding 11 months, only 399 were condemned to death. In other words, the monthly death rate had increased approximately twelve-fold under Robespierre's ministrations. Given our own inurement to high death rates after the depredations of the long twentieth century, these numbers do not lead to instant revulsion. Nevertheless, within the context of the early nineteenth century, writing 41 years after Robespierre's death, "On the basis of these statistics, Croker concluded that the executions 'grew gradually with the personal influence of Robespierre, and became enormous in proportion as he successively extinguished his rivals.' "[44]

On July 25, 1792, the Duke of Brunswick, leader of the forces confronting revolutionary France, declared that if any harm fell to the French king, Louis XVI, Paris would be destroyed.[45] Although that threat was initially scoffed at by the revolutionary leaders, this attitude of complacency would change markedly after the early Austro-Prussian victories. On August 10, the monarchy was abolished, and on August 19, the Duke of Brunswick invaded France, conquering Verdun on September 2. During this period, Robespierre demanded a revolutionary tribunal that "would maintain the peace, satisfy the people's impatience for justice, and investigate promptly all counterrevolutionary activities."[46]

In part, this effort was a political response to the violent popular reactions to the Austro-Prussian victories leading to what is known as the September Massacres. Yielding between 1,000 and 1,500 victims, included among the dead were imprisoned priests, convicts, and royalty, including the queen's friend Princesse de Lamballe.[47]

> She was dispatched with a pike thrust, her still beating heart was ripped from her body and devoured, her legs and arms were severed from her body and shot through cannon… It has been loosely assumed…that most of the other victims were, like herself, aristocrats – an assumption that for some curious reason is often supposed to mitigate these crimes. Very few victims were, in fact, of the former nobility – less than thirty out of the fifteen hundred who were killed.[48]

As the issue of Louis XVI's future loomed large, on December 3, Robespierre was to reflect to the new National Convention on the external threat stimulated by the king's presence:

---

[43] 1835; quoted in Scurr 2006, 3.   [44] Scurr 2006, 3.   [45] Scurr 2006, 213.
[46] Scurr 2006, 222.   [47] Scurr 2006, 220.
[48] Loomis 1964, quoted in Kekes 2005, 31.

Louis was king, and the republic is founded. The great question with which you are occupied is settled by this argument: Louis has been deposed by his crimes. Louis denounced the French people as rebels; to punish them he called upon the arms of his fellow tyrants. Victory and the people have decided that he alone was a rebel. Therefore, Louis cannot be judged; he has already been condemned, else the republic is not cleared of guilt. *To propose a trial for Louis XVI of any sort is to step backward toward royal and constitutional despotism. Such a proposal is counterrevolutionary since it would bring the Revolution itself before the court.* In fact, if Louis could yet be tried, he might be found innocent... If Louis is acquitted, where then is the Revolution?[49]

Robespierre then urged the king's execution without further delay in order "to nourish in the spirit of tyrants a salutary terror of the justice of the people."[50]

By this time, on September 20, the French had won a major victory at Valmy against the enemy coalition, and another at Jemappes on November 6, so that the execution of the king appeared to be less of a calamitous act with grave international consequences. And in this lessening of external threat, the first Revolutionary Tribunal was dissolved.

But now both external and internal events were to conspire against revolutionary tranquility. Ten days after the execution of Louis XVI on January 21, 1793, France declared war on Britain and the Dutch Republic as a pre-emptive act. And insurrection in Paris occurred on March 9–10. On March 10, the Revolutionary Tribunal was now revived. Later that month, on March 18, a major defeat of French forces occurred at Neerwinden in Belgium. This was an especially bitter defeat because (1) the French invasion of the Low Countries initially appeared to have been proceeding on course, and (2) General Charles Dumouriez in command at Neerwinden, earlier the hero of Valmy, defected to the Royalists. Soon after this defeat and a now heightened conscription, the Vendée, a traditionally conservative Roman Catholic region, would erupt in a counter-revolutionary revolt. It would last the better part of the year and lead to the mass murder of approximately 117,000 victims.[51]

The combination of military reversal and subsequent treachery would prove consequential for Robespierre. Despite the repeated efforts of Georges Danton to retain Dumouriez, he nevertheless deserted to the Austrians. Thoroughly alarmed, Danton, then a close colleague of Robespierre, urged the Convention to create a Committee of Public Safety to exercise ministerial power more quickly and effectively. It was this agency, ultimately led by Robespierre that was to freely, peremptorily, and capriciously impose the death sentence on many innocents. In his own mind, Robespierre connected "Prime Minister Pitt with General Dumouriez, the Girondin faction [moderate revolutionaries], property owners in France fearful for their assets, and the nobility hoping to recover their old regime privileges."[52]

[49] Emphasis added; quoted in Scurr 2006, 244.   [50] Quoted in Scurr 2006, 245.
[51] Secher 2003.   [52] Scurr 2006, 263.

In less threatening times, Robespierre had supported freedom of the press, even for his enemies, the moderate Girondins. Now he supported the destruction of print shops as the source of "counter-revolutionary" propaganda. And he supported the crowd of Parisian petitioners who, on May 31, arrived early at the Convention (which had been moved to new quarters) and occupied the seats of Girondins who had not yet arrived. Concluding his speech in support of the petitioners, Robespierre stated:

> Against you who, after the revolution of 10 August [monarchy deposed] wanted to bring to the scaffold those who had accomplished it, against you who have never ceased to provoke the destruction of Paris, against you who wanted to save the tyrant [Louis XVI], against you who conspired with Dumouriez, against you who have rabidly pursued the same patriots whose heads Dumouriez demanded [the Jacobins], against you whose criminal vengeance had provoked the same cries of indignation that you want to proscribe in those who are your victims. Ah yes! My conclusion is the decree of accusation against all the accomplices of Dumouriez and all those whom the petitioners have designated.[53]

Robespierre now advocated the triumph of a revolutionary mentality that would pay little heed, if any, to the rights of the individual: "Let us not trouble about this or that individual, but only about the country."[54]

On August 8, the siege of Lyon began; on August 29, Toulouse surrendered to the British; and on September 5, 1793, the Convention declared terror to be the "order of the day."[55] The Terror remained the official regime for the next 9 months. During this period, Lyon would fall to the Royalists, and the revolt in the Vendée proceeded with great intensity.

The climax of Robespierre's terror would come with his advocacy of the Law of 22 Prairial (revolutionary date corresponding to June 10). The Committee of Public Safety and the larger Committee of General Security now were not the only venues for accusation. The Convention itself, its representatives in the provinces, and the public prosecutor could try anyone accused of "seeking to reestablish the monarchy, discredit the Convention, betray the republic, communicate with foreign enemies, interfere with food provision, shelter conspirators, speak ill of patriotism, suborn officials, mislead the people, spread false news, insult morality, deprave the public conscience, steal public property, abuse public office, or plot against the liberty, unity, and security of the state. The punishment for all these crimes was death."[56]

But in the Battle of Fleurus on June 26, 1794, the French won a decisive victory over the Austrian army. The road to Paris was now secured against enemy forces. In response to many proponents in the Convention, Robespierre opposed disbanding the revolutionary government in favor of the republican constitution

[53] Quoted in Scurr 2006, 268.   [54] Quoted in Scurr 2006, 302.
[55] Scurr 2006, 284.   [56] Scurr 2006, 328.

that had been accepted in December 1793. Despite support for his position by allies in the Jacobin club such as Saint-Just, Robespierre's political position in the Convention deteriorated until he, Saint-Just, and others were sent to the guillotine on July 28, one day after their arrest.

The Committee of Public Safety, even the entire French revolutionary government, was a war government. Earlier, when the Revolution was embattled, attempts to disband it in favor of the constitution of 1793 were unsuccessful.[57] But now that the Austrians had been defeated, the counter-revolution in Lyon failed, Toulon recaptured in December and at the same time the rebellion in the Vendée crushed, the threat and fear of reversion to the *ancien régime* was vastly diminished. Robespierre's fall followed the establishment of relative security for the French Revolution. We now turn to an examination of the second possible pathway to extremism.

Anger, loss, and the perception of injustice

Ephemeral gains, especially in the form of defeats (or other sources of loss) entailing massive loss of life by the defeated, may appear to be grossly unjust, leading to our second pathway to extremism. Indeed, Aristotle equated the origins of anger with perceived injustice. To have lost more than a million men in war, as did Germany in World War I, and then in addition to have lost substantial territories that had been part of the German polity for more than a century, was seen to be unjust by major portions of the German population. This was especially the case after Woodrow Wilson's promise of the incorporation of the Fourteen Points of a just peace was unwisely transformed into the Treaty of Versailles.

At Versailles, denial of territory along the Adriatic Coast to Italy, promised earlier in the Treaty of London of 1915 leading to Italy's accession to the Allied cause in World War I is another illustration. Although the city of Fiume (today's Rijeka) was not promised in that treaty, nevertheless it became a burning issue after the November 1918 plebiscite of the ethnic Italian population in Fiume declared for union with Italy.[58] According to Mark Thompson,[59] "Fiume became the first neuralgic point created by the Paris conference. Like the Sudetenland for Hitler's Germany and Transylvania for Hungary, it was a symbol of burning injustice. A sense of jeopardised identity and wounded pride fused with a toponym to produce an explosive compound."[60]

Italy's loss of 689,000 men in that war was a consequence that would weigh heavily on the Italian political mind. The Japanese participation in World War I entailing the loss of Japanese lives was not matched by the Treaties of Washington (1922) and London (1930) specifying a subordinate condition of

---

[57] Scurr 2006, 272.   [58] Thompson 2008, 368.   [59] Thompson 2008, 381.
[60] For an analysis of the core identities of people and their consequences for international politics, see Midlarsky 2000b.

the Japanese navy relative to those of Great Britain and the United States. The latter treaty was especially unfortunate, as we shall see. Many other examples could also be provided.

An essential antecedent of extremism is the anger at an injustice that leads to the placing of blame on specific targets. Justice as fairness,[61] in many instances identified with equity,[62] is the understanding of justice adopted here. The idea of a reference point or frame is important, because it provides a specific context for the evaluation of fairness or its absence. A loss, territorial or otherwise, can be measured against what might be considered to be fair or equitable in that context.

Anger has been found to be associated with loss.[63] Equally important, anger has been shown to be a significant emotional response to injustice.[64] Aristotle[65] in his *Rhetoric* (Bk2, Ch2) defined anger as, "an impulse, accompanied by pain, to a conspicuous revenge for a conspicuous slight directed without justification towards what concerns oneself or toward what concerns one's friends." Commenting on Aristotle's definition, Jonathan Haidt[66] notes that "anger is not just a response to insults, in which case it would be just a guardian of self-esteem. Anger is a response to *unjustified* insults, and anger can be triggered on behalf of one's friends, as well as oneself." Thus, anger is categorized by Haidt[67] as one of the "moral emotions," those "that are linked to the interests or welfare either of society as a whole or at least of persons other than the judge or agent."

People in a state of anger are "more apt to blame others for mishaps that occurred."[68] Further, persons of an ethnicity different from one's own are more likely to be targeted.[69] Anger in response to loss has also been associated with the desire to obtain restitution or compensation,[70] or revenge.[71]

Following this normative theme, Frijda[72] amplifies: Anger is provoked by a violation of what "ought to be" in the agent's view. Thus, a normative order has been violated, which justifies a challenge to this changing of the rules by the offending party. "Anger implies nonacceptance of the present event as necessary or inevitable; and it implies that the event is amenable to being changed."[73] Or as a consequence of loss, "anger often carries with it a desire not only to reinstate the goal, but also to remove or change the conditions that lead to goal blockage in the first place."[74]

Thus, loss generates anger at the injustice of the loss, which in turn can be mobilized by extremist groups that seek not only to retrieve or redress the loss (as in territory), but also to direct their anger at helpless civilian targets who are

---

[61] Rawls 2001.   [62] Deutsch 1985.   [63] Stein, Trabasso, and Liwag 1993.
[64] Haidt 2003.   [65] 1991.   [66] Emphasis in original; Haidt 2003, 856.
[67] Haidt 2003, 853.   [68] Berkowitz 2003, 816.
[69] Bodenhausen, Sheppard, and Kramer 1994; DeSteno *et al.* 2004.
[70] Stein, Trabasso, and Liwag 1993.   [71] Frijda 1994; Nisbett and Cohen 1996.
[72] 1986.   [73] 1986, 199.   [74] Stein, Trabasso, and Liwag 1993, 291–4.

somehow implicated, often in the most indirect fashion, in the origins of the loss.[75]

Justice as fairness

Ever since the writings of John Rawls,[76] justice as fairness has been increasingly used as a basis for understanding the genesis of conflict or cooperation. At the same time, we may note the obverse. Lack of fairness can be perceived as an injustice. Hence, it is to our advantage to understand the conditions under which fairness evolves in dyadic relations. It turns out that in the ultimatum game, fairness evolves as a stable solution when the past behavior or reputation of individual players becomes available.[77]

In the ultimatum game, two players are asked to split a sum of money. The proposer suggests how to divide the sum. If the proposal is accepted, both receive their agreed-upon shares. If the division is rejected, both players receive nothing. The closer the split is to 50–50, or a division in excess of even-handedness in favor of the responder, the more likely it is that the deal will be accepted. Typically, an equal division is perceived as fair, with perceived unfairness increasing as the proposed inequality of division increases. Many responders reject low offers of 80–20, or even 70–30, despite the fact that they will lose everything, suggesting that decisions having a strong component of justice as fairness are independent of any rational calculations of cost-benefit. According to Marc Hauser,[78] "When reciprocity fails or the offer is unfair, imaging studies reveal significant activation of the anterior insula, an address of the brain known to play a role in negative emotions such as pain, distress, anger, and especially disgust."

Stable solutions to the ultimatum game depend on player reputation, suggesting that, "When it comes to group level activity, reputation fuels cooperation and provides a shield against defection."[79] But for victims of political extremism such as Jews in Germany during the early 1930s and thereafter, or for Tutsis in Rwanda in the early 1990s, there was no opportunity for reputation to conform to reality. Distorted propaganda efforts were centered on the encapsulation of Jews or Tutsis (Hate Radio in Rwanda is a prime example) so that an accurate record of the actual behavior of the potential victims would not be available to a majority of the population.

An extraordinary example is the infamous "stab in the back" calumny against the Jews, accusing them of undermining the German war effort during World War I, leading to Germany's defeat. As Kaiser Wilhelm II put it in a letter to General August von Mackensen on December 2, 1919: "The deepest, most

---

[75] Midlarsky 2005a, 2005b.   [76] 1971, 1999, 2001.
[77] Nowak, Page, and Sigmund 2000; Sigmund, Hauert, and Nowak 2001.
[78] 2006, 287.   [79] Hauser 2006, 79.

disgusting shame ever perpetrated by a people in history, the Germans have done onto [sic] themselves. Egged on and misled by the tribe of Juda [sic] whom they hated, who were guests among them! That was their thanks! Let no German ever forget this, nor rest until these parasites have been destroyed and exterminated [*vertilgt und ausgerottet*] from German soil! This poisonous mushroom on the German oak tree!"[80] When there exists the appearance or actuality of exploitation, "We are driven by something deeper and hotter than sheer reason – by a feeling of moral indignation, of just grievance."[81] Revenge and retribution can then follow. All of this despite the reality of 100,000 Jewish men under arms (80,000 having served in combat), 12,000 Jewish dead at the front, and 35,000 decorated for battlefield bravery. These statistics are out of all proportion to the roughly 500,000 Jewish citizens living in Germany in 1914.[82]

Extremist leaders excel in undermining potential support for targeted populations. Stable cooperation between majorities and minorities therefore is made impossible. As Hauser[83] puts it, "the only way to guarantee stable, cooperative societies is by ensuring open inspection of reputation and providing opportunities for punishing cheaters." The ultimatum game provides an opportunity for both. Reputation can be introduced in the form of information on players' past performance in the game, and punishment inheres in the ability of the responder to turn down an unfair offer.

If we view justice as fairness, as does John Rawls,[84] arguably the leading political philosopher of the twentieth century, then the connection between loss and reactions to perceived lack of fairness (injustice) can be specified physiologically. Two recent studies have suggested that levels of serotonin, influencing feelings of wellbeing, affect perceived fairness or its absence. In both studies, the ultimatum game was used to elicit reactions.

In the first study, in early morning the serotonin levels were depressed by giving volunteers a cocktail of amino acids needed by the human body, excepting tryptophan required for the production of serotonin. Although there was no measurable impact of the reduction of serotonin on general mood, 82 percent of those with depleted serotonin rejected an 80–20 division, meaning no money was gained for either player. In contrast, 67 percent of subjects in a control condition given a placebo rejected that same proposal.[85]

A different manipulation of the serotonin level yielded essentially the same findings in another study.[86] Since loss very likely will depress serotonin levels, then under conditions of loss even irrational judgments (based on criteria of individual utility maximization), such as rejection of any compromise in the face of perceived injustice, become more probable.

---

[80] Quoted in Röhl 1994, 210.   [81] Wright 2000, 24, quoted in Schroeder *et al.* 2003, 382.
[82] Fischer 1998, 120.   [83] 2006, 81.   [84] 2001.
[85] Crockett *et al.* 2008.   [86] Brondino *et al.* 2008.

Even animals have been shown to react badly to perceived injustices in the form of inequities. When dogs were paired with one receiving a reward and the other not, the latter refused to obey already learned commands.[87] In earlier studies of primates, Capuchin monkeys displayed similar behavior, reacting even to unequal reward distribution.[88] If even animals will refuse to cooperate under conditions of inequity, then how much more intensely will humans react to similar circumstances?

Related to justice as fairness but still forming a conceptually distinct category is justice as the freedom to pursue capabilities.[89] From this perspective, the discrimination against minorities and women that prevented their freedom to pursue capabilities is understood as a form of injustice. Here, the restrictions of the Treaty of Versailles on Germany and those of the later Naval Treaties of 1922 and 1930 limiting Japanese building of capital ships, even heavy cruisers, can be understood as injustices. And the social psychologist Paul Rozin and his colleagues[90] found that violations of autonomy tended to be most directly associated with the emotion of anger.

Justice and honor

Perceptions of international justice can also yield considerations of national honor, especially that form of honor emphasizing national autonomy. This is the first conception of honor to be considered here; in the following section a different form of honor will be considered in relation to shame, an emotion stemming from dishonorable conduct based on existing societal norms.

In a recent meditation on the meaning of the term, the philosopher Alexander Welsh[91] concluded that:

> Honor is a morality founded in respect. The respect of a peer group and the event of coming of age are the necessary spatial and temporal conditions for honor's hold on individual behavior… That a morality of respect entails coming of age helps to explain certain kinds of motivation associated with honor: a scorn for following orders and threats of punishments; an exultation, for a while at least, in putting the body at risk; a belief in personal autonomy.

Simply by modifying these characteristics to reflect national autonomy instead of (or in addition to) personal autonomy, this is a striking characterization of the policies of extremist leaders such as Hitler or Stalin. Several items are noteworthy: (1) the necessity for the respect of a peer group (national or personal), (2) the willingness to disobey (international) orders and risk (international) punishment, (3) insensitivity to the risk of death, and (4) an emphasis on

---

[87] Range *et al.* 2009.   [88] Brosnan and de Waal 2003.
[89] Nussbaum and Sen 1993; Sen 2000.   [90] 1999.   [91] 2008, 22.

national and personal autonomy. This description could also apply to other risk-acceptant national leaders.

Issues of honor generally are found where the laws of the state, or indeed any other political organization, are absent or behave dysfunctionally. This is the principal conclusion drawn from studies of a variety of settings including Pakistani immigrants in Norway, Danish outlaw bikers, areas of the American South, the Hindu Kush Mountains, and Kurdistan.[92] Codes of honor function as a replacement for the absent or dysfunctional laws. In this sense, one can interpret the emphasis on honor in extremist groups (e.g., the *SS* slogan *Meine Ehre heisst Treue*, My Honor is Loyalty) as a replacement for international arrangements such as the Treaty of Versailles in Europe, or the Treaties of Washington and London vis-à-vis Japan. All of the characteristics of honor listed above are found. The dysfunctional military and economic arrangements incorporated in these treaties, widely seen as injustices in the affected societies, are to be opposed by the new sense of honor. Perceived injustice then can yield efforts to counter the injustice by emphasizing national honor. The "dark stain" (cf. Stalin on the Russian defeat by Japan in 1905) of an earlier shame will have been removed.

Or as in the case of radical Islamism, the perceived injustices of the reigning (in their view) international political paradigm – democracy – require a vigorous response. Accordingly, Mohammad Sidique Khan, the presumed leader of the London underground bombing of July 2005, stated: "Your democratically elected governments continuously perpetuate atrocities against my people all over the world. And your support makes you directly responsible, just as I am directly responsible for protecting and avenging my Muslim brothers and sisters... Until you stop the bombing, gassing, imprisonment and torture of my people we will not stop this fight."[93]

Perceptions of injustice in settings such as Versailles or Trianon (1920; relevant to Hungary) yield an emphasis on national autonomy. Even without evidence of international dysfunction as at Versailles, when faced with the offer of arbitration between two states, the historian Heinrich von Treitschke[94] remarked, "Were we to commit the folly of treating the Alsace-Lorraine problem as an open question, by submitting it to arbitration, who would seriously believe that the award could be impartial? It is, moreover, a point of honor for a State [sic] to solve such difficulties for itself."

But Treitschke, lecturing at the University of Berlin in the late nineteenth century (leading to the book, *Politics*, containing these excerpts) went further. Referring to interstate war, he declared, "Modern wars are not fought for the sake of booty. Here the high moral ideal of national honour is a factor handed down from one generation to another, enshrining something positively sacred, and compelling the individual to sacrifice himself to it. This ideal is above all price

---

[92] Aase 2002.   [93] Quoted in Jones 2008, 38.   [94] [1916] 1963, 17.

and cannot be reduced to pounds, shillings, and pence."[95] He then quoted the great philosopher, Johann Gottlieb Fichte: "Individual man sees in his country the realization of his earthly immortality."[96] Elsewhere, Treitschke commented on the diminished importance of Jews as a cosmopolitan force uniting national cultures and economies. "After a nation has become conscious of its own personality there is no place left for the cosmopolitanism of the Semites; we can find no use for an international Judaism in the world today."[97] Here, the interests of national honor and minority rights collide.

Earlier, after the end of the American Civil War, when US claims against the British-built commerce raider *Alabama* were put forward for arbitration, Lord Russell responded that, "England's honor can never be made the subject of arbitration."[98]

More generally, according to Henry Kissinger, "No serious policymaker could allow himself to succumb to the fashionable debunking of 'prestige,' or 'honor' or 'credibility.' "[99] And the military historian Donald Kagan wrote, "The reader may be surprised by how small a role…considerations of practical utility and material gain, and even ambition for power itself, play in bringing on wars, and how often some aspect of honor is decisive."[100]

And for the Nazis, honor was extremely important, as we saw in the SS slogan. Honor is to be found in the "best" of national traditions, however defined. Identification with the nation is exhibited by virtually all of our extremist leaders, even famously (or infamously) by Stalin, the Georgian-cum-Russian, in his victory toast to the Russian people in 1945, as we shall see in Chapter 5. And in this instance, to be anti-Soviet – increasingly to Stalin, anti-Russian – was a mortal sin to be expiated frequently only by death.

Anger and the placing of blame

Several studies help us understand the emergence of anger and the placing of blame from ephemeral gains. Among the earliest is that by Keltner, Ellsworth, and Edwards[101] that investigated whether anger would lead to the attributing of blame to persons or to situations. Sadness was hypothesized to yield precisely the converse attribution. Forty-eight psychology students at Stanford were divided into groups that received either an anger or sadness induction of mood. The anger induction consisted of students imagining themselves to be instructed by a teaching assistant who was considered by many to be "dogmatic and condescending." After submitting a paper that had required substantial time and research effort, in an area of inquiry in which the student had considerable competence and fully expected a high grade, he or she received a C minus. Note

---

[95] von Treitschke [1916] 1963, 9–10.
[96] Quoted in von Treitschke [1916] 1963, 10.   [97] von Treitschke [1916] 1963, 133.
[98] Quoted in O'Neill 1999, 88.   [99] O'Neill 1999, 85.
[100] Quoted in O'Neill 1999, 85–6.   [101] 1993.

the clear perception of injustice embedded in the scenario that, although not necessarily intended by the experimenters, nevertheless resonates strongly with Aristotle's description of anger as an emotion derived principally from perceptions of injustice, as we saw. The sadness induction centered on the illness of a mother, as conveyed to the student by his sibling.

Although all subjects thought that situational agency events were far more likely to occur than their human agency counterparts (in evaluating the causality of mishaps such as missing a flight, buying a new car "lemon," or a plane crash that could be attributed either to pilot error or to lightning), the majority of students in the anger condition were more likely to blame human agency than situational.

Because of the specificity of events asked to be evaluated for their etiology in the first experiment, another was generated in which blame could be attributed either to situational or to human agency. An imaginary social situation was created in which, at a party, a student was embarrassed when a girl (boy) that he/she had invited and expected to woo, arrived with a boy(girl)friend. An ambiguous situation was generated in which blame could be attributed either to situational factors (absence of knowledge as to the invitee's state of affairs) or to human agency (a duplicitous act by the invitee). Again, angry subjects were more likely to blame other people for this (essentially sad) situation, than the sad inductees. Further experiments found that the induced emotions were the likely cause of human or situational blame, not cognitive appraisal of these scenarios.[102] A separate study of the effect of blame attributions on feelings of anger found that perceived injustice was central to the process.[103]

But the specifics of blame need to be investigated. And here the work of Galen Bodenhausen, Lori Sheppard, and Geoffrey Kramer[104] is important. Using an affect induction, students were asked to vividly recall experiences that made them either very angry or very sad. Stereotypic judgments were rendered by the former group, but not the latter. Students in both groups were asked to evaluate the guilt or innocence of a "Juan Garcia" who was accused of assault, and a "John Gardner," a "well-known track and field athlete on campus" who was accused of cheating. In that student population, prior studies had revealed that male Hispanics were typically viewed as aggressive and student athletes as more prone to cheat than others. In both instances, the angry subjects were far more likely to perceive the guilt of the stereotypical target than students who were sad or in a neutral condition where no mood induction occurred.

A variation on this theme has strong implications not only for automatic stereotypical responses, but also for the ability of extremists to attract supporters

---

[102] Keltner, Ellsworth, and Edwards 1993.   [103] Quigley and Tedeschi 1996.
[104] 1994; also see Bodenhausen *et al.* 2001.

in a hierarchical fashion. An essay that advocated raising the legal driving age from 16 to 18 was read by all students, but for some the essay author was said to consist of "a group of transportation policy experts at Princeton University" and for the remainder, the essay was attributed to "a group of students at Sinclair Community College in New Jersey." Angry subjects exhibited a "strong and significant tendency to agree with the high-expertise source." Sad subjects actually reversed the pattern, agreeing with the low-expertise source but to a non-significant extent. Those in the neutral condition (no mood induction) demonstrated no significant difference in their preferences. A case in point within the political realm was the very likely strong impact on future Nazis by Kaiser Wilhelm II blaming the Jews for the defeat in World War I, as we saw earlier in this chapter.

More recently, the effects of emotion on automatic intergroup attitudes was investigated. As in the Bodenhausen *et al.* studies, the emotions of anger and sadness were induced. All students were asked the affectively neutral question "How many people ride the New York subway every day?" Subjects were informed that they were either "overestimators or underestimators." In reality, subjects were randomly assigned to these two groups and were asked to wear wristbands designating their group. When shown pictures of these groups, subjects were slower to associate positive attributes to the "outgroup" than negative ones. However, "there was no difference in the speed in which [angry participants] associated positive versus negative attributes with the ingroup."[105] And in the neutral or sad conditions no significant differences of any kind were found in the speed of associating positive or negative attributes with any group. A second experiment using a somewhat different measure of automatic attitudes as well as a self-reporting measure gave similar results. These findings successfully built on the work of the experimenter and his colleagues.[106]

Even hypocrisy is subject to group identity. When subjects were asked to evaluate the morality or fairness (or lack of it) of another person, and that individual was a member of the subject's "ingroup" (created by the experimenter), the fairness evaluation was higher than when that individual was a member of an "outgroup."[107] According to David DeSteno,[108] "Anyone who is on 'our team' is excused for moral transgressions. The importance of group cohesion, *of any type*, simply extends our moral radius for lenience."

The third pathway to extremism, humiliation-shame, will now be detailed. More on the rise of Nazism and other genocidal regimes is found in later chapters, specifically on genocide (Chapter 13) and ethics and morality (Chapter 15).

---

[105] DeSteno *et al.* 2004, 321.   [106] DeSteno *et al.* 2000.
[107] Valdesolo and DeSteno 2007, 689–90.   [108] Emphasis added; quoted in Tierney 2008, F6.

Humiliation-shame

Humiliation and shame at the loss and threatened or actual reversion, are frequently unexpected. Humiliation refers to the emotion experienced upon an abrupt diminution of pride. In the instance of extremists, pride almost always stems from the national or ethnoreligious experience. As such, humiliation is temporally based and therefore can (but does not have to) inhere in a diachronic model. The current humiliating treatment is unfavorably compared with that which *should* exist, based on wishful considerations of what might have been in another time, sometimes in another place. In the model proposed here, humiliation would be prominent only in the case of a much earlier national experience greatly at variance with the current parlous condition.

Shame, on the other hand, is not temporally based. Instead, it derives from the violation of a code of honorable conduct (in contrast to honor expressed in the form of national autonomy emphasized in the preceding section). Honor is the obverse of shame, which is essentially a dishonorable condition. Existing societal norms govern the sense of shame. According to Jonathan Lear, "Shame is one of the basic emotions by which we regulate our sense of what is and what is not appropriate behavior."[109] Shame is what keeps us within the limits of the social contract.[110] Distinguishing between prospective and retrospective shame, Alexander Welsh[111] states: "The first, avoidance of shame at all costs, translates as a motive of honor; the second, a state of shame, occurs already too late, with loss of honor." Honor was to be a major concern of German society after World War I, culminating in the SS slogan, "Meine Ehre heisst Treue" (My Honor is Loyalty). Indeed, the Treaty of Versailles was widely called the Treaty of Shame.

When fair rules are not followed (or such is the appearance), a victim can claim a just grievance requiring retribution. The violation of social norms yielding shame can also generate a desire for retribution. If during a major war a group has been accused, rightly or wrongly, of defecting to the enemy, as happened to the Armenians during World War I, the Jews prior to World War II, and the Tutsi after the RPF invasion of 1990, then the strong norm of cooperation during wartime has been violated.

An incident reveals the extent of Heinrich Himmler's reaction to any form of defection from accepted norms of cooperative behavior. It occurred in September 1916, as food shortages were making themselves felt in wartime Germany. A clipping from a local newspaper kept by Himmler denounced the hoarding behavior of a woman known to him. She had complained to the Himmler family about the food restrictions in Germany that she was circumventing by her hoarding behavior in Passau. Food she collected there was being sent home. Bradley Smith[112] concluded from this incident "that the Himmlers – perhaps

---

[109] Lear 2006, 61.   [110] Braithwaite 1989.   [111] 2008, 35.   [112] 1971, 43.

Heinrich himself – were directly involved in the denunciation of the hoarders. The boy's wealth of information on the incident certainly suggests that he played some part in its exposure."

If simple food hoarding, as distasteful as it may seem, could generate such a reaction by the Himmlers, then the presumed Jewish responsibility for the loss of World War I could yield far more dire consequences for the presumed defectors. Accordingly, Himmler in his Posen speech of October 4, 1943, justifying the mass murder of the Jews, stated: "If the Jews were still lodged in the body of the German nation, we would probably have reached by now the stage of 1916–17."[113]

The manufacture of shame

Ideation can serve as a vehicle for the manufacture of codes of honorable conduct that can be used to identify the shameful. An emphasis on purity, racial or otherwise, can establish such a code. Upon reading a nineteenth-century book about Yiddish, Heinrich Himmler comments, "One sees that Yiddish is a form of middle high German…Shame to our beautiful language."[114] Himmler's reaction illustrates the philosopher Jesse Prinz's[115] understanding of the intimate relationship between morality and shame. Accordingly, "Moral shame is a species of aversive embarrassment that has been calibrated to norms having to do with the natural order." The "natural order" here of course is the superiority of the Aryan over the Jew. And as we shall see in Chapter 15 on ethics and morality, Himmler never ceased to consider himself a moral person.

But purity often has biological referents, as in Hitler's racial laws that criminalized any sexual contact between Jews and "Aryans." Thus, consorting with Jews in any intimate way could (and did) lead to the accusation of shame in violating the racial codes. A new criterion had been established against which conduct could be measured as shameful.

Mussolini not only defined himself as an Italian nationalist, but even more so as a Roman, heir to the glories of ancient Rome. The Punjabis, Pashtuns, Sindhis, and other western Pakistani peoples identified only with their own region and cognate ethnies, and were not to be governed by the Bengalis of East Pakistan, even if, like them, they were mostly Muslim in religion. And al-Qaeda's identification, although to a casual observer exclusively Islamic, nevertheless has a substratum of Arab nationality to which most of its leaders and members belong. The humiliation and shame of defeat by a former *dhimmi* (subordinate non-Muslim) people in the old Ottoman Empire – the Jews – in the 1948–49 Arab-Israeli war and again in the Sinai campaign of 1956 was a powerful stimulus to the thinking of Sayyid Qutb. Although writing as a Muslim, nevertheless it is clear that much of his attention was devoted to the parlous condition of contemporary Arabs,

---

[113] Quoted in Burleigh 2000, 660.   [114] Quoted in Smith 1971, 143.
[115] 2007, 78.

especially in comparison with their earlier triumphal period. Given the origins of Islam in the Arabian Peninsula, this is hardly surprising.

Although conceptually distinct, humiliation and shame frequently are coeval, stemming from the same event. Thus, for the nationalists, although humiliation is measured against the much earlier period of national glory, the descent from that height can also be considered shameful if it simultaneously violates a code of honor. Stalin's reaction to the defeat of Russia by Japan was not only a humiliation at the first Russian defeat of the twentieth century after the 1878 victory over the Ottoman Empire and earlier tsarist successes, but was also shameful in the sense that a non-European country simply was not supposed to defeat a European power. The code of European-white supremacy was ubiquitous at that time. Certainly, Germany's defeat in World War I and consequent territorial contraction was humiliating when measured against the expanse of the Holy Roman Empire (the first Reich). But it was also soon to be shameful since Nazi ideology would shortly manufacture racial codes of conduct in which Jews (as the presumed source of the Allied victory in World War I) were inferior to Aryans; thus it is shameful to allow any intimate contact with them, certainly not allow "their" victory to stand.

The experience of humiliation-shame can lead to the adoption of new behaviors that would not have been considered appropriate within the earlier context of gain prior to defeat. Many of these new behaviors directly defy the codes of conduct of traditional political authorities who are now held accountable for the defeat leading to loss, and are to be replaced by extremists. Later, in confronting issues of ethics and morality (Chapter 15), the concept of "honor-shame" stemming from an example given by Herodotus will be developed. This form of shame derives from the violation of a collective norm, such as that required by nationalist extremists. Honor-shame will be contrasted with worth-shame,[116] in which the code of conduct stems from the individual conscience, independent of any collectivity such as the nation.

China

Although not associated with a *sui generis* ephemeral gain, China's lost wars, indicated in the closing chapter of this Part, suggest the magnitude of humiliation that can be incorporated into the national experience. Indeed, a new literature has arisen in China around the idea of 100 years of national humiliation. According to William A. Callahan,[117] "the national humiliation narrative is [still] painstakingly reproduced in textbooks, museums, popular history books, virtual exhibits, feature films, dictionaries, journals, atlases, pictorials and commemorative stamps." A crucial Chinese narrative specifies the "century of humiliation" from the mid-nineteenth century to the mid-twentieth.[118] Thus,

---

[116] Kekes 1993.   [117] Quoted in Schell 2008, 31.   [118] Gries 2004, 45.

the choice of an ideologically cognate Stalinist template, itself stemming from an ephemeral gain, is made more probable.

The Chinese-born filmmaker, Chen Shi-zheng, has directed *Dark Matter*, a film based on the murder of five faculty members and administrators, as well as a rival graduate student at the University of Iowa by a humiliated Chinese graduate student. He was forced by his dissertation committee to make computation corrections in his physics dissertation that would deny him the possibility of receiving an award. Although not intended as a direct explanation of Chinese extremism, nevertheless Chen commented, "We Chinese carry the burden of our history with us and the question of Western humiliation is always unconsciously inside us… Thus, we feel sensitive to any kind of slight and often have a very sharp reaction to perceived unfair treatment or injustices. On an emotional level we cannot help but associate treatment in the present with past injuries, defeats, invasions, and occupations by foreigners. There is something almost in our DNA that triggers autonomic, and sometimes extreme, responses to foreign criticism or put-downs."[119]

The Chinese experience may be a special case of the philosopher Avishai Margalit's[120] general observation that, "In remembering torture, the victim dwells on the humiliation, whereas in experiencing torture he dwells on the pain…we remember insults better than pains in the sense of reliving them."

As early as 1947, writing in his book, *China's Destiny*, Chiang Kai-shek, leader of the Nationalist Chinese opposed to the communists, stated, "During the past hundred years, the citizens of the entire country, suffering under the yoke of the unequal treaties which gave foreigners special 'concessions' and extra-territorial status in China, were unanimous in their demand that the national humiliation be avenged, and the state be made strong."[121]

Upon the formation of the People's Republic of China in 1949, Mao Tse-tung is said to have declared, "Ours will no longer be a nation subject to insult and humiliation. We…have stood up."[122] The power of the anecdote is in its survival. One of the most widespread slogans of 1997 was: "Celebrate Hong Kong's return, erase the National Humiliation."[123] A Chinese multivolume series is titled, "Do Not Forget the National Humiliation Historical Series."[124] After 1991, these issues were raised repeatedly in the "Patriotic Education Campaign."[125]

A central theme of the present book is revealed in China's emphasis on territorial integrity, as it was for Russia in Stalin's time, as we shall see. Chinese patriots have viewed China as having been "cut up like a melon."[126] Thus, a concern for territorial restoration and integrity has led to a dream "of reunifying China as a multiethnic state composed of *Han* (central Chinese), *Man* (Manchurians), *Meng* (Mongolians), *Hui* (Muslims), and *Zang* (Tibetans), as well as bringing

---

[119] Quoted in Schell 2008, 30.   [120] 2002, 119–20.   [121] Quoted in Schell 2008, 31.
[122] Quoted in Schell 2008. See also Gries 2004, 163, n 30 in which the power of this anecdote is understood not in its veracity but in its survival.
[123] Gries 2004, 52.   [124] Gries 2004, 70.   [125] Wang 2008.   [126] Schell 2008, 31 .

back into the fold of 'the sacred motherland' those parts of the old Chinese Empire that had either been pried loose by imperialist powers or had broken away during times of weakness. (Those included Hong Kong, Macao, Taiwan, the Spratly Island in the South China Sea, and the Diaoyu Islands near Japan. And, of course, it also meant holding onto Tibet and Xinjiang, whose peoples have long flirted with independence)."[127]

The loss of Chinese territory to Japan is especially emphasized. A volume in the "National Humiliation Historical Series" is titled, *Extraordinary Humiliation at Shimonoseki*, the name (and location) of the treaty ending the Sino-Japanese war of 1894–95 and yielding Taiwan, the Liaotung Peninsula and the Pescadores Islands to Japan. In the recent controversy between China and Japan over the Diaoyu (Senkaku) Islands, currently occupied by Japan, a book, *Be Vigilant Against Japanese Militarism*, declares, "Confronted by the Japan threat, China cannot give an inch... No Chinese should be willing or dare to relinquish sovereignty over Chinese territory, leaving a name to be cursed for generations."[128] At the same time, as we shall see, Mao relied heavily on Stalinist methods as precedents for the establishment of successful communist states.

Polarization

The ephemeral gain itself as a historical trajectory (see Figure 1.1) maps onto the human psyche in singular ways. In the mind's eye, it can be seen as a dichotomous condition in which gain is precipitously followed by a disastrous fall. A major consequence follows: first, the national or ethnoreligious experience is divided into two polarized conditions that can be summarized as exquisite and catastrophic. In the former, all was beautiful prior to the recent disaster, as it was in an earlier triumphal period prior to subordination. Sayyid Qutb, the pre-eminent theorist of radical Islam had just such a polarized view. Recalling the period of *jahiliyyah* as the state of ignorance prior to the advent of Islam (the triumphal period), "The callers of Islam should not have any superficial doubts in their hearts concerning the nature of *jahiliyyah* and the nature of Islam... Indeed, there is no Islam in a land where Islam is not dominant and where Shari'a is not established... There is nothing beyond faith except unbelief, nothing beyond Islam except *jahiliyyah*, nothing beyond truth except falsehood."[129]

Alas, according to Qutb, *jahiliyyah* as a form of subordination exists once again in the form of "apostate" rulers of Muslim lands too heavily influenced by Western ideas. He did not live to see the victory of the *mujahadin* over the Soviets in Afghanistan that would constitute a later ephemeral period after the 1991 Gulf War and the "occupation" of Saudi Arabia.

Just as the ephemeral gain in its stark contrast between ascendancy and defeat does not admit the possibility of gradualism or ambiguity, neither does the

---

[127] Schell 2008, 31.   [128] Quoted in Gries 2004, 123.   [129] Quoted in Jones 2008, 134.

consequent polarization. A rigid dichotomization follows, in which good must pursue and destroy evil. The rapidity of the latest transformation from gain to subordination beggars the imagination. How could this happen?

One answer is the presence of agents of evil directly responsible for the precipitous decline. This is the second consequence of the dichotomized international trajectory. Directing his remarks to terrorists of the extreme left, Ehud Sprinzak[130] remarked: "Individuals who are identified with the rotten, and soon-to-be destroyed, social and political order are depersonalized and dehumanized. They are derogated to the ranks of subhuman species. Dehumanization makes it possible for the radicals to be disengaged morally and to commit atrocities without a second thought. It bifurcates the world into the sons of light and sons of darkness, and makes the 'fantasy war' of the former versus the latter fully legitimate."

David Vital[131] recounts the experience of tsarist troops of the Volunteer Army in the midst of the Russian Civil War fighting the Bolsheviks:

> All ranks within it were politically united in their dedication to the re-establishment of the Autocracy and genuinely imbued with the connected, driving conviction that at the root of Russia's tragedy and their own political discomfiture as a military class lay the Jews. If their Russia was ever to rise again from the ashes in which it now languished, the Jews, so ran their common and exceedingly tenacious belief, needed to be punished, indeed destroyed… In the view of the thinking members of the Volunteer Army, there lay upon them a positive duty to rid Russia, and by extension Christian Europe generally, of "the Jew" – "the Jew" in general, that is to say, conceived generically and without regard to his or her actual sex, or age, or station in life, or political affiliation (if any at all).

In addition to perceptions of injustice and the feelings of anger, blame (including stereotypic judgments), fear of reversion, humiliation-shame, and other intense reactions to the losses entailed in the ephemeral gain, there may be the simple desire to maintain the feelings of elation, even exualtation at the moment of victory that are now vitiated by the later loss, suggesting that the earlier gain is now ephemeral. An intense desire to avoid or reverse the ephemeral can fuel the extremist response, for the descent from elation to subordination is precipitous. Indeed, Gabriele D'Annunzio, the behavioral prototype for Mussolini's fascism, as we shall see later, declared that the "constant feeding of one's own exaltation"[132] should somehow be captured and directed into the political arena. And Sir John Elliott,[133] remarking on the psychological impact of the Spanish Empire on its population within the metropole, with all its vicissitudes of territorial gain and loss, indicated that it was "so dramatic, and so overwhelming in its consequences, that it is not surprising if the mood of Castilian society in

---

[130] 2006, 165–6.   [131] 1999, 324–5.   [132] Quoted in Mosse 1966a, 15.
[133] 2009, 148.

the age of the Baroque oscillated violently between moments of exaltation and profound despair."

Summary of the three pathways

The path leading from humiliation-shame to anger is easily understood, as the Chinese case attests. In Chapter 15 on ethics and morality, a more personal instance drawn from Herodotus is also illustrative. A perception of injustice as another pathway leading to anger is also explicated clearly. Not so easily understood is the pathway from threat and fear of reversion to anger, yet as we shall see in the case of Poland after World War II, that pathway is important for understanding the unprovoked attacks by Poles on Jews returning to their homes after the defeat of the Nazis.

Each of the three pathways from the ephemeral gain requires a referent. Humiliation is frequently measured against an earlier period of triumph and glory occurring in a distant historical past, but also against a more recent time of gain. Shame can be manufactured, as in the adoption of new codes of conduct that make relations with other racial or other ethnoreligious ethnies "shameful." Injustice can be measured against a norm of "justice as fairness" or the freedom to pursue capabilities, but can also be magnified through the adoption of extreme national, racial, or religious interpretations of history in response to the dysfunction of the international setting, all in the service of national honor. And the threat and fear of reversion to an earlier subordinate condition is explicitly contained within the theory of the ephemeral gain. These pathways are shown in Figure 2.1 at the end of the following chapter, which explicates the final component of the theory – mortality salience.

Mortality Salience: Intimations of
the Corporeally Finite

This chapter establishes the connection between intimations of mortality, or mortality salience as it is known in the social psychological literature, and the rise of political extremism. Mortality salience is the companion variable to the ephemeral gain, whose pathways to extremism were explored in the preceding chapter. War is not only a clear processual incubator of violence, but ultimately can yield political extremism. World War I is the seminal event of the twentieth century, which, despite important antecedent events like the Russo-Japanese War of 1904–05 that will be explored elsewhere in this book, nevertheless exerted its unique and extraordinary impact.

On the whole, the immediate origins of European fascism are not in dispute. Virtually all major analysts of the etiology of this phenomenon agree that World War I was crucial.[1] Fundamental causes, or more precisely long-term processes, as well as ideational content tend to be disputed,[2] but the immediate importance of World War I is seldom contested. Reasons for this emerging consensus are not hard to find. Virtually all of the important fascist leaders of the interwar period experienced battle at the front, or were close to those who did. According to the cognitive psychologist, Seymour Epstein,[3] "Experientially derived knowledge is often more compelling and more likely to influence behavior than is abstract knowledge." Simply the return of large numbers of battle-hardened veterans could destabilize societies already exposed to significant economic, social, and especially political strains associated with maintaining the home front intact. For countries that lost the war, these strains would be magnified enormously.

But there is more than simply a general destabilizing impact. For countries that lost the war, or were part of a victorious coalition but were deprived of promised territory at the war's end (Italy), the consequences were severe. Men at the front, who saw their friends die violent deaths, or themselves had debilitating wounds inflicted upon them, would be infuriated at the sacrifice in vain. That fury could be mobilized by leaders with political agendas that appeared to address the major concerns of the angry war veterans. The first political organization headed by Mussolini after the war, and a direct precursor of the Italian

---

[1] E.g., Weber 1964; Payne 1995; Lyttelton 1966; Mann 2004; Paxton 2004.
[2] E.g., Gregor, 1979, 1999, 2005; Sternhell *et al.*, 1994; Laqueur 1996.   [3] 1994, 711.

fascist party, was called *fasci di combattimento*, or fraternities of combat, made up of war veterans and other nationalists.[4] As early as 1916, Mussolini advocated governance of Italy by a "*trenchocracy*, a new and better elite."[5] Fascists in Germany, Hungary, and Romania also were disproportionately involved in the war.

The Russo-Japanese War of 1904–05 and the even more consequential World War I and ensuing Civil War followed by the Russo-Polish War were to play a similar role in the rise of Russian extremisms of both left and right. The enormous numbers of Russian dead in these wars, followed by the widespread famine of the early 1920s, were to establish a mortality salience beyond measure. All of the leading Bolshevik protagonists, as well as their rightist counterparts, were to play leading roles in one or more of these conflicts. The mass murder of Jews and other presumed enemies of tsarism by the rightists during the Civil War was to be more than matched by the later depredations of Stalin.

A similar process occurred in the development of radical Islamism. The rise of al-Qaeda can be traced directly to the organization of veterans of the Afghan war against the Soviets.[6] According to Gilles Kepel,[7] "The dispersion all over the world, after 1992, of the jihadist-salafists formerly concentrated in Kabul and Peshawar, *more than anything else*, explains the sudden, lightning expansion of radical Islamism in Muslim countries and the West. These hardened veterans of the Afghan jihad excited the enthusiasm of zealots around the globe, who saw 'heavy blows' being struck at the 'godless' and the 'apostates.'" Osama bin Laden himself was one such veteran,[8] who, like Hitler and Mussolini, thought that he had distinguished himself on the battlefield. As the current war in Iraq winds down, the likelihood of international terrorism increases, with radical Islamists dispersing throughout the Middle East and elsewhere.[9]

At the same time, the cognitive polarization induced by the ephemeral gain (see the preceding chapter) is reinforced by the experience of fighting as the German *Frontkämpfer* (later to form the backbone of the *Freikorps*), Italian *squadristi*, Bolshevik Red armies, and radical Islamist jihadi groups, who together during their respective wars and thereafter, could develop common extreme worldviews. The years of common fighting, with its frequent lulls entailing group discussion to alleviate the boredom, provided ample opportunity for that initial polarization to evolve into something far more extreme than it was at the outset. Even without significant war involvement in the immediate past, groups within the Japanese military during the 1930s could evolve increasingly extreme positions in response to international events. A major finding across

---

[4] Bosworth 2002, 122; Paxton 2004, 5.

[5] Emphasis in original; quoted in Thompson 2008, 388; *trincerocrazia* in Italian, Bosworth 1998, 38.

[6] Andersen and Aagaard 2005.   [7] Emphasis added; 2002, 299.

[8] Bergen 2001; Gunaratna 2002; Burke 2003.   [9] Mazzetti 2006.

virtually all studies of group polarization is for the basic premise of the group at its founding to be reinforced by later discussion within the group.[10] Thus, moderate feminists, for example, following group discussion would take more militant stands on feminist issues.[11]

Mortality salience and worldview defense

But in addition to this shared war experience, there exists a powerful stimulus to extremism in defense of a particular worldview. It is called mortality salience by Jeff Greenberg, Tom Pyszczynski, and Sheldon Solomon, who have written widely on its impact. Mortality salience is understood by them to mean a height-ened awareness of mortality, typically induced by thoughts of one's death.

In their social psychological experiments, mortality salience has been shown to be powerful in its impact. The first such experiment[12] was conducted in Tucson, Arizona using twenty-two municipal court judges who volunteered to participate in a study of personality traits and bail decisions.

One group of judges was administered a questionnaire that asked them to write about: "(a) what will happen to them as they physically die, and (b) the emotions that the thought of their own death arouses in them."[13] The remaining judges in a control group did not receive this questionnaire. All of the judges were then given a hypothetical case in which they were asked to set bail for a prostitute who was claimed by the prosecutor to be a flight risk. The absence of established community ties led the prosecutor to oppose the granting of bail. Each of the judges was then asked to set bail for this defendant.

Despite the fact that judges are typically trained to be fair, and dispassionate (and in this sense rational) in their decision making, the average bond set in the mortality salience group was $455, but in the control group, $50. This is a huge difference, well beyond the need for any inferential measure of statistical significance.

More directly now, Jeff Greenberg *et al.*[14] tested the impact of mortality sali-ence on patriotism, a common worldview. American college students were asked to read essays in an apparently authoritative but fictional political sci-ence journal authored by an ostensible Nobel Prize-winning political scientist (actually two exist in real life, but both Elinor Ostrom and Herbert Simon won it in economics). One essay, a pro-American piece, acknowledged some mis-takes in US foreign policy but was generally positive and ended with: "In this country, the people and not the government will be the final judges of the value of what I have to say. That is what makes this country a great place in which to be a free thinker." An anti-American essay acknowledged some virtues of the American political system, but was mostly negative and ended with: "Morality

---

[10] Isenberg 1986.   [11] Myers 1978.   [12] Rosenblatt *et al.* 1989.
[13] Rosenblatt *et al.* 1989, 682   [14] 1990.

has absolutely nothing to do with our foreign policy. That's why the idea that the U.S. is a promoter of world democracy and freedom is a total sham."[15] The *violent* overthrow of the US government was also suggested. Likeability and knowledgeability of the author of each of the two statements was then evaluated by the students.

All participants responded more favorably to the pro-American than to the anti-American author, but those in the mortality salience condition diverged more sharply in their judgments. In that condition, the pro-American author was evaluated much more positively and the anti-American author much more negatively than in the control condition, where mortality salience was absent.

In a more recent volume, Pyszczynski, Solomon, and Greenberg[16] conclude that "this finding has become the most commonly replicated effect of thoughts of one's own demise, the prototypic demonstration of what we refer to as *world-view defense*: more positive evaluations of those who help validate one's world-view and more negative evaluations of those who challenge the validity of that worldview."

As one might expect, worldview defense can lead to intergroup prejudice. The embrace of people with similar worldviews can also be coupled with the derogation of those who hold different worldviews. Christian college students who were exposed to mortality salience tended to have more positive reactions to a description of another Christian college student than to a description of a Jewish student. In the control condition, without mortality salience, there was no difference in their evaluations of the two students.[17] And stereotypic think-ing, a hypothesized consequence of the anger induced by the ephemeral gain, is also enhanced by mortality salience.[18]

The findings of additional studies were consistent with these results. Under conditions of mortality salience (watching videos of deadly automobile acci-dents), American students tended to blame the auto manufacturer, but only if that manufacturer was Japanese.[19] In another study, social distance between German and Turkish participants was increased substantially under conditions of mortality salience. The control condition exhibited no increase in social dis-tance. This result is important because it demonstrates a *behavioral* consequence of mortality salience instead of the typical attitudinal response.[20]

A personality variable of interest is self-esteem. This is especially important since, as we have seen, the ephemeral gain (victory) induces an unstable self-esteem associated with a heightened probability of violence. As self-esteem can serve as an anxiety buffer, its effects were examined. When subjects had their self-esteem raised in an experimental condition, the effects of mortality salience were eliminated. Another iteration of this study found that disproportionately high self-esteem, as well as the induced effect of the need for worldview defense,

[15] Greenberg *et al.* 1990, 315.   [16] Emphasis in original; 2003, 51.   [17] Greenberg *et al.* 1990.
[18] Schimel *et al.* 1999.   [19] Nelson *et al.* 1997.   [20] Ochsman and Mathy 1994.

was diminished after the mortality salience induction.[21] Apparently, the stability of high self-esteem is crucial, for in its absence (that is an unstable self-esteem) violence is more likely to occur.

Finally, of the relevant findings of this research program, a belief in symbolic immortality (as in an afterlife, generational continuity, or a belief that one's work will live on after death[22]) has import here. In one element of the study, as one might expect, fear of death was found to correlate negatively with belief in symbolic immortality. In the second, the classic mortality salience induction[23] was found to yield higher bond assessments only for those in the low belief condition.[24] Thus, the impact of mortality salience was eliminated under conditions of high belief in symbolic immortality.

Yet the findings raise an important question concerning radical Islamists or any other extremists like Hindu Jaffna Tamils of the LTTE who may believe (or had believed) in an afterlife or reincarnation. Mortality salience may be mitigated by these belief systems. But if the belief system can be manipulated to justify acts of violence, as bin Laden, Zarqawi, or others like them have done, then mortality salience as a result of experience in war can be made consistent with the belief in symbolic or even real immortality. The writings of radical Islamists tend to interpret Islam in this fashion, after tortuously attempting to reconcile the wanton killing of civilians, even women and children, with the tenets of Islam. Here the impact of mortality salience on worldview defense, especially violent defense, is made consistent with religious belief as a major form of belief in symbolic immortality.

Two additional studies speak directly to the origins of extremism. In the first, when subjects were asked to evaluate political candidates as a function of leadership style, the charismatic leader was strongly preferred under conditions of mortality salience, while the leaders who were task-oriented or relationship-oriented (compassionate and sensitive to the needs of the public) were preferred under conditions of the absence of mortality salience.[25] Charismatic leaders are more prone to extremes, since many of the legislative and judicial obstacles to extremist behavior can be more easily subverted or removed under their aegis (e.g., Hitler). In the second study, Iranian students exposed to mortality salience were substantially supportive of martyrdom attacks, while those in a control condition without mortality salience were opposed to these attacks. This finding is consistent with another experiment in the same study in which American conservative college students exposed to mortality salience were more supportive of the use of extreme military force in support of US policy goals than were those in other experimental conditions.[26] A related finding is one obtained by Cohen et al.[27] in which mortality salience was found to strongly increase support

---

[21] Harmon-Jones et al. 1997.   [22] Lifton 1968.   [23] Rosenblatt et al. 1989.
[24] Florian and Mikulincer 1998.   [25] Cohen et al. 2004.
[26] Pyszczynski et al. 2006.   [27] 2005.

for George W. Bush in voting for the 2004 US presidential election. John Kerry was preferred in the control condition.

In a summary of Italian Fascism that could serve well as a generic explanation of its development, A. James Gregor[28] averred that, after his experience in World War I, "Mussolini was convinced that human beings, particularly when they found themselves facing special difficulties, would instinctively respond to confident leadership, authority, and hierarchical control – in an arrangement that might best be depicted as *military*" (emphasis in original). Further, "Mussolini was convinced that such arrangements, accompanied by dramatic ceremony and quasireligious liturgy, were essential to the achievement of purpose when a people is called to *sacrifice and protracted effort*."[29]

Finally, there exists the connection between mortality salience and fairness or equity. According to Kees Van den Bos,[30] "when people have been thinking about their own mortality they react more strongly to fairness of treatment than when they have not been thinking about this subject." This finding is important for establishing a further connection between mortality and the ephemeral victory. If people thought that losses in war led to an approximately fair outcome, as in Allied territorial gains after World War I, then extremism is much less likely to be adopted, as it was not in Great Britain and France. But if in a war leading to substantial losses of life and territory after an earlier gain, then the reaction to this loss of life and territory in the absence of fairness of this outcome would be far more intense, thereby increasing the likelihood of political extremism, as occurred in Germany after World War I.

Considerations of justice become paramount. Given interpretations of justice as fairness[31] or justice as the freedom to pursue capabilities,[32] then countries that lost considerable territory, like Germany at Versailles, Italy (based on the 1915 Treaty of London), and Hungary at Trianon (1920), were reacting to the absence of international justice. Certainly, territorial loss after an immense loss of life can be easily understood as an injustice, as can a limitation on national capabilities. A reliance on national honor in the form of greatly increased autonomy from the international environment was a consequence. Fascism and Nazism were exemplars of this process, but as we shall see, even a particularistic national honor can be emphasized in the presence of perceived injustice.

Precipitants

In addition to the numerous earlier findings on the salience of mortality and its significance here in the explanation of political extremism (e.g., the role of international warfare), there is another reinforcing perspective. It emerges from the understanding of injustice as an unacceptable limitation on personal or national

---

[28] 2006, 44.   [29] Emphasis added.   [30] 2004, 170.   [31] Rawls 2001.
[32] Nussbaum and Sen 1993; Sen 2000.

autonomy, including restrictions on the pursuit of capabilities.[33] Death can be understood as the ultimate limitation. Beyond that event, concepts of autonomy or capability are rendered meaningless. Thus one would expect that the deaths of others, especially if perceived as unwarranted or incurred in a futile endeavor, can be a final spur to extremist action. We will shortly witness this process in the decision of young Moroccans to journey to Iraq for the sake of jihad, sparked by the knowledge that Iraqi Muslims were dying in a confrontation with the West.

World War I was a massive incubation of fascism, as well as communism as it evolved in the Soviet Union. It would be difficult to underestimate the influence of Mussolini's concept of "trenchocracy" on the rise of Italian Fascism, or Hitler's distinguished service on the blood-soaked Western front in the genesis of Nazism. The deaths of so many comrades at the front were decisive in the formation of the paramilitary Italian *squadristi* and German *Freikorps* as progenitors of European extremism. Massive human losses were also salient in Russia during World War I and the subsequent Civil War, followed by the Russo-Polish conflict. The etiology of Stalinism certainly was not independent of this butchery.

Even the death of one person, however important, can yield consequences far beyond those envisioned by the perpetrator(s). Of course, the assassination of Franz Ferdinand, heir apparent to the throne of Austria-Hungary, is prototypical; the political implications of an interregnum (Franz Joseph, the Austro-Hungarian emperor, was aged) in the most unstable of the European empires was painfully apparent. Certainly, we cannot discount the impact of his brother's execution by the tsarist government on Lenin's later support of state terror, as we shall see in Chapter 5.

Another killing that sparked a conflagration was the death of an Israeli by Hamas rocket fire in the town of Nativot, deeper inside Israel than the former Hamas target of choice, the Israeli town of Sderot, close to Gaza. The location of the killing was near to the heart of Israel, as are Ashkelon and Ashdod, locations also struck by rocket fire. The implications for the sovereign control of Israeli territory were profound, enhanced here by mortality, and the 2008 Israeli incursion into Gaza then followed.

Less obvious in its consequences for outbursts of potentially extremist violence is the December 2008 killing of a 15-year-old boy by police in Athens. This event led to riots in Thessaloniki, Istanbul, London, Paris, Rome, Berlin, Madrid, Barcelona, Bordeaux, Copenhagen, Seville, and Nicosia, the Cypriot capital. Clearly, a common disaffection among the youth of many cities was triggered by the killing of Alexandros Grigoropoulos by the police, the agents of authority. But without that introduction of mortality and in one so young, it is extremely unlikely that these disturbances would have occurred.

---

[33] Nussbaum and Sen 1993; Sen 2000.

Necessity for the two components of the theory

Which of the two, the ephemeral gain or mortality salience appears to be more consequential for understanding the rise of political extremism? Answers can be found in two quarters. First, in the case of the ephemeral *victory*, mortality salience is found intrinsically, for the losses at the end of the process always include dead fighters or murdered innocents. The ephemeral victory is a special case of the ephemeral gain. Gains can occur without battles entailing the loss of life, indeed as will be seen later in the analysis of the Tamil gain within the Ceylonese (later Sri Lankan) civil service prior to 1956. The victory in war or other forms of political violence entails death, and to that extent both analytic components – the ephemeral gain and mortality – are incorporated within the ephemeral victory.

But what of the ephemeral gain, which in itself does not *necessarily* imply mortality? Can this analytic condition be said to be more consequential than mortality salience alone? The case of Sri Lanka will demonstrate that the formation of extremist groups did not begin until *after* the killing began, suggesting the requirement of mortality to spur the ephemeral gain into the extremist condition. Neither condition alone will yield extremist behavior. Mortality alone certainly does not yield extremism; if mortality would have that consequence, then most parts of the world would be perpetually governed by extremists. The ephemeral gain itself does not yield extremism, as evidenced by the dissolution of the British Empire after its victory in World War II. That decline was not precipitated by a war entailing death, but by the diplomacy of the post-World War II period that saw Britain unable to maintain its grip economically and politically on its former imperial realm. Consequently, political extremism in Britain was not to be expected and did not occur.

The interface between individual and nation

When considering the link between the individual and the nation – an important interface in this analysis – an additional dimension appears. The worldview of the individual not only consists of a set of ethical, religious, or political beliefs that might appear to be threatened by intimations of mortality, but national continuity also might appear to be at risk. Major wars that take on existential overtones as the combat proceeds and intensifies are cases in point. Virtually all extremists, especially fascists and radical Islamists, have expressed deep concerns about their respective national conditions (the 'umma understood here as a nation of the Islamic faithful). And communists, of course, at least nominally expressed continuing concerns about the future of the working class.

The chasm between pre-war national optimism and post-war pessimism subsequent to the loss has profound implications. Where once the national future *finally* appears to be secure and on track to further accomplishments, whether through additional territorial aggrandizement or domestic economic achievements, that future is now cast in serious doubt. And after repeated ephemeral gains, these fears are amplified considerably. In other words, after repeated failures to establish the desired level of national continuity, each additional failure becomes even more threatening, for the earlier ones were still in mind, especially if the time intervals between the ephemera are short. And as we saw in the preceding chapter, according to the cognitive neuroscientist, Daniel Schacter,[34] "Reminders of difficult experiences can slow the normal fading of painful emotions over time."

Mortality salience therefore not only extends easily to concerns about the national welfare, but also intersects with the ephemeral gain as a harbinger of threats to national continuity. Mortality can sensitize an individual to the ephemeral condition of his nation, thereby intensifying the consequences of the ephemeral gain. The greater the identification between the interests of an individual and those of the nation, the more likely the onset of extremism for that individual when mortality has been made salient in the presence of an ephemeral gain. As we shall see, German history will provide a fruitful area of inquiry. Nazism, of course, demanded that the line between the interests of the individual and the Nazi state be blurred, even erased.

A case in point

Although mortality salience has not been theorized to be a continuous variable in the research of social psychologists, having been generally induced as a binary experimental condition (either the subject is in that condition or not), the *extent* of the salience can be important. It may matter significantly if the mortality of concern is remote geographically or temporally, or very close to home in space and time. Of course, the returning battlefield veterans of defeated countries in World War I are cases in point, having experienced the death of comrades at the front or recovering from serious wounds.

Yet there can be other sources of mortality salience that are nearby and palpable. The experience of young North African Muslims traveling to participate in the Iraqi insurgency after the Madrid bombings is instructive, for it suggests that the salience of nearby death made the war in Iraq of much greater concern and resulted in their participation. The proximity of Spain to North Africa was a factor in that salience, but as we shall see, even more important was the participation in the Madrid bombings of townspeople from Tenouan in northern Morocco that attracted the soon-to-be jihadis from that town. (I use the term *jihadi* to signify active radical Islamist combatants or suicide terrorists, while the term radical Islamist is reserved for the larger group consisting either of active fighters or supporters within the radical Islamist movement.) Mortality of

---

[34] 2001, 165.

a more intense variety is here found within the reinforced ephemeral victories that will be described shortly. The decision to wage jihad can reveal the intimate connection between the ephemeral gain and mortality in their dual impact – the ephemeral victory – yielding extremist behavior.

In one of the more extensive microanalyses of jihadi origins, Andrea Elliott[35] seeks to understand why a small neighborhood in the northern Moroccan city of Tetouan gave rise to a disproportionate number of radical Islamists. Her answers stem mostly from the importance of friendship and worship networks in the town suggested by earlier analyses such as that of Marc Sageman.[36] Yet in her narrative, evidence is found for the transformative importance of the conjunction of nearby death and a perceived ephemeral gain(s). Her question of disproportional participation is rendered here as: Why did a group of typically disinterested North African Muslims seek to wage jihad in a distant country, not typically associated in any meaningful way with the Maghreb, especially its western portion?

The Madrid bombing of March 2004 was the transforming event. Jamal Ahmidan and four friends from the neighborhood of Jamaa Mezuak in Tetouan, along with an Algerian and a Tunisian, were implicated in the train bombings of March 11. The attacks were deadly, leaving 191 dead and over 1,800 injured. On April 3, the police surrounded the building in which the conspirators were hiding. Upon a forcible entry by the police, a huge explosion took the lives of the seven terrorists along with a policeman, apparently the result of a mass suicide. Examination of the debris revealed plans for future attacks, including suicide belts. The impact of these events on future jihadis in Iraq would soon be felt.

Four of the five young Moroccan subjects of Elliott's narrative who would soon leave for Iraq were Hamza Akhlifa, Younes Achbak, and the brothers Bilal and Muncif Ben Aboud. According to Elliott,[37] "Before the Madrid bombings in March 2004, Hamza, Younes, and the Ben Abouds would chat casually about the day's news. Their attention drifted from topic to topic. Sometimes it was soccer; sometimes politics. *But after the bombings they became consumed by one subject: the war in Iraq…* The friends became obsessed with the war. They traded details of the day's news, stirring the anger in one another. They were outraged by the graphic deaths they saw on television and by the American contractors they heard were profiting from the occupation."

Muncif Ben Aboud, a superb student and by far the most accomplished among the future jihadis, also perceived the potential for future loss. According to a relative, Muncif thought, "If they do not have someone to help them, maybe this will happen to all Muslims. Maybe if Iraq doesn't have sovereignty, Morocco will be the next country invaded."[38]

---

[35] 2007.   [36] 2004.   [37] Emphasis added; 2007, 79.   [38] Elliott 2007, 79.

The young Moroccans now began to pray at the same mosque, where they met the fifth radical Islamist, Abdelmunim Amakchar Elmamrani, who was to join them in Iraq. Younes left for Syria in June 2006, followed by Muncif, Bilal, and Hamza in July. Abdelmunim left in September. Bilal and Hamza apparently did not make it to Iraq, having been detained in Syria for possible extradition back to Morocco for trial. Muncif, Younes and Abdelmunim were probably killed in Iraq.

It is uncertain, of course, if the killing of 191 Spaniards in March 2004, or the later apparent mass suicide of the conspirators in April was most consequential in inducing mortality salience among the travelers to Iraq. One or another, or both could have been influential. But the fact that five of the seven Madrid conspirators and one of its two leaders, Jamal Ahmidan, hailed from the Jamaa Mezuak neighborhood of Tetouan, and were possibly even known to these later jihadis, in itself could have been decisive. The proximity of death in space and time makes the mortality more salient. As Andrea Elliott makes clear, the jihadist sentiment dates only from the period after the Madrid bombings and apparent mass suicide. And the later jihadis did not travel to Madrid or some other European location, but chose Iraq, where ephemeral victories were already being played out.

A similar case

Another case in point is that of an 18-year-old Pakistani named Mudasar, who journeyed to Afghanistan and became a suicide bomber. Although intensely religious and deeply concerned about the "martyred people of Afghanistan"[39] after the US invasion, it was the *immediacy* of the killing that sparked Mudasar's political engagement. "In January 2006, the Americans maneuvered a Predator drone across the border into Pakistan and fired a missile at a building they thought contained Ayman al-Zawahiri, al-Qaeda's deputy leader. The missile reportedly missed Zawahiri by a couple of hours, but it killed his son-in-law and several other senior al-Qaeda members. A number of civilians died as well, including women and children. Television footage from the scene, showing corpses lying amid the rubble, sparked protests across Pakistan."[40] More on that shortly.

Presence of the ephemeral gain and mortality

Important here is the ephemeral victory perceived by many Muslims after the successful bin Laden-organized attacks of 9/11. Andrea Elliott[41] reports on the prevailing attitudes toward bin Laden of the residents of Jamaa Mezuak, in

---

[39] Filkins 2008, 116.   [40] Filkins 2008, 116.   [41] 2007, 73.

northern Morocco, expressed by a "spunky" 13-year-old, among other boys. "He's very courageous. Nobody did what he did. He challenges the whole world. He even challenges George Bush." In a similar vein but with more determination, Jaber, the brother of the Madrid bombing organizer, Jamal Ahmidan, quoted Jamal, "The soldiers of bin Laden are soldiers of God. Because the world was looking for them" – "And couldn't find them," said another brother.[42]

This victory, albeit limited to tall, symbolically important buildings and a militarily important building, including their inhabitants, was now imperiled by the invasion of Iraq and the threat to capture bin Laden in Afghanistan or in the tribal Pakistani borderlands. Much as Mohammed Atta leading the 9/11 attack was influenced by the ephemeral victory of the Chechens defeating the Russians in 1996, followed by a new Russian occupation in 2000, so too were the soon-to-be Iraqi jihadists influenced by the apparent success of the 9/11 attacks and the renewed threats to bin Laden and al-Qaeda.

It is worth considering the extent to which the events of 9/11 indeed constituted a victory. These attacks can be compared with another surprise attack, and one that is widely considered a victory. The Japanese air assault on Pearl Harbor in 1941 was also thoroughly unexpected and revealed the weak American defenses of that period. Although the Japanese attack yielded mostly military casualties and the destruction of military targets, the loss of human life actually was less than that of 9/11. Both attacks achieved their respective goals. The US battleship fleet destroyed at Pearl Harbor was a deterrent to Japanese expansion in the South Pacific, while the destruction of the World Trade Center had enormous symbolic value for the radical Islamists. Now they had shown that the attempted destruction of 1993 was merely a dress rehearsal for the far more consequential events of 9/11, and they had demonstrated the vulnerability of the world's only superpower. The fact that bin Laden still eludes capture or death also casts a victorious glow around the event.

The importance of the combination of ephemeral gains (in this case two) and mortality yielding ephemeral victories is emphasized. The first of these ephemeral victories is that of the *mujahadin* in Afghanistan over the Soviets beginning in 1986, followed by the "occupation" of Saudi Arabia by Christian and Jewish soldiers and the defeat of Iraq in the first Gulf War (1991). The second ephemeral period was framed by the successful attacks of 9/11 followed by the fall of Afghanistan and then Iraq in 2003. What were remote events to these residents of Tetouan in northern Morocco, suddenly became salient through the Madrid bombings and deaths, indeed martyrdom of their townspeople. Jihad was extended to the Middle East where al-Qaeda and other jihadists central to the ephemeral victories were prepared to accept them. Through the mortality of both the Spanish victims and their murderers, these ephemeral victories were now seen as their own by the young latter-day jihadis of Tetouan.

---

[42] Quoted in Elliott 2007, 76.

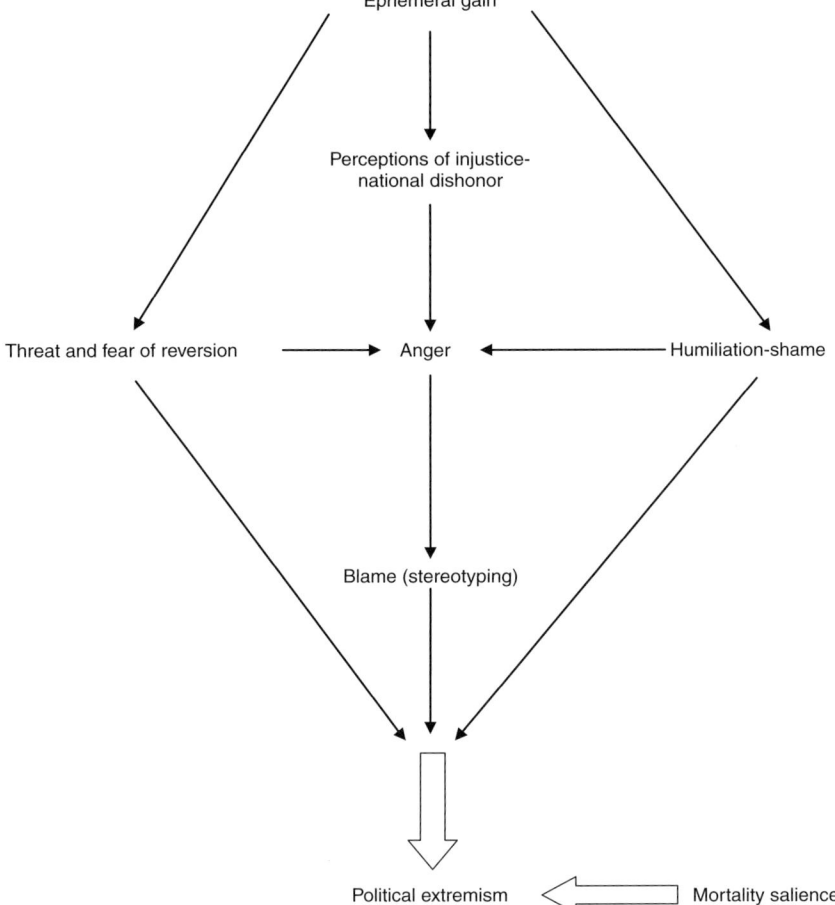

Figure 2.1: The model

Our young Pakistani jihadi, Mudasar, also was exposed to the ephemeral victory of 9/11, followed by the successful invasion of Afghanistan and its own death toll. The victorious Americans had even ventured into Pakistan in pursuit of the displaced leaders of al-Qaeda, yielding additional dead, including civilians.

Summary of the theory

Figure 2.1 summarizes the theory. Political extremism is suggested to be a consequence of an initial ephemeral gain that leads to three possible pathways: (1) the threat and fear of reversion, (2) perceived injustice leading to anger, followed by blame, including stereotyping of the "other," and (3) humiliation-shame. These paths to extremism may occur concurrently in some cases, whereas in others a single path may dominate to the virtual exclusion of others. However, the latter instance of single-pathway dominance is relatively rare. In most cases, at least two of the pathways will combine to yield the outcome of political extremism. Because of its enormity, the onset of extremist behavior generally will require the simultaneous occurrence of two or more sources, as Theda Skocpol[43] originally discovered in her analysis of social revolutions, and also extraordinary occurrences.

The second major component is mortality salience, which is independent of the ephemeral gain, but nevertheless is required to establish the ephemeral victory. Specific pathways are suggested for the ephemeral gain because its consequences have not been explored elsewhere. Mortality, on the other hand, can occur in myriad ways that do not require detailed presentation here. All that is needed is that the mortality be politically salient. Hence, the larger double arrows appear just prior to the occurrence of political extremism.

Yet, in a larger sense, the structural components of the overall theory are related. Although the two theoretical roots of the ephemeral victory stemmed from entirely different literatures, a connection exists that will be made more explicit in the introduction to Chapter 15. Temporal human existence clearly incorporating mortality is itself ephemeral. Any political reminder of that ephemerality is bound to be salient, especially when national existence has been made to appear ephemeral. Here, the strong identification between individual and nation comes into play. Intimations of the politically and corporeally finite merge.

[43] 1979.

3

Cases

How does one test the theory of ephemeral gains systematically? Three strategies are adopted in identifying cases for analysis. First, a systematic method of selection will be based on the principal independent variable, the ephemeral gain or victory.[1] This involves a diachronic process for each case, including at least one loss and a prior victory, as well as earlier subordination. We begin with an examination of interstate wars involving territorial transfer as a major outcome of lost wars. Given the theory specifying subordination, then gain preceding later loss (see Figure 1.1), the possibility of prior gain will be examined for all European cases beginning in 1807, the nadir of Prussian fortunes prior to its expansion leading to the unification of Germany in that century. Later losses will be identified for the period 1894–1997, the last year that data appear in the source.

Second, after World War II, especially toward the end of the twentieth century, transnational movements emerged facilitated by new and powerful forms of global communication. Cross-border identifications among affine populations have intensified in recent years because of the growth of various forms of mass communication, the internet constituting one example, the Al-Jazeera Arabic-language television station providing another. Interstate war no longer was the only vehicle for societal gains and losses. Conflicts stemming from transnational processes in the post-World War II period will be examined.

Finally, comparisons with cognate instances of mass murder *not* stemming directly from the ephemeral gain will be introduced. This is a form of paired comparison to test the limits of the theory's explanatory power. Obvious cases are found in the realm of the rampaging military.

The ephemeral gain in war

Hence, two lists of interstate war outcomes will be compiled, one ending just prior to the end of World War II, and the other thereafter; these dates span 1894–1944 and 1945–1997. The opening year was chosen to approximate the beginning of the modern period of warfare, with the inclusion of Japan as an

---

[1] For a general treatment of case studies, see George and Bennett 2005. For additional, wide-ranging issues of political methodology, see Box-Steffensmeier, Brady, and Collier 2008.

emerging great power. The year 1944 was chosen to end this period because it was clear by this time which countries were to be the winners and losers in World War II. Using 1943 as an alternate break point made no difference in the case selection outcome.

The Correlates of War (COW) Interstate Wars (version 3.0) was the initial data set examined and compared with a listing of territorial transfers (1900–2000[2]). This led to the classification of war outcomes for countries experiencing at least two interstate wars involving territorial transfer during the two periods 1894–1944 and 1945–1997, approximately a century in length, essentially the Century of Extremes in Hobsbawm's treatment.

Three categories emerged: (1) countries that never experienced territorial loss as a result of interstate war in this overall period, (2) those that had one loss alternating with a victory, and (3) countries with two or more consecutive losses in war involving territorial transfers, separated by at least 5 years of peace in order to allow for the possibility of an extremist government to emerge between the two wars. If a loss occurred during the earlier time period (1894–1944) without any intervening victory, then one additional loss in the second period (1945–1997) counted as a consecutive loss. These categories are shown in Table 3.1.

Examination of the table reveals, unsurprisingly, that the United States and Great Britain have never relinquished state territory in time of war. Japan is also included in this category during the first time interval, but not in the second. The story of this transition will occupy much of Chapter 12 on the rampaging military. Victories can be muted, even transformed into perceptions of loss (or "mutilated victories") as we shall see in the case of Italy, and later Japan. If not for the 1941 Yugoslav defeat in World War II and the direct German occupation of the Serbian portion of Yugoslavia, that country might have remained in the first column of the table as the result of its earlier successive victories. Here too, this transition is of interest, especially in its impact on the later Serbian extremist behavior during the recent intra-state wars of Yugoslav succession.

Clearly the center column is the location of candidate countries for the ephemeral gain yielding political extremism. (China in the third column had the Stalinist template for Mao to adapt and utilize without an ephemeral gain. Effectively, the choice of this template was to be a direct communist response to the perceptions of injustice and humiliation engendered by China's losses.)

Europe after World War I

Drawn from the center column of Table 3.1, Table 3.2 below effectively locates potential extremism in Europe during the first time period (1894–1944), with the partial exception of the Ottoman Empire (analyzed in Chapter 13), which was only partly located in Europe. With only one exception, Greece, the

---

[2] Tir 2006.

Table 3.1 *Countries experiencing two or more interstate wars involving territorial loss, 1894–1997*[1]

No Losses	Alternating Gains[2] and Losses	Two or More Successive Losses[3]
	1894–1944	
United States	Germany	Austria-Hungary[4]/Austria
United Kingdom	Ottoman Empire	Bulgaria
Japan	Russia/Soviet Union	China
	Greece	
	Italy	
	Hungary[5]	
	Poland[6]	
	France	
	Serbia/Yugoslavia	
	Romania[7]	
	1945–1997	
Israel	Japan	Germany[8]
	India[9]	Hungary[10]
	Pakistan	Egypt
		Iraq
		Syria

1. Gains are measured from 1807, the nadir of Prussia's territorial extent in the nineteenth century, after which the Prusso-German expansion began.
2. The data source is the Correlates of War (COW) Interstate Wars data set (version 3.0). Countries listed are based on participation in two or more wars.
3. Separated by at least 5 years of peace to allow for the possibility of the formation of extremist groups after the first loss. Wartime generally does not allow additional political movements to develop.
4. Austria-Hungary ceased its imperial existence in 1919 and was transformed into successor states, of which only Hungary and Serbia/Yugoslavia experienced extremism. Neither is Belgium included because of its peripheral importance, especially in World War II. Austria's successive territorial losses were first, the necessity to form a dual monarchy in 1867 after the losses to Prussia in 1866 and, second, World War I. The exceptional status of Bosnia-Herzegovina is treated in footnote 24 below.
5. Hungary's earlier gain stems from its emergence as an equal participant with Austria in the Austro-Hungarian Empire in 1867, especially after the bloodletting of 1848 that reinforced Hungarian subordination. Its loss occurred at the end of World War I.

Notes to Table 3.1 (*cont.*)

6. Poland's loss occurred at the start of a major war – World War II – that did not allow extremist groups to form during the German occupation. However, extreme Polish nationalism did express itself violently at the end of the war, as will be seen in Chapter 10.

7. Romania's territorial gain in 1919 was mostly surrendered to Hungary and the Soviet Union in 1940.

8. If a loss occurred in the second time period after a preceding loss in the first, it was counted as a consecutive loss. The same principle applies to alternating gains and losses.

9. India gained territory in Kashmir as a result of the 1947–48 war with Pakistan, but lost a bit of territory in the Rann (salt marsh) of Kutch as a result of the 1965 war. However, because of the minuscule territorial gain by Pakistan in that war, it was seen as a "mutilated victory" (like Italy and Japan) after the stellar performance of the Pakistani air force and armor early in the war. COW records the 1965 war as a loss for India, but one without much significance for India in light of the failure of Pakistan to gain any territory in Kashmir, the principal Pakistani objective. Pakistan of course lost East Pakistan, now Bangladesh, in 1971.

10. Hungary's successive losses are the 1919 war between Hungary and the states allied against it, and World War II.

European countries in the table (drawn from the center column of Table 3.1) experienced substantial political extremism.

Fascism, proto-fascism, and communism

Examining the most recent gains and losses of the fascist, proto-fascist, and communist states, in all instances these losses were found to be preceded by gains, and still earlier, by subordination to other political entities. Unifications of Germany and Italy in themselves were giant leaps in the expansions of authority space, after the earlier limitations on their authority as the result of foreign occupation (Italy) and/or small state factionalism (Germany) that allowed for French domination, especially in the West. The rate of German economic growth was outstanding after unification in 1871, bettered only by the United States in this time period. Between 1871 and 1890, Otto von Bismarck, the German chancellor, was at the heart of European diplomatic activity, serving as the "honest broker" at the crucial (for Southeastern Europe) Congress of Berlin in 1878. Afterward, Germany continued in its central role within European diplomatic activity.[3]

---

[3] Albrecht-Carrié 1958.

Italy, after unification in 1870, also progressed very rapidly both economically and politically, and now was counted among the great powers of Europe for the first time since the height of Venetian power in the fourteenth to the sixteenth centuries.[4]

But all of the cases of governmental fascism considered here experienced territorial losses prior to their first entry of fascist government. The German experience was dramatic. If, as did many Germans, one measures the territorial losses from June 1918, when much of Eastern Europe and Ukraine, and portions of France and Belgium were under German and Austro-Hungarian authority, then the contraction would appear to be immense.[5] Eastern territory that had been German governed for nearly a century and a half now was to be handed over to newly independent Poland. The eastern border with Poland was to be one of the driving forces of German foreign policy until the invasion of Poland in September 1939. And reversal of these losses, in tandem with abrogation of the Treaty of Versailles that mandated them, would constitute the major Nazi political demand of the interwar period.[6]

Italy did not experience any direct territorial loss from its boundaries of 1914. However, territory promised to Italy in the Treaty of London of 1915 was not forthcoming at Versailles. According to that treaty, northern Dalmatia was to become Italian territory after the war, but was not granted to Italy at Versailles. Additionally, the city of Fiume, not granted in the Treaty of London, nevertheless became a burning issue after the November 1918 plebiscite of the ethnic Italian population in Fiume declared for union with Italy.[7]

When Fiume still was not granted to Italy at Versailles, so incensed was the nationalist Gabriele D'Annunzio, speaking of the "mutilated victory,"[8] that he and his followers entered Fiume with the intent of ultimately forcing its annexation. This irredentism was to be intensified by memories of the catastrophic military loss by Italy at Caporetto in October 1917, with German forces advancing to territory just north of Venice. A total of 294,000 soldiers having been captured, this was by far the most serious defeat that newly independent and unified Italy had ever experienced.[9] Thus, territory promised but not delivered would be seen as more of an insult and humiliation than would otherwise have been the case.

Interestingly, without an earlier period of subordination prior to its defeat of 1870–71, France behaved very differently from Germany upon her own defeat. Contrasting Germany's sudden collapse in 1918 with France's *levée en masse* in response to French defeat by the Prussians at Sedan in 1870, Wolfgang Schivelbusch[10] suggests that:

> The most important difference between the two was that the collapse of
> 1870 did not leave France in a free fall. France's safety net was its sense of

---

[4] Braudel 1984, 124–38.   [5] Evans 2004, 52–3.   [6] Evans 2004.
[7] Thompson 2008, 368.   [8] Knox 1996, 123.   [9] Knox 1996, 120.
[10] Emphasis added; 2003, 196–7.

national pride, which had developed over the course of two centuries of European hegemony. The vanquished Germans of 1918 lacked any comparable heritage. *The memories of centuries of national inferiority, supposedly relegated to the past by the victory of 1870–71, by the founding of the empire, and by forty years of power politics, now reappeared like an unwelcome guest on Germany's doorstep.*

The burden of the past helps explain the response to the news of German defeat. People reacted not with manly composure, as the heroic vision would have it, but with everything from bewilderment to literal paralysis and nervous breakdown.[11] France, however, did experience subordination to Germany after the defeat of 1871 and the loss of Alsace-Lorraine.

Having lost Alsace-Lorraine to the Germans in 1871, France regained that territory as a key victor of World War I. After the defeat of 1940, three-fifths of pre-war French territory was forfeited to German occupation, with the remainder constituting Vichy France as a formal neutral, but effectively an ally of the German war effort. Many of the ideas of Charles Maurras' proto-fascist[12] *Action française*, including non-democratic centralized control of the state, state-sponsored anti-Semitism, and a penchant for violence, were characteristic of the Vichy regime. French and Russian proto-fascism are developed in more detail in Chapter 4.

Hungary prior to World War I, and Romania after that war, boasted substantial gains. After subordination to Austria, in 1867 Hungary was admitted formally to equal participation with Austria through establishment of the Austro-Hungarian (Dual) Monarchy, also one of the European great powers. Hungarian territory now included portions of Croatia, Slovenia, Slovakia, Transylvania, and Bukovina.[13] Interestingly, one of the states to gain most from the post-World War I dismemberment of the Dual Monarchy was Romania. As of 1920, the territory of Romania doubled, absorbing Transylvania, Bessarabia, Bukovina, and Crişana.[14] Prior to 1878, Romania was incorporated within the Ottoman Empire.

Dismemberment of the Austro-Hungarian Empire at the end of World War I led to large swaths of territory being ceded to Romania, Czechoslovakia, and the Kingdom of Serbs, Croats, and Slovenes (soon to be called Yugoslavia) as stipulated by the Trianon Treaty of June 4, 1920. Accordingly, Hungary lost "71.4 per cent of her prewar territory, and 63.5 per cent of her population. (Of the 325,411 square kilometers that had comprised the lands of the Holy Crown, Hungary was left with only 92,963. Of the population of 20,886,486 [1910 census], Hungary was left with only 7,615,117.) Of the persons of Magyar tongue, no fewer than 3,200,000 became the subjects of Romania, Czechoslovakia, Yugoslavia, and Austria."[15] Many of them, especially those who had been in the

---

[11] Schivelbusch 2003, 196–7.   [12] Weber 1965a, 125; Nolte 1966, 26.
[13] Nagy-Talavera 2001, 85.   [14] Jelavich 1983, 122–4.   [15] Deák 1965, 372.

Hungarian military or civil service, fled to the now truncated Trianon Hungary and provided a strong stimulus to the formation of the Szeged fascist movement. The later loss of Hungarian territory to the westward-bound Soviet army in mid-1944 would act as a spur to the abandonment of Horthy's newly declared neutrality in the war, and the accession of the Arrow Cross government on October 16, 1944.[16]

Romania in 1940 lost Bessarabia and northern Bukovina to the Soviet Union in June, northern Transylvania to Hungary in August, and southern Dobrudja to Bulgaria in September.[17] These territories were substantial in size, equaling roughly one-third of Romania at that time. The particular reasons for these territorial transfers do not concern us here; the consequences, however, were immense. These losses were felt deeply by most Romanians, leading to an immediate increase in popularity of the Iron Guard and their entry into the government shortly thereafter.

Following subordination to the West indicated by the loss of the Crimean War (1856), the Russian gains from the 1877–78 Russo-Turkish War ceded by the defeated Ottomans amounted to: southern Bessarabia, Kars, Ardahan, and Batum (as a free port[18]). But as the first European great power to be defeated by a non-European one in the modern period, and with the loss of territory to Japan (southern half of Sakhalin Island and the Liaotung Peninsula[19]), Russia felt humiliated. The extent of that humiliation can be gauged by Stalin's victory address on the occasion of Japan's unconditional surrender on September 2, 1945:

> The defeat of the Russian troops in 1904 in the period of the Russo-Japanese War left grave memories in the minds of our peoples. It was a dark stain on our country. Our people trusted and awaited the day when Japan would be routed and the stain wiped out. For forty years have we, men of the older generation, waited for this day. And now this day has come![20]

Apparent exceptions

Austria

Although not appearing in the center column of Table 3.1, it is still appropriate to ask why Austria did not experience a home-grown governmental fascism as did Italy and especially Germany. After all, Austrian territorial losses after World War I were much greater than those of Germany, yet an overtly fascist party did not gain political power until after the *Anschluss* of 1938, accomplished by a German military invasion. Despite deep cultural commonalities with Germany, what did happen in Austria was quite different from events in Germany. After a political crisis led to the resignation of the Austrian parliamentary leaders in

---

[16] Nagy-Talavera 2001, 321.   [17] Jelavich 1983, 226.   [18] Mazour 1962, 303.
[19] Mazour 1962, 338.   [20] Quoted in Wolfe 1984, 279.

March 1933, the Christian Social leader, Engelbert Dollfuss, assumed full power, establishing a dictatorship based on his own party and the *Heimwehr* (home guard), a rough equivalent of the paramilitary *Freikorps*, a major source of Nazi recruits in Germany.[21]

However, "Though both Dollfuss and the Heimwehr leader Starhemberg had promised Mussolini late in 1933 that they would move toward 'fascism,' the Austrian regime developed a different profile... This represented among other things an attempt to realize the Catholic ideals of the recent papal encyclical *Quadragesimo Anno* (1931), which endorsed corporative forms of organization and representation for Catholic society."[22] Or as Mann[23] describes the Austrian dictatorship: "Though it drew some doctrines from Italian fascism, it most resembled the Franco [Spain] and Salazar [Portugal] regimes."

The major difference in etiology between the Austrian and German variants is to be found in the general absence of gain for Austrian society prior to World War I, especially in comparison with Germany.[24] Instead of the unification of Germany and its triumphal march to continental European leadership, or Hungary's joining Austria in the Dual Monarchy and governing an empire of its own, Austria had to relinquish power to the Hungarians, thereby experiencing a vastly truncated authority space. Thus, when the Austro-Hungarian Empire was dismantled after World War I there was widespread sentiment for an *Anschluss* with Germany even at that time and surprise, vividness, and the urge to act quickly in order to restore the status quo ante were decidedly absent.

Initially, few German speakers within the territory soon to be the Republic of Austria wanted to have a separate republic. Indeed, Article 2 of the 1918 constitution stated explicitly that German Austria is part of the German republic. "This declaration of loyalty to a German identity and to the union with the German republic was common to all political persuasions."[25] But the Allies at Versailles sought to limit German expansion, not endorse it, and so they insisted on the permanence of the Austrian state despite the wishes of the majority of its population.

It is the experience of earlier loss, not gain during this period prior to World War I, even to the extent of advocating state extinction upon further loss after World War I, which strongly distinguishes Austria from the extremist cases.

---

[21] Payne 1995, 248.   [22] Payne 1995, 249.   [23] 2004, 209.

[24] An exception is the administration of Bosnia-Herzegovina (hereafter abbreviated as Bosnia) as a result of the Congress of Berlin in 1878. However, this was not a territorial gain as the result of victory in war, but a consequence of diplomacy in Berlin that awarded Bosnia to Austro-Hungarian administration, but with formal sovereignty retained by the Ottoman Empire. Bosnia was annexed unilaterally by Austria-Hungary in 1908, but the ensuing crisis of that year and the assassination of the Austro-Hungarian heir to the monarchy in 1914 stemming from that annexation ultimately yielding dissolution of the empire in 1919, nullified any sense of gain as the result of the Bosnian imbroglio.

[25] Fellner 1981, 9.

Greece

Greece was part of the Ottoman Empire until 1832, did permanently gain territory in 1919 (western Thrace), yet did not develop a fascist regime despite its 1922 loss of some Anatolian territory occupied since 1919 in the Greco-Turkish War. The remaining, larger portion of Anatolian territory was lost in the fortunes of war. At most, Greece suffered the dictatorial rule of General Ioannis Metaxas starting in 1936. It was a military dictatorship like that of Franco's Spain. Indeed, during the period of governance by Metaxas, there was never any sign of his abandoning the traditional Greek alliance with Britain in favor of the fascist powers.[26] Extended discussion of the Greek exception is found in Chapter 11 on the Balkans.

Poland

Poland at first appears to be a candidate for extremism because of its alternating victory (1920) and defeat (1939). However, German occupation immediately after the defeat did not allow for any home-grown extremist movement to emerge. Nevertheless, as we shall see, extremism in the form of mass murder did emerge *after* World War II had ended. The mass murder of Polish-Jewish refugees returning from the Soviet Union requires explanation that can be found within the theoretical framework offered here.

Japan, India, Pakistan, and the Ottoman Empire

The four non-European powers in the second column are Japan, India, Pakistan, and the Ottoman Empire. The first two will be analyzed along with Indonesia as a cognate comparison of the rampaging military. Extremism in the Ottoman Empire, by the end of the nineteenth century a mostly non-European entity, will be analyzed in the chapter on genocide.

The third column

Bulgaria

Examining the third column of Table 3.1, Bulgaria generates interest because of its militaristic stance during the Balkan Wars and World War I, held in common with states like Serbia, later to be extremist. Formerly part of the Ottoman Empire, attaining autonomy in 1878 and independence in 1908, Bulgaria also experienced loss after World War I, specifically western Thrace to Greece and small border corrections to Serbia, at this time in Yugoslavia.[27] But this loss

---

[26] Clogg 1992, 119–20.   [27] Jelavich 1983, 123.

occurred after an earlier loss (not gain) in the Second Balkan War of June–August 1913, in which Bulgaria lost significant territories in Macedonia gained in the First Balkan War (October 1912–May 1913), and southern Dobrudja.[28]

Interestingly, in his exhaustive survey of fascism worldwide, Stanley Payne appears to have expected that the defeats and territorial losses of Greece (in 1922) and Bulgaria would have led to the mobilization of at least one significant fascist movement. Accordingly, "Bulgaria, like Greece…seemed to possess a number of the prerequisites for significant fascist mobilization. As the so-called Prussia of the Balkans, it had been at war almost continuously between 1912 and 1918, suffering great social and economic stress as well as loss of life. Defeated twice within five years, it was despoiled of territory after both the Second Balkan War of 1913 and World War I. Yet the only mass movement to emerge in post-war Bulgaria was the Agrarian Union – a peace movement par excellence."[29]

What Payne did not recognize was the importance of these losses within an earlier context of gains and still earlier subordination in order to yield the sur-prise, vividness, and emotional intensity that would lead to a call for urgent action in a Bulgarian fascist mass movement, which, of course, did not eventu-ate. Alternatively, as in the case of Greece, significant loss compensation for the state can deter the rise of fascism, as we shall see in the chapter on the Balkans.

As expected, Germany appears in the third column in the lower portion of the table, after having lost both World Wars I and II. Hungary also lost two con-secutive wars, that of Hungary versus Czechoslovakia and Romania (1919) and World War I. Bulgaria already had appeared in the third column during the ear-lier of the two time periods as the result of its losses in the Second Balkan War followed by World War I. Once again, Bulgaria was on the losing side in World War I, until its *volte face* in September 1944. Until 1949, China was not yet ruled by the revolutionary communist government that was later to stalemate the United Nations forces in Korea and win a hotly contested war with Vietnam, with no territorial transfers at its end. Hence, China appears in the top half of the third column, with its territorial losses to Japan in 1895 and 1932.

Table 3.2 presents these contrasts between earlier gains and later losses, as well as apparent exceptions prior to the rise of fascism, proto-fascism, and com-munism in Europe. *All* of these cases (except Austria) experienced subordin-ation prior to their gains; hence this earlier condition is not shown explicitly in the table because of its near-uniform occurrence.

---

[28] The loss here is that experienced at the end of World War I not that of the Second Balkan War just prior to World War I. Although Bulgaria experienced a brief territorial gain in the First Balkan War followed by loss in the Second, that loss was followed immediately by the start of World War I. Fascism must have an opportunity to take hold after a territorial loss and this was not possible during the enormous societal strains imposed by that war; Jelavich 1983, 99, 166; Shaw and Shaw 1977, 297.

[29] Payne 1995, 326.

Post-World War II and transnationalism

The three Arab states in the third column of Table 3.1 suggest two things: (1) Absent an ephemeral gain, Arab *governments*, on the whole, have not gone the way of fascism or communism in the extent of their genocidal extremism (excepting Hafez al-Assad's destruction of Hama in Syria and Saddam Hussein's genocidal acts in the Kurdish and Shi'a areas of Iraq). Sudan will later be treated as a separate case with its own ephemeral gain (Chapter 7). (2) We now have the basis of transnational Arab reaction to the Israeli victories of 1948–49 and 1956 that most likely provided an impetus to Sayyid Qutb's writings in Egypt and the start of contemporary radical Islamism. The Israeli victories of 1967 and 1973 (both occurring after Qutb's death) of course accelerated this pattern. Thus, a major extension of the findings emerging from the COW Interstate Wars data leads to an analysis of radical Islamism. Of course, fascism and communism will also be analyzed at length.

Radical Islamism is not the only transnational phenomenon of interest. Communism, as we saw, is another, and there are transnational elements in the spread of fascism, but somewhat less so than the other "isms." Therefore, all of the countries in the second and third columns will be analyzed in one form or another in the succeeding chapters.

Two additional cases of transnationalism will be identified. One is, in part, a consequence of the nexus between the communist and Islamic worlds, much as was the highly consequential 1979–1989 war in Afghanistan. This is the extended government massacre of Indonesian communists and suspected sympathizers in 1965. The strong Islamic (and Hindu on Bali) reaction to the threat of domestic communist rule in cooperation with Communist China is one element, but another equally important factor is the ephemeral gain of Indonesia in its region, especially in its relations with Malaysia, and with Malaysia's principal supporter, the United Kingdom, as we shall see. The COW Militarized Interstate Disputes (MID) data suggest the importance of this regional context in the form of at least three serious disputes rising to the level of the display of force against neighboring countries (Japan, Malaysia), and the United Kingdom as the principal supporter of Malaysia. Territory here was at issue.

Another type of transnationalism appears in the form of identical ethnicities residing among three neighboring countries, Rwanda, Uganda, and Burundi. The MID data suggest the importance of this additional transnational element in the form of a dispute between Rwanda and Uganda rising to the level of the use of force after the invasion of Rwanda by the predominantly Tutsi Rwandese Patriotic Front (RPF), initially based in Uganda and largely English speaking. Territorial gain by the RPF was a critical factor leading to the genocide of Rwanda's Tutsis, as was Burundi's massacre of Hutus prior to the RPF invasion and the subsequent Rwandan genocide.

Table 3.2 *Gains and losses of extremist cases in Europe and apparent exceptions*

	Fascist Italy	Germany	Hungary	Romania	Proto-Fascist France	Russia
Gains*	Unification (completed 1870) Treaty of London (1915; South Tyrol, Trentino, Trieste, Istria, Fiume, northern Dalmatia)	Unification (1871)	Formation of Dual Monarchy (1867)	Doubling of territory (1920; Transylvania, Bessarabia, Bukovina, Crişana)	Versailles (1919; Alsace-Lorraine)	Congress of Berlin (1878; southern Bessarabia, Kars, Ardahan, and Batum [as a free port])
Losses**	Caporetto (1917) Versailles (1919; Fiume, northern Dalmatia)	Versailles (1919; West Prussia [most], Danzig, Eupen, Malmedy, N. Schleswig, Upper Silesia [part])	Trianon (1920; Transylvania, Slovakia, Ruthenia, Croatia, Slovenia, Banat) Territorial losses to Soviets (1944)	Territorial cessions (1940; Bessarabia, Transylvania [northern], Bukovina [northern], Dobrudja [southern])	Defeat (1940; 3/5 of pre-war territory, Alsace-Lorraine)	Portsmouth (1905; south Sakhalin Island, Liaotung Peninsula)

	Apparent exceptions		
	Austria	Greece	Bulgaria
Gains*	See footnote 24	Neuilly (1919; western Thrace)	See footnote 28
Losses**	Versailles (1919; Bohemia, Moravia, Tyrol, Carniola, southern Poland, Galicia, and all of Hungary)	Defeat (1922; all of occupied Anatolia)	Neuilly (1919; western Thrace, small border concessions)

*Latest gains prior to losses.
**In 1900–45 (Europe).

Both the Indonesian and Rwandan conflicts with their transnational origins are also included among the highest-intensity mass murders of the post-World War II era, approximately 500,000 in Indonesia, and 800,000 in Rwanda.[30] As we shall see, the Indonesian case will serve as a cognate comparison with two other instances of the rampant military – Japan and Pakistan – as will the Rwandan genocide supplement the Holocaust and genocide of the Armenians in the Ottoman Empire, shown in the second column, consisting of the most vulnerable countries to extremism stemming from the ephemeral gain.

At the same time, the shadow of the present will be analyzed briefly in three cases of the rampant military that have different origins from the ephemeral gain as a coincidence between the shadows of the past and of the future. These cases are the Congo, Guatemala, and Afghanistan, which, in one form or another, experienced regional spillover of neighboring violence. They will establish the limits of the theory's applicability.

India presents a special case, for it is unique in its earlier history of increasing ascendancy of Hindus over Muslims within the British Raj, signified by the independence efforts of the Hindu-dominated All-India Congress Movement preceding the formation of the All-India Muslim League. Thus, the pattern for India is not that of Figure 1.1 (subordination, gain, and loss), but an inverted one in which the earlier ascendancy within the Raj is then followed by the victorious incorporation of most of Kashmir. The narrow defeat by Pakistan in 1965 (it is recorded as such in the COW Interstate Wars data) leading to a small territorial loss in the mostly barren Rann (salt marsh) of Kutch, was relatively insignificant from India's perspective. No Indian territory in Kashmir – Pakistan's target – was lost. This defeat was to be followed by the resounding victory over Pakistan in 1971. Pakistan of course illustrates the pattern suggested in Figure 1.1, as will be seen in Chapter 12.

In contrast, the formation of the Liberation Tigers of Tamil Eelam (LTTE) in Sri Lanka, another South Asian country, indeed conforms to the pattern of the ephemeral gain. This group also arose in part as the result of transnational processes between the state of Tamil Nadu in India, where the LTTE fighters were first trained, and Sri Lanka.

Clearly, the period between the two world wars of the twentieth century was extraordinarily fertile for the rise of extremism. Fascism, communism (especially in its Stalinist form), even the basis for radical Islamism, burgeoned during this period. Fascism as the most widespread form of extremism during this period will be analyzed first, followed by communism, and radical Islamism in the five succeeding chapters.

---

[30] See Chapters 12 and 13, respectively.

PART II

The Secular "Isms"

4

Fascism

The concept of fascism has a long and tortuous history. In its descriptive mode it has been used to characterize a set of European countries during the interwar and World War II periods. In its pejorative form, it has been used to condemn anyone vaguely associated with what is typically called "the right," even if the targets of the accusation are simply centrist liberals. Supporters of the US war in Vietnam, and even to some extent the wars in Afghanistan and Iraq, come to mind.

But fascism also has had a conceptual history that is fairly clear in its contours and logically consistent in its development.[1] A logical consistency in development as understood by analysts does not imply that logic or rationality were especially valued in the theory or practice of fascism, as we shall see.

After discussing several of the more prominent definitions, commonalities among the four cases of European fascist movements that actually achieved governmental power during the interwar period – Italy, Germany, Hungary, and Romania – will be presented. Germany and Italy, as the largest and politically most important, will be emphasized. As we saw in the introductory chapter, the focus here is on the leaders who form the extremist groups, but the only cases analyzed are those in which the ephemeral gain was sufficiently robust to generate a following large enough to ensure capture of the government. Thus, the only fascist movements to be incorporated here are those that experienced some period of state governance. Proto-fascism in France and Russia will also be discussed because of its later impact on the rise of fascist regimes. Excluded are several cases that, despite conventional understandings, were only marginally fascist. Spain and Portugal had autocratic governments during the interwar period that had at most a fascist patina. Austria presented a form of Catholic corporatism,[2] which in some respects bore a strong resemblance to the Franco and Salazar regimes in Spain and Portugal.

Definitions

Fascism has been defined simply as "a genus of political ideology whose mythic core in its various permutations is a palingenetic form of populist

[1] Gregor 1999; 2005.   [2] Payne 1995, 248.

ultra-nationalism."[3] Here we see an emphasis on populism and extreme nationalism as well as the palingenesis that demands a national rebirth in matters of culture, society, and *esprit de corps*. These ideas will be developed more fully later.

In his article on *fascismo* in the *Enciclopedia Italiana*,[4] Emilio Gentile provides a much more expansive definition consisting of ten items. Because of its centrality, I will quote only the first. Thus, fascism is "a mass movement with multiclass membership in which prevail, among the leaders and militants, the middle sectors, in large part new to political activity, organized as a party militia, that bases its identity not on social hierarchy or class origin but on the sense of comradeship, believes itself invested with a mission of national regeneration, considers itself in a state of war against political adversaries and aims at conquering a monopoly of political power by using terror, parliamentary tactics, and deals with leading groups, to create a new regime that destroys parliamentary democracy."[5] In the last of his ten items, Gentile emphasizes the foreign policy of imperial expansion based on a myth of national greatness that Stanley Payne[6] incorporates and expands into his own typology as the "goal of empire, expansion, or a radical change in the nation's relationship with other powers." A final important element of fascism consists of a set of fascist negations: "antiliberalism, anticommunism, [and] anticonservatism (though with the understanding that fascist groups were willing to undertake temporary alliances with other sectors, most commonly with the right)."[7]

A less comprehensive but nevertheless valuable approach is taken by Robert Paxton[8] in which fascism is defined as "a form of political behavior marked by obsessive preoccupation with community decline, humiliation, or victimhood and by compensatory cults of unity, energy, and purity, in which a mass-based party of committed nationalist militants, working in uneasy but effective collaboration with traditional elites, abandons democratic liberties and pursues with redemptive violence and without ethical or legal restraints goals of internal cleansing and external expansion."

In their totality, these definitions suggest something unique about fascism, which requires explanation. Nevertheless, certain commonalities will emerge between fascism and other forms of political extremism such as radical Islamism, or rampant militarism. A major commonality, as we shall see, is found in A. James Gregor's[9] suggestion (incorporated in Paxton's definition above) that "although 'fascist ideas' may surface anywhere and at any time, fascism is a function of a collective sense of intense and protracted national humiliation. Without that pervasive and inclusive sense of humiliation, 'fascist thought' has appeal to only a small minority of any population."

---

[3] Griffin 1991, 44.   [4] 1992.   [5] Quoted in Payne 1995, 5–6.
[6] Payne 1995, 7.   [7] Payne 1995, 7.   [8] 2004, 235.   [9] 1999, 21.

Some behavioral characteristics

As is now obvious, most these definitions contain either the implied or explicit origins of fascism. It would also be useful to indicate various behavioral characteristics that fascist movements held in common, apart from their etiology that will be examined separately in some detail. These are the willingness to kill, paramilitarism, politics as theater, the search for unity, and confrontations with modernity.

Willingness to kill

The willingness to kill is a principal characteristic of fascism. As we shall see, all of the cases of extremism considered here, whether fascist, communist, radical Islamist, militarist, or extreme nationalist, were extremely bloody.

Paramilitarism

In his very brief definition, Michael Mann[10] emphasizes paramilitarism as a distinctive element of fascism. But expanding on this theme, according to Mann:[11]

> Paramilitarism was both a key value and the key organizational form of fascism. It was seen as "popular," welling up spontaneously from below, but it was also elitist, supposedly representing the vanguard of the nation. Brooker[12] homes in on the comradeship of fascist movements as their defining characteristic, and they certainly viewed their battle-hardened comradeship as an exemplar of the organic nation and the new man. Violence was the key to the "radicalism" of fascism. They overturned legal forms of killings. Through it, the people would effect class transcendence, "knocking heads together." Its elitism and hierarchy would then dominate the authoritarian state that it would bring into being.

All of the fascist governments employed groups like the German *SA* (Nazi paramilitary assault divisions) and *SS* (Nazi defense echelons), Italian *squadristi*, Hungarian Arrow Cross paramilitaries, and Romanian Iron Guardists not only to effect "class transcendence," but also as terror machines to achieve desired political outcomes. The "knocking heads together" was a form of physical intimidation designed to terrorize the population into effective political impotence.

Politics as theater

Public theatricality is another important uniformity. Even before the rise of fascism, the template for fascist politics as theater was set by Gabriele D'Annunzio.

---

[10] 2004, 13.   [11] 2004, 16.   [12] 1991.

Poet, novelist, military hero, and, most important, a fervent Italian nationalist, in 1919 he led a group of nationalists into the city of Fiume (today's Rijeka in Croatia) on the Adriatic coast. Territory on the Adriatic coast had been promised to Italy in the Treaty of London (1915) by which Italy entered the war, but was not awarded to her at Versailles. Although not granted in the Treaty of London, the city of Fiume nevertheless became a burning issue after the November 1918 plebiscite of the ethnic Italian population in Fiume declared for union with Italy.[13] D'Annunzio would play on this theme of the "mutilated victory," as later would Mussolini. Emblematic here was the haranguing speech from a balcony overlooking a huge crowd of supporters surrounded by flags representing either a political party or the nation.

According to Robert Paxton,[14] "Declaring Fiume the 'Republic of Carnaro,' D'Annunzio invented the public theatricality that Mussolini was later to make his own: daily harangues by the *Comandante* from a balcony, lots of uniforms and parades, the 'Roman salute' with arm outstretched, the meaningless war cry *'Eia, eia, alalà.'"* Or according to the Dutch historian Michael Ledeen:[15]

> Virtually the entire ritual of Fascism came from the "Free State of Fiume": the balcony address, the Roman salute, the cries of "aia, aia, alala," the dramatic dialogues with the crowd, the use of religious symbols in a new secular setting, the eulogies to the "martyrs" of the cause and the employment of these relicts in political ceremonies. Moreover, quite aside from the poet's contribution to the form and style of Fascist politics, Mussolini's movement first started to attract great strength when the future dictator supported D'Annunzio's occupation of Fiume.

All of the European fascist parties employed these public displays, the Nazis perhaps foremost among them. The Nuremberg night rallies by torchlight, the SS uniforms with death's-head insignia, the Hitler salute, and the swastika all were intended to heighten the emotional attachment to Nazism. Black shirts in Italy, brown shirts in Germany, or green shirts in Romania were intended to unmistakably signify fascism to the relevant public. (In Hungary, a flag with crossed arrows was used to symbolize the Arrow Cross party.) Symbolism in all cases was strong and laden with emotional content.

Unity in opposition to liberalism

An important outcome of World War I was the feeling of unity in battle and equality before death of many of the combatants. Indeed, these sentiments were expressed by both Hitler and Mussolini, as well as by many of the respondents to the survey of early Nazi Party members by Theodore Abel,[16] reanalyzed

---

[13] Thompson 2008, 368.   [14] 2004, 59.   [15] Quoted in Glenny 1999, 376.
[16] [1938] 1986.

extensively by Peter Merkl.[17] In all instances of extremism considered here, unity was exhorted in the battle against Western liberalism and/or elements of modernity. Liberalism is understood to mean the emphasis on individual civil liberties, in contrast to the perceived needs of the collectivity. All instances of extremism considered here had a distinctly collectivist orientation.

Party uniforms in Germany and in any of the fascist countries served as an equalizer that established unity among the party members. All of the fascist parties considered here were "catch-all" parties, in contrast to the traditional class-based, ethnoreligious-based, or sectional political parties.[18] All members of the nation or *Volk* were to be accepted as equal affiliates of the fascist party, as long as they met certain criteria of "race," religion, or nationality.

Equality was to be a major vehicle for the establishment of unity in Nazi Germany. From a practical standpoint, German unity was absolutely required if the Nazis were to continue to govern and then successfully defeat their enemies on the battlefield. For these reasons, the spirit of 1914 was continually invoked as the one moment in recent German history when all of the historical German divisions (Catholic vs. Protestant, liberal vs. conservative, industrialist vs. agriculturalist) disappeared, and were replaced by a German people united against a common enemy. The nation rose as one to the challenge of the new war. And according to Wolfgang Schivelbusch:[19] "To call upon the unity of the nation in the form of folk community was henceforth identical with reviving the spirit of 1914." Bands of Italian war veterans organized as fascist *squadristi*[20] in the early 1920s also represented the unity in political action derived from the World War I experience, as did groups of the Hungarian Arrow Cross, and Romanian Iron Guard.

As Heinrich Himmler himself remarked,[21] "The war is precisely as surely to be won as the world war was in November 1918, January 1919, if only we had had a firm leadership then, a loyalty pervading the whole *Volk* up to the top, and good nerves." Justifying the mass murder, Himmler continues, "We are in the fortunate position that we have no more Jews within, so the scum of all revolts has been eradicated in the mass of the people." Thus, only the Jews were to blame for the presumed home front disunity leading to the German defeat in World War I; the unity and equality of comradeship on the battlefield had been secure, and undermined only from within the "Jewish-infested" state.

Interestingly, although it is debatable whether 1930s Japan was a fascist state (see Chapter 12), unity was a major concern. According to the highly influential Sadao Araki, army minister in 1931–34, "Ninety million people must become one and join the emperor in spreading the imperial virtue. For this we must unite and advance until the very last minute (of the battle). In this way, we will secure the glory of final victory."[22] And in Serbia, unity too was a major concern

---

[17] 1975. [18] Kircheimer 1966; Paxton 2004, 49–50. [19] 2003, 222–3.
[20] See Tannenbaum 1969. [21] Quoted in Padfield 1991, 519.
[22] Quoted in Bix 2000, 276.

from the very first emergence of the independent Archiepiscopat in the thirteenth century. According to St. Sava, the *ocila* symbol on the flag of the Serbian Orthodox Church meant "Only Unity Saves the Serbs."[23] In neither of these two instances do we find much sympathy with liberalism.

Confrontations with modernity

The desire for unity fed into the confrontation with modernity experienced by all of the fascist movements. This confrontation contained an inherent ambiguity. On the one hand, technology as a principal component of modernity was to be used to maximize state or societal power. On the other hand, the socioeconomic consequences of modernity were abhorrent. Both capitalism and communism carried with them seeds of extreme disunity, class inequality in the former, and class hatred or even class destruction in the latter. Liberalism, with its penchant for argument and skepticism, also was to be eschewed. Only the integrative efforts of fascism could avoid these extremes. Corporatism, with an appearance (if not the reality) of unity, or at least a form of managed capitalism, was a common solution to this problem.

As Adrian Lyttelton[24] remarked, "Fascism was inspired by the modernity of war, not the modernity of peace, and can perhaps best be understood, if one looks at its whole historical trajectory, as the attempt to impose on a peacetime society the techniques of wartime mobilization. Technology, in this perspective, was seen as an extension of the 'will to power', and as a means to renew the 'primacy of politics'." Or according to Robert Paxton,[25] "it was an alternative modernity that Fascist regimes sought: a technically advanced society in which modernity's strains and divisions had been smothered by fascism's powers of integration and control."

Italian Fascism

Despite a well-deserved reputation for restraint during the Holocaust that had Italian troops in occupied France and Yugoslavia protecting Jews (and Serbs) from annihilation,[26] at least until the Allied invasion of Sicily in July 1943,[27] this is not the whole story. Fascist governance of Libya (an Italian colony since 1912), in the 1920s resulted in the suppression of resistance in the inland Cyrenaica region that entailed gassing of civilians and confinement of 80,000 Libyans in concentration camps where many perished. It is estimated that approximately one-tenth of the Libyan population died during the period of fascist rule. The

---

[23] *Flags of the World* 2007.   [24] 1996, 18.   [25] 2004, 13.   [26] Steinberg 1990.
[27] Several days after the invasion and the almost immediate realization that the loss of Sicily was a near certainty, for the first time Mussolini granted Germany's request for the deportation of Jews from Italian-occupied France; Zuccotti 2000, 132.

Italian invasion of Ethiopia in 1935, which, as in Libya, employed chemical weapons of mass destruction, led to the large-scale murder of civilian populations. Between 1935 and 1939, 617 tons of gas were shipped to Ethiopia. Altogether, by 1938, 250,000 Ethiopians were dead as a result of gassings and the use of conventional weaponry by the Italians.[28] As we shall see, murder on such a grand scale clearly places fascist Italy in the same category as Hungary and Romania, although not at the same level of annihilation as Nazi Germany.

Ideational roots

For now, we need to examine the historical sources of fascism that will suggest certain differences in the historical development of Italian Fascism and German Nazism, but as separate points on a continuum of fascist practice, not in their fundamental cores described adequately by the preceding definitions. Intellectually, Nazism in Germany simply got a much later start than did Italian Fascism, which had its earliest roots in Marxist socialism.

In contrast to Nazism, Italian Fascism had deeper roots. Specifically, the birth of fascism was facilitated by the crisis in Marxism, the reigning intellectual framework of the European Left at the end of the nineteenth century. According to Zeev Sternhell and his colleagues,[29] "the Fascist ideology represented a synthesis of organic nationalism with the antimaterialist revision of Marxism." From this point on, generic fascism will be denoted by the lowercase "f," while Italian Fascism will receive the uppercase notation.

By this time, at the end of the nineteenth century, the economic predictions of Marxism simply had not come to pass. Instead of a deepening crisis of capitalism predicted by Marx, despite periodic recessions, capitalism appeared to be in robust shape. Industrialization and trade were rapidly increasing in all of the capitalist economies of the West, especially in Germany and the United States. Pauperization of the working class and class conflict had not worsened. Indeed, the material conditions of the worker actually had improved during the last third of the nineteenth century. Incipient forms of social security, common in Germany under Bismarck had already established the precedent of a worker safety net. A Sickness Insurance Law was passed in 1883, compulsory accident insurance in 1884, and old age pensions were introduced. Moreover, the Marxist image of the capitalist state as the "instrument of repression by the industrialist owners of the means of production" also had not materialized. Western legislatures were increasingly accommodating liberal parties, and even to some extent, albeit fitfully, socialist ones such as the German Social Democratic Party. As a consequence, not only were workers far better off than they had been earlier in the nineteenth century, but the long-expected polarization of society did not occur. When Eduard Bernstein published his liberal

[28] Ben-Ghiat 2001, 125–6.   [29] 1994, 6.

critique of classical Marxism, the German Socialists were already "fighting for the democratization of political life in Germany. [They] believed in the virtues of democracy and in the possibility of attaining the objectives of socialism by democratic means."[30]

The contradictions between classical revolutionary Marxist theory based on pauperization and class struggle, and the reality of an increasing worker stake in the welfare of capitalist societies, led to further attacks on Marxist theory. Among the many were those of Wilfredo Pareto in the economic realm, and Georges Sorel in the more general societal bailiwick. It is in the latter that we see the most distinctive and consequential contributions to Fascist theory. Although Pareto lent a unique social scientific legitimation to his critique of Marxism and subsequently was co-opted by Fascist theorists, it was Sorel who would make the stronger mark politically. Fascist doctrine and practice did not occur principally in the economic realm but had a more general societal orientation, as indicated by virtually all of the preceding definitions.

I concentrate on Sorel because Mussolini was quite open in acknowledging his debt to Sorel. Accordingly, "I owe most to Georges Sorel. This master of syndicalism by his rough theories of revolutionary tactics has contributed most to form the discipline, energy, and power of the fascist cohorts."[31] That admiration was reciprocated by Sorel: "Mussolini is not an ordinary socialist. You will perhaps see him one day as the leader of a consecrated battalion, saluting the flag of Italy with his sword. He is an Italian of the fifteenth century, a condottiere. He is the only man with the strength to correct the weaknesses of the government."[32]

Starting with a firm commitment to Marxist theory "the greatest innovation in philosophy for centuries,"[33] and a firm commitment to the preservation of Marxist purity, Sorel slowly began to change. He was especially excited by the moral arguments that he saw expressed in *Das Kapital*. When the Dreyfus affair erupted, convinced that the moral dimension of Marxist theory demanded that he do so, Sorel became a firm Dreyfusard, vigorously arguing for a reversal of the official guilty verdict of treason on an innocent man.

The first major change in his adherence to Marxist thought was a critique of its economic base. This led to a Marxist revisionism that was still within the bounds of Marxist tradition, writ large. Especially important was the retention of the violent struggle of the workers that was being marginalized by liberal Marxists. But Sorel's revisionism was already beginning to appear as revolutionary, antirationalist, and mythical in its core. Sorel saw that the claimed scientific aspects of Marxism (e.g., the theory of surplus value) would not inspire the workers to revolt. Only the antirational elements of national myth could achieve that revolutionary goal. Accordingly, the myth is "a body of images capable of

---

[30] Sternhell, Sznajder, and Asheri 1994, 15.   [31] Quoted in Shils 1961, 24.
[32] Quoted in Gregor 1979, 129.
[33] Quoted in Sternhell, Sznajder, and Asheri 1994, 39.

evoking instinctively all the sentiments which correspond to the different manifestations of the war undertaken by Socialism against modern society."[34]

The general strike was to be the instrument for a declaration of war of the
proletariat against the middle-class supporters of parliamentary democracy. In
itself the general strike constitutes the mythological embodiment of the class
struggle that is assumed to animate all of history. But it is important to note that,
according to Sorel, such a myth is not equivalent to an affirmation of utopia:

> A myth cannot be refuted, since it is, at bottom, identical with the convic-
> tions of a group, being the expression of these convictions in the language
> of movement; and it is, in consequence, unanalyzable into parts which
> could be placed on the plane of historical descriptions. A Utopia [sic], on
> the contrary, can be discussed like any other social constitution; the spon-
> taneous movements it presupposes can be compared with the movements
> actually observed in the course of history, and we can in this way evaluate
> its verisimilitude; it is possible to refute Utopias by showing that the eco-
> nomic system on which they have been made to rest is incompatible with
> the necessary conditions of modern production.[35]

Thus, in his rejection of utopia, Sorel clearly demonstrates his departure from
Marxist economics, which was presumed to yield a utopian society in which
both the state as an institution and class conflict would be absent. But the incon-
trovertible myth, based not on the examination of social reality but on firmly
held conviction, was to remain the centerpiece of Sorel's thought.

Sorel advocated the political separation of groups in society; in this, he was at
one with the Syndicalists, who supported autonomous workers' actions against
the industrialists. These class enemies were not to negotiate with each other.
Like Lenin, whom he admired, and the fascists who were to be his intellectual
heirs, he rejected compromise. Marxism was to be an ideological instrument
of an apocalyptical societal war through the vehicle of the general strike. The
democratic heritage was to be relinquished. To that end, individualism, liberalism, and worker reforms within democratic capitalist society were also to be
dispensed with. The worker syndicates were to serve as the only social authority that would "take the worker out of the control of the shopkeeper, that great
elector of bourgeois democracy."[36] The existing order was to be destroyed by the
general strike. According to Edward Shils[37] in his Introduction to the American
edition of *Reflections on Violence*, "in [Sorel's] political philosophy, fine grada-
tions escaped him or were viewed as insignificant. It was always an affair of all or
nothing." This political inclination would foreshadow Hitler's far more extreme
anti-Semitism in his comment: "With the Jew, there can be no negotiation, but
only the decision: all or nothing!"[38]

---

[34] Sorel [1906] 1961, 127.   [35] Sorel [1906] 1961, 50.
[36] Sternhell, Sznajder, and Asheri 1994, 51.   [37] 1961, 18.
[38] Quoted in Burrin 1994, 30.

And Sorel became increasingly anti-Semitic, especially in comparison with his early Dreyfusard position. Between 1911 and 1913, he edited
L' Indépendance, which expressed the themes of "nationalism, anti-Semitism,
the defense of culture, classicism, the Greco-Roman heritage, and the struggle
against the university and secular education."[39] He collaborated with Charles
Maurras, editor of *L' Action française*, who wrote "Everything seems impossible
or terribly difficult, without the providential appearance of anti-Semitism. It
enables everything to be arranged, smoothed over, and simplified. If one was
not an anti-Semite through patriotism, one would become one through a simple sense of opportunity."[40] Sorel himself threatened the Jews and accused them
of ritual murder. As early as 1906 and publication of *Reflections on Violence*,
he used the term "big Jew bankers."[41] In this he was closer to the German variant of fascism to develop – Nazism – than to Mussolini's Fascism that was to
pre-date it. However, recent research has suggested that, contrary to conventional assumptions, Mussolini in the late 1930s turned to anti-Semitism as
state policy not out of a desire to emulate Hitler or in response to his requests,
but as the result of Mussolini's own domestic and foreign concerns.[42] The general, although not universal, hostility of both Italian and foreign Jews to Italy's
bloody colonial venture in Ethiopia was to be a critical element in fostering
Mussolini's growing anti-Semitism.

But what lay at the historical root of Sorel's preference for apocalyptical violence? Just as Charles Maurras, founder of the proto-fascist *Action française*, after
the French defeat by the Prussians in 1870 described the Prussians as "wicked
men, barbarians wearing spiked helmets,"[43] Sorel, too, likely was influenced by
that critical event. He observed that "The disasters of 1870 brought the country
back to practical, prudent, and prosaic conditions… After 1871 everybody in
France thought only of the search for the most suitable means of setting the
country on its feet again."[44] In place of an emphasis on the glorious, legendary,
revolutionary, and military epic of the turn of the nineteenth century, a crass
opportunism became the norm. Sorel, in turn, became "a moralist distressed
with the dissolution of traditional morals into rationalistic individualism and
hedonism."[45]

A return to national glory required a societal cleansing of these prosaic and
allogenic elements. Only violence by the proletariat incorporated into the general strike could accomplish that goal. Yet, Sorel did initially welcome the onset
of World War I. As early as January 1914, he quoted William James that "on the
stage, only heroism has the great roles."[46] Sorel soon became disillusioned with

[39] Sternhell, Sznajder, and Asheri 1994, 84.
[40] Quoted in Sternhell, Sznajder, and Asheri 1994, 85.
[41] Sorel [1906] 1961, 68.   [42] Sarfatti 2006, 97–9.   [43] Nolte 1966, 59.
[44] Sorel [1906] 1961, 101.   [45] Shils 1961, 20.
[46] Quoted in Sternhell, Sznajder, and Asheri 1994, 89.

the Allied coalition that would "finish off everything serious, grand, and *Roman* that is still in Europe."[47]

The war, however, would give rise to political outcomes that were unexpected in their propensity towards violence. The rise of Nazism also followed from the war as an extension of the politics of human destruction. Camaraderie of the military squad dominated much post-war thinking in Europe, leading to a collectivist orientation in both literature and politics. Ernst Jünger, for one "described the faces of soldiers, peering from their steel helmets, faces that had lost much of their individual distinction but were nonetheless sharply defined, as though molded from steel. This, he continued, 'is the face of a race that is beginning to develop under the peculiar demands of a new landscape, a race that no longer represents the lone figure as a person or individual, but as a type.' "[48] Henri Barbusse's novel *Under Fire*[49] was in many respects a paean to the camaraderie of the squad. And as George Mosse observes, unity above and beyond social class was a consequence:

> The battle of Verdun was said to have transformed the struggle of men and machines into a new kind of community which liberated man from his own self and transcended the individual... Front-line soldiers... follow[ed] the example of Barbusse's veterans' organization, the *Arditi* in Italy or the German storm-troopers – well-defined bodies of men claiming to act as elites on behalf of the nation. They had provided the cadres of D'Annunzio's Legions, the fascist squadristas and the shock troops of the German political right, inspired by the spirit of 1914 and the ideals of wartime camaraderie.[50]

In many respects, the defeat of France and its lost territory as the result of the Franco-Prussian War of 1870–71 was a source of French anti-Semitism verging on but not yet entering the realm of extremism, which World War I would later diffuse throughout the European countries that had lost territory at its end. Susan Zuccotti[51] explicitly states, "As would occur again…in 1940 but in different chronological order, the resurgence of anti-Semitism in France in the 1880s was preceded by a catastrophic military defeat… The lightning German victory in the Franco-Prussian War in 1870–71 severely wounded French national pride and self-confidence. The consequent loss of Alsace and Lorraine to the newly unified German state created a sense of rancor, an upsurge of exaggerated chauvinism, and a thirst for revenge that festered for decades." And Marrus and Paxton[52] aver that during the 1880s, Paris became "the spiritual capital of the European Right." anti-Semitism was a consistent staple of this political orientation.[53] Of course, anti-Semitism was a salient characteristic of proto-fascist organizations ranging from *Action française* to the Russian Black Hundreds.

---

[47] Emphasis in original; quoted in Sternhell, Sznajder, and Asheri 1994, 90.
[48] Buruma 2006, 15.   [49] 1916.   [50] Mosse 1986, 497–8.   [51] 1993, 11.
[52] 1995, 21.   [53] Soucy 1966.

With the Sorelian basis already established and with the additional contri-butions of Roberto Michels ("Iron Law of Oligarchy"), the events surrounding World War I were to be decisive. Adopting the increasingly nationalist senti-ment of Sorelian Marxism, Mussolini commented, "to fight for one's fatherland is to fight for one's love."[54] Effectively, a revolutionary nationalism was adopted that would soon become a hallmark of fascism. Michels added a distinctive element to this ideology:

> A "secular religion," a dedication to the interests of the nation in its struggle for equity and justice in a modern competitive world, would provide the "ideal" ingredients of revolutionary mass-mobilization. *Ideally, that pur-pose, the pursuit of justice and equity, should find its embodiment in a tribune, a "charismatic leader," who would articulate the "ultimate interests" of the collectivity – who could orchestrate the energy of the masses.* Corporativism [sic] served as an instrumentality within that orchestration.[55]

Much earlier, Machiavelli, despairing of the domination of Italy by foreigners and the disunity within Italian society, had enunciated a similar hope for Italy. In his "Exhortation to Liberate Italy from the Barbarians," the last chapter of *The Prince*, Machiavelli expressed the fervent "hope that some individual might be appointed by God for her [Italy's] redemption;…now, almost lifeless, she awaits one who may heal her wounds and put a stop to the pillaging of Lombardy, to the rapacity and extortion in the Kingdom of Naples and in Tuscany, and cure her of those sores which have long been festering. *Behold how she prays God to send some one to redeem her from this barbarous cruelty and insolence. Behold her ready and willing to follow any standard if only there be some one to raise it.*"[56]

Following the contours of Figure 1.1 and the information contained in Table 3.2 (omitting the earlier triumphal period, which in this case clearly is Rome), Figure 4.1 presents the ephemeral gain within Italian authority space. Measurement of the ephemeral gain is based on the existence of events suffi-ciently important to be memorialized historically and in public awareness. Interstate and civil wars or major international agreements typically, but not always, are prime examples. Clearly, these moments in time vary across countries and so a uniform metric cannot be imposed upon them. As a result, Figure 4.1 and all remaining figures are not drawn to scale.

German Nazism

The mass murder of 6 million European Jews by the Nazis during World War II has few, if any, historical parallels.[57] Yet the Nazis *in extremis* shared with remaining European fascist governments the willingness to engage in large-scale

---

[54] Gregor 1979, 85.   [55] Emphasis added; Gregor 1999, 90.
[56] Emphasis added; Machiavelli 1950, 95.   [57] Hilberg 2003.

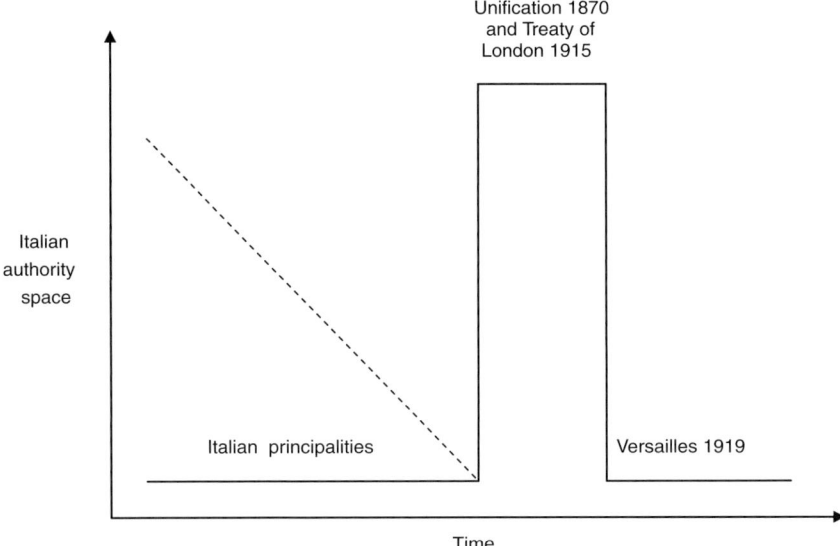

Figure 4.1: Changes in Italian authority space over time*
*Not to scale

killing. As in the Italian case, political momentum was accelerated by invasion and war. And despite the virulence of Nazi ideology, it was only after the German invasion of the Soviet Union in June 1941 that Nazi policy was radicalized sufficiently to initiate the genocide of Europe's Jews.[58]

Ideational roots

Like Italy, we can also learn much from the German historical experience. Several themes are intertwined within this German history. Humiliation, self-sacrifice, and resurrection through national unity are among the most prominent. The earliest theme to appear in widely disseminated material is that of humiliation. Writing in the late eighteenth century, the German poet and dramatist Friedrich Schiller laments the tyrannies imposed in the absence of German national freedom:

> So we have to cringe and sneak about on our own soil,
> like murderers, and take what is rightfully ours by
> night, whose dark cloak lends itself only to
> criminality and conspiracy, but which in our case is as
> bright and clear and majestic as the noonday sun.[59]

[58] Browning 2004; Midlarsky 2005b.   [59] Quoted in Baird 1990, 21.

German history reflects the frequent inverse relationship between culture and politics. Norbert Elias, the great German historical sociologist, comments:

> Embedded in the meaning of the German term "culture" was a non-political and perhaps even an anti-political bias symptomatic of the recurrent feeling among the German middle-class elites that politics and the affairs of state represented the area of their humiliation and lack of freedom, while culture represented the sphere of their freedom and their pride. During the eighteenth and part of the nineteenth centuries, the anti-political bias of the middle-class concept of "culture" was directed against the politics of autocratic princes... At a later stage, this anti-political bias was turned against the parliamentary politics of a democratic state.[60]

In the face of petty autocracies in the German principalities before unification, and later the wrangling of parliamentarians, culture became the refuge of the German intellectual. Or as Thomas Mann[61] suggested, there exists "the specifically German antithesis of power and intellect; in the fact, namely that seen historically these two, intellect and power, seem to miss each other with apparent regularity, that blossoming of the state and blossoming of culture seem to exclude one another – and this is why the conviction could and did settle among artists and believers in culture that a politically powerful Germany would necessarily be opposed to intellect and culture, that German intellectual blossoming would never be united with the flowering of the state." Later, Mann will present a fascinating illustration of the tendency toward extremism under conditions of war and national mobilization.

In Germany, as Fritz Stern argued, "Culture was the arena of the absolute, a realm without compromise. Its exaltation nourished the illusion that culture could be a substitute for power and therefore a substitute for politics."[62] With the radical decline of political power as a major societal value in the wake of Germany's defeat in World War I, German culture was to be emphasized in the new Weimar Republic, but "A cultural renaissance that was enhanced by democratic ideals and liberal values could be vilified as profiting from the military disaster of the First World War and the political collapse of the Reich. It was this tension between politics and culture that would contribute to the rise of National Socialism and the fall of the Weimar Republic. As Peter Gay wrote at the beginning of his book on Weimar Culture (sic), 'to found a country in the city of Goethe did not guarantee a country in Goethe's image. It did not even guarantee its survival.' "[63]

But in his otherwise splendid account of the seduction of culture in German history, Wolf Lepenies missed a critical point. This is the *unity* of culture and politics in time of national crisis wherein selected cultural elements are transported directly into the realm of politics. These elements are often of recent

---

[60] Elias 1996, 126–7.   [61] [1918] 1983, 183.   [62] Lepenies 2006, 16.
[63] Quoted in Lepenies 2006, 26.

origin, having their genesis during a recent war, and yield extremism and brutality. The culture of war becomes the template for the new politics, or as an editorialist for the *Frankfurter Zeitung* wrote on Hitler in 1928, "It is a matter of a manic idea of atavistic origin that pushes aside complicated reality and replaces it with a primitive fighting unit... Naturally, Hitler is a dangerous fool... But if one asks how the son of a petty Upper Austrian customs officer arrives at his craze, then one can only say one thing: he has taken war ideology perfectly literally and interpreted it in almost as primitive a way that one might be living in the era of the *Völkerwanderung* – the period of Barbarian invasions at the end of the Roman Empire."[64]

And upon the Nazis' accession to power in 1933, the publisher Paul Suhrkamp, a veteran of World War I and an anti-Nazi, wrote in the spring of 1933:

> I was repeatedly struck by the similarity to my memories of the summer of 1914. The similarity extended to the smallest details. Uniformed SA and SS men and regular army soldiers now marched alongside private citizens, some wearing medals. There were children and older women and servant girls, and between the marchers and the spectators standing on the sidewalks or perched on fences or trees or on the roofs of the electric streetcars there ran a current of unanimity and heartfelt openness... At the center of it all were always young men in uniform – and men in uniform always seemed young. Great columns of young men in neatly pressed uniforms marching in lockstep and taut, disciplined faces dominated the scene. Cities, towns, and country roads...all were filled with the presence of the army. The astonishing thing, however, was that although the soldiers sang war songs they seemed not warlike but rather, at that moment, thoroughly peaceful. Not complacent or collegial or clubby, though; the impression was of earnest readiness. What we experienced was an active army filled with the determination, zeal, and excitement of our old forces in the field, but without the threat of war or even the prospect of war on the horizon. *What we were witnessing was something that made no rational sense and can scarcely be imagined: the military as an end in itself, as the fulfillment and satisfaction of a feeling for life... Without the past war, such a pure military phenomenon would hardly have been possible.* But what we saw did not necessarily require a war.[65]

Ironically, the spirit of 1914 is neatly summarized by a leading jurist, lawyer, and co-founder of the Central Association of German Citizens of the Jewish Faith, Eugen Fuchs. At the start of World War I, "A great flood of enthusiasm arose...a tremendous wave that swept up everyone in its path. Our hearts thumped and our eyes shown [sic] with anticipation... Everyone was filled with an irrepressible hope that we would, that we had to win. Germany, as the Emperor said in

---

[64] Quoted in Kershaw 1998, 302.
[65] Emphasis added; quoted in Schivelbusch 2003, 240–1.

his rallying cry to the German people, had never been conquered when it was united. And united we were indeed."[66]

These emotions stand in stark contrast to those evoked by the later losses in 1918 that were to prove so devastating, especially in comparison with the extraordinarily hopeful beginnings. Indeed, in one exhibit in the Deutsches Historisches Museum in Berlin, the Treaty of Versailles was called by Germans the "Treaty of Shame." Heightened anticipation, determination to win the war, even enthusiasm at its coming were to be again reflected in the later enormous successes of German arms early in World War II, with consequences to be detailed in a later chapter (13) on genocidal variation.

The search for unity

The German desire for unity had deep historical roots. It eventuated in Carl Schmitt's *The Concept of the Political*,[67] which based virtually all of politics on the collective friend–enemy distinction. Essentially a political justification for genocide was established.

The beginning of the Wilhelmine period witnessed the writings of Paul de Lagarde, a widely read social critic who was deeply pessimistic about Germany's future, despite the public euphoria in the immediate aftermath of the formation of imperial Germany. In 1880, he wrote, "I have no use for abstract truth. I want to bind and liberate my people."[68] Moreover, the unity of his people was paramount.

With the competing loyalties of North and South Germans, Protestants and Catholics, liberals and conservatives, as well as tensions among classes signified by the rapid rise of the Social Democrats, Lagarde emphasized the most critical problem facing the newly established Germany. Continuing divisiveness was, in many respects, the hallmark of the new Germany.

How then could the disunity and the increasing role of Jews as promoters of toxic ideologies such as capitalism be combated? In his *Deutsche Schriften* (German Writings), Lagarde argued that a *Führer* was required, a leader who could command the loyalty of all "true" Germans and who also could exterminate the Jews as the apostles of capitalism and disunity. He used the analogy of bacilli and trichinae to justify the mass murder of all enemies of German unity. Himmler's use of the word "bacterium" in his infamous Posen speech justifying the genocide (see Chapter 15), obviously has a historical root in Lagarde's lexicon, and also serves as clear evidence of dehumanization. It is not surprising that in 1944, in the midst of the extermination campaign, the German army distributed an anthology of Lagarde's work, which enunciated his sanctioning

---

[66] Exhibit in Jüdisches Museum Berlin, 2009.
[67] [1932] 1996.   [68] Stern 1974, 36.

of mass murder. As Fritz Stern comments, "Few men prophesied Hitler's work with such accuracy – and approval."[69]

Lagarde, Julius Langbehn, an advocate of the need for a "Germanic" art, and later Moeller van den Bruck, effectively advocated the idea of national socialism, in which German solidarity would be firmly established, and would not necessarily be based on economic principles. But this desired unity was to be coupled with sacrifice. Two cases are especially relevant. In 1923, Leo Schlageter, a highly decorated veteran of World War I and a former member of the *Freikorps* who earlier had fought against the Russian Communists in the Baltic, the German Communists in the Ruhr, and the Poles in Upper Silesia, was executed by the French for attempted sabotage during their occupation of the Ruhr. He was immediately canonized as a hero of the German battle for unity in the face of enemies both to the East and West. He was especially prominent in Nazi martyrology.

The second instance is that of Moeller van den Bruck's suicide. Although not anti-Semitic as were Lagarde and Langbehn, he nevertheless wrote *Das Dritte Reich* (The Third Reich) as an expression of his extreme nationalism, emphasis on unity, and hatred of liberalism.[70] His suicide in 1925 was seen by both friend and foe as a "Germanic" suicide. His despair over Germany's future was said to have been the source of his suicide.[71] The Nazis later appropriated the name of his book for their new Germany. Although seemingly far less dramatic in the overt level of self-sacrifice, Himmler, in his efforts to enhance German unity and cooperation, follows this "Germanic" tradition. In the end though, the nihilism that pervaded the Nazi Party was to find its ultimate expression in the suicides of Hitler, Himmler, Goering, and Goebbels, the most prominent architects of the Final Solution.

Schlageter was one of a rich pantheon of martyrs to the German people developed by the Nazis. Upon the French invasion of the Ruhr in 1923, he engaged in the sabotage of railways bringing coal to France as part of the reparations agreement. After his death at the hands of a French firing squad, he was immediately canonized by the Nazis. The Schlageter Memorial Museum was opened on May 26, 1933. A massive commemoration of the tenth anniversary of his death witnessed Hermann Goering speaking to a crowd of 185,000 men of the *SA* and *SS*:

> When the shots rang out ten years ago at dawn at this spot, they were heard through the German night and awakened the nation in her weakness and humiliation. In those days the memory of Schlageter inspired us and gave us hope. We refused to believe that his sacrifice had been in vain. Schlageter demonstrated in the way he died that the German spirit could not be destroyed. Schlageter, you can rest in peace. We have seen to it that

[69] Stern 1974, 63.   [70] Stern 1974, 261–2.   [71] Stern 1974, 266.

> you were honored here and not betrayed like your two million comrades
> [casualties of World War I]. As long as there are Schlageters in Germany,
> the nation will live.[72]

In this brief message, we see the combination of humiliation, sacrifice, betrayal by allogenic elements (mainly the Jews), and ultimate redemption through German unity achieved by means of the revival of the German spirit.

Finally a pep talk by a *Wehrmacht* Captain Wesreidau in autumn 1943 is quoted at length in order to reveal the relationships existing among the search for unity, risk, and inverted morality, especially the need for sacrifice:

> We are now embarked on a risky enterprise, with no assurance of safety.
> We are advancing an idea of unity which is neither rich nor easily digest-
> ible, but the vast majority of the German people accept [sic] it and adhere
> to it, forging and forming it in an admirable collective effort. This is where
> we are now risking everything. We are trying, taking due account of the
> attitudes of society, to change the face of the world, hoping to revive the
> ancient virtues buried under the layers of filth bequeathed to us by our for-
> bears... We shall be suffering not only in the interests of ultimate victory,
> but in the interests of daily victory against those who hurl themselves at us
> without respite, and whose only thought is to exterminate us, without any
> understanding of what is at stake.[73]

In addition to ideological and societal calls for German unity, the demands of economic growth after World War I also required it. Not only was economic growth needed to compete with other European powers and the United States, but the Nazis understood that their continued tenure in power rested, in part, on German consumer satisfaction.[74] And the path to rapid economic growth was seen as a rationalization of industry along American lines, specifically with Henry Ford's assembly-line innovations as a model. An analysis of German economic efforts by Robert Brady just prior to the Nazi accession to power suggested that:

> Rationalization will be retarded in Germany as long as national, political,
> social, and other barriers stand in the way of technological and economic
> forces... There are definite limits set to rationalization and economic plan-
> ning so long as Germany remains a house divided against itself – so long as
> Catholic Bavaria is pitted against Protestant Prussia, the right against the
> left, the industrialists against the agriculturists, the urban against the rural
> districts, the cartels against consumers, the states against the Reich.[75]

Thus, from a practical standpoint, German unity was absolutely required if the Nazis were to continue to govern, and then successfully defeat their enemies on the battlefield. For these reasons, the spirit of 1914 was continually invoked as

---

[72] Quoted in Baird 1990, 37.   [73] Quoted in Sajer 1971, 217–18.
[74] Schivelbusch 2003, 285.   [75] Quoted in Schivelbusch 2003, 283–4.

the one moment in recent German history when all of the divisions mentioned by Lagarde and Brady disappeared, and were replaced by a German people united against a common enemy. The nation rose as one to the challenge of the new war. And according to Wolfgang Schivelbusch: "To call upon the unity of the nation in the form of folk community was henceforth identical with reviving the spirit of 1914."[76]

Ernst von Salomon, implicated in the 1922 assassination of the liberal Jewish Weimar foreign minister, Walther Rathenau, wrote upon observing the French entry into Essen:

> At that moment the French moved into the city. I heard their trumpets blowing, and hurried down to the street and watched… I saw the arrogance of the victors, the elegance and the smiles of contempt which bespoke punishment and revenge. The city was delivered to the will of the enemy, its honor sullied, and it was unbearable for those of us who had to suffer through it… *Elemental, proletarian rage rushed through me… To think that they could march in their military splendor while we stood there humiliated, that set my heart afire with rage.* The whole morning I walked through the city, totally beside myself.[77]

And Joseph Goebbels, Nazi propaganda minister, would boldly articulate the theme of national humiliation to be followed by national resurrection. At the funeral of Horst Wessel, an *SA* officer killed by a communist in 1930 and whose poem "Die Fahne hoch" (the respected flag) was set to music and became the anthem of the *Nationalsozialistische Deutsche Arbeiterpartei* (NSDAP), Goebbels said: "I can see columns marching, endless, endless. A *humiliated* people rises up and begins to stir… It joins in step behind the standards… The flags wave, drums resound, the pipes are jubilant; and a million flutes join in the song of the German revolution: 'Die Fahne hoch!' "[78] Self-sacrifice was to be the vehicle for this resurrection. According to Goebbels, "When in the future, in a German Germany [sic], workers and students march along together, then they will sing his song, and he will march with them… The brown [uniform of the *SA*] soldiers are already singing it in every corner of the country. In ten years children in the schools, workers in their factories, and soldiers along the roads will sing it. His song has made him immortal!… A soldier of the German revolution! Just as always, hand on his belt, proud and upright, with his youthful smile, striking out ahead leading his comrades, always ready to sacrifice his life, he will remain with us in this way."[79] And Hitler intoned on this self-sacrifice in the midst of despair:

> Every people which strives to purify and free itself from desperation and defeat brings forth its muse, who transmits in words what the masses are

---

[76] Schivelbusch 2003, 222–3.   [77] Emphasis added; quoted in Baird 1990, 20–1.
[78] Emphasis added; quoted in Baird 1990, 84–5.   [79] Quoted in Baird 1990, 84.

feeling deep in their souls… With his song, sung today by millions, Horst Wessel has won a place in history which will last much longer than this stone and iron memorial. Even after millennia have passed, when there isn't a stone left standing in this huge city of Berlin, the greatest of the German freedom movements and its poet will be remembered. Comrades, raise the banners, Horst Wessel, who lies under this stone, is not dead. His spirit is with us every hour of every day, and he is marching in our columns.[80]

The battle of Langemarck and German martyrdom

On the night of October 26, 1914, a poorly prepared but supremely overconfident group of young German soldiers were sent into battle against a battle-hardened British unit. Without supporting artillery barrages, the young Germans were mowed down by the thousand. The German commanders who ordered this futile disaster were not blamed, instead the dead became enshrined as the sacrificial heroes of Langemarck, the battlefield's location in Flanders. In *Mein Kampf*, Hitler recorded his own experience in this same sector:

> We marched silently through a wet, cold night in Flanders, and just as the sun began to disperse the fog, an iron greeting was sent our way and shrapnel and shells exploded all around us; but before the smoke had cleared, the first hurrahs welled up from two thousand voices as the first messengers of death. Then we heard the crack and roar of gunfire, singing and yelling, and with wild eyes we all lunged forward, faster and faster, until suddenly man-to-man fighting broke out in turnip fields and thickets. We heard the sounds of a song from afar which came closer and closer to us, passing from one company to another, and then, just as men were dying all around us it spread into our ranks, and we passed it on: "Deutschland, Deutschland über alles, über alles in der Welt!"[81]

In July 1932, a monument to the 11,000 Langemarck dead was dedicated. A well-known writer on World War I, Josef Magnus Wehner, later one of "Hitler's poets," gave the dedication speech in which the deeds of the fallen were immortalized:

> The dying sang! The stormers sang. The young students sang as they were being annihilated: "Deutschland, Deutschland über alles, über alles in der Welt." But by singing this song, they were resurrected once more, a thousand times, and they will rise again a thousand times until the end of the Reich. Because the sacred German Reich is not a question of boundaries or countries, *it is as infinite as the world itself, created by God, and given to the Germans as an immortal commission.* Their song did not perish when they

---

[80] Quoted in Baird 1990, 87.   [81] Quoted in Baird 1990, 4.

died at Langemarck. The dead heroes became an omen for the German people.[82]

When the Third Reich was established, the fallen of Langemarck were merged with those of the Feldherrnhalle, the Nazi dead in the November 9, 1923 Munich uprising. As Hitler affirmed, "one can serve God only in heroic raiment."[83] And Jay Baird[84] comments, "In his demented ideological world based on racial struggle, heroic death was more beautiful than life itself… *Five years of humiliation had taken its toll on the insurgents. The terrible disappointment of defeat in the Great War, coupled with abuse on their return from the front, was more than they could bear.* Further, they were traumatized by unemployment, Bolshevik insurgency, inflation, governmental instability, and the French occupation of the Ruhr."

At his trial in 1924, Hitler returned in spirit to the fields of Flanders where the battle of Langemarck was fought. The sixteen dead as the result of the failed Munich uprising had not died in vain, for their sacrifice, along with those of Langemarck, and Leo Schlageter, would contribute to the unification and resurgence of the German people. Accordingly, "The army, which has formed behind us, is growing from day to day, and from hour to hour. I have the proud hope, that the time is coming again when these small battle-ready units will become battalions, then regiments, and will grow to divisions, and that they will raise our old standards out of the filth, and our old flags will wave proudly in the wind once more."[85]

Later, in November 1933, after the Nazis had won their election victory, there was a massive celebration of the 10-year anniversary of the abortive Munich uprising. At the celebration, Hitler stated: "We were determined to put an end to that *regime of shame*… On that night and on the next day our young Movement opened the eyes of the entire German people, and set an example of heroism which it needed later. We can say tonight ten years later joyfully and with pride – we were victorious and as a result the year 1923 has become one of the sweetest memories of our whole lives, a memory which moves us to the quick."[86]

In 1935, a Temple of Honor was built in which the disinterred bodies of the "martyrs" were reburied. The Temple of Honor was to be the center of a complex of party and official buildings. The wife of one of the dead, Frau Gerdy Troost, stated:

> The Temple of Honor of the first martyrs of the Movement lies between the broad granite Forum, the "community space" of our Volk, and the Führerbau. Faith and the readiness for self-sacrifice represent the eternal bonds between a Volk and its leadership. The fallen stand as an "Eternal Guard" for the ideals for which they died. They help guide the decision

---

[82] Emphasis added; quoted in Baird 1990, 8.   [83] Quoted in Baird 1990, 41.
[84] Emphasis added; Baird 1990, 41–2.   [85] Quoted in Baird 1990, 45.
[86] Emphasis added; quoted in Baird 1990, 53.

making in the Führerbau next to them. They inspire those who take their
oaths here and the people who make pilgrimages to this sacred place year
after year. The greatness and living power of ideology have found their worthy incarnation in this structure.[87]

And when the bronze sarcophagi were raised into their places and the horses
hooves of the Wehrmacht honor guard resounded strongly, cannons were fired.
The official script of the event stated, "The sarcophagi are in place. The fallen of
9 November 1923 have been resurrected and have taken their positions as
Eternal Guards, directly between the two buildings of the Führer. The drum roll
commences, just as it does with the ordinary changing of the guard."[88]

Baird[89] comments, "Viewers are immediately swept into a world of German
heroes who offered themselves in sacrifice, were resurrected, and returned to
live on with their comrades... The flow of German history, and their place in
its future development, was clear. The sacrifice of the two million dead in the
Great War had been fulfilled by the martyrs of 1923. Hitler showed the way to a
glorious future."

Josef Magnus Wehner ties together the themes of despair of the mothers
of the fallen, sacrifice, and resurrection through German unity. "[The mothers'] sacred grief, the tears of the widows and orphans, will lead to the pain of a
new birth, and finally there will arise out of blood and death the new man, the
Führer, on whose shoulders rests the construction of the future... They died,
that we might become. Without their sacrifice we would not have been transformed, our hearts beat with their blood. The true meaning of their death is our
resurrection in the Reich."[90]

The Volksstaat

The parlous condition of the German *Volk*, at least in the Nazi view, also led
to a thoroughly distorted politics of virtue based *only* on the perceived needs
of the *Volk*. Accordingly, Hitler stated in October 1935: "I view myself as
the most independent of men...obligated to no one, subordinate to no one,
indebted to no one – instead answerable only to my own conscience. *And this
conscience has but one single commander – our Volk!*"[91] German "morality,
customs, sense of justice, religion, etc." were to be protected by the Nazis.[92]
Whenever a key decision was to be made, only the needs of the *Volk* were to
be considered: "To do justice to God and our own conscience, we have turned
once more to the German *Volk*... We are not fighting for ourselves, but for
Germany."[93]

---

[87] Quoted in Baird 1990, 58.   [88] Quoted in Baird 1990, 62.
[89] Baird 1990, 65.   [90] Quoted in Baird 1990, 90.
[91] Emphasis added; quoted in Koonz 2003, 4.
[92] Quoted in Koonz 2003, 21.   [93] Quoted in Koonz 2003, 31.

Earlier during World War I, the august literary figure Thomas Mann reflected this orientation. Writing during that war and the mobilization of the state during an unexpectedly long war, Mann[94] wrote: "The *Volksstaat*, the politicization of the people, to say it once more, is necessary because Germany has been put 'into the saddle' and must not fall off; it is necessary for the sake of the governmental tasks she feels called to." Mann came perilously close to the *völkisch* ideas of the Nazis and their National Socialism. During wartime, Mann articulated, and Lepenies[95] concurs, that "when culture was accepted as a substitute for politics, the absence of morality in the public sphere was easily accepted as well." According to Mann,[96] "realizing that, one should not overestimate the significance of legal order for national life, with all intellectual reservations, by the way, and in the quiet confidence that the German *Volksstaat* will show important and quite national differences from the democracy of the rhetorical bourgeois."

Recall that Thomas Mann became a dedicated anti-Nazi, fled Germany in 1933 almost immediately after the Nazi accession to power, and in the US, while accepting its citizenship, argued strongly for democratic principles. Yet the earlier Mann, the acclaimed author, future Nobel Prize winner,[97] and cultural icon, understood the undemocratic (or even anti-democratic) *Volksstaat* as the preferred political organization for Germany. It was only upon observing the extraordinarily dangerous consequences of the Nazis' uniting of politics with war-derived cultural elements that he ultimately arrived at his democratic ethos.

This was ethno-nationalism at its most extreme and primitive, yet evoked the devotion of even the most sophisticated German thinkers. After the rise of Hitler to power, Martin Heidegger, for one, sought now to incite "a spiritual renewal of life in its entirety."[98] Sacrifice for the *Volk* was deeply admired by Heidegger. Indeed in one of his first public lectures, Heidegger spoke of Leo Schlageter's "hardness and clarity" on the tenth anniversary of his execution by the French. Following the increasingly prominent theme of martyrdom and regeneration, Heidegger urged his audience to allow Schlageter's memory to "stream through them."[99] Claudia Koonz reproduces a Nazi poster showing the spirit of a dead soldier of the Great War virtually passing into the body of a contemporary[100] Nazi storm trooper. It is titled "The Front Soldier: Your spirit restores my honor!"[101]

Carl Schmitt, the initial self-appointed ideologue of the Nazi Party, was a political theorist who sought German unity in contrast to the Germany of 1916 in which "the *Volk* pushes itself on, instinctively wanting to submit and letting itself be whipped."[102] "Homogeneity" and "authenticity" were the two most important constituent qualities of the new German community. The former

---

[94] [1918] 1983, 197.   [95] 2006, 47.   [96] [1918] 1983, 196.   [97] 1929.
[98] Quoted in Koonz 2003, 50.   [99] Quoted in Koonz 2003, 52.
[100] 1933.   [101] Quoted in Koonz 2003, 225.   [102] Quoted in Koonz 2003, 57.

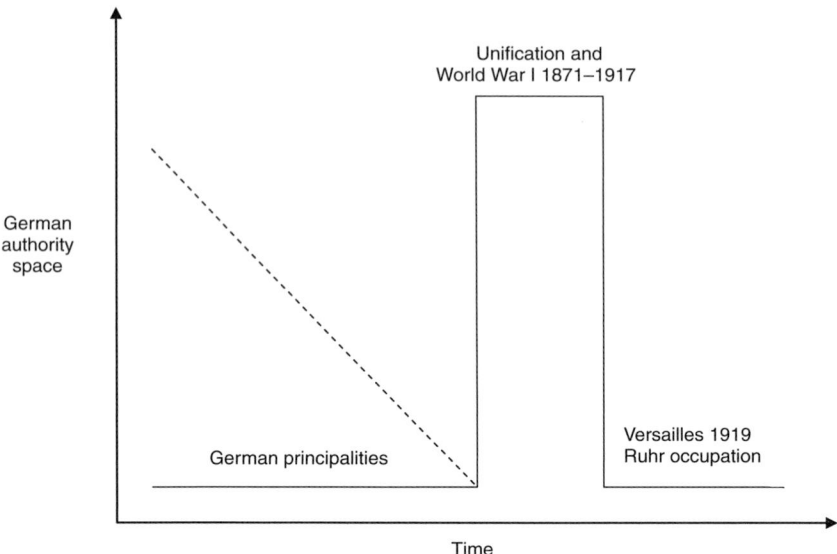

Figure 4.2: Changes in German authority space over time

demanded the exodus of those (principally Jews) who did not belong to the *Volk*. Public life was to be "purified" of non-Aryans. "Authenticity" was understood to be "allegiance to one's *volk*."[103] In 1933, a well-known actress praised the rescue of morality from the "'totally and essentially alien' Jewish rationalism. 'Now reason stops leading us…a heroic Germanic passion commands. And it's high time, too!'"[104]

The ephemeral gain for Germany is shown in Figure 4.2. Schiller, like Machiavelli for Italy, laments the state of national disunity. But unity did come in 1871, to be followed by a near hegemony on the European continent. Alas, World War I would eventuate in loss of territory (see Table 3.2) and the humiliation of the French occupation of the Ruhr. But successive ephemera will later appear in the German case first as a result of its participation in World War I and then a perception of its impending loss in World War II, as will be shown in Chapter 13.

Having illustrated the trajectory of Italian and German history in these figures, no further graphic material is necessary in this chapter. The conformity to the theory of the following cases of fascism and proto-fascism has already been shown in Table 3.2. The important exception of Greece will be discussed at length in Chapter 11 on the Balkans. In succeeding chapters, graphic illustrations

---

[103] Koonz 2003, 59.   [104] Quoted in Koonz 2003, 81.

will be presented either when no tabular material has been presented, or the appropriate table does not present all of the relevant information.

Hungary and Romania

Hungary and Romania were much smaller states that in themselves could not initiate major warfare and invasions leading to large-scale killing, yet did participate in the mass murder of perceived internal enemies, especially the Jews. The Hungarian government actually had two fascist incarnations. The first occurred immediately after World War I with the rise of the "Szeged Idea," a form of native Hungarian fascism that included a reversal of massive territorial losses by Hungary in the Trianon Treaty of 1920 and virulent anti-Semitism.

Nicholas Nagy-Talavera[105] elaborates: "Of the 325,000 km² territory of the lands of the Holy Crown of St. Stephen (Croatia and Slovenia included), only 92,000 km² were left under Hungarian control. Some 103,000 km² went to Romania, 61,500 km² to Czechoslovakia, 20,500 km² to Yugoslavia (in addition to 43,000 km² of Croatia and Slovenia), and about 4,000 km² to Austria. Fiume, Hungary's only port, became Italian; even Poland acquired a small piece of Hungarian territory. Of a prewar population of 21 million, Hungary was left with 7.6 million." Commenting further, "This situation was not made easier by the ill-treatment meted out by the Successor States to their large, newly acquired Hungarian minorities… And in all this, one must keep in mind that Hungarian thought centered much more around historical rights, dating back a continuity of a thousand years, than around the relatively new and roughly enforced principle of self-determination of peoples. Hungary had one answer for Trianon: 'No, no, never!' (*Nem, nem, soha!*)."[106]

As early as 1919, Gyula Gömbös, a former captain on the Austro-Hungarian general staff[107] and a leader of the Szeged group, spoke of himself as a Hungarian National Socialist.[108] After assuming the post of prime minister in 1932 (but not as a representative of the Szeged group), Gömbös did not initiate any anti-Semitic activity, but did lay the political foundations for later collaboration with the Germans in deporting several hundred thousand Jews after March 1944.[109] According to Michael Mann,[110] "He [Gömbös] moved steadily toward fascism. He declared violence to be 'an acceptable means of statecraft…to shape the course of history, not in the interest of a narrow clique, but of an entire nation.' He now embraced corporatist solutions to national unity and moved closer to Mussolini. After Hitler's coup he promised Göring he would introduce totalitarianism and he wrote to Hitler describing himself as a 'fellow racist.'" Or as Nicholas Nagy-Talavera[111] avers: "The full responsibility for the year 1944 lies

---

[105] 2001, 85.   [106] Nagy-Talavera 2001, 85–6.   [107] Deák 1965, 377.
[108] Weber 1964, 90.   [109] Braham 2000, 23.   [110] 2004, 243.   [111] 2001, 341.

with the Szeged Idea – the line that can be traced from Gömbös straight to Imrédy [Hungarian prime minister at the time of the deportations]. Most of the protagonists of 1944 also came from Szeged."

But the Arrow Cross became the Hungarian fascist political party with the largest electoral mass base, proportionally larger than that of the Nazis in Germany at the height of their electoral success. The Arrow Cross was directly responsible for the deaths of at least 50–60,000 Hungarian Jews during its brief tenure in office.[112] It was founded in 1935 by Ferenc Szálasi,[113] a veteran of World War I and later a member of the general staff, as the Party of the National Will that later, in 1938, was transformed into the Arrow Cross party. Shortly after the collaborating government of Admiral Horthy (the Hungarian Regent) declared an armistice, effectively withdrawing from the Axis coalition in October 1944, the Arrow Cross staged a successful coup. It was this government that would be directly responsible for handing over 50,000 Jews to the Germans, who did not have the manpower to carry out the deportations themselves. Additional thousands of Jews in Budapest and elsewhere were murdered by Arrow Cross thugs. Only the completed conquest of Hungary by Soviet forces ended this reign of terror.[114]

Romanian fascism was represented by the Legion of the Archangel Michael – more commonly known as the Iron Guard – formed in 1927 as an offshoot of the League of National Christian Defense founded by Corneliu Codreanu in 1923.[115] Of all the major European fascist organizations that attained political power,[116] it was the only one with a strong religious base, Eastern Orthodoxy.[117] During the approximate period in which the Iron Guard directly participated in the Romanian government (September 1940–March 1941), more than 600 Jews were killed.[118] But the influence of the Iron Guard would extend later to the Iaşi pogrom of June 1941, shortly after the German invasion of the Soviet Union. The number of Jewish dead was estimated at 3–4,000.[119] When the war got well underway, Romanian collaboration with Nazi Germany, again with strong individual Iron Guard participation, would lead to the deaths of 250,000 Jews in Romania and neighboring conquered Soviet territories. According to Raul Hilberg,[120] "no country, besides Germany, was involved in massacres of Jews on such a scale."

---

[112] Braham 2000, 253.

[113] Payne 1995, 273.   [114] Nagy-Talavera 2001.   [115] Weber 1965b, 517–27; 1966.

[116] For an important fascist movement with religious trappings that did not attain political power, see Brustein (1988).

[117] An earlier regime with fascist leanings was formed in December 1937 (lasting only until February 1938) by a mentor of Codreanu, Alexander Cuza, and Octavian Goga of the National Christian Defense Party. But Cuza disapproved of illegality and violence (Weber 1965b, 526), and the party ultimately did not achieve the mass base of the Iron Guard (Jelavich 1983, 206).

[118] Ioanid 2000, 61.   [119] Ioanid 2000, 77.   [120] 2003, 809.

In common with other forms of fascism, especially Nazism, the Iron Guard emphasized extreme sacrifice. Its newspaper once wrote: "The most beautiful aspect of Legionary life is death. The Legionary death has nothing in common with ordinary death. Through his death the Legionary becomes one with Eternity; through his death the Legionary becomes the earthly incarnation of history. He becomes a legend. The Legionary must not hesitate before death. Legionary death is dear to his heart; a goal is achieved through it; it becomes a symbol. The death of the Legionary is a symbol, a cult."[121]

Prototypical fascism

Russia

Certainly, paramilitarism as one of the behavioral attributes of fascism existed in Russia in the form of the Black Hundreds, as well as willingness to kill, theatricality, an emphasis on unity in opposition to liberalism, and confrontations with modernity. An etiology deriving from origins in war and contraction of authority space after the Russo-Japanese War are also characteristic of this instance. As the first European great power to be defeated by a non-European one in the modern period, and with the loss of territory to Japan (southern half of Sakhalin Island and the Liaotung Peninsula[122]), Russia felt humiliated. The extent of that humiliation can be gauged by Stalin's victory address on the occasion of Japan's unconditional surrender on September 2, 1945. Mentioned in Chapter 3, it is worth repeating here:

> The defeat of the Russian troops in 1904 in the period of the Russo-Japanese War left grave memories in the minds of our peoples. It was a dark stain on our country. Our people trusted and awaited the day when Japan would be routed and the stain wiped out. For forty years have we, men of the older generation, waited for this day. And now this day has come![123]

And this defeat came after the earlier gains of the 1877–78 Russo-Turkish War in which territory was gained from the defeated Ottomans: southern Bessarabia, Kars, Ardahan, and Batum (as a free port[124]).[125] Earlier still, Russia's performance in the Crimean War (1853–56) against Britain and France, which led to an imposed peace settlement entailing the loss of the mouth of the Danube River, southern Bessarabia, and the demilitarization of the Black Sea, highlighted her

---

[121] Quoted in Glenny 1999, 447.   [122] Mazour 1962, 338.
[123] Quoted in Wolfe 1984, 279.   [124] Mazour 1962, 303.
[125] Although the Congress of Berlin in 1878 frustrated the major Russian political goal of massive Bulgarian expansion at Ottoman expense, the territories conquered by Russia remained almost entirely intact (only Batum became a free port). Afterwards, as Bulgaria drifted steadily out of the Russian orbit, ultimately siding with the Central Powers during World War I, the "loss" of territory by Bulgaria was seen by Russian policy makers as a salutary consequence of the Congress of Berlin.

backwardness relative to the other states of Europe.[126] Further, prior to their victory, the Japanese apparently had financially assisted various revolutionary forces in the Russian Empire in the interests of its weakening. Jewish revolutionaries *and* capitalists, both representing elements of modernity, were to be blamed by the emerging rightist movements for these presumed accelerants of the Russian defeat.[127]

This defeat and the succeeding revolution were to be firmly linked in the public mind. On December 20, 1904 Port Arthur fell to the Japanese after a long siege. This was to be followed almost immediately on January 9 by Bloody Sunday, in which the tsar's troops fired on a peaceful crowd of demonstrators approaching the Winter Palace.[128] It was this event that most clearly indicated the state insecurity pervading the tsarist government at that time; it was also the event that was to signal the start of revolution in earnest, to be followed by the rightist reaction.

In the spring and summer of 1905 there appeared a "veritable mushroom growth of right-wing groups in dozens of towns all over the country."[129] When the tsar issued his October 17 manifesto granting civil liberties and an elected assembly in order to stem the tide of revolution,[130] the counter-revolutionary Black Hundreds, blaming the Jews for this "liberal declaration," initiated a series of disturbances during the week of October 18–25, with Jews as the primary targets. About fifty pogroms were enacted against Jewish communities throughout Russia, including those in Kiev, Odessa, and Kishinev.[131] The Odessa pogrom was described by Hans Rogger[132] as committed by "yellow-shirted bands that terrorized the entire city of Odessa for three days."[133]

Most important among the Black Hundreds was the "Union of the Russian People" (URP), founded on October 22 to establish a firm political base for the violent counter-revolutionary activity.[134] Among the organizers of the URP at that time and later were a Dr. A. I. Dobrovin, N. E. Markov, and V. M. Purishkevich. When the organization broke up in 1909, it was Purishkevich, probably the most violent of the lot, who was to found the Union of the Archangel Michael as a successor organization.[135] Note the similarity of this organizational title with the later Romanian fascist Legion of the Archangel Michael (Iron Guard). And as Purishkevich[136] exclaimed concerning his political participation in the Duma (the newly established Russian national legislature): "To the right of me there is only the wall." He was also prone to the outbursts and theatricality that we now associate with fascism.[137]

On December 23, Tsar Nicholas II accepted a medal from the URP and wished it "total success" in its efforts to unify the Russian people.[138] Many Orthodox

---

[126] Mazour 1962, 251.   [127] Wolfe 1984, 280.   [128] Rawson 1995, 10–11.
[129] Rogger 1965, 483.   [130] Rogger 1965, 483.   [131] Dubnov 1973, 739.
[132] 1965, 483, 492.   [133] 1965, 483, 492.   [134] Rogger 1964b, 402.
[135] Rawson 1995, 230.   [136] Quoted in Rogger 1965, 494.   [137] Rogger 1965.
[138] Rawson 1995, 143.

clerics joined the Union, or (as in the case of one distinguished priest, Father Ioann of Kronstadt, dean of St. Andrew's Cathedral at that important naval base near St. Petersburg) accepted honorary membership in the Union.

Thus, indicative of the anti-liberal purposes of the URP as the largest organization associated with the Black Hundreds is the affiliation of like-minded organizations such as "The White Flag," "People's Union," "League of Struggle against Sedition," "Autocracy and Church," and "For Tsar and Order."[139] Because of these more traditional associations, the URP has not been considered by many to be a true fascist organization.[140] Yet even Rogger[141] admits that "paramilitary organizations (such as the 'Yellow shirts' in Odessa and secret combat groups, the *druzhiny*)...are reminiscent of the *fasci di combattimento*."

Perhaps the most accurate assessment of these organizations, especially their leaders, Markov and Purishkevich, is that they can be considered to be "proto-fascist."[142] This is especially the case in light of the apparent influence on the Romanian Iron Guard, and the fact that many of the Black Hundreds later escaped the Bolshevik Revolution of 1917 by fleeing to Germany, particularly Bavaria, where they were to be deeply involved in the Nazi cause.[143]

The Protocols of the Elders of Zion, the infamous forgery prepared by the tsar's secret service agents, first published in serialized form in Russia in 1903, and reprinted in book form in 1905,[144] was to become a staple of Nazi belief and propaganda throughout the rise of that movement. It is this ability to exert influence in democratic Germany more than in increasingly autocratic Russia (but traditionally so) that suggests the importance of Juan Linz's[145] concept of a political space in which fascists or their prototypes can maneuver to gain political influence.

France

In the *Action française*, we have another movement that Eugen Weber[146] calls "proto-fascist"; Ernst Nolte[147] agrees: "The practice of the Action Française anticipates, in the clear simplicity of the rudimentary, the characteristic traits of the infinitely cruder and more wholesale methods used in Italy and Germany."

Like the Russian (URP) case, *Action française*, under the leadership of Charles Maurras, was rigorously monarchist and prone to street violence. As a nationalist French movement it was anti-Dreyfusard[148] and anti-German. Maurras' early ideas very possibly were influenced by the French defeat in the Franco-Prussian

---

[139] Rogger 1964a, 78.   [140] e.g. Rogger 1964b.   [141] Rogger 1964b, 404.
[142] Rawson 1995, 230.   [143] Malia 1999, 351.   [144] Baron 1976, 55.
[145] 1980.   [146] 1965a, 125.   [147] 1966, 26
[148] A Jewish officer on the French general staff, Alfred Dreyfus, was falsely accused of treason and imprisoned until ultimately exonerated. Anti-Dreyfusards were those who opposed that process of exoneration.

War when he was roughly two and a half years of age. He described Prussians as "wicked men, barbarians wearing spiked helmets."[149]

When France was defeated in May 1940, in stark contrast to its victory in 1918 but consistent with the humiliation of 1870, and the independent Vichy regime under Maréchal Philippe Pétain was established only in the two-fifths of France not occupied by Germany, Maurras and *Action française* became even more extreme. After the first Vichy anti-Semitic legislation was passed in October 1940, Maurras remarked that an opportunity had now arrived to rid France of its "Jewish scourge."[150] Even into late 1944, he refused to countenance any effort to save the East European Jews in France, or even French-Jewish citizens that were continually under threat of deportation, yielding a total of approximately 72,500 Jewish dead.[151] This, despite his opposition in principle to German occupation.

And like the tsar in relation to the URP, Pétain called Maurras "le plus français des Français."[152] Maurras reciprocated in his complete support for Pétain and the Vichy regime as the apotheosis of monarchism in the twentieth century. Nolte[153] concludes: "The Action Française [sic] was the first political grouping of any influence or intellectual status to bear unmistakably fascist traits."[154]

This review of European fascism and proto-fascism is now followed by that other great European invention – communism. As Russia spawned strong proto-fascist movements, it even earlier developed socialist groupings, culminating in Bolshevism and Stalinist communism. In many respects, these latter forms of extremism were more consequential than fascism because of their later influence on Maoism and the Cambodian Khmer Rouge.

---

[149] Nolte 1966, 59.   [150] Nolte 1966, 82.   [151] Marrus and Paxton 1995, 343.
[152] Nolte 1966, 80.   [153] 1966, 25.   [154] Also quoted in Payne 1995, 47.

5

Communism

This chapter examines the etiology of communism as it evolved in Russia both before the Bolshevik Revolution and thereafter; it later emphasizes the genesis of Stalinist extremism.[1] In contrast to fascism's, especially Nazism's, departure from European (Western) political traditions, communism will be seen to emerge from native ideational roots, especially as it was evolving among the intelligentsia. Tsarist authority space was contracting slowly during the nineteenth century, well before the defeat by Japan in 1905 was to accelerate this process. As we shall see, the impact of this defeat on Stalin was to be consequential for his later extremism. Indeed, Stalin's entire personal development as a Bolshevik revolutionary is crucial to understanding the formation of his later extremist policies.

Because the Soviet, especially Stalinist template, was so important for later communist developments in, say, China[2] or Cambodia,[3] this initial communist model will be emphasized. For example, according to Vojtech Mastny,[4] a prescient observer of the communist scene, "There cannot be a doubt that Mao Zedong on his first visit to Moscow treated Stalin as the supreme authority of world communism, with a reverence that was not merely pretended but rooted in a perception of common interests, to which the Chinese leader repeatedly and cogently alluded." Russia also is unique in being the crucible both for the formation of proto-fascism, as we saw in the preceding chapter, and Bolshevism, which would later evolve into communist and Stalinist extremism.

Communism is singular in its extremist program involving mass murder carried out during peacetime, in contrast to mass murders by the fascists during wartime or colonial insurrection. How do we understand these processes? The origins of Soviet communism conform approximately to the pattern identified in Figure 1.1 (see Chapter 1), in which the initial defeat in the Crimean War (1853–56) was followed by the victory over Turkey in the Russo-Turkish War of 1877–78. A stunning defeat by Japan in the Russo-Japanese War of 1904–05 was followed by an even more stellar collapse of the Russian forces when confronted

---

[1] A portion of this chapter is reprinted from Midlarsky 2009b with the kind permission of the publisher, Taylor & Francis.
[2] Chang and Halliday 2005.   [3] Jackson 1989; Chandler 2000.   [4] 1995/96, 22.

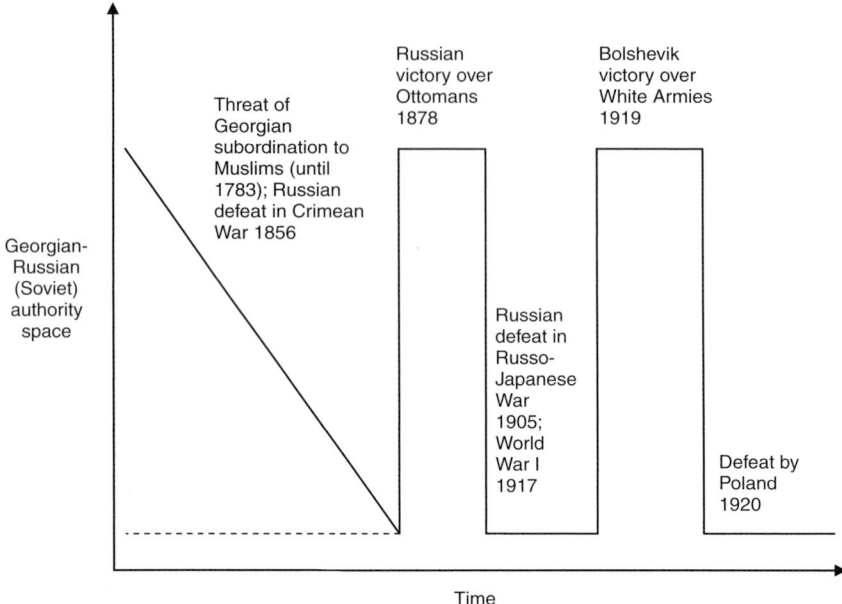

Figure 5.1:   Changes in Georgian-Russian (Soviet) authority space over time

by those of Germany during World War I. A victory of the Bolshevik armies over those of the counter-revolutionary Whites was quickly followed by a defeat of the Bolsheviks by the newly organized nationalist Poles in 1920. This pattern of successive ephemera, later to be specifically applied to the rise of Stalinism, is seen in Figure 5.1.[5]

This approximately 65-year history indicated one overriding conclusion. When confronted by non-Western armies like the Ottomans, or hastily organized counter-revolutionary armies drawn from a newly defeated mass of peasants and their tsarist leaders, the Russians (now in Bolshevik form) could emerge victorious. But Western European or even rapidly moderniz-ing Eastern states like Japan, or highly motivated (and mobilized) Eastern European nationalists such as the Poles could defeat the Russians. In the absence of a concerted effort to modernize, and to do it quickly, Bolshevik Russia could easily go down to defeat once again at the hands of European, American, or Japanese forces.

This constellation of potential external victors in a future war was supple-mented by the recognition that political power was only insecurely held by the Bolshevik minority. True, the Marxist-Leninist dialectic stated unequivocally

---

[5] See also Midlarsky 2009b.

that the representatives of the working class, i.e., the Communist Party, although unelected, were historically ordained in that role. The New Economic Policy (NEP) initiated by Lenin in 1921 as a form of state capitalism to blunt peasant resentment and potential organized opposition was a successful palliative restoring Soviet production in 1926 to its pre-war level.[6] However, "The NEP years relaxed the non-political atmosphere, but not the feeling that the party was a beleaguered minority which might have history on its side, but was working against the grain of the Russian masses and the Russian present. The decision to launch the industrial revolution from above, automatically committed the system to imposing authority, perhaps even more ruthlessly than in the Civil War years, because its machinery for exercising power continuously was now much greater."[7]

Without that industrial revolution, two things were more likely to happen: (1) another defeat by a modernized power (or coalition of them), and (2) a loss of domestic authority to a rising opposition from conservative groups that could mobilize peasant opposition. In any event, a conviction permeated the Bolshevik cadres that power must not be relinquished and the Revolution not be reversed.

Goals were routinely set too high in the expectation that massive exertions would be required to meet them. As in the pre-NEP "War Communism" period, cruelty was used as a way to accelerate the rate of economic growth. The massive famine of 1932–33 was a consequence, as was an anti-Stalin reaction to the unrealistic goals and the cruelties inflicted in this process. The absence of limits gave the terror an inhuman face that many of the Old Bolsheviks could not stomach. Accordingly, "The seventeenth Congress of the CPSU(b) revealed a substantial opposition to him [Stalin]. Whether it actually constituted a threat to his power we shall never know, for between 1934 and 1939 four or five million party members and officials were arrested on political grounds, four or five hundred thousand of them were executed without trial, and the next (eighteenth) Party Congress which met in the spring of 1939, contained a bare thirty-seven survivors of the 1827 delegates who had been present at the seventeenth in 1934."[8]

Russian roots of Soviet extremism

Because of its centrality, it is worthwhile repeating the summary observation by Pierre Pascal of late nineteenth-century Russian governance under Alexander III (1881–94): "an accentuated divorce between authority, resting on an artificially consolidated nobility, and the country in full economic and social evolution."[9] During the 1860s and 1870s, Alexander II emancipated the serfs, established an

---

[6] Hobsbawm 1994, 379.   [7] Hobsbawm 1994, 387.   [8] Hobsbawm 1994, 391.
[9] Quoted in Mazour 1962, 306.

independent court system including trial by jury, and created local elected assemblies (Zemstvos), as well as municipal legislatures in major cities. In the 1890s the finance minister Sergei Witte promoted an industrial growth that was "more rapid and revolutionary than any previously experienced by a Western nation."[10] For the first time Russia had a genuine urban working class. Introduction of the gold standard in 1897 made Russia a prime locus of Western investment. Also for the first time, Russia now had the basis for a civil society.[11]

In stark contrast, as late as 1905, the Criminal Code regarding sedition was the same as that which existed in 1845:

1. All attempts to limit the authority of the sovereign, or to alter the prevailing system of government, as well as to persuade others to do so, or to give overt expression to such intentions, or to conceal, assist, or fail to denounce anyone guilty of these offenses, carry the death penalty and the confiscation of all property;

2. The spreading by word of mouth or by means of the written or printed word of ideas which, without actually inciting to sedition, as defined above, *raise doubts about the authority of the sovereign or lessen respect for him or his office*, are punishable *by the loss of civil rights and terms of hard labor from four to twelve years, as well as corporal punishment and branding*.[12]

When a Zemstvo delegation approached the new tsar with requests for greater responsiveness of the national government to local needs in January 1895, Nicholas II responded that he would "maintain the principle of autocracy just as firmly and unswervingly as did my late and unforgettable father [Alexander III]."[13] This statement would soon give rise to an unyielding response by popular forces as in "You first began the struggle and the struggle will come."[14]

The nineteenth century witnessed a florescence of political extremism directed against the increasingly sclerotic tsarist state. After the failed Decembrist uprising of westernizing army officers in 1825, as early as 1830 Mikhail Lermontov wrote the poem "Prediction":

> The day will come, for Russia that dark day
> When the Tsar's diadem will fall, and they,
> Rabble who loved him once, will love no more,
> And many will subsist on death and gore.
> Downtrodden law no shelter will provide
> For child or guiltless woman, Plague will ride
> From stinking corpses through the grief-struck land
> Where fluttering rags from cottages demand

---

[10] Malia 1999, 172.   [11] Malia 1999, 163.
[12] Emphasis added; quoted in Pipes 2003, 27.
[13] Quoted in Mazour 1962, 314.   [14] Quoted in Mazour 1962, 315.

> Help none can give. And famine's gnawing pangs
> Will grip the countryside with ruthless fangs.
> Dawn on the streams will shed a crimson light.
> And then will be revealed the Man of might
> Whom thou wilt know; and thou wilt understand
> Wherefore a shining blade is in his hand.
> Sorry will be thy lot, grief melt thine eyes
> And he will laugh at all thy fears and sighs.[15]

As Nicolas Berdyaev[16] comments: "This romantic poem written in 1830 foresees the horrors of a revolution which took place almost a century later." It is incredible, yet true, that the conditions ultimately yielding the Revolutions of 1905 and 1917 and their horrific totalitarian legacy were apparent nearly a century earlier.

Another prominent individual to recognize the savage nature of the forthcoming revolution was Konstantin Leontiev. "He foretold that the revolution would be tyrannical and bloody, that it would not be liberal but communist, that it would bring no proclamation of rights and of freedom and that the liberal radical intelligentsia would be overthrown. The revolution would not be humane and it would [heed] the old instincts of domination and submission."[17] In Leontiev's view, the revolution was not to be prevented. Hence, he withdrew to the center of Russian monasticism, Optina Pustyn', where in comfort, he lived the rest of his life.[18]

Konstantin Pobedonostsev

Intransigence of the tsarist autocracy during the nineteenth century inspired these reactions of anger (Lermontov) and resignation (Leontiev). The response of tsarist autocracy towards the end of the nineteenth century, in turn, was still more intransigence. Central to this effort was Konstantin Pobedonostsev, director general of the Most Holy Synod of the Russian Orthodox Church from 1880 until 1905, a position with ministerial status, and tutor to Tsars Alexander III and Nicholas II. In his intellectual and political tutelage, he provided the justification for unbridled autocracy. In this, he was the precursor of Vyacheslav Plehve, his draconian policies, and perhaps even of Lenin himself. According to Berdyaev:

> Like Pobedonostzev [sic] he [Lenin] thought that it was only possible to
> organize human life by coercion and force. As Pobedonostzev despised the
> ecclesiastical hierarchy over whom he had control, so also Lenin despised
> the revolutionary hierarchy which he controlled. He referred to the com-
> munists in mocking language and had no belief in their human qualities.

[15] Quoted in Berdyaev 1937, 92.   [16] Berdyaev 1937, 92.
[17] Berdyaev 1937, 104.   [18] Pipes 2005, 146–7.

> Both men alike believed in regimentation, in the forcible organization of
> the people, as the only way out. Society cannot be based upon human qual-
> ities. It must be so organized that the hopelessly bad human material shall
> be subjected to regimentation and made accustomed to the conditions of
> life lived as a community.[19]

Suffused with a passionate belief in Russian Orthodoxy, both as a religion and as
the only appropriate ideational basis for societal cohesion, he imbued his young
charges with the necessity for autocracy emanating from the Russian Orthodox
Church. Finnish and Baltic Lutherans, Polish and Lithuanian Roman Catholics,
and Jews in their Pale of Settlement simply could not have the same status as
Russian Orthodox citizens. Although at first he viewed the Jews as simply one
more non-Russian sector of the empire to be treated accordingly, he gradually
became more anti-Semitic, to the point where his principal intellectual partners
were the well-known anti-Semites Konstantin Aksakov and Mikhail Katkov.

Pobedonostsev became convinced that "our great ulcer has penetrated
everywhere."[20] Jews and liberals were virtually synonymous to him. All of the liberal newspapers and foreign interests in Russia were believed to be either Jewish
owned or in the service of Jews.[21] He expressed the hope that "one-third of the
Jews would emigrate, one-third would be assimilated, and one-third would die
out."[22] Exactly how this "dying out" was going to happen of course is crucial,
especially given the very rapid Jewish population growth at that time.

Despite Pobedonostsev's aversion to pogromist violence for fear of its spread
to other societal sectors, the beginnings of an annihilationist sentiment are
apparent that ultimately would be expressed in the deadly pogroms of 1919–20,
leading to as many as 150,000 Jewish dead.[23] Pobedonostsev consistently supported policies that would restrict Jewish access to the centers of Russian life,
whether it be in the form of quotas on university admissions, or limitations on
residence to the old Jewish Pale in the southwest of the country.[24]

Most consequential was Pobedonostsev's successful opposition to the Loris-
Melikov proposals for governmental reform. Mikhail Loris-Melikov was minister of the interior under Alexander II and was acutely aware of the desperate
need for reform. Perhaps his Armenian origin, and long successful service in
the Caucasus away from the power centers of Russia sharpened his perception of the necessity for change. In any event, although these proposals were
not at all radical even by nineteenth-century standards, they aroused the strong
opposition of Pobedonostsev. A General Commission would be elected by the
Zemstvos and local councils. These elected officials would then suggest reorgan-
izations of national finance and administration to be, in turn, recommended to
the Council of State.

---

[19] Berdyaev 1937, 188–9.   [20] Quoted in Byrnes 1968, 205.   [21] Byrnes 1968, 206.
[22] Byrnes 1968, 207.   [23] Vital 1999, 722.   [24] Byrnes 1968, 207.

On the same day that Tsar Alexander II approved these proposals, he was assassinated,[25] thereby providing Pobedonostsev with the opportunity to once again vigorously oppose these reforms, this time to the new tsar, Alexander III, his former student. He believed that these proposals would undermine and destroy Russian autocracy. The possibility that the General Commission might soon emerge as a national parliament and Russia as a representative democracy was abhorrent to Pobedonostsev. In a letter to a close friend, he wrote, "I tell him [Loris-Melikov] 'remember, I am in the position of a believer who cannot agree with idolaters. You are all idolaters, you worship the idols of freedom, and they are all idols, idols…'. But he only smiles."[26] Within 2 months the new tsar rejected the proposals for reform. The Manifesto of the new sovereign declared "that the chief aim of Alexander III was to uphold and consolidate the autocratic power entrusted to him by Divine Providence."[27]

Revealing in its detail is an interchange between the liberal B. N. Chicherin and Pobedonostsev in the summer of 1882. Prior to this meeting the two had been on friendly terms. Chicherin said to Pobedonostsev:

> You are the only serious man among all those surrounding the tsar; he (the tsar) must trust you more than the rest. Therefore, Russia considers you to be more responsible for what is being done; from you we Russians may rightfully demand an accounting. Where have you led us? After 1 March [the assassination of Alexander II] everyone without exception was ready to gather around the throne and to obey every wave of the tsar's hand. But now what kind of a position have you put us in? You have surrounded the throne with mud, so that it is now bespattered. You have pulled out of the mob all kinds of trash, and entrusted to it the governance of Russia. All decent people are forced to turn away with indignation. You object against a zemsky sobor [assembly of the land including clerical, military, merchant, town, and even peasant representatives], but you are driving us by compulsion toward a zemsky sobor.[28]

According to G. M. Hamburg:

> Pobedonostsev stopped Chicherin and exclaimed: "A zemsky sobor – that is chaos!" Chicherin answered, "I know that it is chaos, but from chaos comes a new world, and out of a rotten tree nothing will come, except decay." "And who will give it (a zemsky sobor) to you?" Pobedonostsev asked. Chicherin then reached up and grabbed the Ober-Procurator of the Synod by the shoulders and said: "We will take it, Konstantin Petrovich, we will take it. And for this we don't even have to move a muscle; it is enough to sit with an open mouth and everything will fall into it. Do you really imagine that you, with your Petersburg rot, can lead Russia onto a proper course?" Chicherin concluded this account of his conversation with Pobedonostsev,

[25] Mazour 1962, 274–5.   [26] Quoted in Byrnes 1968, 147.
[27] Mazour 1962, 305.   [28] Quoted in Hamburg 1984, 83–4.

by observing that "Pobedonostsev dolefully listened to my indignant reproaches. He considered me an irretrievably fallen man."[29]

Two fundamental beliefs provided the foundation for Pobedonostsev's political views. I examine them at some length because they will provide a useful comparison with the political outlook of contemporary radical Islamists. The first was the indissolubility of the connection between church and state. Accordingly, on the first page of his *Reflections of a Russian Statesman*, he writes "However powerful the State may be, its power is based alone upon identity of religious profession with the people; the faith of the people sustains it; when discord once appears to weaken this identity, its foundations are sapped, its power dissolves away."[30] The need for community is great; "it finds satisfaction only in the Church."[31] Of course, "Christianity is the source of every right in political and civil life, and of all true culture."[32] Interestingly, the communitarian function of religion is a major source of stability. "In our churches all social distinctions are laid aside, we surrender our positions in the world and mingle completely in the congregation before the face of God... The poorest beggar feels, with the greatest noble, that the church, at least, is his."[33] In this fashion, while the church satisfies the egalitarian impulse, political hierarchy can be maintained in the traditional autocratic manner.

Pobedonostsev's second fundamental belief was in the extreme danger of democracy. Thus, "Democracy now aspires to universal suffrage – a fatal error, and one of the most remarkable in the history of mankind."[34] Or, "Among the falsest of political principles is the principle of the sovereignty of the people, the principle that all power issues from the people, and is based upon the national will."[35] He distrusted the people, considering them "vulgar" and essentially unable to discriminate between good leaders and bad. Democracy might work more or less well in countries such as Britain, with its long history of individual participation in public life, but in Russia, with its communal forms of peasant organization and high levels of illiteracy, democracy simply would not do. In any event, democratic opinion, however consensual in its expression, cannot substitute for basic truths handed down from the one true Christian church. In Russia, of course, it is the Russian Orthodox Church that is the only legitimate source of Christian doctrine.

Compare these views with those of Sayyid Qutb (see Chapter 6), the apostle of Muslim extremism. If one substitutes "mosque" for "church," "Islam" for "Christianity," and the "Muslim world" for "Russia," then these autocratic and theocratic views of Pobedonostsev could just as easily have been stated by Qutb. The notion of fundamental truth uncompromised by popular belief or fashion

---

[29] Quoted in Hamburg 1984, 84.   [30] Pobedonostsev [1898] 1965, 1.
[31] Pobedonostsev [1898] 1965, 3.   [32] Pobedonostsev [1898] 1965, 19.
[33] Pobedonostsev [1898] 1965, 206.   [34] Pobedonostsev [1898] 1965, 26.
[35] Pobedonostsev [1898] 1965, 32.

is common to both. Religion and politics are indissoluble; indeed, as Patricia Crone[36] indicates, "As believers *and* as citizens they [Muslims] were members of the *umma*." It is no accident that Pobedonostsev's desire for the disappearance of one-third of Russia's Jews (in addition to the assimilation and emigration of the remainder) and bin Laden's murderous activities based very much on Qutb's thought, are rooted in visions of the ineffable as the basis for politics.

Continuities

Continuity of communist thinking and practice with that of earlier Russian revolutionary thought is suggestive of the deep roots of the Bolshevik Revolution in Russian history. This continuity stands in contrast to the novelty of fascism and radical Islamism in comparison with the earlier histories of European and Middle Eastern societies. Lenin, in particular, rooted his ideas in earlier Russian thought. Perhaps his most important contribution was advocacy of the formation of a professional and secret revolutionary organization that would seize the moment and lead the masses in a communist revolution. Spontaneity of the masses was not to be relied upon; instead, the small band of professional revolutionaries would constitute the revolutionary vanguard. In this, Lenin explicitly acknowledged his debt to Nikolai Chernyshevsky. Indeed, the title of Lenin's most important work *What is to be Done?* is an exact copy of Chernyshevsky's *What is to be Done?* written in the 1860s. Only the subtitles differ.

In that novel, Chernyshevsky describes his hero Rakhmetov who sleeps on a bed of nails to harden himself in order to better endure pain and suffering. He eats only semi-raw beef steak and black bread and works as a Volga boatman in order to build up his strength. Rakhmetov's purpose was to liberate himself from social conventions, lies, and oppression in order to prepare for prodigious revolutionary activity that was to establish a cooperative socialist commonwealth based on collective ownership of the soil.[37] Indeed, according to Anatole Mazour,[38] "It can be safely stated that the germinal ideas of the future collective agrarian economy were planted by the generation of Chernyshevsky." This prototypical radical would give rise to Lenin's notion of the professional revolutionary, just as it inspired the People's Will, a radical terrorist group that assassinated Tsar Alexander II. Lenin even confided to friends in a Geneva café in 1904 that Chernyshevsky's novel had deeply influenced his thinking about the ideal professional revolutionary.[39] Accordingly, Lenin stated that Chernyshevsky was:

> the greatest and most talented representative of socialism before Marx… Under his influence hundreds of people became revolutionaries… He plowed me up more profoundly than anyone else… After my brother's execution, knowing that Chernyshevsky's novel was one of his favorite books,

---

[36] 2004, 13; emphasis in original.   [37] Berlin 1978, 228.
[38] 1962, 277.   [39] Tucker 1975, xxxix.

I really undertook to read it, and I sat over it not for several days but for several weeks. Only then did I understand its depth... It's a thing that supplies energy for a whole lifetime.[40]

Karl Marx at the age of 50 taught himself Russian in order to be able to read Chernyshevsky's work.[41]

In the 1870s Pyotr Tkachev even more specifically established the template for a Russian revolution. Tkachev was not a democrat and his socialism was not of the democratic variety. He was a *political* revolutionary who, in contrast to Marx, set politics above economics on the path to revolution. The revolution was to be made by a dedicated minority of revolutionaries who were to employ terrorism, if necessary, in order to overthrow the Russian monarchy.[42] In describing him, Berdyaev[43] uses the term "the will to power," very much in the Leninist mode. Hence, Lenin drew on the pre-existing patterns of Russian revolutionary thinking and practice in his own revolutionary development. According to Robert Tucker,[44] "Trotsky described Lenin as a blend of Marxist internationalist and Russian revolutionary statesman with 'something about him that is strongly suggestive of a peasant.'" More generally, upon the failure of the populist People's Will after the assassination of Alexander II, according to Malia[45] "Marxism did not come to Russia because industrialization had produced a proletariat; it came to Russia because, after Populism's failure, the radical intelligentsia needed a new theory of revolution." And "Beneath Lenin's Marxist veneer, therefore, he was a throwback to the unscientific and conspiratorial People's Will, even to the idea of 'preventive revolution' against capitalism advocated by Petr [Pyotr] Tkachev in the mid-1870s; and the Bolshevik regime had in consequence turned out to be the mirror image of the backward autocracy it replaced."[46] It was Lenin's acceptance of Tkachev's advocacy of the revolutionary vanguard combined with elements of Marxist theory that would distinguish his leadership.

Lenin implemented these revolutionary ideas after the Bolshevik seizure of power both in his mode of decision making, and in his sponsorship of the Cheka (Soviet secret police). Lenin advocated the establishment of a proletarian dictatorship. What did he mean? "Dictatorship...is a big word, and big words should not be thrown about carelessly. Dictatorship is iron rule, government that is revolutionarily bold, swift and ruthless in suppressing both exploiters and hooligans. But our government is excessively mild, very often it resembles jelly more than iron. We must not forget for a moment that the bourgeois and petty-bourgeois element is fighting against the Soviet system."[47] Lenin's modus operandi was that of the final authority. Thus, according to a participant in sessions of the Council of People's Commissars, "Lenin was not merely a chairman but a

---

[40] Quoted in Katz and Wagner 1989, 32.   [41] Malia 1999, 183.
[42] Berdyaev 1937, 82.   [43] Berdyaev 1937, 83.   [44] 1975, lxi.   [45] 1999, 270.
[46] Quoted in Malia 1999, 271.   [47] Lenin [1918] quoted in Tucker 1975, 452.

recognized chief to whom everyone brought his thorny problems. The commissars quarreled among themselves in their daily work, but here Lenin had the last word; and all alike left these meetings reassured, as though their quarrels had been those of children now pacified by a wise parent."[48]

The impact of the tsarist police state

Given the intellectual foundations of Bolshevism during the nineteenth century, it is important that we explore the proximate pathways to the tsarist police state. According to Richard Pipes,[49] the immediate antecedent of this authoritarianism and the subsequent 1905 Revolution was the general university strike of February 1899, in itself a consequence of limitations placed on university students.

Following the assassination of Alexander II in 1881, the liberal University Statute of 1863 was substantially revised. University autonomy was now limited by placing all universities under the direct supervision of the Ministry of Education. Student organizations were declared illegal. The not unrealistic view held by the authorities that Russian universities were the seat of anti-tsarist activity was reinforced. And a forthcoming celebration of the anniversary of the founding of St. Petersburg University on February 8, 1899 was to provide the stimulus for the student strike. A well-known and popular rector of the university was persuaded by governmental authorities to post the following warning to students. It is quoted at length to suggest the flavor of the growing police state in tsarist Russia:

> On February 8, the anniversary of the founding of the Imperial St. Petersburg University, it has been not uncommon for students to disturb peace and order on the streets as well as in public places of St. Petersburg. These disturbances begin immediately after the completion of university celebrations when students, singing and shouting "Hurrah!," march in a crowd to the Palace Bridge and thence to Nevsky Prospect...
>
> On February 8, the police are obliged to preserve peace in the same manner as on any other day of the year. Should order be disturbed, they are obliged to stop the disturbance *at any cost*. In addition, the law provides for the use of force to end disorders. The results of such a clash with the police may be most unfortunate. Those guilty may be subject to arrest, the loss of privileges, dismissal and expulsion from the university, and exile from the capital. I feel obliged to warn the student body of this. Students must respect the law in order to uphold the honor and dignity of the university.[50]

This warning by the police is an effective illustration of the shrinking of tsarist authority space from an important, even critical, societal sector – the university

---

[48] Quoted in Tucker 1975, lv.   [49] 1990, 4.
[50] Emphasis added; quoted in Pipes 1990, 5–6.

students. Sanctions including the use of force were threatened in the absence of sufficient authority to prevent the occurrence of the more violent demonstrations by students. In point of fact, the students were infuriated and frequent clashes with the police ensued. As was becoming increasingly common in late Imperial Russia, protests were co-opted by the more extreme student elements. Socialists dominating a Mutual Aid Fund sought to politicize the student body. Among them were "Boris Savinkov, a future terrorist, Ivan Kaliaev, who in 1905 would assassinate Grand Duke Sergei, the governor-general of Moscow, and George Nosar (Khrustalev), who in October 1905 would chair the Petrograd Soviet."[51] They assumed leadership of what quickly became a widespread strike of some 25,000 students in national universities. A Manifesto of the students declared that the clashes were: "one episode of the regime that prevails in Russia, (a regime) that rests on arbitrariness, secrecy (*bezglasnost*), and complete lack of security, including even the absence of the most indispensable, indeed, the most sacred rights of the development of human individuality."[52] Vyacheslav Plehve, at that time the director of the Police Department, remarked that "almost all the regicides and a very large number of those involved in political crimes" were students.[53]

Six years later, in January 1905, after additional strikes by students and workers took place throughout the major cities of the empire, the shrinking of tsarist authority and a consequent state insecurity would lead to the massacre of innocents on Bloody Sunday. Tsarist Russia was already so autocratic in 1904 that Richard Pipes[54] concludes that, after Plehve's assumption of the office of minister of the interior in 1902: "During Plehve's two-year tenure in office, Russia came close to becoming a police state in the modern, 'totalitarian' sense of the word."

According to Leonard Schapiro, the Bolshevik organization at that time consisted of "a disciplined order of professional committee men, grouped around a band of conspirators who were all linked by personal allegiance to their chieftain, Lenin, and ready to follow him in any adventure, as long as his leadership appeared sufficiently radical and extreme."[55] A strong historical continuity exists between the Bolshevik movement and its socialist predecessors. As Malia remarks about the German Social Democratic Party (SPD), "This organization, even after its legalization in 1891, remained something of a bunker party – no longer underground but still a beleaguered subsociety in the Kaiserreich and thus structurally mobilized for survival. It was this model that the Russian Marxists adopted for their own party in 1903. And this structure can readily be adapted to top-down bureaucratic authoritarianism, as Robert Michels was the first to demonstrate in his classic study of the German SDs in 1911."[56]

Secrecy surrounding the activities of the professional revolutionary organization was mandated.[57] Lenin frequently argued for the "ruthless destruction of

---

[51] Pipes 1990, 6.   [52] Quoted in Pipes 1990, 7.   [53] Pipes 1990, 8.
[54] Pipes 1990, 9.   [55] Quoted in Pipes 1990, 361.   [56] Malia 1999, 272.
[57] Lenin [1902], cited in Zile 1992, 45.

the enemy."[58] He spoke of the "conquest of political power."[59] When power was seized, the state would be, in Lenin's words, "the machinery of suppression."[60] And an important Menshevik (social democratic) leader, Pavel Akselrod, wrote in June 1904 that Leninism was "a very simple copy or caricature of the bureaucratic-autocratic system of our Minister of the Interior [Plehve]."[61] The 1918 constitution of the Russian Socialist Federative Soviet Republic (RSFSR) explicitly stated that "the RSFSR deprives individual persons and groups of rights which they use to the detriment of the socialist revolution."[62] In an interview with Feliks Dzerzhinsky,[63] leader of the Cheka, Lenin averred, "We stand for organized terror – this should be frankly admitted. Terror is an absolute necessity during the times of revolution." In a supreme irony, if a prisoner was suspected of opposing the Soviet government, the interrogator was supposed to ask "what class he belongs to, his origin, education, and occupation. These questions should decide the fate of the prisoner. This is the meaning and essence of Red Terror."[64] A more concrete throwback to the more egregious elements of the pre-1864 judicial code could not be imagined.

The Cheka was to be the instrument of terror and consolidation of the Soviet state. Essentially, the Cheka was an augmented imitation of its tsarist predecessor, the Okhrana. Successes of the Okhrana, such as the use of Roman Malinovsky, leader of the Bolshevik deputies in the Duma, as an Okhrana informant led to the expressed need to imitate where appropriate "'bourgeois' intelligence agencies."[65] But the necessity of defending the revolution would greatly expand the Cheka in contrast to its predecessor. According to Andrew and Mitrokhin,[66] "In 1901, 4,113 Russians were in internal exile for political crimes, of whom only 180 were on hard labour. Executions for political crimes were limited to those involved in actual or attempted assassinations. During the Civil War, by contrast, Cheka executions probably numbered as many as 250,000, and may well have exceeded the number of deaths in battle."

Bureaucratization under communism

The contractions of authority space, although traversing somewhat different pathways, had similar consequences for both German Nazism and Soviet Communism. Valentin Berezhkov, a Soviet interpreter working in Berlin in 1940 as a consequence of the trade agreement between the two countries, observed:

> The same idolization of "the leader," the same mass rallies and parades where the participants carried portraits of the Führer and little children

[58] Quoted in Overy 2004, 644.   [59] Lenin [1899], quoted in Zile 1992, 43.
[60] Lenin [1918], quoted in Zile 1992, 65.   [61] Quoted in Pipes 1990, 361.
[62] Constitution of the RSFSR of 1918, quoted in Zile 1992, 66.
[63] [1918], quoted in Zile 1992, 102.   [64] Latsis [1918], quoted in Zile 1992, 103.
[65] Andrew and Mitrokhin 1999, 31.   [66] 1999, 37.

presented him with flowers. Very similar, ostentatious architecture, heroic themes depicted in art much like our socialist realism. Having eliminated all opponents or sent them off to detention camps, Hitler, just like Stalin, persuaded the crowd to idolize him through massive ideological brainwashing.[67]

These similarities resulted from the necessity to construct a new authority in place of the old one that was obviously failing. In Russia, that new authority was already firmly established within important elements of the intelligentsia. It appeared as a Marxism that would take many forms ranging from the moderate (Menshevik-social democratic) to the extreme (Bolshevik-communist). In much of the rest of Europe, especially after World War I, there was no such agreement. Liberalism, of course, was increasingly ascendant in Western Europe until the onset of World War I. Thereafter, the experience of the war itself would be ideationally formative, yielding the rise of fascism almost immediately at the war's end.

The vision of the Soviet Union as a "model socialist state where all people would be equal and happy"[68] was the driving impetus of Stalin's policies, however violent and barbaric. The contrast with Nazi Germany may be seen in the extent of bureaucratization of the Soviet state. According to Ian Kershaw,[69]

> Stalin's rule, for all its dynamic radicalism in the brutal collectivisation programme, the drive to industrialisation, and the paranoid phase of the purges, was not incompatible with rational ordering of priorities and attainment of limited and comprehensible goals, even if the methods were barbarous in the extreme and the accompanying inhumanity on a scale defying belief. Whether the methods were the most appropriate to attain the goals in view might still be debated, but the attempt to force industrialisation at breakneck speed on a highly backward economy and to introduce "socialism in one country" cannot be seen as irrational or limitless aims.

In keeping with fascism's origins in war, mass murder would be even more central to the Nazi state. It is useful to examine the records of labor camps in both states that were non-exterminatory in intent. In the Soviet Union,

> During the war, camp labour made up around one-tenth of the entire non-farming workforce. The prisoners produced 8.9 million tonnes of coal, 30.2 million mortar shells (13 per cent of all production), 25.5 million large-calibre shells, 9.2 million anti-personnel mines and 1.7 million un-needed gas masks. They also produced food for the prisoners and guards, and for the wider population, on prison farms: in 1941 alone this amounted to 140,000 tonnes of grain, 203,000 tonnes of potatoes, 225,000 tonnes of fodder and 366,500 animals.[70]

During the war the death rate for the camps in the Gulag was approximately 14 percent. In contrast, that for the German (non-exterminatory) camps was 40

---

[67] Berezhkov 1994, 7.   [68] Overy 2004, 39.   [69] 1997, 95.   [70] Overy 2004, 609.

percent, a difference of nearly 300 percent. The purpose of the Soviet camps was to keep production moving; that of the German camps was to punish the inmates and in many instances to work them to death. Mostly non-Germans were found in the German camps, reflecting the outward impulse of Nazi imperial policies; in the Soviet Union, the majority of inmates were either Russian or Ukrainian, "class-aliens" who were incarcerated for reasons of state.[71] This fundamental difference suggests the racial animus of the Nazis, in contrast to a more pragmatic view, at least in wartime, of the Soviet state.

In the absence of issues of national defense thrust upon the Soviet state by external enemies, it is clear that economic issues preoccupied the Bolshevik rulers. This outcome was to be expected. Until the second half of the 1930s, when Nazi Germany was emerging as a military threat, neither the commissar of international affairs, Litvinov, nor the commissar of the NKVD (successor to the Cheka), Yagoda, were members of the Politburo, the chief Soviet decision-making body at that time. The leading members of the Politburo were the economic controllers, Kuibyshev, Mikoyan, and Kaganovich.[72] This economic predominance further suggests the primacy of the communist template over and above any war-related issues that gave rise to fascism. Only after war became a distinct possibility in the late 1930s, thereby also raising issues of internal security, did the Commissariat of Defense and that of the NKVD begin to predominate. Only after 1935 did defense outlays begin to escalate, reaching 18.1 percent of labor incomes in 1940 (from 5.7 percent in 1935).[73] While Hitler's early war policies were almost always formulated in the aggressive mode, the evidence suggests that Stalin's were defensive, in an effort to curb Hitler's colonial ambitions.[74]

Even the Great Famine of 1932–33 resulting from the agricultural collectivization drive begun in 1930 was not entirely a consequence of Stalin's mendacity and desire to suppress Ukrainian nationalism,[75] but also had economic roots in the communist template. R. W. Davies[76] provides evidence that there actually were efforts to ameliorate the famine then occurring principally in the Ukraine. Accordingly, "In the following year, 1932…a number of piecemeal Politburo decisions again reduced the grain collection plan. The initial quota for the Ukraine was already lower than in 1931, and three separate Politburo decisions reduced it by a further 35 percent; it was referred to in the secret discussions about quotas as 'the thrice-reduced already reduced plan.' These cuts, though substantial, were insufficient to avoid the onset of severe famine in the spring of 1933."[77]

And if anyone doubts the ultimate effectiveness of this industrialization program, one has only to reflect that during World War II the Soviet Union

[71] Malia 1999, 333–4. [72] Rees 2001. [73] Harrison 2001, 85.
[74] Harrison 2001, 88; Gorodetsky 1999. [75] Conquest 1986.
[76] 2001, 71. [77] Davies 2001, 71.

was the "*only* country to undergo a serious [Nazi] invasion without collapsing promptly."[78] Further, "However one evaluates their efficiency compared with other possible arrangements, such incentive mechanisms created sufficient conditions for the Red Army to be supplied with the rockets, tanks, aircraft, guns, and shells that defeated Hitler's *Wehrmacht,* and for the postwar Soviet Union to compete effectively in atomic weaponry and aerospace. For a relatively poor country, regardless of its size, this was a story of success."[79]

Finally, three fundamental characteristics underlie the distinctions between the Soviet and Nazi cases. The first is ideological. When the Nazis chose Aryan political dominance as their fundamental desideratum, this desire clearly implied the necessity for military conquest. Non-Aryans (or "lesser" Aryans, i.e., non-German ones) would not readily submit to an imposed rule by Hitler. The concept of socioeconomic class, on the other hand, is universal and inclusive. All workers, and peasants as they are sometimes included among the oppressed, can join in the march to the communist utopia.

Second, as Malia[80] put it, "The aim of Hitler's revolution was to forge a monolithic national community in order to resume the First World War, and to do so before he was fifty, while he was still young enough to win the second round. There was no time for his projected internal revolution, which would have been disruptive of society on the eve of battle." In contrast, as we have seen, the Soviet path was first to make the internal social and economic revolution, basically as a vehicle for catching up with the competing Western capitalist systems. Here the threat and fear of reversion to a subordinate status is a principal impetus for extremism, as will be seen shortly.

Finally, while the *Führer* was necessary to the Nazi system, as strong and charismatic leaders were necessary for other fascist systems, it was the Communist Party as the organizational vanguard of the proletariat that was essential. The "primitive fighting unit" identified by the *Frankfurter Zeitung* editorialist cited earlier, needed a specific leader. When the chieftain dies, typically the fighting band itself dissolves, in the absence of some hereditary or other principle of succession. Although Stalin developed a cult of personality, it was politically manufactured because of the distinct absence of charisma in Stalin's personality.[81] Nevertheless, in contrast to the fascist cases, the Communist Party continued to govern well after Stalin's death, providing another 38 years of communist rule, much to the detriment of the Soviet peoples.

Stalin

Yet when we examine the life of the most extreme and murderous Soviet Communist – Stalin – the etiology put forward here also helps explain the

---

[78] Emphasis in original; Harrison 2001, 90.   [79] Harrison 2001, 109.
[80] 1999, 332.   [81] Malia 1999, 331.

origins of the most extreme period of Soviet governance. Because of its earlier occurrence, it provided a model for later extremism practiced mainly in China and Cambodia. Instead of a *sui generis* explanation for the eruption of extremist behavior in the famine associated with the Chinese Great Leap Forward of the late 1950s, the Cultural Revolution of the mid to late 1960s, or the Cambodian mass murders of 1975–79, these events can be understood as following a template established in the Soviet Union of the 1930s.

Stalin's behavior after consolidating power can be understood as providing a communist model for all of these events. Agricultural collectivization and its associated atrocities are first seen in the Soviet Union of the early 1930s and later in China and Cambodia. Massive purges of the party faithful again are found first in the Soviet Union in the 1930s and later in China and Cambodia.

I do not claim that mimesis occurred here. But when faced with problems similar to those experienced by the Soviet Union in roughly comparable revolutionary situations accompanied by external threat (e.g., US vis-à-vis China; Vietnam vis-à-vis Cambodia), similar solutions were chosen, justified in part by the communist script originally found in Lenin's writings, behavior, and draconian dictates of the War Communism period (cf. Lenin's justifications in his "Immediate Tasks of the Soviet Government"[82]). These policies would be carried to much further extremes by Stalin during the late 1920s.

What are the origins of Stalin's (born Iosef Dzhugashvili) murderous behavior? This has been a matter of intense debate among historians and biographers of the Soviet period. Explanations have varied from a "psycho-historical" approach originally championed by Robert Tucker[83] to a societally based understanding of Stalin as a bridge between the pre-modern world of *ancien régime* Russia and the demands of modernity.[84] In the former, the particularities of his upbringing – a brutal drunken abusive father failing at his chosen occupation, a mother working as a domestic, a seminary education that was stultifying to a gifted child, and exposure to violence-ridden Caucasian society – meshed with a revolutionary ideology that brooked no opposition and legitimated mass violence. In the latter confrontation with modernity approach, Russia was confronted with the need to modernize rapidly and create the "New Soviet Man" who could comfortably fit into the socialist-communist state then envisioned.

More recently, a more balanced view has been put forward by Robert Service:[85]

> Stalin in many ways behaved as a "normal human being." In fact he was very far from being "normal." He had a vast desire to dominate, punish and butcher. Often he also comported himself with oafish menace in private. But he could also be charming; he could attract passion and admiration both from close comrades and from an immense public audience. On occasion he could be modest. He was hard-working. He was capable of

---

[82] Tucker 1975, 450–2.   [83] 1973.   [84] Hoffmann and Kotsonis 2000.   [85] 2004, 12.

kindliness to relatives. He thought a lot about the good of the communist cause. Before he started killing them, most communists in the USSR and in the Comintern judged him to be functioning within the acceptable bounds of political conduct.

Of course, they overlooked the other side of Stalin. It was a side that had been plentifully evident after the October Revolution. He had killed innumerable innocents in the Civil War. He had gone on to cause hundred, of thousands of deaths in the First and Second Five-Year Plans. He was a state murderer long before instigating the Great Terror.

At the same time, Richard Overy[86] could remark that "the one consistent strand in all his activity was the survival of the revolution and the defence of the first socialist state. Power with Stalin seems to have been power to preserve and enlarge the revolution and the state that represented it, not power simply for its own sake."

What most or all of these views of Stalin have in common is the existence of an "imperative" that drove this man beyond the bounds of "normal" conduct. An understanding of this imperative can be found in the theoretical framework put forward here. Using this framework singles out important elements of Stalin's youth that shed light on his later behaviors – the structuring of that imperative at an early age.

As we saw in the instances of Hitler, Mussolini, and others, there was a clear identification with the nation, whether ethnically or religiously defined. Hitler, for example, in World War I chose to serve in the German army, not the Austro-Hungarian, the army of his native country. After service at the front, comradeship with other soldiers, and awareness of the broad contours of German history, including the massive human and territorial losses of World War I, he could identify with and be emotionally affected by the historical trajectory shown in Figure 4.2.

But what of Stalin, the Georgian raised in the shadow of Russian domination of the Caucasus, both Christian and Muslim? Here existed a complex social and political milieu. But several things stand out. First, there existed (then and now) a Georgian nationalism at the local level that chafed against a sometimes too oppressive Russian presence, especially in the gymnasium and Orthodox seminary where Stalin studied. Yet a historical reality intruded in the form of a necessity in the eighteenth century for the Georgian polity to ally with and ultimately be absorbed into the imperial Russian state in the face of threats from Turkey and Iran, both of course predominantly Muslim in religious orientation. Isaac Deutscher[87] quotes a Georgian historian, "There was no other way out. George XII [the last king of eastern Georgia] had to lean either on Turkey or on Iran or on Russia in order to save Georgia… He had to make the choice quickly. George naturally turned towards co-religionist Russia. This was dictated to him

---

[86] 2004, 13.   [87] 1960, 10.

by the will of his ancestors, who had ever since 1491 repeatedly negotiated with Russia, hoping to obtain her support." Service[88] dates the request for Russian protectorate status from 1783. A steady accretion of Russian control followed that event; even the Georgian Orthodox Church's autocephaly was abolished in 1811. Russian control was complete.

At the same time, Shamil, the Islamist rebel from Daghestan (see Chapter 7) was finally subdued in 1859, establishing Russian dominance over the non-Christian sectors of the Caucasus. Deeply versed in Georgian and Caucasian history generally, Stalin would have been aware of these events.

His personal experiences support the claims of the present theory: that Stalin was aware of the earlier Muslim domination of much of the Caucasus (one period of subordination), as well as the loss of the Crimean War including the cession of Russian territory (a second period of subordination, this time to the West); that during a critical period in his life he resided in an area recently (1878) conquered by Russia from the Ottomans, thereby accentuating the ascendant (gain) portion of Figure 1.1, but he would then be personally exposed to elements of the first great shocking Russian loss of the twentieth century, the Russo-Japanese War. This pattern would later be supplemented by Stalin's witnessing the abject Russian defeat by Germany in World War I, but direct participation in many of the bloody but ultimately victorious episodes of the Civil War (against White armies and Allied interveners), followed by the defeat of Soviet forces by the Poles in 1920, in which Stalin also was intimately involved. Thus, there are two successive reinforcing ephemera over time, and they stem initially from two elements of past subordination. This pattern can be seen in Figure 5.1.

It was in Batum (today's Batumi), ceded to Russia by the Ottoman Empire in 1878 as a result of the Russian victory of that year, that Stalin would find his revolutionary persona. Deutscher[89] tells us that, "His stay at Batum had lasted only four and a half months, but these were months of intense activity." And it was in Batum that Dzhugashvili took the name Koba, his first *nom de guerre* that in fact many of his intimates used until the 1930s. The name Koba means "indomitable" in the Turkish vernacular.[90] Koba was a Georgian literary hero and outlaw in the novel *The Patricide* by A. Kazbegi. Whether this name was chosen to reflect Koba's beginning identification with Russian-Christian dominance, newly achieved in Batum, we cannot say. But his awareness of that dominance, especially over Muslim must have been augmented by his stay with an Abkhazian Muslim, Hashim Smyrba, who sheltered him from the tsarist authorities who had become aware of his revolutionary activities. Smyrba apparently tried to convert the young Stalin to Islam[91] saying that, "Because if you adopted the Moslem faith, I'd find you seven beautiful women to marry."[92] It was here that Stalin probably received his first intimation of the importance of

[88] 2004, 14.   [89] 1960, 47.   [90] Deutscher 1960, 46; McDermott 2006, 19.
[91] Deutscher 1960, 47.   [92] Service 2004, 49.

maintaining territorial integrity as an instrument of domination that he would later amplify at a Kremlin reception in 1937.

According to Service,[93] "If anyone sought to detach the smallest piece of Soviet territory, he [Stalin] declared, 'he is an enemy, an accursed enemy of the state and the peoples of the USSR.' Then came the climax: 'And we will annihilate every such enemy, even if he were to be an Old Bolshevik! We will annihilate his entire clan, his family! We will mercilessly annihilate everyone who by his actions and thoughts (yes, thoughts too) assails the unity of the socialist state. For the total annihilation of all enemies, both themselves and their clan!'"

Batum was also the place where Stalin witnessed the first massacre of workers. Fifteen were killed on March 8, 1902 by government forces confronted by a mass of 6,000 workers demonstrating for the release of strike leaders. In hiding from tsarist troops, Stalin was captured on April 5 and imprisoned in Batum. Prior to the massacre, Stalin had suggested taking a fairly moderate approach in dealing with the authorities. But afterward, "All then changed: 'The tone was altered.' Never again did Dzhugashvili hold back in contest with the opponents of Marxism in Georgia or the Russian Empire as a whole."[94]

And here we see the beginnings of the transition from a local Georgian or at most Caucasian concern to an identification with Russia in its entirety, but of course excluding its tsarist government. Earlier, Stalin had advocated a territorially demarcated Marxist party, but in 1904, after escaping his first exile in Siberia, he wrote a "credo" forsaking this early parochialism.[95] Stalin's parochialism was transcended by the influence of more Russified and cosmopolitan early friends such as Lev Kamenev, who would later collaborate closely with Stalin until murdered by him in 1936. Ultimately, "According to his daughter, Soso [another diminutive for Stalin] would become 'completely Russian' to the extent that his son Vasilii once said to her, 'You know, Papa used to be a Georgian once.'"[96]

By the end of World War II this Russophile identification would go so far as the infamous toast of May 24, 1945 at a victory celebration for Red Army commanders. Stalin declared:

> Comrades, allow me to propose one last toast.
> I would like to propose a toast to the health of our Soviet people and, above all, of the Russian people because it is the outstanding nation of all the nations forming part of the Soviet Union.
> I would propose this toast to the health of the Russian people because in this war it earned general recognition as the leading force of the Soviet Union among all the people of our country.[97]

[93] 2004, 340. [94] Service 2004, 50. [95] Kuromiya 2005, 6.
[96] Kuromiya 2005, 6. [97] Quoted in Service 2004, 479.

Thus far, Stalin's intimate association with territorial gain has been established (in Batum), as well as his concerns about territorial integrity. We have also seen his growing identification with the Russian nation, over and above that of Georgia. But what would sensitize him to loss, especially territorial loss? Here, once again, as in the instance of territorial gain, Stalin was exposed very early to the intimations of loss. This occurred during his first exile to Siberia which took him to Novaya Uda near Irkutsk in eastern Siberia, not far from the Manchurian border.

In Caucasian prisons for over a year and a half, without sufficient legal evidence against him, Stalin was "administratively" condemned to a 3-year deportation to the Irkutsk region beginning in November 1903. Irkutsk was one of the major stops on the Trans-Siberian railroad carrying Russian troops and materiel to the South Manchurian railway that had just been completed under Russian auspices in July 1903. And Port Arthur, the terminus of that railway, was to be the site of one of the most important battles of the Russo-Japanese War.

As Stalin and his fellow exiles moved eastward, "the exiles felt more and more closely the breath of the impending Russo-Japanese war. There was far too much excitement and fever in the air for Koba to put up with the prospect of being cut off from politics for three long years. No sooner had he arrived at his destination than he began to prepare his escape. In the eve-of-war confusion, the vigilance of the authorities near the Manchurian frontier was weakened. The underground was able to organize escapes on a mass scale."[98]

We are certain that Stalin was deeply affected by the loss of that war and the territories ceded to Japan (Liaotung Peninsula, Port Arthur, and half of Sakhalin Island), as well as the South Manchurian railroad. As we have seen, a victory address by Stalin upon the unconditional surrender of Japan on September 2, 1945 stated:

> The defeat of the Russian troops in 1904 in the period of the Russo-Japanese War left grave memories in the minds of our peoples. It was a dark stain on our country. Our people trusted and awaited the day when Japan would be routed and the stain wiped out. For forty years have we, men of the older generation, waited for this day. And now this day has come![99]

Thus, the interstate war that was to leave the first decisive impression on Stalin was not World War I, as claimed by Kevin McDermott[100] in his War-Revolution "model" of understanding Stalin's behavior, but the Russo-Japanese War of 1904–05 and its associated losses and humiliation. When the Japanese began their advance into Manchuria in 1931–32, the Soviet fear of war escalated dramatically.[101] Even suspected agents of the Japanese – the Koreans – were to be deported. According to the NKVD head in the Far East, Genrikh Liushkov, Stalin stated explicitly: "It is necessary to clean up the army and its rear in the most determined manner from hostile spy and pro-Japanese elements…the Far

---

[98] Deutscher 1960, 57–8.   [99] Quoted in Wolfe 1984, 279.
[100] 2006, 161.   [101] Kuromiya 2007, 2.

East is not Soviet, there the Japanese rule… Stalin resumed the conversation by saying that it was necessary in cleansing the rear to terrorise the [Korean] district and the frontier so as to prevent any Japanese [espionage] work."[102]

To be sure, the losses to Germany during World War I, complementing the earlier losses to Japan, were also important. The Russian Civil War, with its associated "siege mentality," and immense brutalities but ultimate victories over the White armies and Allied interveners, in which Stalin played a significant role, was to be critical in establishing the later pattern of victory to be followed by defeat in the Russo-Polish War of 1920, with French commanders advising the Poles. And, as Stalin was in physical proximity to the impending Russo-Japanese War, he was actually political commissar and effective co-commander (with Aleksandr Yegorov) of one of the two Soviet armies fighting in the Russo-Polish War.[103] The solidification of Finnish, Estonian, Latvian, and Lithuanian independence, as well as, of course, the creation of newly independent Poland including large portions of the Ukraine and Byelorussia followed from the defeat of 1920.

Here, as in the Russo-Japanese War, there also exists evidence of Stalin's hostility toward the agents of defeat – the Poles as architects of the first major territorial loss in war of the soon to be constituted Soviet Union. According to Niall Ferguson:[104]

> He [Stalin] regarded few minorities with more suspicion than the Poles. Even before the outbreak of war, 10,000 ethnic Polish families living in the western border region of the Soviet Union had been deported. Now the entire Polish population of the Soviet-occupied zone was at Stalin's mercy. Beginning on the night of February 10, 1940, the NKVD unleashed a campaign of terror against suspected "anti-Soviet" elements… By the spring of 1940, around 14,700 Poles were being held in prisoner of war camps, of whom the majority were officers of the vanquished army. But there were also police officers, prison guards, intelligence personnel, government officials, landowners and priests. In addition, 10,685 Poles were being held in the western region of the Ukraine and Byelorussia, including not only ex-officers but also landowners, factory owners and government officials… In the forest of Katyn, near Smolensk, more than 4,000 of them were tied up, shot in the back of the head and buried in a mass grave, a crime the Soviets subsequently sought to blame on the Nazis. This was only one of a series of mass executions. All told, more than 20,000 Poles were killed. Further "liquidations" followed, notably the emptying of the prisons of Lwów, Pińsk, and other towns in the summer of 1941.

The territorial losses of the immediate post-World War I period undoubtedly were to be critical in yielding Stalin's emphatic pronouncements on the

---

[102] Kuromiya 2007, 126.   [103] Service 2004, 180–2.
[104] 2006, 418–19.

inviolability of Soviet territory, as we saw. Indeed, it is possible that the later Brezhnev Doctrine of the inviolability of communist revolution (any territory that was now governed by a communist government cannot be lost to noncommunist authorities) stemmed at least in part from similar sources. Born in 1906, Leonid Brezhnev was an impressionable teenager at the time of the disintegration of the tsarist empire and Russian Civil War, and defeat of the Soviets by the Poles leading to major territorial losses.

And there is another element in the 1878 Treaty of Berlin essentially abrogating the earlier Treaty of San Stefano that ended the Russo-Turkish War. Instead of a vastly enlarged Bulgaria envisioned by the Russians at San Stefano, Bulgaria, then a close ally of Russia, was to be truncated. Thus, one of the Russian goals of that war was not realized as a result of Western pressure in Berlin to minimize the impact of the defeat on the Ottoman Empire. There existed a fear in Western capitals (especially London) that the Ottoman Empire could be on the verge of disintegration, thereby facilitating further Russian expansion into Central Asia. Stalin must have been aware of this frustration of Russian policy as another outcome of the war that had yielded Batum for the Russians. Western humiliation of Russia had occurred and was to be vastly exacerbated by the defeat of Russia by Japan, then a close ally of Britain. Indeed, the ships used by the Japanese to annihilate the Russian fleet at Tsushima were built in British dockyards.

It is no wonder then that very early in his life Stalin learned to distrust the West, apart from any ideological convictions that also would have inspired an anti-Western ethos. The Molotov-Ribbentrop Pact of 1939 allowing the possibility of Hitler's invasion of Poland should then have held no surprise, for it was essentially an alliance between two profoundly anti-Western governments that had both suffered territorial losses at the hands of the West, or countries oriented toward the West.

And as will be developed in more detail in Chapter 7, four peoples – the Chechens, Ingush, Kalmyks, and Karachai – on Stalin's orders were deported from their homes in February 1944. Yet the Avars of Daghestan, not only Muslim but traditionally active in opposition to Russian rule, were not deported, nor were the predominantly Christian Ossetians. Moreover, the Ingush, who, as noted later did not participate in the great rebellion of 1920–22 nor that of Shamil in the preceding century, indeed were deported.

Territorial considerations distinguish among peoples chosen to be deported and those allowed to remain. The furthest advance of the German army in 1942 includes all of the Karachai and Balkar territories in its zone of occupation, as well as most of the North Ossetian ASSR, a portion of the Chechen-Ingush ASSR, and a small part of Daghestan. But the small portion of Daghestan occupied by the Germans was well to the north of the Terek River, and the vast majority of the Avar population was located principally to the south of that river.[105] Earlier,

[105] Conquest 1970, 33; Kisriev 2004, 109; S. Smith 1998, map 5.

the Kalmyks, many of whom were found within the line of maximum German advance, were deported in December 1943.[106] In their eastward march, proximity to the Avars was not at all achieved by the Germans. At the same time, the portion of the Chechen-Ingush ASSR to the west occupied by the Germans was entirely Ingush in ethnicity.

Thus, experience of German occupation either in whole or in part was a key factor in deciding which Muslim ethnicity to deport, in addition of course to the centrality of resistance to the Soviets found in Chechnya proper. Christian Ossetians not implicated either in dissidence or suspected collaboration with the Germans were exempt from deportation, despite their partial German occupation. Clearly, revenge for suspected, if not actual collaboration with the Germans was a determinant, but lingering uncertainty as to German capabilities for a counter-offensive (the Normandy landings had not yet occurred opening the second major front in Europe) must have played an important role. As we shall see, security considerations in the maintenance of Soviet territorial integrity played a key role in the Russian demand for the maximum possible security before initiating the deportations one year after they were planned.

Orlando Figes[107] avers that, "By 1937, Stalin was convinced that the Soviet Union was on the brink of war with the Fascist states in Europe and with Japan in the East. The Soviet press typically portrayed the country as threatened on all sides and undermined by Fascist infiltrators – 'spies' and 'hidden enemies' – in every corner of society." According to Hiroaki Kuromiya,[108] "Foreign factors were the leitmotiv of the Great Terror."

Stalin's behavior is one important instance of political extremism understood through the prism of the ephemeral gain. Given his depredations, it is amazing that the Soviet Union persisted for another 38 years beyond his death. Perhaps it was a combination of the reversal of earlier humiliations, ostensible correctives by the communist system for earlier class injustices, and the ascendance to superpower status in place of the earlier threatened reversion that combined to prolong the existence of a brutal and inefficient form of governance. And there still are Russians who mourn the passing of the Stalinist era,[109] for it gave back to Russia what had become only a dim memory of earlier tsarist glories. But when humiliation appeared once again in the form of defeat of the Soviets by the *mujahadin* in Afghanistan, the Soviet system was revealed to be corrupt and elitist, and reversion to international second-class status occurred upon the loss of communist East-Central Europe, the system finally expired.

Whether these factors that in earlier form gave rise to Stalinist excesses will also yield future Russian extremism is an open question. Reversal of the 1996 Chechen victory over the Russians by Vladimir Putin in 1999, and the Russian

---

[106] Conquest 1970, 89.   [107] 2007, 236.   [108] Kuromiya 2007, 258.
[109] A sign of that nostalgia can be seen in the restoration of a statue of Feliks Dzerzhinsky to a public place in Moscow (Randolph 2005).

economic resurgence fueled mainly by petrodollars, if continued, may mitigate this tendency. Nevertheless, there is cause for concern, if only as demonstrated by the 2008 Russian invasion of Georgia, and effective annexation of Abkhazia and South Ossetia. Ironically, the Russian ability to retain these territories, as in Chechnya, may augur well for the prevention of future Russian extremism, for territorial gains will have been consolidated.

PART III

An Ostensibly Sacred "Ism"

6

Radical Islamism: Foundations

Any comparison among the forms of extremism comes up against a formidable distinction between radical Islamism and the remaining types such as fascism or communism. The latter two avowedly secular ideologies did not find their intellectual roots in sacred theologies (although Hitler did say at one point that in his viciously anti-Semitic policies he was *"fighting for the Lord's work"*).[1] Indeed, one of the first acts of the Nazi regime was to demand the dissolution of the Catholic Center Party as the heretofore highly successful political instrument of 27 million German Catholics. In exchange, Hitler would allow the unfettered continuation of Catholic worship and education in the new, essentially pagan environment of Nazism. Neither the political imagery nor the ideation of Nazism or Italian Fascism was rooted in the sacred. Mussolini took pains to limit the Vatican's political and ecclesiastical influence in fascist Italy. Of course, among the first activities of the victorious Bolsheviks was the looting and destruction of Orthodox churches and monasteries, to such a vigorous extent that it took the untiring efforts of Anatole Lunacharsky, the Bolshevik minister of culture (and of Jewish origin), to rescue major Christian historical antiquities.

In stark contrast, radical Islamists routinely cloak their pronouncements and activities in the language of Islam. Virtually all of bin Laden's statements, long or short, include mention of Allah, the Prophet Muhammad, or some reference to *jahiliyyah*, the state of Arab ignorance prior to Muhammad's arrival, which, according to Sayyid Qutb, is now revived in the form of duplicitous and corrupt ostensibly Muslim rulers of predominantly Islamic countries.[2] How do we understand this seeming disjunction among our cases of extremism? The answer resides precisely in the *actual* disjunction between historic Islam, or the way it has been traditionally understood, and its more recent radical interpreters.

Moreover, the distinction between secular extremists and those who base their actions on sacred scripture is more apparent than real. Long ago, Joseph Conrad saw this clearly. In his last great political novel, *Under Western Eyes*, Victor Haldin, the assassin of the fictional stand-in for Vyacheslav Plehve, the draconian Russian minister of the interior, speaks to his soon-to-be betrayer, Razumov: "Men like me leave no posterity, but their souls are not lost. No man's

---

[1] Emphasis in original; Hitler 1939, 84.   [2] Shepard 2003.

soul is ever lost. It works for itself – or else where would be the sense of self-sacrifice, of martyrdom, of conviction, of faith – the labours of the soul? What will become of my soul when I die in the way I must die – soon – very soon perhaps. It shall not perish."[3] This passage is all the more remarkable because, in real life, Plehve's assassins were the secular Socialist Revolutionaries.

According to Akil Awan, "The crux of the problem appears to lie with the misappropriation of religious labels for violent ends, which in itself is neither new nor confined to the Islamic tradition. Nevertheless, these are rendered moot points, for whatever the theological justification behind such actions (or perhaps a lack thereof) it remains an indelible sociological fact that these individuals considered themselves to be 'true Muslims,' and indeed Islam provided part of the *raison d'etre* for their acts of terrorism." At the same time, "increasing religiosity per se, particularly through intensification experiences, is unlikely to result in radicalization and often requires some further catalyst such as an abrupt transition experience."[4] It is suggested here that the ephemeral gain combined with mortality salience – the ephemeral victory – provides that abrupt transition.

First I will review elements of the traditional understanding of Islam followed by these newer interpretations; this radical change will then be understood in reference to the massively altered sociopolitical circumstances of Muslim populations. Finally I will demonstrate how the theory offered here helps explain the more extreme transition to the indiscriminate use of violence by radical Islamists, even against women and children.

Traditional Islam

This chapter addresses a question that has puzzled observers since the rapid emergence of radical Islamism during the past decade and a half. How could a religion with a glorious past and absolute prohibition against the killing of innocents – non-combatants, women, and children – be transformed at the hands of militants into the justification for acts of sheer barbarism? In a valuable review of the relationship between Islam and politics, L. Carl Brown emphasizes the quietist political tradition within Islamic societies, especially within Shia communities:

> Muslim history has been marked by a de facto separation of state and religious community. Political leadership, often autocratic, has usually tempered its authoritarian potential by leaving the ruled free to live their lives demanding only peace (avoidance of fitna [dissension]) and payment of taxes (which in principle can be manageable since government itself is small and confined to maintaining order.) The ruled, in turn, have been

---

[3] Conrad 1929, 22.   [4] Awan 2008, 13.

satisfied to avoid politics and to accept a fairly distinct separation between rulers and the ruled.[5]

Traditional elements include an emphasis on community that generally is more emphasized in Islam than in, say, Christianity. That emphasis continues. Historically, in comparison with Christian governments, there have been fewer attempts by Muslim rulers to forcibly convert non-Muslim subjects. This reluctance to enter the ecclesiastical arena may have emerged from the desire to preserve the funds provided by "protected communities," who were required to render special taxes to the governing Muslim authorities. Whether this motivation continued into the recent past is moot for our purposes. Suffice it to say that Muslim authorities have generally behaved in a more tolerant manner towards Jewish and Christian minorities than did their Christian counterparts in governing Muslim and Jewish communities in their midst. Forced conversion, expulsion, and massacre characterized many (but not all) medieval Christian policies towards religious minorities, especially Jews. The persistence, even affluence, of the 23,000 member Jewish community in Turkey is a reminder of this tolerant period. On a memorial plaque commemorating the victims of the 2003 Hamas attack on the largest synagogue in Istanbul, Neve Shalom, the number of Muslim Turks murdered actually exceeds that of the Jewish dead.

In the following analysis, I distinguish between Islamism and radical Islamism.[6] Only in radical Islamism is the ready willingness to kill manifest – behaviorally its defining property. Islamism can simply focus on the Shari'a (corpus of Islamic law) as the basis for governance without the necessity for mass murder.[7] It can even provide a constitutional basis for the rule of law in majority Muslim societies heretofore ruled by corrupt autocratic governments.[8] Islamists can capture or create elements of civil society – mosques, primary schools, networks of social services – thereby advancing their cause within a weakening state.[9] Radical Islamism is a far more dynamic political movement, which, like other extremist groups, entails killing large numbers of people as part of its need for sustained or even accelerated political momentum.

Ideational sources of radical Islamism

There are six major ideational sources of radical Islamism that I will explore. They range from Ahmad ibn 'Abd al-Halim Ibn Taymiyya (1263–1328), who represents the earliest emphasis on what have become modern interpretations of jihad, through Muhammad ibn 'Abd-al Wahhab (1703/04–92) who gave impetus to contemporary fundamentalist Islam in the form of Wahhabism. Muhammad Rashid Rida (1865–1935) was the first major Islamic thinker to confront issues

---

[5] 2000, 80.   [6] Burgat 2003; Jackson 2001; Midlarsky 1998.
[7] Roy 2004, 60.   [8] Feldman 2008.   [9] S. Berman 2003, 14–16.

of modernity; Sayyid Abdul 'Ala Maududi (1903–79) dealt with similar issues but principally in the South Asian context. Hasan al-Banna (1906–49) was the founder of the first overtly Islamist political movement in the modern period, the Muslim Brotherhood, while Sayyid Qutb (1903–66) gave rise to the most thoroughly articulated justification for radical Islamism that inspired Osama bin Laden, among others.

What unites all of these thinkers is the assertion that Islam is a complete, sanctified belief system for the resolution of all problems confronting the Muslim world. Ibn Taymiyya argued that "Islam requires state power, the foundational principle for all Islamists."[10] And this state, of course, is one governed solely by Islamic principles, as was the Caliphate, the political model to be resurrected by contemporary radical Islamists. These Islamic principles were those given by God, transmitted by Muhammad, and interpreted later by Islamic jurists. Armed struggle against those not within the fold of Islam was required. Jihad – the struggle against non-believers – was needed, along with the more pacific interpretation of jihad as the internal struggle of each person to obey all of God's commandments. According to Habeck,[11] "After a careful study of the relevant traditions and Qur'anic passages, [Ibn Taymiyya] concluded that not only should the Islamic nation fight all heretics, apostates, hypocrites, sinners, and unbelievers (including Christians and Jews) until 'all religion was for God alone,' but also any Muslim who tried to avoid participating in jihad. His theory about jihad – its significance, necessity, and types of fighting that should be included within its realm – was one of the major contributions that Ibn Taymiyya made to Islamic law."

Effectively, a theory of just war had been enunciated by Ibn Taymiyya that justified a wide range of military activities. Radical Islamists today use Ibn Taymiyya's doctrines as a basis for attacking contemporary Muslim rulers of mostly secular states as sinners, hypocrites, and apostates.

As did Ibn Taymiyya, Wahhab emphasized that the word of God transmitted by Muhammad was paramount, but he added that it was also the responsibility of individual Muslims to think for themselves and not necessarily rely on the rulings of earlier jurists. Wahhab asserted that most Muslims did not fully understand the faith they espoused. Especially important for him was the oneness of God and his sole rule. Any other divinities were forbidden; statues, saints, or any other possible temporal objects of veneration were excluded from authentic Islam. For this reason, among others, Shiism, with its emphasis on holy figures including, of course, 'Ali and his relatives, was to be excluded from this realm of authenticity.

The destruction of the ancient and enormous Bamyan Buddhas in Afghanistan by the Taliban was consistent with Wahhab's writings, as was the destruction by the Saudis of the tombs of Muhammad's earliest companions.

---

[10] Habeck 2006, 19.   [11] 2006, 21.

Saudi Arabia, of course, has become the fount of Wahhabism in the Muslim world, facilitated by the flow of Muslim workers to Saudi Arabia and the use of petrodollars to spread the Wahhabi worldview. Wahhab's forceful rejection of Shiism may have morphed into Abu Musab al-Zarqawi's willingness, even eagerness, to wage brutal war against the Shi'a of Iraq, until he himself was killed.

Initially, Rida, born in Ottoman Syria, urged that Islam reform itself in response to modernity's demands. But the secularization of modern Turkey, and abolition of the Caliphate, led him to condemn Islamic modernizers as "false renewers" and "heretics." Upon the dissolution of the Caliphate, Rida wrote that Islam "does not really exist unless an independent and strong Islamic state is established which could apply the laws of Islam and defend it against any foreign opposition and domination."[12] Rida admired Wahhabism and was among the first to rediscover Ibn Taymiyya and his emphasis on the necessity for a strong Islamic state.

Al-Banna, Maududi, and Qutb were contemporaries of each other and drew on the writings of the earlier thinkers. In his founding of the Muslim Brotherhood, al-Banna also recognized the need for organizational infrastructure to implement Islamism in its confrontation with nationalism, secularism, and other elements of modernity. He declared that, "If [Europeans] mean by 'patriotism' the conquest of countries and lordship over the earth, Islam has already ordained that, and has sent out conquerors to carry out the most gracious of colonizations and the most blessed of conquests. This is what He, the Almighty, says: 'Fight them till there is no longer discord, and the religion is God's.'"[13] Al-Banna sought the elimination of Westernization and its influence on Muslim minds. A united and Islamically educated Muslim population was required to fend off the West and its unwitting, or even deliberate assault on Islam. Al-Banna asserted that:

> Our task in general is to stand against the flood of modernist civilization overflowing from the swamp of materialistic and sinful desires. This flood has swept the Muslim nation away from the Prophet's leadership and Qur'anic guidance and deprived the world of its guiding light. Western secularism moved into a Muslim world already estranged from its Qur'anic roots, and delayed its advancement for centuries, and will continue to do so until we drive it from our lands. Moreover, we will not stop at this point, but will pursue this evil force to its own lands, invade its Western heartland, and struggle to overcome it until all the world shouts by the name of the Prophet and the teachings of Islam spread throughout the world. Only then will Muslims achieve their fundamental goal, and there will be no more "persecution" and all religion will be exclusively for Allah.[14]

---

[12] Quoted in Habeck 2006, 28.   [13] Quoted in Habeck 2006, 29.
[14] Quoted in Habeck 2006, 29–30.

Violence was justified as a form of universal salvation. The rise of an overarching Islamic polity would save all of humanity from the political, social, and spiritual decay that he witnessed. And as we shall see, the Muslim Brotherhood had a secret section dedicated to the violence required to achieve "authentic" Islamist goals.

Maududi also affirmed that jihad was essential for the propagation of the faith, especially in the face of the Hindu majority in British India. His successors established the jihadist Hizbul-Mujahidin in order to free Kashmir from Indian governance. More recently, the group chose political action in order to achieve its goal, a tactic which distinguishes Maududi's more recent political followers from those of other groups such as the Muslim Brotherhood (in its early incarnation), and Lashkar-e-Taiba, a more radical Islamist group of Kashmiri origin.

The last and most influential of the major sources of radical Islamist thinking – Sayyid Qutb – became most influential after his death through the activities of Ayman al-Zawahiri, the Egyptian jihadist, and Osama bin Laden. There were many targets of Qutb's wrath. Among them were the "apostate" leaders of predominantly Muslim societies, liberalism in most any form that undermined God's sole prerogative for lawmaking, separation of religion from the state, and democracy as a "false religion" that seeks to provide legitimacy for laws that can only be the work of God. Without the sacred governance of Islam, Muslims are in a "state of ignorance" (*jahiliyyah*) a term that Muhammad used to describe Arabs before the rise of Islam. Thus, Muslims not in this "state of grace" (to use a Christian metaphor) could be fought and killed.[15]

Qutb saw enemies on all sides. Before his death, he declared that there existed "a final offensive which is actually taking place now in all the Muslim countries… It is an effort to exterminate this religion as even a basic creed, and to replace it with secular conceptions having their own implications, values, institutions, and organizations."[16] This assault was being conducted by Muslims (called "apostates"), the Crusaders (the West, principally the US), and the Jews (mainly in Israel); they needed to be fought vigorously. And this fighting was to be waged by a "vanguard" of Muslims, like Muhammad and his early companions, who made war during the earliest stages of Islam. And whatever the outcome of the latest "offensive" by the West against Islam, this state of conflict is never-ending. After quoting selections from the Qur'an, Qutb declared: "In all these categorical statements God makes it clear that all those in the camp of *jahiliyyah* have the same objectives when it comes to dealing with Islam and Muslims. They pursue their goals with clear persistence that never fades with the passage of time, nor does it change as a result of changing circumstances."[17] Ultimately, a state was to be established that would be governed only by the precepts of Islam.

[15] Habeck 2006, 36.   [16] Quoted in P. Berman 2003, 92.
[17] Quoted in Bergesen 2008, 89.

A basic characteristic of this society is the absence of human servitude in the absence of man-made laws. This Islamic polity was to be for "all human beings, whether they be rulers or ruled, black or white, poor or rich, ignorant or learned. Its law is uniform for all, and all human beings are equally responsible with it. In other systems, human beings obey other human beings and follow man-made laws."[18]

In his determination to maintain the distinction between the Islamic world and that of *jahiliyyah*, Qutb strongly distinguished between the two existential conditions: "Islam did not come to condone people's desires...rather, it has come to eliminate these completely...and to found human existence on a particular basis. It came to organize life once and for all. To construct a life which will spring wholly from [Islam] and which will be firmly united with the very core of Islam itself."[19]

Qutb understood the core of Islam to include the principles of equality and a social solidarity that would be vitiated by capitalism as a competing normative frame. "Islam is not content with the acknowledged, assured, and profitable results of freedom of conscience; rather it emphasizes the principle of equality in word and precept, so that everything may be clear and firm and definite."[20] At the same time, however, Islam "prescribes holy war in the way of Allah as a responsibility incumbent on every one who is able for it. But over and above that it kindles a love for holy wars by inciting the conscience to accept it, by depicting it in glowing terms, and by emphasizing its justice and the glories which it brings to a society."[21]

In the midst of Qutb's concern for social justice, equality, and a benign Shari'a-governed society, there is the requirement for jihad. And dying for the cause of jihad is not really death at all. According to Qutb:

> The Surah tells the Muslims that, in the fight to uphold God's universal Truth, lives will have to be sacrificed. Those who risk their lives and go out to fight, and who are prepared to lay down their lives for the cause of God are honorable people, pure of heart and blessed of soul. But the great surprise is that those among them who are killed in the struggle must not be considered or described as dead. They continue to live, as God Himself clearly states.
>
> To all intents and purposes, those people may very well appear lifeless, but life and death are not judged by superficial physical means alone. Life is chiefly characterized by activity, growth, and persistence, while death is a state of total loss of function, of complete inertia and lifelessness. But the death of those who are killed for the cause of God gives more impetus to the cause, which continues to thrive on their blood. Their influence on those they leave behind also grows and spreads. Thus after their death they

---

[18] Quoted in P. Berman 2003, 95.   [19] Quoted in Tripp 2006, 157.
[20] Qutb 1953, 45.   [21] Qutb 1953, 85.

> remain an active force in shaping the life of their community and giving it
> direction. It is in this sense that such people, having sacrificed their lives for
> the sake of God, retain their active existence in everyday life…
>   There is no real sense of loss in their death, since they continue to live.[22]

Here we have the ultimate justification for death by any means, including suicide bombing, if it is in the service of jihad. One can easily see the influence of
this kind of thinking on those like al-Zawahiri and bin Laden who seek to win at
virtually any cost, either to other Muslims, or to themselves.

Societal sources: the Western ascendancy

What led to the choice of violent solutions? In recent years, many scholars have
criticized the condition of Muslim societies, especially in the Arab world.[23]
Fawaz Gerges identifies the basic problem as one of social structures; he asserts
that: "At the heart of this structural crisis lie entrenched authoritarianism and
a vacuum of legitimate political authority fueling the ambitions of secular and
religious activists."[24] Clearly, contraction of authority space has occurred over
the past several decades. But, in addition to the problems solely originating in
domestic societies, there are critical issues that have an international provenance. Sadik al-Azm, an Arab philosopher, identifies one of the core issues:

> In the marrow of our bones, we still perceive ourselves as the subjects of
> history… We have never acknowledged, let alone reconciled ourselves to,
> the marginality and passivity of our position in modern times. In fact, deep
> in our collective soul, we find it intolerable that our supposedly great nation
> must stand hopelessly on the margins not only of modern history in gen-
> eral but even of our local and particular histories.[25]

In other words, a widespread feeling of humiliation pervades Arab societies.
These themes will be developed more fully in this chapter.

Muslim decline

Beginning in the eighteenth century, the Muslim world lost ground to European
Christian advances. From the high point of Muslim expansion in the near conquest of Vienna by Ottoman forces in 1683 (after an earlier unsuccessful effort in
1529), a steady decline ensued. The year 1774 witnessed the end of a catastrophic
war for the Ottomans, and the Treaty of Kuchuk Kainardji for the first time ceded
Muslim territory in the Crimea to Christians in the form of the Russian Empire.
(Earlier, at the end of the fifteenth century, the Spanish *Reconquesta* ended the
long tenure of Muslim *Andalus*, but this was compensated for by the Muslim

---

[22] Quoted in P. Berman 2003, 101–2.
[23] E.g. Ajami 1998.   [24] Gerges 2005, 273.   [25] Quoted in Gerges 2005, 245.

conquest of Anatolia and the beginnings of the Ottoman Empire.) Further defeats of the Ottomans by the Russians followed in the nineteenth century, culminating in the 1877–78 war leading to the loss of much of the Balkans.

In the Indian subcontinent, the Battle of Plassey (1757) witnessed the British East India Company defeating the Nawab of Bengal. During the following century, the remnants of the Mughal Empire in India were eliminated after the Sepoy Rebellion was put down by British forces. To complete the rout of Muslim states in Asia, after experiencing internal difficulties, the Iranian Safavid Empire came under constant pressure by the Russians, leading to the treaties of Gulistan in 1813 and Turkmanchay in 1828, which entailed substantial territorial losses to the Russians.[26] When we add the British and French nineteenth-century conquests in Africa, and the continuing Dutch control of the East Indies (today's Indonesia), eventually the country with the largest Muslim population, we see a nearly complete Christian-Western domination of the Muslim world.

In tandem with these changes occurred the writings of Islamists. The prototype was Ibn Taymiyyah (1263–1328), who wrote in the wake of the Mongol invasion that in 1258 utterly destroyed Baghdad, the capital of the Abbasid Empire.

The caliph, al-Musta'sim, was put to death; only Christians and some Shi'ites were spared. The heartland of Islam was now a Mongol province. Although the Mongols would eventually convert to Islam, many of the *ulema* regarded the quality of Mongol observance to be syncretic, at best. One can understand Ibn Taymiyyah's emphasis on the absolute Islamic requirement for Muslim state power stemming precisely from its absence during this period. And as we saw, jihad was to be waged on behalf of this Islamic state, even against the nominal Muslims who did not meet the high standards of belief and practice advocated by Ibn Taymiyyah.

Wahhab (1703/4–92) also wrote at the time of Muslim decline. During his lifetime, the Mughal Empire, one of the largest Islamic-governed realms, came increasingly under British domination, and the Ottoman Empire, seat of the Caliphate, was losing territory to the Russians. If the tolerant Mughals, among the most benign Muslim rulers of a diverse population, and the worldly Ottomans were to experience defeat, then a turn to Islamic fundamentalism was required. God's favor could only be found in the most fastidious belief and observance of His laws. To this extent any remnant of the period of *jahiliyyah*, such as the ancient large Buddhist statuary in Afghanistan, later destroyed by the Taliban, could not be tolerated.

Al-Banna, Maududi, and Qutb wrote and acted during the period of Western ascendancy. Al-Banna in Egypt, as we saw, reacted strongly to the British presence, especially in the area of Suez where he first taught (Ismailiya), and where the British had their largest concentration of military forces.

---

[26] Brown 2000, 84.

In his travels in the United States, Sayyid Qutb reflects on the totality of his Islamic heritage, in stark contrast to the liberalism and individual freedom of the Western society in which he temporarily resides. It is this contrast that forms the basis of his voluminous writings on Islam in its confrontation with the West. And Qutb was following closely in the footsteps of Hasan al-Banna, founder of the Society of the Muslim Brothers that was to do so much to lay the foundation for contemporary radical Islamism.

The Society of the Muslim Brothers

The etiology of radical Islamism is found in embryonic form in the formation of the Society of the Muslim Brothers in Egypt in 1928. At its founding meeting, six like-minded individuals approached al-Banna, thanked him for his teachings, then said:

> We have heard and we have become aware and we have been affected. We know not the practical way to reach the glory ['*izza*] of Islam and to serve the welfare of Muslims. We are weary of this life of humiliation and restriction. Lo, we see that the Arabs and the Muslims have no status [*manzila*], and no dignity [*karama*]. They are not more than mere hirelings belonging to the foreigners. We possess nothing but this blood...and these souls... and these few coins... We are unable to perceive the road to action as you perceive it, or to know the path to the service of the fatherland [*watan*], the religion, and the nation ['*umma*] as you know it.[27]

Here, as in the statements of Sadik al-Azm (above), humiliation and failure characterize this period. An Islamic revival in Egypt was to begin the period of Muslim regeneration. Initially, the Muslim Brothers sought to increase membership in the Society, and to combat Christian missionary activity. But "his [al-Banna's] main concern was the 'blind emulation' of the West among Egyptians, which led to a rejection of Islam and Islamic culture."[28] Al-Banna's conception of Islam was total. Accordingly, "Our mission is one described most comprehensively by the term 'Islamic,' though this word has a meaning broader than the narrow definition understood by people generally. We believe that Islam is an all-embracing concept which regulates every aspect of life, adjudicating on every one of its concerns and prescribing for it a solid and rigorous order."[29]

For the first time in the modern period, Islam was explicitly politicized. Al-Banna preaches:

> O ye Brethren! Tell me if Islam is something else than politics, society, economy, law and culture, what is it then? Is it only empty acts of prostration, devoid of a pulsating heart?... O ye Brethren! Did the Koran reveal a complete, perfect and elaborate system in mankind just for this?... This narrow interpretation of Islam and these closed boundaries to which Islam

---

[27] Quoted in Mitchell 1969, 8.   [28] Lia 1998, 31.   [29] Quoted in Lia 1998, 75–6.

has been confined is exactly what the adversaries of Islam want in order to keep the Muslims in place and make fun of them.[30]

In its General Law of 1934, the Society of the Muslim Brothers eliminated its provision requiring non-involvement in politics.[31] According to Brynjar Lia,[32] "The politicization of Islam was one of the Society's most fundamental ideological characteristics."

And a signal event in Egyptian national life, always a factor in the political orientation of the Muslim Brothers, was the withdrawal of the British and the gaining of national independence by Egypt. The revolution of 1919 against British rule led in 1922 to the formation of an autonomous Egypt, in domestic affairs mostly independent of the British.[33] By 1936, remaining limitations on Egyptian independence were eliminated. The fourth general conference of the Muslim Brothers was convened in 1937 explicitly in order "to celebrate the coronation of King Faruq."[34] It was a long and joyful celebration culminating in a traditional oath of loyalty to the new king: "We grant you our allegiance on the Book of God and the Tradition of His Prophet."[35] In the same year, Egypt was accepted as a new member of the League of Nations, thereby internationally legitimating its sovereignty.

Yet, two factors were to move the Society of the Muslim Brothers towards extremist violence. The first was the Arab general strikes and uprising (1936–39) against the British mandate in Palestine and its Jewish population, expanding now because of the Hitlerite persecutions in Europe. Al-Banna and the Society were active in soliciting funds on behalf of the Palestinian Arab population. Later, as we shall see, that essentially benign activity would be transformed into military support within the territory of what was to be the state of Israel after 1948. The second factor was World War II and its impact on Egypt, especially the renewed British occupation, effectively constituting an ephemeral gain.

At the start of the war, most Egyptian political sectors, including the Muslim Brothers did not oppose the activation of the 1936 treaty of alliance and defense between the United Kingdom and Egypt. That support was confined to a strict interpretation of its provisions that, among other things, allowed the British to assume control of Egyptian ports. But by February 1942, nationalist agitation had increased against what appeared to be an increasingly large British military presence. At this time, the British forced the installation of the ministry of Nahhas Pasha, a strong ally of the United Kingdom. "From this time on, many elements of the national government began to develop a new and inordinately bitter focus for their agitation."[36] And the Muslim Brothers' inauguration of the "Special Apparatus" specifically dedicated to violence dates from this time in 1942, according to Richard Mitchell,[37] or even earlier, in 1940, according to Lia.[38]

---

[30] Quoted in Lia 1998, 202.   [31] Lia 1998, 243.   [32] 1998, 283.
[33] Lia 1998, 27.   [34] Mitchell 1969, 14.   [35] Quoted in Mitchell 1969, 16.
[36] Mitchell 1969, 26.   [37] 1969, 30.   [38] 1998, 180.

In order to implement these activities, a system of "families" was instituted, actually amounting to a very large number of cells, each of which was limited to five members. Secrecy from the authorities was thus enhanced. The British imperialist presence in Egypt was to be strongly opposed, for according to al-Banna: "We have now before us a proud tyrant who enslaves God's worshippers, despising them as weaklings and using them as servitors, attendants, slaves and chattels, while on the other hand we have a noble and glorious people enslaved by this overbearing despot."[39]

The formation of the Special Apparatus was facilitated in part by the support of the Palestinian Hajj Amin al-Husayni, the Grand Mufti of Jerusalem, and funds supplied by the German legation in Cairo. Documents were found which implicated Wilhelm Stellbogen, director of the German News Agency, in granting funds to the Muslim Brothers – subsidies that were substantially larger than those offered to other anti-British groups. Transfer of these funds was coordinated by al-Husayni and Palestinian contacts in Cairo, although this German subvention was to cease after the internment and deportation of Stellbogen by British military authorities in late 1939.[40]

At the war's end, even as the British military presence was only slowly diminishing, the Palestine issue loomed large. Even before the November 1947 United Nations decision to partition Palestine into two states, one Arab and the other Jewish, al-Banna ordered the various branches of the Society to prepare for jihad.[41] And even before the arrival of official "Volunteers of the Arab League" in Palestine, the Muslim Brothers were militarily attacking some of the Jewish settlements in the Negev (the south of Israel). Upon the later invasion of Israel by the Egyptian army, the Muslim Brothers were most notably involved in supplying the "Faluja pocket" in late 1948.

Meanwhile in Egypt itself, the Muslim Brothers were active in the actual or attempted assassination of governmental officials. In June 1948, houses were blown up in the Jewish quarter of Cairo. In July, two Jewish-owned department stores were partly destroyed. From September through November, other buildings in the Jewish quarter or owned by suspected Zionist sympathizers were destroyed, leading to much property damage and loss of life. In early 1949, these and other disturbances widely attributed to the Society of the Muslim Brothers led to its dissolution by the Egyptian government.[42] In the early 1950s, in response to persistent extremist attacks on their barracks in Ismailiya within the Suez Canal zone, British forces shot and killed fifty Egyptian police conscripts. Now the remainder of the British occupation in Egypt was targeted, leading to the destruction of British-owned clubs and hotels. Thirty people were killed and 750 buildings were destroyed.[43] Note that al-Banna began his Islamist career in

---

[39] Quoted in Lia 1998, 81.   [40] Lia 1998, 179–80.   [41] Mitchell 1969, 56.
[42] Mitchell 1969, 63–5.   [43] Wright 2006, 25–6.

Ismailiya,[44] leading to a strong residue of Muslim Brothers sentiment, which likely sparked the initial attacks against the British.

This strong tendency toward violence in the name of Islam marks the Society of the Muslim Brothers as the prototypical radical Islamist movement. Carl Brown[45] describes the origins of the Muslim Brotherhood within the context of the British occupation: "Located on the Suez Canal, Isma'iliyya in those years was replete with the signs of alien military, economic, and cultural domination. British military bases, the foreign officialdom of the Suez Canal Company, foreign economic denomination of all major businesses and public utilities, even street signs in English brought home to al-Banna the colonized status of his fellow Muslims. It was in this environment that he organized his Muslim Brethren, the first members being, significantly, six Egyptian workers from the British military camp."

The violent orientation of the Muslim Brotherhood came into existence along the lines of the trajectory indicated in Figure 1.1, as shown here in Figure 6.1. The early period of subordination prior to 1928 is overcome by the newly found Egyptian independence from British control that the Islamist Muslim Brothers celebrated. But the wartime return of the British occupation, combined with the ongoing difficulties of the Egyptian army in Israel and ultimate defeat by the nascent Israeli forces, was to reverse this trajectory. Instead of a continued independent and successful Egyptian polity, renewed British occupation and humiliating defeat by another newly created power, perceived to be Western in origin, led to a widespread perception of Arab subordination. Violence was now the preferred solution. This was to be an early prototype of the etiology that would lead to 9/11 and other attacks by radical Islamists, analyzed in the succeeding chapter.

Activities of the Society of the Muslim Brothers also served as a prototype of contemporary Islamist groups' concern for social welfare, as practiced, say, by Hamas and Hizbollah. Al-Banna was particularly exercised by the enormous gap between living conditions in cities such as Cairo and the countryside.[46] As his group served as an example of political extremism, it also provided a model for the peaceful amelioration of the living conditions of the peasantry.

From these humble beginnings in 1928, Richard Mitchell[47] records explosive growth. At its peak, the Brotherhood's membership was about 500,000, with an approximately equal number of sympathizers. As we shall see later, evidence will be provided for Brown's[48] contention that the Brotherhood "is best labeled an Islamist totalitarian movement. As such it cultivated 'true believers' with a mindset dividing the world into the good and the bad, the saved and the damned. Given this orientation, it was easy to sanctify any means, including

---

[44] Mitchell 1969, 9–11.   [45] 2000, 143.
[46] Lia 1998, 109.   [47] 1969, 328.   [48] 2000, 148.

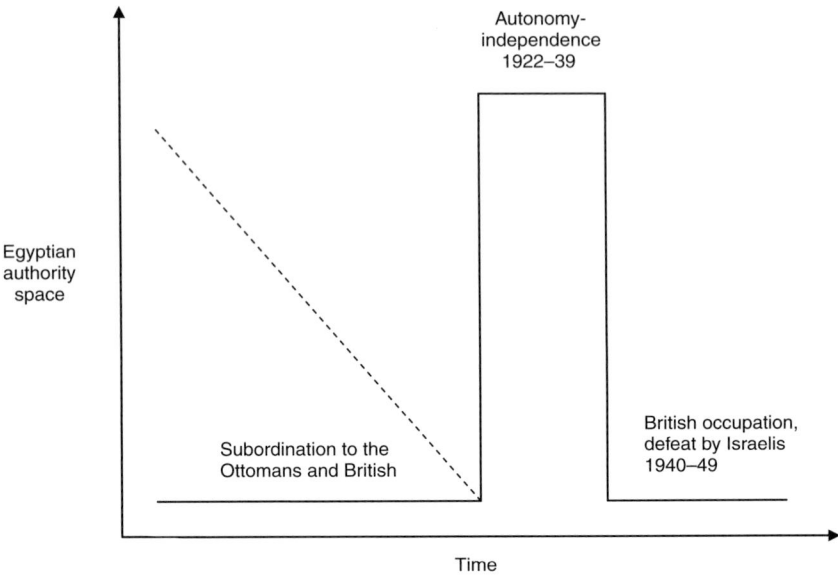

Figure 6.1:   Changes in Egyptian authority space over time

violence, used to advance God's plan and to oppose God's enemies. As such, it was the prototype of many later Islamist movements." However, given the nomenclature adopted in this book, I prefer to use the term "political extremism" in place of totalitarianism.

The Caliphate

Because al-Qaeda is not tied to a particular territory, there is a tendency to deny its political aspirations. In his declaration of war against the United States in 2001, Osama bin Laden states: "The walls of oppression and humiliation cannot be demolished except in a rain of bullets. Without shedding blood no degradation and branding can be removed from the forehead."[49]

As a faithful acolyte of Sayyid Qutb, bin Laden looked to the restoration of the Caliphate as an instrument that would unify all of Islam, presumably under his banner. Indeed, as does Qutb, he harks back precisely to the disappearance of the Caliphate as the time when the "humiliation" and "desecration" of Islam began. Bin Laden called Mullah Omar of Afghanistan's Islamist Taliban "a caliph."[50] Remarking that the United States was "filled with horror" after the attacks of September 11, bin Laden goes on to say, "Our Islamic nation has been tasting

[49] Quoted in Devji 2005, 133.   [50] Devji 2005, 22.

the same for more [than] 80 years, of humiliation and disgrace, its sons killed and their blood spilled, its sanctities desecrated."[51]

How realistic is the re-establishment of the Caliphate as a political goal? One way to answer this question is through comparison with other "history seeking" movements. In 1928, when an editorialist in the *Frankfurter Zeitung* described Hitler as a "fool,"[52] who would have dreamt that 5 years later he would be chancellor of Germany and on the brink of establishing near-total control of its society? Or during the interwar period, in the midst of the French Third Republic, when Charles Maurras and *Action française* were demanding a return to monarchy as part of their proto-fascist platform, who would have suggested that several years later with German "help," a latter-day version of such a regime would be established at Vichy by Henri Pétain and Pierre Laval. The emergence of Russia as the seat of the first communist state was surprising, even shocking, given its underdevelopment relative to the West. In other words, unanticipated events, especially the violent and chaotic, can lead to surprising outcomes. Indeed, reading bin Laden carefully, we can discern the strategy he is using to achieve his desired Caliphate, or at least the political unity of Muslims that is required to establish it.

Although seemingly quixotic, the resurrection of the Muslim Caliphate is indeed a possibility. Historically, the Caliphate was a synthesis of political and religious Muslim governance; more recently, until 1922, the Ottoman sultan was the caliph, occupying both ecclesiastical and temporal seats of power. After the destruction of the Abbasid Empire and Caliphate as the political center for unified Muslim rule in 1258, the Ottoman Empire assumed that function, at least for the majority Sunni Muslims. Since that time, the Caliphate has functioned as a major source of unity for Sunni Muslims. I will illustrate this function in several instances to impart a sense of the way unity has been pursued using the Caliphate as a principal vehicle.

I will use colonial India as an example, partly because it has been outside the mainstream of Muslim politics after the British arrived as colonizers, hence suggestive of the strong societal processes operating even at the constrained periphery of the Muslim world. At the same time, combining all of today's India, Pakistan, Bangladesh, and Assam, colonial India (the British Raj) had one of the largest Muslim populations in the world at the turn of the twentieth century. (During the period of Mughal governance prior to the British, the Mughal ruler assumed the title of caliph within India.[53]) This moment in history at the start of the twentieth century is critical because it witnessed the rise of the All-India Khilafat (Caliphate) movement that expressed widespread support for the Muslim Caliphate in the Ottoman Empire in the interests of Muslim unity.

---

[51] Quoted in P. Berman 2003, 117.   [52] Kershaw 1998, 302.
[53] Minault 1982, 4.

The importance of this period is signaled by international events, as well as those occurring within the Raj. In 1912, Italy invaded Ottoman-controlled Libya, establishing it as an Italian colony. The 1912–13 Balkan Wars witnessed the loss of almost all of the Ottoman Empire's European territories (excepting Thrace). These territories were now governed by Christian rulers, and after the emigration of much of the Muslim population, both forced and voluntary, had substantial Christian majorities. To an interested observer, it must have seemed as if there had occurred a massive European Christian effort to continue the dismantling of the Empire, a process that had been ongoing since the eighteenth century. If Constantinople were to fall into European hands – a major Russian goal for centuries – then the Caliphate itself, situated in that city, was in danger.

These perceived international threats to Islam were complemented by internal ones within the Raj. In 1909, separate Muslim electorates were established, but as a consequence of nationalist opposition, in 1911 the Muslim majority province of Eastern Bengal and Assam was eliminated, thereby removing a major source of Muslim political influence.[54] Shortly thereafter, a Muslim University Constitution Committee was established by Muslim notables with the purpose of founding a university dedicated to the education of Muslims and administered entirely by Muslim leaders. But despite a positive recommendation by the colonial government, the government in London rejected this project. Thus, even from the local perspective within India, it must have seemed that here, too, Islam was under attack.

As a consequence of these events, two highly prominent Muslim brothers, Mohammed and Shaukat Ali, became increasingly partisan in favor of Turkey as the seat of political Islam. But during World War I, largely as a result of their pro-Turkish stand, the two leaders were interned under the Defence of India Act, and then confined to a remote corner of central India. Among other notables, at the end of the war they were to found the Khilafat movement, principally as an effort to maintain intact the now defeated Ottoman Empire as a way of safeguarding the Khilafat in Constantinople. In March 1919, the Khilafat Committee was formed during a public meeting of 15,000 Muslims in Bombay.[55] In September of that year, an All-India Muslim Conference was held in Lucknow that resolved to hold an All-India Khilafat Day on October 17; this event turned out to be a major success. Special prayers for the maintenance of the caliph's temporal powers were offered in Bombay, including by Shi'ites, who themselves were concerned about the decline of political Islam in both the Middle East and India. Earlier, in December 1918, at a meeting of the Muslim League that foreshadowed the Khilafat movement, a resolution was passed stating:

> The Indian Musalmans take a deep interest in the fate of their coreligionists outside India…[T]he collapse of the Muslim powers of the world is bound

---

[54] Minault 1982, 10.   [55] Minault 1982, 73.

to have an adverse influence on the political importance of the Musalmans in this country, and the annihilation of the military powers of Islam in the world cannot but have a far-reaching effect on the minds of even the loyal Musalmans of India.[56]

To implement a plan of action, an All-India Khilafat Conference was assembled in Delhi in November 1919. Four important resolutions were passed, including (1) a Muslim boycott of peace celebrations scheduled for December until Turkey received a just settlement of the war, (2) a withdrawal of cooperation from the government if the Khilafat was jeopardized by an unjust settlement, (3) a boycott of European goods if the peace was unjust to Turkey, and (4) further representations of the Muslim cause to be made in London.[57] "Justice" for Turkey was to consist of a minimization of territorial loss in order to safeguard the Caliphate in Constantinople. All of this activity, of course, was rendered moot first by the Greco-Turkish War that had its own settlement in Lausanne, and second by Kemal Atatürk's 1922 abolition of the Ottoman sultanate, thereby removing the caliph's temporal powers.

When, in 1923, Indian Muslims expressed support for the caliph's temporal powers, they appealed to Atatürk to place the Khilafat "on a basis which would command the confidence and esteem of Muslim nations, and thus impart to the Turkish state unique strength and dignity."[58] Instead of supporting the caliph, the delegates to the National Assembly in Constantinople were infuriated at this perceived effort to undermine the newly proclaimed Republic of Turkey by advocating a restoration of the Ottoman dynasty. On March 1, 1924, the Caliphate was abolished by the National Assembly, stating that this action was needed to "cleanse and elevate the Islamic faith, by rescuing it from the position of a political instrument."[59]

Although the Khilafat movement in colonial India was a failure, it illustrates the unifying effect of a central religious institution in the face of manifest political failure. The decisive defeat of the Ottoman Empire at the hands of Christian Europe and its disappearance as a political entity, as well as political losses at home in India, led to the concentration on a traditional focus of Islamic life – the Caliphate. If political failures within the Muslim world continue as they have until the present, then it is possible that such religio-political symbolism may once again emerge as a major focus of the Islamic future.

Colonial India was not the only Asian location populated by many Muslims to engage the issue of the Caliphate. The Dutch East Indies, today's Indonesia, the state with the largest number of Muslims in the world, also witnessed serious consideration of the future of the Caliphate. Prominent among writers, even emblematic of them, was Rashid Rida who, although not Indonesian, contributed original thinking to the debates. Rejecting the secular nationalism that

[56] Quoted in Minault 1982, 62.   [57] Minault 1982, 77–8.   [58] Quoted in Minault 1982, 203.
[59] Quoted in Minault 1982.

increasingly was in vogue as the twentieth century progressed, Rida emphasized an Islamic response to the problem of colonialism. The Caliphate, separated by Atatürk from all executive roles in 1922, could be restructured to satisfy the demands of modernity. Instead of a dynastic succession established by the first of the Umayyads over the centuries, leading to a state of inertia and ossification, Muslims should now elect a new caliph. In this fashion, the popular focus of the Muslim world would be shifted from the everyday problems of colonialism (that would appear to require secular solutions in the form of individual nationalisms developing within the separate Muslim nationalities) to a more cosmopolitan emphasis on the *'umma*. In other words, an Islamic solution should be decided upon; the caliph should represent all Muslims, regardless of their individual national aspirations. Foreshadowing the contemporary use of the internet and other advanced forms of communication, Rida commented in 1923:

> The time is upon us in our age as was faithfully foretold in many *hadīth*,... countries (*aqtār*) are linked to each other, by land and sea, with steam-ships and railroads. Airships have begun to transport mail and people hundreds and thousands of miles within an hour or a few hours. News is carried through the power of electricity from the beginning to the ends of the earth in a few seconds. *Had our ancestors possessed these means in their day, then they would have gained possession of the entire world!*[60]

With some minor changes of language needed to reflect contemporary modernity, Osama bin Laden could have written these words. Muslims in the Middle East, North Africa, India, and Java could unite in ways simply not imagined in ancient times. Bin Laden obviously was not the first Muslim leader to emphasize the international nature of the *'umma*, but is the first to have acted in emphatic ways, using violent means and modern technology, to realize the goal of Islamic unity. Certainly he would agree with Rida's summary observation that "possession of the entire world" could now be within the grasp of Muslims willing to unite and act decisively.

In addition to theatricality and ostensible religiosity, suicide bombing is one of the most effective ways to establish unity among a fractious population. It is a spectacular form of self-sacrifice which, if carried out successfully, takes many "enemy" lives as well. Instead of a "metaphysical" form of activity – one with its own interiority – as claimed by Devji, in social psychological experiments this form of altruistic punishment has been shown to yield cooperation.[61]

Having reviewed the ideational and societal foundations of contemporary radical Islamism, we can now turn to an examination of specific cases. All of these manifestations of the principles developed in this chapter occurred during the past three decades.

---

[60] Emphasis added; quoted in Laffan 2003, 205.   [61] Fehr and Gachter 2002.

7

Contemporary Radical Islamist Movements

In the post-World War II period, we have seen the rise of radical Islamists that have committed mass violence. Al-Qaeda, al-Muhajiroun (in Britain), the Sudanese government, and the Shamil-led Chechen Islamists are cases in point that will be reviewed in this chapter. The last of these groups committed the Beslan school massacre that was mind-numbing in its murder of 186 children, among others. This and the centrality of Chechnya in the radical Islamists' worldview have led this case to receive more attention in this chapter than others.

Al-Qaeda

The regimentation of politics also characterizes the origins of late twentieth-century radical Islamism. Abdullah Azzam is generally recognized as the first of the prominent jihadists who ventured into Afghanistan immediately after the Soviet invasion of 1979. Earlier, as a Palestinian born in Jenin, he fought in the Six-Day War of 1967 and in the Palestinian resistance. But Arab oppositional movements like the Palestine Liberation Organization (PLO) were insufficiently religious for him. He joined the Muslim Brotherhood and later was among the founders of Hamas, before obtaining higher degrees in institutions of Islamic learning. According to Terry McDermott,[1] in Peshawar, the emerging capital of the Afghan resistance headquartered in Pakistan's Northwest Frontier, "Azzam found his cause: Afghanistan would be the incubator for a new, muscular Islam, a religion of warriors like that of the Prophet's time." Violent revolt against the "apostate" Muslim regimes was required; as Assam said,[2] "Jihad and the rifle alone: no negotiations, no conferences, and no dialogues." Azzam quoted the Qur'an in support of his position:

> Then, it is obligatory upon the whole of creation to march out for jihad. If they fail to respond, they are in sin… The light, the heavy, the riding, the walking, the slave, and the free man shall all go out. Whoever has a father, without his permission and whoever has not a father, until Allah's religion

---

[1] 2005, 94.   [2] Quoted in McDermott 2005, 94–5.

prevails, defends the territory and the property, humiliates the enemy and rescues the prisoners. On this there is no disagreement. What does he do if the rest stay behind? He finds a prisoner and pays his ransom. He attacks by himself if he is able, and if not he prepares a warrior.[3]

As in 1933 Germany, an anachronistic regimentation of society would be required to achieve either the goals of secular ideology, or those of sacred belief. Azzam became the mentor of Osama bin Laden upon the latter's arrival in Afghanistan. Later, in 1989,[4] he and two of his sons would be assassinated by a remote control bomb as they were journeying to Friday prayers.

War and self-sacrifice

The actual experience of war would be the cauldron in which this Arab "band of brothers" would cement their allegiance to jihad. In 1987, bin Laden, Azzam and other Arabs, as well as Khalid Sheikh Mohammed (Pakistani organizer of the 9/11 attacks) withstood a Russian assault on the village of Jaji. The small group of Arabs held off the Soviets for weeks until they left the field. It was here that bin Laden's reputation as a battlefield warrior was first established. Arabs who took part in the Battle of the Lion's Den, as bin Laden was wont to call it, would later become part of his close entourage. It was here too that bin Laden first began to think of himself as not simply a liberator of Afghanistan from the infidel Soviet presence, but as a potential leader of global jihad.

Bin Laden now renewed Azzam's "call for martyrdom in a pan-Islamic international jihad against oppression, from the very real experience of the brutal violence and chaos of modern warfare and from the empowering confidence founded in the belief, however wrong, that Islam alone had defeated the Soviets and their munafiq stooges among the Aghans."[5] Note here too bin Laden's assumption of Azzam's earlier explicit preference for a vanguard of radical Islamists to lead the jihad. As he stated: "Every principle needs a vanguard to carry it forward and [to] put up with heavy tasks and enormous sacrifices. There is no ideology, neither earthly nor heavenly, that does not require…a vanguard that gives everything it possesses in order to achieve victory… It carries the flag all along the sheer, endless and difficult path until it reaches its destination in the reality of life, since Allah has destined that it should make it and manifest itself. This vanguard constitutes the strong foundation (*al qaeda al-sulbah*) for the expected society."[6]

This is the first recorded usage of the term *al qaeda* as at least an ideological buttress, if not an organizational vehicle for Islamic revolution. One may conclude that in his organizational thinking, Azzam was to Qutb, as Lenin was to Marx. But martyrdom was to be the vehicle or vocabulary of political expression. An important *mujahadin* leader recalls the behavior of Arabs in Afghanistan

---

[3] Quoted in McDermott 2005, 95.   [4] Burke 2003, 77.
[5] Burke 2003, 77.   [6] Quoted in Burke 2003, 8.

ordered to hold a position: "They fought all day then when I went to relieve them in the evening the Arabs were crying because they wanted to be martyred. They were saying, 'I must have committed some sin for Allah has not chosen me to go to heaven,' I told them that if they wanted to stay…and fight then I wasn't going to stop them. The next day they were killed. Osama said later that he had told them that the trench was their gate to heaven."[7]

Osama bin Laden and Ayman al-Zawahiri, leaders of al-Qaeda, also are no strangers to political theater. In addition to the horrific and spectacular images of the destruction of the World Trade Center carried by the visual media,[8] televised interviews of both leaders have featured the traditional medieval Arab costume dress[9] to emphasize their Islamic purity.

Building on the idea of equality found in traditional Islam,[10] and the experience of unity among the Muslim *mujahadin* in the Afghan war against the Soviets, radical Islamism seeks to establish unity within the entire *'umma*, or Muslim nation. According to bin Laden,[11] "if it is not possible to push back the enemy except by the collective movement of the Muslim people, then there is a duty on the Muslims to ignore the minor differences among themselves." Following Sayyid Qutb, arguably the single most influential philosopher of Muslim extremism, bin Laden's goal is nothing less than the re-creation of the Muslim Caliphate that once sprawled over the entire Middle East and North Africa a millennium ago.[12]

Beginning in the 1940s, Qutb argued for a vast Muslim rejection of Western liberalism, especially its cornerstone of separation of church and state. With the dissolution of the Ottoman Empire in 1921 and the emergence of secular Turkey under Kemal Atatürk as a successor state, the empire unifying the Muslim peoples of the Middle East had been replaced by a horrendous model to be avoided at all costs. Qutb's solution, enthusiastically adopted later by Egyptian fundamentalist groups and still later by al-Qaeda, was resurrection of the Muslim Caliphate whose institutional vestiges had been destroyed by Atatürk's regime.[13]

The self-sacrifice of leaders such as bin Laden in his hideaway, bereft of any civilized amenities, and of followers in their suicide bombing is intended to achieve cooperation/unity among the currently divided Muslim populations. Surveys following 9/11 suggest that he succeeded admirably, at least in his core constituency. Between 2003 and 2005, proportions of the population which had confidence in Osama bin Laden increased in Jordan and Pakistan, although in regions less central to the Muslim experience and to bin Laden's earlier activities (e.g., Indonesia, Morocco), confidence decreased during this time period. On the whole, most Muslim populations welcomed the greater role of Islam in politics.[14] Without the events of 9/11 and their sequelae – the invasions of

---

[7] Quoted in Burke 2003, 76.   [8] Baudrillard 2002.   [9] Kepel 2002.
[10] Jackson 2001.   [11] 1996, 29.   [12] Gunaratna 2002, 21.   [13] P. Berman 2003.
[14] Pew Global Attitudes Project 2005.

Afghanistan and Iraq, Abu-Ghraib, Guantanamo, and multiple suicide bombings all yielding a raised Islamic consciousness – it is unlikely that the Danish
cartoon controversy would have yielded so many worldwide Muslim protests,
both peaceful and violent.

Most recently, bin Laden stated that he will never be captured alive, thereby
choosing the ultimate sacrifice. "I have sworn to only live free," he is reported
to have said. "Even if I find bitter the taste of death, I don't want to die humiliated or deceived."[15] In this avowal of self-sacrifice, bin Laden was following his
ideological mentor Sayyid Qutb, who was also on the same sacrificial path.
According to Ayman al-Zawahiri, bin Laden's Egyptian second in command at
al-Qaeda, "Qutb's words acquired a deeper resonance because of his defiance
and refusal to appeal to President Nasser to spare his life, which provided activists with an example of steadfastness and sacrifice."[16]

Qutb's example was followed in the early 1970s by Salah Sirriya, a Palestinian
Islamist who conspired with Egyptian students to stage a coup d'état against
President Anwar Sadat. Upon the failure of this attempt, and Sirriya's subsequent death sentence, he steadfastly refused to petition Sadat for clemency. So
determined was he on the path of self-sacrifice, that when his wife and nine
children visited him shortly before his execution, he told her, "If you petition for
amnesty, consider yourself divorced."[17] In his writings, Zawahiri tells this tale
approvingly.

Zawahiri himself, along with bin Laden, appears to have chosen the path
of self-sacrifice. Why he did so is explored at length in Gerges.[18] Although I
have no quarrel with his conclusions, the analysis here will shed a different light
on Zawahiri's decision to depart from the religious nationalism – that which
is devoted to establishing a national Islamist government – of Tanzim al-Jihad
(Islamic Jihad) and join bin Laden in transnational jihad. From the 1970s until
the late 1990s, as the leader of Islamic Jihad, his focus was almost exclusively on
the overthrow of the Egyptian government. Even the Palestinian issue, always of
central importance in the Arab world, was secondary. Importantly at this time,
bin Laden and his mentor in Afghanistan, Azzam, were dedicated to jihad only
within the regional Middle Eastern–Central Asian environment.

What transformed the Islamist devotees of domestic change to the transnational mode? Gerges[19] emphasizes the failure of the religious nationalists
such as Islamic Jihad and the substantially larger Egyptian Islamic Group, and
the Algerian Islamic Salvation Front (FIS). After years of violent confrontations with their respective secularist governments, these organizations were
decisively defeated. Not only was the defeat palpable as the result of the combined impact of growing popular revulsion at the violence (especially the 1997
Luxor Massacre of sixty-two foreigners and Egyptians), improved government

---

[15] *New York Times* 2006, A5.   [16] Paraphrased in Gerges 2005, 7.
[17] Quoted in Gerges 2005, 8.   [18] 2005.   [19] 2005.

intelligence, and the willingness of the Europeans and Americans to aid the besieged governments, but many of the imprisoned jihadis later openly rejected violence. In 1997, the Egyptian Islamic Group initiated a cease fire. Shortly thereafter, several books were written that repudiated virtually all of its earlier ideology and violent practices.

Writing from their Egyptian prison cells, the Islamists assumed responsibility for the violence that began in the 1980s and relinquished their earlier claimed right to commit jihad against Muslim rulers who do not govern by the Shari'a. Individual leaders cannot initiate jihad; this is left only to the *ulema* (Islamic scholars) and the appropriate state leaders. These writers also affirmed the traditional Islamic injunction against killing civilians of any religion.[20]

Al-Qaeda, in particular, receives serious criticism from members of the Islamic Group. Mohammed Derbala, for example, criticizes al-Qaeda for violating Islamic law on the killing of civilians. Instead of the outraged condemnation of the United States typical of earlier years, these Islamic leaders recount instances where the United States aided Muslims. Support of the *mujahadin* in Afghanistan, the expulsion of Iraqis from Kuwait, and the use of Western force to compel the Serbs to cease their massacres of Muslims in Bosnia and the ethnic cleansing of Muslims in Kosovo were all said to be positive elements of US foreign policy. Derbala criticized al-Qaeda for needlessly making enemies, especially powerful ones such as the United States, and "Al Qaeda has to understand that jihad is only one of the Muslim's duties. Jihad is a means, not an end."[21]

Why then did Zawahiri join his Islamic Jihad with bin Laden's al-Qaeda in the late 1990s? Gerges[22] reports that former associates and jihadis credit this change to Zawahiri's increasing financial dependence on bin Laden, and the latter's influence over him. The defeat and volte face of so many Egyptian jihadis also suggested that by the mid-to-late 1990s Zawahiri simply had nowhere to go.

The ephemeral gain

But there is more to this than the difficult corner in which Zawahiri found himself. Both he and bin Laden had served in Afghanistan, Zawahiri arriving in 1986, just at the start of the turn to victory of the *mujahadin*. It was this victory of the transnational jihad in Afghanistan that was exhilarating, especially in contrast to the defeat at home. The following account of Nasir al-Bahri, who later became bin Laden's bodyguard after his service in Bosnia, is suggestive of the impact of the transnational experience. In Bosnia:

> We began to have real contact with the other trends, the enemies of the ummah, and the ideology of the ummah began to evolve in our minds. We realized we were a nation [ummah] that had a distinguished place among

---

[20] Gerges 2005, 200.   [21] Quoted in Gerges 2005, 203.   [22] 2005, 121.

nations. Otherwise, what would make me leave Saudi Arabia – and I am of Yemeni origin – to go and fight in Bosnia? The issue of [secular] nationalism was put out of our minds, and we acquired a wider view than that, namely the issue of the ummah. Although the issue was very simple at the start, yet it was a motive and an incentive for jihad.[23]

And later, upon joining bin Laden in Afghanistan, al-Bahri exults in the victories over the Serbs, Russians, and now the Americans:

> In view of our military experience and our experience in carrying arms, we said:
> What is America? If we had succeeded in many armed confrontations and military fronts against the Serbs, the Russians, and others, America will not be something new. We often sat down with the brothers who fought the Americans in Somalia, and we used to hear about the brothers who struck the Americans at the Aden Hotel in the early 1990s and about the brothers who blew up American residences in Riyadh and al-Khobar. We reached the conclusion that America is no different from the forces we have fought because it has become a target for all and sundry. All of its foes have dealt blows to it. So I decided to join sheikh Osama bin Laden. That was the beginning of my work with Al Qaeda.[24]

This thoroughly distorted view of the prospects for future victory over the United States will shortly be demonstrated in bin Laden's own statements.

There is the temptation to credit bin Laden's declaration of jihad against the United States to the humiliation of US troops during the 1993 aid effort in Somalia. The remaining superpower, the United States, just like its defeated Soviet counterpart, would appear to have clay feet. As Bruce Lawrence[25] suggests in his Introduction to the public utterances of bin Laden, "If one superpower could be defeated, and even ultimately destroyed, by warriors for the faith, why should not the other, which had proved much less resilient in Mogadishu?" Hence, a steely resolve and bold but judicious tactics could lead to the humiliation, even destruction of the remaining superpower.

Yet, the pre-eminent factor yielding bin Laden's declaration of jihad is the affront to Islam of US troops on Saudi soil after 1991. This is clear from bin Laden's statements. Prior to this declaration, bin Laden specifically addressed the issue of the "occupation" of Saudi Arabia. He refers to "a calamity unprecedented in the history of our *umma*, namely the invasion by the American and western Crusader forces of the Arabian Peninsula and Saudi Arabia, the home of the Noble Ka'ba, the Sacred House of God, the Muslim's direction of prayer, the Noble Sanctuary of the Prophet, and the city of God's Messenger, where the Prophetic revelation was received."[26] Nowhere is Somalia mentioned.

---

[23] Quoted in Gerges 2005, 63.   [24] Quoted in Gerges 2005, 65.   [25] 2005, xxi.
[26] Quoted in Lawrence 2005, 15–16.

And in the later declaration of jihad itself, the occupation of Saudi Arabia is once again mentioned as "the greatest disaster to befall the Muslims since the death of the Prophet Muhammad."[27] Here, Somalia is mentioned only once and in a long list of presumed massacres of Muslims having occurred in places such as Tajikistan, Burma, Kashmir, Assam, the Philippines, Eritrea, and, of course, Somalia.[28] Still later, in his 1997 interview with Peter Arnett, Somalia is mentioned at some length but only in response to a question about Mogadishu put to bin Laden by Arnett.[29]

And if one accepts that the first World Trade Center bombing of 1993 was an al-Qaeda-linked operation, then the events in Mogadishu could have had nothing to do with bin Laden's initiation of violence against the United States. The bombing occurred on February 26, 1993, while the battles of the marines in Mogadishu cited by bin Laden occurred in October of that year.[30] Ramzi Yousef, supervisor of the bombing, apparently stayed in a house funded by bin Laden in Peshawar. Yousef's uncle, Khalid Sheikh Mohammed, was described by the 9/11 Commission as "the principal architect of the 9/11 attacks."[31]

At bottom, the violation of Islamic authority space by the presence of US troops in Saudi Arabia after 1991, combined with the further humiliation of Arabs in the defeat of Saddam Hussein, was the precipitant of the declaration of jihad by bin Laden. After a comprehensive review of bin Laden's and Zawahiri's statements, Gerges[32] concludes: "More than any other variable, bin Laden frequently used the American military presence in the 'land of the two holy places' (Islam's two holiest cities in Mecca and Medina) as a rallying cry and an effective recruitment tool to lure young Muslims to join his anti-American network." At the same time, it is clear that events in Somalia were salient to him.

Here is bin Laden in a 2000 recruitment tape describing the impact of Somalia:

> Using very meager resources and military means, the Afghan mujahedeen demolished one of the most important human myths in history and the biggest military apparatus. We no longer fear the so-called Great Powers. We believe that America is much weaker than Russia; and our brothers who fought in Somalia told us that they were astonished to observe how weak, impotent, and cowardly the American soldier is. As soon as eighty American troops were killed, they fled in the dark as fast as they could, after making a great deal of noise about the new international order.[33]

It is also clear that faith in God's rule yields a distorted view in the militants' underestimation of US power. According to Gerges,[34] "Militants like bin Laden, Zawahiri, and their associates believe that the power asymmetry with the United

---

[27] Quoted in Lawrence 2005, 25.   [28] Lawrence 2005, 25.   [29] Lawrence 2005, 54.
[30] Lawrence 2005, 53–4.   [31] Lawrence 2005, 53.   [32] 2005, 56.
[33] Quoted in Gerges 2005, 85.   [34] Gerges 2005, 199.

States is of little consequence because they are armed with faith – God is watching over them so they will ultimately prevail."

Instability of the cognitive frame

Consistent with other instances of radicalism, it is the aggrieved or frustrated upwardly mobile minority group member experiencing discrimination that is more likely to be oriented towards violent change, not the poorly educated or marginally employed laborer. Thus, the great radical leaders of the twentieth century experienced discrimination and/or humiliation in their native societies (e.g., Jews such as Leon Trotsky, Grigori Zinoviev, or Lev Kamenev experiencing intense anti-Semitism in tsarist Russia). Although Osama bin Laden did not experience discrimination directly, his participation with the Afghan *mujahadin*, including encounters with Western-born participants, must have intimated to him the disappointments of their Western experience. Further, his personal identification with the *'umma* and its bitter defeats in its twentieth-century confrontations with the West also must have imbued bin Laden with deep feelings of humiliation on behalf of the *'umma*.

Radical Islamist leaders identify with the *'umma*, which, in bin Laden's usage, is equivalent to the Muslim nation. For these leaders, success of the nation is linked with their own egos, as is national failure. Hence, threats to their egos in the form of national losses can be enormously consequential.

Contrary to conventional wisdom, people with low self-esteem are not the most likely to be aggressive and commit violent acts. Instead, those with high self-esteem and who experience threats to their egos are the most likely candidates for violent aggression. Summarizing a large body of research, Baumeister *et al.*[35] conclude that "violence appears to be most commonly a result of threatened egotism – that is, highly favorable views of self that are disputed by some person or circumstance. *Inflated, unstable, or tentative beliefs in the self's superiority may be most prone to encountering threats and hence to causing violence.*"

People with high self-esteem tend to be continually aspiring upward. When their egos are threatened, they are highly reluctant to revise their opinions of self downward. Decreases in self-esteem are aversive. Instead, individuals with high self-esteem direct their attention to the source of the ego threat. Frequently, violence can be a result of this confrontation.[36] High self-esteem individuals who have inflated, unstable or tentative beliefs in their own (or the nation's) superiority are most prone to violence.

The case of Osama bin Laden is emblematic of this process. Identifying with the *'umma*, and himself having contributed to the victory in Afghanistan, he clearly identified with this success, even to the extent of inflating its significance

[35] Emphasis added; 1996, 5.   [36] Baumeister, Smart, and Boden 1996, 8.

for the *'umma*. Accordingly, "After the collapse of the Soviet Union – in which the US has no mentionable role, but rather the credit goes to God and the *mujahadin* in Afghanistan – this collapse made the US more haughty and arrogant, and it has started to see itself as a Master of this world and established what it calls the new world order."[37] By deflating the actual US role – *mujahadin* victory in Afghanistan beginning only after neutralization of the Soviet air force with US-supplied Stinger missiles – bin Laden inflates the *mujahadin* and, by implication, his own importance. This is symptomatic of the unstable and uncertain high self-esteem acquired through the victory in Afghanistan occurring only 8 years before the interview with Peter Arnett, from which the previous passage is quoted.

Indeed, the instability and uncertainty are realistic. The victory in 1989 over the Soviets was the only one in a long line of military calamities that befell the Muslim world in its confrontation with non-Muslims. Western colonization of virtually the entire Muslim world, including the Middle East (after World War I), North Africa, South Asia, and Indonesia, was followed by four major military defeats of Arab armies by tiny Israel, and the one-sided victory of India over Pakistan in the last of three wars between the two protagonists. The one exception to this pattern, important to self-esteem of members of the *'umma* despite US aid, was the *mujahadin* victory in Afghanistan.

Gain and loss

As Lawrence Wright[38] indicates, "bin Laden and his Arab Afghans believed that, in Afghanistan, they had turned the tide and that Islam was again on the march." All of these events occurred against the backdrop of the dissolution of the Muslim Caliphate in 1924 by the relentlessly secular Atatürk. Hence, at the time of the 1991 Gulf War, entry of the US and other Western troops into Saudi Arabia (home of the two most sacred mosques in all of Islam) leading to another Arab military defeat, this time of Saddam Hussein by the West, must have been deeply consequential. An insecurely held high self-esteem as the result of the victory in Afghanistan was seriously threatened, thereby leading to the subsequent al-Qaeda-inspired extremist violence.

Osama bin Laden's loss was to be found in the occupation of portions of Saudi Arabian territory to house Western, especially American, military forces at the time of the 1991 Gulf War. According to Islamic fundamentalists, Saudi territory, and most importantly the mosques of Mecca and Medina, were to be free of any "infidel" contamination. The presence of Christian Bibles and Jewish Torah scrolls on Saudi territory in some proximity to these mosques was a provocation and humiliation to bin Laden. In his declaration of 1996, bin Laden states that "Americans and their allies, civilians and military" are to be killed because of the

---

[37] bin Laden, quoted in Lawrence 2005, 50–1.   [38] 2006, 171.

need to liberate "the holy mosque [Mecca] from their grip, and in order for their armies to move out of all the lands of Islam, defeated and unable to threaten any Muslim."[39] Further, the defeat of Saddam Hussein by the US-led coalition forces in the Gulf War was seen as another major loss by radical Arab movements,[40] especially in light of certain commonalities between the goals of Baathists and radical Islamists in the Middle East.[41]

These losses are suggestive of an even earlier loss, namely the dissolution of the Ottoman Empire in 1921, the emergence of secular Turkey, and elimination of the Muslim Caliphate by Kemal Atatürk in 1924. Bin Laden explicitly harks back to this time of Muslim "humiliation" after World War I. Remarking that America was "filled with horror" after the attacks of 9/11, bin Laden goes on to say, "Our Islamic nation has been tasting the same for more [than] 80 years, of humiliation and disgrace, its sons killed and their blood spilled, its sanctities desecrated."[42] As a faithful acolyte of Sayyid Qutb, bin Laden would look to the restoration of the Caliphate as an instrument that would unify all of Islam, presumably under his banner. Indeed, as does Qutb, he harks back precisely to the disappearance of the Caliphate as the time when the "humiliation" and "desecration" of Islam began. Bin Laden called Mullah Omar of Afghanistan's Islamist Taliban "a caliph,"[43] in recognition of his leadership of a Sunni Muslim regime.

Figure 7.1 traces this process through time. To the left of the figure, we see the Russian defeats of the Ottomans throughout the nineteenth century, followed by the disappearance of the empire, and especially significant for radical Islamism, the rise of modern secularized Turkey and dissolution of the Caliphate as the institutional seat of ecclesiastical Islam. To the right, the victory in Afghanistan over the Soviets, the first significant such victory for Islam versus non-Muslim powers, is followed by a most significant defeat – the presence of Christians and Jews on Arabian soil, effectively, in bin Laden's view, a direct Western attack on the holiest sites of Islam, supplementing the attack on Saddam Hussein.

Al-Muhajiroun

Al-Qaeda, of course, is not the only manifestation of radical Islamism. The bombing of Mike's Place, a Tel-Aviv bar popular with English speakers, was carried out not by Saudi or Egyptian radical Islamists, but by British Muslim citizens of Kashmiri extraction, born and raised in the United Kingdom. As British citizens posing as tourists crossing the Allenby Bridge from Jordan to the West Bank, they were subject to far less scrutiny than others. On April 30, 2003, Asif Mohammed Hanif detonated his bomb killing three and injuring fifty-five outside the bar (the security guard blocked the entrance). The other suicide bomber,

---

[39] bin Laden 1996, 46.   [40] Randal 2004, 164.   [41] P. Berman 2003, 56–8.
[42] Quoted in P. Berman 2003, 117.   [43] Devji 2005, 22.

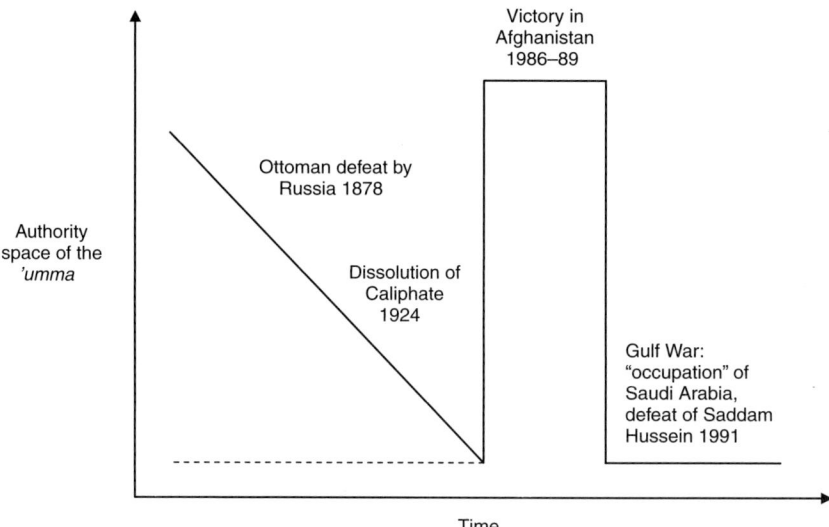

Figure 7.1:   Changes in authority space of the *'umma* over time

Omar Khan Sharif, could not detonate his bomb successfully and temporarily escaped; his body was later found floating in the water near the bar.

What would make two British-born citizens, one from a wealthy background and the other an excellent student, want to immolate themselves and commit multiple murders for the cause of Palestinians (not a common ethnic background for either)? Other Muslims from Western countries numbering in the thousands also fought in foreign places such as Bosnia, Chechnya, and Afghanistan. The answer, at least initially, is found in the organization al-Muhajiroun, originating in the United Kingdom, that subscribed to radical Islamist principles. The organization was founded by a radical imam of Syrian origin, Omar Bakri Mohammed, educated at Islamic institutions in Saudi Arabia, he ultimately migrated to the United Kingdom.

Earlier, al-Muhajiroun did not advocate open violence against non-Islamic targets. Instead, its program included the conversion to Islam of Queen Elizabeth, or failing that, a non-violent Islamic military coup in Britain and other countries where Muslims are found.[44] However, after 9/11, the movement became more radicalized. Upon the death of Hanif but before the finding of Sharif's body, Bakri proclaimed "These two brothers have drawn a divine road map, one which is drawn in blood. We pray to God to accept one brother as a martyr [Hanif]. I am very proud with the fact that the Muslims grow closer

---

[44] Wiktorowicz 2005, 9.

every day, that the Muslim land is one land and there is no more nationalism or Arabism."[45] Here we see a process critical for the making of radical Islamists – identification with the 'umma as a whole, not simply a portion of it.

This emphasis on Islamic faith as the key cement uniting all Muslims over and above ethnicity such as "Arabism" marks a fundamental similarity with al-Qaeda. For like al-Qaeda, al-Muhajiroun had as one of its basic tenets the essential need for re-establishment of the Caliphate as the seat of international Muslim governance.[46] This demand was based on the oft-quoted (among Islamist groups) command in Qur'an 3:104: "Let there rise from among you group(s) calling society to Islam, commanding society to do what Allah orders and to refrain from what He forbids and these (group(s)) are the ones who are successful."[47]

Examining the characteristics of members of al-Muhajiroun can provide clues to understanding the sources of radical Islamism, at least in the West. First, these activists tend to be university graduates having the expectation of upward mobility. Here, we have a version of the ephemeral gain. Initially, from a Western-colonized portion of the Islamic world – Kashmir – still colonized by India in the Islamist view, nevertheless the two jihadis rose to some prominence in their youth. Yet, as Omar Bakri comments, "You find someone called Muhammad, who grew up in western society, he concedes a lot so people accept him. He changes his name to Mike, he has girlfriend, he drinks alcohol, he dances, he has sex, raves, rock and roll, then they say, 'You are a Paki.' After everything he gave up to be accepted, they tell him he is a bloody Arab or a Paki."[48] As such there exists an identity crisis for these Muslims leading to the attempt to provide an "identity of empowerment" through radical Islamism.[49] Instead of belonging to a despised group of immigrants or their recent descendants, radical Islamists can now proclaim their adherence to a 1,300-year-old religion, which through its political institutions at one time governed the Middle East, North Africa, and portions of Europe and South Asia. And the final stimulus to the emergence of a radical Islamist suicide bomber was not only the mortality salience and "victory" of 9/11 as we saw in the Moroccan example in Chapter 2 and in the preceding chapter, but now the invasion of Iraq during March 20–May 1, 2003, still ongoing at the time of the Tel Aviv suicide bombing, but with Iraq clearly losing. Note the date of the Tel Aviv suicide bombing as April 30.

Figure 7.2 illustrates the ephemeral gain for members of al-Muhajiroun. The experience of British colonialism and subsequent Indian domination of Kashmir is followed by the brief experience of personal success in Britain and the "victory" of 9/11, followed by the invasion of Iraq.

---

[45] Quoted in Wiktorowicz 2005, 6–7.   [46] Wiktorowicz 2005, 178.
[47] Quoted in Wiktorowicz 2005 179.   [48] Quoted in Wiktorowicz 2005, 91.
[49] Wiktorowicz 2005.

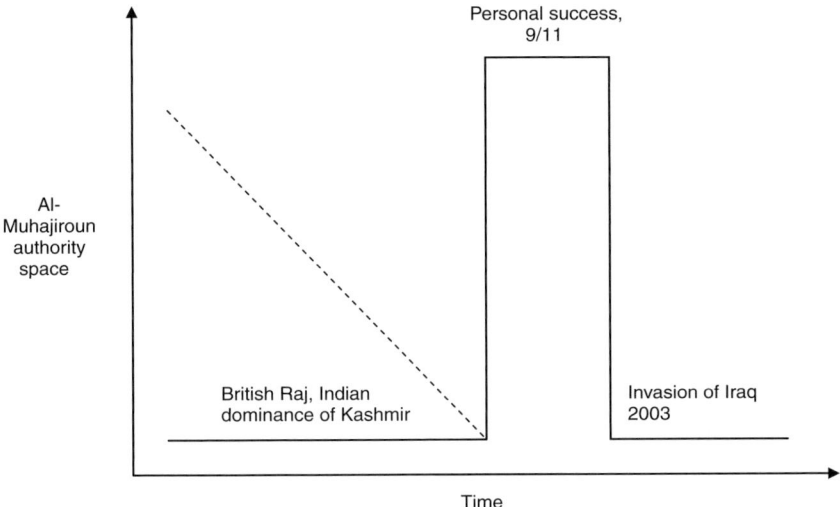

Figure 7.2: Changes in al-Muhajiroun authority space over time

In addition, the identity crisis in itself can provide a cognitive opening for the radical Islamist recruiter to exploit. Social networks can be used to attract the identity- or religion-seeking candidate, and then once engaged, the candidate can be gradually indoctrinated in the principles of the movement, especially its commitment to practice jihad. Accordingly, in a survey of al-Muhajiroun members, "While those who were attracted to al-Muhajiroun did not see themselves as religious prior to seeking and therefore were unlikely to have adopted a religious identity, respondents in the control group survey view themselves first and foremost as Muslims."[50]

Based on this analysis, although one cannot distinguish among individual members *within* a group in their propensity towards extremism, one can distinguish *between* groups in the likelihood of extremist behavior of their members. British Muslims of South Asian descent, for example (especially if Kashmiri), if they have achieved a certain degree of personal accomplishment, as did Hanif and Sharif and, if they identify with the 9/11 success, because their current humiliation evokes earlier subordination of their forebears as British (and now Indian) colonial subjects, are more likely to commit extremist violence than say, British citizens of French or German extraction. For such a British Muslim, the threat and fear of reversion to a subordinate condition is far more palpable than for the British citizen of European descent. At a pro-immigrant rally in London some 25 years ago, one person held up a sign that

---

[50] Wiktorowicz 2005, 102.

read "We are here because you were there." This succinctly summarizes the dilemma of these British citizens.

Yet, comfortable with their Muslim identity, the vast majority of British Muslims, 68 percent of whom in a control group survey indicated that "Muslim" was their first identity, do not subscribe to radical Islamism. In that same survey, the control group respondents were less intensely concerned with racism in British society and more satisfied with their lives than members of al-Muhajiroun.[51]

Sudan

In contrast to al-Qaeda, European radical Islamism and Chechnya, Sudan is not an especially important part of radical Islamism's worldview, or indeed its historical development. For this reason, this case is given less attention than others. Nevertheless, it is worthy of mention because of the large number of people who have suffered in recent Sudanese history.[52]

After June 30, 1989, one may consider Sudan to be an extremist state, the first on the African continent.[53] A radical Islamist government was introduced that created paramilitaries in the form of the People's Defense Forces[54] that were to constitute a vanguard of Islamization, especially in the rebellious Christian and animist South. Whether or not one considers their violent activities to be wanton mass killing, occurring as they did in the midst of a civil war that has taken approximately 2 million lives since 1983,[55] Sudanese extremism can be explained by an etiology involving early British colonization, followed by the experience of nearly constant warfare since independence in 1956 and early gains in the incorporation of the South into the Sudanese state at independence – the first modern rule of Muslims over Christians in the Horn of Africa – and the Islamization efforts begun in 1983.

These gains were threatened by the battlefield successes of the mainly southern Sudan People's Liberation Army (SPLA) at Kurmuk and Qaysan in the Arabized northern portion of the country and later at Kapoeta.[56] The "unrelenting successes by the SPLA and serious humiliations of the [Sudanese] army"[57] led the government of Sadiq al-Mahdi to negotiate with the SPLA, promising at least a suspension of Islamization, if not its complete abrogation.[58] This threatened loss on top of the SPLA military successes led to the Islamist coup. Thus, the first Islamist government on the African continent was to take power after an ephemeral gain experienced by its outgoing predecessor. This pattern is similar

---

[51] Wiktorowicz 2005, 102–3.
[52] For a general treatment of Sudanese conflicts, see Deng 1995.
[53] Burr and Collins 2003.   [54] Woodward 1996, 54.
[55] Burr and Collins 2003, 254.   [56] Anderson 1999, 108–10.
[57] Anderson 1999, 110.   [58] Woodward 1996, 54.

to those found in the preceding illustrations and indeed in the following case, and so will not be separately presented as a figure.

Beslan

Turning now to our concern with the school massacre at Beslan in North Ossetia, the following narrative will illustrate two things: (1) the conformity of the school takeover and its lethal consequences to the theory put forward here, and (2) the tendency for extremists to commit ever more horrific acts as they sink further into the domain of losses. The importance of Chechnya is indicated not only by the mind-numbing brutality of the school takeover, but also by Chechnya's centrality in the worldview of radical Islamists. Mohammed Atta, Marwan al-Shehi, and Ziad Jarrah, three of the four suicide pilots on 9/11, and Ramzi Binalshibh, the coordinator of the attacks, initially in 1999 were journeying to fight in Chechnya, but a chance meeting on a train in Germany deflected them to Afghanistan.[59] According to Khalid Sheikh Mohammed, the organizer of the 9/11 attacks, several of the Saudi "muscle" hijackers were also diverted to Afghanistan from their target jihad in Chechnya.[60] To fully understand any of these violent events, the historical context is essential. As we shall see, early in Chechnya's violent history, deportations were employed by the tsarist regime as a means of quelling dissidence. The massive deportations of 1944 by Stalin in many respects set the stage for the current impasse between the Russians and Chechens.

Chechnya: a brief history

Located in the North Caucasus, Chechnya is a landlocked, almost entirely Muslim enclave sandwiched between Ingushetia to the west and Daghestan to the east, both also predominantly Muslim. Comparisons among the three with their differing propensities toward extremism will be introduced later. All are currently members of the Russian Federation after the demise of the Soviet Union in 1991, but in contrast to neighboring peoples, Chechen militant groups waged war against the Russians and their mostly Christian allies such as the Ossetians. (During the school takeover in North Ossetia, an indignant mother said to one of the terrorists: "Your children rest in our sanatoriums. Your women give birth here." To which the terrorist replied: "Not our wives and children. They are the spawn of Kadyrov."[61] According to Chivers,[62] "The word stung. *Kadyrov* – the surname of former rebels who aligned with Russia and became the Kremlin's proxies. The separatists despised them with a loathing reserved for traitors.")

---

[59] National Commission on Terrorist Attacks upon the United States 2004, 165.
[60] National Commission on Terrorist Attacks upon the United States 2004, 233.
[61] Quoted in Chivers 2006, 146.   [62] Emphasis in original; Chivers 2006.

Ever since Peter the Great's 1722 incursions, Russia had been at war with one or another of the peoples of the Caucasus, most frequently the Chechens, their close ethnic relations, the Ingush, or their coreligionists, the Daghestani Avars.[63] However, the most brutal phase of Imperial Russia's expansion is associated with the name of General Aleksei Yermolov (1777–1861). Even before the current difficulties, on two occasions in 1969 Chechens attempted to blow up a statue of Yermolov located in Grozny, then the capital of the combined Soviet Republic of Checheno-Ingushetia.[64] Before Yermolov's leadership of his campaign, bribes and subsidies were used to obtain the loyalty of indigenous groups. Under Yermolov, severe punishment was meted out to dissidents. Massacres and mass rape were not uncommon. In one instance, in September 1819, a demand for surrender was refused by a Chechen village. The stone walls surrounding each of the houses was battered by artillery and "Some of the natives, seeing defeat to be inevitable, slaughtered their wives and children under the eyes of the [Russian] soldiers; many of the women threw themselves on the latter knife in hand, or in despair leaped into burning buildings and perished in the flames."[65] The village then was looted.

Yermolov also adopted a policy of deporting Chechens from their lowland villages occupying fertile land to mountainous areas from which many had originally migrated. This policy reversed the long-standing tendency of Chechens to migrate from the mountains with a livestock-based economy to one predominantly agricultural in the lowlands.[66] Effectively, the state of Chechen economic development was retarded by these policies, thereby ensuring additional grievance and hostility toward the Russians. Some Chechens were also deported to Siberia. The much later Chechen deportations of 1944 were to be far more complete. But Yermolov's policies not only yielded an implacable hostility to the invading Russians, but also an increased Islamization of Chechen society, which heretofore had only been superficially Muslim.

This Islamization process continued throughout the Caucasus War of 1817–64. Although there had been earlier imams, interestingly Avars from Daghestan that served as leaders of the Chechens and other Muslims, the most successful was Imam Shamil, also an Avar from Daghestan. Initially, it appeared as if the Chechens would be subdued in 1839–40, but an attempt to disarm them led to a rapidly escalating support for Shamil and his unification of the Chechen clans under the aegis of strict Muslim orthodoxy. In 1841, a Russian General Golovin averred that, "We have never had in the Caucasus an enemy so savage and dangerous as Shamil."[67] Ultimately though, he was defeated by the sheer force of Russian arms. At the end of the Crimean War in 1856, Russia had a 200,000-man force in the Caucasus region that was used to crush Shamil's forces.

[63] Dunlop 1998, 6.   [64] Dunlop 1998, 14.   [65] Baddeley 1908, 131.
[66] Dunlop 1998, 16.   [67] Quoted in Dunlop 1998, 26.

Deportation once again was used to minimize the Chechen threat by removing them from the lowlands of western Chechnya; by 1850, these areas were cleared of Chechens. A third deportation occurred after the final defeat of the Chechens and Daghestanis in 1859. At the instigation of the tsarist government, huge numbers of Muslims left the Caucasus for the Ottoman Empire. Although almost the entire Chechen population departed from the Caucasus, within a few years after the Russo-Turkish War of 1877–78, they would return. Horrible conditions awaited them in the Ottoman Empire, leading to many deaths from disease and as high as a 33 percent mortality rate.[68] Overall, during the Caucasus War the Chechens lost almost half of their population, and inherited a ruined economy.

After a year-long rebellion in 1877, brutally suppressed by the tsarist regime, the next significant period for Chechnya was that of the Bolshevik Revolution and consequent Civil War, calamitous for all peoples residing in Imperial Russia, but particularly for those of the North Caucasus. Shortly after the seizure of power by the Bolsheviks, a North Caucasus state called the Mountain Republic was declared to be independent of Russia on May 11, 1918. Arabic and Turkish became the official languages, although local languages, like Chechen, were also used. Somewhat earlier, in mid-1917, a meeting of religious leaders took place in the mountainous Avar region of Daghestan at which it was decided to re-establish an imamate that had not existed since the time of Shamil. The imam was to govern Daghestan and Chechnya. "The goals pursued by the revived *tariqat* were the restoration of a theocracy governed by the Shari'a; the expulsion of the Russians from the region; and the liquidation of Muslims who were supporting 'infidel' rulers."[69]

However, a White army led by the former tsarist General Anton Denikin occupied portions of the region. In a sense, this was a reprise of the older Cossack-Muslim wars of the eighteenth and nineteenth centuries, since most of Denikin's troops were Christian Cossacks. Although defeated by the mountaineers in late 1919, liberating the mountains of Daghestan, Chechnya, and Ossetia, among other regions, Denikin was soon replaced by the now victorious Bolsheviks who greatly outnumbered the local defenders. Despite the vigorous defense by the indigenous forces, they were ultimately subdued.

As Bolshevik people's commissar for nationalities, Joseph Stalin met with the founders of the Mountain Republic and acknowledged its internal independence and sovereignty. But by late 1922 the Bolsheviks severed Chechnya, site of the most intensive resistance in 1920–22, from the remainder of the Republic. An attempted disarming of the population then followed, leading to Chechen resistance ending only in 1925.[70]

In Daghestan and in the Ingush region, on the other hand, the Bolsheviks were successful in dividing the Muslim communities, having their own appointed

---

[68] Dunlop 1998, 30.   [69] Dunlop 1998, 37–8.   [70] Dunlop 1998, 44.

Islamic leaders occupying powerful ecclesiastical positions. The Ingush in particular did not participate in the great rebellion of 1920–22, nor indeed did they side with the Shamil movement during the nineteenth century.[71] As we shall see, these historical differences will factor into our contrast between the tendencies toward extremism of the Chechens, on the one hand, and the Ingush and (to varying extents) the Daghestanis, on the other.

A Russification policy was instituted for the entire North Caucasus region. In 1928–29, the Latin alphabet replaced the Arabic script then in use; as early as 1923 a Latin alphabet had already been devised for the Chechens. In 1938, a shift to the Cyrillic alphabet was required, the hiatus between the two alphabet changes emerging from the necessity to disguise at least to some extent the Russification process.

Forced collectivization then followed in 1929, coinciding with an effort to eliminate Islam as a major religious force in the region. Rebellion against collectivization occurred here, as well as in other portions of the Soviet Union, but the tradition of revolt in Chechnya, combined with logistical difficulties of the Russians, led to much greater initial success. Once again however, Chechnya was subdued by the Soviet regime in 1930.[72]

The rebellion against Stalin

During the Great Purges beginning in 1937, numerous Chechens were caught in the NKVD (communist secret police) net. Nearly 14,000 men or 3 percent of the population of Checheno-Ingushetia were rounded up and shipped to Grozny. Mass executions took place throughout the city. Further arrests then followed; an entire generation of writers, artists, and academics was being eliminated. In 1938, 490 *kolkhozes* (collective farms) were established throughout that republic, leading to peasant revolts and intensification of violence. The guerrilla groups that were formed began to be led by Hasan Izrailov, one of the Chechen artists caught up in the purges and jailed twice. Upon his second release, he saw that Finland was actually defeating the Soviet Union in the early stages of the Winter War, raising possibilities for Chechen independence. In January 1940, he published the following:

> For twenty years now, the Soviet authorities have been fighting my people, aiming to destroy them group by group: first the *kulaks*, then the Mullahs and the "bandits", then the "bourgeois-nationalists". I am sure now that the real object of this war is the annihilation of our nation as a whole. That is why I have decided to assume the leadership of my people in their struggle for liberation… I understand only too well that Chechnya-Ingushetia – indeed, the whole of the Caucasus – will find it difficult to get rid of the yoke of Red imperialism. But a passionate faith in justice and hope that

---

[71] Bennigsen and Wimbush 1986, 189.   [72] Dunlop 1998, 50–1.

the freedom-loving people of the Caucasus and of the world will come to our assistance inspires me in this enterprise which you may consider foolhardy and senseless but which I believe to be the only possible path. The brave Finns are proving that this great empire built on slavery is devoid of strength when faced with a small freedom-loving nation. The Caucasus will be a second Finland and will be followed by other oppressed nations.[73]

Like the Finns, he too was extremely successful at the outset. Although Finland ultimately fell, Germany invaded the Soviet Union with stunning initial success, yielding a new opportunity for the assertion of independence. And here, under conditions of an extraordinary threat to the Soviet state engendered by the Nazi invasion of 1941–42, the Chechens apparently made their approach to the Germans.

Izrailov had accumulated a total of 24,970 men ready to rebel upon his orders. One of the leaders of his organization was the people's commissar for internal affairs of the Chechen-Ingush Autonomous Soviet Socialist Republic (ASSR), Albogachiyev. Upon the beginning of the uprising in September 1941 (the German invasion having begun on June 22), Albogachiyev allegedly wrote the following letter to Izrailov containing the following passage: "You are not familiar with the Gestapo agents in Ordzhonikidze through whom, as I told you, we have to send all the information about our anti-Soviet activity. Sum up the results of the present revolt and send them to me. I shall be able to forward them to Germany immediately. Tear my letter to pieces in the presence of my messenger. The times are dangerous and I am afraid."[74]

Either independently or in concert with Izrailov, Mairbek Sheripov, the former chief prosecutor of the republic, initiated his own insurrection and then joined Izrailov. Although "not a major threat, the rebels' activities, which drew a considerable Soviet force, seriously constrained and complicated the Soviet Army's efforts against the German advance into the Caucasus."[75] However, by early 1943, the areas of the North Caucasus occupied by the rebels had been returned to Soviet control. Izrailov himself, on the run, was trapped and killed in late 1944. Moshe Gammer[76] concludes:

> "My enemy's enemy is my friend" is a proverb common to all humanity and nothing is more natural than to follow it when one is at war. Germany was at war with the Soviet Union. Thus Izrailov and his fellow Chechen rebels, like many other Soviet groups, including Russians, regarded Germany as their liberator. They might have been suspicious of Berlin, they might have disliked the Nazi regime, but this was their only way to win. One can dispute the number of ties and the nature of the collaboration with Germany as well as the significance of their contribution to its war effort, but not deny them.

[73] Quoted in Gammer 2006, 160.   [74] Quoted in Gammer 2006, 161–2.
[75] Gammer 2006, 162.   [76] 2006, 165.

Stalin's reaction

Stalin's reactions were emphatic in the extreme. On February 23, 1944 the deportations of the Chechen and Ingush were carried out in only a few days as the result of a massive operation, obviously well rehearsed and conducted under conditions of extreme surprise.[77] The actual decision to deport the Chechens and others apparently was made a year earlier on February 11, 1943,[78] but was deferred until the Germans had been pushed back farther from their maximum penetration into the Caucasus. From that point of view, security considerations were paramount, as was the choice of peoples to deport. Along with the Chechens and Ingush were the Karachai and Balkars, also Muslim peoples of the North Caucasus. Yet the Avars of Daghestan, not only Muslim but traditionally active in opposition to Russian rule, were not deported, nor were the predominantly Christian Ossetians. Moreover the Ingush, who did not participate in the great rebellion of 1920–22 nor that of Shamil in the preceding century, indeed were deported. Although noted in Chapter 5, the following analysis is relevant here.

Security considerations distinguish among peoples chosen to be deported and those allowed to remain. The furthest advance of the German army in 1942 includes all of the Karachai and Balkar territories in its zone of occupation, as well as most of the North Ossetian ASSR, a portion of the Chechen-Ingush ASSR, and a small part of Daghestan. But the small portion of Daghestan occupied by the Germans was well to the north of the Terek River and the vast majority of the Avar population located principally to the south of that river.[79] Earlier, the Kalmyks, found very close to or actually within the line of maximum German advance in Daghestan were deported in December 1943.[80] In their eastward march, proximity to the Avars was not at all achieved by the Germans. At the same time, the portion of the Chechen-Ingush ASSR to the west occupied by the Germans was entirely Ingush in ethnicity.

Thus, experience of German occupation either in whole or in part was a key factor in deciding which Muslim ethnicity to deport, in addition of course to the centrality of resistance to the Soviets found in Chechnya proper. Christian Ossetians not implicated either in dissidence or suspected collaboration with the Germans were exempt from deportation, despite their partial German occupation. Clearly, revenge for suspected, if not actual collaboration with the Germans was a major determinant, but lingering uncertainty as to German capabilities for a counter-offensive (the Normandy landings had not yet occurred, opening the second major front in Europe) must have played an important role.

It would be difficult to minimize the impact of the deportations on the Chechens. Over a third of the Chechen and Ingush peoples were lost as a result

[77] Tishkov 2004, 25.   [78] Conquest 1970, 88.
[79] Conquest 1970, 33; Kisriev 2004, 109; S. Smith 1998, Map 5.
[80] Conquest 1970, 89.

of the harsh conditions of deportation and exilic settlement in foreign climes.[81] Most returned only in 1957 and thereafter subsequent to Khruschev's reforms. But the judgment of Sergei Artyunov, a Caucasus specialist, implicates not only the 1944 deportations but earlier ones as well. Accordingly: "For a Chechen to be a man is to remember the names of seven generations of paternal ancestors… and not only their names, but the circumstances of their deaths and the places of their tombstones. This constitutes an enormous depth of historic memory, and in many cases the remembered deaths occurred at the hands of Russian soldiers – under Catherine the Great, under Nicholas the First, under Stalin. Even the smallest Chechen boy, already knows well the whole history of the deportations [of 1944] and the entire history of the sufferings of his people."[82] As late as the 1990s, a poem about the 1944 deportations was put to song and broadcast on the local television channel. It went as follows:

> Of our dark days the mountains told me,
> A darker story no highlander ever heard,
> No time can heal the pain felt in the Vainakh [Chechen and Ingush] land
> When it saw its people rounded up
> And banished from their homes in contempt
> By a cruel order they couldn't understand.
> We were like cattle driven into freight trains –
> What had we done that we were punished so
> By our country in that wartime year?
> We passed through horrors and starvation,
> We prayed, and we heaped our curses on Stalin's head,
> He paid no heed, wading knee-deep in blood
> Toward his pinnacle over the frightened crowd.
> We were like cogs in that well-oiled machine,
> What woeful time we had to live through,
> Torn from our dear mountains of the Caucasus!
> Once on my way back there I met a friend:
> I asked him what he carried in his bag.
> He said he'd dug out his mother's ashes
> To take them home to be buried in our land.
> Our train arrived at dawn, and as we got off
> We saw an old man in a worn beshmet [wool placket]
> Alight and fall down upon his knees
> To touch his native land and give it a kiss.[83]

The threat and fear of reversion

The early humiliations and their memory required by the theory are amply satisfied by this catastrophic history. The second requirement of Figure 1.1 – victory

---

[81] Tishkov 2004, 27.   [82] Dunlop 1998, 211.   [83] Quoted in Tishkov 2004, 53.

and an enhanced authority space – was rarely achieved by the Chechens, but was indeed accomplished in spectacular fashion by the retaking of Grozny after the costly (for the Russians) capture of the city in 1995.[84]

In August 1996, between 2,000 and 3,000 Chechen fighters assembled for a counter-attack led by Shamil Basayev[85] against the roughly 12,000 Russian troops holding the city. Through the use of clever ambush and enveloping tactics, as well as the later appearance of Chechen volunteers and part-time fighters, the Russians were rendered helpless. According to Sebastian Smith,[86] "It was easy to see the new battle for Grozny as glorious. Surviving each day felt good, and seeing the Chechens win, after so many defeats and so much suffering, felt good." The Russian humiliation was complete. On November 23, President Boris Yeltsin ordered a complete Russian withdrawal from Chechnya. Smith[87] described the scene of Russian retreat: "When the battle for Grozny is over, the Russian soldiers leave the city and mountains in columns of hundreds of trucks and APCs [armored personnel carriers] flying white flags and escorted for their own safety by jeeps of Chechen *boyeviks* [warriors]. The Chechens go back to their villages in buses, jeeps, trucks and captured armoured vehicles packed with cheering men and flying the rebel flag."

Here was the first decisive victory of the Chechens in the twentieth century, indeed of any of the Muslim peoples of the North Caucasus over the historic Russian adversary. And as we have seen, it came after an unrelenting series of humiliations of the Chechens by the far larger forces of the Russian tsarists and communists. Yet, this was not to be the end of the story. Instead of a consolidation of the victory and the establishment of a working government under the elected presidency of the rebel leader Aslan Maskhadov, the Chechens experienced instability and radicalization. Within a year of Maskhadov's election, he split with his former ally Basayev, hero of the June 1995 Budennovsk hospital attack, resulting in the deaths of over 100 people among the more than 1,000 hostages, and a Russian escort home for the rebels after the Russian failure to lift the siege by force.[88] Basayev was also acclaimed as a hero for his extraordinarily successful command of the central sector in the first Chechen war.[89] Without Russian aid, the economy collapsed, and the kidnapping of presumably wealthy people, Westerners, Jews, or local notables became a cottage industry.[90] Four telecommunications engineers from Great Britain and New Zealand were kidnapped, beheaded, and their severed heads shown on television.

In August 1999, Wahhabis occupied two villages in Daghestan. Basayev and the Saudi, Emir Khattab, seeing this as an opportunity to declare an Islamic republic in Daghestan, crossed the border with 1,000 Chechen militants in support of the Wahhabis. The Chechens were quickly expelled by Russian and

---

[84] S. Smith 1998, 165.   [85] S. Smith 1998, 241–6.   [86] 1998, 248.
[87] 1998, 257.   [88] Bowker 2004, 259.   [89] Gammer 2006, 212.
[90] Tishkov 2004, 118–19.

Daghestani forces, suggesting little support for Wahhabism in Daghestan at that time. In September, the targeting of apartment blocks in Moscow, Volgodonsk and Buinaksk in Daghestan, killing 300 civilians and Russian servicemen, led immediately to the second, now more successful Russian invasion of Chechnya. Whether or not the Russians were somehow complicit in the apartment bombings to facilitate the now decided upon second invasion of Chechnya (as has been alleged),[91] the attack by Basayev is significant for understanding extremist behavior.

The victory over the Russians in 1996 was an unique event in Chechen history, yet the country was not stable. This instability in a very real sense mirrored the instability of Chechen history, and the psychological necessity to reinforce the recent victory by further victories in the Wahhabi Islamization of Daghestan. If all were to go well, the success in Daghestan could then be exported to Chechnya. An additional advantage was to have a refuge in nearby Daghestan in the event of a Russian invasion. But principally, the new victory(ies) was intended to be a reinforcement of the salience of the earlier one; not a singular occurrence in a national history otherwise replete with humiliation and failure; but the beginning of an upward trajectory in which the first victory would establish a strong momentum leading to many additional triumphs.

Note that Basayev's first military effort in Daghestan after the Russian defeat did not involve hostage taking and the widespread killing of civilians. Instead, a military victory was anticipated, much as other political extremists have first chosen the straightforward military option and then, seeing its failure, have descended to more extreme and bloody mass murder. Later we shall see that other extremists such as Hitler followed a similar pattern. Reflecting a global understanding of Osama bin Laden's popularity among Muslims, very much like that of Basayev's among Chechens and other North Caucasians, Michael Scheuer[92] comments, "as bin Laden and his ilk defend the things they love – a love held by most Muslims – they are themselves loved not just for defending the faith, but as symbols of hope in a Muslim [Chechen] world conditioned to massive military defeats."

For a brief period between 1996 and 1999, it appeared as if the subordination had ceased and would be reversed. Alas, the domain of losses would once again engulf the Chechen militants after the more unsparing invasion of October 1999. The role of an unstable and shaky self-esteem conditioned by these fluctuations in Chechen history applies to Shamil Basayev as well as to Osama bin Laden. After the lost war with Russia and the October 2002 (Basayev-organized) terrorist attack on a Moscow theater leading to 120 hostage deaths,[93] he wrote:

---

[91] Baker and Glasser 2005, 55; Goltz 2003, 269; Politkovskaya 2001.
[92] 2005, 19.   [93] Tishkov 2004, 211.

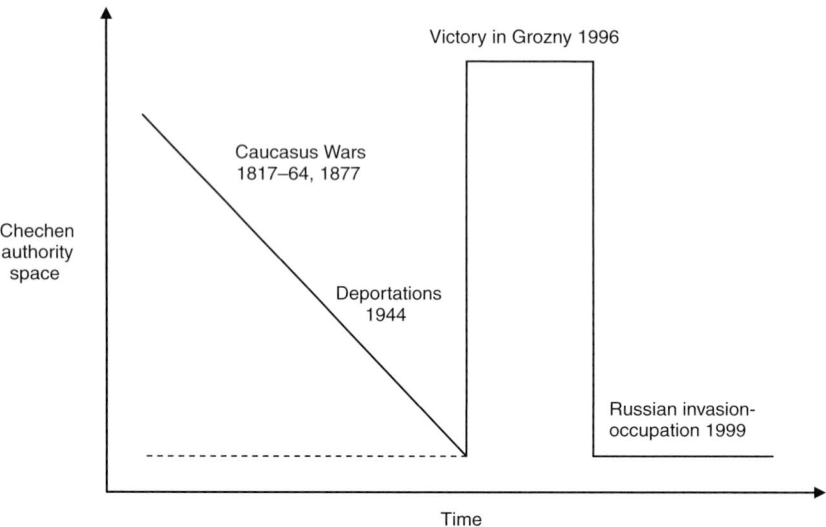

Figure 7.3:   Changes in Chechen authority space over time

> In this regard, you have to ask yourself: Who are the more than three thousand children aged under ten who died during the three years of the brutal and bloody war in Chechnya? Who are the more than four thousand children who lost their legs, arms, eyes, who ended up paralyzed? Who are the thirty-five hundred missing people who have been abducted from their homes or detained in the streets by the Russian occupiers and whose fate remains a mystery? Who are the two hundred thousand [actually between 50,000,[94] and 100,000[95]] slain women, elderly, ill, children, and men? Who are they?[96]

The Beslan school takeover of September 1–3, 2004 in its unthinkable brutality, even more than that of the Moscow theater takeover, had the nominal goal of forcing a withdrawal of federal Russian forces from Chechnya in exchange for safety of the hostages. Extreme brutality became the modus operandi in the face of unacceptable loss. The capture of the school led to the deaths of 321 hostages and 10 soldiers of the Russian Special Forces, in addition to the 31 terrorists. Among the dead were 186 children; the majority of the more than 700 injured were children.[97]

Figure 7.3 traces this process through time. To the left of the figure are the successive nineteenth-century encroachments of tsarist Russia onto Chechen

---

[94] Bowker 2004, 265.   [95] Goltz 2003, 5.   [96] Quoted in Chivers 2006, 149.
[97] Chivers 2006; Baker and Glasser 2005.

lands, culminating in the Soviet deportation of the Chechen people in 1944. Victory over Russia in 1996 was a much-celebrated event that was followed by the more unsparing Russian invasion of 1999. The threat and fear of reversion to Russian rule was now the overwhelming source of Chechen extremism.

Why Chechnya?

In the entire Muslim North Caucasus, why are the Chechens distinguished from other nationalities in their propensity to extremist violence? First, consider the differences between the Chechens and the Ingush, their close Vainakh relatives. In contrast to the Chechens, as we saw, the Ingush participated neither in the Shamil-led revolt of the nineteenth century, nor in the great rebellion of 1920–22.[98] And at the same time as the Chechens were declaring their independence from Russia, the Ingush, in contrast, on September 15, 1991, declared an "Ingush Autonomous Republic *within* the RSFSR."[99] Thus from the outset, a more moderate path was chosen by the Ingush.

A more recent phenomenon has been the rise of Wahhabism in the North Caucasus, especially in Daghestan.[100] Although still a small minority preference in Daghestan, it nevertheless adds another dimension to the many differences among Daghestani peoples. Despite the common Islamic cement unifying the Muslim peoples of the North Caucasus, an increasing radicalization of many, and the declared goal of the initial Chechen leadership under Dudaev to create a union of Caucasian ethnicities,[101] thus far this union has not come to pass. Why? Several observers agree that the divisions within Daghestani society will not permit amalgamation with Chechnya or other North Caucasus entities. Accordingly, "The Chechen pro-independence drive is shared neither by the elites nor by large segments of the population of Daghestan. Separatism is not on the political agenda, and those advocating the creation of an Islamic state and separation from Russia, are in a tiny minority."[102]

Dmitri Trenin, Alexey Malashenko, and Anatol Lieven[103] refer to "a fragile ethnic balance" that could erupt in civil war if either separatism within Daghestan, or trans-Caucasus integration were pursued too vigorously, especially should these impulses emerge principally from Chechnya, genuinely unique in its Caucasian historical trajectory, as shown in Figure 7.3.

---

[98] Bennigsen and Wimbush 1986, 189.
[99] Emphasis added; quoted in Dunlop 1998, 108.   [100] Tishkov 2004, 172–9.
[101] Dunlop 1998, 140.   [102] Matveeva 2004, 130.   [103] 2004, 81.

8

Muslims in India

Let us now examine the tendencies toward extremism, or lack of same, among the upward of 130 million Muslims of India, the third largest population of Muslims after those of Indonesia and Pakistan. The question immediately arises: excluding the unique circumstances of Kashmir, why has not this Muslim population engaged in terrorism as have those from Saudi Arabia (al-Qaeda), Egypt (Muslim Brotherhood and Islamic Group), Algeria (Salafist Group for Preaching and Combat (GSPC)), or even Britain (al-Muhajiroun).

An immediate answer lies in the obvious non-conformity of Indian Muslim history to the pattern of Figure 1.1. The Muslim population, subordinate under the British, has continued in a minority status, in certain respects (e.g., economically) also subordinate to the majority Hindus after Indian independence in 1947. Certainly there has been no Muslim ascendancy, ephemeral or otherwise, and losses have been incurred but on a sporadic basis, such as the 1984 intrusion of the Indian Supreme Court in Islamic personal law,[1] the riots and Muslim deaths after the destruction of the Babri mosque in 1992,[2] or the rise to power of the Hindu nationalist Bharatiya Janata Party (BJP). The workings of Indian democracy have mostly reversed these Muslim losses, as in the limits imposed on the government's ability to regulate personal Islamic law, the prevention of additional attacks on Muslim holy places, and the decline in the political fortunes of the BJP. Communal strife still exists,[3] but it is generally local in nature and does not reflect state policy, the most dangerous condition for threatened minorities. Certainly all is not well in the political and especially economic circumstances of Indian Muslims, but no evidence exists for ephemeral gains in the recent past.

The roots of the relative passivity of the Muslim community go deeper still and suggest two different paths for the Hindu and Muslim communities. The first of these is state centered. While Mughal (essentially Muslim, while strictly meaning Mongol) power was in rapid decline beginning in the early eighteenth century, the Marāthā (Hindu) kingdom was in its ascendancy. The last of the great Mughal leaders, Aurangzeb (ruled 1658–1707), expanded the empire and imposed a much more stringent form of Islam than had his predecessors,

[1] Sikand 2004, 41.   [2] Sikand 2004, 42.   [3] Varshney 2002.

but some of his conquests were transitory (Assam), and his brutality, as well as attempts to convert large numbers of Hindus, led to insurgencies that sapped the imperial power. By the end of his reign, the Mughal Empire was on the verge of a long and steady decline. By 1739, the government was so weak that it was virtually powerless to prevent the invasion by Nāder Shāh, an Iranian adventurer. He inflicted defeat after defeat on the Mughals, sacked Delhi, massacring 30,000 in the process, and annexed Kabul province to Iran. Ultimately, the much diminished Mughal successor of Oudh in northern India succumbed to British power in 1801.

While the Mughal Empire was being humiliated by Iranians, the Marāthās were reaching the zenith of their ascendancy. The great Marāthā hero Śivajī (1627–80) waged successful war against the Mughals, among others, establishing the basis of Marāthā power in western India. By 1740 and the death of Bājī Rāo, the last of the great Marāthā leaders, the kingdom had spread all over India. In 1785, the Marāthās even captured the Mughal capital, Delhi, which, with a small territory surrounding it, was all that remained of the once extensive empire. Ultimately, the Marāthās also were too weak to successfully oppose British military force and finally succumbed in 1818, but only after two wars that taxed the British army in India to the limits.

This differential trajectory between Hindu and Muslim communities is reflected in the second of our two paths, the formation of organized political action under the British Raj. The Indian National Congress had its first meeting in December 1885 in Bombay, significantly a principal city of the old Marāthā lands. Also significant, perhaps much more so, was the predominance of Hindu delegates. While fifty-four of the delegates were Hindu, only two were Muslim, the remainder mainly Parsi and Jain. In the Muslim view, Hindu dominance of the Congress movement would continue even after strenuous efforts of Hindus such as Ghandi to eliminate or at least attenuate that perception. Ghandi even adopted as his own the All-India Khilafat movement, a Muslim effort to revive the Caliphate that was eliminated in 1924 by Kemal Atatürk, but to no avail. This initial perception of Hindu dominance was to yield the formation of the All-India Muslim League in 1906. Of course, the Congress movement was to result in the formation of a secular Indian government that would later have strong Hindu overtones, while the Muslim League would eventuate in the formation of a nominally Muslim Pakistan under Mohammed Ali Jinnah, which would later become increasingly fundamentalist under his successors.

Crucial here is the relatively powerless state of Muslims within India, beginning at the end of the eighteenth century and continuing throughout the British Raj. The formation of Pakistan was intended to ameliorate that subordinate condition, and was partially successful within the borders of Pakistan, despite the lost wars with India. But within the borders of India, notwithstanding the striking accomplishments of individual Indian Muslims (richest man in India, leading movie stars), communal subordination persists to this day.

One could leave it at that and claim that the absence of a principal antecedent of political extremism, an ephemeral gain, explains the absence of that extremism. But that would be too cavalier an approach, for we also need to understand why any sort of generalized extremism is not expected *even* among Islamist elements of the Indian population.

As a first cut, we must note a key difference between Indian Muslims that collectively do not govern a state, and others such as Arabs or Persians that do. Indeed the origins of Islamic theology, which claims no distinction between politics and religion, are coterminous with the rise of Arab (or Arab/Persian) states in the form of the Umayyad and Abbasid Empires.[4] Islamic jurisprudence was developed mostly within the context of Muslim political supremacy. Thus, according to Zaki Badawi, a leading Muslim scholar residing in Britain, "Muslim theology offers, up to the present, no systematic formulations of the status of being in a minority."[5]

Clearly, British Muslim extremist groups such as al-Muhajiroun had set as their goal the Islamization of Britain, or the conversion to Islam of the Queen and royal family, but they have been a tiny minority of British Muslims, without any widespread support. For most Muslims existing in the relatively recent status of minorities without direct political power, the expectation of Islamic governance is virtually nonexistent. Instead, India offers up a wide range of potential responses to this minority status, all of them short of governmental domination.

And here lies the crux of the matter. Without the realistic expectation of state governance, there is little connection with one of the principal tenets of current Islamic radicalism – restoration of the Caliphate.[6] Once, as we have seen, the Caliphate or Khilafat movement was strong in India, but that was before establishment of an Islamic state in the region, Pakistan, and the independence of India. With these emergent states, one of them explicitly Islamic, the Khilafat movement, already in decline, virtually disappeared. Removing "apostate" Muslim rulers in predominantly Islamic countries like Egypt or Saudi Arabia, is another goal of these Islamist movements, but again has little salience for the majority of India's Muslims.

Figure 8.1 presents the trajectory for the Indian Muslim community. It clearly bears no resemblance to the contours of Figure 1.1.

Indian Muslim thinkers

What does concern the majority of India's Muslim thinkers and writers? As might be expected, the confrontation between tradition and modernity is of major importance today, as it once was at the time of the nineteenth-century writings of Sayyid Ahmad Khan, who attempted to reconcile Islam with the

[4] Hodgson 1974.   [5] Quoted in Sikand 2004, 8.   [6] Habeck 2006, 151.

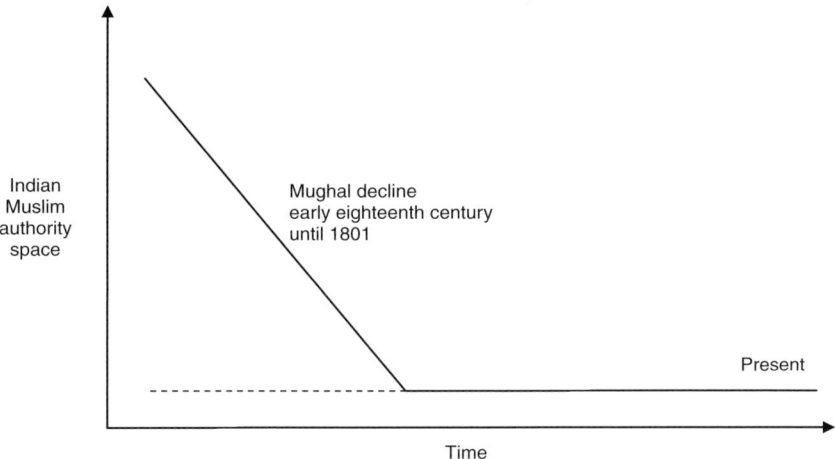

Figure 8.1:   Changes in authority space of Indian Muslims over time

demands of contemporary life.[7] He argued that Islam was compatible with reason and with "nature." Khan was very much an advocate of science and posi-
tivism. In 1877, he created a Westernizing Muslim College at Aligarh, now the
Aligarh Muslim University (AMU).[8]

A contemporary Indian public intellectual is Asghar 'Ali Engineer, who
interprets the Qur'an in liberal ways. He understands the Qur'an not as a book
of specific laws, but "above all, a call for a just social order based on a new
value system, and the institutional forms that express these values can, and
indeed must, radically differ across space and time."[9] Engineer understands
that the fundamental values of the Qur'an are eternally valid, but specific laws
do not possess that validity, for they are more than anything a reflection of
societal need at a given point in space and time. Legal context-specificity is
a cornerstone of his theory. Hence, the pronouncements of the traditional
ulema (Islamic legal scholars) or *fiqh* (Islamic legal rulings) represent a "fos-
silized religion" and had given rise to a "feudalized Islam" incapable of dealing
with modernity.

A significant component of modernity is pluralism, especially in the Indian
context. Instead of the monochromatic Islam of the Arabian Peninsula as Islam
rose to power, and which gave rise to much of the body of Islamic law, the religious diversity of the contemporary period must be addressed. Hence, interpret-
ive dialogue is essential. Moreover, all religions are to be addressed as equals, for
the Qur'an is clear on the lack of "compulsion in religion" and that people vie

---

[7] Brown 2000, 94–5.   [8] Brown 2000, 95.   [9] Sikand 2004, 15.

with each other "in virtuous deeds."[10] The fact that religious diversity exists must be part of God's plan and must be respected, for he must have ordained its presence on this Earth. Accordingly, "he [Engineer] writes that, while Islam stresses justice, Buddhism stresses non-violence and Christianity love. By dialoguing with Buddhists and Christians, then, Muslims can gain new insights that can be used to evolve new interpretations and understanding of their own religion."[11]

Engineer even argues that Hinduism, although polytheistic, filled with statues and images, and therefore utterly opposed to Islam's rigorous monotheism and prohibition of idolatry, nevertheless has theistic cores that must be respected by Muslims. An emphasis on peace, justice, and equality can provide a common framework for dialogue among all of the major faiths of the Indian subcontinent. The idea of an Islamic state, however, has no place in this dialogue, for it is a product of another time and another place. The best that Muslims in India can hope for is a state, nominally secular, that is neutral regarding all religions. Although reviled by many Islamists, democracy is the best protector of any religion mistreated by the state. Engineer points to the Treaty of Medina between the Prophet and his followers on the one hand, and Jews and Pagan Arabs on the other, that defined all of them as part of one 'umma. The idea of a single Muslim "nationality" (a more restricted meaning of 'umma) therefore is unacceptable, for people of many different faiths can be part of the same nation, as in the Qur'an. Clearly, Engineer has a very different interpretation of Islam from that of Islamists, especially of the radical variety.

Another addition to this corpus of writing comes from the prolific pen of Sayyed Hasan 'Ali Nadwi. He was descended from a line of Islamic scholars; even his mother had memorized the entire Qur'an. Writing in the colonial period, he analyzed the state of Islam in the Arab world, exhorting Arabs to return to their Islamic roots. He also criticized pan-Arabism, communism, and nationalism as false ideologies seeking to displace the pre-eminence of Islam. "However, he stood apart from most Islamists by arguing that the Islamic political order could come about in India only in some remotely distant future. Rather than directly struggling for it in the present, he believed that the Muslims of the country should focus their energies in trying to build what he saw as a truly Islamic society, on the basis of which alone could an ideal Islamic political order come into being."[12]

Nadwi also opposed the creation of Pakistan as a separate state for Muslims. Only in a united India could Muslims continue their required missionary activity. Although initially active in the Jama'at-i Islami founded by Sayyid Abdul 'Ala Maududi (see Chapter 6), Nadwi became disillusioned both with its emphasis on the struggle to found an Islamic state and with the apparent "cult of personality" having grown up around Maududi. "At Maududi's hands, he [Nadwi] says, 'God' (ilah), 'the Sustainer' (rabb), 'Religion' (din) and 'Worship' (ibadat) have

---

[10] Quoted in Sikand 2004, 21.   [11] Sikand 2004, 22.   [12] Sikand 2004, 33.

all been reduced to political concepts, suggesting that Islam is simply about political power and that the relationship between God and human beings is only that between an All-Powerful King and His subjects. However, Nadwi says, this relationship is also one of 'love' and 'realization of the Truth', which is far more comprehensive than what Maududi envisages."[13] Instead of this preoccupation with politics, "love" and "the realization of the Truth" are to be emphasized. Only a "silent revolution" is conceivable in order to "prepare people's minds" for a genuinely Islamic government in the distant future.

After Indian independence, in contrast to most Islamists, Nadwi was willing to accept democracy and secularism in the face of potential Hindu extremism that could deprive Indian Muslims of their civil rights, including freedom of worship. He feared "cultural genocide" of the Muslim population in which Islam would disappear. Cooperation with Hindus was a means of preventing this outcome. He became active politically, proclaiming that Muslims were indeed the *khair ummat* (the best community) based on their beliefs and rigorous observance. For this purpose, Nadwi, along with other leading Muslim figures, established the All-India Muslim Consultative Assembly in 1964. Only in a climate of peace and cooperation could Muslims best make their religion inviting to the potential Hindu or Christian convert. When the Babri mosque controversy erupted in the early 1990s, Nadwi counseled restraint and dialogue, instead of retaliation and conflict. When Hindu temples were attacked after the destruction of the Babri mosque, he bitterly criticized the actions of these militants.

Summarizing his own views, Nadwi stated:

> If you make Muslims one hundred per cent mindful of their supererogatory prayers (*tahajjud guzar*), making them all very pious, but leave them cut off from the wider environment, ignorant of where the country is heading and of how hatred is being stirred up in the country against them, then, leave alone the supererogatory prayers, it will soon become impossible for Muslims to say even their five daily prayers. If you make Muslims strangers in their own land, blind them to social realities and cause them to remain indifferent to the radical changes taking place in the country and the new laws that are being imposed and the new ideas that are ruling people's hearts and minds, then let alone [acquiring] leadership [of the country], it will become difficult for Muslims to even ensure their own existence.[14]

At the same time, he exhorted Muslims to observe their faith rigorously and never compromise it for social or political expediency.

The last of our Islamic thinkers to react strongly to the Muslim minority status within India was Maulana Wahiduddin Khan. He, too, was early influenced by Maududi and the Jama'at-i Islami Hind, the Indian branch of the Jama'at. But like Nadwi, he became disillusioned. According to Khan, Maududi was more

---

[13] Sikand 2004, 36.   [14] Quoted in Sikand 2004, 43.

influenced by Western imperialism than by any authentic interpretation of Islam. A political understanding of Islam had emerged in his thinking to counter the spread of Western influence. Very much in agreement with the theory offered here, "this understanding of Islam Khan now began to see as a result of a sense of loss, of defeat suffered by the Muslims at the hands of the West, rather than as emanating from a genuine spiritual quest."[15]

Khan became increasingly concerned with Hindu–Muslim relations in India, specifying a personalized Islamic faith and efforts at individual reform. Accordingly, like other faiths, Islam is prepared to welcome modernity, pluralism, and inter-faith dialogue. Muslims must leave their ghettos and shed their "persecution complex" and separatist thinking. Following the Islamic tradition, the Prophet Muhammad is said to have insisted on "respect for every human being," and required Muslims to "honour one of another creed."[16] When the Muslim community was small and without much power, the Prophet sought peaceful relations with surrounding communities that would allow the propagation of the faith. The situation of Muslims in India as a minority is directly analogous:

> Khan repeatedly refers to what he calls the "Hudaibiyah principle" as a model for Muslims to follow. In the nineteenth year of his prophethood Muhammad entered into a ten-year no-war treaty with his Meccan Qur'aish opponents at Hudaibiyah, which contained what some of his followers thought were conditions particularly humiliating for the Muslims. The Qur'an, however, announced it as a "great victory" (fateh mubin), and so it proved itself to be. The Qur'aish refused to allow the Prophet to sign his name as "the Messenger of Allah" on the document of the agreement and, instead, forced him to write simply "Muhammad, son of Abdullah." Further, they did not allow the Muslims to enter Mecca that year to perform the 'umra, and insisted that if any Meccan Muslim was to take refuge in Medina, he would have to be returned to them. Yet the Prophet accepted these seemingly humiliating conditions, for he had, Khan says, a "deep missionary plan" in mind. Peace with the Qur'aish opened up new possibilities of daw'ah [peaceful struggle for the propagation of Islam] work for the Muslims, as a result of which in a few years' time not just the Qur'aish alone, but, in fact, almost all of Arabia, turned Muslim. This shows, Khan argues, that "the power of peace is stronger than the power of violence," a valuable lesson for the Muslims of contemporary India to profit from.[17]

Further, Khan argues for abandoning the "Islam of pride" and recovering the "Islam of humility and balance." A position of modesty is desirable. In this way, like the Prophet in Mecca, Islam would turn out to be ultimately victorious. Opposed to an Islamic state like Pakistan, Khan argued that the focus of Islam should be the "inner transformation" of the individual. Then and only then, as

---

[15] Sikand 2004, 50–1.   [16] Sikand 2004, 54.   [17] Sikand 2004, 57.

a gift from God, an Islamic state may come into being. To attempt to establish such a state by force is effectively to usurp a privilege for God alone. According to Yoginder Sikand,[18] "This principle of peaceful 'gradualism' tempered with 'pragmatism' is seen as being in complete contrast to the efforts of Islamist groups to establish an Islamic state by force. Religiously sanctified violence, Khan believes, has only given Islam, a 'religion of peace and mercy,' a bad name, making it synonymous for many with violence and terror, thus gravely damaging the cause of Islamic *da'wah*." Science and scientific rationality also should be part of Islam, although revelation is always superior to reason.

Clearly, these Indian Muslim thinkers establish a paradigm for majority–minority relations when Muslims are in the minority. The most important element here is the absence of a realistic expectation of state formation without some sort of cataclysmic outcome. Failing the "Armageddon" alternative, gradualism is required. Even if this program were to fail in its ultimate purpose of converting all non-Muslims in the Indian subcontinent, still the goal would continue to exist as a major preoccupation of the Muslim community. In the collective view of these thinkers, this alternative is vastly preferable to the mass political violence effectively advocated by the radical Islamists.

Communal violence

Although radical Islamism has not taken strong hold in the Indian subcontinent, with the possible exception of Kashmir, nevertheless, violence has occurred principally in the form of Hindu–Muslim communal rioting. This is not to say that this violence is trivial, nor that political extremist tendencies in the form of the BJP, or the Jama'at-iIslami do not exist. Instead, even when communal violence has been on the upswing, as Ashutosh Varshney[19] chronicles in great detail, it is generally not the result of extremist tendencies but of intercommunal relations, often of a routinized political nature.

The state is crucial, not so much in daily practice, but in the imagination of the potential perpetrators of violence. In the case of al-Qaeda or other radical Islamist groups, the Caliphate as the sovereign political expression of authentic Islam must be re-created. And when Osama bin Laden called Mullah Omar of the Taliban a "Caliph," it was his recognition that Taliban rule in Afghanistan was an incarnation of authentic Islamic governance that hopefully could be extended to other Muslim societies. In India, on the other hand, there is little room for Muslim speculation on the existence of a future Caliphate. That expectation had already been manifested in the Khilafat movement of 1919–24[20] that petered out without significant immediate consequence. A long-term consequence may have been the movement to found Pakistan as an independent state begun in

[18] 2004, 64.   [19] 2002, 95–102.   [20] See above; Hasan and Pernau 2005.

the 1930s,[21] but having established one such state, it was extremely unlikely that another could be founded.

More important is the not uncommon perception of Muslim neighborhoods in India as mini-Pakistans. According to Rowena Robinson,[22] "In the north Indian plains, it is common to hear a man going to the toilet – that impure *sandas* often outside or behind the home – refer to his visit as 'going to Pakistan'. In the brutal communal discourses we have been made to countenance, more so over the last decades, the Indian Muslim *is* a Pakistani, a scorned being who should 'go to Pakistan'. Indeed, as the social geography of Indian cities manifests, the Muslim in fact *lives* in Pakistan, *many* Pakistans, *mini* Pakistans."

And the space allotted to Muslim neighborhoods has been contracting, especially after communal riots involving Hindus and Muslims. In many areas of India, Muslims have experienced a contraction of space, especially after the occurrence of communal strife. The following example is taken from Jogeshwari (East) where:

> Muslims have been systematically pushed, over the last two decades, into a smaller and smaller settlement area at the peak of a hill, surrounded by Hindu settlements all around and having almost no access routes out of their pocket except through these Hindu areas. In the 1970s, Muslims and Hindus were interspersed throughout the area as a whole, though there were larger and smaller religion-based pockets here and there. Each riot has, however, led to the further concentration of Muslims. As Muslims tried to move inwards from the boundary line with each bout of violence, the boundary itself shifted further towards the interior, thereby reducing considerably the space available for habitation. Today Muslims are largely ghettoized in Prem Nagar which is, of course, East Jogeshwari's "Pakistan" and the road that divides it from the Hindu area is, ironically enough, Gandhi Market road.[23]

Another limitation on Muslim neighborhoods is the heightened police presence after each riot. Thus, the area of habitation is increasingly circumscribed, and the police further limit the movement of Muslims. Given this steady processual loss, in the absence of any realistic expectation of state formation for Indian Muslims, the only option is fortitude (e.g., Nadwi, see above) or the occasional act of revenge (e.g., the Gujarat train fire killing some fifty Hindus) that yields many more Muslim deaths after the subsequent more intense communal violence. "Given the minority position and the geographical dispersion of Muslims, 'devotion for political ends' has, right from the outset, very little potential of fulfillment regardless of the ambitions of individual persons or particular subgroups."[24]

---

[21] Niemeijer 1972, 178.   [22] Emphases in original; 2005, 13.   [23] Robinson 2005, 51–2.
[24] Robinson 2005, 156.

Constructive approaches have included proactive networks of cooperation between Hindus and Muslims in locations where riots have been largely absent (Calicut in Kerala in southern India), in contrast to the absence of such networks where riots have typically occurred (Aligarh in Uttar Pradesh in northern India).[25] The presence of the AMU in that city may be thought to heighten Muslim consciousness, thereby increasing the probability of violence. However, Calicut also has its respected Muslim institutions. According to Varshney,

> although they restrain politicians in the short and medium run, the inter-communal civic networks in Calicut were *politically* constructed in the long run. Caste injustice within Hindu society rather than communal antagonism between Hindus and Muslims has historically formed the master narrative of Kerala politics. Caste was more central to the ascriptive hierarchy in Kerala than was religion. Hence ethnic conflict historically took the idiom of caste. Hindu–Muslim politics functioned within a larger context of intra-Hindu caste differences. In Aligarh, the reverse has been true. Communalism has been the dominant political narrative for a century, and caste politics within Hinduism has historically functioned within the larger framework of Hindu–Muslim antagonisms.[26]

Interlocking intercommunal dependence exists in the former instance but not in the latter, where violence has been endemic.[27] Lest geography appear to be compelling (as in the proximity of Aligarh to Pakistan, but the remoteness of Calicut from Pakistan), the case of Ajmer in central Rajasthan, close to Pakistan but peaceful in its relations between Hindus and Muslims, belies this assumption. "Over time it became a major nucleus for Hindu and Muslim pilgrimage and for the activity of numerous tribes, castes, and sects that have been classified as Hindu, Muslim, Jain, Christian, Sikh, Parsi, and others."[28]

Among the sources of ethnic coexistence are a shared mythico-religious space.[29] A Sufi shrine, for example, has served as a locus for the expected healing of the sick of virtually all sects in Ajmer. Historically, both Mughal and Hindu princes patronized the shrine.[30]

Everyday life reinforces the significance of this essentially multicultural shrine. The market near the shrine has both Hindu and Muslim traders, the prosperity of both hinging on the steady flow of pilgrims. According to Shail Mayaram, "the Sindhi-Muslim interface derives from the activity centred on the shrine. Sindhi traders dominate the Dargah Bazar and benefit considerably from the annual Urs turnover of something like Rs 80–100 million. Their post-Independence economic prosperity is, hence, dependent on the continuous flow of pilgrims."[31] Thus, the rapid settlement of disputes is in the interests of

---

[25] Varshney 2002, 122–5.   [26] Emphasis in original; Varshney 2002, 122.
[27] Varshney 2002, 128.   [28] Mayaram 2005, 150.
[29] For a game theoretic analysis of inter-ethnic cooperation, see Fearon and Laitin 1996.
[30] Mayaram 2005, 154.   [31] Mayaram 2005, 159.

both Sindhis (local Hindu population) and Muslims. Further, it is the "unheroic quality of everyday life" that reinforces pluralism.[32] And "Muslims remark on the marked absence of ideas of purity–pollution among Sindhis"[33] that further sustains these cooperative relationships, as one might expect given the emphasis on purity as a major accelerant of political extremism.

We turn now to an examination of extremism in a more particularistic mode – extreme nationalism. The first of these cases is also found in South Asia, the Liberation Tigers of Tamil Eelam (the LTTE) that waged a 25-year insurgency in Sri Lanka, and was only recently defeated by the Sri Lankan army.

---

[32] D.R. Nagaraj, quoted in Mayaram 2005.   [33] Mayaram 2005.

PART IV

Extreme Nationalism

9

Sri Lankan Tamils

In Part IV, extreme nationalism is represented by a diverse set of populations and geographical regions, ranging from Europe (Germany, Poland, the Balkans) to the Middle East (Ottoman Empire), Africa (Rwanda), South Asia (Pakistan, Sri Lanka), East Asia (Japan), and Southeast Asia (Indonesia). Extreme nationalism is understood to be the condition under which the perceived needs of the nation are to be maximized at any cost, including the mass murder of presumed opponents. As such, extreme nationalism is a particular kind of political extremism that can be directly activated during interstate war, or some other threat to the nation. Although Nazi ideation initially was a response to perceived injustice and humiliation-shame, as discussed in Chapter 4, it was the threat and fear of reversion during World War II that directly influenced many of the Nazi perpetrators, as will be seen in Chapter 13. The case of the Liberation Tigers of Tamil Eelam (LTTE) in Sri Lanka provides a striking comparison with the Indian condition analyzed in the preceding chapter and so will begin the investigation of extreme nationalism.

A stark contrast with India is found in the trajectory of the neighboring island state of Sri Lanka. Since the passage of the Language Bill of 1956 designating Sinhalese as the official language of Sri Lanka, thereby relegating Tamil to the limbo of official nonexistence, communal relations between the two principal ethnicities have deteriorated. According to Patrick Peebles,[1] the LTTE had "created an authoritarian quasi-state in the northeast. It govern[ed] under permanent wartime conditions with heavy-handed propaganda, universal conscription (even of children and elderly people), and ruthless suppression of dissent."

How did this extremist, terrorist organization evolve to the point of governing a portion of Sri Lanka under these conditions? In particular, the resort to suicide bombing by the LTTE, with its potential for mass murder, requires explanation. The theory of ephemeral gain, especially the fear of transitory governance, will go far to explain this extremist behavior. To do this effectively, the political histories of the two communities need to be addressed, even in pre-colonial times. As we shall see, a political substitutability[2] during the colonial period will be

---

[1] 2006, 5. [2] Most and Starr 1989.

encountered that will do much to set the stage for Sinhalese nationalism and Tamil extremism.

Pre-independence

The history of the earliest periods prior to the arrival of the Europeans is murky, but certain basic facts are known. During this time, there were indigenous Sinhalese and Tamil kingdoms vying for control of the island. This process settled into a Tamil-governed kingdom in Jaffna in the northern portion, and one governed by the Sinhalese in the southern sector, especially the interior of the island. But the Portuguese arrived in 1505 and displaced Muslim merchants who had earlier dominated regional trade. Through a process of gradual expansion, the Portuguese began to dominate the northern region and expanded beyond it. By 1519, the Jaffna kingdom, although still independent, was substantially reduced in strength. In 1591, after a Portuguese invasion of the Jaffna Peninsula, a local puppet monarch was installed under Portugal's tutelage. After a revolt of Christian subjects and an attempted suppression of that rebellion by the Tamil authorities, in 1619 the Portuguese annexed the kingdom outright.[3] This kingdom now lost its independence, never to be revived until some facsimile of that earlier condition was restored after 2000, only to be ended in 2009.

After 1621, the only surviving indigenous polity was that of Kandy, situated in the interior. Earlier, in 1581, after an invasion by a neighboring indigenous opponent, the kingdom lost its sovereignty for a decade. After independence was re-established, the Portuguese attempted to conquer the Kandyan kingdom, weakening it. It was the British arrival in the nineteenth century (after the Dutch expulsion of the Portuguese), that would end the independence of Kandy for good. The British raided Kandy in 1803 but were unsuccessful at that time. In 1815, however, a convention was signed between the British and the Kandyans that preserved local autonomy for Kandy while recognizing British sovereignty. A rebellion of highland Sinhalese (the backbone of Kandy) in 1818 was suppressed, leading to limitations on Kandyan self-governance, and "The suppression of the Kandyan Rebellion unified the entire island under a single government for the first time in its history."[4]

As K. M. de Silva[5] suggests, "There had been a long and successful tradition of Sinhalese resistance to Western colonial powers, Portugal first, then Holland and Britain itself. The years 1815–18 when the British established their control over the whole island constitute, in every way, a decisive turning point in the country's history. This time was the first since the early and mid-fifteenth century, when a Sri Lankan (Sinhalese) ruler had effective control over the whole island for about fifty years, that the process of unification had been successfully introduced."

---

[3] Peebles 2006, 36.   [4] Peebles 2006, 53.   [5] 1995, 75–6.

A reorganization of the island colony in 1832 that effectively ended a Buddhist religious hegemony, also allowed Christian missionary activity. American missionaries were to be critical in this effort and, "The best schools in the island – some say the best schools in Asia – were in the Jaffna Peninsula. American missionaries supported education as a means to convert students; the people of Jaffna responded enthusiastically to the opportunity. Jaffna Tamils used education to move into the English-speaking occupations in government, the private sector, and the professions. Many Tamils migrated to the southern and central regions for employment, leading to Sinhalese protests that the British favored Tamils over the majority Sinhalese."[6] Hereafter, English-language education was controlled largely by Christian missionaries. "The gap in prestige and income between the English-educated and the *swabasha*-educated was immense,"[7] and "The biggest beneficiaries of British colonialism were those who spoke English."[8]

In addition to the Dutch Burghers, left over from the colonial period, missionary-educated Jaffna Tamils were to constitute an administrative elite. An additional consequence was the study of Jaffna history and culture by English-speaking Tamils; the sense of a unique Jaffna Tamil identity was enhanced. Although as of 1938, Indian civil servants comprised 25 percent of all government workers in Ceylon (as the colony was called under the British), by 1941, they were reduced by more than half. Correspondingly there was a net emigration of some 65,000 people of Indian origin to India. Increasingly, the English-speaking Jaffna Tamils assumed many of these vacated positions, so that by 1957, when the effects of the 1956 Language Bill had not yet been felt, the percentage of government employees identifiably Jaffna Tamil was approximately 50 percent.[9] This percentage is out of all proportion to the 12.71 percent (as of 1981[10]) of this Sri Lankan population that was Jaffna Tamil. Not having been granted citizenship, the Indian ("Plantation") Tamils (comprising 5.51 percent) of the population were not eligible for these positions.

Although Patrick Peebles, possibly calculating on a different database, indicates that only 30 percent of the jobs in the administrative services at that time were occupied by Tamils, still "by 1975, that number had fallen to 5%,"[11] a substantial reduction, whatever the initial estimate.

Here we see the now familiar trajectory of an initial Jaffna Tamil subordination to colonial powers after 1619 (two centuries before the demise of the Sinhalese Kandyan state), followed by a gain of Tamil domination of the colonial civil service during the nineteenth century. Effectively, a substitution of civil service authority – the only kind allowed indigenous peoples within a colonial setting – for political power in an independent state had been achieved by the

---

[6] Peebles 2006, 63.   [7] Peebles 2006, 63.   [8] Peebles 2006, 65.
[9] DeVotta 2004, 120.   [10] Fair 2004, 19.   [11] 2006, 113.

Jaffna Tamils. But after 1956, when this authority was removed from the Tamils by the Sinhalese-only Language Bill, the descent was rapid.

Rise of the LTTE

Initially, intercommunal violence was the protest norm. The Sinhalese character "Sri" was defaced on license plates; in response, Tamil language signs were painted over. But soon, in 1958, the violence took the form of "rape, beating, arson, and murder directed at Tamils, but Tamils soon retaliated against Sinhalese."[12] By May 26, attacks had become a general ethnic war. A state of emergency was finally declared and law and order resumed, especially after a Tamil Language Special Provisions Bill (1958) was enacted.

Along with the "nationalization" of language in favor of Sinhala, many Tamil-owned industries were nationalized. For example, shipping companies owned by Tamils were displaced in 1967 when the port of Trincomalee in the eastern sector was nationalized.[13] At around this time, the communal pressure for an independent Tamil state began to grow. Additionally, only militarized pressure was deemed to have any chance of success.

In part to palliate Sinhalese nationalists who were dissatisfied with the (minimal) conciliatory alleviation of Tamil grievances, the 1972 Constitution of the First Republic of Sri Lanka "Declared Sri Lanka 'a Unitary State,' gave 'Buddhism the foremost place' and made it the state's duty 'to protect and foster Buddhism,' instituted Sinhala as the 'Official Language of Sri Lanka,' and mandated that the regulations drafted under the Tamil Language Act of 1958 were 'subordinate legislation.'"[14]

By the late 1970s and early 1980s, several insurgent organizations were formed. The most important of these were the Tamil Eelam Liberation Organization, the People's Liberation Organization for Tamil Eelam, the Eelam People's Revolution Liberation Front, and last but certainly not least, the LTTE, the only one of these organizations to survive. Founded by Velupillai Prabhakaran in Jaffna in the mid-1970s, it became among the most brutal of the Tamil nationalist groups, ultimately assassinating members of other such groups until the LTTE was the only one remaining.[15]

Slowly increasing violence became a standard part of the Sri Lankan landscape, but after 1983 it escalated dramatically.[16] Earlier, in 1977, anti-government activity by Tamil youths sparked riots that were inflamed by the police and armed forces. In May 1978, the government proscribed the LTTE and in July 1982, the Prevention of Terrorism Act that had been enacted on a temporary basis in 1979 now became permanent throughout the island. Essentially, this

---

[12] Peebles 2006, 111.   [13] Peebles 2006, 116.   [14] DeVotta 2004, 134.
[15] Fair 2004, 18.
[16] For a graph of violence occurring between 1948 and 1990, see Richardson 2004, 42.

bill empowered the police and other security forces to violate the civil rights of virtually all persons suspected of committing terrorist acts or simply harboring separatist sympathies. "The new law explicitly contravened the International Covenant on Civil and Political Rights, to which the country was a signatory, and led to many young Tamils being abused and tortured, which merely deepened their determination to secede. With the police and security forces in the Jaffna Peninsula also continuing to harass, beat, and rape Tamils with impunity, Tamil rebels stepped up their violent acts."[17]

Violence during a period of contentious elections to District Development Councils in Jaffna led to the destruction of the Jaffna Municipal Library by government forces in 1981. The library contained approximately 100,000 ancient and irreplaceable documents pertaining to that community; virtually all were destroyed in the fire. Sporadic anti-Tamil riots followed the library fire, many sparked by government agents. Inescapably, many if not most Tamils came to the conclusion that in the name of Sinhala nationalism, the Sinhalese government intended to annihilate their cultural heritage, even their very lives.

But in 1983, riots broke out that effectively transformed the existing ethnic conflict into civil war. In July 1983, the LTTE ambushed a patrol in Jaffna, killing thirteen soldiers. After the bodies were flown to Colombo for a mass funeral, an anti-Tamil rampage ensued. Shops and businesses owned by Tamils were targeted. According to an *Economist* article, written in 1983, "Two weeks ago Tamils owned 60 percent of the wholesale trade and 80 percent of the retail trade in the capital. Today that trade is gone."[18] The death toll was officially estimated at 367, but unofficial estimates ran as high as 3,000. In addition, fifty-three Tamil prisoners were murdered in Welikada Prison and 135,000 Tamil refugees were generated, 30,000 of them immigrating to the Indian state of Tamil-Nadu.[19]

Gradually and ruthlessly, the LTTE established its control over Jaffna. A major fillip to their efforts actually came from the Sinhalese-dominated government. Reacting to the riots of 1983, the majority Sinhalese party effectively banned members of the Tamil United Liberation Front (TULF) from the legislature. The sixth amendment to the Constitution read "No person shall directly, or indirectly, in or outside Sri Lanka, support, espouse, promote, finance, encourage or advocate the establishment of a separate State within the territory of Sri Lanka."[20] Since the TULF was formally committed to the establishment of a separate Tamil state, its members could not stand for office. Thus, the only nonviolent avenue for the expression of Tamil grievances was now closed. Tamil youth now flocked to the paramilitary organizations, thereby clearing the path for paramilitary rule in the North (86 percent Tamil population in 1981), and attempted such rule in the East (40 percent Tamil, 32 percent Muslim, 25 percent Sinhalese in 1981[21]).

---

[17] DeVotta 2004, 149.   [18] Quoted in DeVotta 2004, 151.
[19] Peebles 2006, 135–6.   [20] Quoted in Bush 2003, 137.   [21] Bush 2003, 41.

Between March 1, 1985 and January 31, 1986, Amnesty International confirmed 2,578 murders, 12,105 arrests, and 547 disappearances. Approximately 55,000 people, including 30,000 mainly Muslims from Trincomalee in the Eastern Province, were displaced. In November 1984, the LTTE massacred over eighty Sinhalese men, women, and children in the Kent and Dollar Farms in the Eastern Province. Another LTTE massacre, this time of 70–75 Sinhalese (including women and children) occurred in Anuradhapura, presumably in response to the earlier murder of forty-three Tamil males in Jaffna. In Vavuniya in August 1985 nearly 100 Tamils were murdered after an army patrol narrowly escaped a land mine explosion.[22]

By 1986, the LTTE had established effective military control over most of the Tamil areas of northern Sri Lanka by silencing or co-opting the competing paramilitaries and effectively opposing the Sri Lankan Army (SLA). The final stages of this process began in January 1983, when the Sri Lankan government reacted to increasing paramilitary activity by imposing a fuel and economic blockade on all of these Tamil areas. Simultaneously, the SLA began a campaign of air raids and artillery shelling of the Jaffna Peninsula. An LTTE response in April 1987 was to stop vehicles on the Colombo to Trincomalee road and massacre over a 100 Sinhalese passengers. Shortly thereafter, the Colombo bus station was bombed, killing between 100 and 200 people and injuring hundreds more.[23] The SLA campaign continued with military thrusts into the region. And on July 5, with its power over Jaffna increasingly in jeopardy, the LTTE carried out its first suicide bombing, in which forty SLA troops were killed in the Nelliyadi army camp.

Figure 9.1 illustrates the historical trajectory of the Jaffna Tamil community. In common with the Stalinist and, as we shall see, Nazi, Ottoman, and Serbian contours, that of the Jaffna Tamils displays successive reinforced ephemera.

Note the increasing willingness to kill civilians by the LTTE and its first use of suicide terrorism *only* after the possibility of a major loss appeared on the horizon. The stiffening military opposition of the SLA and the willingness of the Sri Lankan government to establish a blockade of the Jaffna region suggested that the LTTE might be defeated and perhaps even destroyed if many of its cadres could not escape into the jungle. At the very least, the loss of Jaffna, "the symbol of LTTE power and authority, one that had weathered all SLA attempts to capture"[24] would be a crucial defeat. The LTTE had now entered the camp of authoritarian extremism, permitting no Tamil rivals, and engaging in deadly violence against civilians and military alike.

Striking in its implications is the absence of any religious or even ideological motivation for the suicide attacks of the LTTE. And suicide bombing had been

---

[22] Bush 2003, 139.   [23] Bush 2003, 141.   [24] Fair 2004, 21.

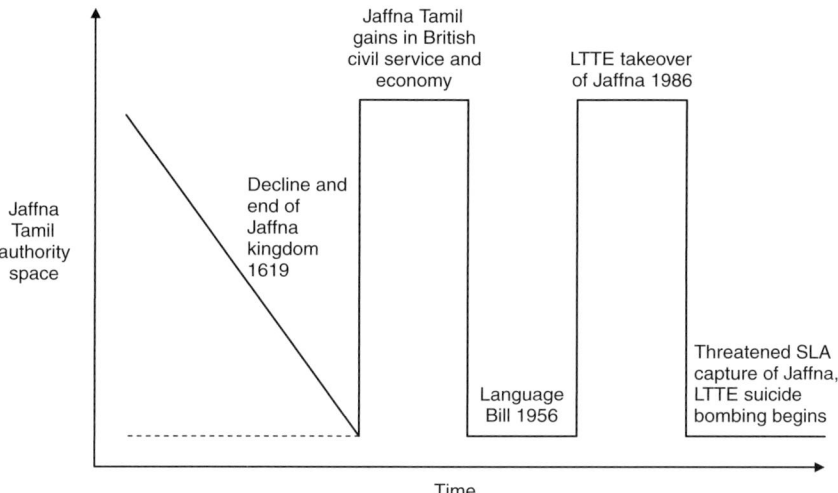

Figure 9.1:   Changes in Jaffna Tamil authority space over time

a much-used tactic of the Tigers. Between 1980 and 2000, when the LTTE was most active in its terror campaigns, its 168 suicide attacks comprised the preponderance of all such events.[25] Since that time, the Palestinian Intifada II and the Iraq insurgency have added many new suicide bombings,[26] but the LTTE still stands prominent in this activity. According to Christine Fair,[27] "In some ways, the entire LTTE could arguably be declared a suicide force of sorts. Each cadre is required to wear a cyanide capsule, which is distributed by the local commando leader in the celebration that follows the completion of training. LTTE cadres have shown little hesitation in consuming the capsule if their mission is compromised."

But the elite of all of the cadres were the Black Tigers, the suicide arm of the LTTE. They were the most honored of the Tigers. After applying for admission, they were selected for the Black Tigers only after the most thorough vetting; many applicants were rejected. Every year their sacrifices were honored in a major celebration called Great Heroes' Day (often incorrectly translated as "Martyrs' Day"). Black Tiger elite status was signified in their access to Velupillai Prabhakaran, the LTTE leader, who hosted a meal with them before their final mission. It was not a religion or a specific ideology that motivated the Black Tigers. "Instead, the mythology and reverence attached to the sacrifice of the Black Tigers serve[d] to motivate the cadres."[28]

---

[25] Fair 2004, 41.   [26] Pape 2005, 253–64.   [27] 2004, 37.   [28] Fair 2004, 47.

Indian intervention

Given the large Tamil population in the Indian state of Tamil Nadu across the Palk Strait from the Jaffna Peninsula, it might seem inevitable that India eventually would intervene in the Sri Lankan violence. Actually, it was the Indian external intelligence agency, the Research and Analysis Wing, which began training the LTTE and other Tamil rebel groups from Sri Lanka. The Indian government strongly opposed the post-1977 pro-Western policies of the Sri Lankan government and sought to undermine it.[29]

Training camps were set up in Tamil Nadu, but as hostility to the LTTE increased in India, the Tigers began moving their bases to the Jaffna Peninsula. In the midst of the SLA offensive (begun in February 1987) against the LTTE in Jaffna, the Indian air force began dropping food and medicine to the rebels, after a refusal by the Sri Lankan government to allow such shipments by sea. In July, an agreement to allow Indian forces to enter Sri Lanka essentially was imposed upon the Sri Lankan government; soon 6,000 Indian troops of the Indian Peace Keeping Force (IPKF) were in the Jaffna region.[30] Almost immediately, the IPKF and LTTE came into conflict as the former tried to disarm the Tamil rebels, and the violence quickly escalated.

By the time the IPKF withdrew from Sri Lanka in 1990, it had lost 1,157 troops in combat and nearly 3,000 wounded in India's longest war.[31] Clearly, the initial decision to arm the Jaffna Tamil rebels had become a "blowback" for the Indian government, as had the CIA's strategy to arm Islamic militants in fighting the Soviets in Afghanistan during the mid-1980s. The role of suicide bombing in the Indian decision to ultimately withdraw *all* support from the LTTE should not be minimized, for in March 1991 Rajiv Gandhi was assassinated by an LTTE female suicide bomber.

The first suicide bombing by the LTTE occurred just prior to the Indian intervention; the LTTE suicide bombing of Rajiv Gandhi would also put an exclamation point to the end of that action. And the reinforcing ephemera experienced by the Jaffna Tamils would set the stage for that unfortunate intervention. Nothing of that sort has happened internally in India (again excluding Kashmir); violence at this level involving government forces has been avoided.

Why are ephemeral victories, especially reinforcing ephemera so dangerous for international stability, at least at the regional level, even beyond. First, anger associated with these ephemera is intense. As a consequence, the violence that erupts tends to be severe and long lasting in the absence of the massive external force needed to quell the violence. If the ephemera are reinforced, as in the Sri Lankan case, then the intensity of the ethnic conflict is increased to the point that external intervention becomes more likely. As we shall see in the chapter on

---

[29] DeVotta 2004, 171.   [30] Peebles 2006, 157.   [31] DeVotta 2004, 173.

the Balkans, the Serbian aggression after 1991 resulted from three reinforcing ephemera that yielded massive conflict within the former Yugoslavia, including genocide at Srebrenica. Western, especially American intervention was required to end the violence. Alas, the size of the Indian force needed to decisively defeat the LTTE, and the political will to continue the IPKF mission in Sri Lanka were absent, and so the violence continued until the recent past.

10

Poland

An especially egregious case of murderous ethnic cleansing will now occupy our attention. Why does ethnic cleansing, and especially this particular case, deserve study as an example of political extremism? It is simply because the goal of a Poland free of its Jewish population, enunciated by nationalist extremists like the National Democrats and National Radical Camp as early as the beginning of the interwar period, came to fruition after World War II. This is an egregious case because the earlier massive persecution of Jews by the Nazis was now to be revisited by Poles, albeit in much attenuated form. If ever there appeared to be a case where extremist behavior should have been tempered by compassion for the victims, this was a prime candidate. Yet this was not the case. Why?

Post-war anti-Semitism in Poland

One of the striking features of the post-World War II period is the emergence of a murderous anti-Semitism in Poland. Between 500 and 1,500 Jews were killed by Poles in the immediate post-war period.[1] The Jews who had barely survived the war either as inmates of Nazi concentration camps, hidden by Polish gentiles, or escaped to the Soviet Union, were now returning to Poland. In virtually all cases, they had experienced devastating family losses in addition to their own extraordinary personal hardships.

After a pogrom in Kraków in 1945, according to Wincenty Bednarczuk, a returning Polish émigré writing in an important political-literary weekly *Odrodzenie*: "We hypothesized that the frightening tragedy of the Polish Jews would cure the Poles of anti-Semitism. It cannot be any other way, we thought, but that the sight of massacred children and old people must evoke a response of compassion and help. The common fate suffered under the occupation must somehow reconcile them. But we didn't know human nature... It turned out that our notions about mankind were naïve. The country surprised us."[2]

---

[1] Gross 2006, 35.   [2] Quoted in Gross 2006, 130.

Supporting this view is that of Jerzy Andrzejewski, one of the greatest writers of post-war Poland. In a long essay in *Odrodzenie*, he wrote:

> I wish I could honestly say [that] yes, anti-Semitism in Poland is disappear-ing… Unfortunately, after many years of thinking about this matter as an open, infected wound festering within our organism, witnessing all that happened in Poland before and during the war, and what is taking place at present; listening to people from various milieus and of different lev-els of intelligence, noticing their often unconscious gestures and reactions, observing how certain gestures and reactions automatically follow, I am not able to conclude, I cannot conclude, anything else but that the Polish nation in all its strata and across all intellectual levels, from the highest all the way down to the lowest, was and remains after the war anti-Semitic.[3]

Two related puzzles are posed by post-war Polish anti-Semitism. First, why did there occur pogroms in *post-war* Poland after the presumably common enemy of both Jews and Poles, Nazi Germany, had been soundly defeated? Traditional Polish anti-Semitism is the most often-cited explanation, but the exceptional violence of the Kielce pogrom of July 4, 1946, in which forty-two Jews were bru-tally murdered, contrasts sharply with traditional Polish patterns of personal beatings, business discriminations, legal exclusions, and other less violently expressed forms of anti-Semitism.

The second related puzzle is quoted by Jan Gross.[4] In response to efforts to condemn perpetrators of the pogrom leading to condemnatory statements in the press, strikes were called at factories and workshops in Łódź. Refusal to sign such statements by workers and others was widespread, even resulting in vio-lence used against those who wanted to resume work. Strikes spread to other cities and "In Lublin during a mass meeting of 1,500 railwaymen in this matter people were screaming, 'Down with the Jews,' 'Shame, they came to defend the Jews,' 'Bierut [the President of Poland at the time] will not dare to sentence them to death,' 'Wilno and Lwów have to be ours.'"[5]

Puzzling, if not striking here, is the juxtaposition of the typical anti-Semitic statement of "Down with the Jews" with the boundary-related "Wilno and Lwów have to be ours." Why this combination of seemingly unrelated elements? Yet they are related through the particular theoretical prism of territorial loss. For these cities with majority Polish (and Jewish) populations before the war were now to be incorporated within the new borders of the Soviet Union. Effectively, the Polish state was to be moved westward in its entirety, receiving former German lands in the west but relinquishing a much larger portion of territory in the east. A net territorial loss of 20 percent was experienced in this massive tran-sition.[6] And since much of the western territory had been occupied by Germans,

---

[3] Quoted in Gross 2006, 131–2.   [4] 2001.   [5] Gross 2001, 149.
[6] Davies 1982, 189.

representing historically a much more powerful political entity than Poland, the formerly German lands were only insecurely held until the very recent past.

Yet, despite these territorial losses, the population density of Poland actually decreased from 1939 through 1945. This decrease resulted from the loss of nearly one quarter of its pre-war population due to death (3 million Jews, 3 million Poles) and the post-war exodus of large numbers of Germans and other minorities. With a reduced population density, why then the concern over the loss of territories in Wilno and Lwów, coupled with overt anti-Semitism? The locations of these strikes and protests suggest an answer.

Both Łódź and Lublin had very large Jewish populations before the war. Lublin, where the quoted anti-Semitic statements were made, was an especially important Jewish center prior to World War II. When in 1928, a large Orthodox Jewish gathering was convened in Vienna to select a location for the building of a new major Yeshiva (center of Jewish higher learning), Lublin was chosen. And when surviving Jews, having escaped to Russia, returned to Poland after the war to reclaim their stolen property or simply to assess the current situation, their destination was frequently Lublin. At one point in 1946, approximately 200,000 Jews were to be found in the Lublin vicinity. Thus, to the railwaymen of Lublin and other Poles in the region, it must have appeared as if the Jews were returning en masse; earlier efforts by individual Poles tacitly or actively supporting the Nazi genocide had seemingly come to naught. Here, the tradeoff between external territory and the immediate environment becomes apparent. The loss of Wilno and Lwów to the Soviet Union, unlikely to be recouped, is to be compensated by the sustained exclusion of Jews from Polish society.

In this, the Polish railwaymen and sympathizers were successful. The vast majority of returning Jews left Poland permanently, leaving only about 25,000 concentrated in the capital city of Warsaw. Most of these remaining Jews would also leave after the governmentally inspired anti-Semitic campaigns of the late 1960s. The extremist goal of eliminating the Jews from Poland, entertained for many years by the anti-Semitic National Democrats, and later, before the war, by the openly fascist and violently anti-Semitic National Radical Camp, was finally achieved.[7]

Jewish exclusion

As early as 1943, a Polish official affirmed the necessity of a sustained Jewish exclusion from Polish society. Roman Knoll, head of the Foreign Affairs Commission in the apparatus of the Government Delegate (Polish underground state) said that non-Jewish Poles had by now assumed formerly Jewish positions in the socioeconomic structure, and this change was "permanent in character... Should Jews attempt to return en masse people would not perceive

---

[7] Gieysztor *et al.* 1979, 595; Michlic 2006, 112–13.

this as a restoration, but as an invasion, which they would resist even by physical means."[8]

Another distinguished official, Jerzy Braun, declared that:

> Today there is no place for a Jew in small towns or villages. During the past six years (*finally!* [emphasis in the original]) a Polish third estate has emerged which did not exist before. It completely took over trade, supplies, mediation, and local crafts in the provinces… Those young peasant sons and former urban proletarians, who once worked for the Jews, are determined, persistent, greedy, deprived of all moral scruples in trade, and superior to Jews in courage, initiative, and flexibility. These masses…are not aware what an important historic role they play by *conquering for Poland a new territory, formerly occupied by aliens.* Those masses will not relinquish what they have conquered. There is no force which could remove them.[9]

Here, Braun affirms the importance of new internal "territory" to compensate the Poles for their territorial losses in the post-war reconfiguration.

Even Władysław Gomułka, first secretary of the communist Polish Workers' Party (PPR), at a time shortly after the Kraków pogrom, met with Stalin and "pleaded during the meeting with the Soviet leader for a ban on the repatriation of a quarter million Polish Jews who would soon be eligible to return to Poland. Stalin was noncommittal and in the end did not oblige, but he commiserated with his Polish colleague about how each Jew taken separately was such a wonderful fellow, but as a group, taken altogether, Jews were a problem."[10]

Gomułka was not exceptionally anti-Semitic. His wife was Jewish but also headed a commission for the polonization of Jewish-sounding names for the PPR. A Jewish head of the regional Office of Press Control in Olsztyn understood the significance of this practice:

> It is becoming ever clearer to me that there is no future for us on this path, and that I am here only by accident, as an unwanted and alien intruder. Please do not misunderstand me: I did not have the slightest problems on account of my ethnic background; my views derive from more general reflections… [A member of the] Jewish intelligentsia employed in high positions is an intruder, an undesirable phenomenon, tolerated even in the most democratic milieus only with deep regret because this is against proper "tactics." We know how closely our comrades investigate the sound of people's names, their facial features, etc., from the point of view of "Aryan" characteristics before they decide to appoint someone to an important assignment. How often they advise people to hide nationality, or even to change or polonize their names. This is everyday stuff.[11]

As late as 1992, I personally witnessed a related phenomenon. When the convener of a conference in Lublin having a German/Jewish sounding name (he

---

[8] Quoted in Gross 2006, 46.   [9] Emphasis added; quoted in Gross 2006, 47.
[10] Gross 2006, 213.   [11] Quoted in Gross 2006, 215.

claimed German origin) introduced the chancellor of the university with a clearly Polish name, the convener declared that the chancellor was "an authentic Pole." To my astonishment, there was no visible or aural reaction from anyone. The chancellor simply continued smiling as the introductory remarks were completed. According to Joanna Michlic,[12] "In the early 1990s the conflation of ethno-nationalism with homogeneity in Polish society was a serious obstacle to improvement of the position of national and ethnic minorities in Poland."

At a press conference in 1990, Lech Wałęsa, a founder of the political reformist labor movement Solidarity, in obvious reference to a liberal Catholic political rival, Tadeusz Mazowiecki, asked that "persons of Jewish origin should not conceal [their] origin."[13] On several occasions, Wałęsa described himself as "a full-blooded Pole with documents going back to his great-grandfathers to prove it."[14] In the presidential election of the late 1990s, a Roman Catholic cleric, highly placed in the hierarchy, investigated Mazowiecki's background and declared that he had Jewish ancestry; therefore he was a "hidden Jew."[15]

This treatment of Jews as outside the Polish universe of moral concern was noted in the immediate post-war period, although it had strong resonance in the pre-1939 reference to the Jews as "the Fourth Partition."[16] Thus, the Jews were portrayed as equivalent to the three partitioning powers of the late eighteenth century – Austria, Prussia, and Russia – that eliminated Polish sovereignty. In Gross's[17] judgment, "Jewish experience was bracketed off and removed from consideration when the story of 'Polish society under the German occupation' was narrated." In September 1945, Bednarczuk wrote that anti-Semitism in Poland was "no longer an economic issue, it is no longer a political issue either. It is a moral problem pure and simple. Today, it is not a question of saving the Jews from misery and death, it is a problem of saving the Poles from moral misery and spiritual death."[18] And from a Jewish perspective, in Kraków, Mordecai Gebirtig wrote in February 1940:

> ... It hurts!
> It hurts terribly!
> When it isn't a foreign foe,
> But they –
> Poland's sons and daughters,
> Whose land will some day
> Be ashamed of them,
> But who now chuckle, gasp with laughter,
> Seeing down in the street
> How our common enemy
> Ridicules the Jews,

---

[12] 2006, 266.   [13] Quoted in Michlic 2006, 263.   [14] Quoted in Michlic 2006, 263.
[15] Quoted in Michlic 2006, 263.   [16] Michlic 2006, 247.   [17] 2006, 185.
[18] Quoted in Gross 2006, 29.

Strikes and torments the old,
Then plunders them undisturbed,
Cutting off the beards of Jews
Like they were slices of bread…
And they,
Who are left like us
Without a land,
Who feel now like us
The crazed enemy's hand –
How can they heckle, laugh, rejoice
At such a time
When Poland's pride and honour
Are so disgraced,
When Poland's white eagle
Is dragged on the ground,
Between the beards,
The grey and black hair
Of Jewish beards –
Is this not eternal shame
For all of them?
Isn't it like spitting
Right in their own faces?
It hurts!
How terribly it hurts![19]

Jan Karski understood the import of this circumstance for the Poles under German occupation. Accordingly,

> "The solution of the Jewish question" by the Germans – I must state this with a full sense of responsibility for what I am saying – is a serious and quite dangerous tool in the hands of the Germans, leading toward the "moral pacification" of broad sections of Polish society. It would certainly be erroneous to suppose that this issue alone will be effective in gaining for them the acceptance of the populace. However, although the nation loathes them mortally, this question is creating something akin to a narrow bridge upon which the Germans and a large portion of Polish society are finding agreement.[20]

Fear

The title of Jan Gross's 2006 book is *Fear: Anti-Semitism in Poland after Auschwitz.* And the reader initially assumes that the fear is that of the Jews confronted with murderous anti-Semitism. This conclusion is true, in part, for many of the returnees were literally in fear for their lives. Yet, Gross also

---

[19] Quoted in Gross 2006, 256–7.   [20] Quoted in Korzec and Szurek 1993, 388–9.

points to the fear that Poles felt upon once again seeing the Jewish presence. Accordingly, "The Jews who survived the war were not threatening just because they reminded those who had availed themselves of Jewish property that its rightful owners might come back to reclaim it. They also induced fear in people by reminding them of the fragility of *their own* existence, of the propensity for violence residing in *their own* communities, and of *their own* helplessness vis-à-vis the agents of pseudospeciation who now invoked class criteria for elimination from public life."[21]

More specifically, Polish nationalists feared anyone who arrived from the East, including Polish-Jewish refugees, most of whom had survived the war in the Soviet Union. The returnees from the Soviet Union comprised 70 percent of the total number of Jews in post-war Poland.[22] According to Krystyna Kersten and Paweł Szapiro,[23] "There was anxiety, even fear, in the face of everything that came from the East, because of a series of painful experiences stretching back to 1939. It is not surprising, then, that the imperative of biological and spiritual survival and of the defence of national identity were instilled into the behaviour of Poles, and that the call for resistance, variously conceived, remained alive, and was directed against everything seen as *subjugation* and, consequently, against those perceived as its perpetrators."

Jews were perceived as perpetrators, not only because of their immediate origins in the Soviet Union as they returned to their homes, but also because of the association between Jews and communism – also originating in the Soviet Union. Many of the earliest Polish communists were Jewish, and as we saw, temporarily accepted administrative positions especially in the security services[24] that later would be assumed by Poles, or at least thoroughly Polonized Jews, including their names. Efforts by high communist leaders to combat anti-Semitism only reinforced the connection between Jews and communism in the public mind.

The myth of Judeo-communism was further enhanced by the vastly better treatment that Jews received upon arrival of the Russians in eastern Poland in 1939. In an earlier work, Gross affirmed that, "The changes which began to occur in the village after the Russians' arrival were a total surprise… To the Jews, they could only consider it a dream, as if the Messiah had come. The Russians raised their status, they gave them something – a status that they had never had in their lives."[25]

A wave of 300–400,000 refugees fleeing the eastward march of the Germans gave a tumultuous welcome to the advancing Soviet forces. Almost all of the refugees were Jews who felt that their freedom, even their lives, were in danger before the Russians' arrival. Paweł Korzec and Jean-Charles Szurek[26] conclude

[21] Emphases in original; Gross 2006, 256.   [22] Michlic 2006, 198.
[23] Emphasis added; 1993, 459.   [24] Kersten and Szapiro 1993, 463.
[25] Quoted in Korzec and Szurek 1993, 398.   [26] Korzec and Szurek 1993, 389.

that, "It is clear that the German danger and the Soviet presence did not weigh on Jews and Poles to the same degree."

Yet in her excellent and thoroughly researched book on Poland and its Jews, Joanna Michlic pinpoints ethno-nationalism as the principal source of anti-Jewish hostility and violence. Beginning after the failed Polish revolution of 1863–64, a modern form of ethno-nationalism took hold which targeted the Jews as the purveyors of industry, capitalism, socialism, secularism, and all the other elements of modernity that were to make the Jew into "Poland's threatening other." Polish self-identification was to be generated by this societal division – increasingly a yawning chasm. And according to Michlic, ethno-nationalism, somewhat modified in reaction to the new communist realities, but still in its organic Polish form was to be blamed for the murderous anti-Semitism of the post-war period. Indeed, the title of her chapter on the years 1945–49 when most of the killings took place is "Old Wine in a New Bottle."

Certainly, Polish ethno-nationalism was a major factor in the anti-Semitism of this and many of the older historical periods. But was it alone sufficient for the onset of anti-Semitic mass murder? Considerations stemming from the present theory are relevant in understanding the advent of *murderous* anti-Semitism. And despite framing of the puzzle at the outset of this chapter as centered on killing in the *post-war* period, some elementary calculations suggest that the puzzle should be centered on the appearance of spontaneous Polish violent anti-Semitism, without German instigation or participation, soon after the retreat of the Russians from Soviet-occupied Poland in June 1941. The Jedwabne massacre, made famous by Gross's *Neighbors*, is one case in point, as are the massacres at Radziłów, Wąsosz, and Wizna. In these instances, deaths have been estimated to be respectively, 1,600, 800, 600, and 82, including corrections in *Neighbors* for some initial exaggerations.[27]

These numbers sum to 3,082 Jews killed by Poles in the formerly occupied zone of Poland. I chose to use only the number of Jews killed in that zone, because the vast majority of murders of Jews by Poles occurred in that region. (In deference to the sensitivities of survivors and relatives of the murdered, I hesitate to engage in what would appear to be a "numbers game." One human being killed in a pogrom or massacre is certainly one too many. Yet, if it helps understand the sources of extremism that lead to mass murder, the analysis of percentages killed at least will have some analytic utility that may be useful in devising future preventive measures. The dead will not have died completely in vain.)

On a percentage basis, given the approximately 1 million Jews in the formerly Soviet zone at that time,[28] this amounts to 0.3 percent of the available number of Jews. As we saw, an approximation to the number of Jews killed in the

---

[27] Gross 2001, 7, 57, 70.   [28] Michlic 2006, 139.

immediate post-war period was 1,000[29] which, given the roughly 200,000 Jews in Poland in 1946,[30] yields a killing percentage of 0.5 percent.

Contrast these two percentages with that of the percentage of Jews killed between 1935 (Piłsudski's death) and 1937, the most deadly time for Polish Jews between independence and World War II, and a period at least as long or longer than those used in the preceding calculations. According to Michlic,[31] "between twenty and thirty" Jews were killed at that time. Given the 3.5 million Jews living in Poland before the war[32] and the approximation of 25 Jews killed, the killing percentage is a minuscule 0.0007 percent, or three orders of magnitude less than either the 1941 or post-war killing percentages. Even assuming inaccuracies in reporting, the vast difference between the 1941 and post-war values on the one hand, and that of the 1935–37 period on the other, cannot be ignored.

Now, one can argue that the post-war killing, despite occurring during peacetime (as was the interwar period), was only a continuation by the Poles of what the Nazis had begun. But that response still begs the question of why the Poles should emulate their hated enemies, the Nazis. Certainly the Poles did not imitate the Ukrainian and White (tsarist) Russian killing of Jews in the aftermath of World War I, despite close proximity of Poles to the killing. Approximately 150,000 Jews died in the Ukrainian and White Russian massacres (including deaths due to massacre-induced disease and starvation), roughly 10 percent of Ukrainian Jewry.[33] In 1918–19, in Polish-controlled areas of that region, 230 Jews were killed,[34] again a comparatively minuscule percentage. Why did not the Poles at that time even remotely approach the killing rate of Jews by the Ukrainians and White Russians?

The answer, interestingly, is found in a statement attributed to a Ukrainian at the time of the massacres: "What, you want to rule over us?"[35] This statement obviously refers to the relatively large number of Jews in the Bolshevik leadership, and the perception of Jews as communists, or at least as sympathetic to communism. In post-World War II Poland, a similar phenomenon occurred in which issues of governance by Jews, largely absent in 1918–19 Poland, but clearly present in the Ukraine at that time, became paramount.

After World War II, old-time communists of Jewish origin such as Jakub Berman, Hilary Minc, and Roman Zambrowski returned from the Soviet Union and were elected members of the Politburo and Central Committee of the PPR. They were highly visible. Berman was an undersecretary in the Ministry of Foreign Affairs, Minc was minister of industry, and Zambrowski was deputy chairman of the Polish Parliament. To make the situation even more threatening, at least in the Polish view, was the fact that 26.3 percent of the leaders of

---

[29] Gross 2006, 35.   [30] Gross 2006, 28; Michlic 2006, 198.
[31] 2006, 114.   [32] Gross 2006, 28.
[33] Gergel 1951, cited in Vital 1999, 722; Baron 1976, 184–5.
[34] Michlic 2006, 111.   [35] Heifetz 1921, 8.

the political police in 1945–46 were ethnically Jewish.[36] And Michlic[37] herself acknowledges that: "Poles reacted to the presence of Jews in their own government the same way they had to the presence of Jews in the Soviet Communist Party and the state apparatus in the eastern territories under the Soviet occupation, between 1939 and 1941. The presence of Polish Jews like Minc, Berman, and Zambrowski in high state and party positions in the early postwar period must have seemed to many ethnic Poles a 'reversal of the natural order.'"

This situation stands in stark contrast to that which existed during the interwar period. At that time only two of the approximately 600 high governmental positions were occupied by Jews – Szymon Aszkenazy, a distinguished professor and an official Polish representative at the League of Nations in 1920 and 1923, and Anatol Muelstein who served in the Polish Foreign Office.[38] Note that both were serving in an "external" capacity and did not directly influence domestic policy.

Constituting 10 percent of the Polish population and a much higher percentage of its literate population before the war, Jews were vastly under-represented in the occupation of sensitive governmental positions, especially in comparison with the post-war period and its massively reduced Jewish population. The killing rates during the three time spans, interwar, wartime (Soviet zone), and postwar closely correspond to the differential visibility of Jews in key governmental positions. Ethno-nationalism therefore must be understood in conjunction with the equally, perhaps even more, important perceived "reversal of the natural order" in explaining the post-war violence against Jews. Effectively, issues of governance trump those of compassion and morality when the governed assess the value of human life of the "threatening" governors.

Conclusion

The appropriate referent for understanding the immediate post-war onset of murderous anti-Semitism is the 1939–41 Soviet occupation of eastern Poland and the elevation of Jews to administrative positions. Neither the 90 percent killing rate of the Nazi Holocaust nor the minuscule killing rate of the interwar period is appropriate. The similarities in the calculated percentages of Jews killed immediately after the Soviet occupation and post-war periods are striking in comparison with that of the interwar period, or for that matter the pogroms of 1918–19. Fear of subordination to Jews and Jewish communists not only in trade and crafts but, importantly, in governance, first appeared not in 1945, but during the Soviet occupation of 1939–41. The puzzle of the post-war anti-Semitic murders, even after the horrors of the Jewish experience during the Holocaust, is but an extension of the earlier puzzle presented by the 1941 killings. The theory offered here is one suggested explanation.

[36] Michlic 2006, 204.   [37] 2006, 201.   [38] Michlic 2006, 201.

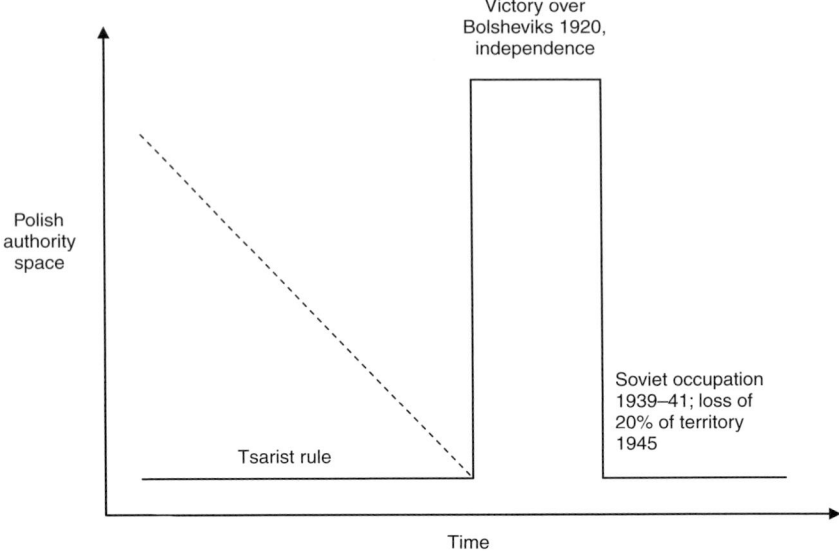

Figure 10.1:   Changes in Polish authority space over time

Once again, as during the 125-year period before the Polish victory of 1920 over Soviet forces (often called "the miracle on the Vistula") yielding an independent Poland, the Russians, or at least their form of political organization and ideological handmaidens would be in charge. The Polish Partitions of the late eighteenth century extinguishing Polish sovereignty, and the failed Polish revolutions of 1830–31 and 1863–64 against the Russians constituted a pattern of national subordination broken only briefly by the independence period of 1920–39. The threat and fear of reversion was palpable. Any reminder, indicator, or suspected agent of this renewed subordination and lost territory – the Jews ("the Fourth Partition") – was to be treated harshly.

The 20 percent of pre-war Polish territory lost in 1945 was roughly coterminous with that occupied by the Soviets in 1939. Concerns over lost territory and returning Jews – in the Polish nationalist mind welcome hosts of the Soviets in 1939 – were to be merged in the post-war murderous ethnic cleansing. Figure 10.1 presents this ephemeral gain for Poland.

11

The Balkans

The Balkans as a region has contributed disproportionately to the advance of political extremism in the twentieth century. The assassination of Archduke Franz Ferdinand in Sarajevo, setting off the conflagration of 1914, and the strong fillip to fascism in Fiume (today's Rijeka in Croatia) after World War I are but two cases in point. The Balkan Wars of 1912–13 also were extraordinarily bloody and affected this extremist trajectory.

This chapter examines four cases in the Balkans, two of which exhibited strong evidence of extremism, while the remaining two did not. Serbia not only gave rise to the extreme nationalist Chetniks, but was the only country to be complicit in a European genocide after 1945. Croatia, in its quasi-independent existence under Nazi tutelage in World War II, was led by the extraordinarily bloody fascist Ustaše. In strong contrast, Bulgaria and Greece were never led by extremist governments. This chapter will explore these contrasts, but after a brief discussion of the work of Ivo Andrić that will serve as an introduction. Romania has also exhibited extremist tendencies, especially in the form of the Iron Guard; this organization and Romanian electoral behavior are discussed elsewhere in this book (see Chapters 3, 4, and 13).

Ivo Andrić

"No better introduction to the study of Balkan and Ottoman history exists," exclaims the distinguished historian, William McNeill,[1] in his Introduction to the Nobel Laureate Ivo Andrić's *The Bridge on the Drina*. Although historical fiction, the book nevertheless hews so closely to the historical record that a historian of McNeill's stature can praise it unqualifiedly. Indeed although Andrić probably did not coin the term "the will to power," an important antecedent of the extremist enterprise, the phrase appears at a salient point in the narrative.[2]

I refer to this work at some length because it so clearly delineates the ethnic fault lines in turn of the twentieth-century Bosnia-Herzegovina. Equally, if not more important for contemporary concerns, Andrić highlights the debates

---

[1] 1995, 1.　　[2] Andrić [1959] 1995, 242.

within the Muslim community about the value of human life. As a Roman Catholic Croat growing up in a predominantly Muslim, Serbian (Eastern Orthodox), and Jewish town, he could write presciently about the society around him, much as did Joseph Conrad in his writings about Russia, albeit raised as a member of the Polish Roman Catholic minority in the Ukraine.

It is obvious that the author is most sympathetic to two characters. One is Lotte, a Jewish migrant from Galicia to Bosnia-Herzegovina after the Austrian occupation began in 1878. She is beautiful, is successful at business investments, establishes a thriving hotel, and is immensely dedicated to her large extended family in Galicia. But as matters begin to decay as the twentieth century unfolds, Andrić[3] describes her anguish. "Life was bursting asunder, was crumbling, was disintegrating. It seemed to her that the present generation attached more importance to its views on life than to life itself. It seemed to her mad and completely incomprehensible, yet it was so. Therefore life was losing its value and wasting away in mere words. Lotte saw this clearly and felt it at every step."

The rise of Serbian nationalism in Bosnia that would lead ultimately to the assassination of the Archduke Franz Ferdinand and his pregnant wife Sophie in Sarajevo in June 1914 was one of Lotte's (and Andrić's) concerns, as was the increasing popularity of revolutionary Marxism. Lotte is life affirming. All guests at her hotel, as well as her large extended family, should enjoy life to the fullest without impinging on the rights of others. Belligerent drunks were not welcome at her hotel.

The other sympathetic character is Alihodja Mutevelić, a "Turkish" (in the parlance of the time, but Bosnian Muslim) shopkeeper and a leading member of the *ulema* (Muslim jurists). When the Austro-Hungarian occupation of Bosnia-Herzegovina began in 1878 with the agreement of the Ottoman sultan demanded by the Treaty of Berlin, there was talk of armed opposition to the Austrian troops. This movement was led locally by a *mufti*, Osman Effendi Karamanli. Opposed to him was Alihodja. After much argument to and fro in the midst of a large gathering, Karamanli,

> in the end, completely beside himself…replied with scarcely concealed disdain to every question of the *hodja*: "The time has come to die", "We will lay down our lives", "We shall all die to the last man."
>
> "But," broke in the *hodja*, "I understand that you wanted to drive the Schwabes [Austrians] out of Bosnia and that was the reason why you were collecting us. If it is only a question of dying, then we too know how to die, Effendi, even without your assistance. There is nothing easier than to die."
>
> "*Ama*, I can see that you will not be one of those who die," broke in Karamanli, harshly.

[3] [1959] 1995, 258.

"I can see that you will be one," answered the *hodja* sarcastically, "only I
do not see why you ask for our company in this senseless attempt."[4]

Later, at the start of World War I, when there is talk among Muslims about
joining the *Schutzkorps* [local defense forces] directed principally at the Serbs,
Alihodja comments to one Muslim enthusiast, "I see that you have made up
your mind to go. You too want to die... But remember that long ago old men
said: 'The time has not come to die but to let it be seen of what stuff a man is
made.' These are such times."[5]

Although clearly averse to Serbian nationalism (there are no sympathetic
Serbian characters comparable to Lotte and Alihodja), nevertheless Andrić establishes the early basis for Serbian extremism in response to Ottoman excesses.
When the Ottoman government decides to facilitate transport by building the
bridge over the Drina in the early sixteenth century, Serbian peasants, led by
Radisav, successfully sabotage its construction. When finally caught by the local
Ottoman leader, Radisav is slowly and with immense cruelty impaled on a large
stake that is then raised so that his body is exhibited vertically for all to see, as in
a crucifixion. This process is described by Andrić in great detail, as if to establish
the political climate that would later give rise to Serbian extremism.

Serbia

In the case of the Serbs, we have at least three such ephemeral periods in which
gain is followed by loss with great regularity, beginning in the nineteenth century. At the same time, the ethnic cleansing by Serbs principally of Muslims,
including one genocidal occurrence at Srebrenica during the mid-1990s, is the
only example of such extremist behavior in Europe since the end of World War
II. I argue that this Serbian extremism was a consequence of Serbian exceptional history in the occurrence of cyclical and reinforcing ephemera, really
unmatched by any other European country. If in the minds of many Serbs, history projected the Serbs into the untenable position of having to repeatedly conquer their neighbors in several political or military contests yielding many Serb
deaths, then ethnic cleansing, even mass murder and genocide, is required to
effect the "Final Solution" of this chronic problem.

To begin with, I shall exclude detailed consideration of the Battle of Kosovo
of 1389 and its even more consequential (but less memorialized) defeat of the
Serbs by the Turks at the Battle on the Maritsa of 1371. Although clearly fitting
the criteria of defeat following an earlier period of expansion, against the background of still earlier national failure during the period of tribal dissension, the
Battle of Kosovo was used extensively by ethnic entrepreneurs such as Slobodan
Milošević or Vuk Drašković to mobilize public opinion in favor of the war with

---

[4] Andrić [1959] 1995, 116.   [5] Andrić [1959] 1995, 285.

Croatia and ultimately the ethnic cleansing of Muslims in Bosnia-Herzegovina. Indeed on the monument commemorating the Battle of Kosovo, a portion of an epic folk poem is engraved:

> Whoever is a Serb, and of Serbian seed,
> And doesn't come to fight the Battle of Kosovo,
> Let him never father a child,
> Neither male nor female,
> Let whatever he grows never yield fruit,
> Neither red wine nor white wheat,
> Let him rot in evil shame till his last progeny.[6]

The efforts of politicians like Milošević, pandering to nationalist sentiment, were required to keep such memories alive. But the question then becomes why so much of the population was receptive to these bellicose, even extremist ideas? Ethnic entrepreneurs tend to gain political advantage if their appeals are given a favorable reception, but why should the populace be so persuaded? Cvijeto Job[7] answers this question in part: "One of the more unfortunate traits in Yugoslav provincial culture is the worship of intellectuals, or, more correctly, those who pass for intellectuals. Academic and professional titles suffice to assure their holders a special authority, whatever the subject. Their pronouncements on the vital issues of the day are accepted without question." But clearly there is more, for these "authenticated" pronouncements must fall on fertile political soil.

It was Ilija Garašanin, arguably the most influential Serb politician of the nineteenth century, who established the foreign policy for Serbian programmatic territorial acquisition.[8] In his *Načertanije*, effectively a blueprint for Serbian expansion based on his model of earlier Serbian grandeur (see Figure 1.1), he wrote that Serbs should be seen by others as:

> the true heirs of our great forefathers, and they are engaged in nothing new but the *restoration of their ancient homeland*. Our present will not be without a tie with our past, but it will bring into being a connected, coherent, and congruous whole, and for this Serbdom, its nationality and its political existence as a state, stands under the protection of sacred historic right. Our aspiration cannot be accused of being something new, unfounded, out of revolution and rebellion, but everyone must admit that it is politically necessary, that it is *founded upon the distant past, and that it has its root in the past political and national life of the Serbs*, a root which is only bringing forth new branches and beginning to flourish anew.[9]

And in 1847, Prince-Bishop Petar II Petrović-Njegoš published an epic poem *The Mountain Wreath* that inspired generations of younger Serbs and Montenegrins

---

[6] Quoted in Job 1993, 65–6.   [7] 1993, 67.   [8] Glenny 1999, 45–6.
[9] Emphasis added; quoted in Judah 2000, 58.

by its glorification of Miloš Obilić, a legendary hero of Kosovo who was thought
to have killed the Ottoman sultan:

> Who, Miloš would not envy thee?
> A victim thou to thine own truth and worth!
> All-puissant spirit in the things of War;
> A thunder mighty which did shatter thrones!
> The deeds thy knightly soul hath wrought,
> Outshine all luster of the Past, –
> The fame of Sparta and of mighty Rome!
> Their valiant and heroic feats
> Are all surpass'd by thy proud arm.[10]

Serbian expansion required a militarism that led Leon Trotsky (then a war correspondent) to observe Belgrade during the Balkan Wars. It has, said Trotsky,
"a special air about it – on the alert like a military camp… The streets are full of
mobilized men and men about to be mobilized. The shops are empty… Industry
is at a standstill, apart from the branch that serves the needs of mobilization
and the coming war… For ten days already railway travel has been suspended
in Serbia: the trains carry only soldiers and war materials… If Belgrade is an
armed camp, the railway station is the heart of this camp. Military authority
reigns there exclusively."[11]

At the same time, as we saw earlier, the symbol on the flag of the Serbian
Orthodox Church proclaims according to St. Sava, a founder of the independent
Serbian Orthodox Church, "only unity saves the Serbs."[12]

After a long period of subordination to the Ottomans after the Battles of
Maritsa and Kosovo, the Serbs finally gained a measure of autonomy in 1817.
Successive expansions of Serbian holdings occurred in 1833, 1878, and 1912–
13.[13] (Serbian armies were defeated in 1876 by the Ottomans and in 1885 by the
Bulgarians, but none of these defeats entailed the loss of Serbian territory.[14]) All
of the gains followed wars that the Ottomans or neighboring Balkan states lost
to the Russians or Serbs. This period of uninterrupted expansion of the Serbian
state, the first ephemeral period, was followed by the crushing defeats of 1915
during World War I. Although the Serbs did a masterful job of stopping initial
Austro-Hungarian thrusts into Serbia, and even counter-attacked into Bosnia,
matters were to turn decidedly against them. After the loss of Belgrade to the
enemy but its recapture by the Serbs, Bulgaria entered the war on the side of the
Central Powers. Shortly thereafter, a combined Austro-Hungarian, Bulgarian,
and German armed force conquered all of Serbia, leading to a long march of
the remains of the Serbian army to northern Albania and, after evacuation by
the French, from there to the Isle of Corfu.[15] They would return to fight well at

---

[10] Quoted in Judah 2000, 63–4.   [11] Quoted in Glenny 1999, 232.
[12] *Flags of the World* 2007.   [13] Jelavich and Jelavich 1977, 57.
[14] Glenny 1999, 132, 177.   [15] Judah 2000, 98–101.

Salonika and then to help establish the Kingdom of Serbs, Croats, and Slovenes in 1918, to be formally renamed Yugoslavia in 1929.[16]

The costs of war to the Serbs during this period were colossal. "During the Balkan Wars Serbia lost some 30,000 men. The First World War cost it 275,000 men and wartime diseases another 800,000 civilians. These losses amounted to a quarter of the population and two-thirds of its male population between the ages of fifteen and fifty-five."[17]

These events were not to be lost on the contemporary Serbian population. During the 1970s, the Serb writer Dobrica Ćosić published a four-volume novel, *Time of Death*, recounting the horrors suffered by the Serbs in 1915. In her classic observations on Yugoslavia, Rebecca West remarked in 1937 how "defeat had taken all":

> [S]habby, empty hills in Milutin's [early Serb leader] time had been covered with villages...receded into distances that were truly vast, for a traveler could penetrate them for many miles before he came on life that was gentle, where the meals were full and delicate... Yet when Grachanitsa was built the people...had eaten game and fine fattened meats off gold and silver... But because the Christians had lost the battle of Kossovo (sic) all this life had perished... Nothing...was left...the residue was pitifully thin, thin as a shadow cast by a clouded sun.[18]

But matters on the whole were on the upswing for the Serbs after establishment of an independent Yugoslavia. Although Yugoslavia was a melancholy place for many during the interwar period, especially for Macedonians, Albanians, and Croats, it was the Serbs "who dominated the state in every respect."[19] Yet despite the Kosovo defeat recorded by West and other despoliations, a sense of this Serb dominance can be seen in her comments on the Serbs themselves through the light of the monastery at Gračanica: "From the immense height of the cupolas light descends on three naves, divided by three gigantesquely sturdy columns, and arrives there multicolored, dyed by the frescoes which cover every inch of the wall. There is here a sense of colossal strength, of animal vigor, of lust so lusty that it can sup off high pleasures as well as low, and likes crimson on its eye as well as wine on its tongue and a godhead as well as a mistress."[20]

A less grandiloquent early estimate of future Serb dominance within Yugoslavia is provided by the July 1917 statement of Stojan Protić, a Serbian representative negotiating with the Croat Ante Trumbić about the future South Slav state. "'We have the solution to Bosnia,' Protić announced to Trumbić, in one of their discussions. 'When our army crosses the Drina we will give the Turks [Bosnian Muslims] 24 hours, well, maybe 48, to return to the Orthodox faith. Those who won't, will be killed, as we have done in our time in Serbia.' The

---

[16] Judah 2000, 106–8.   [17] Judah 2000, 101.   [18] Quoted in Kaplan 1993, 40.
[19] Judah 2000, 109.   [20] Quoted in Judah 2000, 23.

Croatian delegation fell silent in astonishment. 'You can't be serious.' Trumbić said at last. 'Quite serious,' the Serb replied."[21] The reference here, of course, is to Slavic landowners (mostly Orthodox) who, after the Ottoman conquest, had converted to Islam in order to retain their holdings.

But it was World War II that would provide a more immediate prism for the justification of political extremisms of all stripes as Yugoslavia imploded during the early 1990s. From a dominant ethnicity in the 1920s and 1930s, the second ephemeral period, the Serbs became a hunted minority, much as had occurred during the previous world war. With the rapid defeat of the Royal Yugoslav Army by the combined German and Italian armies supported by Hungarian and Bulgarian Axis forces, the government capitulated. The Axis attack was carried out swiftly and ruthlessly because of Hitler's rage at the initial adherence of the Yugoslav government to the Axis, followed by an almost immediate military coup that yielded a government reneging on that agreement. A large Independent State of Croatia (NDH) was carved out of Yugoslavia, including the territories of Croatia (excepting Dalmatia) and Bosnia-Herzegovina.[22] Ante Pavelić, leader of both the Croatian Ustaša fascist movement and the new NDH, was said to proclaim regarding the Serbs: "kill a third, expel a third, convert a third [to Catholicism]."[23] This statement, of course, is virtually identical to Pobedonostsev's proclamation regarding the Jews in tsarist Russia (see Chapter 5). The infamous Jasenovac concentration camp was the location of the mass murder of many Serbs by the Croatian Ustaše.

After the formation of the Ustaša-run NDH in 1941 under Nazi tutelage, one of the new ministers, Milovan Žanić, stated: "I say this openly, this state, this our homeland, must be Croat and nothing else. Therefore those who have moved in must go. The events of centuries, and especially of the past twenty years, show all compromise is impossible. This must be the land of the Croats and no one else, and *there are no methods that we Ustashe will not use to make this land truly Croatian*, and cleanse it of the Serbs who have endangered us for centuries."[24]

Of course the Serbs were not only victims, but also perpetrators. In response to the German occupation, an organization of Serbian nationalists, the Četnici (Chetniks), was formed under the leadership of Draža Mihailović, a royalist and Serb nationalist officer in the Yugoslav army. Croats and Muslims were to be targeted by the Četnici, just as Serbs and Jews were targeted by the Ustaše. Estimating deaths from political violence of all sorts within Yugoslavia during World War II, a Serb scholar, Bogoljub Kočović, records 487,000 Serbs, 207,000 Croats, and 86,000 Muslims killed. A Croatian scholar, Vladimir Žerjavić, estimates 530,000 Serb, 192,000 Croat, and 103,000 Muslim deaths.[25] These figures most certainly are reliable within statistical margins of error, for the Serb and

---

[21] Tanner 2001, 116.   [22] Judah 2000, 114–16.   [23] Silber and Little 1996, 93.
[24] Emphasis added; quoted in Tanner 2001, 151.   [25] Quoted in Cigar 1995, 9.

Croat scholars, relative to each other's numbers, tended to underestimate deaths in their own ethnicity and overestimate them for the opposing one. Clearly the nationalistic purpose of recent victimization was not satisfied by these accounts. Nevertheless, these are horrendous losses that would be used to stoke ethnic passions within Yugoslavia as its end neared.

Despite these losses by all major ethnic groups (approximately 60,000 Jews were killed as well), "the overarching cause of [the 1990s wars of Yugoslav dissolution] was the discontent, which emanated from Serbian communities in all three regions about the implications of the disintegration of the Communist state and the loss of their 'protection' from Belgrade."[26] As the biggest loser in the imploding state, the Serbs would now hark back to the losses of World War II and, before that, World War I.

The third ephemeral period of gain occurred between 1945 and the early 1960s. Although not entirely dominant in all areas of society as before the war, nevertheless the Serbs were relatively satisfied with their lot. The capital of the state still was Belgrade in the heart of Serbia. The army was still Serb (and Montenegrin) dominated and increasingly so. At the time of the break-up of Yugoslavia, 70 percent of the officers were either Serbs or Montenegrins.[27] In part this situation stemmed from the fact that the earliest partisans in Tito's forces were from Serbia or Montenegro.

The period of Serbian decline may be dated from the mid-1960s. One of Tito's closest advisers, Aleksandar Ranković, a Serb who tended to protect Serbian interests, was removed from office in 1966.[28] With his departure, there was no Serb to be found at the highest level of government. At the same time, demographic trajectories were not operating in favor of the Serbs. While Serbs were a plurality (42.8 percent) of the population of Bosnia-Herzegovina in 1961 and Muslims a distinct minority at 25.6 percent, by 1991 that relationship was reversed. Muslims now constituted 43.7 percent of the population and Serbs 31.4 percent. As the former dominant ethnicity in the imploding state, the Serbs would now look back to their earlier losses. In Kosovo, the spiritual heartland of the Serbian nation, the minority status of the Serbs worsened. While Serbs went from 23.5 percent of the population to 10 percent between 1961 and 1991, Albanians grew from 67 percent to 90 percent of the population during this time period.[29] Whereas in the early 1960s an increasing number of Yugoslav citizens defined themselves as Yugoslavs over and above their particular ethnicities, an early 1970s survey in Serbia found that, "64 percent of high school students described their nationality as Serb and 32 percent as Yugoslav – a much higher figure for the latter category than was recorded in either the preceding or following censuses of 1971 and 1981."[30]

---

[26] Carmichael 2002, 17.   [27] Glenny 1996, 134.   [28] Sell 2002, 42.
[29] Woodward 1995, 33–4.   [30] Sell 2002, 35.

These data imply the earlier increasing satisfaction with the Serb position within Yugoslavia, but by 1981 that satisfaction was eroding. Aside from an increasing awareness of the demographic issue, one of the principal causes of that erosion was the Constitution of 1974. The two already de facto autonomous regions within Serbia – Kosovo to the south abutting Albania, and Vojvodina to the north on the Hungarian border – were to become legally co-constituent units of the federal government. They had separate delegations to the federal parliament, with nearly the same powers as republics such as Serbia. Both regions acquired seats in the collective presidency of the Yugoslav Federation.[31] Thus, demographics were now to directly affect governance to the detriment of Serbian power within the federation. Of all the republics, only Serbia had autonomous regions that were sometimes called "federal."[32]

Economically, by 1984 unemployment was becoming a serious problem, officially established at 14 percent. While Slovenia experienced full employment and Croatia nearly so, the unemployment rates were 23 percent in Bosnia-Herzegovina and large parts of Serbia including Belgrade, 27 percent in Macedonia and 50 percent in Kosovo. Inflation was an additional problem – it rose to 50 percent a year and more than that after 1984. Because of the different economic performance rates between the north and the south of the federation, "The Slovene and Croatian governments, basing their reasoning on trickle-down orthodoxy, opposed expenditures for defense and development credits in the south, justified withholding tax monies from the federal government, and opposed moves to strengthen federal capacities."[33] Thus, from an economic perspective, Serbia was fast losing its pre-eminence as the "first among equals" even in the area of defense and the Yugoslav National Army (JNA). Sufficient monies for the JNA simply were not being approved by the federal government.

And when the federal government began to fail, Serbian and Montenegrin officers of the JNA provided military help to their ethnic kin in the various portions of the federation in which they were found. Paramilitaries also arose to defend their own communities and attack others, often in concert with the JNA. "The most hawkish member of the Serbian government, Budimir Košutić, advocated a crusade of retribution against Croats. As a child in Croatia, Košutić watched how his father was told to divide his children into two groups, one group would be shot, the other allowed to live."[34] The commander of the JNA's Knin Garrison, Ratko Mladić, lost his father in a partisan raid on the birthplace of Ante Pavelić, the Croatian leader of the Ustaša. Mladić's extremist views are illustrated by the following statement: "Regardless of what we decide, the west will continue to implement its infernal plan. What is at stake is an attempt to disunite the Orthodox world, and even annihilate it."[35] Mladić was to be the commander of the Bosnian Serb force that would commit the genocide of

[31] Job 2002, 76.   [32] Woodward 1995, 65.   [33] Woodward 1995, 69.
[34] Glenny 1996, 122.   [35] Judah 2000, 231.

approximately 8,000 Muslim males in Srebrenica, after realizing that Knin (his earlier command) and the Krajina region of Croatia populated by Serbs could no longer be held in the face of a massive Croatian offensive.

The Serb paramilitary fighters from Croatia and Bosnia called themselves Četnici (Chetniks), as did the earlier Serb nationalist fighters of World War II and the much earlier Balkan Wars.[36] Here, the old Serbian fighting tradition was renewed in the face of national loss and the need to overcome it. Croatian neo-fascist paramilitaries took the form of the Croatian Defense Forces (HOS), wearing black uniforms and sporting insignia reminiscent of the fascist Ustaše of World War II that were responsible for hundreds of thousands of Serb dead, especially within the borders of Croatia and Bosnia-Herzegovina.[37] In this fashion, memories of the ethnic cleansings and mass murders not only of World War II but even of the Balkan Wars and World War I were to be activated.

The widespread sense of national victimization was manifest. This is perhaps the main consequence of the repeated pattern of ephemeral gains. When the Serbs appeared to be finally achieving a substantial degree of national security, even dominance, either alone (before World War I) or within a larger Slavic community (interwar and post-war periods), that security either vanishes (World War I and World War II) leaving large numbers of Serbian dead, or is threatened (since the mid-1960s and the dissolution of Yugoslavia). This was especially true for Serbian communities residing outside of Serbia proper. The largest proportions of murdered Serbs were found in these relatively unprotected areas in Bosnia and Croatia both during World War II and in the more recent troubles. Resort to ethnic cleansing, even genocide, was a consequence of the understanding at least by many Serbs that communal security, let alone ascendancy, could not be achieved without extreme action. The three periods of ephemeral gain are shown in Figure 11.1.

Croatia

Extremism in Croatia, especially during World War II, was a direct consequence of a pattern identified in Figure 1.1. The much anticipated and welcomed (by Croats) Kingdom of Serbs, Croats, and Slovenes (SHS) established in 1918 came after a period of subordination of Croatia to Austria and later Hungary within the Dual Monarchy of Austria-Hungary.

After a period of early Croatian independence, the Hungarians secured the Croatian throne in 1097;[38] the union between Hungary and Croatia would persist despite intermittent Ottoman conquests that ceased in the seventeenth century. Virtually all traces of the Ottomans in Croatia have been eliminated.[39]

---

[36] Carmichael 2002, 42.   [37] Carmichael 2002, 43–4.   [38] Goldstein 1999, 20.
[39] Goldstein 1999, 46.

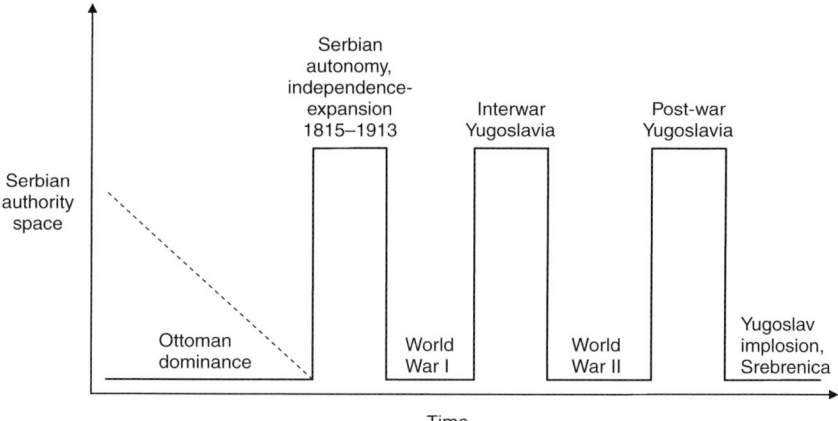

Figure 11.1:   Changes in Serbian authority space over time

Croatian restiveness under the Hungarians (within the earlier Austrian Empire) was intensified by Hungarian plans to reduce the size of the Croatian administrative unit, eliminate its outlet to the sea, and replace Croatian with Latin as the official language.[40] In the immediate turmoil surrounding the revolution of 1848, a Croatian military force led by the new Croatian *Ban* (leader) Josip Jelačić, essentially sided with the Austrian emperor against Hungarian insurgents. Significantly for the future formation of the Kingdom of SHS, the new *Ban*, Jelačić, had his oath of office administered by the Serbian Metropolitan, Josip Rajačić, in the absence of the Catholic Bishop of Zagreb who had fled the turmoil. The Orthodox cleric was in Zagreb as part of a Serbian mission to attempt to seal a Serbo-Croatian alliance against the Hungarians.[41]

Although Russian intervening forces quashed the Hungarians, Austria realized that it had to seek a rapprochement with Hungary. The result was the Austro-Hungarian Empire with Croatia and Slavonia (still separate administrative entities) under Hungarian rule, and Dalmatia and Istria under Austrian governance.[42]

Croatian nationalism, still of a liberal pan-Slav variety, was now led by Bishop Josip Strossmayer of Zagreb. Unsurprisingly, his view of the Hungarians was negative: "The Hungarians are a proud, egotistical and in the highest degree tyrannical race, and my poor nation is persecuted, oppressed and ill treated."[43] Yet Strossmayer was also appalled by agreements between Budapest and Vienna

[40] Goldstein 1999, 67.   [41] Tanner 2001, 88.   [42] Goldstein 1999, 82.
[43] Quoted in Tanner 2001, 95.

that, for example, detached Rijeka and the Međimurje region from Croatia and incorporated them into Hungary. This was a reversal of Empress Maria Theresa's decision of 1776.[44] Strossmayer then began increasingly to woo Slav leaders from around Europe with special attention to the Serbs, for, of course, they had a closely related language. This was the "linguistic nationalism" that was to do so much to lay the foundations of the Kingdom of SHS.

While suspicious of the Serbian government, Strossmayer sought to use ethnic Serbs within Austria-Hungary as allies against the Hungarians. In contrast, his great rival, Ante Starčević, as early as 1852 began attacking Serbs as inferior to Croats. He began agitating for an independent Croatia, including Dalmatia, Slavonia, Istria, and even Slovenia.[45]

The conflict between Strossmayer and Starčević would have an impact on the rise of Croatian extremism. While Strossmayer was lauded even by Tito as an exemplar of inclusive politics, Starčević's group would, in unexpected fashion, yield the beginnings of the fascist Ustaša. Upon his death, followers split into two factions, one of which was founded by Josip Frank, a Jewish convert to Catholicism. He founded the Party of Pure Rights that was implacably hostile to the Serbs and later became opposed to the unified Yugoslav state. The Ustaša claimed the Frankist heritage, for Olga, Frank's daughter, married Slavko Kvaternik, one of the Ustaša leaders.[46]

Right from the start of the Kingdom of SHS, Serbs were dominant. Although the Serbs were only 38.8 percent of the population in 1918, "13 of the 20 ministers constituting the first cabinet (65%) were Serbs, with four Croats, two Slovenes, and one Bosniak completing the lineup."[47] And for all of the interwar period lasting some 268 months, 264 of them witnessed a Serb occupying the post of prime minister. For the remaining 4 months, a Slovene occupied that position.[48]

Early during the interwar period, radical paramilitary organizations were formed that had fascist inspiration, and did not hesitate to use street violence to enforce their views. Among them, the Organization of Yugoslav Nationalists (ORJUNA), was established by a government administration to oppose communists, Croatian separatists, or any other presumed opponents of the state. A more extreme Serbian nationalist version was the Serbian National Youth (SRNAO) with a Croatian counterpart, the Croatian National Youth (HANHO). All of these groups would establish an ever more threatening climate to the interwar period. One of the most violence-prone was an interwar version of the old Chetniks who had committed terrorist acts in the name of Serbian nationalism.

Although this group split into factions in 1924, the leader of one of the groups, "The Union of Serbian Chetniks," was Puniša Račić, who in 1928 slaughtered five deputies of the National Assembly in a shooting spree that included Stjepan Radić and his nephew, Pavle.[49] Radić survived for several months but then

---

[44] Tanner 2001, 99.   [45] Tanner 2001, 104.   [46] Tanner 2001, 106.
[47] Ramet 2006, 45.   [48] Ramet 2006, 38.   [49] Ramet 2006, 59.

succumbed to his wounds. This assassination was a signal event of the inter-war period, for Radić was the single most popular (or at least well known) Croat politician of this period. In his leadership of the Croatian Republican Peasant Party (HRSS), he opposed Serbian hegemonic ambitions within the Kingdom. In the March 1923 election, this party received the second largest percentage of the vote, 21.8 percent. Soon after the election, the HRSS demanded that Serbian political figures recognize the Croats' "complete and unlimited right of national self-determination."[50] This was in keeping with Radić's image as Croatia's advo-cate and protector. Radić's assassination immediately threw the entire country into turmoil. A large demonstration in Zagreb demanded that "the Croatian parliament be convoked for the purpose of demanding separation 'from bloody Serbia.'"[51]

A response to the turmoil was King Aleksandar's 1929 proclamation of a dic-tatorship. The Kingdom of Serbs, Croats, and Slovenes was officially proclaimed now to be the Kingdom of Yugoslavia. New administrative units were estab-lished that were intended to foster a unitary government. Essentially, increased centralization under Belgrade's governance was the order of the day.

Paralleling this governmental policy of unitary rule was the complementar-ity of an attempted Serbian Orthodox hegemony. Ante Ciliga, a major Croatian political figure commented:

> What is least understood is that [in the interwar kingdom] war was being waged against the Catholic Church and in favor of the Serb Orthodox Church at the same time. The Catholic Church accepted loyally the new state, departing from its universalistic idea in the hope of assuring the rap-prochement of the two Christian Churches. The Orthodox Church, unfor-tunately, followed the opposite path, desiring [to use] the new State as a point of departure "to create first a national Catholic Church," that is, sepa-rated from the Roman Pontiff, in order in the second phase to unite it to the Orthodox Church. So it came to the singular fact that as a state, where almost half of the population was Catholic, did not permit the construction of [a] Catholic Cathedral in Belgrade, as was said, "in order not to break the Orthodox appearance of the city."[52]

Sabrina Ramet[53] adds: "Strikingly, the official organ of the Serbian Orthodox Church wrote explicitly that what it wanted to achieve was 'the victory of Serbian Orthodoxy' throughout the country."

Just before the assassination of Radić, Josip Predavec, an official of the Peasants Party, gave this striking account of Croatian perceptions:

> Right up to 1918 we lived under the guidance of native Croatian officials. The four main internal departments of government were housed in Zagreb,

---

[50] Quoted in Ramet 2006, 61.   [51] Ramet 2006, 73.   [52] Quoted in Ramet 2006, 95.
[53] 2006, 95.

and in all internal matters, even under the Habsburgs, the Croat people
were their own masters. Now, if you want to find those government depart-
ments, you must search for them at Belgrade…you will further find that all
the police, the civil service and even the railwaymen on the state system are
Serbs. Every post is reserved for the predominant race, despite the fact that
the Croatian people are by common consent a century ahead of the Serbs
in civilization.[54]

Now after the assassination and immediately upon proclamation of the dictatorship, a Croatian deputy from Zagreb, Ante Pavelić, in January 1929 established an
illegal paramilitary organization, the Ustaša Croatian Liberation Organization
(an Ustaša referring to a person taking part in an *ustanak*, an uprising[55]). Pavelić
already had been arrested as early as 1912 in connection with the attempted
assassination of *Ban* Cuvaj. Pavelić was a follower of the Frankists, among the
most extreme of Croatian nationalists and haters of the Serbs.

Forced to flee Yugoslavia by the authorities, Pavelić and his followers found
refuge in Fascist Italy, where paramilitary training camps were established.
In addition to disturbances within Yugoslavia fomented by the Ustaše, they
cooperated with a Macedonian revolutionary organization to assassinate King
Aleksandar in 1934 in Marseilles. Faced with this scandal, the Italians interned
the Ustaše, ultimately releasing Pavelić in 1936. Slavko Kvaternik continued
to recruit and expand the organization in Zagreb, until, with the invasion of
Yugoslavia in 1941 and the establishment of an "independent" and expanded
Croatia (including much of Bosnia) under Nazi tutelage, the Ustaše emerged at
its head.

Hatred of the Serbs was endemic even among mainline Croat supporters of
Yugoslav unity, such as the former foreign minister, Ante Trumbić. In 1935, in
a conversation with a French writer, he stated: "You are not going to compare,
I hope, the Croats, the Slovenes, the Dalmatians whom centuries of artistic,
moral and intellectual communion with Austria, Italy and Hungary have made
pure occidentals, with these half-civilised Serbs, the Balkan hybrids of Slavs
and Turks. They are barbarians, even their chiefs, whose occidentalism goes
no further than their phraseology and the cut of their clothes. *Between us and
the pan-Serb camarilla which directs Yugoslavia today, it is not a question of
force, for they are by far the strongest, but it is a question of time, a question of
patience, until the day arrives when accounts will be settled.*"[56] The menace here
is palpable.

Now in control of much of Yugoslav territory, including most of Bosnia,
in June 1941, the proclamation of one of the new Ustaša ministers, Milovan
Žanić, cited earlier, came to pass. Serbs (and Jews) would be slaughtered

[54] Quoted in Ramet 2006, 127.   [55] Tanner 2001, 125.
[56] Emphasis added; quoted in Tanner 2001, 127–8.

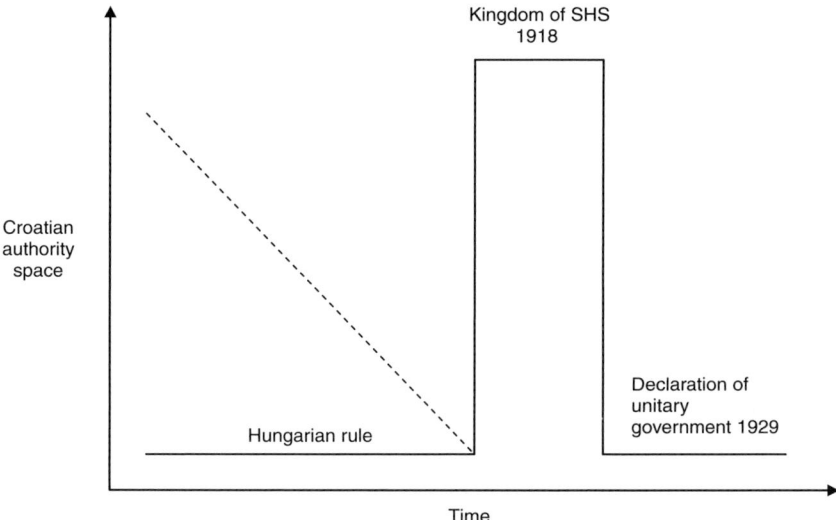

Figure 11.2:   Changes in Croatian authority space over time

en masse for the sake of creating an ethnically homogeneous Croatian state shorn of its Serbian (and Jewish) constituents.[57]

Trumbić's prediction was now to be borne out in draconian form. As we saw earlier, at least 487,000 Serbs and 192,000 Croats were killed. Thus did the pattern of extremist behavior incorporate not only Croats, with their recent historical trajectory conforming to that of Figure 1.1, but also Serbs, with their reinforcing ephemera already detailed in this chapter. This Croatian pattern can be seen in Figure 11.2.

Bulgaria

Bulgaria also experienced loss after World War I, specifically western Thrace to Greece and small border corrections to Serbia, at this time in the Kingdom of SHS.[58] But this loss occurred within the context of an earlier loss (not gain) in the Second Balkan War of June–August 1913, in which Bulgaria lost significant territories in Macedonia gained in the First Balkan War, and southern Dobrudja

---

[57] Tanner 2001, 151.

[58] Jelavich 1983, 123. The loss here is that experienced at the end of World War I not that of the Second Balkan War just prior to World War I. As was seen in Chapter 3, fascism must have an opportunity to take hold after a territorial loss and this was not possible during the enormous societal strains imposed by World War I. Hence, the brief ephemeral gain entailing gain in the First Balkan War but loss in the Second did not have the political space to yield an extremist movement.

(October 1912–May 1913[59]). Interestingly, in his exhaustive survey of fascism worldwide, Stanley Payne appears to have expected that the defeats and territorial losses of Greece (in 1922) and Bulgaria would have led to the mobilization of at least one significant fascist movement, as we saw in Chapter 3.

What Payne did not recognize was the importance of these losses within an earlier context of gains and still earlier subordination in order to yield the surprise, vividness, and emotional intensity that would lead to a call for urgent action in a Bulgarian fascist mass movement, which, of course, did not eventuate.

Thus, we can conclude correctly that the reason for the absence of Bulgarian extremism is to be found in the absence of an ephemeral gain. But this begs the question posed at the outset: why the stark contrast with Serbian extremism? Of course, Serbia experienced several ephemeral gains detailed in this chapter, as the Bulgarians did not, but then why, given other similarities of history, confessional faith, ethnic, and linguistic commonalities (Balkan Slavs using the Cyrillic alphabet) would they diverge so radically?

As the famous historian of the Balkans, L. S. Stavrianos remarked: "there are few areas in the world where geography has influenced history as profoundly as in the Balkan Peninsula."[60] Although quoted by Misha Glenny to suggest the proximity of Bulgaria to the Ottoman Empire, hence its ability to control Bulgaria for a time, this statement by Stavrianos has a different significance here. The proximity of important ethnically mixed areas to both Serbia and Bulgaria was to be crucial for both countries. In effect, the poly-ethnic Bosnia-Herzegovina (hereafter Bosnia) was to be critical for the Serbs, as was ethnically mixed Macedonia for the Bulgarians. And it was the Serbs' ability to incorporate Bosnia into the Yugoslav domains during the interwar period that was to distinguish Bosnia from Macedonia, which did not eventually fall under Bulgarian governance despite strenuous Bulgarian efforts during both the Balkan Wars and World War I.

Bosnia was crucial to Serbia's interests because of its proximity to Serbia and later, during the interwar period and beyond because it occupied the central portion of the Yugoslav state under Serb tutelage. In order to achieve the union of the South Slavs, including Slovenes, Croats, Bosnian Muslims, Montenegrins, Macedonians, and Serbs, Bosnia needed to be incorporated within the Kingdom of SHS at the end of World War I. The valor and horrendous losses of the Serbian army, even in defeat against the combined Austro-Hungarian, Bulgarian and German forces, only to fight victoriously later in World War I was to strongly influence the Allied victors to suggest the formation of the South Slav Kingdom. Effectively, the army had done its job of helping to establish a "greater Serbia" at the end of the Great War.

Bulgaria's relationship with Macedonia was to be entirely different, despite the many casualties suffered by the Bulgarians in the Balkan Wars and in World War I. In the latter, 101,224 were killed, "the highest per capita toll of any country

---

[59] Jelavich 1983, 99, 166; Shaw and Shaw 1977, 297.   [60] Quoted in Glenny 1999, 111.

in the war."[61] But in contrast to Serbian troops who were, among other Allied forces, racing for Skopje, the principal Macedonian city, the Bulgarians in the fall of 1918 were in full retreat from Macedonia. The critical significance of these events for the Central Powers is captured by General Erich von Ludendorff's regret at not having reinforced the Bulgarian front when requested. Accordingly, "August 8th [the start of the Allied offensive in France] was the black day of the German army in the history of this war. This was the worst experience that I had to go through, except for the events that, from September 15th onwards, took place on the Bulgarian front and sealed the fate of the Quadruple Alliance."[62]

Macedonia was lost to the Bulgarians, and this defeat, combined with the inordinate number of battle casualties, led to the overthrow of Tsar Ferdinand. He had joined the Central Powers alliance in the expectation of territorial gain to compensate for the losses at the end of the Second Balkan War in 1913. This second loss in 1918 was to complement the first, 5 years earlier; an ephemeral victory was denied to Bulgaria.

At the same time, Macedonia, now incorporated chiefly within Yugoslavia, was a source of deep instability within Bulgaria. The Internal Macedonian Revolutionary Organization (UMRO), founded in 1905 in order to achieve independence (or at least significant autonomy) for Macedonia, was now located mainly in southwest Bulgaria. An extraordinarily violent organization, with several factions at war with one another, it would in 1934 cooperate with the Ustaše in assassinating King Aleksandar of Yugoslavia.[63] Earlier, UMRO had cooperated with the army in the 1923 overthrow of the Bulgarian government led by Alexander Stamboliiski, whose body was dismembered after the coup.[64]

By the early 1930s, UMRO was implicated in hundreds of shootings, murders, and bombings. The new Tsar Boris I now cooperated with a new government determined to rid Bulgaria of the sources of endemic violence and territorial revisionism. Within several weeks of the start of a campaign against UMRO, it was virtually wiped out, and in the process relinquished control of Petrich in southwestern Bulgaria. The government cooperated with the officially outlawed Military League to effect this outcome.

At the same time, although temporarily cooperating with the Military League, Tsar Boris "was convinced that as long as the army felt able to intervene in Bulgarian politics at will, then the country would be unable to develop any coherent political structures. The Tsar's distrust of the military contrasted with King Aleksandar's belief that the army was the very essence of his power and of Yugoslav identity."[65]

Here we have the two most important outcomes of the successive Bulgarian defeats of 1913 and 1918. First, Macedonia as a source of territorial revisionism was simply removed from the important agenda items of Bulgarian foreign

---

[61] Glenny 1999, 357.   [62] Quoted in Glenny 1999, 354.   [63] Glenny 1999, 435.
[64] Glenny 1999, 398–9.   [65] Glenny 1999, 440.

policy. Defeated twice in its efforts to conquer and annex Macedonia, Bulgarian policy makers would have to be extremely incautious in once again trying to annex it, especially in light of its strongly destabilizing influence in the form of UMRO. Second, in contrast to King Aleksandar's strong reliance on the Serbian-led Yugoslav army, highly successful in the later stages of World War I, Tsar Boris could not place such faith in the Bulgarian army. Without that militarist orientation, territorial revisionism really was not a viable option for Bulgarian policy makers. As revisionism lay at the heart of European fascism, indeed European extremism in general, the likelihood of Bulgaria developing a successful extremist movement was small indeed.

Greece

Greece did not develop a fascist regime despite its 1922 loss of Anatolian territory in the Greco-Turkish War. At most, Greece suffered the dictatorial rule of General Ioannis Metaxas starting in 1936. It was a military dictatorship like that of Franco's Spain. Indeed, during the period of governance by Metaxas, there was never any sign of his abandoning the traditional Greek alliance with Britain in favor of the fascist powers.[66] Moreover, in contrast to the vast majority of European fascist states (even including Mussolini's Italy after 1938), Metaxas did not engage in the anti-Semitism common to virtually all of them. He actually eliminated a low-level anti-Semitism that pervaded the earlier republic. "It was only in 1936 that the Metaxas dictatorship reportedly 'brought a change for the better in the lives of the Jews of Salonika' and offered them the last years of peace and security before the Nazi holocaust, which was to destroy them almost completely."[67]

As a result of the Balkan Wars (1912–13), Greece expanded greatly. The acquisition of most of Macedonia, Crete, southern Epirus, and many Aegean islands led to a 68 percent increase of Greek territory and a population increase from 2.7 to 4.4 million people.[68] But after the Greek invasion of Anatolia in 1919 (advancing more rapidly in 1921–22) and its decisive defeat in the summer of 1922, a massive loss was incurred.[69] A consequence of that defeat was the expulsion of Anatolian Greeks, leading to the resettlement of approximately 1 million of their number in Greece, and the 1923 Treaty of Lausanne that stipulated a population exchange resulting in approximately 350,000 Muslims from Greek territory and 200,000 additional Anatolian and Thracian ethnic Greeks to be resettled respectively in Turkey and Greece.[70]

The "Great Idea" of incorporating portions of western Anatolia with its large ethnic Greek population into greater Greece had driven Greek foreign policy

---

[66] Clogg 1992, 119–20.   [67] Mavrogordatos 1983, 255.
[68] Couloumbis, Petropulos, and Psomiades 1976, 35.   [69] M. Smith 1998, 181.
[70] Hirschon 2003, 14.

for decades.[71] It was now dead. Instead, a large Greek army, defeated and dispirited, returned to Greece along with the 1.2 million (total) ethnic Greek refugees. Approaching the point of embarkation, Smyrna (today's Izmir), the last large Greek-held city in Anatolia, the devastated state of the Greek army is described by a witness: "Then the defeated, dusty, ragged Greek soldiers began to arrive [in Smyrna], looking straight ahead, like men walking in their sleep... In a never-ending stream they poured through the town toward the point on the coast at which the Greek fleet had withdrawn. Silently as ghosts they went, looking neither to the right nor the left. From time to time, some soldier, his strength entirely spent, collapsed on the side-walk or by a door."[72] And later, as the Anatolian-Greek refugees began pouring into Greece, their plight is vividly portrayed by Ambassador Henry Morgenthau:

> In one case, which I myself beheld, seven thousand people were packed into a vessel that would have been crowded with a load of two thousand. In this and many other cases there was neither food to eat nor water to drink, and in numerous instances the ships were buffeted about for several days at sea before their wretched human cargoes could be brought to land. Typhoid and smallpox swept through the ships. Lice infested everyone. Babes were born on board. Men and women went insane. Some leaped overboard to end their miseries in the sea; Those who survived were landed without shelter upon the open beach, loaded with filth, racked by fever, without blankets or even warm clothing, without food and without money. Besides these horrors the refugees endured every form of sorrow – the loss of husbands by wives, loss of wives by husbands, loss of children through death or straying, all manner of illnesses. If ever the Four Horsemen of the Apocalypse rode down upon a nation it was when this appalling host appeared upon the shores of Greece, that was trampled by the flying hoofs of their chargers and scourged by the spectral riders of War, Famine, Pestilence, and Death.[73]

Figure 11.3 illustrates this historical trajectory for Greece that might be expected to yield an extremist government.

Yet, despite this apparent similarity, there are three fundamental distinctions between Greece and our cases of extremism. First, the earlier period of Greek history prior to the successes of the Balkan Wars was *also* replete with territorial increases as the result of a steady expansion, as indicated in Figure 11.3. Greece achieved independence from the Ottoman Empire in 1832, earlier than any other Balkan state, indeed almost a half century earlier. Thus, the period of subordination was shorter and in the more distant past relative to our cases of extremism. Second, the Greek occupation of Anatolian territory was short, less than 3 years and contested militarily by the Turks, especially after the Greek

[71] Clogg 1992, 97–9.   [72] Quoted in Gallant 2001, 143.   [73] Quoted in Gallant 2001, 146.

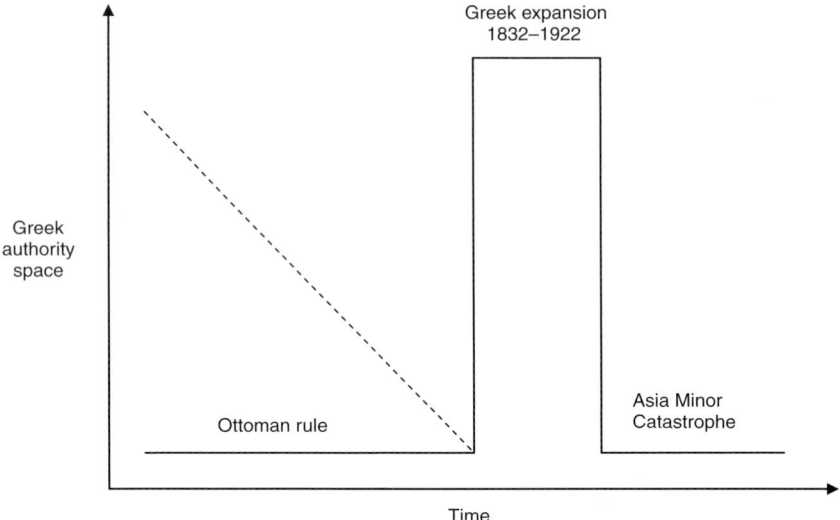

Figure 11.3:   Changes in Greek authority space over time

invasion of the Anatolian heartland. Third, important for the failure to generate the anger necessary for the urgent irredentist impulse was the simultaneous
gain that accrued to Greece. While refugees typically constitute a burden on
both the economy and society, in this instance they actually served a positive
function for the Greek state.

A consequence of the earlier territorial gain at the end of the Balkan Wars was
an insecurely held Macedonia populated by a heavily slavophone population.
Bulgaria and Yugoslavia after World War I could have forcefully laid claim to
these territories. Indeed, there were such disputes, especially with Bulgaria.[74] By
resettling most of the ethnic Greek refugees in Macedonia and western Thrace,
the new territory, heretofore vulnerable to slavophone expansion, could be
rendered safe and secure for the Greek state. In 1912, only 43 percent of the
population inhabiting the Greek state was ethnically Greek; in 1926 it was 89
percent.[75]

Here is the mitigation of loss in the form of significant loss compensation.
Security of the Greek state was enhanced by the addition of these refugees.
While not fulfilling the "Great Idea," nevertheless the ingathering of this
Greek diaspora, homogenizing the population of Greece through the forced
emigration of its Muslim population from western Thrace, and securing the
earlier expanded state boundaries was increasingly recognized as a salutary,

---

[74] Veremis 2003, 61.   [75] Mavrogordatos 1983, 226.

if painful, outcome of the defeat of 1922.[76] Effectively, the loss portion of the ephemeral gain was nullified by the security attained for these earlier only insecurely held conquests. Here we have an illustration of the transformation from the affective to the instrumental. Affective attachment to territory in Anatolia as a fulfillment of the "Great Idea" was transformed into the instrumentality of securing national borders in the face of the potential secession of an ethnically different population. This theme will be further developed in the final chapter of this book.

Yet, there is more. First, the refugees not only populated areas with significant slavophone populations, but also brought with them skills that were badly needed in the underdeveloped Greece of that period. Many had been professionals or entrepreneurs before the population exchange and helped expand the industrial sector. "The Greek economy between 1924 and 1930 witnessed its highest level of industrialization to that time."[77]

Second, a major external threat to Greek territorial integrity emerged not from Turkey as might be expected, but from the Soviet-sponsored Comintern that decided in 1924 that Greek, Bulgarian, and Serbian parts of Macedonia should be incorporated into an autonomous state within a Balkan confederation.[78] Newly acquired Greek territory as the result of the Balkan Wars therefore would have to be surrendered in the event this Comintern policy prevailed in the region. Virtually all of the refugees opposed this policy. "The fear of again becoming an ethnic minority in a united Macedonia with a hostile Slavic majority determined the political choices of the rural settlers for years to come."[79]

Instead of the Greek Communists (KKE), the refugees (especially those settled in rural areas) supported the Venizelists, who not only were opponents of ceding any newly conquered territory, but also were not responsible for the Asia Minor Catastrophe, as the 1922 Greek debacle was called. It was King Constantine, a staunch opponent of the prime minister at the time, Eleftherios Venizelos, who had made the decision to attack inland Anatolia leading to the ultimate defeat.[80] And Venizelos made a political comeback in 1928, capturing 63.5 percent of the popular vote and 90.4 percent of the parliamentary representatives. The vast majority of the refugees (91 percent) supported him.[81] One of his first foreign policy successes was the Treaty of Ankara (October 1930), in which "Greece and Turkey officially recognized the existing territorial boundaries and accepted naval equality in the eastern Mediterranean."[82]

Although many of the refugees were upset that no compensation was to be paid to either side for abandoned property in Greece and Anatolia (far more

---

[76] Kontogiorgi 2003, 65.   [77] Gallant 2001, 148.
[78] Koliopoulos and Veremis 2004, 133.   [79] Koliopoulos and Veremis 2004, 134.
[80] Koliopoulos and Veremis 2004, 133.   [81] Gallant 2001, 151–2.
[82] Gallant 2001, 153.

extensive for Anatolian Greeks than for Thracian Turks), nevertheless the Treaty not only eliminated the possibility of a Turkish military threat, never again to be manifested against the Greek mainland, but also precluded the possibility of a renewed subordination to Turkey. Given the centuries-long political dominance of Greece by the Ottoman Empire and the communal inferiority in political rights of Christians, including of course Anatolian Greeks, to the Muslim Turks, this treaty was a critically important event, especially to those who had most recently experienced that political inferiority in Anatolia. Only in Cyprus would military engagements involving the Turks take place after 1955, but not directly involving mainland Greeks.

Of course, the Megali Idea of incorporating much of Anatolia into an expanded Greece was dead. As early as August 17, 1922, on the eve of the final Turkish offensive, Georgios Vlachos, a major newspaper editor, proclaimed: "The blood of Greece does not flow in her veins to be spilled in farthest Asia Minor. It flows to warm Greece and move her into action, for herself, and for the Greece of tomorrow. The German iron chancellor once said: 'Not one Pomeranian for the East.' And Greece must no longer give her Pomeranians for the East which is beyond her designs. Not one evzone [member of elite shock units] for new adventures."[83]

Two substitutes were found for the Megali Idea. The first was cultural, which eventuated in an important political consequence – an emphasis on Hellenism within a larger European context. As early as 1929, the influential Greek writer George Theotokas wrote of the individual characteristics of European countries as comprising a "European garden." But Greece must throw "all its byzantine and Balkan traditions into the sea as it searches for a new way."[84] In advocating for a Hellenism beyond Greek borders, he wrote, "Hellenism is something more than a geographical region and a sum of mores and customs. Hellenism is primarily a way of 'thinking and feeling,' a certain stance toward the world and life, an attitude, a spirit, indeed a spirit that is universal, born to conceive of ideas and forms higher than any borders."[85]

In his 1932 *Forward with our Social Problems*, Theotokas called for a European Economic Assembly that recognized the independence of nations and classes.[86] Theotokas opposed communism as a panacea for Greece's ills, contrasting it with a Europeanized Hellenism: "Greece will claim its European identity not by a geographical claim, but by a cultural one based on its contribution to European identity over two thousand years."[87]

And in 1940 Theotokas wrote, "our admission into Europe…will bring about in Greece new sources of activity and creative energy, which exist all around us but which are today invisible, because they have never been given the chance,

---

[83] Quoted in Mavrogordatos 1983, 200.   [84] Calotychos 2003, 163.
[85] Quoted in Calotychos 2003, 161.   [86] Calotychos 2003, 164.
[87] Calotychos 2003, 165.

the context, the horizon that they need to express themselves – multifarious sources of life, be they economic, social, cultural… For the young who feel the lack of a contemporary and fruitful ideal which might inspire and activate their creative powers, *this could very well be a new Megali Idea.*"[88]

Of course, Greece's entry into the European Community in 1981 and its subsequent acceptance into the EU's Economic and Monetary Union (EMU or Eurozone) in 2002 were a consequence, in part, of this European orientation beginning in the late 1920s.

The second substitute was, like the Megali Idea, still a territorial or boundary-related concern, but one much more limited in scope. This was a concern with the Aegean and its largest island, Cyprus, not under Greek authority. Odysseas Elytis, a Greek from one of the easternmost Aegean islands and a Nobel Prize winner for literature in 1979 was to romanticize the Aegean in his poetry beginning in the 1950s. It was this eastern orientation that was to find political expression in the writings of George Seferis, a poet and Greek diplomat. Born in Asia Minor, he shared the trauma of the Anatolian Greeks. As the director of the Second Political Bureau of the Ministry of Foreign Affairs (1956–57) and as Greek ambassador to Great Britain in 1957–62, he was "unswerving in his belief that the Hellenicity of Cyprus could be safeguarded only by its incorporation into the Greek state."[89]

Enosis, or union of Cyprus with Greece, became a critical Greek political issue that, with the decision to grant Cypriot independence by Great Britain in 1960, ultimately led to the 1974 Turkish invasion of Cyprus and partition of the island. However, because of the location of Cyprus as an eastern island far removed from the Greek mainland and geographically much closer to Turkey, there was little opportunity to militarily challenge this invasion. The condition of Cyprus has remained a critical issue to this day, in part preventing Turkish accession to the EU, but in no way generating the sort of Greek response that led to the invasion of 1919–22 and the Asia Minor Catastrophe. Greece gravitated towards the European center, increasingly requiring democracy as a *sine qua non* of entry into European economic and political organizations, which precluded any political extremist response to Turkish military activity.

Thus, the cultural and geopolitical reinforced each other. Substituting an overtly European cultural orientation for the Asia Minor-centered Megali Idea was to lead ultimately to the full Europeanization of Greece within the EU. At the same time, the differences between Greece and Turkey over Cyprus have been contained both by enormous tactical difficulties entailed in a Greek military response, and by the need to maintain cordial relations within Europe that would be vitiated by any Greek military adventurism. Indeed, the path to entry into the EC was smoothed considerably by the 1974 removal of the Greek

---

[88] Emphasis in original; quoted in Calotychos 2003, 165–6.
[89] Calotychos 2003, 185.

military junta that had ruled since 1967, with *enosis* a major goal of the junta. Of course, it was precisely that policy, along with Greek Cypriot agitation and repression of the island's 20 percent Turkish population, that led to the 1974 invasion.

But of all of the consequences of the Asia Minor Catastrophe and the resulting population exchanges, increased security of the Greek state within its expanded 1913 borders was to be paramount. This vastly increased security as a form of loss compensation precluded the rise of native Greek fascism. In turn, the European orientation and ultimately democratization of Greece was to eventuate in its full incorporation into the European Union, whatever the fiscal difficulties that Greece, along with Ireland, Spain, Portugal, and Italy recently experienced.

12

The Rampaging Military

Thus far, I have examined the incidence of violent extremism stemming from organized political movements of the extreme left and right, secular and sacred, and forms of extreme nationalism. Yet there are types of sociopolitical organization that can yield mass murder on a scale equaling, even surpassing many of the movements already considered. Without an extremist ideology or even a political program that they can call uniquely their own, military organizations have killed large numbers of innocent civilians, usually in time of interstate or civil war (sometimes both taking place simultaneously).

Three cases in point are Japan, Pakistan, and Indonesia. In his analyses of mass killing, the former two are treated by Rudolph Rummel[1] in separate chapters, thereby indicating their importance. Japan and Pakistan developed different political cultures and traditions; their religious heritages also differ sharply. Whereas the Japanese religious tradition most relevant to politics, including a form of emperor worship – Shintoism – was essentially reinvented after the Meiji Restoration of the late nineteenth century, political Islam in Pakistan emerged from a much older tradition and one that was only obliquely relevant to the 1971 massacres in East Pakistan, today Bangladesh. More than anything else, religion provided a vehicle for emphasizing ethnic difference that justified the killing of one group of Muslims by another, as well as Hindu citizens of East Pakistan. Both the massacres initiated by the Japanese and Pakistani militaries will be found to conform to the model put forward in Chapter 1. In Indonesia, we find another illustration of transnational effects mentioned in Chapter 3, as well as a clash of ideologies between Islam and the relentlessly secular communists. This case also conforms to the model of the ephemeral gain. Later, we shall see that the shadow of the present is an additional explanation appropriate for understanding the rampaging military in three other cases, briefly considered.

Japan

Can wartime Japan be properly included among the extremist states? We are now exploring the power of the theory at the margins. If it applies even in this

---

[1] 1997.

seemingly doubtful case, then we can have additional confidence in the theory's validity.

Japanese fascism?

There has been much debate about the inclusion of Japan among the *fascist* states, fascism being understood by many[2] as principally a European phenomenon that experienced its florescence during the interwar period. Japan, despite its alliance with Fascist Italy and Nazi Germany would therefore likely be excluded. And that exclusion is supportable on empirical grounds beyond those of geographic propinquity. The absence of a single paramount mass mobilization party with paramilitaristic tendencies is one such characteristic.[3] Further, the domestic Japanese system was never completely dominated by the dictator, General Hideki Tōjō. According to Gerhard Weinberg,[4] "While the army subsidized an approved list of candidates [for] election, it was still possible for many others to run and for some of those not approved to win seats in the Diet. There were pressures, restrictions, censorship, and police persecutions, but the system was still characterized by roles for old political and economic elites, an occasionally stubborn bureaucracy, and a more than nominal adherence to prior forms and procedures." A rampant militarism appears to be the most salient characteristic of the Japanese government during the 1930s and 1940s.

Yet there are indicators of Japanese fascism at that time. Despite Mann's exclusion of Japan from the fascist category, he does acknowledge that the Japanese imperial government "contained fascist elements."[5] Further, although there were no politically ascendant fascist movements in Japan during this period, there existed right-wing groups such as Kingoro Hashimoto's Great Japan Youth Party and Seigo Nakano's Eastern Way Society.[6] Neither party was paramount in the sense of attaining substantial electoral support; additionally the more popular Eastern Way Society repudiated political violence and accepted the monarchy. In this, it was substantially different from the European fascists. At most, these parties could be considered to be proto-fascist.[7]

But Richard Samuels[8] has compared Japan and Italy during the 1930s and 1940s, and explicitly places Japan under the fascist rubric. His arguments are many, but in the main boil down to the adoption of corporatism in both countries. On this dimension, there is a strong similarity between Italian Fascism and Japanese economic policy. According to Stanley Payne,[9] Nazi Germany's corporatism also was imitated by the Japanese. Whether or not this similarity alone justifies using the term fascism to apply to Japan, especially in light of the similar economic policies followed in Austria, Spain, and Portugal that to varying extents were non-fascist, is an open question.

---

[2] E.g., Paxton 2004.   [3] Mann 2004, 24.   [4] 2005, 62.   [5] Mann 2004, 46.
[6] Payne 1995, 333.   [7] Payne 1995, 331.   [8] 2003.   [9] 1995, 335.

Abandoning the concept of fascism and turning to the more inclusive concept of political extremism, incorporated in the definition is the willingness to engage in mass murder as a principal criterion. Now, matters become considerably less opaque. Here we see a generalized pattern of mass murder undertaken throughout the theater of Japanese military operations. Rummel's compilation of democide statistics (the killing of unarmed and helpless men, women, or children[10]) yielded a total of 5,964,000 deaths as a relatively conservative estimate of the number of innocents killed by the Japanese military between 1937 and 1945. Beginning in 1937, the war in China alone accounted for 3,949,000 of the total number of deaths, while during World War II, prisoners of war, internees, foreign laborers, and civilians in occupied areas accounted for another 2,015,000 deaths.[11] Although not quite in the same category as Nazi Germany (20,945,000 total[12]), accompanied by the horrific legacy of gas chambers and crematoria, nevertheless the Japanese record is not significantly less appalling. Certainly when compared with Fascist Italy's killing of 224,000 between 1922 and 1943, Rummel's[13] (somewhat less than Ben-Ghiat's numbers cited earlier) estimate suggests that Japan's record is sanguinary in the extreme.

The instrument of the killing was the army or, as Rummel titles his chapter in *Statistics of Democide*, "Japan's Savage Military."[14] Why was the army – the only Japanese military component to come into contact with large numbers of civilians or prisoners of war – determined to engage in this savage behavior? Despite differences with other extremist states, namely the absence of a dominant mass party or totalitarian rule, the Japanese military behaved as extremists typically do when confronted with political or military opposition. They killed massively. In this respect, the etiology of Japanese extremist behavior does not differ substantially from our European cases. Here, as in the remaining cases, the incidence of loss, but differentially experienced at least initially by the Japanese army and navy, will prove to be crucial.

Subordination

An early period of subordination to Western commercial interests characterized Japanese foreign relations after Admiral Perry's "opening of Japan" in 1853–54. Largely closed to the West by the Tokugawa Shogunate since the beginning of the seventeenth century, matters would change radically in the 1850s. Not only the United States, but Britain, France, Russia, and the Netherlands were interested in trade with Japan. And China played a pivotal role in this scenario, as it would much later in the 1920s and 1930s. Indeed, it was the example of China's defeat in the Opium Wars of 1839–42 with Britain and again in 1856–60 (this time with French participation against China) that signaled the possible fate of

---

[10] Rummel 1997, vi.   [11] Rummel 1997, 46.   [12] Rummel 1997, 352.
[13] 1997, 353.   [14] 1997, 32.

Japan. The net result of the two wars was the opening of many ports to Western interests, rights of foreigners to travel freely in China, and the legalization of the opium trade. Most important, at least to the Japanese, was the size of the naval squadrons sent to guard the merchant vessels in the treaty ports. As early as 1854, and Perry's second entry into Edo (Tokyo) Bay with eight ships instead of the four appearing the previous year, the Japanese recognized their weakness in the face of a modern Western naval squadron. Although Perry did gain concessions from the Japanese, the Russians under E. V. Putiatin actually obtained territorial gain in the division of the Kuril Islands between Russia and Japan.[15]

In 1856, American Consul Townsend Harris arrived to negotiate a proper commercial treaty that would open additional ports to US trade. Matters dragged along without conclusion until the Treaty of Tientsin was signed with China in 1858 temporarily ending the Second Opium War, thereby freeing British and French forces to attack Japan, if they so desired. On July 29, Townsend Harris had his treaty accepted, including principles of extra-territoriality and the opening of five ports to the US, in addition to the two existing treaty ports. Foreigners were to be admitted to Edo and Osaka.[16] Britain, France, Russia, and the Netherlands soon made similar agreements with the Japanese authorities. According to W. G. Beasley:[17] "Thus despite the Bakufu's [Japanese administrators] diplomatic rearguard action and the strong criticism coming from many influential Japanese, Japan had at last been brought – in a *subordinate condition* – into the world of what scholars now call Free Trade Imperialism."

Victory and loss

The events of 1858 set in motion a process leading to the Meiji Restoration of 1868 that in turn led to the reform and modernization of much of Japan. Japanese society and its military component now experienced considerable success. From the status of serving as a near vassal of Western commerce during the Tokugawa Shogunate, around the turn of the twentieth century, victories over China in 1895 and especially Russia in 1904–05 established both the Japanese army and navy as pre-eminent military institutions. The defeat of a major European power both on land (Port Arthur) and at sea (Tsushima) was stunning. Prior to the massive naval battles in the Pacific during World War II, the annihilation of the Russian fleet in the Straits of Tsushima was held to be the classic naval victory of the modern period. Yet despite this stellar accomplishment and Japan's creditable performance during World War I, especially its anti-Bolshevik activities in Siberia at the war's end that exceeded those of any other Allied power, the authority space craved by the Japanese army, and in its view warranted by Japanese military successes, was to be denied.

---

[15] Beasley 2000, 29.   [16] Beasley 2000, 31.   [17] Emphasis added; Beasley 2000, 34.

The Washington Naval Conference of 1922 was the first of the setbacks that would augment Japanese nationalism within the military. Although Japanese naval authorities "viewed the Washington Conference with some satisfaction"[18] because of its prevention of the onset of a costly and potentially dangerous (to Japanese society) naval arms race, the army had a different view. The increase of Chinese nationalism threatening Japan's privileged position in Manchuria, and the emergence of the aggressively communist Soviet Union after the war were both viewed with alarm by army leaders. But even more important was the relinquishing of territory by Japan required at the Washington Conference. In addition to Article I of the Treaty requiring all signatories to respect the sovereignty and independence of China, as well as maintaining equality of access to commerce, Japan also was required to restore the earlier German-leased territory in Shandong to China, withdraw from North Sakhalin and Eastern Siberia, and permit an international consortium to cooperate in the development of Manchuria and Inner Mongolia.[19] Kazunari Ugaki, soon to be army minister in 1924–27 and again in 1929–31, remarked shortly after the Washington conference:

> The removal of troops from Shandong, the evacuation of Hankou, and now the withdrawal from Siberia have become realities. Those independent actions of the empire have all come to nothing. Nay, as in the case of our stationing troops in Shandong, which was our right by treaty, there is the tendency to relinquish the great proportion of our special rights and withdraw. *Thus we further contract our noticeably diminished national prestige and national rights.* The realization, flashing before our eyes, that the Japanese government is abandoning its responsibilities in China is truly unbearable.[20]

Soon after the Washington conference, the Soviet Union remained the number one enemy, "But now, for the first time in Japan's history, both chiefs of staff named the United States as the second main enemy after the Soviet Union."[21] But however difficult the consequences of the Washington Conference were for the Japanese military, these would soon pale before those of the London Naval Conference of 1930. At the time of its signing, the Washington Treaty at least maintained the existing ratio of capital ships among the major naval powers. Effectively, the Treaty guarded Japan's naval hegemony in the Western Pacific in exchange for a commitment to honor the integrity of China. Japanese naval and army leaders therefore diverged in their reception of the Treaty. However, the London Naval Treaty of 1930 united army and navy leaders in their opposition to the Treaty system, for it utterly transformed naval ratios in one important area – the construction of heavy cruisers deemed to be essential for Japanese security in the Western Pacific.

[18] Crowley 1966, 31.   [19] Crowley 1966, 29.
[20] Emphasis added; quoted in Humphreys 1995, 130.   [21] Bix 2000, 151.

Following World War I, while the United States did not initiate much naval construction, Japan did so in the category of heavy cruisers, most likely to be effective in the Western Pacific, close to the Japanese homeland. The United States sought to reverse the temporary supremacy of the Japanese in this naval category.

At the London Naval Conference, an Anglo-American condominium forced the Japanese to accept a ratio of 10 to 6 in heavy cruisers (the same ratio as specified for capital ships in the Washington Treaty), a ratio that was below the Japanese minimum requirement of 10 to 7. Without the British support that Japanese leaders could formerly count on in international negotiations, they felt obliged to accept these terms in lieu of a naval arms race and consequent international instability.[22] Anti-war sentiment was rife in the civilian-led Japanese government of that era. However, "most officers believed that the London Treaty had endangered the security of the empire."[23]

According to Maruyama Masao, after centuries of isolation, "an awareness of equality in international affairs was totally absent. The advocates of expulsion [of the barbarians] viewed international relations from positions within the national hierarchy based on the supremacy of superiors over inferiors. Consequently, when the premises of the national hierarchy were transferred horizontally into the international sphere, international problems were reduced to a single alternative: *conquer or be conquered.*"[24] From this perspective, high-level military officers suggested that the 1930 London Treaty essentially amounted, at the very least, to a potential loss. Indeed, that term was used by fleet Admiral Tōgō, as quoted by Admiral Kanji Katō, chief of the naval general staff:

> Once we conclude the treaty, it will create an irreparable loss, just as the acceptance of the 60 percent ratio at the Washington Conference did. From the beginning we made a concession and offered 70 percent in the heavy cruiser [class], but the United States has not made the slightest concession. This being the case, there is no way but to break up the conference and come home. Even if we fail to obtain a treaty, it would not lead to great naval expansion, so there is no financial worry. Originally I wondered whether 70 percent was enough, but I agreed to it because I was assured…that the 70 percent was the absolute minimum below which we would not go. Since we have taken the position that our national defense cannot be assured with anything less, there is no use haggling over one or two percent. If they don't accept our demand, there is no way but to resolutely withdraw from the conference.[25]

In other words, the serious loss potential embodied in the Washington and London Treaties required radically new thinking about the role of the navy in the emerging scenario of "conquer or be conquered." Surprise attack by the

---

[22] Crowley 1966, 76–81.   [23] Crowley 1966, 74.
[24] Emphasis added; quoted in Anderson 2006, 97.   [25] Quoted in Asada 2006, 143.

navy without a declaration of war was to be the modus operandi as meticu-
lously developed by Isoroku Yamamoto and Minoru Genda at Pearl Harbor, just
as army officers also would resort to radically new methods, especially in their
treatment of civilians and prisoners of war. Formerly in World War I, Japanese
officers were scrupulous in their treatment of non-combatants.

And in November 1930, the Japanese prime minister, Yūkō Hamaguchi,
ultimately responsible for signing the treaty, was fatally shot by an extreme
nationalist.[26] According to the assassin, Hamaguchi had violated "the right of
supreme command" in negotiating the treaty.[27] This was to be the first of many
violent attacks on the legally appointed political leaders that would characterize
1930s Japan.

Even before the 1930 Naval Treaty, dissident and extremist elements were taking root in the army. At least two major factions eventually developed. The first,
made up largely of senior officers dissatisfied with the accomodationist foreign
policy of Baron Kijūrō Shidehara and party politics of the Japanese government,
formed the Issekikai on May 19, 1929. Itself comprising two prior dissident
organizations, this combined unit was dedicated to finding a solution to the so-
called Manmō (Manchuria-Inner Mongolia) problem. Apprehension over the
northward march of the Chinese Nationalist Guomindang led by Chiang Kai-
shek generated sentiments for unity among the dissidents to confront the ruling
Nationalist Party. According to Leonard Humphreys:[28]

> The ultimate power and influence of the men of the Issekikai must not be
> underestimated. They provided Japan with 1 prime minister (Tōjō Hideki),
> 2 ministers of state (Obata Toshishirō and Suzuki Teiichi), 6 (full) generals
> (Tōjō, Itagaki Seishirō, Doihara Kenji, Okamura Yasuji, Okabe Naosaburō,
> and Yamashita Tomoyuki), 30 lieutenant generals (including Nagata
> Tetsuzan, who was appointed posthumously), 8 area army commanding
> generals, and 14 army commanding generals. Five (Tōjō, Itagaki, Okada
> Tasuku, Mutō Akira, and Yamashita) died as war criminals, and 4 others
> were imprisoned for war crimes. Four remained war prisoners of the
> Russians or Chinese until they died.

Hence, China, especially the Manchuria-Inner Mongolia problem, was the
source of much of the extremist behavior of the Japanese army, as Rummel's
statistics of mass murder indicate.

Almost immediately after the London Naval Treaty had been negotiated
(but not yet formally approved on October 2), on September 30, the Sakurakai
(Cherry Society) was formed by a Lieutenant Colonel Kingorō Hashimoto,
who was influenced by the Turkish military reforms, after having served in that
country. Although composed of captains, majors, and lieutenant colonels in the
army, senior officers tacitly, and in some cases actively, supported the Sakurakai.

[26] Shillony 1973, 8.   [27] Quoted in Crowley 1966, 78.   [28] 1995, 112.

A parallel naval group was also formed called Seiyōkai.[29] A coup was planned for March 1931, but was called off at the last moment because the war minister, General Ugaki, who would have been installed as the new Japanese leader after the coup, ultimately declined to participate.

In addition to the organization of the Sakurakai in the fall of 1930, and the aborted coup of March 1931, dissidence among the military after the London Naval Treaty was indicated by political and strategic plans developed by the war ministry. As early as 1927, Japanese troops were dispatched to Shandong, ostensibly to protect "Japanese lives and property" (approximately 17,000 Japanese people lived in this area), but with the rather obvious purpose of preventing the Guomindang army of Chiang Kai-shek from penetrating into Manchuria. Additionally, the Soviet five-year plan of economic development was perceived to be a major threat. "By 1931, the operations division was convinced of the historical inevitability of a Soviet-Japanese conflict, and consequently these officers favored a program of direct military action in Manchuria as essential to Japanese interests in the area."[30]

In the war ministry, the concepts of "total war," "general mobilization," and "internal army reorganization" were put forward as methods of transforming Japan into a world power. Because of the poverty of natural resources on the Japanese islands, access to the resources of Manchuria was seen to be essential for the industrial development required to achieve the historic goal of first-class military capability.[31] The staff of the Japanese Guangdong Army (in South Manchuria since 1919) was especially active in drawing up plans for the seizure of all of Manchuria. By late August 1931, operational plans were drawn up by Colonels Seishiro Itagaki and Kanji Ishiwara to effect this purpose. In addition to Itagaki, two more soon-to-be war criminals, then Colonels Hideki Tōjō and Akira Mutō were assistants to the chief of the operations division in Tokyo. When called to Tokyo as part of a normal rotation, Ishiwara informed the staff of the operations division of the elaborate plans for the seizure of Manchuria. He received a tacit endorsement.[32]

The murder of a Captain Nakamura by elements of Marshal Chang Hsüeh-liang's army was a precipitant of the seizure of Manchuria. A peaceful resolution of the Nakamura incident was envisioned by the Japanese government. But on his own authority, Itagaki initiated an attack on barracks of the Chinese army, and manipulations by Ishiwara and others led to the government's acquiescence in the beginning of the conquest of Manchuria.[33] Friction between the Japanese and Chinese armies on the border of what was now called Manchukuo continued, leading to the Japanese invasion of China in 1937 and the Greater East Asia War that was to blend into World War II. Humphreys[34] concludes that, "The

---

[29] Shillony 1973, 26.   [30] Crowley 1966, 111.   [31] Crowley 1966, 112.
[32] Crowley 1966, 117.   [33] Crowley 1966, 119–21.   [34] 1995, 180–1.

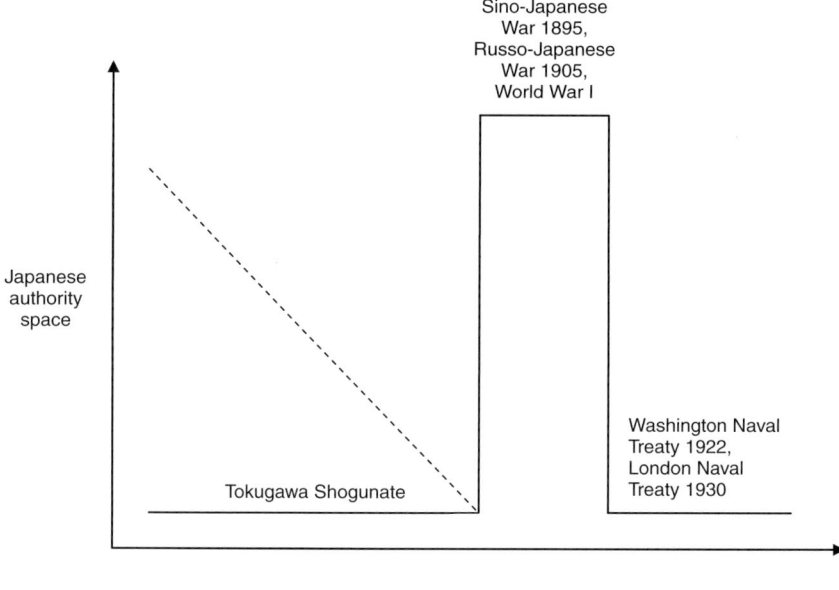

Figure 12.1:   Changes in Japanese authority space over time

Japanese army of the 1920's presents a strange and contradictory picture – a mixture of pride, arrogance, and hubris on the one hand, and the haunting fear of impending calamity on the other... The army's problem was to re-create the lost consensus of the Russo-Japanese War."

If we understand that these extremely discordant elements of "arrogance" and "haunting fear" arise from earlier gains (Sino-Japanese and Russo-Japanese Wars) contrasted with later losses (Washington and London Naval Treaties), and the possibility of future losses and reversion to a still earlier period of sub-ordination prior to the Meiji Restoration, then we can specify the origins of the "strange and contradictory picture" identified by Humphreys. Figure 12.1 presents this ephemeral gain.

Another abortive coup, that of the Young Officers Movement on February 26, 1936 had the explicit purpose of initiating a Shōwa (name of Emperor Hirohito's reign) Restoration that "was meant to restore a moral order in which all parts of society were believed to be members of one family, with the Emperor as its head."[35] The earlier highly successful Meiji Restoration was the model for this new restoration. This latest political intervention was designed to prevent the "calamity" that many felt was fast approaching. As early as May

---

[35] Shillony 1973, 61.

1930, American Ambassador William Castle suggested the contours of these potential future losses:

> Opinion is virtually unanimous among Japanese that the only possibility of war occurring between the United States and Japan lies in the present state of China… There is no doubt whatever that if China should attempt to wrest the South Manchurian Railway from Japan, Japanese opinion would force the government to resist the attempt by all means at its command. In such an event, it is likely the Chinese would appeal for sympathy to the United States. So long as the Treaty to Outlaw War has not been seriously tested and found to be capable of restraining a third nation from participating in a quarrel of this nature, the Japanese feel no assurance that the United States would not be obliged by an inflamed American public to take the part of China.[36]

Note the desire for the restoration of lost worlds as a similarity between the Japanese case and the remaining instances of extremism. A Shōwa Restoration would presumably lead Japan back to an earlier "state of grace" at the time of the Meiji Restoration. More specifically, the harking back to the Japanese unity and martial spirit evidenced during the Russo-Japanese War is a direct parallel to the Nazi desire for a return to the unity of the battlefront experienced by so many German soldiers during World War I. Humiliation at the treatment of Japan in 1922 and 1930 was to be measured against this earlier time of glory.

A major difference between the German and Japanese cases is found in the source of the desire for restoration. While in Germany such sympathies were found throughout elements of German society that gave the Nazis pluralities at the polls in 1932, it was the Japanese military that principally harbored these sentiments. Thus, while in Germany brutality toward civilians could be found among the ordinary police, as in "Reserve Police Battalion 101" murdering Jews in the East,[37] or even among the German civilians who killed Jews on the death marches at the end of the war,[38] it was the Japanese military that was responsible for almost the entirety of civilian and prisoner of war deaths at Japanese hands.

Finally, although not widely known, the Japanese case is similar to others in the prevalence of the concept of "holy war." Japanese ideologues of this period emphasized the sacred nature of imperial Japanese rule. Accordingly:

> The emperor was a living god, the descendant of Amaterasu Ōmikami; Japan was the incarnation of morality and justice; by definition its wars were just and it could never commit aggression. Hence its effort to establish the "imperial way" (kōdō) in China and bring people there under the emperor's benevolent occupation by means of "compassionate killing" – killing off the few troublemakers so that the many might live – was a blessing upon the occupied people, and by no means colonial expansion. Those

---

[36] Quoted in Crowley 1966, 81.   [37] Browning 1992.   [38] Goldhagen 1996.

who resisted, naturally, had to be brought to their senses. But formally there was no "war," only an "incident." Consequently, from early on in the war the Japanese government regularly referred to the "China Incident" as its "sacred struggle" or "holy war" (*seisen*).[39]

Pakistan

Between 1 million and 3 million non-combatants died at the hands of the Pakistani military during the civil war and Indo-Pakistani war of 1971. As an approximation, Rummel[40] arrives at a figure of 1.5 million. Rummel[41] also tells us that from extant sources it is difficult to provide separate estimates of Hindus and Muslims killed by the Pakistani military (virtually all from West Pakistan). But from the number of refugees fleeing East Pakistan to Hindu-majority India – in excess of 10 million[42] – and statistics on the percentage of Hindus in East Pakistan at that time (nearly 20 percent according to Mohammed Ayub[43]), then certainly a significant proportion of those who were killed were Hindu, although probably not a majority.

From independence through 1971, India and Pakistan engaged in three wars with each other. Additionally, in 1962, India and China waged a border war, the outcome of which will be important in the following analysis.

The first Indo-Pakistani war

The first of the Indo-Pakistani wars was over Kashmir, as was the second. In 1947, at the time of partition, Kashmir had a Hindu ruler, but a predominantly Muslim population. The monarch of Jammu and Kashmir, Maharaja Hari Singh refused to join either newly sovereign state, despite pressures emanating from both. But a tribal rebellion against the maharaja's governance forced him to choose India as a source of military aid. Interestingly, it was not only the maharaja who signed the Instrument of Accession, but also Sheikh Mohammed Abdullah, leader of the largest popular secular political organization. Both signatures were required by Jawaharlal Nehru, the newly installed Indian prime minister, before military aid would be forthcoming. Indian troops were airlifted into Kashmir and stopped the tribal incursions, but only after they had severed about one-third of the princely state from the remainder.[44]

What is more important for our story is the introduction first of Pakistani troops disguised as local tribesmen, followed by the appearance in Kashmir of

---

[39] Bix 2000, 326.
[40] 1997, 160. But Sarmila Bose 2010 arrives at a much lower number, somewhere in the six-figure range.
[41] 1997, 153.   [42] Rummel 1997, 162.   [43] 2005, 177.
[44] Ganguly and Hagerty 2005, 23.

the regular Pakistani army. These units would be effective enough to threaten the links between important Indian cities such as Amritsar in the Indian state of Punjab, and Jammu, Pathankot, and Poonch in the state of Jammu and Kashmir. To counter this strategic advantage, India would have to expand the conflict, but the necessary resources simply were not available. India referred the dispute to the United Nations, thereby concluding the conflict. Approximately two-thirds of Jammu and Kashmir remained in Indian hands.[45] The ceasefire became effective on January 1, 1949, and came in the midst of Pakistani advances. According to Major General Fazal Muqeen Khan:

> By accepting the cease-fire, Pakistan lost a golden chance to liberate more territory in Kashmir, while the morale of the Indian troops was low. [The] Indian Army was scattered in the valley and the mountains were still covered with snow. India had only two reserve Armored Brigades and one Infantry Brigade left to reinforce their troops. Even if Indian [sic] wanted to mobile [sic] them (from India), Pakistan could have the whole Kashmir. High-ranking Pakistan military officers as well as a senior British officer… agree[d] that the plan was workable, but no one listened to them.[46]

And Hafeez Muhammad Saeed, founder of one of the leading organizations fighting the Indian occupation of Kashmir, declared that, "The acceptance of the cease fire in 1948 was a grave mistake. If that would not have happened, the Kashmir problem would have [been] solved [a] long time ago."[47]

Although the Correlates of War Project lists the outcome of this war as a tie, there was a high level of morale among the Pakistani troops, for not only had they demonstrated considerable accomplishments on the battlefield, but had done so against a much larger Indian army with greater resources at its disposal. The division of the old British Indian army between the new states of India and Pakistan had led the lion's share to be allocated to India (70 percent of the army, and 83 percent of the revenue), the more populous of the two entities.[48] Stephen Cohen[49] observes, "the army acquitted itself well and quickly assumed its place as one of Pakistan's central institutions."

"Victory into defeat": the second Indo-Pakistani war

This self-congratulatory mood would be carried over into the second Indo-Pakistani war of 1965, not only as a consequence of the outcome of the first war, but also as a result of the poor performance of Indian troops versus Chinese counterparts in their border war of 1962. Caught by surprise by the Chinese after Indian troops had gradually begun infiltrating disputed territory in the Himalayas, the "war proved to be a complete military debacle for India."[50]

---

[45] Ganguly and Hagerty 2005, 25–6.   [46] Quoted in Ayub 2005, 73.
[47] Quoted in Ayub 2005, 73.   [48] Haqqani 2005, 26.   [49] 2004, 47.
[50] Ganguly and Hagerty 2005, 27.

Following this defeat, India sought to modernize and expand all of its armed forces. The scale of this expansion (a million men under arms and a forty-five squadron modern air force), although directed principally at China, nevertheless greatly alarmed the Pakistanis.[51] Importantly, the scale of this military buildup implied that the status of Kashmir as principally an Indian state would be rendered permanent by this expanded force capability.[52] A window of opportunity was closing, during which the Pakistanis might have their last chance at gaining control of all of Kashmir. This opportunity was enhanced by the 1964 death of Nehru, India's long-standing prime minister. Lacking firm leadership, India might be more easily coerced into relinquishing control of Kashmir.[53] Indeed, there is a long history of territorial wars occurring precisely during interregnum periods.[54]

Thus, the sense of accomplishment by Pakistan's military leaders stemming from the first Indo-Pakistani war over Kashmir, the poor performance of the Indian military in the Sino-Indian border war, potential Indian governmental instability after the death of Nehru, and the apparent closing of a window of opportunity for seizing Kashmir outright combined to generate Pakistani military optimism in early 1965. In that summer, Pakistan began infiltrating irregular forces into Kashmir in the hope of fomenting rebellion. When the local population proved to be less than enthusiastic, on August 14 Pakistani regular forces breached the Cease Fire Line (CFL).[55]

The opening stages of this second Indo-Pakistani war justified the initial Pakistani optimism. Launched on September 1, operation "Grand Slam" made good progress in capturing Jaurian, and was on the verge of capturing the strategically important town of Akhnur that would cut India off from Kashmir. Pakistani pilots also won victories in air combat with the Indian air force. Yet, whether the outcome of an ill-timed Pakistani change of command or of the threat of an Indian attack on West Pakistan itself, the advance on Akhnur was delayed. According to Mohammed Ayub,[56] this delay was the result of replacing Major General Akhtar Hussain Malik with Major General Yahya Khan (later to be a full general and state president). General Gul Hassan affirmed that:

> Had there been no delay in the capture of Chhamb [sic] and the Operation had gone as planned on September 1, Jaurian would have been secured on September 2 or 3, because the enemy was retreating in total disarray. As things turned out, the place was captured on September 5, and ad interim the enemy had been given precious breathing space to reinforce his garrison, and more importantly, time to recover from the pounding meted out to him earlier.[57]

---

[51] Ganguly and Hagerty 2005, 28.   [52] Sathasivam 2005, 8.   [53] Haqqani 2005, 47.
[54] Blainey 1988.   [55] Ganguly and Hagerty 2005, 29.   [56] 2005, 89.
[57] Quoted in Ayub 2005, 89.

At the same time, on September 4, a message from Pakistani sources in New Delhi was received by the foreign office, indicating that an attack on Pakistan itself could be expected on September 6.[58] On that date, the Indian army crossed the border and now threatened the large Pakistani city of Lahore. This threat was sufficient to relieve Pakistani pressure on Akhnur, and ultimately ensure that Kashmir would remain predominantly under Indian control. Several major tank battles would be fought, one at Khem Karan in Punjab yielding a major Pakistani defeat,[59] and another at Chawinda involving over 600 tanks, the outcome of which was inconclusive.[60] On September 21 and 22, India and Pakistan respectively accepted a United Nations Security Council ceasefire resolution.

There are conflicting claims concerning numbers of casualties incurred by each country, quantities of tanks and aircraft destroyed, and amount of territory conquered.[61] The most recent estimate has Pakistan occupying 1,600 square miles of Indian territory (1,300 of it desert). India conquered 350 square miles of Pakistan, but "of greater strategic value, as it was located near the West Pakistani capital, Lahore, and the industrial city of Sialkot as well as in Kashmir."[62]

At the Tashkent conference in January 1966, both sides agreed to exchange conquered territory, thereby returning to the CFL existing prior to August 5, 1965.[63] Although the fighting ended in a stalemate, and the main Pakistani goal of acquiring more territory in Kashmir was frustrated, the army was thought to have performed well against heavy odds. According to Hasan Rizvi,[64] "the September War between India and Pakistan brought the prestige of the Armed Forces to its peak. This was clearly reflected in the debates of the National Assembly and Provincial Assemblies, statements of the political leaders, various articles, poems and short stories." And the Correlates of War Project declared Pakistan the winner of the 1965 war.

In many quarters, the Tashkent agreement yielding a relatively large parcel of territory in return for a much smaller one was seen as a defeat at the negotiations table, despite the later award of additional territory to Pakistan in the Rann of Kutch in 1968. The United States, Britain, and the Soviet Union all to varying degrees supported India; the weakened US-Pakistani relationship was the most significant outcome. And

> the public found it difficult to understand why "objective reality on the ground" had forced an "unfavorable" settlement on Pakistan. The Tashkent agreement also made no mention of Pakistan's demand for a plebiscite in Kashmir, which made the people wonder why Pakistan's "military victory" did not bring it any gain in territory or at least the promise of a future favorable settlement. Ayub Khan's foreign minister, Zulfikar Ali Bhutto, resigned

[58] Ayub 2005, 90.   [59] Ganguly and Hagerty 2005, 30.
[60] Ayub 2005, 94.   [61] E.g., Rizvi 1974, 163.   [62] Haqqani 2005, 49.
[63] Ayub 2005, 112.   [64] 1974, 167.

from the cabinet and led critics in suggesting that "political surrender" at
Tashkent had converted a military victory into defeat.[65]

This theme is precisely embodied in the title of Ayub's[66] chapter analyzing the
outcome of the 1965 war: "Victory into Defeat."

Here we have the ephemeral victory with origins in the creditable performance of the Pakistani military in the first Indo-Pakistani war that was continued,
even enhanced, in the early stages of the second such war. It was the "defeat" at
the negotiations table, in part a response to international pressures, which set
in motion a malaise that would culminate in the mass murders of 1971. In this
sense, the Pakistani experience was akin to that of Japan during the interwar
period. Although the Japanese military victories around the turn of the twentieth century preceding the 1922 Naval Conference were far more clear cut, even
spectacular relative to those of Pakistan, nevertheless feelings ran high among
the Pakistani military and within a public subjected to considerable governmental propaganda extolling the battlefield victories. Cohen[67] avers: "Pakistanis were
to be told that the 1965 war demonstrated their martial superiority over Hindu
India, and some of the worst racism and cultural arrogance seen since Partition
emerged under official sponsorship in a number of articles and books. This self-
delusion was fostered by a powerful and effective public-relations machinery
under the control of the commander-in-chief." Pakistanis felt something like the
humiliation of Italian nationalists after World War I that "a mutilated victory"
had occurred, as D'Annunzio and Mussolini put it. A summary comment is
given by Cohen:[68] "The 1965–71 period came to be known as the 'sawdust years,'
in which military honor and professionalism slipped away from the Pakistan
Army. The experience of 1965 was not subject to analysis, and this professional
failure contributed to the disaster of 1971, as did the military's involvement in
'the mire of politics.' "

The debacle of 1971

An additional consequence of the 1965 war was a rapidly growing separatist
movement in East Pakistan. The Pakistani military slogan that the "defense of
the east lies in the west"[69] did not sit well with the Bengalis of the east. They
saw themselves open to the mercies of the Indian military during the 1965 war,
for there was little direct military provision for the defense of East Pakistan. In
part, this was a consequence of the overwhelming control of the army by West
Pakistan. According to Asghar Khan,[70] East Pakistanis constituted 56 percent
of the country's total population, but only 7 percent of its military. Whatever
the sources of this anomaly, whether a sense of superiority over Bengalis by

---

[65] Haqqani 2005, 50.   [66] 2005, 100.   [67] 1984, 69.   [68] 1984, 72.
[69] Ganguly and Hagerty 2005, 31.   [70] 2005, 24.

the Punjabis who dominated the Pakistani officer corps, shorter average height of the Bengali applicants compared with westerners, or simply the myth of an absence of a military tradition in East Bengal relative to that of Punjab, this heavy imbalance would further alienate the citizens of East Pakistan. It would appear to East Pakistanis as if an army of occupation was in their midst, not their own national army.

The immediate precipitant of the civil war was the election of 1970. Founded by Huseyn Shaheed Suhrawardy to implement the earlier vision of Pakistan as a secular state, the Awami League proposed a loose confederation between East and West and better relations with India.[71] For its part, the army viewed the League as a Trojan Horse implementing Indian policy within Pakistan, especially the dissolution of the Pakistani state as then constituted. In reality, however, an accurate characterization of the views of supporters of the Awami League, as well as those of most citizens of East Pakistan, stated, "Alongside their commitment to Islam they possessed a deep loyalty to their Bengali culture, and they were schooled in parliamentary traditions and the practice of the rule of law. In every way except their common faith, the attitudes of the East Bengalis differed from those of their fellow-Pakistanis in the western provinces."[72]

Because of this confluence between policies of the League and political sentiments of the East Pakistani electorate, the Awami League won more than 72 percent of the overall Pakistani popular vote in the 1970 election, leading to its control of 160 out of 300 contested seats. By gaining even uncontested seats for women, the League now controlled 167 seats of the 313-member National Assembly. Shortly after the election, a general visiting Dhaka said to his military colleagues, "Don't worry…we will not allow these black bastards to rule over us."[73] Figure 12.2 presents this Pakistani ephemeral gain.

On March 1, 1971, General Yahya Khan, head of the Pakistani military regime, announced that the session of the National Assembly would be indefinitely postponed. The Awami League then called for civil disobedience. The new flag of Bangladesh now replaced that of Pakistan for several days in many locations, and Awami League supporters ruled the streets, even in the face of military opposition. The military crackdown began on March 25, according to the following guidelines:

> A. L. [Awami League] action and reactions to be treated as rebellion and those who support [the League] or defy M. L. [Martial Law] action to be dealt with as hostile elements… As A.L. has widespread support even amongst E. P. [East Pakistani] elements in the Army the operation has to be launched with great cunningness, surprise, deception and speed combined with shock action.[74]

---

[71] Haqqani 2005, 51.   [72] Quoted in Haqqani 2005, 63.
[73] Quoted in Haqqani 2005, 65.   [74] Quoted in Haqqani 2005, 71.

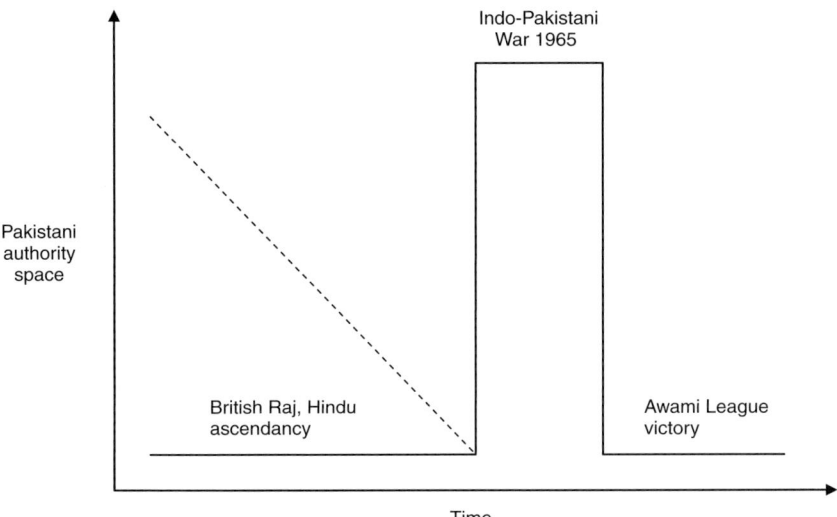

Figure 12.2: Changes in Pakistani authority space over time

And the mindset of the Pakistani officer corps was described in the following manner:

> A sort of "trigger-happiness" was setting in: young officers went about in full combat gear, the *jawans* twirled their moustaches and looked down disdainfully upon the Bengalis. A colonel proudly told a gathering of friends that he had been able to shed his reluctance to shoot and kill. I knew the fellow and there was no doubt that he was bragging and talking nonsense but there was also [no] doubt that the soldiers had lost all respect and regard for the Bengalis – their life and honour. In the same country there were now two nations torn asunder by deep mutual hostility and hatred. Even the common bond of religion, which had survived the many political vicissitudes in one form or another, had finally snapped. The army had moved in not just to control an immediate law and order situation but also to brainwash the people, to wean them off their native Bengali mores, and make them *true* Pakistanis. "Pakistanization" of the Bengalis, was the objective of the exercise. Hindu influence and customs must be done away with once and for all.[75]

According to US Ambassador Joseph Farland: "Army officials and soldiers give every sign of believing they are now embarked on a jihad against

---

[75] Emphasis in original; Siddiqi 2004, 110–11.

Hindu-corrupted Bengalis."[76] Or as Major General Khadim Hussain Raja remarked: "I will muster all I can – tanks, artillery and machine guns – to kill all the traitors and, if necessary, raze Dacca to the ground. There will be no one to rule; there will be nothing to rule."[77]

It was this destructive purpose of the Pakistani army that was to lead to so much of the ethnic cleansing and bloodshed of the 1971 civil war. It quickly morphed into the Indo-Pakistani war, following Indian support, training, and arming of the Mukti Bahini (liberation force) consisting of former Pakistani officers and others of Bengali origin. Failure to control the insurgents led to an air strike by Pakistan on Indian bases on March 3, 1971. Indian air and naval forces responded forcefully, and on December 6, the Indian army entered East Pakistan. In all some 90,000 Pakistani troops were forced to surrender to the victorious Indian army. The former East Pakistan, now Bangladesh, declared independence.[78]

This military trajectory was paralleled by one directed at the East Pakistani civilian population. As the civil war appeared to be imminent, the Pakistani army created a *razakaar* (volunteer force consisting of at least 50,000 men). Two special brigades of Islamists were formed, Al-Shams (in Arabic, "the sun") and Al-Badr ("the moon"). General Niazi, commander of the eastern front, described the origin and purpose of the *razakaars*:

> A separate *Razakaars* Directorate was established… Two separate wings called *Al-Badr* and *Al-Shams* were organized. Well educated and properly motivated students from the schools and madrasas were put in *Al-Badr* wing, where they were trained to undertake "Specialized Operations," while the remainder were grouped together under *Al-Shams*, which was responsible for the protection of bridges, vital points and other areas.
>
> The *Razakaars* were mostly employed in areas where army elements were around to control and utilize them… This force was useful when available, particularly in the areas where the rightist parties were in strength and had sufficient local influence.[79]

According to Bangladeshi sources, the two militias acted as the Pakistani army's death squads that murdered left-wing professors, journalists, *littérateurs*, and doctors. Al-Badr was reported to have killed "10 professors of Dacca University, five leading journalists (including the BBC correspondent), two littérateurs and 26 doctors in Dacca alone."[80] For their part, the Mukti Bahini were active in attacking members of the Islamist groups, leading to an estimated total of 150,000, non-Bengali, non-combatant dead.[81]

---

[76] Quoted in Haqqani 2005, 83.   [77] Quoted in Haqqani 2005, 71.
[78] Ganguly and Haggerty 2005, 33–4.   [79] Quoted in Haqqani 2005, 79.
[80] Quoted in Haqqani 2005, 79–80.   [81] Rummel 1997, 162.

Indonesia

The last case of a rampaging military is that of Indonesia in 1965 and East Timor between 1975 and 2002. Most estimates agree that at least 500,000 people were killed in 1965, mostly civilians and for the most part communists, suspected communists, or any individual that could be remotely associated with communism such as the ethnic Chinese. On Bali alone, 80,000–100,000 people were murdered.[82] Other areas of intense killing included East and Central Java, where the Indonesian Communist Party (PKI) was strong.[83] Not only the military, but also civilian groups were active in killing. Principally, these included Muslim organizations such as the Ansor Youth of the Nahdatal Ulama (Muslim Teachers' Party), or many traditional Hindus on Bali who were deeply offended by the communist disdain for their religious values.[84] But it was the military that unleashed the anti-communist purge, and later stood by while civilians joined in the carnage.

Night of the generals

These cataclysmic events were initiated by the *Gestapu* (Gerakan Tiga Puluh September, or 30 September Movement[85]). On the evening of September 30, six high-ranking Indonesian army officers were either killed in their homes, or were taken to the Halim Airbase, where they were later murdered. Although the most important intended victim, General A. H. Nasution, escaped capture, his 5-year-old daughter was wounded in the kidnapping attempt and later died, while an aide to Nasution was captured instead and later murdered at Halim.[86] Nasution, along with General Suharto, commander of the army's strategic reserve (KOSTRAD), not a kidnapping target, put down the coup in short order.

Among the conspirators were other army leaders, as well as the head of the Indonesian Communist Party, Dipa Nusantra Aidit. Much controversy has emerged concerning the *extent* to which the PKI was involved in the attempted coup, although virtually all observers agree that there was *some* involvement. After extensive interviews with observers and participants on both sides, John Hughes[87] concludes that, "There is no question, of course, that the Indonesian Communist Party was up to its neck in the coup attempt. But still open to debate is whether the Communists planned the whole thing and gave the actual signal to jump, or whether the Communists jumped at somebody else's beckoning." A more cautious estimate, but still roughly in the same ballpark, is one given recently by Steven Drakeley:[88]

> The most likely explanation is that the affair was cooked up between Sukarno [then President] and a few of his closest confidants, including

[82] Vickers 2005, 159.   [83] Hughes 1967.   [84] Hughes 1967, 154.
[85] van der Kroef 1970/71, 557.   [86] Hughes 1967, 31–2.   [87] 1967, 114.
[88] 2005, 111.

D. N. Aidit, the leader of PKI. It was intended to be a delicate and limited operation that would allow Sukarno to rid himself of the senior generals who were impeding his political objectives without himself appearing to take the initiative. The operation was not intended to bring PKI to power, at least not immediately, but to create a political environment whereby Sukarno could bequeath power to a like-minded, radical, nationalist regime in due course.

But even given the heinous nature of the assassination of six high-ranking army officers, including allegations of the torture of those kidnapped by members of the *Pemuda Rakjat* (People's Youth) and *Gerwani* (Communist Women's Organization), as well as the horrible death of a 5-year-old girl, why was the response so extreme that at least 500,000 people, most of them innocents, lost their lives? To begin to answer this question, we must first turn to the theory of the ephemeral gain incorporating mortality salience, and its applicability to this case.

Mortality salience, subordination, gain and loss

First, mortality salience is easily satisfied by the fact that people, including a child, had been murdered under horrendous conditions. Even if the claim of torture and mutilation prior to death was untrue or exaggerated,[89] nevertheless both the army and public were led to believe that it was true. Further, and relevant to the theory of the ephemeral gain, is the anti-colonial battle with the Dutch in West Irian (West New Guinea) that ended only in 1962,[90] and the *Konfrontasi* (confrontation) with Malaysia that was still ongoing at the time of the attempted coup. The army, of course, was especially aware of deaths associated with both battlefronts.

Equally important to the theory are the earlier period of gain, when the Dutch agreed to allow Jakarta to assume control of West Irian, but a later loss occurred in the failure of *Konfrontasi* to prevent the formation of Malaysia in 1963 as envisioned by the British, then the colonial power in Malaya. British troops were especially successful in fending off Indonesian military efforts that, with the passage of time, became more desultory than determined.

Here, we have the ephemeral gain satisfied by the Indonesian success in displacing the Dutch, beginning with Indonesian independence in 1949, and ending in 1962. But *Konfrontasi*, begun in December 1962 with Indonesia's full support for the Brunei rebellion against incorporation within Malaysia, was clearly failing in 1965 when the *Gestapu* attempted coup took place. In the interim, violent attacks by Indonesia began in April 1963 in Sarawak and continued throughout this period.

---

[89] Anderson 1987.   [90] Drakeley 2005, 133.

The larger threat of reversion

Yet, though the empirics already satisfy the demands of the theory, there is clearly more to the story of the *Gestapu* violence and its horrific aftermath that provides additional confirmation of the theory. The army had lost its taste for *Konfrontasi* when the British began their successful defense, so that defeat in this campaign might not be as significant as it might first appear. The roots of the mass murder in Indonesia *do* reside in the failures of *Konfrontasi* and *Gestapu*, but their significance needs to be explored in some greater detail. The international conditions surrounding both events will prove to be crucial, for ultimately it was the threat of loss far beyond some Malaysian territory that was to be crucial. The looming image of a victorious PKI fully supported, even dominated by Communist China, a nuclear power as of 1964, would be absolutely critical in unleashing the mass killing.

By 1961, the PKI had emerged as arguably "the most powerful political party in Indonesia."[91] In the last national election before the September 30 coup, that of 1955, the PKI ranked fourth among political parties and had developed allies within the largest party at the time, the Nationalists (PNI) and its left-wing affiliate, the Partindo. In local elections that were held 2 years later, the PKI was first in central Java.[92] And in 1965, Sukarno appointed Njoto, second deputy chairman of the Communist Party, to the post of minister in the cabinet Presidium. Aidit, the Party chairman, already held the post of coordinator-minister and M. H. Lukman, the first deputy chairman of the Party, was a minister. Njoto also was editor of the *People's Daily*, the official newspaper of the PKI.[93] And in an editorial in that paper shortly after the coup, on October 2, Njoto wrote that, "we the People, fully comprehend what the leaders of the coup were trying to accomplish with their patriotic movement...to preserve the Revolution and the People."[94]

Thus, the highest level of leadership of the Communist Party also was firmly ensconced at the highest level of government under Sukarno. On May 23, 1965, at a rally celebrating the forty-fifth anniversary of the formation of the PKI, Sukarno embraced Aidit, proclaiming, "See, I, Sukarno, embrace the PKI."[95] And according to J. M van der Kroef:[96] "Indeed, by January 1965, Sukarno was saying openly that 'of course' he would have no objection if Indonesia were to evolve into a Communist state." The PKI itself had grown from 7,910 cardholders in 1952 to more than 3 million in 1965. It also boasted "a youth organization, *Pemuda Rakjat*, of three million; a federation of trade unions, SOBSI, of 3.5 million; a peasant organization, BTI, of nine million; a women's organization, Gerwani, of three million; a cultural association, *Lekra*, of a half million; and a student movement, CGMI, of more than 70,000 members."[97]

---

[91] Sutter 1966, 524.   [92] Hughes 1967, 85.   [93] Brackman 1969, 34.
[94] Quoted in van der Kroef 1970/71, 559.   [95] Quoted in Brackman 1969, 32.
[96] 1972, 277.   [97] Brackman 1969, 29.

By any standards, this was phenomenal organizational growth, making the PKI the third largest communist party in the world, after those of the People's Republic of China and the Soviet Union. And the *Pemuda Rakjat* and *Gerwani* members were undergoing military training at least since July 1965.[98]

Threatening as the PKI was to conservative elements in the army, the international situation ramped up that threat considerably. Beginning in the early 1960s, the People's Republic of China increasingly supported Indonesia's *Konfrontasi* policy. All of the Chinese Communist leaders, including Chairman Lin Shao-chi, Premier Chou En-lai, and Foreign Minister Ch'en Yi actively cultivated Sukarno and his foreign minister, Subandrio. On April 1963, Lin visited Indonesia and proclaimed that Indonesia and China were "comrades in arms." Chinese youths who had been receiving paramilitary training in Sarawak crossed into Kalimantan to support the Indonesian effort. To make matters worse from the army's perspective, *Konfrontasi* was making enemies of Australia, Great Britain, and the United States, who opposed Communist China.

A communist, Djawoto, was now Indonesian ambassador to Beijing. By the end of October 1964, Indonesia now had diplomatic ties with North Korea and North Vietnam, and had recognized the National Liberation Front (NLF) of South Vietnam. Generous support from Beijing enabled local Chinese residents of Indonesia to contribute massively to the PKI, making it the richest political party in Indonesia. According to John Sutter:[99]

> The Soekarno-Subandrio Government, with strong P.K.I. backing, shared certain strategic goals in Southeast Asia with Peking, including: (a) the discrediting of Great Britain and the United States through a campaign of agitation and vilification against these "neo-colonialist, old established forces," in order to force removal of their troops from Southeast Asia; (b) the fragmentation of Malaysia and replacement of its government by "anti-imperialist" regimes; (c) the victory of the "Liberation Front" in Vietnam; (d) the elimination of the remnants of anti-communist or anti-Soekarnoist influence inside Indonesia; and (e) the division of Southeast Asia into spheres of influence under Peking, Hanoi, and Djakarta. The P.K.I.'s goals (with which the C.C.P. [Chinese Communist Party] was in agreement) went a shade further in certain instances, namely: the communization of Vietnam; the communization of Malaysia; the takeover of the Indonesian Government – by force, if necessary – by the Party; and the division of Southeast Asia among the Communist parties in Peking, Hanoi, and Djakarta.

So committed was Sukarno to the *Konfrontasi* policy in an effort to fragment Malaysia that as late as July 1966, after the failure of the September 30 coup and the waning of his power, he could still insist that, "Malaysia must be destroyed and wanted to know when Sabah and Sarawak would be invaded."[100]

---

[98] Hughes 1967, 23.   [99] 1966, 531–2.
[100] Quoted in Easter 2004, 190; see also Jones 2002, 272–3.

To facilitate the PKI's efforts domestically, Beijing agreed to secretly ship small arms to Indonesia to arm the *Pemuda Rakjat, Gerwani*, and other affiliates of the PKI. Further, Chou En-lai and Ch'en Yi supported the formation of a "Fifth Force" that would constitute a "people's militia" to supplement the regular armed forces and police. Sukarno himself in August 1965, with Ch'en Yi as an honored guest, openly supported the formation of a Fifth Force.[101] When the PKI, with Beijing's public support, suggested that political commissars be placed in the army, its leaders, Generals Nasution and Yani (who later was to be among those slaughtered by *Gestapu*) reflected on that proposal. According to one leading general, "We agree with the President that our struggle is against Necolim [public abbreviation for neocolonialism]. The only thing is, he looks at Washington and London when he talks about Necolim. When we talk about Necolim, we're beginning to look much, much harder at Peking."[102]

Worse, the growth in Chinese power abroad and influence at home within Indonesia was thoroughly consistent with the historic role of China as the leader of an East (and Southeast) Asian hierarchy. Before the onset of the Cold War, China had close relations with neighboring countries. Earlier still,

> the traditional international order in East Asia encompassed a regionally shared set of norms and expectations that guided relations and yielded substantial stability. In Chinese eyes – and explicitly accepted by the surrounding nations – the world of the past millennium has consisted of civilization (China) and barbarians (all other states). In this view, as long as the barbarian states were willing to kowtow to the Chinese emperor and show formal acceptance of their lower position in the hierarchy, the Chinese had neither the need to invade these countries nor the desire to do so. Explicit acceptance of the Chinese perspective on the regional order brought diplomatic recognition from China and allowed the pursuit of international trade and diplomacy.[103]

Although the long period of Dutch colonial rule and Chinese weakness prevented the assertion of direct Chinese influence, independent Indonesia, especially via its large communist party was ripe for Chinese penetration.

Only the army stood directly in the way of Sukarno and his PKI allies. His Independence Day speech mentioned "corruptors and swindlers" who would be destroyed by "the people."[104] Since the term *kabir* (bureaucratic-capitalist) was already being used to describe "uncooperative" army officers, this was obviously a veiled reference to them. On September 25, three days before the coup, Sukarno stated that "we are now about to enter the second stage of the Indonesian Revolution, namely the implementation of socialism."[105] And on that same day, the foreign minister, Subandrio, declared, "The time has come to exterminate the

---

[101] Sutter 1966, 536.   [102] Quoted in Hughes 1967, 140.   [103] Kang 2007, 43.
[104] Sutter 1966, 538.   [105] Quoted in Sutter 1966, 538.

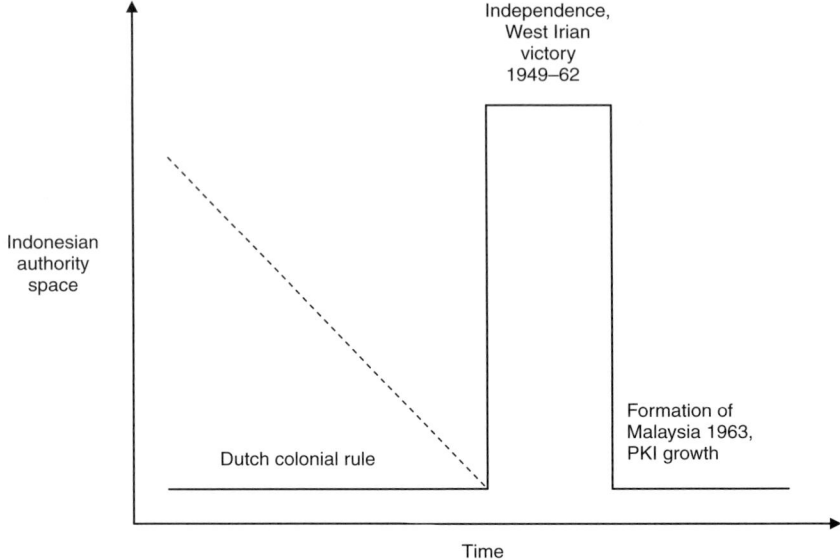

Figure 12.3:   Changes in Indonesian authority space over time

kabir.[106] On September 30, the *Gestapu* coup had begun, followed by the mass killing. Thus domestic and international threats coalesced within Indonesia, leading to the extreme reaction. Figure 12.3 presents this ephemeral gain.

A violent sequel to the events of 1965 was to begin a decade later, under the now entrenched Suharto government: the invasion of East Timor in 1975, after the 1974 Portuguese withdrawal from that colony. As a consequence of that invasion and civil war between the East Timorese, a minimum of 125,000 died,[107] while other observers place the number as high as 200,000.[108] This is an incredibly high proportion of the 650,000 East Timorese population, comparable to the 1975–79 mass murders in Cambodia.

The case of Indonesia presents an interesting transition to the shadow of the present. Certainly, Communist China posed a contemporaneous threat to conservatives within the Indonesian military. Yet in contrast to the cases soon to be considered, there was little ongoing violence nearby to be opposed or emulated. Here, the violence was largely *sui generis*; the extremist response yielding at least 500,000 dead cannot be attributed to an external violent stimulus. The enormity of the military response can be understood, however, by the earlier subordination to a foreign power, a burgeoning independent state with considerable international prestige but recent failures in territorial acquisition, and

[106] Quoted in Sutter 1966, 538.   [107] Vickers 2005, 167.   [108] Lamoureux 2003, 49.

the extreme anger that a current combined external and internal threat yielded within this context.

The shadow of the present

Thus far, the analysis has focused on the shadow of the past, the shadow of the future, and coincidence of the two in the ephemeral gain, especially the threat and fear of reversion. But when examining cases of military excesses and the ability of command structures to act quickly in the face of threat, the shadow of the present emerges. Here, instead of diachronic change, which occupies most of this book, cross-sectional dynamics appear.

Unlike the ephemeral gain, the shadow of the present does not require a gestation period, nor does it need an opportunity structure provided by the political space identified by Juan Linz.[109] It is a direct military threat entailing simultaneous but independently generated violence in a neighboring country (typically absent in the onset of the ephemeral gain) that can engender an immediate response. In the ephemeral gain, on the other hand, the past "percolates" in the formation of extremist groups, even at times inchoate within the military, who then enact their murderous impulses at the (or, in the case of successive ephemera, another) threat and fear of reversion. Emotions also are more heavily engaged. In other words, a politically subordinate recent past is largely irrelevant in these cases of a present threatening agent. Three cases will now be considered that reflect different forms of a military response to presumed threat, but all stemming from a neighboring country enmeshed in violence.

The first type is that of a direct spillover of military confrontations from one country to its immediate neighbor. A particularly deadly form occurred in the Democratic Republic of the Congo (formerly Zaire). Hutu *génocidaires* escaping the victorious Rwandese Patriotic Front (RPF) spilled over the borders into Zaire, followed by troops of the RPF and other Tutsis seeking vengeance. Attempts to depose the Laurent Kabila government led to civil war involving local political and tribal groups, with substantial external involvement, principally Rwandan. French-led troops came as peacekeepers, to be replaced more recently by a force of Bangladeshi, Pakistani, Nepalese, and Uruguayan composition. Given the magnitude of the killing (up to 5.4 million dead, including otherwise preventable deaths from disease and starvation[110]) and the involvement of so many African countries signifying Congo's size and geographic centrality, it is doubtful that we have seen the last of the consequences of the Rwandan genocide.

A second case takes the form of an interstate response to developments within a neighboring country. Between 1978 and 1996, anywhere between 60,000 and 200,000 innocent people were killed in Guatemala, principally by the military.

[109] 1980.   [110] McGreal 2008.

They were mostly peasants, frequently Maya, who appeared to be influenced by the burgeoning guerrilla movement against the military government.

Central to the instigation of the violence during the late 1970s and early 1980s were political developments within Nicaragua. There, the Sandinista movement was making considerable headway against the Somoza government, leading to the Sandinista accession to power in 1979. According to Charles Brockett,[111] "Guatemalan contention occurred in a larger regional context...From the fall of 1978 Nicaragua was in a state of mass insurrection, with dictator Somoza's power coming to an end in July 1979."

So determined was the Guatemalan military to prevent a Sandinista-like revolution in Guatemala that international opinion was incautiously flouted. When, on January 31, 1980 the Spanish embassy was occupied by protesters attempting to alert the world to the escalating violence, the president, minister of the interior, and police chief met, and decided to use force. The embassy building was attacked by police using incendiary devices that exploded the Molotov cocktails brought in by the protesters. Refusal of the police to unlock the doors or allow firefighters to control the blaze led to the deaths of thirty-nine people, protesters, and hostages, all screaming in agony. Patrick Ball and his colleagues[112] comment, "In Nicaragua, only a few months before the Spanish embassy occupation, Sandinista rebels had, prior to their victory, gained enormous credibility internationally and within the country by forcing the Somoza regime to negotiate a hostage release at the national Congress." This, the Guatemalan military regime was determined to prevent.

Finally, the third case, that of Afghanistan, illustrates a cross-border invasion of a neighboring country in support of its beleaguered allied government. As a result of this invasion, up to 1.8 million innocents were killed between 1979 and 1992. As in Guatemala, external events were to play a critical role. "The revolution in Iran...had implications for the Soviet Union's southern, Muslim republics. If Islamic fervor became a new threat, it was preferable to extend that front line to the Hindu Kush rather than wait for it on Soviet territory after a further Islamic triumph in Afghanistan. A socialist humiliation just across the Amu Darya would echo throughout Soviet Transoxiana."[113]

Regional foreign policy was pre-eminent. After examining Soviet documents available after the dissolution of that government, Odd Arne Westad of the Norwegian Nobel Institute concluded: "The primacy of regional foreign policy over socialist ideology accelerated in mid-1979, as the Soviets watched the events in Tehran with glowing alarm, and led them to increase their aid to the *Khalqi* [local communist] regime. This, in turn, increased the Soviets' stake in its survival."[114] And "the Kremlin's decisions about Afghanistan were not guided

---

[111] 2005, 215.   [112] 1999, 23.   [113] Tanner 2002, 234.
[114] Westad 1994, 66.

primarily by the image of a hostile United States but by one of a regional challenge from militant Islam."[115]

Thus, in all three cases the shadow of the present was addressed brutally with great loss of life. The decades-old Hutu–Tutsi conflict was to be continued in deadly fashion on the killing fields of the Congo, in Guatemala an older repertory of violence against Mayan peasants was resuscitated to confront the Sandinista-like challenge, and in Afghanistan, once again (see Chapter 7), Russians (Soviets) were committing enormities against a Muslim population. History mattered, but the contemporaneous regional threat was paramount. These cases exemplify the finding of Karen Rasler and William Thompson[116] that the "neighborhood" matters for the spread of civil violence, a result that emerged from a test of Idean Salehyan's[117] general hypotheses.

Conclusion

Both Japan and Pakistan are notable for the military brutalization of civilian populations within contested territories. This is not uncommon when invading or occupying forces encounter uncooperative civilian populations. However, the *extent* of the brutality sets these two cases apart; they also conform to the theoretical expectations advanced here. The turn of the twentieth century witnessed extraordinary successes by the Japanese military. But these victories were "mutilated" at the Washington (territorial loss and naval limitations) and London (unacceptable naval limitations) Naval Conferences. It would appear to Japanese nationalists, especially those in the military, as if these victories never occurred. The international naval community centered in Washington and London simply would not allow the Japanese to receive the appropriate rewards for their many victories and cooperation during World War I.

Similarly, Pakistan appeared to be on a victorious trajectory, beginning with independence in 1947 and continuing at least through the early stages of the 1965 Indo-Pakistani war. Intense government propaganda managed to convince most Pakistanis, including those in the military, that here, too, a "mutilated" victory had occurred, for these victories had not been appropriately recognized at the negotiations table, in part a consequence of international pressure. As in the Japanese case, extreme brutality followed. In both cases, there existed a fear of reversion to an earlier subjugation to foreign entities: Japan's subordination to the West (especially the US), Pakistan's under British colonial rule within Hindu-dominated India.

Indonesia's fear of reversion was not to the West but to Communist China, in league with the third largest communist party in the world, the PKI. Until the

---

[115] Westad 1994, 68.   [116] 2009.   [117] 2009.

mid-1960s, Indonesia was on a track of consolidating its independence and add-ing new territory to its domains (e.g., West Irian), but then failing in its consid-erable efforts to disallow the formation of Malaysia, including territory claimed by Indonesia. The threat of Chinese Communist dominance was now palpable.

Yet at the same time, we see the shadow of the present as a complement to the diachronic ephemeral gain. Together they explain a very large proportion of the number killed in the genocides and mass murders of the recent past.

13

Variations in Genocidal Behavior

In the pantheon of extremist behavior, genocide is emblematic. It would be difficult to imagine a more brutal example of extremism, and one that defies the traditional moral precepts of almost any code of human conduct, sacred or secular. The three most extensive genocides of the twentieth century, those that as a matter of state policy aimed at the annihilation of a particular group, were the Armenians (1915–16), the Holocaust (1941–45), and the Tutsi in Rwanda (1994). These are the principal cases examined in *The Killing Trap*, but now are to be investigated from the perspective of the elaborated framework offered here. (The massacre of the Herero in 1904 did have a genocidal consequence, but was not German state policy.[1])

The Armenians

If the theory of the ephemeral gain is valid it should be applicable to these cases, and here, in the instance of the Armenian genocide, at first glance it would seem to be inapplicable. By the turn of the twentieth century, the history of the Ottoman Empire would appear to have been one of inexorable decline. After the Treaty of Kuchuk Kainardji signaled the first loss of Ottoman territory to the non-Muslim world, in this case Russia, no instance of victory or reversal of this pattern appears at a cursory inspection of the historical record. The identification of loss as a progenitor of genocide appeared in *The Killing Trap*,[2] but no indication of a preceding victory was noted.

Yet a power of the present theory is to be found in its more fine-grained approach to political history. Informed by the concept of ephemerality and its consequences, anomalies begin to be clarified. Why, for example, were so many Armenians killed – over 200,000 – between 1894 and 1896? Certainly, we would treat that today as a major genocide. At the same time, the tendency of scholars has been to concentrate on the more extreme case of 1915–16, in which approximately one million died.

---

[1] Midlarsky 2005b, 30–4.   [2] Midlarsky 2005b.

A clue is found in the petition of 306 inhabitants of the Anatolian Khnouss district prepared for presentation to the "humane and noble people of England" by E. J. Dillon, an Irish journalist, linguist, and scholar:

> We now solemnly assure you that the butchery of Sassoun [1894] is but a drop in the ocean of Armenian blood shed gradually and silently all over the Empire since the *late Turko-Russian war*. Year by year, month by month, day by day, innocent men, women and children have been shot down, stabbed, or clubbed to death in their houses and their fields, tortured in strange fiendish ways in fetid prison cells, or left to rot in exile under the scorching sun of Arabia. During the progress of that long and horrible tragedy no voice was raised for mercy, no hand extended to help us. That process is still going on, but it has already entered upon its final phases, and the Armenian people are at the last gasp. Is European sympathy destined to take the form of a cross upon our graves?[3]

[t]he "late Turko-Russian War," of course was a critical loss, but the present theory suggests that the extent of the butchery was preceded by a gain that proved to be ephemeral. Although initially unexpected by me because the Ottomans were not assigned a central role in the 1853–56 Crimean War in Western accounts, nevertheless the outcome of that war was perceived to be a major victory by the Ottoman Muslim population. Demilitarizing the Black Sea and guaranteeing the independence and territorial integrity of the Ottoman Empire,[4] according to Kemal Karpat:

> The Crimean War also had a lasting psychological impact on the Ottoman Muslims. The war and the Paris treaty, which appeared for a time as Ottoman victories, came after a long series of Ottoman military defeats and humiliating peace treaties with Russia during the period from 1768 to 1839. The ignoble treaty of Hunkiar Iskelesi of 1833 even allowed Russia to station troops in the vicinity of Istanbul to protect the sultan from his own vassal, Mehmet Ali of Egypt... The Ottoman victories in Crimea (on land in eastern Anatolia the Ottoman troops were actually defeated) shattered a prevailing belief among many Ottomans that the Empire was headed toward inevitable doom at the hands of Russia. Indeed, the defeat of Russia in the war of 1853–56 apparently gave many Muslims and leading Ottoman statesmen confidence in the political future of the Ottoman state and led them to *view England and France and other European powers not as the enemies of Islam but as saviors and as trustworthy friends and allies... It is essential to emphasize that the de facto Ottoman alliance with Europe in the Crimean War was the first of its kind in the long, troubled history of Ottoman relations with Christian Europe.*[5]

---

[3] Emphasis added; quoted in Dillon 1895, 184.   [4] Shaw and Shaw 1977, 140.
[5] Emphasis added; Karpat 2001, 74–5.

Note the earlier humiliation by Mehmet Ali and Russian troops stationed near Istanbul to protect that city, which was now eliminated by the Treaty of Paris. Alas, the Russian victory over the Ottomans in 1878 restored their earlier sense of loss.

Yet, a small but highly significant reversal of decline again occurred during the Second Balkan War. This was the reconquest of Adrianople (today's Edirne) by the Ottoman forces led by Enver Paşa, who was to be minister of war during the later genocide.[6]

Talât Paşa, who was minister of the interior during the genocide and responsible for organizing the deportations, also had a personal connection with Adrianople. He was born there and worked for the telegraph company in that city and then became deputy for Adrianople in the Ottoman parliament.[7] Talât's personal history is especially important because he not only organized the deportations, but was responsible for appointing his personal satraps to do his bidding in the face of a frequently unsympathetic Turkish Muslim population, as the genocide unfolded.[8]

In addition to these personal connections of the Ottoman leaders most intimately connected with the later genocide, the city Adrianople itself was extraordinarily important in Ottoman history. It was the capital of the Ottoman Empire between 1413 and 1458, again for 40 years after 1663, and even during Constantinople's ascension to that status, Adrianople continued as an administrative center. Its status was further enhanced by the presence of two historic mosques. The Bayezid mosque of 1488 is the oldest in that city, but of even greater fame and renown because of its architectural grandeur is the Selimiye mosque, built between 1569 and 1575. It is the only building whose photograph appears in the *Report of the International Commission to Inquire into the Causes and Conduct of the Balkan Wars* (1914).

Politically, the "recapture of Edirne stimulated a *mass Ottoman exaltation so intense* that the CUP's [Committee of Union and Progress] right to rule unopposed was accepted and confirmed without further discussion or opposition."[9] Or as Barbara Jelavich[10] comments, "Although [the young Turk regime] had been challenged by opposition parties from 1909 to 1911, it attained a full victory in June 1913 and established a dictatorship. The other parties were suppressed." Of course, Enver Paşa's position was immensely strengthened by his command of the troops that retook Adrianople.[11]

But now at the beginning of the Ottoman Empire's participation in World War I, the potential for horrendous loss loomed once again from two directions. First, upon the Ottoman declaration of war, the Russian army pushed across the border, and after a major Turkish defeat at Sarşkamiş in December 1914 and a

---

[6] Shaw and Shaw 1977, 299.   [7] Shaw and Shaw 1977, 295.   [8] Balakian 2009.
[9] Emphasis added; Shaw and Shaw 1977, 298.   [10] 1983, 100.
[11] Shaw and Shaw 1977, 299.

Russian successful counter-offensive in January 1915, the Ottoman army scattered with over three-quarters of the men lost as they retreated. The way was now open for a Russian push into eastern Anatolia.[12]

It was precisely at this time (December 1914 or January 1915) that a document was prepared by the CUP called "The Ten Commandments" ordering the deportation and extermination of the Armenians.[13]

The second extreme threat was posed by the Dardanelles campaign begun in February 1915. Because of difficulties in passing through the straits easily, the British-led Australian and New Zealand contingents began to land on April 25.[14] Extensive preparations for these landings were known to the Ottomans prior to that date, if only because of Liman von Sanders' correspondingly extensive preparations on the Turkish side begun on March 25.[15] On April 24, the Interior Ministry authorized the arrest of the Armenian political and community leaders suspected of anti-government tendencies. In Constantinople alone, nearly 2,000 such leaders were arrested; eventually most were executed.[16] The following month, in late May, widespread deportations of Armenians were ordered. The genocide had begun.

Note the proximity in time and place of the threat of loss and genocidal response. Constantinople, with its large Armenian population (nearly 10 percent of the total[17]), lay close by the Dardenelles now under attack. The largest concentration of Armenians in the empire was found in eastern Anatolia, near to the expected Russian military advances after the Ottoman defeat of January. Further, many of the Ottoman defeats in battle were attributed by the Turks to the Armenian volunteer movement fighting with the Russians, comprising Armenians from Russia, Persia, Europe, and the United States. Armenians from Turkey were also involved. Antranik, an Armenian hero of the Balkan Wars, was a leader of this movement; he was instrumental in inflicting a major defeat on much larger Turkish forces (a ratio of nearly 10 to 1) on April 18, 1915.[18] A successful uprising, later to be reversed, in the heavily Armenian city of Van in eastern Anatolia also began on April 15.[19] Note the beginning of the arrests from Constantinople on April 24.

As Kamuran Gürün put it, "In short, Armenians residing in the provinces bordering the area of military operations and in proximity to the Mediterranean Sea would be relocated."[20] The risk of state dissolution at the hands of powerful British and Russian forces was palpable. Approximately a million Armenians were deported to their deaths in 1915–16. And both Enver and Talât, who ordered the deportations, were intimately tied to the victory in Adrianople and its soon-to-be ephemeral status, as it would have appeared to them early in 1915. The overall pattern of Armenian mass murder is shown in Figure 13.1.

---

[12] Shaw and Shaw 1977, 159.   [13] Balakian 2003, 189–90.   [14] Hickey 1995, 109.
[15] Erickson 2001, 81.   [16] Dadrian 1997, 221.   [17] Karpat 1985, 188–9.
[18] Dadrian 1999, 115.   [19] Dadrian 1999, 116.   [20] Gürün 1985, 207.

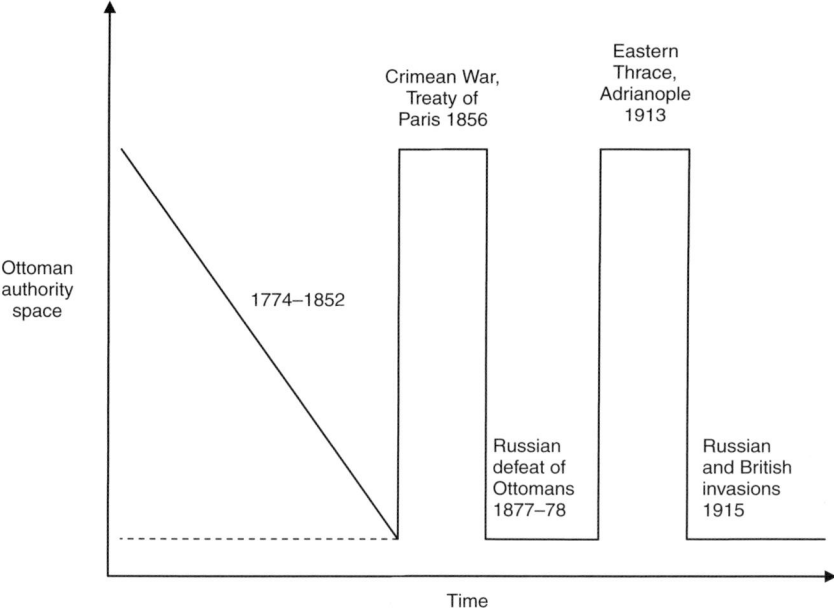

Figure 13.1: Changes in Ottoman authority space over time

Rwanda

Turning now to the case of Rwanda, a similar pattern prevails. The gains of the revolution of 1959 that for the first time since the eighteenth century put the Hutu in power over the Tutsi were threatened by the Rwandese Patriotic Front's (RPF) invasion of 1990 and continued Rwandan territorial loss in February 1993. In excess of 800,000 Tutsi and moderate Hutu were murdered.

In place of the combination of "Hutu supernatural powers with Tutsi military powers"[21] in the early Rwandese state, and agriculturalists as well as pastoralists of both origins living side by side, a gradual polarization set in. Beginning in the mid-eighteenth century, political power was increasingly defined as a Tutsi prerogative, with the Hutu correspondingly degraded in status.

This process would be rapidly accelerated under Belgian colonial rule. While there existed impoverished Tutsi or "petits Tutsi,"[22] and some Hutu who could accumulate cattle and thereby rise in socioeconomic status in the pre-colonial period, thus minimizing social differences, the arrival of the Europeans rigidified the Hutu–Tutsi distinction. In particular, the Tutsi pastoralists were treated

---

[21] Mamdani 2001, 62.   [22] Mamdani 2001, 57.

as "Hamites" having arrived from the Hamitic northeast carrying with them civilizational attributes that justified their rule over the indigenous Hutu. Seen as more "European" in appearance and presumed origins, the Tutsi were racialized into an elite class to be the handmaidens of Belgian colonial rule. With the revolution of 1959 entailing the emergence of the Hutu majority as the dominant political force, status relations between Hutu and Tutsi were reversed, at least in the political arena.[23] Yet the invasion of Rwanda by the Tutsi-led RPF (initially based in Uganda) in October 1990 threatened to reverse these Hutu gains. Early RPF military successes led to the convening of the Arusha peace talks beginning in July 1992.

Four factors then led to an extraordinary evocation of the domain of losses. First, very early in the talks, it became clear that the presidential system that had favored Hutu power would be replaced by a parliamentary system combined with a council of ministers. Later in the talks, the strongest advocate of Hutu power, the *Coalition pour la Défense de la Republique* (CDR) was to be excluded from any transitional political institutions. At about the same time, it was decided that the number of seats in the new assembly and government ministries would favor the opposition to the earlier Hutu-led government party, the *Mouvement Révolutionnaire National pour la Démocratie et le Développement* (MRNDD).

Second, after the massacre of several hundred Tutsi, the RPF renewed its offensive in February 1993, and within two weeks had doubled the amount of territory under its control.[24] A consequence of this success was the agreement to allow 50 percent of the armed command of the RPF to be composed of Tutsis, despite the 15 percent representation of Tutsis in the population at large. Refugees abroad, including of course many Tutsis in Uganda and elsewhere in Africa, were to be allowed back in the country as envisioned by the earlier Dar-es-Salaam declaration on the Rwandan refugee problem.

Third, the assassination on October 30, 1993 of Melchior Ndadaye, the first Hutu president of Burundi (along with the Rwandan president, Juvénal Habyarimana, in their common aircraft) by the Tutsi-dominated army began a series of killings of thousands of Hutu in that country. According to Bruce Jones,[25] "The assassination and killings were rich material for the extremists in Rwanda, who used the events to lend credence to their claims that the Tutsi of the RPF were returning to Rwanda to reestablish their historic dominance over the Hutu."

As in our other two cases of genocide, the presence of refugees grievously accentuated the dimensions of loss. The refugees were of two types, both Hutu, but from different locations. First, were Hutu from Burundi who fled the Tutsi-led massacres of 1972 and again in 1993.[26] Second, in 1988, poor harvests led to near starvation in Burundi, leading to an additional refugee influx.[27] The latest

[23] Prunier 1995.   [24] Jones 1999, 141.   [25] 1999, 144.
[26] Mamdani 2001, 204.   [27] Pottier 2002, 21.

of these, however, was to be the most consequential. After the assassination of President Ndadaye of Burundi in 1993, waves of violence spread that led to some 400,000 refugees from Burundi, mostly Hutu, crowding into Rwanda. Many of the *génocidaires* would be drawn from this group.[28] According to Gérard Prunier,[29] "The psychological impact of the Hutu President's murder and of the arrival in Rwanda of hundreds of thousands of Hutu refugees spreading tales of terror and massacre at the hands of the Tutsi army of Burundi had enormous negative consequences on the already overcast Rwandese political weather."

The assassination and refugee arrivals solidified the position of the extremist "Hutu power" advocates. Supporters of a hard-line approach suggesting virtually a "final solution" of the Tutsi, now secured additional public support. Many of these Burundi Hutu participated in the genocide, even to the point of committing extraordinary torture and atrocity.[30]

After the RPF invasion of 1990, the number of refugees climbed from 80,000 in that year to 350,000 in 1992, and 950,000 after the February 1993 offensive.[31] Territories in Rwanda were cleared of Hutu as they fled before the advancing RPF forces, under the assumption that Hutu peasants themselves would be massacred. After earlier Hutu massacres of Tutsi, the RPF forces did take revenge on some Hutu communities.

The Arusha Accords of July 1993 threatened the "sociological majority" principle of the 1959 revolution,[32] namely that political power was to be held by the Hutu as the majority ethnicity in Rwanda. These agreements stipulated that the ruling MRNDD party would be guaranteed only one-third of the parliamentary seats, thereby rendering it a minority party. Further, the RPF would receive a 40 percent share of the troops in a combined armed forces, in addition to the 50–50 split of the officers with the existing Hutu-led army.[33] The loss of political and military power would be accompanied by the right of return of all refugees to Rwanda. As these were mostly Tutsi, the political power base of the Tutsi in a multiparty system would be considerably enhanced at the polls. Despite the fact that only refugees who left the country 10 years earlier or less had the right to recoup lost properties,[34] the threat of numbers in an increasingly democratic system was substantial. By destroying the Tutsi demographic base, political power might be retained by the MRNDD and its extremist allies. The Arusha Accords and even a likely RPF victory in a renewed war might be nullified by the act of genocide. A return to the old condition of subordination to the Tutsi might be avoided.

In addition, there also exists an extensive evidentiary base of the personal histories of the *génocidaires*. It exists in two forms: (1) interviews with Hutu mass murderers that individually shed light on sources of the genocide, especially if

---

[28] Newbury 1995, 16.   [29] 1995, 200.   [30] Mamdani 2001, 205.
[31] Mamdani 2001, 204.   [32] Prunier 1995, 161.   [33] Jones 2001, 93.
[34] Pottier 2002, 187.

they were more highly placed in the genocidal enterprise, and (2) a systematic quantitative analysis of the largest subset of these interviews. While the one study[35] consists of a set of interviews concentrating on a gang of Hutu killers in the Nyamata commune, the second is more wide ranging across the country and consists of interviews with 206 *génocidaires* from eleven prefectures. From these interviews we can derive individual statements as well as systematic findings.[36]

It is important to emphasize that these interviews occurred after the invasion of Rwanda in 1990 by the RPF, an organization formed by Tutsi exiles then serving in the Ugandan army. The invasion was increasingly successful, with the capital city of Kigali nearly falling to the RPF in February 1993, but for the intervention of French troops that stopped the RPF advance.

A reading of the interview materials suggests that the more highly placed the individual *génocidaire*, the more feared the ephemeral gain. Of the thirteen individuals in Jean Hatzfeld's study, only one was an *interahamwe* (militia that did much of the killing) leader, Joseph-Désiré Bitero, who declared: "I was raised in the fear that the *mwami* – the Tutsi kings – and their commanders might return; that was because of all the stories old folks told us at home about unpaid forced labor and other humiliations of that sad period for us."[37] And according to François Karera, a former prefect: "The president was Hutu. When he was killed, in the Hutu mind, they thought the Tutsis were going to bring back their regime and that we the Hutus were going to work for them again."[38] Or on Radio Rwanda early in the genocide: "Soldiers, gendarmes, and all Rwandans have decided to fight their common enemy... The enemy is still the same. He is the one who has always been trying to return the [Tutsi] monarch who was overthrown... The Ministry of Defense asks Rwandans, soldiers and gendarmes the following: citizens are asked to act together, carry out patrols, and fight the enemy."[39]

A member of the extremist CDR describes his own process of awareness that the current Hutu ascendancy might be ephemeral: "Before the war of 1990, I did not know how to differentiate Hutu from Tutsi. I even had a Tutsi wife. My father-in-law had two Tutsi wives. DID THE WAR CHANGE YOUR VIEWS? Before, I had heard the history of the Tutsis, but I was never interested. With the 1990 war, I began to think about it, but not really. But with Juvénal Habyarimana's death, I became interested."[40]

Thus in his own mind, first the war and then the assassination of Habyarimana were to engage this extremist. And the two themes are well represented; mortality salience is evident. An RTLM (hate radio) broadcast

[35] Hatzfeld 2006.   [36] Lyons and Straus 2006; Straus 2006.
[37] Quoted in Hatzfeld 2006, 166.   [38] Quoted in Straus 2006, 171.
[39] Quoted in Straus 2006, 169.   [40] Quoted in Lyons and Straus 2006, 75.

stated: "This war that we bring is a very important war… They can call it what they want, it's a war of extermination, a war unleashed by the *Inkotanyi* [RPF soldiers], because it was they who unleashed it in order to exterminate the Hutu."[41] According to interim Prime Minister Jean Kambanda, "All of us, together, must wage this war… It is a final war, it must be finished."[42] And the interim minister of health, Casimir Bizimungu, wrote to *African Rights*: "The destruction of the presidential [plane]…is the straw that broke the camel's back… For four years, the RPF has used the gun, the grenade, mines, rope, the hoe, the mortar and I don't know what else to sow desolation and terror. The ripping open of pregnant women and the massacres of innocent civilians by a blow of the hoe to the head… Isn't it evident that the RPF had put everything in place to implement an ethnic purge from the [moment of the] assassination of the President?"[43]

The term *Inkotanyi*, typically used to describe the RPF fighters, is variously defined as "invincible"[44] or "fierce warrior."[45] It is found throughout both interview sets, suggesting the fear that the RPF inspired. Indeed, the fear and anger, intensified by the assassination of Habyarimana, frequently referred to as "the parent of Rwanda"[46] is one of the principal findings of Scott Straus's systematic analysis of his interviews. Accordingly, "The most powerful predictor of why one perpetrator committed more violence than another was whether a respondent described himself as motivated by *war-related fear or anger*. The qualitative testimony briefly presented above also showed how killing Tutsis was inseparable from the language of war. Killing Tutsis in fact was equated with fighting the enemy."[47]

The idea of the Hutu people as an army fighting the Tutsi is contained in the interviews, such as that of the CDR party member who declared, "All the Hutus were like an army."[48] As reflected in many of the interviews, all Tutsis were considered to be "accomplices" of the RPF. Even Hutu who did not participate in the killing were thought to be accomplices, therefore subject to sanction, even murder.[49] According to Léopord Twagirayezu, one of Hatzfeld's thirteen *génocidaires*: "Our Tutsi neighbors, we knew they were guilty of no misdoing, but we thought all Tutsis at fault for our constant troubles. We no longer looked at them one by one; we no longer stopped to recognize them as they had been, not even as colleagues. They had become a threat greater than all we had experienced together, more important than our way of seeing things in the community. That's how we reasoned and how we killed at the time."[50] Figure 13.2 presents the ephemeral gain for Rwanda.

[41] Quoted in Straus 2006, 170.   [42] Quoted in Straus 2006, 171.
[43] Quoted in Straus 2006, 171.   [44] Hatzfeld 2006, 32.
[45] Lyons and Straus 2006, 180.   [46] E.g., Lyons and Straus 2006, 81, 92.
[47] Emphasis added; Straus 2006, 151.   [48] Quoted in Lyons and Straus 2006, 71.
[49] Straus 2006, 142.   [50] Quoted in Hatzfeld 2006, 121.

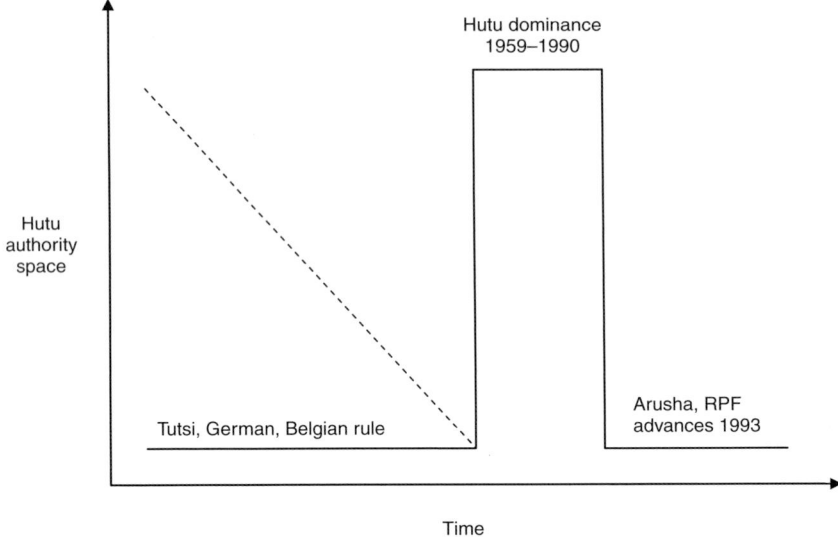

Figure 13.2:   Changes in Rwandan Hutu authority space over time

The Holocaust

In the case of the Holocaust, the ephemeral gain for the rise of German extremism (Nazism) was shown in Figure 4.2, but it is important to detail the dimensions of German loss – the threat and fear of reversion – in World War II,
yielding successive reinforced ephemera and the onset of genocide. Brutality
first evidenced against Jews in the invasion of Russia begun on June 22, 1941,
later escalated to full-fledged genocide after the probability of loss increased.
Because of the fear of an American intervention in the war that would vastly
increase the probability of loss, and a reversion to at least second-ranked status,
extreme brutality was seen to be necessary in order to achieve a quick victory.

Thus, at the outset, all male Jews, assumed to be communists and political
commissars, were to be shot by the *Einsatzgruppen*.[51] Jews in any sort of leadership capacity were especially targeted. Yet even in Lithuania, for example, site of
the most brutal and extensive killing, women and children were not yet subject
to mass murder. According to Christoph Dieckmann,[52] "When on 30 June 1941,
the Lithuanian police chief of Alytus, a town in the south of Lithuania, offered
to kill all of the Jews in the whole region with a squad of 1,050 Lithuanian police
and partisans in a few days, it was rejected by the German side." However, as
the extent of Soviet opposition became apparent in July, the killing began to be

---

[51] Burleigh 2000, 602.   [52] 2000, 245.

extended to all Jews, including women and children. A summary of the German view at that time is given by Jürgen Matthäus: "Beginning in late July, as a result of the failure to win a quick victory over the Red Army, German obsession with security increased. The Reich was, as Hitler put it, forced 'to rule areas extending over 300 to 500 kilometers with a handful of people.' The army leadership compensated for that lack of manpower by an even more massive use of force."[53]

Events were making Nazi state security even more uncertain and the "killing, though horrifying, was on nothing like the scale that it reached from August onwards."[54] On August 11, Prime Minister Winston Churchill of Great Britain and President Franklin Roosevelt of the United States issued the Atlantic Charter, as a consequence of their meeting at sea off the coast of Newfoundland. Although several provisions pertained only to the two signatories, at least three must have been of deep concern to the Nazi leadership: (1) No territorial changes would be made without the freely expressed wishes of the people concerned. (2) Sovereignty rights and self government would be restored to peoples forcibly deprived of them. (3) All countries who threaten or commit aggression would be disarmed.[55] This agreement was a further solidification of the developing Anglo-American alliance that had already witnessed the Lend-Lease Act of March 1941 and the sale of fifty American destroyers to Britain in return for ninety-nine-year leases on bases in British possessions in the Atlantic. The greatly feared two-front war was becoming a reality for Hitler.

All of this was so upsetting to Hitler that on August 18, much to Goebbels' surprise, Hitler raised the possibility of peace with Stalin.[56] Although the terms potentially to be offered to Stalin would likely have been unacceptable to him, nevertheless thoughts of peace on the Eastern front must have been generated by the growing fears of defeat at the hands of the combined Soviet and Anglo-American forces. Failing such a peace with Stalin, the war would grind on and a "rough estimate would show about 50,000 Jews killed up until mid-August, in nearly two months of activity. An impressive figure, ten times higher than the one for Jewish victims of the Polish campaign; but a modest figure compared to the total, ten times higher still, that would be achieved by the end of the year, in four more months."[57]

Significantly, August 15 is the date after which women and children were being killed en masse.[58] Risk minimization – the killing of male Jews and new stricter controls on Jews ordered on July 22 in response to Stalin's earlier July 3 call for partisan activity against the German occupiers – had now been transformed into loss compensation. The Jews would now have to pay not only for the "stab in the back" of World War I and the consequent German loss, but would now have to pay for German blood shed on the Eastern front and the likely opening soon of other fronts. On August 26, Goebbels noted that "as long as Germany

---

[53] Matthäus 2004, 278.   [54] Kershaw 2000a, 467.   [55] Albrecht-Carrié 1958, 565.
[56] Kershaw 2000a, 412.   [57] Burrin 1994, 113.   [58] Burrin 1994, 110.

was fighting for her life, he would make sure the Jews neither profited from the war nor were spared by it."[59] And on January 30, 1942, Hitler stated that, "For the first time, other people will not be the only ones to spill their blood; this time, for the first time, the old Jewish law will be in effect: an eye for an eye, and a tooth for a tooth."[60]

But how did the order to destroy *all* of European Jewry come about? Thus far, into the autumn of 1941, only Soviet Jews, presumably infected by the Bolshevik bacillus, were being murdered en masse. Now the certain, not merely probable, opening up of new fronts and extreme dangers to the Nazi state eventuated. On November 29, 1941, Dr. Fritz Todt, minister for armaments and war production of the Nazi government, after returning to Berlin from the Russian front, reported to Hitler: "Given the arms and industrial supremacy of the Anglo-Saxon powers, we can no longer militarily win this war."[61] On November 30, General Franz Halder recorded in his diary: "The eastern army has a shortage of 340,000 men, i.e., 50 percent of the combat strength of its infantry. Company combat strength is 50–60 men… In Germany we have only 33,000 men available. The bulk of the replacements are not yet broken in to the front-line routine and so have limited combat value. Trucks: Serviceability, at most 60 percent."[62]

The contrast with the summer of 1940 after the fall of France is startling. In the Deutsches Historisches Museum in Berlin, several exhibits on the early period of World War II alternately described the "wave of enthusiasm" after the fall of France, the "euphoria of victory" and a "triumphal exaltation" in Germany. Given the relentless honesty and meticulous historical presentation of the Holocaust in this museum (at least to this observer), there is little reason to doubt the accuracy of the German historians who rendered these judgments on this earlier period.

On December 7, 1941, Japanese forces attacked the United States naval base at Pearl Harbor. True to the Axis alliance, Hitler declared war on the United States on December 11. These critical events occurred just prior to Hitler's address to the NSDAP leaders on December 12. Again, Goebbels notes:

> Regarding the Jewish question, the Führer is determined to clear the table. He warned the Jews that if they were to cause another world war, it would lead to their own destruction. Those were not empty words. Now the world war has come. The destruction of the Jews must be its necessary consequence. We cannot be sentimental about it. It is not for us to feel sympathy for the Jews. We should have sympathy rather with our own German people. *If the German people have to sacrifice 160,000 victims in yet another campaign in the east, then those responsible for this bloody conflict will have to pay for it with their lives.*[63]

---

[59] Quoted in Burrin 1994, 152.   [60] Quoted in Burrin 1994, 152.
[61] Quoted in Gilbert 1989, 265.   [62] Halder 1988, 571.
[63] Emphasis added; quoted in Gerlach 2000, 122.

Hitler of course was referring to his Reichstag speech of January 30, 1939, in which he warned: "If the world of international financial Jewry, both in and outside of Europe, should succeed in plunging the nations into another *world war*, the result will not be the Bolshevization of the world and thus a victory for Judaism. The result will be the extermination of the Jewish race in Europe."[64]

Now a world war had come about, and the Jews would have to pay for German blood spilled in the war. Later, speeches such as that of Hans Frank, the leader of the General Government of Poland, on December 18 spoke of Hitler's "prophecy" and the efforts to realize its goals of the liquidation of European Jewry now that a world war had actually come to pass. Accordingly, "as far as the Jews are concerned, I would therefore be guided by the basic expectation that they are going to disappear. They have to be gotten rid of."[65] Additional evidence is found in Christian Gerlach's comprehensive treatment that has been cited approvingly by historians such as Ian Kershaw and Michael Burleigh.

Despite the Germans' imperative need for rolling stock immediately after the successful Soviet counter-offensive before Moscow began on December 5, 1941, transport thereafter was principally allocated to the mass murders.[66]

A grisly indicator of the importance of the December dates is the following change in the construction of large gas vans intended for the *Einsatzgruppen*. Whereas in early October, vans with the capacity of approximately thirty people were ordered, in December the killing capacity was raised twelve-fold, according to Götz Aly, "a clear qualitative leap."[67] Peter Longrich concurs with these facts. Accordingly, "In the fall of 1941 the decision for the immediate murder of all European Jews had not yet been taken. In the fall of 1941 the murder of hundreds of thousands, but not millions of human beings was being prepared."[68] As late as November 30, evidence exists for the absence of a generalized policy for the liquidation of Jews, whether confined in ghettoes or not.[69]

The successive reinforced ephemera are shown in Figure 13.3.

Nazi war criminality

Another perspective on the Holocaust and one with important implications for the theory of ephemeral gains is supplied by the personal histories of perpetrators. Just as we saw Enver's and Talât's personal experiences in Adrianople as important for understanding their later command of the Armenian genocide, or the personal histories of Hutu leaders shedding light on their emergence as *génocidaires*, so too are these biographical elements critical for explaining

---

[64] Emphasis in original; quoted in Gerlach 2000, 122.
[65] Quoted in Gerlach 2000, 122, 125; also see Kershaw 2000b, 125–6.
[66] Braham 1981; 2000, 136.   [67] Aly 1999, 232.   [68] Quoted in Browning 2004, 373.
[69] Matthäus 2004, 305. Evidence exists in the form of Himmler's direct order on November 30 not to kill Berlin Jews transported to Riga.

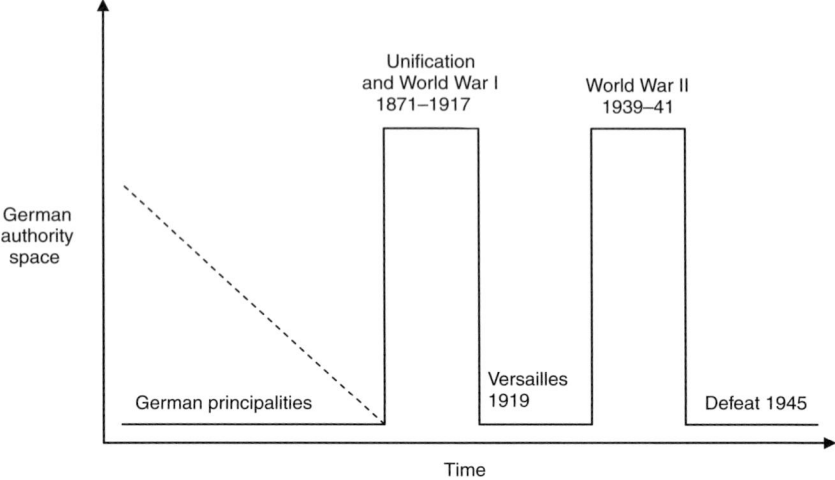

Figure 13.3:   Changes in German authority space over time: extended

perpetrator behaviors during the Holocaust. And in Chapter 5 we already saw Stalin's personal involvement in interstate and civil wars as central to understanding his later initiation of mass violence.

A study of 1,500 perpetrators revealed important connections with subordination, gain, and loss, also following the pattern of Figure 1.1. A unique perspective on the Holocaust is supplied by these personal histories.

A data set generated by Michael Mann[70] is salient because it allows us to distinguish between locations that gave rise to disproportionately high percentages of war criminals, and others associated with much lower percentages of perpetrators. Mann's study of 1,581 German war criminals identified by war crimes trials reveals patterns indicating the ephemeral gain at the highest levels of perpetrator density. Two-thirds of the 1,581 individuals (1,054) served either as concentration camp personnel, members of the *Einsatzgruppen* (mobile machine-gun squads murdering Jews and suspected communists during the invasion of Russia), or security police, suggesting their intimate connection with the Holocaust. This proportion is a conservative estimate because it does not include doctors and dentists (e.g., the infamous Dr. Josef Mengele), who are included within a separate category.

What is most striking about the findings of Mann's study is the overrepresentation of perpetrators born in areas that conform to the pattern of subordination, gain and loss shown in Figure 1.1. Germans born in Alsace-Lorraine and Malmedy account for by far the highest proportion of war criminals.

[70] 2000, 2005.

Table 13.1 presents the ratios calculated by Mann in order of percentages of war criminals using his descriptive categories (some are truncated to fit comfortably into the map that he uses to present his data), with the exception of the first, which he calls "Alsatians and other Western Germans."[71] His numbers constitute "a *ratio of representation*, the percentage of perpetrators with a given characteristic [e.g., born in Alsace-Lorraine] divided by the percentage contribution of people with this characteristic in the German population...as a whole."[72]

Proceeding to the right of the table, the first column records the presence of territorial loss by German residents immediately after World War I, signified by a "+," and the absence of such loss, indicated by a "−." In apposition to loss, territorial gain for Germans (Prussians) between 1807 (the nadir of nineteenth-century Prussian territorial extent after the defeat by Napoleon)[73] and 1914 is signified by a "+." Gain here is interpreted as any addition to the territory of the Prusso-German state as part of the process of Prussian expansion or German unification in which citizens of a smaller principality now could see themselves as part of a larger German national entity. Starting at a relatively early point in the modern period allows us to see the national expansion unfold. It is understood here that in a burgeoning nationalistic age, belonging to a larger, more powerful national unit is preferable to being part of a feeble, smaller unit subject to domination by neighboring powers such as France or Austria (-Hungary).

An early date for the measurement of gain has an additional advantage. The longer a territory is held by a national entity, the more likely the widespread anger and outrage at its violent dispossession. In the 1990s, the extreme Serb reaction to the potential imminent loss of long-held Kosovo as the result of increasingly strident Albanian efforts is one case in point. By the same token, in 1922 Turkey's loss of very recently conquered territory by Greece in Anatolia elicited no appreciable extremist response.[74] Thus, areas that became part of Germany (or Prussia) after 1807 were given a "+," while all areas governed by Prussia prior to 1807 were coded with a "−," signifying simply that no gain for that region was achieved in the process of Prusso-German unification. The third column lists subordination prior to 1807 in the form of rule of a territory by a government having an ethnoreligious composition substantially different from that of the German population being governed. A "+" signifies a subordinate condition; absence of subordination is indicated by a "−."

---

[71] According to Mann 2005, 224: "The most overrepresented are the westerners, almost all from Alsace-Lorraine and areas lost to Denmark and Belgium."

[72] Mann 2005, 223–4; emphasis in original. There are two other norming procedures that Mann used, but the one recorded in the table here is the one that is most comparable across the various cases, and the one that he lists first.

[73] Information concerning the gain and loss of territory is found in Treharne and Fullard 1969.

[74] Clogg 1992; Payne 1995.

Table 13.1 *Nazi war criminals:*[1] *loss, gain, and subordination*

Birthplace	Ratio	Loss	Gain	Subordination
1. Alsace-Lorraine, Malmedy	4.37	+	+	+
2. Other Eastern Ethnic Germans[2]	2.37	+	−	+
3. Ethnic Germans in Poland[3]	2.20	+	−	−
4. Catholic Bavaria	1.72	−	+	−
5. Upper Silesia	1.70	+	−	−
6. Austria[4]	1.37+	+	+	−
7. Schleswig-Holstein[5]	1.31	+	+	+
Mean	1.29			
8. East Prussia	1.17	−	−	−
9. Baden, etc.	1.09	−	+	−
10. Rhineland	.94	−	+	−
11. East Pomerania, Brandenburg	.87	−	−	−
12. Saxony	.80	−	+	−
13. Franconia, Württemberg	.77	−	+	−
14. Lower Silesia	.74	−	−	−
15. Hanover, etc.	.73	−	+	−
16. West Pomerania, Brandenburg,[6] Mecklenburg[7]	.63	−	+	−
17. Westphalia, Hesse	.62	−	+	−
18. Thuringia, etc.	.57	−	+	−
19. Sudeten Germans (Czechoslovakia)	.55	−	−	−

1. Adapted from Mann 2005, 225.
2. Territorial loss in this instance was manifested quite directly in the form of German-owned large estates nationalized by newly independent states such as Estonia and Latvia, in addition to the dispossession of German homes and property.
3. In contrast to the "Other Eastern Ethnic Germans," most ethnic Germans in Poland had been part of imperial Germany prior to 1919.
4. The number of Austrian perpetrators probably was underestimated because of the later and much smaller number of war crimes trials in Austria in contrast to West Germany.
5. Only North Schleswig was lost to Denmark in 1920, but the data are recorded as Schleswig-Holstein, thereby underestimating the impact of North Schleswig's unique trajectory.
6. Apparently, Brandenburg was divided into two, west and east, for purposes of indicating birthplace, but this division had no effect on the findings of this study.
7. A value for Berlin (.66) was calculated separately by Mann, but as Berlin itself is not a region and this number is close to that obtained for this region as a whole (.63), it was omitted here.

Alsace-Lorraine, Malmedy, Schleswig-Holstein. Only three areas fully meet the criteria shown in Table 13.1, namely subordination followed by gain, in turn followed by loss, signified by three "+" signs in the respective columns. Alsace-Lorraine was effectively governed by France after 1648, and full French control was established by Louis XIV, lasting until 1871. Between 1871 and 1919 this territory was incorporated into imperial Germany, only to be returned to France in 1919. During World War II, Alsace-Lorraine was once again part of the German state. Malmedy was first governed by France, but after the Napoleonic Wars, the Congress of Vienna in 1815 awarded it to Prussia; after 1871 it continued as part of the Imperial Germany. In 1919, as stipulated in the Treaty of Versailles, Malmedy was allocated to Belgium, only to be joined to the Reich during World War II, but lost in the fall of 1944.

Schleswig-Holstein was controlled by Denmark from the thirteenth century, but after the Danish defeat of 1864, was annexed by Prussia in 1866 and later became part of the German Empire. As the result of a plebiscite after World War I, North Schleswig, but not the remainder of Schleswig-Holstein, was awarded to Denmark in 1920. During World War II, North Schleswig was incorporated into the Reich.

Calculating a mean of 1.29 in the war criminal ratio yields an immediate divide in the table. All regions above the mean (excepting "Catholic Bavaria") experienced loss, while those below that value did not. Thus, territorial loss clearly is a predictor of excess war criminality, confirming the critical importance of territorial loss or the threat of its imminent occurrence in the explanation of genocide.[75] But what of the extraordinary position of Alsace-Lorraine and Malmedy, firmly ensconced at the head of the table? Mann[76] expressed surprise at this finding, but gives no reason for the outlier status of these territories (they sit at 3.35 standard deviations above the mean). The theory presented here singles out these regions as those with the greatest potential for extremist violence.

As a region once governed by France, but with many German speakers, the annexation of Alsace-Lorraine by the newly constituted German Empire was welcomed by many. An indicator of the favored status of German speakers was the rapid immigration to France, Switzerland, and elsewhere by many French speakers. Small, almost exclusively francophone areas (e.g., Metz) were annexed by Germany along with the remainder. Within 5 years of annexation, approximately 100,000 residents of Alsace-Lorraine had emigrated.

Immediately after signing of the Armistice, French troops quickly occupied this region, arriving in Strasbourg on November 21. Alsace-Lorraine was incorporated into the centralized French system, much as had existed prior to 1871. Almost immediately, the French government began a campaign to make Alsace-Lorraine into a thoroughly francophone area. All Germans who had arrived in the region after 1870 were deported. German-language newspapers

---

[75] Midlarsky 2005a, 2005b.   [76] 2005, 227.

no longer could be published.[77] Hence, immediately after the French defeat of 1940 and the re-annexation of Alsace-Lorraine, the tendencies toward extremist revanche became evident. Under these conditions, despite whatever civilizing tendencies existed in the region, an extraordinary participation in war crimes occurred during World War II. And this despite the earlier absence of pogroms or any other manifestations of extreme anti-Semitic sentiment.

We need to examine the ephemeral gain more carefully, particularly regarding the condition of Jews, after all the principal targets of the perpetrators. What is the connection between perpetrator and victim? The answer resides in the image of the Jew as a defector, responsible for the German loss of World War I, one of the main canards of Nazi ideation.

Shortly after the end of World War I, no less a personage than Kaiser Wilhelm II remarked in a letter to General August von Mackensen on December 2, 1919: "The deepest, most disgusting shame ever perpetrated by a people in history, the Germans have done onto [sic] themselves. Egged on and misled by the tribe of Juda [sic] whom they hated, who were guests among them! That was their thanks! Let no German ever forget this, nor rest until these parasites have been destroyed and exterminated [*vertilgt und ausgerottet*] from German soil! This poisonous mushroom on the German oak-tree!"[78]

In the hierarchal society of early twentieth-century Germany, such sentiments would have had considerable weight. Certainly, Hitler agreed completely. Speaking to the Czechoslovakian foreign minister, František Chvalkovský, on January 21, 1939, Hitler stated: "The Jews have not brought about the 9 November 1918 for nothing. This day will be avenged."[79] All of this despite the reality of 100,000 German Jewish men under arms during World War I (80,000 having served in combat), 12,000 Jewish dead at the front, and 35,000 decorated for battlefield bravery. These statistics are out of all proportion to the roughly 500,000 Jewish citizens living in Germany in 1914.[80]

The claim that the Jews were defectors resonated strongly in Alsace-Lorraine, for many Jews in this region fled to France in 1914, just as earlier emigration was a principal source of the decline in Jewish population amounting to 10,500 persons between 1871 and 1910.[81] Among the many reasons for choosing France over Germany was the image and reality of France as the liberator of Jews after the French Revolution, establishing strict legal equality between Christians and Jews. In contrast, until the turn of the twentieth century, there still remained limitations on Jewish participation in German public life.

Pro-French Jewish sentiment in Alsace-Lorraine during World War I was not only visible but in one instance actually was memorialized publicly. David Bloch was born in Alsace-Lorraine in 1895. After working several years in France, instead of returning to Alsace in order to fulfill his military obligation,

---

[77] Silverman 1972.   [78] Quoted in Röhl 1994, 210.   [79] Quoted in Kershaw 2000a, 127.
[80] Fischer 1998, 120.   [81] Caron 1988, 76.

he joined the French army. Because of physical weakness, he was not sent to the front, but volunteered for special reconnaissance in Alsace. Captured by the Germans shortly after arriving, and sentenced to death for high treason, Bloch proclaimed: "I am a French soldier, I have done my duty. My country [*patrie*] will revenge me."[82] After the French entry into Alsace-Lorraine, the French government commissioned the well-known sculptor Emmanuel Hannaux to construct a monument to honor Bloch, who then became a folk hero not only to Alsatian Jews but to all pro-French Alsatians. Other Jews who aided France also were well known.

Overall, although only 1.6 percent of the total population of Alsace-Lorraine (as of 1910),[83] Jews "constituted at least 6 percent of all Alsace-Lorrainers condemned for high treason, approximately 7 percent of those charged with anti-German offenses, and about 10 percent of those stripped of their citizenship in 1915 and 1916 for not responding to the imperial government's appeal to Germans abroad to return home."[84] And in November–December 1918, synagogues throughout Alsace-Lorraine openly celebrated the French victory and expressed their enthusiasm at the prospect of rejoining the French-Jewish community.

Here we see the dynamics of the ephemeral gain and its influence on perpetrators from Alsace-Lorraine. In their view, the Nazis must be correct in their claim that the Jews were defectors from the German nation, for had not the Alsatian Jews and those of Lorraine behaved precisely in the way understood by Nazi ideation? Because these territories were so joyously acquired by the German-speaking population in 1871 after a long period of French governance, their loss, presumably at the hands of Jewish defectors, among others, was especially bitter. Not recognized, of course, was a very natural consequence of this territorial transfer: the blurred loyalties that made such defection much more likely, especially when the Jewish population was treated more civilly by one protagonist (France) than by the other (Germany).

The periods of German subordination (1648–1871), gain (1871–1919), and loss (1919–40) conform to the expectations of Figure 1.1, shown in Figure 13.4.

Malmedy presents another instance of an unexpected disproportionate participation in war crimes. In addition, it is distinguished by the location of the only recorded large-scale massacre of Western prisoners of war following the Normandy invasion of June 1944. Governed by the French until the Congress of Vienna awarded it to Prussia, as late as 1853, Malmedy's francophone status was recognized by the Prussian administration despite its governance since 1815 (formally annexed in 1822). But in 1863, the newly appointed chancellor, Bismarck, required the suppression of the French language in all administrative documents. Although soon rescinded after intense protest, upon the formation

---

[82] Quoted in Caron 1988, 181.   [83] Caron 1988, 76.   [84] Caron 1988, 182.

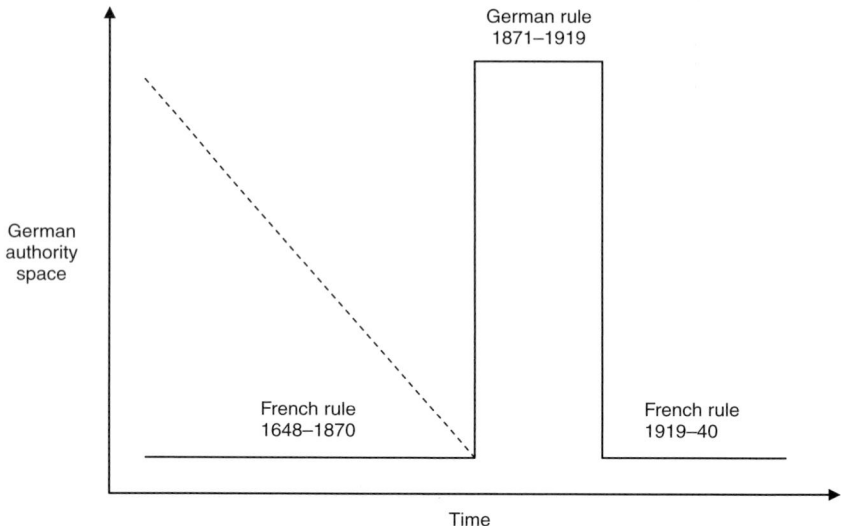

Figure 13.4:   Changes in German authority space over time: Alsace-Lorraine

of the German Empire, the suppression of French in administrative documents was once again demanded in 1878. And the teaching of French was soon to be forbidden. Malmedy's return to francophone status was celebrated after the entry of the Belgian army in 1919. And in 1925 Malmedy was incorporated into the Belgian province of Liège.[85] During World War II, the German language was once again emphasized, under a new German administration.

Thus we see a similar pattern of change of governance as that experienced by Alsace-Lorraine. And Malmedy was the location of the massacre of eighty-four American prisoners of war; although not genocide, this atrocity can also be explained by the present framework. The German invasion of the Ardennes on December 16, 1944 was the heralded beginning of the reconquest of Malmedy on the road to Antwerp, after this region had been lost to the Allies during the fall of 1944.[86] This constitutes another ephemeral period to add to the earlier one.

The men of *Leibstandarte-SS Adolf Hitler* (an archaic description of Hitler's SS bodyguard unit), all volunteers under the overall command of Hitler's personal friend, Sepp Dietrich, must have been keenly aware of the significance of this territory. It was soon to be once again conquered as it had been in 1940, but lost in the Allied campaign after the Normandy invasion. On September 16, 1944, Hitler himself had voiced his desire for an Ardennes

---

[85] Enssle 1980.   [86] Murray and Millett 2000, 435.

offensive focused on the Malmedy region. Planning for this offensive took place despite strategic advice by Hitler's confidantes to counter-attack against the Soviets, although they were not yet on German soil, nor would be for a foreseeable period.[87] In contrast, it was obvious that the Allied eastward advance would soon incorporate formerly German territory in the Malmedy region, which it did.

As the planning proceeded, "Hitler had issued orders that every inch of German soil should be defended by the most radical means; that nothing of value should be allowed to fall into enemy hands."[88] If German territory was sacrosanct to Hitler, then how much more important would be German territory held for over a century, lost to Belgium, regained, and lost again in the fall of 1944, but soon to be recouped? And the statistics for 1920 (both Belgian and German) showed 60,000 residents of the region, only 10,000 of whom were French speakers. *Most of this francophone population was found in and around the city of Malmedy.*[89]

Even before the rise of Hitler, this region, lost to Belgium in 1920, was to be a major concern of the last effective foreign minister of the Weimar Republic, Gustav Stresemann, as evidenced by his extraordinary emphasis on this territory in a speech to the Eupen-Malmedy *Landsmannschaften* on December 16, 1925.[90]

Further indications of Malmedy's exceptional status were given at the trial of perpetrators of the massacre. "Multiple German witnesses testified to the absence of formal directives to murder prisoners of war... Fritz Kraemer, Dietrich's former chief of staff and the first of the defendants to testify, denied that orders distributed by the Sixth Panzer Army had contained directives to engage in illegal killings but admitted that tactical orders had referred to the possibility of resistance by the Belgian guerrillas and that such resistance, when encountered, was to be broken 'at all costs.' Far from having killed its prisoners, Kraemer testified, Dietrich's army had taken captive between five and seven thousand American soldiers during the offensive."[91]

Thus, in addition to the many surviving American prisoners of war taken elsewhere during the German offensive, the Malmedy region is also distinguished by the implied, if not explicit, permission to kill Belgian civilian "resisters." Like Alsatians (Jewish or otherwise) who helped the French army during

---

[87] Murray and Millett 2000, 449. [88] Kershaw 2000a, 737.

[89] Enssle 1980, 20. It is perhaps no accident that the commander of the unit responsible for the Malmedy massacre and atrocities against Belgian civilians, Jochen Peiper, was killed in the midst of a francophone population while residing in France in 1976. Having his death sentence by American judges commuted, he spent ten years in prison after which his employment with Porsche and Volkswagen was later terminated because of his notorious past. Peiper's self-imposed exile in eastern France ended when his house was fire-bombed. See Weingartner 2000, 225.

[90] Enssle 1980, 124. [91] Weingartner 2000, 83.

World War I, Belgian citizens of the Reich in December 1944 were to be treated ruthlessly. And this outcome came to pass. According to Joseph Weingartner:[92]

> Not only had American prisoners of war fallen victim to the guns of Kampfgruppe Peiper [the unit responsible for the Malmedy massacre] but also, according to the sworn statements of the SS prisoners, a substantial number of Belgian civilians. Thus, a member of the Eleventh Company, Second SS Panzergrenadier Regiment, stated in a deposition of March 12, 1946, that on December 18 between Stavelot and La Gleize, he had witnessed a member of his company fire his machine pistol from an SPW at two Belgian civilians working along the road, hitting both. The commander of Tank 101 of the First Company, First SS Panzer Regiment, affirmed in a sworn statement of March 13, 1945, that the radio-man/machine-gunner of his vehicle had fired three to four machine-gun bursts into a group of women while passing through Stavelot on the morning of December 18. A member of a penal group attached to the Ninth Panzer Pioneer Company admitted, in a statement of March 26, 1946, to having blown out the brains of a forty-year-old woman as she stood in her kitchen in Büllingen [easternmost point of the Malmedy region]. Other depositions indicated that civilians had been killed at many other locations.

This behavior is consistent with an earlier Nazi reaction to the activities of the Malmedy priest Joseph Peters who helped young people hide and desert the German army. After his arrest in October 1942, Peters was beheaded in Aachen on July 1, 1943.[93] It is only a short step from these atrocities to the killing of unarmed prisoners of war.

The Malmedy massacre occurred under conditions of successive reinforced ephemera that the theory predicts would lead to atrocity over and above that which would be expected in wartime. Nowhere else in the West was a large-scale massacre of Allied prisoners of war committed, despite the many opportunities. Even the especially hated Allied bomber crews, when captured, although frequently beaten, generally survived, as did Western Jewish prisoners of war after the Normandy invasion. Followers of the same extremist ideology as the SS-Totenkopfverbände who guarded the concentration camps and who comprised a significant portion of the 1,581 war criminals analyzed here, the Waffen SS combat units also varied in their propensity to kill wantonly, as demonstrated by the large-scale massacre of prisoners of war in the Malmedy region, but nowhere else in the West. The reinforced ephemera are shown in Figure 13.5.

An interesting comparison is that between Alsace-Lorraine, Malmedy and another component of the German Empire shorn from it in 1920, North Schleswig. However, a problem of comparability immediately arises. Mann's data presentation includes the entire state of Schleswig-Holstein, not North Schleswig alone. And North Schleswig indeed might be predicted to yield

[92] 1979, 87.   [93] Sache 2008, 3.

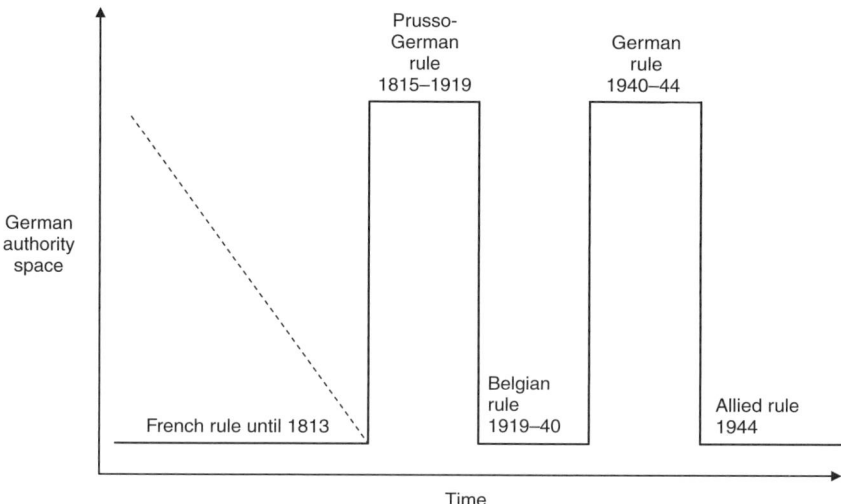

Figure 13.5:   Changes in German authority space over time: Malmedy

a high level of extremist behavior comparable to that of Alsace-Lorraine or Malmedy, based on expectations of the present theory. After the incorporation of Schleswig-Holstein into Prussia in 1866, the German language and culture were heavily emphasized. German was substituted for Danish in the churches, schools, and playgrounds. The only region of this area to resist this forced assimilation, at least somewhat effectively, was North Schleswig. After World War I, a referendum was held in 1920 and 75 percent of voters opted for reunification with Denmark, while 25 percent supported remaining in Germany.[94] Thus, when Hitler occupied Denmark, at least 25 percent of the North Schleswig population could have been sufficiently affected to engage in extremist behavior. Despite underestimation of this impact by data aggregation with the whole of Schleswig-Holstein, this entire state still appears above the mean, signifying the regions with disproportionately large contributions to war criminality.

As in the case of Alsace-Lorraine, Schleswig-Holstein's trajectory can be mapped onto Figures 13.2 or 13.4, with Danish rule until 1864 constituting the subordination period, followed by German ascendance (1866–1919), and loss consisting of the forfeiture of North Schleswig to Denmark in 1920.

Loss in other regions. The remaining regions exhibiting disproportionately high levels of victimization all reflect the presence of material loss, with the exception of "Catholic Bavaria." Many Germans falling into the second category

---

[94]   Steefel 1932, 262.

consisting of "other Eastern ethnic Germans" lost large estates or were otherwise dispossessed of their homes and property. Here, even without a prior gain and only a formal subordination to the tsarist empire, the *direct* loss of property can have a large impact on future extremist behavior. Ethnic Germans in Poland, most of whom were former citizens of imperial Germany, also experienced a profound sense of loss. Most of this German population had been governed by German rulers since the late eighteenth century, at the latest.

After World War I, Austria was a rump state after being shorn of its imperial expanse. Gone were Hungary, Bohemia, Moravia, Slovakia, Croatia, and Bosnia-Herzegovina, among other territories. The sense of loss was so pervasive that virtually all political factions were in agreement on the desirability of joining the German Republic.[95] The Allies at Versailles prevented that outcome. But because Austria was not nearly as thorough in pursuing war criminals as was West Germany, many perpetrators likely slipped through the cracks. Mann adds the "+" to his calculated value suggesting that it is indeed an underestimate of the real figure.

The only apparent exception to this pattern is "Catholic Bavaria."[96] Although exceptional among smaller German states in its long history of independence prior to unification, nevertheless Bavaria was not lost to a foreign power after World War I, as were Alsace-Lorraine, Malmedy and North Schleswig. Nor were Bavarians (unless serving on the Eastern front during World War I) exposed to the rampant anti-Semitism and deadly pogroms in Eastern Europe at the end of that war, as were the Eastern Germans and some from Poland. Nor was Bavaria's geopolitical position on the German periphery consequential, as it was for ethnic Germans in the East. Bavaria's neighbors were the "unthreatening Swiss, Sudetens, and Austrians."[97] Yet Bavaria appears in this high category of extremist behavior, and there are at least three reasons for this outcome.

First, an external threat was experienced more directly by Bavaria than any other German state not directly transferred to foreign rule. In November 1918, a socialist revolution occurred in Bavaria headed by Kurt Eisner, a journalist of Jewish origin and agitator against German participation in the war. Upon his assassination in April 1919, a communist government was established under the leadership of emissaries from the Soviet Union – Lewien, Levine-Niessen, and Axelrod – also of Jewish origin.[98] Despite having been put down readily by troops of the newly born Weimar Republic, the consequences of this revolutionary

---

[95] Fellner 1981, 9.

[96] Mann 2005, 225, 229–30 records Bavaria in this fashion to indicate that, in addition to Bavaria itself, "Catholic Bavaria" includes parts of neighboring regions that are heavily Catholic. This mapping suggests his finding that Roman Catholics were somewhat over-represented among the war criminals in his sample.

[97] Mann 2005, 228.

[98] In contrast, the Spartacist uprising in Berlin (January 1919) led by the extreme left-wing Karl Liebknecht and Rosa Luxemburg was domestic in origin.

period were substantial. Before their soviet republic was quashed, one of the final acts of the revolutionaries was to execute a number of hostages. Among them were seven members of the Thule society, a conservative aristocratic society that gave rise to the German Workers' Party, later to become the NSDAP under Hitler's leadership.[99] Four of the murdered Thule society members were nobles. Heinrich Himmler himself was the namesake of Prince Heinrich of the Bavarian house of Wittelsbad and a student of Professor Himmler, Heinrich's father. The prince's death from wounds suffered at the front during World War I was deeply felt by the Himmlers. According to Peter Padfield,[100] a major Himmler biographer: "It's against this background that Heinrich Himmler's views were formed."

These events imply the second reason for Bavaria's disproportionately large contribution to the stock of war criminals. Although the pogrom-inspired model for mass murder was not a part of the Bavarian landscape, the Jewish presence was to be blamed for threats to the existence of Bavaria's traditional Roman Catholic way of life. In 1923, all Jews who had settled in Bavaria since 1914 were expelled.[101] Finally, as a consequence of this turmoil and proximity to Austria, from which Hitler and other early Nazis originated, Munich became the capital of Nazism. This is not to say that all of Bavaria was pro-Nazi. Nevertheless, Munich's standing in this region must have been influential in stimulating an excess participation of Bavarians in war criminality.

The Sudetenland. In the lower portion of the table, we find just the opposite pattern from that found at the top. Instead of the presence of loss, and in the case of Alsace-Lorraine, Malmedy, and North Schleswig preceded by gain and a still earlier subordination, we find the absence of loss in all cases below the mean. Many of these areas are situated in the German interior, with only one surprising exception, the Sudetenland. Mann[102] calls this a "striking" finding.

This finding is indeed striking and puzzling, for the Sudeten Germans at first appear to exhibit greater similarity with the Germans in Alsace-Lorraine, Malmedy, Austrians, Germans in North Schleswig, or German communities in the East than with those of the traditional Reich. Yet their distinct under-representation among the perpetrators appears to derive from the absence of any extraordinary changes in political circumstance throughout their recent history.

At the dissolution of the Austro-Hungarian Empire in 1919, the Sudetenland, populated by ethnic Germans within the northern portions of Bohemia and Moravia (termed Historic Provinces of the multiethnic Empire),[103] became part of newly independent Czechoslovakia. Earlier, when part of Austria-Hungary, all voters in this region could choose among an array of parties. The most popular, as of data from 1907, were the Social Democrats, Christian Socialists,

---

[99] Kershaw 1998, 135–6.   [100] 1991, 36.   [101] Ascheim 1982, 243.
[102] 2005, 228.   [103] Komjathy and Stockwell 1980, 17.

German Clericals, and German Agrarians.[104] Within Czechoslovakia, these parties now became the German Social Democrats, German Christian Socialists, and German Agrarians.[105]

In other words, approximate continuity existed between the old Austro-Hungarian array of political choices for the ethnic German population and that which existed in the new Czechoslovakia. And in democratic Czechoslovakia these choices actually could have had more political impact than in the tolerant but nevertheless autocratic Austro-Hungarian monarchy. Indeed, in many respects, the situation for most Germans was better. Constituting 23.4 percent of the Czechoslovakian population in 1921 and comprising a disproportionately large share of the literate and industrial worker population, the Czech and Slovak political leadership sought their cooperation. These leaders awarded "more privileges to the German minorities than the [very liberal] minority treaties had proposed."[106]

Only after the Great Depression struck in the early 1930s and their own economic circumstances had worsened considerably, especially in comparison with the less industrialized sections of the interior populated by Czechs and Slovaks, did the majority of Sudeten Germans turn to autonomy as a preferred solution. The election of 1935 was the turning point at which the old, mostly leftist parties were abandoned by most Sudeten Germans, preferring instead the recently formed Sudeten German Party (SDP) winning by a two-thirds majority. And the leader of this party, Konrad Henlein, was initially quite moderate. After meeting with various Reich officials in 1934, Henlein's orientation was close to that of Admiral Wilhelm Canaris, who believed that "Hitler's way may lead to an effective catastrophe."[107]

Henlein sought to maximize Sudeten German autonomy, but only within the framework of a united democratic Czechoslovakia, something that Hitler increasingly opposed. Henlein eventually supported Hitler's policies toward Czechoslovakia, but only because he saw Hitler's Germany as the most effective international avenue of support for the Sudeten Germans, all others being closed to them. Despite this increasingly pro-German orientation, at the time of Hitler's occupation only 1.76 percent of the German population in the Sudetenland and Czech areas were Nazi Party members.[108] One-third of the Sudeten German electorate did not support the SDP, and when in 1938 the Czechoslovak government ordered a partial mobilization, Sudeten Germans responded when called.[109] These facts suggest a fairly low level of dissatisfaction of Sudeten Germans with their political situation within Czechoslovakia. Indeed, as the crisis with Nazi Germany deepened, all political demands of the Sudeten Germans were met by the Czechoslovak government, suggesting the

---

[104] Ogg 1913, 482.   [105] Komjathy and Stockwell 1980, 18.
[106] Komjathy and Stockwell 1980, 18.   [107] Quoted in Komjathy and Stockwell 1980, 25.
[108] Komjathy and Stockwell 1980, 158.   [109] Komjathy and Stockwell 1980, 38.

possibility of even better circumstances for this community just prior to Hitler's entry. An approximate functional political continuity had been constructed for the Sudeten Germans, in stark contrast to the marked discontinuities of the ephemeral gain.

Romania

Another prime candidate for micro-analysis is Romania, responsible for the killing of approximately 250,000 Jews under its jurisdiction.[110] According to Raul Hilberg,[111] "no country, besides Germany, was involved in massacres of Jews on such a scale." Thus, in the array of Holocaust perpetrators, Germany and Romania occupy the first two ranks.

Although to my knowledge, systematic data on individual Romanian perpetrators comparable to those on the German killers is not available, election data indicating popular preferences have indeed been collected and analyzed. The status of Romanian territories such as Bessarabia and Bukovina that conform directly to the pattern of gain and loss identified in Figure 1.1, is directly comparable to that of Alsace-Lorraine and North Schleswig. As we shall see, these Romanian electoral preferences will closely parallel the pattern demonstrated by the Western Nazi perpetrators in Table 13.1.

Prior to 1920, Bessarabia was part of tsarist Russia, while Bukovina was administered by Austria-Hungary. After World War I, these territories were incorporated into an expanded Romanian state as a result of World War I. But in a roughly equivalent pattern to that of the German case, these territories were lost to a foreign power – the Soviet Union – in 1940, prior to the onset of Soviet participation in World War II. Their reconquest after the start of Operation Barbarossa would lead to consequences similar to those found among perpetrators from Alsace-Lorraine and Schleswig-Holstein. We witness a heightened level of popular extremism during the period of threat prior to the loss of these Romanian territories, and when the territories are regained, the violence against targeted civilians blamed for these losses is extensive.

Two right-wing parties competed in the 1937 election, the last free election held before the war. Both were offshoots of the Christian National Defense League (LANC) founded in 1923 by a professor Alexandru C. Cuza. It advocated the revocation of Jewish rights, and limitations on Jewish education. The party used the swastika as a symbol long before Hitler co-opted it. A speech in 1926 elaborated Cuza's sentiments and goals:

> It is monstrous that the constitution should speak of the rights of the Jews. The solution ought to be to eliminate the Jews by law. The first step ought to be to exclude them from the army. Leases of forests granted to Jews should

---

[110] Ioanid 2000.   [111] 2003, 809.

be canceled. All land held by the Jews should be expropriated. Likewise, all town houses owned by Jews should be confiscated. I would introduce a *numerus clausus* (proportional Jewish representation, participation, and membership) in the schools.[112]

Initially an acolyte of Cuza, Corneliu Codreanu in 1927 founded the Legion of the Archangel Michael as a more dynamic and openly fascist version of the LANC. While Cuza was willing to follow the parliamentary route to power, the Legion was to be a movement, not with a specific political program or purpose, such as the seizure of power, but set up as a venue for the training of men. In 1930, Codreanu created the Iron Guard as a paramilitary unit to combat communism. In many respects, but not all, membership in the Legion and in the Iron Guard eventually became interchangeable identities.

The Legion was anti-communist, anti-Semitic, and anti-parliament. Codreanu boasted that he had adopted these positions well before Hitler, and that during his time in Berlin in 1922, had "shown the light" to several Germans who later became prominent Nazis.[113]

As in many other European extreme right-wing movements of the interwar period, Judaism and communism were seen as inextricably linked. Anti-Semitism and anti-communism functioned virtually as a single ideational theme. Romanian peasant life was exalted, as were elements of Romanian Eastern Orthodoxy, both functioning as authentic components of national identity.

Behaviorally, the main feature of the Legion that distinguished it from the LANC was the willingness to use violence, not only against Jews but also against other Romanians who opposed their political goals, however ill-defined. In 1924, Codreanu shot the police chief of Iași who had tried to limit his anti-Semitic activities. "He was acquitted in a much-publicized trial which only augmented his popularity in anti-Semitic circles."[114]

The Cuzists and the Legionairs would compete in the 1937 election. But in 1935 the LANC and the National Agrarian Party (PNA) joined forces to form the National Christian Party (PNC). The PNA had been founded by the poet Octavian Goga who propounded an anti-Semitic populism. This party was perhaps even closer to the Legion in fascist sympathies, but felt it needed to reinforce its national appeal by combining with the LANC.[115] It was the PNC that would compete with the Legion for the right-wing nationalist votes in the two regions that would soon be lost to the Soviets, but regained after the launching of Operation Barbarossa on June 22, 1941. According to Raul Hilberg,[116] "In the two eastern provinces of Bukovina and Bessarabia, which were ceded in 1940 but reconquered in 1941, the Jews were subjected to the brunt of the Romanian destruction process."

---

[112] Quoted in Ioanid 2000, 16–17.   [113] Roberts 1969, 228.
[114] Roberts 1969, 227.   [115] Rus 1998, 14.   [116] 2003, 811.

Table 13.2 *Percentages of estimated ethnic Romanian vote for the combined Legion and PNC in elections to the Assembly of 1937 in four Romanian provinces*[1]

	Bessarabia	Bukovina	Greater Transylvania[2]	Moldavia
1. Total (all ethnicities)	26.30	32.10	21.49	31.10
2. % Romanians	56.23	44.51	57.82	89.81
3. *Estimated ethnic Romanian vote*	*46.77*[3]	*72.12*	*37.17*	*34.63*
4. % Jews (1930)	7.23	10.91[4]	3.48	6.67

1. Adapted from Enescu 1991.
2. Includes all territory gained from Hungary in the Trianon Treaty of 1920.
3. Based on Romanian ethnicity. Using Romanian as the mother tongue, this value is 47.12.
4. A decline from 12.95 percent in 1910.

Election statistics from 1937 bear out the special status of Bessarabia and Bukovina. Table 13.2 presents the estimated percentage of the ethnic Romanian vote in four provinces, based on the total vote within a province and percentages of ethnic Romanians dwelling in it. These provinces were governed by Russia (Bessarabia) and Austria-Hungary (Bukovina and Greater Transylvania). In 1918 these provinces were occupied by Romanian forces leading ultimately to their annexation. Bessarabia was incorporated into Romania despite Soviet objections, Bukovina was granted by the Treaty of Saint-Germain in 1919, and Greater Transylvania was acquired from Hungary by the Treaty of Trianon of 1920.[117] The last of the provinces considered here, Moldavia, was unified with Wallachia in a single autonomous province of the Ottoman Empire in 1861, and was independent as of 1878 as a result of the Treaties of San Stefano (1877) and Berlin (1878).[118] I use the term "Moldavia" to denote this province in order to distinguish it from the now independent Moldova, which is essentially coterminous with Bessarabia as it was between the wars.

Because of its long-term inclusion within the Romanian polity, Moldavia is represented here to provide a potential contrast with the first three provinces listed in the table that were incorporated within Romania only after World War I. Their status as territories newly acquired from neighboring powers that were forced to relinquish them also distinguishes them from Moldavia. In addition, this province had a significant percentage of Jews, and this have stimulated a

[117] Heinen 1986, 523.   [118] Jelavich and Jelavich 1977, 118, 154.

strong extremist response in the form of votes for the two parties. These percentages are presented in the fourth row of the table to allow for comparisons and possible inferences as to the impact of anti-Semitism alone on the vote, instead of the external threat and ephemeral gain that I hypothesized here to account for extremist voting.

The estimated ethnic Romanian vote in the third row is based on dividing the first row by the second, under the assumption that only ethnic Romanians or those whose native language was Romanian would vote for these parties. Given the overt Romanian nationalist emphases of both parties either in extreme nationalist form (the Legion), or straightforward Romanian anti-Semitism (the PNC), this is a plausible assumption. In any event, this calculation is applied equally to all of the provinces so that whatever error is introduced would fall more or less uniformly across the four provinces.

The two provinces that were most threatened by an external power, the Soviet Union, also had the largest vote for the extremist parties. Bukovina and Bessarabia ranked highest, followed by Transylvania, also obtained from a foreign power, Hungary, but one far less threatening than the Soviet Union. The province that was least threatened, Moldavia, demonstrated the lowest percentage vote for the two parties among ethnic Rumanians.

Regarding Bessarabia, "Soviet Russia did not recognize the new *status quo*. The communists, and pro-Soviet irredentists tried to subvert this union with propaganda throughout the interwar years, as with revolts and rebellions up to 1924. Characteristically, the elements desiring union with the Soviet Union seldom came from among Moldavians."[119] In the case of Bukovina, "The [Marxists] had never officially backed Bukovina's union with Romania. The communists even supported the annexation of the province by the Soviet Union. The Marxists of all kinds received their political and electoral support overwhelmingly from Jews and Ukrainians."[120]

And these attempted annexations by the Soviets were not empty threats. As part of the 1939 Nazi-Soviet rapprochement, Bessarabia and northern Bukovina were ceded by Romania to the Soviet Union in 1940, and much of Greater Transylvania was transferred to Hungary in that year. When Bessarabia and northern Bukovina were restored to Romanian rule after the June 22, 1941 invasion of Russia by Germany, the Jews would pay a heavy price, as we saw. There exists here a striking similarity to the genocidal perpetrators from Alsace-Lorraine, Malmedy and North Schleswig in the West, which had a similar history of initial subordination to a foreign power, annexation of that territory, to be followed by its loss and then restoration. It is in the last of these phases that the genocidal behavior occurs.

A question remains after considering the results presented in Table 13.2. Although the overall ranking of these provinces in extremist voting is predicted

---

[119] Rus 1999b, 18.   [120] Rus 1999a, 23.

by the theory (the three recently acquired more threatened provinces ranking higher than the fourth), why was Bessarabia that much lower in extremist voting than Bukovina? After all, like Bukovina, Bessarabia had a history of virulent anti-Semitism that led to one of the worst pogroms of the tsarist period, Kishinev (today's Chişinau) in 1903. Nor was there a substantially different percentage of Jews in the two provinces, shown in the bottom row of the table, which is an alternate explanation of the increased voting for overtly anti-Semitic parties. Certainly the presence of Jews was a factor (although widespread anti-Semitism in post-World War II Poland, with only a minuscule number of Jews, demonstrates that it does not require many Jews to have anti-Semitism, and the much larger percentage of Jews in the US apparently incurs little anti-Semitism), but was not decisive. One has only to consider the percentage of Jews in Greater Transylvania, which was little more than half that of Moldavia, yet Greater Transylvania had a larger percentage vote for the extremist parties.

One has to look elsewhere for a plausible explanation; unsurprisingly it is to be found in the differential historical experiences of the two provinces. While Bessarabia had a fitful and violence-ridden transition to Romanian rule, the "incorporation of Bucovina had none of the turbulence that accompanied Bessarabia's. A general congress met on November 28, 1918, and voted for union with Rumania."[121]

In Bessarabia, even before the February 1917 Revolution that overthrew the tsar, there was strong opposition to the Moldavian *boyars* (Romanian landowning aristocrats) who were "notoriously obscurantist."[122] Beginning in July of that year, peasants began seizing land, and before long, roughly two-thirds of the property was taken over. And on October 21–23, 1917 a military committee representative of the Moldavian population passed a resolution supporting the "historical and political autonomy" of Bessarabia.[123] On December 2, 1917 a national council (*Sfatul Ţării*, or *Sfat*) pronounced the formation of a "Democratic Moldavian Republic as a self-governing unit in the Federative Democratic Russian Republic." After Romanian troops forced the ouster of the Bolsheviks who had gained power in several urban areas, the *Sfat* announced the independence of the Moldavian Republic (roughly coterminous with today's independent Moldova). Germany favored Romanian national interests in Bessarabia, and under pressure the *Sfat* voted in favor of joining Romania, but with administrative autonomy and a retention of the land reforms already instituted. Over time, however, this autonomy was eroded and Bessarabia became "a disaffected area throughout the interwar period, with much the most corrupt administration of any Rumanian province."[124]

Hence, it is no surprise that in 1937, Bessarabia would only marginally support the extreme Romanian nationalist Legion (5 percent of the total vote), but

---

[121] Roberts 1969, 36.   [122] Roberts 1969, 32.   [123] Roberts 1969, 33.
[124] Roberts 1969, 35.

with much greater support for the overtly anti-Semitic PNC with its somewhat smaller emphasis on Romanian nationalism (21.3 percent of the total vote). Nevertheless the Romanian nationalist origins of the LANC component of the PNC was still likely to have put off many voters.

In Bukovina, precisely the opposite pattern was found. While the PNC got 9.3 percent of the vote, the intensely Romanian nationalist Legion recorded a resounding 22.8 percent. Of course, other factors influenced the vote, not the least of which was the extent to which the Legion campaigned in certain areas, but not in others.[125] Nevertheless, the turbulent and difficult relationship between Bessarabia and the Romanian central government, almost entirely absent in the case of Bukovina, did much to yield these electoral outcomes.

It is useful to consider summary measures of the extent of extremist voting across the four provinces. Comparing the average of votes for the two parties by ethnic Romanians in the first two columns with the average of these votes in the second two yields, respectively, 59.45 percent and 35.90 percent. In other words, Bessarabia and Bukovina, which experienced a potential ephemeral gain in 1937, actualized in 1940, demonstrated an average 66 percent greater voting for extremist parties than did the less threatened provinces of Transylvania and especially Moldavia.

Conclusion

Viewing extremist behavior through the lens of genocide reveals the experience of subordination, gain, and loss in German history, leading to successive reinforced ephemera prior to the genocide. This theoretical perspective also allows us to see the variation in regional histories among war criminals, who might not otherwise have been complicit in these enormities. Certainly, the differing propensity of individuals to participate in genocide and Nazi war criminality is explained in part by the variation in their exposure to the historical trajectories of Figures 13.4 and 13.5. This pattern is also seen in the Romanian election data, anticipating the imminent loss of Bessarabia and Bukovina, after their brief gain, following long incorporation respectively in the Russian and Austro-Hungarian empires.

The threat and fear of reversion to an earlier subordinate condition is also found among Hutu *génocidaires* committing the mass murders of Tutsi in 1994.[126] So too was the ephemeral gain of 1856–78 influential in the initiation of the massacres of Armenians thereafter. And the joyous reception, even elation, at the Ottoman victory at Adrianople in 1913 was to provide so stark a contrast to the fear of an impending defeat in 1915 yielding, as before, subordination, that defeat was to be avoided at all costs. As we saw in Chapter 10, the pogroms

[125] Rus 1999b.   [126] Hatzfeld 2005; Straus 2006.

in post-World War II Poland generated the fear that enveloped Polish-Jewish refugees returning from the USSR. But that fear was matched by the Polish nationalists' excessive fear of a reversion to the 1939–41 subordination at the hands of newly arrived Jewish agents of Soviet Communism. Ultimately, the historical trajectories of states and regions matter, influencing fatefully the political trajectories of future perpetrators of unimaginable atrocities.

PART V

Conclusion

14

Pathways to Extremism

Summary of findings

In all cases of extremist behavior as measured by the willingness to kill massively, the ephemeral gain was an important antecedent. In two cases where extremism might have been expected but did not occur – Indian Muslims and Bulgaria – the ephemeral gain was absent. A third case, Greece, had a brief territorial gain in Anatolia, its loss, but loss compensation in the form of the demographic strengthening of ethnic Greeks within earlier annexed territory of mixed ethnicity in Europe, which, among other factors, avoided the onset of extremism. Mortality salience in all cases was present before the rise of political extremism.

Equally if not more important is the ability of this framework to single out the most extreme of extremists, as measured by their willingness to commit mass murder on a truly unheard of scale. Both the Ottoman and German populations felt a "triumphal exaltation" after their respective victories prior to the perception of impending defeats during World Wars I and II. Ottomans, Nazis, and Stalinists experienced their successive reinforced ephemera, as did the Serbs as the first and thus far only European country to commit genocide (at Srebrenica) after the carnage of World War II. As a consequence of successive reinforced ephemera, the Malmedy massacre, to my knowledge never before examined within a comparative theoretical framework, is here contrasted with other areas of the West in which American prisoners of war were not massacred. Here in the German Ardennes offensive, with the Malmedy massacre its most important component, and only here, were Allied prisoners of war in the West subject to mass murder after the Normandy invasion.

The LTTE in Sri Lanka also gave evidence of these reinforced ephemera just prior to their first suicide bombing, a practice that would soon lead them to become the pre-eminent suicide bombers prior to the rise of al-Qaeda and related extremist groups. And the Stalinist template proved to be seductive to the Maoists and Khmer Rouge, who sought ultimate and rapid solutions to their pressing societal difficulties. Although single ephemera also may yield large-scale mass murder, the successive reinforced variety is associated with the most horrific cases, especially in Europe and the Ottoman Empire.

At the same time, the case of Pakistan illustrates the importance of perception in assessing the presence or absence of an ephemeral gain. Although the COW Project judged that Pakistan had won the 1965 war with India after its earlier 1947–48 tie with India, and had indeed gained some territory in the salt marsh of Kutch, yet Pakistan had not achieved its principal goal of territorial gain in Kashmir. In other words, it had not at all reversed the earlier Indian success in Kashmir. Further, the perception of victory in Pakistan was enhanced by the memories of the early stellar performance of the Pakistani armor and air force that in fact was largely reversed by Indian victories towards the end of the conflict. Pakistan was holding more Indian territory at the end of the war than India was occupying Pakistani lands, but Indian conquests were of greater strategic value, near to large Pakistani cities. Withdrawal of the forces of both sides from conquered territory actually was strategically more advantageous to Pakistan. The later award of the Rann of Kutch to Pakistan was a very minor territorial compensation for the Pakistani withdrawal.

Thus, perception can be affected by selective memory retention, and this influenced the Pakistani view of the 1965 conflict as a gain, and the early events of the 1971 civil conflict and war with India as an entry into the domain of losses, thereby constituting an overall ephemeral gain. The loss of the Pakistani legislative majority to the Hindu and culturally Hinduized Muslims of East Pakistan reinforced the ephemeral gain on the battlefield, and led to the deaths of an estimated 1.5 to 3 million persons in East Pakistan.[1]

Additionally, categories of mass murder have been identified that are not explained directly by the present framework. These include the adoption by communist countries of templates of mass murder employed by earlier communist extremists (e.g., Joseph Stalin) in similar circumstances of serious internal and external threats to their governance. And the shadow of the present reveals cross-sectional dynamics for the onset of mass murder, especially at the hands of military forces. Thus, the coincidence of the shadows of the past and of the future in the ephemeral gain can be supplemented by the shadow of the present under conditions of dominating command structures.

Yet for all its apparent applicability across disparate categories – secular and sacred "isms" and extreme nationalism including genocide – the singular pathways from the ephemeral gain to actual extremism necessarily must differ. And this is precisely what we find. The differential applicability of the three pathways from the ephemeral gain to extremism: (1) humility-shame, (2) perceptions of injustice, and (3) the threat and fear of reversion, all leading to anger, will now be explored. Because of the much greater incidence of mass murder – the *sine qua non* of extremist behavior – within fascist and communist governance, they will be discussed at greater length. These two forms of extremism, along with radical Islamism, reflect universal ambition, and are found (to varying extents) to

---

[1] But see note 40, Chapter 12.

incorporate all of the three pathways to extremism stemming from the ephemeral gain. Extreme nationalism (whether or not of the rampaging military) as the remaining form of extremism reflects particular goals that lead to the threat and fear of reversion as the principal pathway from the ephemeral gain.

But what is striking is that the pathways from the ephemeral gain to extremism vary not only across space (the separate cases) but across time *within* cases. This outcome is less surprising when we reflect that political extremists need to respond to varying conditions over time. Their differing worldviews can condition these divergent responses. A review of the principal findings, indicating the pathways from the ephemeral gain to actual extremism will reveal distinctions among the origins of the extremist movements and their choices to engage in mass murder.

Briefly, perceptions of injustice and humiliation-shame that helped give rise to the extremist groups, in many instances were followed by the threat and fear of reversion as a proximal impetus for mass murder, frequently, but not always, in wartime. Even humiliation-shame can sometimes serve as a precipitant to mass murder, although less frequently than fear of reversion, the most common source of mass murder. Extremism giving rise to mass murder appears to be a two-stage process.

Fascism

Italy and Germany

Changes over time can be seen in two of the principal exponents of extremism, Italian Fascism and German Nazism. It is clear that the origins of the Italian Fascist Party are to be found in Italian perceptions of injustice. Although the Treaty of London of 1915, by which Italy entered the war and lost 650,000 dead, entailed the promise of the Dalmatian Coast, that promise was never fulfilled at Versailles. In addition, as we saw, Gabriele D'Annunzio, the poet and Italian nationalist, made Fiume his cause, and shortly thereafter Mussolini benefitted greatly from this widespread nationalist reaction to a perceived grave injustice.

Left-wing or moderate Allied leaders such as David Lloyd George, the British prime minister, were blamed. Even anti-Semitism raised its ugly head in the utterly false charge that Lloyd George was Jewish, hence his perfidy at Versailles, perhaps in league with eastern Jews such as Trotsky and other Jewish Bolsheviks.[2] By this time, Italian Fascism was deeply opposed to communism. When we examine Mussolini's later decision to invade Ethiopia and eventually kill over 250,000 Ethiopians, involving the use of weapons of mass destruction such as poison gas,[3] a slogan used by General Rodolfo Graziani was: "The *Duce* shall have Ethiopia with the Ethiopians or without them, just as he pleases."[4]

---

[2] Bosworth 2002, 147.   [3] Ben-Ghiat 2001, 125–6.   [4] Quoted in Bosworth 2002, 307.

Why this later venture into extremist behavior? Earlier Fascist atrocities in Libya had come on the heels of similar behavior under the Liberals after 1911. The invasion and atrocities in Ethiopia, however, comprised a new chapter in Fascist adventurism, and one which isolated Italy from the Western powers. Here, in addition to perceptions of injustice, the two remaining pathways from the ephemeral gain come into play. Never forgotten were the humiliations of the Italian defeat in the 1895–96 Italo-Ethiopian War leading to the loss of nearly 9,000 men. This was the only decisive defeat of a European colonial power by non-Europeans in the late nineteenth century, leading to the ignominious withdrawal of Italian forces from Ethiopia. Just prior to the second invasion of Ethiopia in 1935, this earlier humiliation was being recalled at frequent intervals.[5]

The possibility of reversion as the third pathway to extremism also existed. As Germany rose in power after the advent of Hitler, so was Italy being "relegated" (Mussolini himself used this term on more than one occasion) to second-rank status, or even below. Accordingly: "The structure of international relations, put under stress by the Nazis in Berlin, simply refused to fall into a pattern which would benefit Italy or satisfy Mussolini. When, in June 1935, an initiative was made to appease the Italian dictator, it was derisory indeed."[6]

Thus, while the Italian Fascists initially rose to power on feelings of injustice, anger, and the placing of blame, the actual later descent into extremist behavior in the form of mass murder was to be facilitated by the remaining two pathways, the threat and fear of reversion (or "relegation"), and a sense of humiliation over past defeats.

German history also reflects this divergence in pathways to extremism, but in a different fashion. The abandonment of Wilson's Fourteen Points at Versailles and the subsequent loss of substantial territory, not to mention the loss of nearly 2 million men at the front, was perceived as a significant injustice, for which blame was to be placed on the Jews. And the financial and military limitations of the Treaty of Versailles were to be understood by Germans as substantial restrictions on German freedom to pursue capabilities – another form of injustice.

But an important theme was humiliation, especially after the French and Belgian occupation of the Ruhr in 1923–25 (to ensure payment of reparations), a violation of historic German territory. And this occupation was to come on the heels of an earlier French occupation of the coal-producing Saar region at the end of the war.[7] The theme of sacrifice to avenge this humiliation was to be prominent during and after the Ruhr occupation, as we saw in Chapter 4. In Italy, no foreign incursions into Italian territory occurred after the war's end.

Hence, in contrast to Italy, not one (perceptions of injustice), but two of the pathways (perceptions of injustice and humiliation-shame) were to be prominent

---

[5] Bosworth 2002, 302.   [6] Bosworth 2002, 302.   [7] Keynes 1920.

in the rise of the Nazis to power prior to the mass murders of World War II. But the actual onset of German ethnic mass murder occurred during World War II, and was precipitated by the threat and fear of reversion to the status of a defeated power, as it was prior to World War II. That threat began to appear almost immediately after the German invasion of the Soviet Union on June 22, 1941. The unexpectedly strong resistance by the Soviets and the increasingly close collaboration between the United States (not yet a combatant) and Great Britain were to buttress that threat. It was to eventuate in mass murder on a previously unheard of scale, as detailed in Chapter 13.

On December 5, the Russians launched their successful counteroffensive before Moscow, saving the city from German capture. On December 7, 1941, Japanese forces attacked the United States naval base at Pearl Harbor. True to the Axis alliance, Hitler declared war on the United States on December 11. On December 12, Hitler addressed a meeting of the most important sectional and regional leaders of the NSDAP, very likely informing them of his decision to destroy all of Europe's Jews. Thus, the two cycles of the ephemeral gain shown in Figure 13.3 represent the diachronic change in which the first cycle helps generate the Nazi Party, while the second is associated with genocide.

Hungary and Romania

In the case of Hungary after World War I, we find a qualitatively similar situation to that of Germany, but greatly augmented. Not only defeated in World War I as one of the two principal components of the Austro-Hungarian Empire, Hungary itself was defeated in the 1919 war with Czechoslovakia and Romania. Hungary's territorial losses at Trianon in 1920 were proportionately much greater than those of Germany. Here the reversion to small-power status was pronounced.

The Little Entente, formed in 1920–21, was an alliance among Czechoslovakia, Romania, and Yugoslavia directed principally against Hungary and supported by France, which accentuated this sense of Hungarian small-power isolation. These powers were to force the Treaty of Trianon on Hungary. Anger and blame were to be directed at the most Westernized people in Hungary (especially in Budapest), the Jews. In 1920, Hungary was the first European country after the war to promulgate anti-Semitic legislation, limiting Jewish admission to higher education institutions.[8] In 1922, a chief judge in a town near Budapest refused to grant permission to a Jewish entrepreneur to start a new industry. His reasoning was: "The request will be refused because on the territory of truncated Hungary the primary task of officials is to guarantee the living conditions of Hungarians. If he granted the request of a member of a different race, a chief judge would act against his obligations."[9]

[8] Braham 2000, 22.   [9] Quoted in Pók 1997, 151.

Yet humiliation was a factor in the rise of Hungarian extremism. Humiliation was felt by the many military and civilian employees of the now defunct Austro-Hungarian Empire. The counter-revolutionary leaders gathered in Szeged included many of those who had been dispossessed one way or another by the massive contraction: military officers who had lost their positions because of the lost war or the revolutionary communist Béla Kun's purges, civilians affected by the inflationary spiral, and especially the "homeless, propertyless, and embittered [who] first placed their hope in the Károlyi and Kun regimes. Disappointed over the violation of their traditional class interests, subsequently they wholeheartedly embraced the counter-revolution. They were easily swayed by the ideologues of the Szeged movement who placed the blame for their suffering on the 'alien' Jews and Bolsheviks."[10] Former public servants constituted the majority of the 300,000 Magyar refugees who fled into Hungary after 1918.

A sense of great injustice was also felt by these former public servants of the Dual Monarchy. Clearly, criteria of fairness and equity would not have been satisfied by their forced removal from their previous governmental service. Nor would the criterion of freedom to pursue capabilities have been met in these circumstances. The poor treatment accorded Magyar minorities in the Austro-Hungarian successor states also fed into the sense of injustice perpetrated against Hungarians.[11]

While Hungary experienced its enormous losses immediately after World War I and its subsequent defeat by the Allied coalition against it, Romania on the other hand was in that victorious coalition and benefitted greatly from the annexation of territories from Austria-Hungary (Transylvania and Bukovina), Russia (Bessarabia), and Bulgaria (Crișana). Only later would the loss of these lands in 1940 lead to extremist behavior.

As Radu Ioanid[12] observes: "The period between 1923 and 1938 represented a golden age of human rights in Romania." Yet this earlier commitment to human rights arose from Allied pressure to ensure that the vastly expanded Romania, with ethnic Romanians comprising only 70 percent of the population, would treat its minorities fairly. It would be tempting indeed for the Romanian ethnic majority to impose its culture, including even its religion, on ethnic Hungarians, Ukrainians (Ruthenians), Jews, and Germans who now populated the state in large numbers.

At the same time, the sense of foreign, especially Jewish, domination was palpable, amounting to a feeling of humiliation at the foreign presence, and an injustice – a lack of fairness or equity – in a disproportionate Jewish presence in positions of professional leadership. According to a poet of the Iron Guard, the premier Romanian fascist organization:

---

[10] Braham 1981, 18.   [11] Nagy-Talavera 2001, 8.   [12] 2000, 12.

> You've come with foreign laws
> To steal my stock, my song, my poverty;
> Out of my sweat you've built your property,
> And taken from our children for your whores

And even more emphatically, in our second sense of freedom's loss as the inability now to pursue capabilities:

> A herd of foreign bastards
> Hard-hearted heathen band
> Have come to be our masters.
> There's wailing in the land.[13]

As in Hungary, the Jews were disproportionately visible economically and socially. Thus, the Iron Guard was born. But it was to commit its mass atrocities only after the loss of the territories gained in 1920. By 1937, as we saw in Chapters 4 and 13, the Soviets were threatening to take the provinces of Bessarabia and Bukovina, leading to the large vote for the Iron Guard. When in 1940 the truncation to the borders of the Old Kingdom (Regat) existing prior to World War I occurred at Soviet and German (now allied) behest, the first anti-Semitic legislation would be passed. The law of August 8, 1940 defined Jews racially in even more draconian fashion than did the Nazis. Another law forbade marriage between Jews and gentiles while directly citing the 1935 Nuremberg laws as precedent.[14] Further legislation restricted Jewish access to education and entry into both the medical and military professions. Economic legislation severely limited Jewish business activity and further restricted Jewish life circumstances. Jewish rural property was nationalized and Jewish civil servants were purged.

Prior to the German invasion of the Soviet Union, the worst period for Romanian Jewry was that just before and during the Iron Guard government of September 6, 1940 to January 21, 1941. It came to power as the result of the foreign policy reverses suffered by King Carol II, especially the loss of significant territories, and his subsequent forced resignation. Even before the accession of the Iron Guard, as the Romanians were withdrawing from territories ceded to its neighboring acquisitors, massacres of Jews occurred. Bessarabia and northern Bukovina, ceded to the Soviet Union, were scenes of some of the worst atrocities.

Thus, there were two historical periods in the origins of Romanian extremism. The first was a reaction to Allied pressure to ensure minority rights within an expanded nationalistic Romania that yielded Romanian feelings of humiliation at the foreign presence, and a perceived injustice at the disproportionate Jewish domination of the professions, but without appreciable violence against minorities. The second reaction appeared after the loss of the acquired territories and the accession of the Iron Guard to the seat of government, yielding

---

[13] Quoted in Weber 1965b, 529.   [14] Ioanid 2000, 20–2.

significant mass violence. As a result of the lost territories in 1940, the threat and fear of reversion to minor-power status relative to the Balkan region was palpable.

Both Hungary and Romania responded to nationalistic impulses in their anti-Semitism and support of mass murder. In this they shared the threat and fear of reversion with the particularist extreme nationalists discussed elsewhere. But the use of Christian imagery – the Arrow *Cross* in Hungary – and the title, "Legion of the Archangel Michael" as the formal name of the organization including the Romanian Iron Guard suggested a more universal impulse connecting these organizations with European Christianity, in the latter instance echoing the earlier (1909) rise of a Russian extremist organization using virtually the identical name (see Chapter 4). Many of the rituals of the Iron Guard were drawn explicitly from Eastern Orthodox practice. Feelings of injustice and humiliation-shame in all three countries' extremism stemmed at least in part from the traditional belief that Christians must be ascendant over Jews or other non-Christians. Virulent anti-Semitism, a form of Christian xenophobia, was a universal cement that united all European fascists, even including the Italians much later, during the interwar period.

Communism

The USSR

When we turn to communism, especially Stalinism as the most redolent with extremist behavior, we find a pattern that clearly suggests the threat and fear of reversion, with humiliation and a rather distinctive form of perceived injustice also operative. In addition to the perceived injustices of the defeat by Japan – a non-European power – in 1905 and blame for the defeat in Poland in which Stalin was intimately involved, there also existed a specific ideational source of perceived injustice.

Recall (Chapter 5) that Stalin abandoned his relatively moderate Marxist stance in favor of a more confrontational one only after the tsarist violence against striking workers in Georgia led to the deaths of several. (Mortality salience is obviously relevant here.) The injustices of the Russian *ancien régime* were interpretable within a Marxist framework but now required a more potent opposition. Although Marxism is principally an economically based ideology, in which political power necessarily flows from the ownership of the means of production, nevertheless there exists a moral component. This is the injustice of a minority self-perpetuating ruling class that dominates a majority without its consent, resulting in a diminished wellbeing of the majority. That majority was identified by Marx as the proletariat, or industrial working class, but the principle of fairness, equated here with justice, can easily be extended (and was) to any population of workers and peasants dominated by a minority without its consent. Of course, the idea of consent inherent in Marxism and embodied explicitly in Marxism-Leninism was not to be a democratic one demanding a mandate by popular vote, but consent to the "historical necessity" of vesting all power and authority in the Communist Party. This was to be Stalin's ideological preference, consistent with the dictates of Lenin.

Thus, a simple adherence to Soviet Communism, or for that matter the later Chinese or Cambodian variants, entailed the perception of a profound injustice in the pre-revolutionary system and the onus of blame placed on the then ruling class, yielding extremist behavior. Humiliation, as we saw, was present in Stalin's reaction to the Russian defeats by Japan and Poland, and in China's reaction to the defeats and occupation of Chinese territory by foreigners, especially the Japanese. The question remains as to the role of the threat and fear of reversion. The cases of Stalin and Mao need to be examined separately, for their patterns diverge.

Stalin's singular involvement as the commissar of one of the two Soviet armies fighting the Poles in 1920 deeply affected him, in large measure because of the blame heaped on him for the defeat.[15] As we saw, the Japanese defeat of Russia in 1905 was also consequential for him. Both wars witnessed Western involvement, first, in the British-built Japanese fleet that so thoroughly defeated its Russian counterpart at Tsushima, and second, in the French military aid and advice given to the Poles in 1920. Of course, the Allied intervention in the Russian Civil War, although militarily insignificant (as the Russo-Japanese and Russo-Polish Wars were not), nevertheless did have another deep impact in the embedding of a fear of future Western intervention. Hence, the essentially defensive mindset of Stalin in his emphasis on "socialism in one country," i.e., Russia, in contrast to the European-wide revolution sought by other Bolsheviks such as Trotsky. Even the famine of the early 1930s that killed millions was not necessarily calculated to murder, but, at least in part, was generated by the complexity of a massive agricultural collectivization that was incompetently administered (see Chapter 5).

The purpose of that collectivization was to allow for the industrial development that was to make the Soviets ready for a future confrontation with the West. As early as 1925, Stalin stated that: "If war comes we will not be able to sit back and relax. We will have to make a move, but we will be the last to act. We shall throw our weight onto the balance, and that might tip the scales."[16] On January 26, 1934, in his address to the 17th Party Congress, Stalin "said that the next major war would be aimed at the conquest and division of the USSR and the country had to prepare itself appropriately. He even alluded to his own terror and purges to come, which were supposedly needed to root out would-be traitors. Despite the great successes that had been achieved, he warned, they had to

---

[15] Service 2004, 184–5.   [16] Quoted in Gellately 2007, 346.

be wary of being overconfident."[17] By 1937, the purge of Party members was in full swing, adding significantly to the total number of deaths at Stalin's hands.

Shortly after World War II, when faced with the possibility of adding territory in East-Central Europe to the communist world, Stalin did not hesitate. But this offensive political expansion, courtesy of the Red Army, was in marked contrast to his earlier caution and essentially defensive posture.

China

Although Chinese and Cambodian political extremism did not stem directly from a *sui generis* ephemeral gain, emerging instead from a prior Stalinist template, itself a consequence of an ephemeral gain, nevertheless it is useful to consider the independent effects of the three pathways. Whereas the Soviet revolution was insecure as a result of the defeat by Poland and other foreign pressures just prior to its descent into mass murder, the same cannot be said of China. Following the successful communist revolution, China had stalemated the US and its allies in Korea, in stark contrast to the Soviet performance in Poland and the earlier Russian defeats. Hence, as might be expected in a revolutionary state having a cosmic teleology within its ideological framework, Mao was aggressive after the end of the Korean War. With Stalin's help, he embarked on an industrialization program that was, in effect, Mao's "Superpower Program":

> Mao wanted to channel every resource the nation had into this programme. The whole "industrialisation" process had to be completed "in ten to fifteen years," or at most a bit longer. Speed, he said over and over again, was everything – "the essence." What he did not spell out was his real goal: to become a military power in his own lifetime, and have the world listen when he spoke.[18]

Mao wanted to live to see the day when China would surpass Great Britain in industrial output. As early as 1918, he wrote: "Some say one has a responsibility for history. I don't believe it... *People like me are not building achievements to leave for future generations...*"[19]

Thus, Stalin's template for rapid industrialization and consequent world power would become Mao's. In 1953, well before the industrialization process was in place, Mao offered 50 million dollars worth of food to East Germany in order to support that dictatorship facing popular unrest. By 1973, when the world's wealthiest countries were contributing at most .5 percent of their GNP to foreign aid, with the US at about .01 percent, China "reached an unbelievable 6.92 per cent – by far the highest the world has ever known."[20]

---

[17] Gellately 2007, 346–7.   [18] Chang and Halliday 2005, 380.
[19] Emphasis in original; Chang and Halliday 2005, 380.
[20] Chang and Halliday 2005, 384.

In order to back up these foreign policy efforts with raw power, Mao decided to industrialize within a period of 8 years. He called the process "The Great Leap Forward." Its purpose was to "overtake all capitalist countries in a fairly short time, and become one of the richest, most advanced and powerful countries in the world."[21] To an elite army group he stated: "Now the Pacific Ocean is not peaceful. It can only be peaceful when we take it over."[22] Mao's colleague, Marshal Lin Piao, interjected: "We must build big ships, and be prepared to land [sc. militarily] in Japan, the Philippines, and San Francisco."[23]

As in the Soviet Union, the collectivization of agriculture was to be the first step. The Great Famine of 1958–61, in which some 38 million Chinese, mostly peasants, starved to death, dwarfed even that of the Soviet Union some 30 years earlier. The Great Leap Forward was a national program of self-sacrifice beyond all measure in order to achieve great power status and influence the world. But the Cultural Revolution of 1966–76 was aimed not at the peasants but at the elite, Party leaders, bureaucrats, and intellectuals who might bear some animus to Mao or oppose his policies.

Here, the threat and fear of reversion was influential. Three factors fed into this threatening process. First, just prior to the Cultural Revolution, Mao sought to politicize the country by destroying traditional Chinese culture, much as Lenin and Stalin had done in gutting Russian Orthodoxy as a basis of traditional Russian culture. Mao was less successful than he would have liked, for Party functionaries typically dragged their heels and even ignored many of his directives. But it was the realm of foreign affairs that reinforced this internal threat and was to be decisive in launching the internal attack on Mao's presumed enemies.

The Soviet Union under Khrushchev was in the process of de-Stalinization that Mao found to be reprehensible. The official Chinese Communist position now declared that Khrushchev was a "revisionist," a particularly malevolent charge in the communist lexicon. Suspected dissident Party officials at all levels were now to be called "revisionists" and when Khrushchev was ousted in October 1964 and the new leaders (equally revisionist in Mao's view) made overtures to individual Chinese leaders such as the foreign minister Chou En-lai suggesting that a Russo-Chinese rapprochement was possible without Mao, he was especially threatened. Mao's response was to insist that the traditional Soviet Party program must be respected, effectively disavowing de-Stalinization.[24] This, of course, was anathema to the new Soviet leaders, thereby continuing the deteriorating relations between the two countries.

A second failure in China's foreign relations concerned China's role as a leader of the Third World. Whereas China's prominence at the first Third World summit meeting in Bandung, Indonesia, was established and increasing thereafter,

---

[21] Quoted in Chang and Halliday 2005, 426.   [22] Quoted in Chang and Halliday 2005, 426.
[23] Quoted in Chang and Halliday 2005, 426.   [24] Chang and Halliday 2005, 487–9.

the second Third World summit was to feature Russian participation. In the end, this summit never convened.

Finally, Indonesia, site of the first Third World summit, and with the third largest communist party in the world (the PKI), was to terminate its status as China's principal ally in Southeast Asia. As we saw in Chapter 12, the PKI was decimated in 1965–66 as a reaction to the assassination of the generals and presumed attempted seizure of power by the PKI in association with Sukarno. Of course, Beijing was intimately involved, encouraging the PKI to take overt action. "By the end of 1965, Mao's global schemes had suffered one setback after another. In a dark and vehement state of mind, he turned to deal with his foes inside China."[25]

The Cultural Revolution, decimating the Chinese Communist Party (CCP), was to lead to at least 3 million deaths; approximately 100 million people suffered in one way or another.[26] In this sense, the fortunes of the CCP and PKI were to mirror each other, except that the CCP would continue to exist with largely new personnel drawn mainly from the military and beholden directly to Mao. The threat of reversion to second-class international status would, in part, inspire Mao's internal purge, much as, in Stalin's case, the threat of war with Germany and/or Japan after 1933, both of which had defeated Russia in the recent past, was to help generate the decimation of the Soviet Communist Party. The precedent of the Stalinist template would facilitate Mao's excesses in less threatening conditions to the integrity of his communist state.

But, the contrast between the Maoist and Stalinist cases highlights the importance of the ephemeral gain. While the Soviet Union experienced ephemerality in the defeat by the Poles in 1920 (with French guidance), the Chinese did not experience such loss after their revolution, having achieved a victory of sorts in preventing the loss of North Korea to the United Nations forces. The threat and fear of reversion, therefore, was more prominent in the Soviet case than in the Chinese, prompting the conclusion that the Stalinist template was indeed a critical factor in generating the Cultural Revolution, for the threatening external impetus as an alternate explanation of Chinese behavior was far less pronounced.

Cambodia

Cambodia presents an even more cogent example of the fear of reversion, specifically to traditional Vietnamese dominance within Indochina. Difficulties with Vietnam began even before the Khmer Rouge victory in April 1975. In helping the Khmer Rouge win its civil war with the Cambodian government, North Vietnamese troops actually occupied more than 25 percent of Cambodian

---

[25] Chang and Halliday 2005, 499.   [26] Chang and Halliday 2005, 547.

territory in 1970.[27] Although these forces withdrew from Cambodia after the Khmer Rouge victory, a clear sense was conveyed to the Cambodians that they were given the role of the "younger brother," obliged to follow the directives of the "elder brother." Immediately after this victory, several Vietnamese-held islands in the Gulf of Siam were attacked by the Cambodian forces.[28]

Tensions with the Vietnamese were highlighted in September 1976 in a dispute within the Cambodian Communist Party (CPK) over whether the party's origins were to be traced back to 1951, when the "Indochinese Communist Party" was founded essentially under Vietnamese tutelage, or to 1960, when a special congress was called in Phnom Penh, which named Pol Pot and Ieng Sary, among others, to the party's Central Committee.[29] Those who favored the latter date were supporting the independence of Cambodia from the perceived threatening hegemony of Vietnam in the former French Indochina.

That threat was accentuated by the treaty of cooperation between Vietnam and Laos signed in July 1977.[30] Their treaty was seen as a forerunner to a united former French Indochina under Vietnamese tutelage. In August, Pol Pot met with a high-level official of the Thai Communist Party. Pol Pot stated that, according to the idea of a unitary Indochinese revolution, there exists "only one Party, one country and one people – whereas other comrades are not in agreement."[31] Pol Pot continued to reject the idea that Indochina was a single unit undergoing revolution: "Nationalism, he implicitly said, was most important. Pol Pot insisted on the party's own forces, autonomy and independence."[32]

Cambodia appeared to be surrounded by potentially hostile forces. Soon after, in September 1977, the Vietnamese congratulated Pol Pot on his speech announcing the existence of the CPK and its relations to Cambodian history. Vietnamese radio reported that the Vietnamese "always considered their *special relationship* with… Kampuchea as their sacred cause."[33] As David Chandler notes, "with friends like that, Pol Pot may have mused, what would Cambodia do for enemies?"[34]

Thus, in common with other extremists faced with the threat of reversion, mass murder occurred. Beginning in mid-1977 and escalating in early 1978, all Vietnamese, part-Vietnamese, and even ethnic Khmer married to Vietnamese were rounded up and murdered.[35] This process began initially at the border with Vietnam. But after a late 1977 decisive defeat of the Khmer Rouge forces by the Vietnamese army, the killing of ethnic Vietnamese and close associates within Cambodia was extended throughout the country.

The mass murder of Vietnamese occurred within the context of the murder of the many other populations, including ethnic Khmer, who were not sufficiently

---

[27] Mosyakov 2006, 50.   [28] Chandler 1999, 219–20.   [29] Carney 1989, 18.
[30] Chandler 1999, 220.   [31] Quoted in Goscha 2006, 172.   [32] Goscha 2006, 172.
[33] Emphasis added by Chandler; quoted in Chandler 1999, 136.
[34] 1999, 136.   [35] Kiernan 1996, 123–4.

acceptable to the Pol Pot regime on political-economic grounds. Following Mao's earlier emptying of cities to eliminate or re-educate the middle classes, but now in much more thorough fashion, Pol Pot was following a communist script initially established by Stalin but applied to Asia by Mao. "In short, Pol Pot was implementing Mao's plan with Stalin's methods."[36]

But of all the proportions of populations murdered by the Khmer Rouge, only the Vietnamese stand out at 100 percent, none of the others exceeding 50 percent.[37] This fact alone signals the importance of the threat and fear of reversion to Vietnamese dominance.

Radical Islamism

Al-Qaeda

Turning now to radical Islamism, there are at least two major variants and one minor that require analysis. The first is that of al-Qaeda, the second, the Chechen extremists, and the third, Indian Muslims who have not given significant evidence of al-Qaeda-like extremism. Al-Muhajiroun, although not a major source of extremist violence, will also be discussed briefly, as will Sudan. Much of the recent violence, especially the November 2008 attacks in Mumbai, reflect the festering sore of Kashmir, in which the Islamist terrorist group Lashkar-e-Taiba (army of the righteous) originated. This last group further illustrates an important dimension of extremism: the tendency towards universality, or its absence, as in the case of Chechen extremists.

The genesis of al-Qaeda amply illustrates the importance of humiliation and perceptions of injustice, as we have seen. For Muslims who are aware of the historical glories of Islam, the contemporary parlous state of much of the Islamic world (but certainly not all of it) means that humiliation is acute. But the injustices are of two types. One is that of the universal claim of the inherent superiority of Islam trumpeted by the minions or proponents of al-Qaeda. Whether or not this is an inherent element of Islamic belief is not the point. What is important is the belief by radical Islamists that the tenets of Islam and its holy places are sacrosanct, requiring mass murder if violated. Thus, justice is equivalent to religious obedience and injustice equated with opposition or violation. Here, as in other "isms" with universal claims, perceptions of justice and injustice stem from the ideation itself.

At the same time, Western concepts of justice in the form of rights to self-rule and non-interference by external powers also play a role. Much of the debate about the sources of radical Islamism tends to focus on the inherent (traditional Islam) or external (Western) roots of radical Islam. My own view emerging from this research is that, at the very least, Western concepts have been grafted onto

[36] Quinn 1989, 236.   [37] Kiernan 1996, 458.

particular interpretations of Islam (e.g., Ibn Taymiyya and his followers) to yield contemporary radical Islamism. That earlier proponents of Islamism were active during severe times of trouble for Islam, as in Ibn Taymiyya's case, establishes a rough historical parallel with the present time for radical Islamists.

Thus, both humiliation and reactions to perceived injustices of various types lie at the root of extremism stemming from the ephemeral gain. Yet, the threat and fear of reversion also exists in the form of a renewed superpower (i.e., the US) domination of a portion of the Islamic world even after the defeat of the other superpower (the USSR) in Afghanistan by the *mujahadin*. The defeat of Iraq in the Gulf War of 1991, coupled with the "occupation" of Saudi Arabia by Western forces, signaled that reversion was a distinct possibility and perhaps had already occurred.

Al-Muhajiroun

Clearly perceptions of injustice and humiliation-shame were important antecedents of the suicide bombing initiated by British Muslims of Kashmiri origin. Like Lashkar-e-Taiba, the ongoing conflict over Kashmir subsequent to the British Raj was salient, generating these emotions. Yet the threat and fear of reversion must have been present upon the successful invasion of Iraq by Western forces, indicating that whatever success had been achieved by 9/11, the United States, first in Afghanistan and now in Iraq, was emerging victorious over the Muslim world.

Sudan

In contrast to Al-Muhajiroun, which had a universal perspective stemming from identification with the entire Islamic *'umma*, Sudanese history has more particular elements. Among them are racial antipathies between the Arabist north and the indigenous African elements in the south and west. Although the predominantly Christian and animist SPLA was fighting in the south against an Islamist government after 1989, these unique racial elements of Sudanese history contributed strongly to the conflicts that even pitted Muslim against Muslim in Darfur. Thus, in the event of the loss of these territories, the threat and fear of reversion of the Arabist north to a powerless remnant of its former territorial expanse would be reminiscent of the earlier subordination to Britain, followed by Anglo-Egyptian colonialism. Certainly under these conditions, Egypt would emerge as by far the leading Islamic power in the African northeast.

Chechnya and India

Clearer still is the threat and fear of reversion in the case of Chechnya, for that threat was direct; a renewed Russian occupation was being accomplished at the time of the Beslan school massacre. Grozny, the capital city, had already been recaptured by the Russians, while the remainder of national territory was undergoing "pacification." Although perceptions of injustice and humiliation were clear, stemming from nearly two centuries of Russian domination, nevertheless the goals of the extremists were boldly stated: withdrawal of the Russians from Chechnya, effectively reversing what had already become an ephemeral gain. This particularity stands in strong contrast to the more universal goal of restoring the Caliphate as the political seat of the entire Islamic world proposed by al-Qaeda-type radical Islamists. Indeed, Chechnya could have been included in the section on extreme nationalism, but for the prominence of the Chechen cause among radical Islamists.

Where radical Islamism has not been in much evidence, the possibility of establishing a universal Islamic political organization is also absent. This is the case in India, in which a quietist Islam has largely been maintained, apart from the communal violence between Hindu and Muslim, and the festering sore of Kashmir. Indeed, the failure of the Khilafat movement of the 1920s that arose in response to the abolition of the Caliphate in Turkey and sought to restore it, illustrated to many Muslims in India the futility of such efforts.

Extreme nationalism

Sri Lanka

Also clear was the direct threat of reversion in the case of the LTTE in Sri Lanka. Feelings of injustice and humiliation were present after the language laws had removed Tamil speakers from their civil service positions and Tamil businesses were nationalized or destroyed. But the resort to extremism in the form of suicide bombings, even of civilians, by an organization that had formerly used classical guerrilla tactics came only after the threat that the victory of the LTTE in establishing an autonomous Jaffna region would be reversed. The advance of the Sri Lankan Army (SLA) into the Jaffna Peninsula threatened to reverse that newly achieved dominance. Consecutive ephemera were at work here. In contrast, the Indian Muslim community presented no sustained commitment to extremist behavior, and the pattern of ephemeral gain was absent.

Poland

Polish extremism after World War II also presents a clear example of the threat and fear of reversion, in this instance to a form of Jewish-communist dominance that existed during the period of Soviet control of eastern Poland in 1939–41. Although rooted far more in opposition to the pervasive anti-Semitism of the former Polish authorities than in sympathy with the new Soviet occupiers, nevertheless Jewish cooperation with the Soviets, where it existed, was deeply resented. This hostility even led to the spontaneous Polish massacre of entire Jewish villages upon the retreat of the Soviets in the face of the German advance in June 1941. The massacre of Jews by Poles after 1945 stemmed from this threat and fear of reversion to that earlier condition upon the return of hundreds of thousands of surviving Jews, principally from the Soviet Union, even as the threat of Soviet political dominance of the entire country was being actualized.

The rampaging military

In the cases of the rampaging military we find variations in the pathways leading from the ephemeral gain to extremist behavior. Japan, like Germany, reacted strongly to Allied behavior after World War I. In this case, the 1922 Washington naval conference was decisive, followed by the even more injurious (from the Japanese perspective) 1930 London naval conference, which further limited Japanese naval capacities. Feelings of injustice at the treatment by a former ally in World War I, Britain, and a close ally even before that time, and humiliation at the clear second-class status the Japanese were relegated to, sparked the path to extremism. Yet it was the limitation on military capacities, conjuring up the sole alternatives of "conquer or be conquered" in the words of Masao, that was to accelerate the threat and fear of reversion to an earlier subordinate condition vis-à-vis the West. For the first time, extreme military measures such as a surprise attack without a declaration of war were considered, eventuating in the attack on Pearl Harbor of December 7, 1941. Of course, other extreme measures were undertaken that would lead to the deaths of millions of innocents.

In the case of Pakistan, the threat and fear of reversion was, if anything, even more pronounced. With the loss of a legislative majority to the Bengali Awami League based in East Pakistan, in the view of West Pakistani leaders the government would now be dominated by a partly Hinduized Muslim population in cooperation with the large Hindu minority in East Pakistan and even potentially the large Hindu majority within India. Moreover, apart from a formal adherence to Islam, the Bengalis of East Pakistan had little in common, culturally, linguistically, or historically with the Pashtuns, Punjabis, Sindhis, and others of the West. A reversion to something like the past Hindu ascendancy in the British Raj was unacceptable. In the case of a successful secession, the loss of East Pakistan would have led to the loss of 56 percent of the entire Pakistani population and much of its territory of strategic value in threatening India from both east and west. Extreme behavior was to be used in "neutralizing" the Bengali opposition.

Indonesia presents a similar picture of a neighboring great power threat to a recently subordinated population, but here it is China, not India, that was threatening to Indonesia. Although feelings of humiliation and perceptions of injustice could have been harbored, they pale before the dimensions of an internal communist threat in association with a neighboring great power, one that had grown significantly in force capability after the explosion of the first Chinese Communist nuclear weapon. And in 1948 local communists had earlier attempted a coup at Madiun, killing some 240 Muslim leaders before its suppression.[38] Here, for the first time in Indonesia's short period of independence, there emerged a possibility of reverting to a subordinate position vis-à-vis more powerful external forces, a condition that had existed during the period of Dutch colonial rule but had been successfully overcome.

The Balkans

As in our preceding cases, humiliation and perceptions of injustice were present in the instances of Serbian and Croatian extremism, but here again the threat and fear of reversion was paramount. The simpler case, of course, is Croatia, for there was only one ephemeral gain, but it was crucial. The envisioned Kingdom of Serbs, Croats, and Slovenes, in which Croats presumably would at least have a proportionate share of authority with Serbs, was in fact disproportionately governed by Serbs. This was in stark contrast to the autonomy experienced by Croats under Hungarian rule within the decentralized Austro-Hungarian Empire, as we saw. Given the prominence of the threat and fear of reversion to an autocratic rule similar to that experienced under the Austrians prior to the formation of the Dual Monarchy, but this time under the Serbs, Ante Pavelić established his Ustaša Liberation Organization immediately upon proclamation of the Kingdom of Yugoslavia under Serb dictatorship.

Complicating the Serbian picture is the existence of successive reinforcing ephemera shown in Chapter 11, but given this repeated pattern of ephemeral gains, the threat and fear of reversion must have been dominant. The losses of the Balkan Wars and World War I were enormous, occurring after earlier significant gains. Each repetition of this cycle must have reinforced the specter of future reversion: that the threat and fear of reversion for the Serbs was not an imaginary fear, but one based on historical reality. Each time that threat was posed, it must have seemed essential to the Serb leaders that more extreme measures be employed to ensure that such a reversion would no longer be in the realm of future possibility. Further, the fact that Serbian history was associated with continued victimization by more powerful forces in the past, especially the Turks, virtually ruled out the possibility of humiliation (in our sense of a precipitous failure), or even perceptions of injustice as significant historical motifs, except insofar as Serbian leaders later fomented such feelings virtually *ex nihilo*.

Defeat within an ephemeral gain cannot be seen as humiliating or unjust, if, in the process of being defeated, the victimized population celebrates its victimhood as an exalted condition. In contrast to most of our other cases, exaltation of victimhood was a primary characteristic of Serbian historical memory. Instead

---

[38] Vickers 2005, 109.

of the other possible pathways, the threat and fear of reversion to simply one more small Balkan state to exist at the mercy of other small Balkan states like Bulgaria, characteristic of the period prior to World War I, was intolerable to the Serbs. The Serbian overtures to the Bosnian Muslims to remain with Serbia and Montenegro within Yugoslavia highlighted Bosnia's centrality in the Serbian efforts to forestall a complete Serbian reversion. Accordingly, for this and other mainly geopolitical reasons, the Bosnian Muslim rejection was the final spur to Serbian extremism, targeting principally the Bosnian Muslims.

Genocidal variation

Finally, the sources of genocide variability demonstrate continuity with the remaining cases, highlighting the salience of the threat and fear of reversion. In the instance of the Holocaust, we saw that feelings of humiliation-shame, perceptions of injustice, and the threat and fear of reversion were all present in German society during the interwar period. But what the personal histories of Nazi war criminals demonstrate most clearly is that during the war, even among extremists, there existed a far greater propensity for extremist behavior among those who originated in territories lost by Germany after World War I, hence most likely to revert to that condition upon German defeat in World War II. Even beyond that, is a commonality held with the Turks in their genocide of the Armenians in World War I. The elation of Germans upon the rapid defeat of the Allied powers in 1939–40 stood in stark contrast with the later difficulties in prosecuting the war upon the invasion of Russia in 1941. The *immediacy* of the contrast was striking, suggesting the ephemerality of the earlier gains and the real possibility of reversion to an earlier condition. Electoral statistics from 1937 Romania are consistent with this interpretation. The Holocaust in all its brutal dimensions then followed.

The experience of the Ottoman Turks was remarkably similar. Ottoman elation, even exultation, was experienced after the reconquest of Adrianople (today's Edirne) in 1913 and the massive outpouring of public support for the Young Turk regime. But the impending losses suggested by the Russian defeat of Ottoman armies in the East at the start of World War I, and the imminent British invasion in the West, provided a stark contrast, suggesting reversion to the pre-1913 condition, or even worse, a dismantling of the entire country, including Anatolia, the Turkish heartland. A reprise of the reversion of 1878 was being enacted. Genocide of the Armenians, to the Turkish mind the most geopolitically threatening of the Christian minorities, ensued.

In the Rwandan case, the immediacy of the threat and fear of reversion was palpable because of the Tutsi-dominated RPF military successes in the early 1990s, and the memories of the long period of Tutsi political ascendance over the Hutu prior to Hutu governance of independent Rwanda. The 1993 Arusha Accords also stipulated potential Tutsi dominance over the military, hence a probable ascendance in the country as a whole. Thus, on both the military and diplomatic fronts, reversion to earlier Tutsi dominance was a clear possibility.

It is now time to summarize the overarching similarities and differences among our cases. They turn out to be based on claims, whether they are predominantly universal, particular, or a mixed category with no dominant pattern.

Claims

Universalists

Humiliation-shame and perceptions of injustice lay at the root of the formation of European extremist parties, especially Italian Fascism, German Nazism, and Soviet Communism. Radical Islamism has famously been attributed to the humiliation of Muslims, especially Arabs, by the West. Perceptions of injustice also abound.

The etiologies of fascism, communism, and radical Islamism include their universal claims. All assert a cosmic view of the world, whether in Italian Fascism's invocation of ancient Roman imperium, Nazi racialism, Marxist-Leninist class determinacy, or Caliphate supremacy. These universal ideologies also are totalizing in that to varying extents they seek to exert total control over an individual's life, especially his/her belief system.

Honor concerns also help us reflect on the differences between the universal and the particular. Honor can be understood as "a compelling motive to take action, or to refrain from certain actions,"[39] or equivalently as "a moral imperative."[40] In this sense, we can understand Thomas à Beckct, Archbishop of Canterbury, in his confrontation with Henry II when he spoke of the "honor of God" as a primary motivation for his refusal to accede to Henry's demands. Many radical Islamists, including, of course, Osama bin Laden, speak reverently of the honor of Allah and His Prophet Muhammad. For many communists, the moral imperatives of history must be acted upon in the fomenting of revolution. And of course, "racial science" demanded the imperative segregation of "inferior" races from the superior Aryans, and loyalty to the race as in the SS slogan, "My Honor is Loyalty."

These universalizing extremes (or in the case of Becket, simply loyalty to his conception of the faith) differ substantially from the particular nationalisms examined elsewhere in this book. Honor as a moral imperative may be invoked for the sake of the nation, but is less demanding than the requirements of religion, class, or race. One can change one's citizenship from one nationality to another fairly easily through a process of migration and acquisition of the knowledge demanded by citizenship tests. Far more difficult is a change of religion requiring the abandonment of lifelong-held existential beliefs, or the

---

[39] Welsh 2008, 1.   [40] Welsh 2008, 4.

restructuring of class loyalties leading many to relinquish dearly held views on societal structure. (Witness the emigration of large numbers of Russian aristocrats, many of them driving taxicabs in Paris after the Bolshevik Revolution.) And "race" as a category is virtually impossible to change.

Particularists

However, when we turn to cases of greater particularity, not so rooted in universal claims, the presence of humiliation-shame and perceptions of injustice are less prominent. Instead, the onset of the violence occurred almost immediately at the point where the threat of reversion became apparent. A case in point is the school attack at Beslan. Although one can certainly point to feelings of humiliation-shame and perceptions of injustice at the overall history of Russo-Chechen relations, including the massive deportations of 1944, it was the reinvasion of Chechnya by Russian troops in 1999 and the retaking of Grozny that actually spurred the school attack. Indeed, Shamil, the organizer of the attack, was a typical high-level army commander in the earlier successful 1996 war, not known for atrocities against civilians.

Although Shamil was an Islamist, it was the nationalistic drive of the Chechens that was to predominate in virtually all encounters with the Russians for more than a century and a half. (Witness the failure of other Muslim peoples of the North Caucasus to engage the Russians in such overt confrontations.) Indeed, it is possible to speculate that Islamism may have been a useful strategic ploy on the part of Shamil to gain external support from the Islamic world in the face of a relentless and far more powerful Russia.

The remaining cases reveal an even deeper concern for the possibility of reversion. The LTTE adopted suicide bombings, including attacks on civilians, at the moment it appeared that the Jaffna Peninsula was about to be retaken by the SLA. Returning Jews, many of whom fled to and survived the war in the Soviet Union were disproportionately represented in the communist security services immediately after the war. In the Polish mind, they threatened a reversion to communist control of portions of Poland, as occurred in 1939–41. Pogroms against these Jews, as well as assassinations of individual Jews, occurred even after the defeat of the common Polish and Jewish enemy, Nazi Germany.

All of the rampaging militaries gave strong evidence of the threat and fear of reversion prior to their extremist behavior. When the Naval Treaties of Washington (1922) and London (1930) made it clear that Japan was to be treated as a second-class power, later reinforced by the Allied restrictions on trade with Japan, methods not earlier considered such as a surprise attack (Pearl Harbor) were now to be adopted. The brutal treatment of civilians also ensued, when it appeared, as in China, that the war would not be easily or quickly won.

In Pakistan the threat of dominance by the numerically superior Bengalis in East Pakistan was to trigger the onset of invasion by the West Pakistanis and extreme brutality. The fact that many of the Bengalis in East Pakistan were Hindu, or, if Muslim, were tolerant of Hindu culture, threatened a reversion to Hindu cultural, even political dominance. Also in Indonesia, the threat of a reversion to external domination was rife, this time by the Communist Chinese instead of the far less powerful recently displaced Dutch. In the Balkans, particularity was embedded within the exclusive ethnic nationalisms of the region. And as we have seen in all three cases of genocide (the first widespread massacres of Armenians occurred after the military reverses and losses of 1878–79), immediacy of the threat and fear of reversion was apparent in the deportation of the Armenians when the Ottomans were confronted by Russian and British forces in World War I, and the Holocaust began in 1941 during a difficult phase of the invasion of Russia. In Rwanda, when the RPF invasion and Arusha Accords threatened to re-establish Tutsi governance, genocide of the Tutsi ensued.

Universalism and injustice

The question remains why there is this disjunction between origins and immediacy of extremist behavior in certain instances but not in others. More precisely, why do the cases where universal claims are prominent yield a greater presence of feelings of injustice and humiliation than those instances where claimed universality is virtually absent? Italian Fascism, German Nazism, Soviet Communism, and radical Islamism make universal claims, to varying degrees. Even the local Hungarian and Romanian fascists adopted universal symbols such as the cross (Hungary), or Eastern Orthodox liturgical elements (Romania).[41] Respectively, the Roman imperium, Aryan racism, universal equality and dominance of workers, and right to religious domination are sources of these universal claims. Because in all cases they hark back to a much earlier time politically that entailed domination of vast areas of the globe, any retreat from that vision represents humiliation. Clearly, the claims of extreme nationalists have no such global resonance.

Tied to this vision of earlier grandeur are feelings of injustice that people with such a magnificent past are now treated poorly. This also is true in all of the cases of universal claims and much less true of the particularistic nationalists. But interesting here are the sources of ideologies making universal claims. In no case is that claim *sui generis*. All of the ideologies in important ways originated outside the locus of extremism, suggesting the transnational ideation that can predispose believers to universal claims.

As we saw in Chapter 4, Sorel, a French theorist (and activist), was a major source of Mussolini's thought and action, in many respects establishing the foundations of Italian Fascism. Mussolini himself admitted as much, saying: "I

---

[41] Iordachi 2004.

owe most to Georges Sorel. This master of syndicalism by his rough theories of revolutionary tactics has contributed most to form the discipline, energy, and power of the fascist cohorts."[42]

Hitler, of course, was deeply influenced by the racist writings of the French nobleman, Joseph Arthur Comte de Gobineau (*An Essay on the Inequality of the Human Race*[43]), asserting the superiority of the white race. Like Gobineau, the Englishman Houston Stewart Chamberlain also claimed supremacy for the white race, but added the qualifier "Aryan" to those who were most racially fit. Unlike Gobineau, but like his idol, the composer Richard Wagner, Chamberlain was deeply anti-Semitic. He actually joined the Nazi Party and was an admirer of Hitler.

Crucial here is the transformation of the vulgar particularistic anti-Semitism of a Richard Wagner or a Karl Lueger, the anti-Semitic mayor of Vienna around the turn of the twentieth century, to a universal claim of Aryan superiority based on "racial science." In order to correct a seeming injustice to one group (Aryan), another (non-Aryan), typically Jewish, is exposed to epistemic injustice[44] in which wild, inaccurate claims are made about this group.

A Marxism that had been formulated with the workers of advanced Western capitalist societies in mind was transformed by the Bolsheviks into a Marxism-Leninism and ultimately a Maoism that was oriented far more to the peasantry in underdeveloped economies. As shown in Chapter 5, national revolutionary thought had already permeated the intelligentsia and students of Russian society well before the advent of Marxism, either in Menshevik (moderate) or Bolshevik (Marxist-Leninist) form, universalized the singular Russian (or Chinese) predicament. Marxism, with truth claims of universal applicability based on a "science" of history, could be used to magnify many times over the perceived injustices of the *ancien régime*.

Again, in the case of radical Islamism, the external influence is evident. Hasan al-Banna, the founder of the Society of the Muslim Brothers in Egypt and spiritual father to Sayyid Qutb, the philosophical mentor of Osama bin Laden, was deeply influenced by the British presence in Egypt. This Western presence in his homeland led al-Banna to universalize the Islamic predicament. Not only Arabs in Egypt and elsewhere in the Middle East, but all Muslims were to respond to this call for Islamic revival.

Paul Berman[45] has done an especially good job of detailing the direct Western ideational influences on radical Islamism. And as we saw in Chapter 8, Indian Muslim thinkers like Maulana Wahiduddin Khan were opposed to radical Islamism precisely because of its constitution largely in reaction to the Western presence in the Islamic world, in place of anything inherently Islamic.

---

[42] Quoted in Shils 1961, 24.   [43] 1853–55.   [44] Fricker 2007.   [45] 2003.

Ideology and justice

The presence of these external sources of universal claims among extremist groups raises the possibility that these non-indigenous sources were tapped for purposes other than intrinsic merit. Clearly, the charge of injustice can be vastly inflated if there exists an ideational base to support it. Without the national emphasis of Sorel's later writings and the Roman imperium as a model for the future, Mussolini's claims might have fallen on deaf ears. The racial superiority of Aryans, especially Germans, suggests a massive injustice of the Treaty of Versailles that effectively blamed Germany for the war and demanded territorial and financial compensation.

An Islam that in many respects was quietest and oriented to individual piety was now transformed into an ideational justification for mass murder. The vehicle of that transformation was a Western concept of revolt. By using Islam as the ideational base, not only were many more people subject to persuasion than were found in the smaller Arab world where the militancy originated, but claims of injustice also could be amplified because of the violation of universal precepts within Islam, the heir and superseder of earlier monotheistic faiths.

Each of the pathways to extremism has a particular referent. The threat and fear of reversion is found in the earlier subordinate condition of the ephemeral gain. Humiliation can only be understood within the context of a much earlier period of glory that makes the current subordination humiliating. And injustice is measured against a set of ideas that makes the current condition unjust and intolerable. The more universal the claim, the greater the injustice, for justice is to be found now only within the precepts of an all-encompassing explanation of being. An ontological truth transcends all others.

Yet the initial reaction of people to the injustice of a particular act based on Rawlsian criteria of justice as fairness or equity, or restrictions on the opportunity to pursue capabilities can set the stage for the far more extreme universal claims of racial or ethnoreligious superiority. If equity is not forthcoming, then the question remains: why? Answers can be found in the "treachery" of presumed "inferiors" such as the Jews. The path from that point to the assertion of universal racial claims is a clear one.

Clearly, this conception of justice bears no relation to that of John Rawls, which ultimately relies on conceptions of egalitarian liberal democracy. But that is precisely the point. The conception of justice incorporated within the universal claims of extremist groups is authoritarian, even totalitarian. Justice can never be seen as a component of human-concocted positive law, as in liberal democratic societies. Instead, justice inheres in the laws of national, racial, historical, or God-driven determinism.

The importance of perspectives of injustice, whether Rawlsian or based on universal claims, is to be seen in Table 14.1. Here, when examining the cases of extremism, perceptions of injustice are second in importance only to the threat and fear of reversion as pathways from the ephemeral gain. Of course,

Table 14.1 *Pathways to extremism*

	Predominantly Universal	Mixed	Predominantly Particular
Perceptions of Injustice	Nazism, Soviet Communism, Chinese Communism, Cambodian Communism, Muslim Brotherhood, al-Qaeda, Revolutionary France	Italian Fascism, Hungarian Fascism, Romanian Fascism, Chechen Radical Islamism, al-Muhajiroun	LTTE (Sri Lanka), Polish Nationalists, Croatian Ustaše, Japanese Nationalists
Humiliation-Shame	Nazism, Soviet Communism, Chinese Communism, Muslim Brotherhood, al-Qaeda	Italian Fascism, Hungarian Fascism, Romanian Fascism, Chechen Radical Islamism, al-Muhajiroun	LTTE, West Pakistani Nationalists, Ottoman Leaders, Young Turks
Threat and Fear of Reversion	Nazism, Soviet Communism, Cambodian Communism, Muslim Brotherhood, al-Qaeda, Revolutionary France	Italian Fascism, Hungarian Fascism Romanian Fascism, Chechen Radical Islamism, al-Muhajiroun	LTTE, Polish Nationalists, Serbian Nationalists, Croatian Ustaše, West Pakistani Nationalists, Japanese Nationalists, Indonesian Nationalists, Ottoman Leaders, Young Turks, Hutu Extremists, Khartoum Government – Sudan

that table includes the particular sources of extremism that tend to center on the threat and fear of reversion, thereby emphasizing the importance of that category within the overall set. Not shown in the table are the three cases of the rampaging military (the Congo, Guatemala, and Afghanistan) that were better explained by the shadow of the present.

The cases are categorized by universal and particular pathways to extremism, but the mixed category seen in the center column represents those cases where it is difficult to parse the relative contributions of each. Even the first and third columns represent *predominantly* universal and *predominantly* particular pathways, not pure distillations of either.

What is most surprising in that table is the lesser role of humiliation-shame within the entire set. Of course, in individual cases such as al-Qaeda, humiliation-shame was apparent, but despite the ubiquity of humiliation as a claimed source of extremism, in the overall scheme it is less important than I had initially theorized. Humiliation is typically measured against a much earlier triumphal period, as in the earlier glories of the Islamic world. Even Romania, despite its long period of subordination within the Ottoman Empire, gave rise to a fascist extremist organization, the Legion of the Archangel Michael (Iron Guard) that emphasized Eastern Orthodox roots, originally inherited from the Byzantine Empire. Hungary, of course, was the co-ruler of one of the major European powers, the Dual Monarchy. But national extremist groups did not have such a heritage. Among them are the Croatian Ustaše, and Pakistani as well as Indonesian extreme nationalists.

Shame, which frequently requires the manufacture of new codes of conduct (e.g., the "racial" laws of the Third Reich, or Marxist-Leninist "equality" exemplified by the term "comrade"), appears to be even less important as a pathway to extremism. The difficulty in disseminating these codes and having them accepted is illustrated by the necessity during World War II for the Soviet government to emphasize the war for "Holy Mother Russia," or use of the descriptor "The Great Patriotic War," in order to stimulate widespread support for the government. The concepts of equality, communism, or comradeship were earlier proved to be insufficient as exhortations to battle.

Yet even in the cases of universalism, we see that the threat and fear of reversion became prominent in the midst of a difficult war or other imminent threat. And even in the absence of universal claims that can justify mass murder, the demands of the battlefield under conditions of threatened ephemerality can generate mass murder at a rate frequently approximating that of the universalists. Japan, Pakistan, the Ottoman Empire, and the Hutu extremists of Rwanda fall into that category. But in the end, the universalists, especially the communists and Nazis, have the bloodiest records, yielding enormities in excess of any other source.

Stemming from this analysis, the single most prominent emotion yielding extremism is fear. We witness it in all of the cases in Table 14.1, with the exception of Communist China, which, as we saw, was heavily influenced by the Stalinist template. In his insightful study of the Polish nationalist killing of Jews after the end of World War II, Jan Gross perceptively titled it *Fear*. And it clearly was not only the Jewish fear of pogrom and assassination that motivated Gross, but also (perhaps primarily) the palpable Polish fear of reversion to Soviet governance as occurred in eastern Poland in 1939–41, with more than occasional Jewish support. The writings of Jean Hatzfeld[46] and Scott Straus[47] arrive at similar conclusions concerning the role of fear, especially of reversion to Tutsi rule as prime motivators of the Rwandan genocide. Although other scholars are less explicit regarding the role of fear in the origins of extremism, nevertheless this is a leitmotif of their writings. Emblematic is the economist Gerald Feldman's[48]

46 2006.   47 2006.   48 1993.

study of the 1914–24 period in Germany. Titled *The Great Disorder*, it emphasizes the widespread fear engendered by the German defeat, immigration of Jews and other Eastern Europeans into Germany, and ultimately the hyperinflation of 1923 that destroyed the value of the Mark. The life savings of many simply were wiped out.

Interestingly, the ephemeral gain combined with mortality *could* satisfy the demands of a sufficient explanation of the rise of extremism more readily than a necessary one. I refer here to origins, not a diffusion effect as in the Stalinist influence on China and Cambodia. In all cases save one, Greece, the ephemeral gain combined with mortality was associated with the rise of extremism. And that one exception exhibited significant loss compensation in the form of demographic consolidation of earlier territorial conquests that could have been subsequently lost, if not for the Greek refugee influx resulting from the lost war with Turkey. In an important sense, the loss component of the ephemeral gain was nullified.

Universalization as a process

The absence of necessity for the ephemeral gain is seen in cases like China and Cambodia that did not experience the ephemeral gain, yet engaged in extremist behaviors. They adopted an extremist template that earlier had been employed by a cognate form of government facing similar internal and external challenges. First, Mao adopted many of Stalin's policies and then Pol Pot adopted a mix of Mao's and Stalin's tactics in Cambodia. The ephemeral gain may have established the extremist template, but once in existence it can be used by others who perceive themselves to be in similar revolutionary circumstances.

And that sort of diffusion effect was not limited to communism or for that matter (to a lesser extent) to fascism during the interwar period. One cannot comprehend the rise of contemporary Islamist movements without noting the establishment of the first overtly Islamist government in Iran, directly opposed to Western governments such as the US. Hizbollah and later Hamas owe their origins very much to the Iranian model and the aid to these groups provided by that country. Al-Qaeda as a relentless (and sanguinary against Shi'ites) Sunni organization would have been far less influenced by the Iranian example, having experienced its own ephemeral gain, as we saw.

Although the ephemeral gain may not explain the rise of these metastasized organizations, nevertheless one can use the remaining two pathways to extremism as explanations, indeed as was done in the Chinese and Cambodian cases (see Table 14.1). The rise of Hizbollah may be attributed to perceived injustices stemming from years of discrimination against Shi'ites by both Christian and Sunni Arabs in Lebanon, followed by the Israeli occupation of south Lebanon. Humiliation and shame were also a consequence of that occupation.

Contacts between Hizbollah and Palestinians in Gaza later facilitated the rise of Hamas.[49]

The dangers of universalizing extremist messages are increased when there already exist pathways among different nationalities holding similar views. The classic European case, of course, is the anti-Semitism held in common by many Germans, Austrians, Romanians, and Hungarians. This pathway linked these and other European nationalities, even those not directly inclined to fascism, such as the Poles. It was Hitler's genius to effectively mine this deep substratum of hostility to the "international Jew" in an increasingly nationalistic European age. It is no accident that a German ally without a history of such anti-Semitism in the modern period, Italy, was among the most reluctant to release its Jews to Hitler's death camps.

Communism chose a different avenue of near-universal appeal. This appeal was to the working classes of many nations who held in common their hostility to manufacturers who still discriminated against women and generally treated their workers abysmally. But beyond elements of the working class in Russia, Poland, Finland, and other components of the old tsarist empire, the forces of European nationalism were far stronger than those of class solidarity among the nations, as the left-wing socialists and communists discovered much to their dismay in 1914. Only after the Red Army swept westward into Germany in 1945 did an enforced universalization of Soviet Communism occur across Central and Eastern Europe.

Radical Islamism has been able to reach into past interpretations of Islam in times of trouble (cf. Ibn Taymiyya in the thirteenth century) that demonized Jews, Christians, and a variety of other infidels, including the recently converted peoples who did not practice a sufficiently authentic version of Islam. Although historically, Islam had different manifestations ranging from the relatively open mindset of Indonesians to the more austere Berber variant, Islamists seek to impose their own uniformity on Islamic belief and practice. Even the traditional Chinese mosque that for centuries had the appearance of other places of worship in China, now is subject to construction along lines dictated in Saudi Arabia. The syncretic is abandoned for the sake of a presumed earlier authenticity in an attempt to make Islam the basis for extremist action, if need be.

But even contemporary global security concerns may activate the universalizing impulse. Although Pakistan's wars have been exclusively with India, nevertheless a Pakistani nuclear scientist, Sultan Bashiruddin Mahmood, said to be eccentric, had more universal ambitions. According to David Sanger,[50] "Mahmood made it clear to friends that his interest was religious: Pakistan's bomb, he told associates, was 'the property of a whole Ummah,' referring to the worldwide Muslim community. He wanted to share it with those who might speed 'the end of days' and lead the way for Islam to rise as the dominant

---

[49] Mishal and Sela 2000.   [50] 2009, 35.

religious force in the world." There is clear evidence that Mahmood actually met with Osama bin Laden and Ayman al-Zawahiri during a visit to Afghanistan just prior to 9/11.

Judaism too, has within it a basis for extremist action. The Covenant of Abraham that promised the land of Israel (then Canaan) to the Jews has been used by radical Zionists, often religiously Orthodox and settlers in the Palestinian territories, to lay claim to all of Palestine. Because of his willingness to cede occupied territories to the Palestinians under the Oslo Accords, Yitzhak Rabin was assassinated by an Orthodox Jewish extremist. The American-born Baruch Goldstein's massacre of Muslims at prayer in Hebron was animated by a similar concern. For the first time in nearly two millennia, the rise of Zionism as a form of politicized Judaism gave Jews the basis for extremist action.

Yet, it is clear that neither the Covenant of Abraham, nor any religious tenet of Islam *requires* the descent into extremism. Even the concept of jihad, notorious for its recent use as a basis for holy war, also has a much more benign interpretation as a basis for self-purification. In a very real sense, religion is what you make of it, but it still exists as a pathway to potentially unite people of different nationalities in some sort of common extremist enterprise. And religion is typically invoked after other, more secular efforts have failed. When Arab, and more specifically Palestinian, nationalism had failed to overcome Israel in four wars, the Islamic Republic of Iran and its Shi'ite offshoot, Hizbollah, now represented a new model of successful political action to be adopted by Hamas. Indeed, we know that early organizers of Hamas had been among the Palestinian militants exiled to Lebanon and had made numerous contacts with Hizbollah before returning to Gaza.[51]

More generally, if a secular response to political and societal problems is readily available in the modern period, it has generally been preferred initially because it directly addresses those difficulties. But sometimes, even if successful, as in the Zionist formation of Israel and the massive 1967 victory over the forces of Egypt, Syria, and Jordan, elements of the religion begin to intrude. Only with God's help could such a victory have been achieved, said many Orthodox Israelis. Thus was laid much of the foundation for the settler movement in the occupied Palestinian territories. God was now fulfilling His Covenant with Abraham through the medium of the Israeli army. These conquered territories must have been ordained by Him to be settled and ultimately folded into the Israeli state.

God is the most universal of all pathways to extremist behavior. Certainly, it is more universal than either race (limited to a segment of humanity), or class (limited to a sector of society). God knows no limits; hence religion can be among the most potent of universalizing pathways.

---

[51] Mishal and Sela 2000, 656.

A life of its own

Obviously, I have emphasized a materialist explanation of extremism, rooted principally in territorial issues. But, although based initially on territoriality, the extremist impulse can take on a life of its own via subsequent ideational development. The rise of the Egyptian Muslim Brotherhood and its more radical offshoot, al-Gamma al-Islamiyya, is a case in point. Founded by Hasan al-Banna very much in response to the British presence in Egypt, especially in Suez, the Muslim Brotherhood's radical interpretation of Islam later became largely independent of the Western presence. Israeli victories over Egypt and other Arab states clearly exacerbated the problem – the Western presence in a new guise – but the basic tenets of Islam were being invoked in their own right. Thus, despite the territorial gain experienced by the return of Sinai to Egypt by Israel in 1979, and the earlier renunciation of violence by the Muslim Brotherhood in 1971, members of the loosely organized al-Gamma al-Islamiyya assassinated Egyptian President Anwar Sadat in 1981. By this time, the issue of Egyptian territory was insignificant to the radical Islamists. Israel, a non-Islamic country in the Middle East, must not be propitiated by the diplomatic recognition that Egypt offered as a quid pro quo for the return of Sinai.

This is the danger of the rise of unhindered extremism. The violence it commits can be divorced from the issues that initially gave rise to the movement. Thus, territorial gain in 1979 would not mitigate the extremism of al-Gamma al-Islamiyya. The violence would continue in the 1990s, yielding the massacre of sixty-two foreign tourists and their Egyptian guides at the Luxor temple site. Revulsion of the Egyptian people at this unbridled brutality led many of the extremists to renounce violence. Subsequently, this movement declined rapidly. Until such time as extremists have exhausted their core constituency's tolerance for brutality, political extremism can take on a life of its own, largely detached from the originating issues.

15

Ethics and Morality: The Rejection of Traditional Moral Restraints

Ancient civilizations may have appreciated the importance of the ephemeral gain as a potential source of aggression against innocent victims. In the Hebrew Bible, from nothing (*tohu vavohu*) humanity is created in God's image, elevated to live in paradise until the fall from grace and ejection from the Garden of Eden. The loss of paradise and the equally devastating loss of the possibility of living forever (forbidden access to the Tree of Life in the Garden of Eden) were precipitated by Adam and Eve eating from the forbidden Tree of the Knowledge of Good and Evil. Thus, evil and sin are now within the repertory of the human condition. Humiliation-shame, too, is seen in the newly found knowledge of their nakedness that led Adam and Eve to seek fig leaf coverings. The humiliating experience of the Lydian queen seen by a stranger in her nakedness, and its violent consequence, is foreshadowed here. This story will be told later in this chapter.

Earliest of the Abrahamic scriptures, the Hebrew Bible recognized the human potential for sin in reaction to anger and a consequent need for faith-inspired restraints. *Immediately* following the ejection from paradise, the Bible tells the story of Cain and Abel, in which Cain reacts in anger to the perceived injustice of Abel's favored position and kills his brother. Anger and sin are the virtually instantaneous consequences of the knowledge of good and evil. That Cain is an agriculturalist and Abel a pastoralist suggests a keen awareness of the perennial conflict between the two settlement types, not only in ancient times but presently in Darfur, and historically in Rwanda.

Ultimately, the threat and fear of reversion to nothingness ("ashes to ashes, dust to dust") implied by the loss of paradise, including its Tree of Life, animates much of the thinking of the Abrahamic faiths. Eternal life in paradise is to be the reward of the faithful who obey the religious constraints, avoiding at the very least the murder and theft that are among the most egregious of sins. Clearly, mortality, an important component of the present theory, is central to this narrative.

It is no wonder that when the Irish-American author, Thomas Cahill, was asked to select the six most important writings on justice and injustice, he listed the Hebrew prophets first among them.[1]

---

[1] *The Week: The Best of the US and International Media* 2009, 26.

First among the written texts were the Ten Commandments, delimiting the domains of virtue and of sin. Interiority of belief and the need for virtue were to constrain human beings from acting out of anger against their environment in the event of a precipitous loss.

In the face of ephemerality after World War I, note the use of near-sacral language by the German war writer Josef Magnus Wehner in Chapter 4: "Because the sacred German Reich is not a question of boundaries or countries, it is as infinite as the world itself, created by God, and given to the Germans as an *immortal* commission."[2] And as we saw in Chapter 1, the great German philosopher Johann Gottlieb Fichte wrote: "Individual man sees in his country the realisation of his earthly immortality." Thus, the awareness of mortality – an ephemeral existence – has deep roots in German nationalism.

Herein may be found another reason for Hitler's undying hatred of the Jews. The concept of internal restraint generated by the Hebrew Bible in partial response to ephemerality and accepted by Christianity was anathema to him. As we know, World War II, especially in the East, was fought by Hitler in eliminationist fashion, without any regard to constraints, sacred or secular. And when purporting to speak from a religious platform, radical Islamists explicitly choose the interpretation of jihad as an act of war against presumed offenders of their faith, instead of the interior need for religious purification adopted by so many Islamic jurists. Of course, the latter interpretation is far more in keeping with the initial concept of individual responsibility for virtue instead of the collective extremist response. Nevertheless, both secular and sacred moral systems have been constructed that most human beings obey.

This chapter addresses a striking problem in understanding extremist behavior. How are the moral constructs that typically prevent extremist behavior compromised or even obviated? Or in addressing the careers of the philosopher Martin Heidegger, and nationalist writer Ernst Jünger, George Steiner[3] asks: "By what blindness and vanity could men of such stature become enmeshed in the politics of the inhuman?" Because of the salience, even astonishing deviance from traditional morality of the Nazi example, it will be the basis of the majority, although by no means all, of the illustrations used in the following analysis.

Moral issues are extremely important, for extremist groups invariably justify the killing of large numbers of people in the service of political objectives. In order to do so, they must jettison the traditional moral constraints of virtually all sacred and secular moral codes. An understanding of this process occurs at least at two levels: the ideational and the processual. I shall concentrate here on the former, since the processual in the form of terror networks has been analyzed thoroughly by Marc Sageman[4] in his examination of the impact of

---

[2] Emphasis added. For a similar Jewish response to the Holocaust and its threat to Jewish continuity, see Heschel 1969.
[3] 2008, 9.   [4] 2004.

extremist groups on individual members, especially the growing social bonds among them. Al-Muhajiroun, analyzed in Chapter 7, is a case in point. Further, according to Herbert Kelman,[5] routinization of the killing yields a reduction in the effort for conscious decision making, and a focus on the details of the "job" instead of its meaning.

The evolution of morality

The rejection of traditional moral restrictions on mass killing nevertheless is important, for it runs counter to revealed patterns in the evolution of morality in primates. In order to examine this phenomenon systematically, two definitions are required: "Goodness requires, at a minimum, taking proper account of others. Badness, by the same token, includes the sort of selfishness that leads us to treat others improperly by ignoring their interests or treating them as instruments. The two basic premises of evolutionary science and moral reality establish the boundaries of the debate over the origins of goodness."[6]

Frans de Waal has been perhaps the leading figure in establishing the contours of the evolutionary science of primate behavior. Although human morality is certainly more elaborate than that of non-human primates, nevertheless a continuum is said to exist between the two. At one end, we find capuchin monkeys that exhibit a sense of egocentric fairness in "an expectation about how they themselves should be treated, not about how everybody around them should be treated."[7] Intermediate on this continuum are chimpanzees who actually can behave altruistically (by showing sympathy towards members of another species). Nancy Eisenberg suggests that "sympathy is believed to involve an other-oriented, altruistic motivation."[8] Finally, at the extreme end are humans, with their capacity for establishing articulate, detailed, moral codes of behavior.

An example of non-human primate sympathy is that of a bonobo female named Kuni:

> One day, Kuni captured a starling. Out of fear that she might molest the stunned bird, which appeared undamaged, the keeper urged the ape to let it go… Kuni picked up the starling with one hand and climbed to the highest point of the highest tree where she wrapped her legs around the trunk so that she had both hands free to hold the bird. She then carefully unfolded its wings and spread them wide open, one wing in each hand, before throwing the bird as hard she could towards the barrier of the enclosure. Unfortunately, it fell short and landed onto the bank of the moat where Kuni guarded it for a long time against a curious juvenile.[9]

---

[5] 1973.   [6] Macedo and Ober 2006, x.   [7] de Waal *et al.* 2006, 49.
[8] Quoted in de Waal *et al.* 2006, 27.
[9] Quoted in de Waal 1997, 156.

Through previous observation, Kuni apparently understood that birds need to fly, and to the best of her ability she tried to make that happen.

Adam Smith[10] memorably described the empathic component of this sympathy as "changing places in fancy with the sufferer." Elaborating, he stated: "How selfish soever man may be supposed, there are evidently some principles in his nature, which interest him in the fortune of others, and render their happiness necessary to him, though he derives nothing from it, except the pleasure of seeing it."[11]

De Waal tells us that the origins of these sentiments are to be found in the necessity for group loyalty and helping among species – wolves, elephants, chimpanzees, people – that rely on cooperation. Survival required this impulse. "But, as so often, the impulse became divorced from the consequences that shaped its evolution. This permitted its expression even when payoffs were unlikely, such as when strangers were beneficiaries. This brings animal altruism much closer to that of humans than usually thought."[12]

Much of this evolutionary theory, when not inspired by field observations as in the case of Kuni, is of necessity based on experiments (non-invasive) with animals, especially monkeys and apes. But as did Adam Smith, the great Chinese philosopher, Mencius (372–289 BCE), historically second in influence only to Confucius, saw the altruism inherent in human beings:[13]

> When I say that all men have a mind which cannot bear to see the suffer-
> ing of others, my meaning may be illustrated thus: even nowadays, if men
> suddenly see a child about to fall into a well, they will without exception
> experience a feeling of alarm and distress. They will feel so, not as a ground
> on which they may gain the favor of the child's parents, nor as a group on
> which they may seek the praise of their neighbors and friends, nor from a
> dislike to the reputation of having been unmoved by such a thing. From
> this case we perceive that the feeling of commiseration is essential to man.

Experimental evidence suggests that both Smith and Mencius were correct, at least in part. The famous trolley-car and footbridge thought experiments have been used effectively to examine moral problems. Suppose a trolley has veered out of control and is rapidly approaching a group of five people in its path. But if a switch is activated to divert the trolley onto an alternate path, one person will die. Most people, approximately 80–90 percent, support the switch activation.

But in a second, related scenario, no such alternate path exists and the only way to prevent the deaths of the five people in the trolley's path is to throw a heavy man off an overhanging footbridge; his weight can stop the trolley. In contrast to the previous scenario, most people are unwilling to commit this act.

---

[10] [1759] 1966.   [11] Smith [1759] 1966, 9; quoted in de Waal *et al.* 2006, 15.
[12] de Waal *et al.* 2006, 15.   [13] Mencius, n.d., quoted in de Waal *et al.* 2006, 51.

In both scenarios, a person will die, yet most people differ enormously in their reactions to the two cases.[14] Why?

An answer is provided by an fMRI (functional Magnetic Resonance Imaging) investigation of the trolley-footbridge problem. Joshua Greene and his colleagues[15] found an emotional basis for the rejection of directly killing the heavy person on the footbridge: "The thought of pushing someone to his death is, we propose, more emotionally salient than the thought of hitting a switch that will cause a trolley to produce similar consequences, and it is this emotional response that accounts for people's tendency to treat these cases differently."[16] Brain areas exhibited differences in activity suggesting the salience of emotions in thoughts of directly killing another human being.

Yet, we know that there are circumstances that lead people to kill one another. One has only to change the thought experiment to establish that the heavy person is a Jew and the five people in the trolley's path are German. In Nazi Germany, beyond a certain point in time, certainly during the war, most Germans would have opted to throw the heavy Jew off the footbridge and save the five Germans. In large measure, this chapter is an effort to understand the ability of Germans at that time to override their innate moral revulsion at committing such an act.

Whether human behavior advances to the level of altruism or not, the heart of morality is reciprocity or retributive behavior. Reciprocity has been documented among chimpanzees who are more likely to share food with others who had previously groomed them. Food possessors among the chimpanzees also were more likely to protest against approaching individuals who had *not* groomed them earlier than at those who had.[17] In simulation studies of cooperative behavior among humans, Tit for Tat was found to be the most successful strategy.[18]

Edward Westermarck, an ethnic Swede living in Finland, understood the retributive emotion as the basis of morality. Certain retributive emotions stem from resentment and anger yielding punishment and revenge, while others, classified as "retributive kindly emotions" derive from a "desire to give pleasure in return for pleasure."[19] The latter instance is a case of reciprocal altruism.

But political extremists concentrate on the former. Among the most prominent bases of extremism is the desire for punishment and revenge as a form of retribution for perceived defection. As we have seen, as early as December 2, 1919, in a letter to General August von Mackensen, the recently abdicated Kaiser Wilhelm II wrote: "The deepest, most disgusting shame ever perpetrated by a people in history, the Germans have done onto [sic] themselves. Egged on and misled by the tribe of Juda [sic] whom they hated, who were guests among them! That was their thanks! Let no German ever forget this, nor rest until these

---

[14] Appiah 2008, 89; Hauser 2006.   [15] 2001.   [16] Greene *et al.* 2001, 2106.
[17] de Waal 1997.   [18] Axelrod 1984.
[19] Westermarck [1908] 1912, 9; quoted in de Waal *et al.* 2006, 19.

parasites have been destroyed and exterminated [*vertilgt und ausgerottet*] from German soil! This poisonous mushroom on the German oak-tree!"[20]

Worthy of note are several key elements in the Kaiser's letter. First is the violation of an assumed reciprocity in the relations between Jews and Germans. As guests of the German people, Jews were supposed to be thankful and behave in an appropriately cooperative manner. Instead, Jewish left-wing activists like Kurt Eisner, leader of an industrial strike in 1916 and the later post-World War I socialist revolution, "stabbed" Germany in the back. The Jews were now accused of defection, in which "breaking a cooperative relationship is minimally a violation of social norms and maximally an immoral act that represents a breach of a legally binding agreement."[21] The exhortation to "destroy and exterminate" is, of course, an extreme retributive response to a presumed defection of an entire people based on the behavior of a few. In this ideational mode, there was no recognition of the reality of 100,000 Jewish men under arms (80,000 having served in combat), 12,000 Jewish dead at the front and 35,000 decorated for battlefield bravery. These statistics are out of all proportion to the roughly 500,000 Jewish citizens living in Germany in 1914.[22]

Second, the organic nationalism that would later be used to separate Jewish Germans from their Christian counterparts was rife throughout Europe. Because of this worldview in which ethnicities were distinct from each other, reciprocity in the form of cooperation, or at least passivity, could be demanded of *all* members of a "non-German" ethnic group. Defection of even a few then could be blamed on the collective whole. Memories of this "defection" could be maintained, even as a negatively retributive camel remembered very real offenses in an anecdote recounted by Westermarck.

A camel had been severely beaten on several occasions by a young camel driver for disobeying commands. After accepting the punishment, on one occasion the camel found itself unladen and alone with the 14-year-old boy. It "seized the unlucky boy's head in its monstrous mouth, and lifting him up in the air flung him down again on the earth with the upper part of the skull completely torn off, and his brains scattered on the ground."[23]

Thus, revenge as a form of severe negative retribution can occur among animals and humans, as can the retributive kindly emotions that yield a reciprocal altruism. Only major dislocations, such as a severe societal loss strongly violating expectations and evoking fears of renewed subordination, can yield sufficient grievance to withstand the evolutionary process that could otherwise give way to a reciprocal altruism, if not sympathy. "High moral outrage, coupled with a focus on the perpetrator, leads to retributive impulses and to a desire to punish."[24]

---

[20] Quoted in Röhl 1994, 210.   [21] Hauser 2006, 255.   [22] Fischer 1998, 120.
[23] Westermarck [1908] 1912, 38.   [24] Darley and Pittman 2003, 331.

Evidence exists for the importance of negative emotions yielding retribution especially under conditions of the failure of reciprocity. This is especially notable because of the importance placed on it by the German Kaiser Wilhelm II, with Hitler's firm agreement, as we saw. "When reciprocity fails or the offer is unfair [in the ultimatum game, see below], imaging studies reveal significant activation of the anterior insula, an address of the brain known to play a role in negative emotions such as pain, distress, anger, and especially disgust."[25]

Ethics and morality

We must understand that not only are there driving forces that move people towards extremism but for that extremism to take hold and be acted upon, traditional sacred or secular moral restraints must be loosened, even entirely removed. Inhibitions and adherence to universal moral codes stemming from empathy or sympathy must be countered. A disinhibitory process needs to take place. It is almost as if, as Steven Pinker suggests,[26] "there seems to be a Law of Conservation of Moralization, so that as old behaviors are taken out of the moralized column, new ones are added to it." Although not written to understand the origins of extremist behavior, a distinction introduced by Avishai Margalit is helpful. He distinguishes between ethics and morality; the former is based on obligations arising from thick relationships, such as those existing among family members. Morality concerns obligations pertaining to thin relations or those not stemming from the family – the world at large: "Morality is greatly concerned, for example, with *respect* and *humiliation*; these are attitudes that manifest themselves among those who have thin relations. Ethics, on the other hand, is greatly concerned with *loyalty* and *betrayal*, manifested among those who have thick relations."[27]

It was Hitler's genius to transform the German universe of moral obligation into one consisting entirely of ethics. He made it virtually impossible, in the language of neuroscientists, to "instinctively do the right thing when our minds allow us to forget the difference between ourselves and others. Through a 'blurring of identity' caused by the failure of various mechanisms in the brain…we instinctively empathize with another and act altruistically."[28]

In the service of maintaining firm distinctions between "us" and "them," one thinks, for example of the SS slogan "*Meine Ehre Heisst Treue*," (My Honor is Loyalty). Loyalty is a product of thick relations involving the family. Margalit[29] provides an example of a man witnessing two persons drowning, one his wife and the other a stranger. The observer can only rescue one of the imperiled people. Morally, the two victims have equal claims on the rescuer, but ethically,

---

[25] Hauser 2006, 287.   [26] 2008, 34.   [27] Emphasis added; Margalit 2002, 8.
[28] Pelekanos 2008, 19.   [29] 2002, 88.

there is little choice. The man must choose his wife, else he would be "ethically cursed" in Margalit's terminology.

Hitler transformed all Germans into people to whom loyalty was owed. When found in peril, as in the two drowning victims, the German person should be chosen, *even if the second victim is his non-German wife.* In this fashion, the world was dichotomized. Germans were owed loyalty, rescue, and salvation by other Germans, *nothing* was owed to anyone else. In this sense, political extremism is not only the willingness to support draconian political programs and the mass murder of opponents if necessary, but also a dichotomization of the world. There exists *no* universe of moral obligation, only the ethical obligation to an organic entity that is viewed as something very closely akin to a family.

Indeed, the family was the unit of choice in Nazi culture. According to Ludwig Leonhardt:

> Deeply perceiving the source of the renewal of the Volk, National Socialism considers the family to be the foundation of the state. In order to grasp the importance of this statement and to evaluate it properly, we must look more closely at the concept of "family." By family we must not understand only parents and children. To a family, in our sense of the word, belong not only those who bear the name or who possess a piece of land or some other property. Neither do legal relationships alone encompass the concept. Rather, the family embraces everything that existed spiritually and psychically as a living patrimony in a definite circle of persons. What we are, what we accomplish, is not due to our own merit; in the last analysis we owe it to our parents and grandparents, our whole line of ancestors, whose heritage we carry within ourselves. In short, we owe it to the spiritual values which have been transmitted to us and which we are to pass on to our children and the children of our children. All this belongs to the family, whose importance in the life of the nation the new state is ready to acknowledge in the fullest sense.[30]

Arthur Miller's play *Incident at Vichy* can be used to illustrate the moral inversion that this ideation introduced. A prominent French-Jewish psychiatrist and a wastrel aristocrat have been fortuitously caught together in a dragnet, and are to be questioned in a Gestapo police station as to their "racial" origins. Conversations between the two lead the aristocrat to learn of the Jewish psychiatrist's contributions to medicine, hence to society. The Jew's life trajectory therefore stands in stark contrast to his own. At the last moment prior to Gestapo questioning, the aristocrat insists that the psychiatrist and he exchange papers that would now document the Jew as an "Aryan." Instead of the psychiatrist, the aristocrat would be interned, very possibly ending in his death.

From the perspective of traditional morality, the aristocrat would be deemed an altruist who was willing to risk his own life to save another that he deemed

---

[30] Quoted in Mosse 1966b, 34.

more worthy. But in the Nazi dichotomization, the Aryan could not betray his own people by depriving them of his existence. The only obligation of the aristocrat was an ethical one to be loyal to his own "race." The Jew, as well as other non-Aryans of course, had no ethical or moral standing.

Social psychology and morality: authority, purity, and sanctity

From a social psychological perspective, there is yet another theory of morality that can help explain extremist ideation. As we shall see, an emphasis on the moral dimension of authority, as well as purity and sanctity, can sharply reinforce the existing tendencies toward ingroup loyalty. As before, the purpose is to understand the extremist effort to supplant sacred and secular moral restraints on extremism, especially the mass murder of innocents. Jonathan Haidt and Jesse Graham[31] formulated a five-foundation theory of morality based largely on mammalian evolution. These are:

(1) Harm/Care in which the sensitivity to suffering in one's own offspring can be generalized to others.
(2) Fairness/Reciprocity. Fair, reciprocal interactions form the basis of another dimension of morality. Robert Trivers[32] earlier argued for a reciprocal altruism. Robert Axelrod's[33] Tit for Tat is an iterated prisoner's dilemma game that incorporates cooperation as the first move and thereafter simply imitates the opponent's preceding move. It was found to defeat all other programs submitted by experts in two rounds of tournament play.
(3) Ingroup/Loyalty. Having lived for millennia within kin-based structures, trust and cooperation are especially valued within the group. Those who betray the group are seen as especially heinous.
(4) Authority/Respect. The several millennia-long pre-modern history of primates entailed existence principally within hierarchically organized groups.[34] Humans, chimpanzees, and to a somewhat lesser extent, bonobos, have evolved within such hierarchical structures. As such, respect for authority, whether based on fear among non-human primates, or on legitimacy and good leadership in human societies, has been valued highly; without it the group is more likely to be conquered or to disintegrate from within.
(5) Purity/Sanctity. Human evolution began to depart from that of other primates when meat-eating became common in human societies. Initially, carcasses may have been scavenged until meat became a staple of the human diet. At this time, the growth in the human cortex, along with meat-eating appears to have imparted to humans – and only to humans – the emotion of

---

[31] 2007; see also Graham, Haidt, and Nosek 2009.   [32] 1971, 35.   [33] 1984.
[34] de Waal 1997.

disgust.[35] Tainted meat and other impurities may have been excluded from the human diet by this emotion acting as a safeguard. Indeed, early religion may have evolved precisely to incorporate additional safeguards in the form of dietary restrictions that were deemed to foster human health, kosher and halal meat serving as prime examples. Later, microbes that could yield decay became objects of disgust. In the following analysis, instead of a single dimension, purity and sanctity will function as mostly independent sources of political extremism.

Purity, sanctity, and in-group loyalty

The five dimensions are based on earlier work by Richard Shweder *et al.*[36] The third dimension in their study is similar to that of Haidt and Graham, but with the important addition of purity that was not included in the earlier work. Purity can be an important component of extremist ideology.

Now, Haidt and Graham[37] do not ascribe any particular significance to their framework for understanding the rise of political extremism. Instead, they suggest that the first two, harm/care and fairness/reciprocity are typical of liberal societies that emphasize individual rights and welfare, while the latter three are found in more traditional group-oriented societies. One can understand the dawn of modernity with its requirements of property rights and fair transactions among individuals as leading to the emphasis on human rights, with the individual as the principal unit of analysis.

Yet precisely because so much of political extremism has been a reaction against the intrusion of modernity into more traditional societies, there appears to be a connection. Societies that have experienced loss, or the threat of loss, may abjure the rights of the individual for the sake of the collective that has experienced injury. Modernity may be blamed, especially if certain individuals (e.g., capitalists, Americans, Jews) representing modernity also, either realistically or phantasmally, appear to be injurious. As a consequence, the latter three domains of in-group/loyalty, authority/respect, and purity/sanctity may be disproportionately emphasized. The "liberal" dimensions of harm/care and fairness/reciprocity may be said not to apply to those individuals who are proclaimed to be outside the universe of moral obligation.

Actually, we can even gauge the *extent* of extremism by knowing which dimension is chosen for emphasis by the group. There exists a general gradient from the first to the last of these moral dimensions based on the *possibility* of inclusion within its moral safeguard. Clearly the first two dimensions apply to all individuals within the polity. The third, in-group/loyalty, can apply to all who choose to identify with the group and are deemed appropriate to be included,

---

[35] Rozin, Haidt, and McCauley 2000.   [36] 1997.   [37] 2007.

while the fourth, authority/respect, can apply to all members of the polity, also deemed appropriate, who accept the particular authority of the moment.

The dominant form of nationalism reflected by the third and fourth dimensions – in-group/loyalty and authority/respect – is ethnic instead of civic (allowing all citizens to enjoy the same civil and political rights). Citizens of a different ethnicity than the majority can change their names, as many do in Japan, or not identify with any significantly large politically excluded minority, either in customs, language, religion, or other markers of ethnicity. But the last dimension, purity/sanctity, can put a more stringent requirement on individuals. If the purity is based on a "racial" standard, as in Nazi Germany or in 1994 Rwanda, then it may be impossible to resist. All "racial" Jews, whatever their religious profession, or parental, even grandparental conversion to Christianity, were doomed to extinction. In Cambodia, between 1975 and 1979, external criteria such as the wearing of glasses could signal the "wrong" urban-educated class and the likelihood of survival was minimal.[38] If sacred or secular belief is the criterion of choice, then some greater latitude could theoretically be expected, but in practice, not much.

Although conversion from Christianity to Islam was technically an option for Armenians threatened with extinction in the 1915–16 Ottoman Empire, in practice it was offered almost exclusively to young and comely Armenian girls who would then be taken into Turkish homes typically as servants, or in some cases as sex slaves. In almost all cases, they were converted to Islam. Osama bin Laden's extreme version of Islam does not allow much latitude for many Muslims who would be characterized by him as "apostates," even if their belief in Islam is sincere, and religious practice is observed faithfully. On the secular side, communism in the Soviet Union and to a somewhat greater extent in China, offered the possibility of ideological conversion, but in practice the class and sometimes ethnic origins of the individual frequently were to determine the life and death decisions by the authorities. The purity/sanctity dimension is the one that is most central for the more zealous practitioners of political extremism.

As one might expect, given the length of human evolutionary development, ingroup loyalty is perhaps the most easily invoked of the three dimensions most conducive to extremism. Sebastian Haffner, once called the "conscience of Germany" after the war and a firm anti-Nazi who emigrated before the war, nevertheless experienced this heightened sense of in-group camaraderie. Haffner recorded his reaction to the required attendance at an ideological indoctrination camp for soon-to-be-certified lawyers. Although put off by the SA leaders, Haffner soon succumbed to what he called "the trap of comradeship." At the end of the camp session, he comments: " 'We' had become a collective entity, and with all the intellectual cowardice and dishonesty of a collective

---

[38] Midlarsky 2005b.

being we instinctively ignored or belittled anything that could disturb our collective self-satisfaction. A German Reich in microcosm."[39] Yet, ultimately he did not succumb to the adulation of authority, nor the virtual sanctity of that authority that was central to Nazi ideation (not to mention the purity component of racial anti-Semitism).

With the possible exception of purity, all of these elements are found in the following confession of Günter Grass, arguably Germany's best known postwar writer, a Nobel Laureate, and a guardian of left-wing liberal values. This is the same writer who, in *My Century*,[40] could describe with great sympathy and affect the impact of Hitler's rise to power on Max Liebermann, the great German-Jewish artist, the brutal murder of a Jewish communist shortly thereafter, the fate of Jewish children in an orphanage, and the mass murder of Polish Jews in Treblinka and Warsaw.

Yet, in 1943, at the age of fifteen, he volunteered for active duty while serving in the auxiliary consisting of boys too young to actively defend the homeland. After time subsequently spent in the Labor Service, in 1944 he was inducted into the *Waffen SS*, the combat arm of the uniformed cadres of the Nazi Party, in which he was trained as a panzer gunner. But before that induction, while still in the Reich Labor Service, a leader arrived pronouncing accusations of:

> shame and craven betrayal; that is, about the base and insidious plot on the part of a coterie of well-born officers – unsuccessful, thank heaven – to assassinate our dearly beloved Führer, and about merciless revenge, the "extermination of this vile clique." And on and on about the Führer, who – "It was truly a miracle!" – had survived.
>
> *A shiver ran through us. Something akin to piety sent the sweat seeping out of our pores. The Führer saved! The heavens were once more, or still, on our side.*
>
> We sang both our national anthems. We shouted *Sieg heil!* three times. We were irate, we were incensed at the still nameless traitors.[41]

In-group solidarity, of course, is established not only by the singing of the two national anthems, but especially by the extreme anger at the still nameless traitors. This solidarity would later be reflected by Grass's exposure to the song of the *Waffen SS*, "If Others Prove Untrue, Yet We Shall Steadfast Be,"[42] which is a variation on the general SS slogan, "My Honor is Loyalty."[43]

But now there is more than mere solidarity. Authority of the "dearly beloved Führer" is fused with something like sanctity as in the "piety" that "sent the sweat seeping out of our pores." And "extermination of this vile clique" is demanded as if these attempted assassins were Jews, also subject to extermination as infectious "microbes."

[39] Haffner 2002, 283, 288.   [40] 1999, 82–88, 107–10.
[41] Emphasis added; Grass 2007, 73.   [42] 2007, 74.   [43] Smith 1971, 171.

As early as the Russian Civil War between Reds and Whites, we see this analogy of Jews to microbes and the need for their extermination, much as the unsuccessful assassins of Hitler must be liquidated. A White secret service agent during the Russian Civil War reported from the Ukraine: "No administrative step would help; it is necessary to neutralize the microbe – the Jews… As long as the Jews are allowed to do their harmful work, the front will always be in danger… The Jew is not satisfied with corrupting the soldier. Lately he has been paying even greater attention to the officers. But he is most interested in young people. Clever [Jewish] agents, under the cover of patriotism and monarchism, mix with young soldiers, and with the help of cards, women and wine they lure the debauched youth into their nets."[44]

Later, of course, this "microbe," or "bacterium" now embedded firmly within Nazi discourse would be used as a justification for mass murder. In his infamous October 4, 1943 Posen speech to a meeting of senior *SS* officers, among others, Himmler stated:

> Most of you men know what it is like to see 100 corpses side by side, or 500 or 1,000. To have stood fast through this and – except for cases of human weakness – to have stayed decent that has made us hard… We had the moral right, we had the duty towards our people, to destroy this people that wanted to destroy us. But we do not have the right to enrich ourselves by so much as a fur, as a watch, by one Mark or a cigarette or anything else. We have exterminated a bacterium because we do not want in the end to be infected by the bacterium and die of it. I will not see so much as a small area of sepsis appear here or gain a hold. Wherever it may form, we will cauterise it. All in all, however, we can say that we have carried out this most difficult of tasks in a spirit of love for our people. And we have suffered no harm in our inner being, our soul, our character.[45]

Not only the Nazis, but other extremists also used the microbe analogy. To justify the killing of large numbers of Cambodians, including members of the Khmer Rouge itself, in the name of class and ideological purity, the term "microbe" was used. According to a 1976 report of the Communist Party of Kampuchea, "The heat of the peoples' [sic] revolution and the democratic revolution were not enough… The level of people's struggle and class struggle meant that [when] we searched for evil microbes inside the party, we couldn't find them. They were able to hide. Now that we are advancing on an all-embracing socialist revolution… in the party, in the army, among the people, we can find the evil microbes. They emerge, pushed out by the true nature of the socialist revolution."[46] Certainly, Stalin's thinking during the Great Purges of the 1930s and that of Mao in the later Cultural Revolution ran along similar lines.

---

[44] Quoted in Kenez 1992, 304.   [45] Quoted in Burleigh 2000, 660–1.
[46] Quoted in Chandler 1990, 169.

Himmler's references to "bacterium" and "sepsis", as well as the communist and even radical Islamist concerns with ideational "contamination," suggest an organic version of the collectivity. Whether "racially" defined, as in the Nazi case, or ideologically and sacrally specified respectively in the communist and radical Islamist instances, the interests of the collectivity vastly outweigh those of the individual. Thus, in the most radical cases of political extremism, two concerns are meshed: political dominance, even hegemony, and a virtual hermetical sealing of the collectivity to ensure that impure and potentially infectious human or ideational material never intrudes. And when these "impurities" already have appeared, they must be extirpated by whatever means, even in violation of any traditionally accepted moral codes of conduct.

Thus, purity *and* sanctity are embodied in extremist ideation, as well as an emphasis on authority and, of course, in-group solidarity. *All else is excluded*, except as it pertains to harm/care, or fairness/reciprocity, but only among the in-group. Clearly, not all political extremism is founded on such draconian foundations; yet, it is chilling to consider first the political effectiveness of this program within 1930s Germany, and then the military prowess of the Nazi war machine against a coalition of opponents commanding vastly superior resources. Perhaps a measure of this effectiveness is the impact on a youth with the potential for later literary, even moral grandeur, but who during the war, was willing to fight under the double rune insignia of the SS.

The search for authenticity

Another, very different approach to morality is taken by the Canadian philosopher Charles Taylor.[47] By a moral ideal, he means "a picture of what a better or higher mode of life would be, where 'better' and 'higher' are defined not in terms of what we happen to desire or need, but offer a standard of what we ought to desire." In earlier times and in most parts of the world, especially those influenced by the Abrahamic faiths, standards of "higher" or "better" were defined by religious doctrine. The problem identified by Taylor is the not unfamiliar one found in liberal societies in which the societal ethos consists largely of individualism, instrumentality, and a culture of self-fulfillment that eschews transcendental concerns. In the absence of clearly articulated external criteria, how does one achieve self-fulfillment?

Answers have been found in an ethics of authenticity pioneered, for example, by Descartes within a rationality in which each person is responsible for him/herself, or a Lockean individualism dependent on individual will prior to social obligation. Basically, the moral sense of what is right or wrong is an intuitive feeling that all people are endowed with, probably at birth. And as we saw, Smith uses the general term "sympathy" towards others, their joys and sorrows, to

----

[47] 1992.

indicate emotions that lie at the basis of a social order. It is not surprising, then, that in a culture of authenticity (one based on its ethics) "relationships are seen as the key loci of self-discovery and self-confirmation."[48]

These relationships can be dyadic or multiple, but whatever their dimension, they define our identity. In a liberal society of the twenty-first century century, the "authentic self" can develop within a virtually random network of relationships leading to self-fulfillment. Not so within the period of ephemeral victories, in which territorial or other losses dominate the societal landscape. Authenticity, then, is not dependent on individual relationships with other known individuals, but on a larger collectivity that simultaneously experienced this collective loss. In a setting of this type, self-fulfillment becomes far more dependent on the larger societal ambience than on individual relationships. A search for the authentic self necessarily entails some recognition of this societal backdrop.

For example, to some African-Americans living in Newark, New Jersey, the light-skinned black mayor Cory Booker, a graduate of Stanford and Yale law school, and a Rhodes Scholar is insufficiently "black." "The question of who is and isn't authentically black touched a nerve in the community."[49] According to his mother, who campaigned for Booker, "People would say, 'Yea, I know, but can you make him talk like us?' "[50] In the rise of extremism, political orientation is less important than more observable or even simplistic measures of authenticity occurring within the context of mortality salience.

If the individual seeker of authenticity is a returning German combat veteran from World War I, then anger, hurt, and patriotism magnified immensely by loss (territory and persons) occurring within the context of a perceived unjust peace, can also magnify the quest for authenticity. What does it mean to be an authentic German, or for that matter Italian, within this context? Or after the immense losses both during and after World War II, what does it mean to be an authentic Pole?

Often the simplest and most readily available answer is not found in dyadic or multiple individual relationships, but in social movements or political parties that offer a ready and emotionally satisfying version of authenticity. Interpretations of race, nation, social class, or ethnoreligious identity can become extreme in response to the perceived extent of the loss. Here, the trajectories of the individual and nation are together forged in war or simply a common national perception that extreme corrections are required. In the absence of traditional limits imposed, say, by religious doctrine, the search for authenticity itself enters the realm of the extreme: the German national becomes an Aryan born to rule; the Italian nationalist, an heir to Roman imperial expansionism; the Arab Muslim, a radical Islamist demanding restoration of the Caliphate; a Hutu extremist, a

---

[48] Taylor 1992, 29.   [49] Boyer 2008, 46.   [50] Boyer 2008, 46.

seeker of the restoration of an authentic central African indigenous government; or a communist proletarian, a motivator of the dynamics of the cutting
edge of history. In an age of extremes the extreme solution is found.

A corollary to the intense search for authenticity, of course, is the rejection,
even purification, of the inauthentic. The non-Aryan Jew, the Jewish opponent
of Italian Fascist imperialism in Ethiopia, the "apostate" Muslim, a Western liberal democrat, the Tutsi ostensibly of east African origin, or a capitalist-kulak
cannot be tolerated in positions of governance or even as legitimate members
of society.

Loss establishes a crisis of authenticity. While the pre-World War I "authentic" German could take satisfaction in his/her diplomatic and military domination of the European continent, even holding sway socially and economically
in Eastern European countries not governed by Germany (e.g., German landowners in the Baltic provinces of tsarist Russia), after World War I this would no
longer be the case. In his novel, *Memoirs of an Anti-Semite*, Gregor von Rezzori,
himself a native of Bukovina, describes the transition of the main character,
also called Gregor originating in Bukovina. Note the setting of Bukovina, formerly a part of the Austro-Hungarian Empire that after World War I experienced an extraordinary contraction of authority space. Jonathan Beckman[51]
summarizes:

> Gregor suffers from the frustration of German masculinity that followed
> defeat in the First World War. He feels it especially acutely as a colonial set-
> tler in Eastern Europe, cut adrift by the dissolution of the Austro-Hungarian
> Empire. Unable to fulfill his swaggering Germany destiny, seeing himself
> as a spiritual descendant of Charlemagne and his paladins, Gregor feels
> uncomfortably divided. Taking a job as a window-dresser for a cosmetics
> company "made the final schism within my soul…anything connected with
> selling in a store was beyond social acceptance. This was the privilege of the
> Jews." The two social postures available to the Jews tormented his divided
> Germanic self. If they remained aloof, they were prone to "the abrupt
> change from immeasurable arrogance to shamefaced self-debasement."
> Yet, through the history of their oppression, the Jews had developed an
> ironic equanimity towards this parlous state that unnerved Germans like
> Gregor. Alternatively, Jews could assimilate but attempts to do so exposed
> the Germans' own inauthenticity. As Gregor sits in a Bucharest tavern with
> his Jewish mistress, he becomes violently angry because she is "too 'elegant'
> for her own good."

Unwilling to compromise and suffer the discomfort of this diminished status appropriate "only for Jews," emphasis on the superiority of "Aryans" is
a simpler and a more comfortable alternative. The results, of course, would
be disastrous. If the "inauthentic" German would have to be bound by the

---

[51] 2008, 20.

typical moral restraints of the quotidian, then the "authentic" German in Aryan garb could dispense with such niceties. Put another way, without the moral norms that constrain the salesman or other typical societal member dependent on the goodwill of both customer and employment superior, the path is now open for extremist behavior by the Aryan *Übermensch*, including mass murder.

Assuming the new identity

When is identity important, especially in relation to consideration of justice norms? One can argue "that identity becomes more salient when it is fluid, such as when individuals or groups undergo geographical or social change and experience psychological and political shifts in their understanding of who they are and their entitlement to social resources."[52]

These concerns immediately raise two identity issues, especially after defeat and territorial loss. Two forms of identity have been posited by Linda Skitka.[53] They are (1) material, referring to access to resources, and (2) social, entailing acceptance, regard, belonging, honor, respect, and interactional justice. Both are found in the case of Germany after World War I: the consequences of territorial loss for the second, social form of identity, and the massive inflation of 1922–23 for the first, material form. According to Skitka,[54] "The identity threat hypothesis would predict – with some qualification – that people should also be most likely to first look for violations of justice norms that protect the currently activated province of identity. Therefore, when people's material interests are threatened, they will first look for violations of the equity norm, and when their social status or standing is threatened, they will first look for evidence of procedural impropriety (e.g., a biased judge) or violations of group norms." Here, the "procedural impropriety" and "biased judge" are found in the Versailles Conference that was seen to have unfairly treated Germany after the war, and established the conditions for the later massive inflation.

Equally, if not more, important is the finding that under conditions of low levels of conflict, similarity in identities leads to inclusion, but under high conflict conditions similarity leads to exclusions.[55] Similarities between the heavily assimilated German-Jewish communities and their Christian counterparts far outweighed their differences. Prior to 1914 under normal conflict conditions of some intergroup tension, Jews could be accepted politically, as evidenced by the rapid decline of overtly anti-Semitic political parties by 1916.[56] However, during World War I with its intense conflict and immediately thereafter, that condition changed markedly. Similarly, the invasion of Rwanda by the predominantly Tutsi RPF established a high conflict condition that led to the exclusion of the

---

[52] Clayton and Opotow 2003, 300.   [53] 2003, 289.   [54] 2003, 292.
[55] Opotow 1995.   [56] Melson 1992.

Tutsi, who in many parts of the country were increasingly assimilated into the Hutu majority. The Pontic Greeks, who among all of the Greek communities in Anatolia were probably most like the Turks, even speaking a Greek dialect unintelligible to other Greeks, were the most clearly exposed to genocidal activity by the Turks during and after World War I.

In his autobiography, Eric Voegelin, a staunch conservative, but fiercely anti-Nazi political philosopher, suggested the identity change. "A further reason for my hatred of National Socialism (other than its fraudulence) and other ideologies is quite a primitive one. I have an aversion to killing people for the fun of it. What the fun is, I did not quite understand at the time, but in the intervening years the ample exploration of revolutionary consciousness has cast some light on this matter. The fun consists in gaining a pseudo-identity through asserting one's power, optimally by killing somebody – a pseudo-identity that serves as a substitute for the human self that has been lost."[57] Michael Burleigh[58] calls this the "one powerful moral consideration that drove" Voegelin's thought.

Taking on this new identity can indeed have powerful moral implications, even if only in social experiments. In a now-classic experiment by Philip Zimbardo and his colleagues,[59] dividing college-age students into prison guards and inmates, with appropriate uniforms, the guards treated the prisoners in an utterly inhumane manner. They forced the prisoners to defecate in buckets, to clean toilets with their bare hands, and to be utterly submissive to their every whim. Stripped of human dignity, the prisoners became objects of derision and near-sadism by the guards. The social arrangement, not any inherent personality flaws, led to the cruelty. Or as Zygmunt Bauman avers, "What mattered was the existence of a polarity, and not who was allocated to its respective sides. *What did matter was that some people were given a total, exclusive and untempered power over some other people.*"[60]

Given the psychic advantage of being an Ayran *Übermensch* instead of the victim of defeat in the reality of interwar Germany, the narcotic effect of this substitution is nearly irresistible. The shame that many Germans felt upon the defeat in World War I and consequent subordination was erased by a "revision of the self."[61]

The infatuation, even obsession with the "new," was found among those who embraced the new European extremism. "It is no secret that many prominent moderns were attracted by the energy of interwar political extremism and especially by its uncompromising shredding of the past. 'I write *nihil* on anything that has been done before,' declaimed the Bolshevik poet-enthusiast Vladimir Mayakovsky."[62]

---

[57] Quoted in Burleigh 2007, 119.   [58] 2007, 119.
[59] Haney, Banks, and Zimbardo 1973; Zimbardo 2008.
[60] Emphasis in original, Bauman 1989, 167–8.
[61] Doris 2002, 155.   [62] Quoted in Eksteins 2008, 24.

All in a day's work

Yet, even the abominable and barbaric ultimately can become routinized partly as the result of the adoption of new "authentic" identities associated with the new, inverted morality. In December 2006, an elderly former American officer, dispossessing himself of his belongings, offered an album of photographs in and around Auschwitz to the United States Holocaust Museum. Found by this officer in an abandoned apartment in Frankfurt at the end of the war, it was now for the first time to be publicly revealed.

How can we understand the pictures of Auschwitz officers at play in nearby Solahütte, a place of recreation for the Nazis working in that extermination facility? A man with an accordion is leading a group of officers in song, Rudolf Hoess, the first commandant of Auschwitz, and Josef Mengele, the physician "Angel of Death," among them. There is an insouciant spirit in the gathering. According to Alec Wilkinson,[63] "The album's effect is discordant. The people it depicts are engaged in the greatest mass murder ever committed, yet its principal impression is of pleasure; nor do the people portrayed look like villains. 'They haven't got red eyes and horns,' Erbelding [an archivist at the Museum] says. 'They don't look like people you would dislike.'"[64]

The career path of Karl Hoecker, an adjutant to Richard Baer, a later Auschwitz commandant is instructive. The son of a bricklayer who died in World War I, Hoecker's family was impoverished. He joined the SS in 1933. In 1940, he worked at the Neuengamme concentration camp near Hamburg, followed by a transfer to Majdanek, where approximately 300,000 Polish Jews were murdered. Hoecker was adjutant at the time of the "Harvest Festival" of November 1943, when 42,000 Jews from three camps in the area were assembled and killed in 2 days.[65] He arrived in Auschwitz on May 25, 1944 in time for most of the mass murder of approximately 440,000 Hungarian Jews between May 15 and July 8, 1944.[66] The job of the adjutant was to provide detailed information to the commandant concerning all events taking place in the camp. In this, he had to be complicit in virtually all of the crimes committed there.

From a childhood of impoverishment without his working-class father, Karl Hoecker could rise to high-level supervisory status, but only in his new identity as an authentic Aryan *Übermensch*. One photograph shows him standing, cane in hand, on a selection ramp for incoming prisoners. The cane was used to point inmates either in the direction of the gas chambers, or to other, less immediately lethal locations.[67] Without that identity change leading to virtually god-like power over life and death, he would have remained at his nondescript job in a bank to which he returned after the war, and again after his parole

---

[63] 2008.   [64] 2008, 55.   [65] Wilkinson 2008, 52.

[66] Braham 1981, 1143.

[67] Wilkinson 2008, 50. Despite confirmation by precise visual tests of similarily to other photographs, some doubt still exists as to whether this is actually Hoecker because of the insignia on his uniform.

from a several-year sentence in a German prison for war crimes. In this fashion, the personal loss of his father in World War I reinforced the mortality salience associated with national loss in that war (both embedded within the ephemeral victory), and inspired the adoption of a new identity, remediating that loss. This time, the victory of 1871 would not prove to be ephemeral as it became in 1919, and Germans in Aryan garb, armed with their new identity, would march to the permanent ascendancy of the "Thousand Year Reich."

Shame

We have seen how shame can govern our sense of what is appropriate and what is inappropriate, especially for the universalists. Herodotus provides a striking example that has important moral implications. These implications will allow us to distinguish further between men like Hobsbawm who, as we saw in the Introduction, created a new and highly productive life after the destruction of the old, and Hitler who sought the path of revenge and new destruction. Both were shamed, one as a now despised Jew, and the other as the adherent of a defeated would-be hegemon, now subordinate after 1919. But their reactions to shame were to differ markedly.

In his First Book, Herodotus writes of the Lydian king, Candaules, who was besotted by his wife's charms. He was so impressed by his wife's sexual attractiveness that he needed to share this knowledge with Gyges, his close friend and bodyguard. When Candaules asked Gyges to hide in the bedroom where he and his wife were to undress prior to making love, he replied: "Master, what an improper suggestion! Do you tell me to look at the queen when she has no clothes on? No, no: 'when she takes off her clothing, she does away with her shame' – you know what they say of women. Let us learn from experience. Right and wrong were distinguished long ago – and I'll tell you one thing that is right: a man should mind his own business. I do not doubt that your wife is the most beautiful of women; so for goodness' sake do not ask me to behave contrary to custom."[68] Gyges was referring to the shame even male Lydians felt upon being seen naked. Nevertheless, he finally agreed to hide in the bedroom.

Alas, the queen saw Gyges, but instead of reacting immediately to her shame, she kept silent and plotted her revenge. The following day, the queen summoned Gyges, saying, "There are two courses open to you, and you may take your choice between them. Kill Candaules and seize the throne, with me as your wife; or die yourself on the spot, so that never again may your blind obedience to the king tempt you to see what you have no right to see. One of you must die: either my husband, the author of this wicked plot; or you, who have outraged propriety by seeing me naked."[69] Choosing to live, the next evening Gyges hid in the bedroom at the queen's behest, murdered Candaules, married the queen, and reigned for the next 38 years.

---

[68] Quoted in Herodotus 2003 [1954], 6.   [69] Herodotus 2003 [1954], 7.

The philosopher John Kekes[70] explores the queen's "disproportionately violent reaction to [the king's] vulgar sophomoric plot." Her resentment at being seen naked is genuine, but is it sufficient to commit murder? Kekes responds first with the concept of "propriety-shame." In his view, the queen's sense of decency, seemliness, and propriety is violated. But this is too slight a structure upon which to hang serious issues of good or evil.

To understand her sanguinary reaction, Kekes turns to "honor-shame":

> The queen's reaction will seem less excessive if we recognize that she had made a basic commitment to the value Lydians attach to propriety. She was not a superficial person who cared a lot about appearances; rather, how she appeared was for her a question of honor. And given her basic commitment to it, being honorable was crucial to her conception of a good life. This conception dictated that how the queen was and how she appeared to others should not be distinguishable. Her honor, dignity, status, and self-respect all demanded that she should ring true all the way through... Her husband's plot, therefore, was not a superficial offense against her sense of propriety, but a serious damage to her conception of a good life, resulting in her dishonor. Her husband caused her to see herself diminished in her own eyes. Her experience may be called "honor-shame," a feeling much deeper and morally more significant than propriety-shame.[71]

As a public figure, thoroughly identified with the mores of the Lydian people, the queen keenly felt an "honor-shame."

The queen experienced an honor-shame, "But there is nowhere for shame to go. Like a vermin, it eats deeper and deeper into the soul... The self-destructive feeling just sits there and then suddenly explodes in some spectacular action, like the queen's revenge. After which, the feeling spent, she could settle into married life with Gyges."[72]

Yet there is a third form of shame that Kekes elaborates: "worth-shame." In this instance, the only morally significant form of shame is that which violates one's own personal standards of conduct. "This moral possibility is that of having a conception of a good life that is different from the conceptions of others. It is a possibility that depends on pluralism that fosters individual differences and encourages experiments in living."[73] This form of shame, stemming only from an individual's own standards of behavior, follows from Nietzsche's description of Mirabeau, "who had no memory for insults and vile actions done to him and was unable to forgive simply because he – forgot. Such a man shakes off with a *single* shrug, many vermin that eat deep into others... [T]hat is the sign of strong, full natures in whom there is an excess of the power to form, to mold, to recuperate and to forget."[74]

---

[70] 1993, 148.   [71] Kekes 1993, 148–9.   [72] Kekes 1993, 150.   [73] 1993, 151.
[74] Emphasis in original; quoted in Kekes 1993, 149.

Mirabeau, a moderate in the French Revolution who predicted the violent course that would soon overtake it, had a private sphere to which he could turn. It was this interiority that enabled him to recuperate and forget the insults of others. His own self-worth was sufficient to overcome the need for revenge. The queen, on the other hand, identified completely as a public figure without a private sphere that would allow her to forgive insults to her honor.

Hobsbawm, developing the interiority of a self-worth that was dictated by a private hierarchy of values, sought historical truth. Hitler, identifying completely with the German people and later assuming a public life essentially suffused by politics, would dedicate his life to the reversal of the ephemeral and seek his revenge at whatever cost.

Intense identification with a nation is characteristic of all the extremists considered here. Before embarking on their sanguinary paths, both Hitler and Stalin, although born outside their respective national heartlands, thoroughly identified with them. Just as Stalin no longer saw himself as a Georgian (as his daughter so clearly understood when Vasili, her brother, said to her, "you know, papa used to be a Georgian once"[75]), so too did Hitler identify completely with Germany, forsaking any Austrian identity.

The lesson here is that a conception of self-worth *independent* of the nation or other collectivity is required for the avoidance of extremist behavior. Without that identification, the individual can define for oneself acceptable codes of conduct; the violation of these codes would be considered shameful. Collectively generated standards of ethics and morality that violate these internal norms would be disregarded.

Superb examples of those who responded to the demands of worth-shame are Gentile rescuers of imperiled Jews during the Holocaust.[76] Instead of conforming to the preferences of an extreme Polish, Lithuanian, or Ukrainian nationalism that sought *judenrein* polities, they chose to follow the dictates of their own internally generated codes of conduct that disallowed the possibility of Jewish neighbors going to their deaths unaided by any other human being. In their view, it would have been shameful to allow such an event to occur.

In truth, it is difficult to avoid collectivities that generate norms of behavior. But if there are many such collectivities, as in a plural society, all successfully claiming near-equal societal legitimacy, then the individual can be allowed the interior space within which to generate his own norms of behavior. Within democratic plural societies, virtually all such collectivities adhere to Abrahamic (or increasingly in India, Hindu-related) standards of behavior, thereby minimizing the probability of extremism. Even certain non-democratic societies (e.g., China) profess public standards that today depart considerably from yesterday's

---

[75] Quoted in Kuromiya 2005, 6.
[76] Midlarsky and Midlarsky 2004; Midlarsky, Fagin Jones, and Corley 2005; Midlarsky, Fagin Jones, and Nemeroff 2006; Fagin Jones and Midlarsky 2007.

extremist norms. Having suffered through the consequences of extremist behavior, countries such as China and even, to a certain extent, Russia, seek to avoid repetitions of this sort. Identification with national norms stemming from a democratic plural society can be benign, in contrast to the intense identification with the nation that identity change frequently stimulates, as in the emergence of the Aryan *Übermensch* and the resulting enormities.

16

War, Peace, and the Decline of Extremism

At the end of the narrative of *War and Peace*, Leo Tolstoy generates a conversation between two of his main characters, Pierre Bezukhov and Natasha Rostov, 7 years after the Napoleonic Wars of 1812. Tolstoy tells us that Pierre and Natasha "talked as only a wife and husband can talk, that is, grasping thoughts and conveying them to each other with extraordinary clarity and quickness, in a way contrary to all the rules of logic."[1] The conversation:

> "No, what were you saying? Speak, speak."
> "No, you tell me, mine was just something stupid," said Natasha.
> "… And what were you going to say?"
> "Just something stupid."
> "No, but still."
> "It's nothing, trifles," said Natasha, her smile shining still more brightly.[2]

Pierre and Natasha revel in the pleasures of everyday life, the fruits of peace, indeed of victory that saw the death of the dashing warrior, Prince Andrei Bolkonsky, adjutant to the great General Kutuzov. The military genius Napoleon fails in his ambitions, but Pierre, a large bumbling character, and Nikolai Rostov, who lost his impetuous younger brother Petya in the war, survive. The critic James Wood[3] comments, "Nikolai and Pierre, survive into peace, surrounded by women, who do not understand warfare, and by children, who must not. To live, the poet Yehuda Amichai writes, is to build a ship and a harbor at the same time: 'And to finish the harbor / long after the ship has gone down.'"

Perhaps more than any other major writer (with the possible exception of the Nobelist Ivo Andrić discussed in Chapter 11), Tolstoy understood the vast difference between wartime and peacetime. The former cannot persist for very long, precisely because it rules out the quotidian, or at least limits its possibilities. It is only during peacetime, and a durable one, that one can have conversations such as that between Pierre and Natasha.

---

[1] Tolstoy 2007, 1174.   [2] Tolstoy 2007, 1177.   [3] 2007, 166.

Tolstoy provides a clue to reasons for the demise of political extremisms such as fascism and communism, and generates expectations that the life of radical Islamism, at least in its current incarnation, will be short. As we have seen, these forms of extremism have their origins in military experience, or in close facsimiles thereof. Combat creates the sort of brotherhood that can support radical departures from the quotidian, but only for a time. The regimentation of society that has its roots in an earlier militarization cannot persist for very long. Following Amichai, the "ship" of military provenance can sink, but the "harbor" of society persists.

In a larger sense, seeking to reverse the ephemera by extremists is almost always futile. The ephemeral gain raises possibilities in the minds of political extremists (authoritarians, adventurers, or simply the ignorant) that typically are extraordinarily difficult to achieve. Virtually all of the instances of extremism analyzed here ended badly for the perpetrators. Fascism (and Nazism) disappeared from the face of the earth, most likely permanently. Communism survived for several decades after Stalin's death, but ultimately, it too passed from the Russian scene, leaving Russia truncated to an even smaller territory than existed after World War I. Ironically, despite Stalin's Herculean and sanguinary efforts, the territorial limits even of the post-World War I Soviet state were to be further diminished by the recent loss of Ukraine, Belarus, and the Soviet Central Asian states like Kazakhstan and Uzbekistan. Even the Indonesian regime, apparently firmly ensconced after the massacres of 1965, gave way to the current functioning democracy.

Radical Islamism

It is too soon to prognosticate on the future of al-Qaeda, the only ongoing universal extremist organization persisting roughly in its initial ideational and strategic form (excepting a decentralizing tendency). And as we saw in Chapter 14, extremism can take on a life of its own beyond originating conditions like a territorially based ephemeral gain. Yet there are already indications that despite its resurgence in the Pakistani borderlands, al-Qaeda may not survive in the long run. Several prominent Islamists once associated with al-Qaeda, or at least counted among its sympathizers, have parted company with bin Laden and Ayman al-Zawahiri, his principal deputy. Among these defectors from within are two stalwarts of the jihadi cause. The first, Sayyid Imam al-Sharif (known later by his underground name of Dr. Fadl), actually was a classmate of Zawahiri at Cairo University medical school. Early in life he was an extremely observant Muslim, later advocating Islamist political goals. In 1988, he disseminated *The Essential Guide for Preparation* in which his view of jihad was developed at length.

According to Lawrence Wright,[4] "The 'Guide' begins with the premise that jihad is the natural state of Islam. Muslims must always be in conflict with non-believers, Fadl asserts, resorting to peace only in moments of abject weakness. Because jihad is, above all, a religious exercise, there are divine rewards to be gained. He who gives money for jihad will be compensated in Heaven, but not as much as the person who acts. The greatest prize goes to the martyr. Every able-bodied believer is obligated to engage in jihad, since most Muslim countries are ruled by infidels who must be forcibly removed, in order to bring about an Islamic state. 'The way to bring an end to the rules' unbelief is armed rebellion,' the 'Guide' states."

Yet despite this firm, even extreme commitment to jihad, Fadl weighed the probabilities of success. When, as a leader of the Egyptian-based al-Jihad (along with Zawahiri), he was implored by members of this group to imitate the larger rival Islamic Group and attack the Egyptian government, Fadl demurred. In his view, that government was too strong to defeat in any sort of open conflict. And events were to prove him correct as popular support for the Islamic Group plummeted after the massacre of sixty two foreign tourists and their Egyptian guides in Upper Egypt. Most of the leadership was then imprisoned.

After 9/11, Fadl too was imprisoned in Egypt. There, he wrote a major work that repudiates much of his earlier thinking. *Rationalizing Jihad* opens with "There is nothing that invokes the anger of God and His wrath like the unwarranted spilling of blood and wrecking of property."[5] The killing of Muslims is forbidden. Fadl quotes Ibn Taymiyya, one of the earliest supporters of jihad against the infidel, "A Muslim's blood and money are safeguarded even if his creed is different."[6] Additionally according to Fadl, "God permitted peace treaties and ceasefires with the infidels, either in exchange for money or without it – all of this in order to protect the Muslims, in contrast with those who push them into peril."[7] And, "There is nothing in the Shari'a about killing Jews and the Nazarenes, referred to by some as the Crusaders… They are the neighbors of the Muslims…and being kind to one's neighbors is a religious duty."[8]

Zawahiri, Fadl's former ally, responded to these attacks knowing full well that "violence was the fuel that kept the radical Islamist organizations running; they had no future without terror."[9] But the damage had been done, and Zawahiri as well as other unrepentant jihadists were now on the defensive.

Another radical Islamist who was later to break with al-Qaeda was Noman Benotman, a staunch opponent of Muammar Qaddafi, the Libyan dictator. Initially an ally of bin Laden and al-Qaeda, after 9/11 Benotman realized that his Libyan jihadist group would be targeted by the US along with al-Qaeda; the United States would not distinguish between them. In January 2007 Benotman flew to Tripoli to attempt to persuade the imprisoned leadership of the Libyan

---

[4] 2008, 38.   [5] Quoted in Wright 2008, 46.   [6] Quoted in Wright 2008, 47.
[7] Quoted in Wright 2008, 47.   [8] Quoted in Wright 2008, 47.   [9] Wright 2008, 41.

Islamic Fighting Group to enter into peace negotiations with Qaddafi's regime. A tentative agreement was reached, including a provision that al-Qaeda would be publicly repudiated by its former ally. In November 2007, Benotman wrote an open letter to Zawahiri calling for an end to all operations against the West.

A major reason for the growing opposition to radical Islamism is the doctrine of *takfir* adopted by al-Qaeda and other extremists. In this view, some Muslims, especially the extremists, can decide who is a "true Muslim," relegating others to a limbo of non-recognition and vulnerability to murder. And this can be done without consulting the *ulema*, the learned Islamic jurists. According to Peter Bergen and Paul Cruickshank,[10] "First, the radicals deem some Muslims apostates; after that, the radicals start killing them. This fatal progression happened in both Algeria and Egypt in the 1990s.[11] It is now taking place even more dramatically in Iraq, where al-Qaeda's suicide bombers have killed more than 10,000 Iraqis, most of them targeted simply for being Shia. Recently, al-Qaeda in Iraq has turned its fire on Sunnis who oppose its diktats, a fact not lost on the Islamic world's Sunni majority."

In other words, a slippery slope has been reached in which wanton killing can proceed based on the solipsistic judgment of a few self-appointed judges and executioners. Traditional Islamic codes of conduct, in place for centuries in the Qur'an, Shari'a, and Hadith count for nothing. In his *Rationalizing Jihad*, also serialized in an independent Egyptian newspaper, Fadl wrote that "jihad…was blemished with grave Shari'a violations during recent years… [N]ow there are those who kill hundreds, including women and children, Muslims and non Muslims in the name of Jihad!"[12] He further exclaimed, "Zawahiri and his Emir bin Laden [are] extremely immoral… I have spoken about this in order to warn the youth against them, youth who are seduced by them, and don't know them."[13]

Patterns of decline

The slippery slope

These illustrations drawn from the recent history of radical Islamism suggests several patterns in the decline of extremism. First, as we have seen, increasing the scope of mass murder justified by essentially non-traditional extremist doctrine becomes a liability, as it is understood to be a slippery slope ending in an abyss. One has only to witness the decline of support for even non-violent Islamist parties such as the Islamic Action Front (IAF) in Jordan after the 2005

---

[10] 2008, 17.
[11] For the rise of recent Islamic extremism in Algeria, see Hafez 2004 and for contemporary Egypt, see Toth 2003.
[12] Quoted in Bergen and Cruickshank 2008, 18.
[13] Quoted in Bergen and Cruickshank 2008, 18.

bombing in Amman by al-Qaeda killed sixty people, mostly Muslim. The election of November 2007, in which the IAF lost a considerable share of its parliamentary representation, was widely seen as an electoral disaster, even by the Islamists themselves. In a 2004 survey, "68 percent of Jordanians polled viewed al-Qa'ida as a 'legitimate resistance organization.' In 2005, that number had declined to 20 percent."[14] And al-Qaeda, as we have seen, is under doctrinal attack even from within the radical Islamist fraternity.

More generally, when in 2009, Muslim populations were asked, "Are suicide bombing and other forms of violence against civilian targets justified to defend Islam from its enemies?" all of the country populations surveyed showed declines in support for suicide bombing from that disclosed in 2002. These populations comprised Muslims in Turkey, Pakistan, Jordan, Indonesia, Egypt, Lebanon, Nigeria, and the Palestinian territories.[15]

Addressing the fate of another exemplar of suicide tactics, the LTTE, its brutality and disregard for human life eventually led to serious curtailment of its sources of international funding. This diminished resource base, as well as local revulsion in Sri Lanka itself, even among many ethnic Tamils, ultimately led to the defeat of the LTTE in May 2009.

External intervention

Second, the tendency to expand the scope of mass murder by extremists has another consequence: the increased likelihood of intervention by alarmed external actors. The US intervention in 2001 against al-Qaeda and its host, the Taliban in Afghanistan, is one case in point. There are others. In 1979, Vietnam intervened in Cambodia, effectively ending the genocidal reign of the Khmer Rouge. The demand for unconditional surrender of Nazi Germany and militarist Japan by the Allies was in large measure a response to the barbarities perpetrated by both regimes. Of course, that surrender was intended to be a prelude to the dissolution of the perpetrating governments and war crimes trials to take place immediately thereafter. The Allies after World War I contemplated the division of what remained of the Ottoman Empire in Anatolia into strongly autonomous regions. Only the catastrophic defeat of the invading Greek army in 1922, demonstrating the military strength of the Atatürk regime, prevented that outcome.

Although the Soviet regime persisted after Stalin's death, the moderating tendencies of subsequent leaders who relied less on terror and more on persuasion likely went far to diminish Western concerns about the potential wholesale deportation of minorities. Only some 3–4 years after Stalin's passing in 1953, the Chechen and Ingush peoples, among others, were allowed to return to their

---

[14] Ryan 2008, 7.   [15] Shane 2009, 4.

homelands in the Caucasus. The Chinese government itself after the death of Mao Tse-tung has reformed much of its earlier revolutionary sanguinary zeal.

Extremist outbidding

Third, extremist outbidding can lead to the weakening and ultimately even the destruction of extremist movements. A case in point is the adoption of extreme methods by Zawahiri and members of the Islamic Group to scuttle ongoing negotiations between radicals in prison and the Egyptian government, and to gain increased visibility as well as a hoped for popularity among the Egyptian public. (Cf. Zawahiri's comments above on the necessity for terror to ensure the radical Islamist future.) In November 1977, members of the Islamic Group massacred sixty-two tourists and their guides in the Luxor region. Public revulsion in Egypt was immediate, leading to a widespread rejection of violence as an Islamist alternative.[16] In other words, this action, like others of the same ilk, backfired, resulting in a dramatic decline of radical Islamism in Egypt.

The rise of Nazism in Germany and its ultimately catastrophic end can be attributed in some measure to extremist outbidding. After World War I, many conservative circles in Germany railed against the harsh terms of the Treaty of Versailles. Among them was the right-wing nationalist, Alfred Hugenberg. Son of a Prussian politician, trained in the law, and chairman of the Board of Directors of the Krupp Armaments Company, he later helped found the National People's Party. Hugenberg's control of the press in rural areas through his newspaper empire helped solidify the influence of right-wing nationalism, including anti-Semitism, throughout Germany.[17] Although he initially supported the Nazis as allies in their common effort to overthrow the liberal Weimar Republic and was appointed minister of agriculture and economics in Hitler's first cabinet, after 6 months he resigned in protest over the dissolution of his Nationalist Party. He also lost control of his newspaper empire in 1943 when it was appropriated by the NSDAP. Given his Prussian background and legal training, it is extraordinarily unlikely that he would have gone to the lengths that Hitler did in waging unconditional warfare against the Allies, and genocide of the Jews and other "undesirables."

Hugenberg's friend, Gottfried Traub, summarized the anti-Semitic policy of Hugenberg's *München-Augsburger Abendzeitung*: "Anti-Semitism can become no refuge for political narrowness and political unsuitability… With merely shouting, 'The Jew is guilty, kill him!' nothing has yet been accomplished. To govern a state, which should maintain its independence from all alien influences, a higher sense of political responsibility and a slow, determined education of the nation is necessary."[18] John Leopold[19] continues, "Hugenberg

---

[16] Wright 2008, 42.   [17] Snyder and Ballentine 1996.
[18] Quoted in Leopold 1977, 22.   [19] 1977, 22.

considered anti-Semitism a tool which could be exploited and discarded; he himself measured a man by his loyalty to the nation rather than by the purity of his racial pedigree." And most members of the German Nationalist Party, including Hugenberg, "adhered to the principles of the *Rechtsstaat*, a state governed by laws."[20]

Nor does Otto Ohlendorf, an early sympathizer of the German National People's Party and later commander of *Einsatzgruppe D* responsible for the deaths of 90,000 Jews on the Eastern front disagree. During an interview with the American psychiatrist Leon Goldensohn at the war crimes trials in Nuremberg after the war, Goldensohn asks: "Was Hugenberg's the same type of anti-Semitism as Hitler's?" Ohlendorf: "I can't say." Goldensohn: "Did Hugenberg advocate annihilation of the Jews?" Ohlendorf: "I doubt it. It wasn't in Hitler's program until 1942."[21] Ohlendorf had no reason to lie, for as he suspected, he would later be sentenced to death in Nuremberg and hanged in 1951.

Whatever the future consequences of a German Nationalist instead of a Nazi-led Germany, it was clear that in order to win either electorally or later in war, Hitler had to go to more extreme lengths in his quest for victory. Of course it was precisely this unmitigated extremism that would prompt the Allies to fight the war relentlessly until unconditional surrender had been achieved. Doctrinal differences assume importance. A suggestion of this fissiparous tendency is found in the early marginalization by *SS* ideologues of the acknowledged ideologist of Nazism, Carl Schmitt. The consequences for him might not have been so salutary, if not for the intervention of Hermann Goering, who allowed Schmitt to remain at his professorial post until forcibly removed by the Allies in 1945.

Doctrinal disputes over the meaning of Marxism-Leninism led to the exile of Leon Trotsky, and his later 1940 assassination by a Stalinist agent in Mexico City. Stalin's emphasis on "socialism in one country" – the strengthening of the first genuinely socialist state – conflicted sharply with Trotsky's far more universal revolutionary approach that sought to immediately export the revolution to the more industrialized regions of Central and Western Europe. Ironically, although Stalinism as a political program has virtually disappeared, Trotskyism in modified form actually survives in areas of Latin America such as Peru. Communism, of course, is no longer the basis of any major coherent ideological or political program.

We have already witnessed the doctrinal disputes among radical Islamists. The nature of *takfir* allowing individual interpretation of Islam even in opposition to the Shari'a or Hadith and the rulings of the *ulema*, has now been challenged vigorously by respected Islamist figures such as Dr. Fadl or Benotman. The doctrinal basis for radical Islamist violence has been seriously undermined.

---

[20] Leopold 1977, 148.   [21] Quoted in Gellately 2004, 387.

Reversing the ephemeral

Fourth, the unrealistic desire to reverse an ephemeral gain has led to the ultimate decline of extremist movements. The territorial reconstitution of the Soviet Union after 1945 and its satellization of most of Eastern Europe in the post-war period can be viewed as a final effort to reverse the losses of 1920 by incorporating lost tsarist territories (in the Ukraine, Byelorussia, and the Baltic region), and maintaining a political hegemony over other such territories like Poland and even to a moderate extent, Finland. The satellites in Central Europe such as East Germany, Hungary, and Czechoslovakia were intended to provide a geopolitical "cushion" against future territorial reverses. Recognizing that this effort to avoid the consequences of ephemerality was unsustainable economically (in the Soviet confrontation with the West), and especially risky politically in hoping to retain even a minimal loyalty of political elites in Central and Eastern Europe, the Soviet government did not strenuously oppose the withdrawal of the satellites, even the later loss of much Soviet territory in the transition to the Russian Federation.

Defeated in war, Nazism has not experienced any sort of political revival. The defeat and losses of World War I would not be ephemeral but would be accentuated temporarily in the division of Germany between East and West, and permanently in the loss of even more territory relative to 1919 in the westward territorial reconfiguration of Poland after World War II. It was widely recognized in Germany that these losses were to remain permanent, especially after the steady repopulation of the formerly German eastern territories by ethnic Poles.[22]

Yet, there remains the threat of universalizing particularist conflicts. The classic contemporary instance is that of Lashkar-e-Taiba. An insurgent group originating in Kashmir and devoted to that area's emancipation from Indian rule, has adopted some of the doctrine and methods of al-Qaeda (e.g., the attack on an ultra-Orthodox Jewish facility in Mumbai having nothing to do with Kashmir). The November 2008 Mumbai bombings illustrate not only a universalizing doctrinal tendency drawn from al-Qaeda, but most likely actual contact between members of Lashkar-e-Taiba and al-Qaeda supporters in the Pakistani tribal borderlands. Although such a universalizing effort failed in Chechnya largely because of overwhelming Russian force capability (but now may be gaining momentum in Daghestan as well as in Chechnya), there is little guarantee that such a process can be prevented in the Pakistani tribal areas. Failing the unlikely destruction of Lashkar-e-Taiba by motivated

---

[22] Although Nazism itself was not revived, nevertheless there are right-wing parties in Europe that tend to keep alive some of the right-wing tenets of Nazi ideology. See, for example, Capoccia 2005, Art 2006, Mudde 2007, Ignazi 2003.

Pakistani forces, only a political settlement between India and Pakistan concerning Kashmir would provide assurance that this universalizing terror process has been halted.

Preventing extremism

Justice and the ephemeral gain

What are the policy prescriptions that emerge from the present analysis? Are there any actions or precautions that can be taken to prevent the rise of extremist movements or at least to minimize the probability of mass violence, given the existence of these movements?[23]

The ephemeral gain, of course, is a historical condition that cannot be altered. It would even be difficult to predict its occurrence. The German loss of World War I after the heady gains of the late nineteenth century was not predictable. Indeed, it only occurred because of the unwise and provocative policies of the *Kaiserreich* that led the United States to enter the war. Without American troops in defense of the Allies, the German spring offensive of 1918 might well have ended the war in Germany's favor. The Polish defeat of the hitherto victorious Soviet forces in 1920 also was not easily predicted. Without India's intervention in the 1971 "pacification of East Pakistan," also not readily predictable, the Pakistani army likely would not have been defeated and Bangladesh would not have achieved independence. One can multiply these examples many times over to understand that loss after earlier victory and still earlier subordination is a highly uncertain outcome.

The key factor, though, is the *response* to the ephemeral gain, specifically the loss at its end. Importantly, that response often occurs at the international level in which victorious powers, international agencies, or simply neighboring countries, play an important role. Clearly, the Treaty of Versailles was the critical event that would do so much to facilitate the rise of German extremism in the form of the Nazi Party. Even nominally victorious powers like Italy found their hopes dashed on the shoals of Versailles, providing the impetus for the rise of Italian Fascism. The Treaty of Trianon was to generate even more territorial loss for Hungary than was done to Germany at Versailles. Certainly, the French military support for Polish independence and the Soviet defeat of 1920 were harbingers of the Western distaste for the Bolshevik regime. And the appearance, if not the actuality of Western democracies opposed to Islam, radical or otherwise (and "occupied" Saudi Arabia as well as defeated Saddam Hussein), was to do much to inflame the radical Islamists.

National governments experiencing loss can develop policies that minimize the perception of loss, or at least do not dwell upon it. Here, loss compensation

---

[23] See also Midlarsky 2009a.

that Greek governments employed after the defeat by Turkey is relevant. Instead of dreaming of revanche, newly acquired territories in Europe insecurely held after the Balkan Wars (not those lost later in Anatolia) became the focus of integration into the Greek national state. Populating the new territories with ethnic Greek refugees from Anatolia soon to outnumber the slavophone population was to do much to develop a relatively homogeneous national society that would ultimately embrace democracy and enter the European Union. Effectively, loss compensation nullified the loss portion of the ephemeral gain.

Yet there are limits to what national governments can do in the face of perceived injustice, especially if they are weak, lack legitimacy, or exercise only nominal suzerainty over certain territories. Weak and only partially legitimated democracies such as the Weimar Republic or post-World War I Italy allowed the political space for extremists to thrive, even allowing their accession to power by democratic procedures, as in the rise of Hitler to the post of Reich chancellor. Therefore, perceived injustices need to be addressed by concerned international parties. Two strategies are (1) loss compensation effected by international sources, and (2) an effort to directly address the issues of justice as fairness or equity. Certainly, the 1922 French invasion of the Ruhr after significant German territorial losses had already occurred was precisely the opposite of what was required. Instead of loss compensation, *additional* territorial losses were threatened by this action. Of course, the non-payment of reparations required by the Treaty of Versailles in the midst of rampant inflation in Germany was the immediate source of this extraordinarily unwise French response, but the reparations in themselves were ill-conceived and ultimately forgiven. However, by this time the Nazi Party had already been firmly established. Here, the problem of democratically elected governments answerable to war-ravaged electorates rears its head. In the electoral environment of post-World War I France, such jingoist action appeared to be a proper course of action in order to satisfy public opinion.

Justice as fairness or equity also must be evaluated within the context of defeated and victorious powers. More precisely, what does equity consist of in this context? Surely, one can argue that power is an important basis of equity calculations in the relations among nations. To the victor belong the spoils is a maxim of post-war thinking. But that is little consolation to German families who lost loved ones at the front and now in the early 1920s are suffering from a calamitous inflation. Equity, determined by a different calculus would yield an outcome very different from the French invasion of the Ruhr. Instead of the national unit that is aggrieved by the war and deserves its spoils at the war's end, the rights of individual human beings must take center stage. If such a European individual human rights emphasis had existed at that time, then even the French electorates might have paused and reflected seriously on the wisdom, even humanity of an additional assault on German territory.

Forgiveness at least once is a property of Robert Axelrod's successful Tit for Tat.[24]

Justice and terrorist organizations

The problem of weak, only partially integrated territories is manifested most strongly in the continuing presence of terrorist organizations in countries such as Afghanistan or Pakistan. The Federally Administered Tribal Areas (FATA) along the Pakistani border with Afghanistan have been notoriously resistant to the exercise of Pakistani governmental authority. As a result, these territories have functioned as a safe haven for al-Qaeda, the Taliban, and other terrorist organizations, some of which may have quasi-governmental sanction, such as Lashkar-e-Taiba. Not only have these territories been historically resistant to *any* central governmental authority, but the current weakness of the Pakistani government is demonstrated in the lack of a clear consensus *within* the government as to which, if any, of these organizations merit its support. The political and geographical space available to extremists therefore is ample.

In the case of Lashkar-e-Taiba, the claim of injustice that led to its organization also resonates with many ordinary Pakistani citizens. With a Muslim majority but with Indian (read Hindu) political control, the areas of Kashmir east of the line of control ending the 1947–48 Indo-Pakistani war are illegitimately governed, in the view of these Pakistani observers. But the political space in Pakistan that allowed, even encouraged the activities of Lashkar-e-Taiba, also allowed for the universalization of its terror. Thus, not only highly visible Indian structures in Mumbai were targeted in the November 2008 terrorist attacks, but a Jewish organization that catered to Israeli visitors was also invaded.

The cooperation – sharing of common methods and goals – between members of Lashkar-e-Taiba and al-Qaeda was allowed to develop within this political space. Perceptions of injustice in one instance, that of Kashmir, are now universalized to include any and all Islamist claims of injustice, whatever their local origins. This is the danger of festering conflicts with ideational roots. Nationalistic conflicts can be brutal and foster extremism, but they are difficult to generalize beyond the boundaries of the conflict itself. Not so with conflicts that originated in nationalistic claims but later share common ideational ground with other conflicts that stemmed from different sources. The common ideational cement here is a radical interpretation of Islam that implies a common enemy for all Muslims, even for nationalistic supporters of a Kashmir free from Indian political authority. A common sense of Muslim humiliation-shame has also developed.

Short of invading weakly administered areas like the FATA, only negotiation can resolve the problem of perceptions of injustice that can universalize

[24] 1984.

and metastasize. The push for justice as fairness or equity in such negotiations requires a quid pro quo. But the power differential between India and Pakistan, as that between the victors and defeated at Versailles or Trianon, constrains the extent to which the units exchanged are of comparable benefit. This is certainly true of the moment such negotiations transpire at the end of a war with victors and losers. But the shadow of the future nevertheless should be long.[25] This was true at the time of the formation of the initial basis of the European Union: the 1951 European Coal and Steel Community Treaty that was transformed into the 1957 Treaty of Rome establishing the European Economic Community that then ultimately morphed into the contemporary European Union. The long shadow of the future was heavily informed by the past; the highly destructive European wars of 1914–18 and 1939–45 must not be repeated. Although France was nominally victorious while Nazi Germany and Fascist Italy were defeated in 1945, nevertheless these countries together constituted the basis for such a union. Even Britain, with its own commonwealth as a trading unit, ultimately was persuaded to join, despite its status as a successful combatant in World War II.

Although initially it might be difficult to persuade India, as the victor of the most recent 1971 Indo-Pakistani war, to join a regional consortium, nevertheless possibilities for trade enhancement within a common South Asian tariff-free zone, including not only India and Pakistan but other countries in the region, could prove attractive. India would be the leading power within such a zone, much as Germany has become one within the EU, without substantial negative consequences for the organization.

Transformations from the affective to the instrumental

Loss compensation either in the form of monetary gain or other desiderata to replace that which is lost can do much to abate the rise of extremism. Greece after 1923 and its territorial losses in Anatolia illustrates the instrumental compensation of increased national security in the form of ethnic Greeks from Anatolia populating formerly slavophone majority territories conquered in 1913. The Megali Idea of greater Greece in Anatolia in all its affective territorial dimensions died, in part, as a result of this transformation of the affective into the instrumental. An example of the obverse condition, wherein extremist behavior was facilitated by the failure to provide adequate compensation for territories about to be lost is given by recent events in Darfur.

As a result of protocols signed on May 26, 2004 (ratified in 2005), between southern Sudanese leaders of the black, predominantly Christian Sudan People's Liberation Army (SPLA) and the Arabized Muslim leaders of the north, a 6-year interim period would be specified, after which a referendum would take place

---

[25] Keohane 1984; Keohane, Nye, and Hoffmann 1993.

allowing for the possibility of independence for the oil-rich south. This outcome would lead to the loss of approximately one-third of Sudanese territory, including its oil. The possible presence of oil in the Darfur region as well makes this territory potentially as valuable economically as the oil-rich south. If Darfur were to be Arabized through the massacre and ethnic cleansing of its black population, then it could serve as compensation for losses in the south, especially in the face of an incipient rebellion by black Africans in Darfur.

Encouraged by the success of the black southern rebels both on the battlefield and at the conference table, two groups of black Muslims from Darfur rebelled, apparently representing black populations persecuted through raids and other violence by nomadic Arabized tribes. Confronted by another separatist rebellion like that of the SPLA, ethnic cleansing of another black population was unleashed, with a possible genocidal component of tens of thousands dead. One purpose of this effort has been to compensate for the potential losses in the south by ensuring that another potentially valuable territory, Darfur, remains within an Arab-dominated Sudan.

As in the Rwandan case, the international community was intensely concerned that a settlement between the Khartoum government and the SPLA be reached. Colin Powell, the US Secretary of State, visited the negotiations between the SPLA and Khartoum leaders in October 2003 and Darfur itself in June 2004. The United Nations has also taken an active role. And like Arusha in the Rwandan case, an international agreement implying heavy losses in the future, whether in political power (Rwanda, territory already having been lost to the RPF) or valuable territory (Sudan), may have spurred this effort at loss compensation. Also like the *interahamwe* in Rwanda, much of the killing and ethnic cleansing has been carried out by government-supported militia, the *Janjaweed*, an Arabized military group.

These considerations suggest that even more active intervention is required to stem these massacres and ethnic cleansing. A pairing of the two regions of Sudan, Darfur and the south, should be a focus of international diplomacy, without forsaking one region for the other. Unfortunately, just the opposite appears to have occurred. According to John Prendergast, a former African affairs director at the National Security Council under President Clinton, "When the secretary [Colin Powell] was in Naivasha [location of the negotiations between the Khartoum government and the SPLA], and a major problem was getting worse in Darfur, everyone agreed to deal with the southern problem first and with Darfur later. That was a monumental diplomatic error."[26]

In *The Killing Trap*,[27] I wrote that "Integration of Sudan into elements of the international economy, including appropriate financial incentives (e.g., firmly guaranteed access to oil in the south in the event of southern independence), might serve at least as a partial loss compensation to offset the loss of one or

---

[26] Quoted in Weisman 2004.   [27] Midlarsky 2005b, 387.

both regions." In the summer of 2009, I was gratified to see that such an outcome came to pass. On July 22, an arbitration panel in The Hague awarded the Khartoum government control over virtually all major oil reserves in the disputed region of Abyei, where many of the most profitable large oil fields are located.[28] Although grazing lands in that region were awarded to the SPLA, the northern government declared the outcome a victory. According to Dirdeiry Mohamed Ahmed, the head of the northern government delegation, "We welcome the fact that the oil fields are now excluded from the Abyei area, particularly the Heglig oil field."[29] The affective attachment to territory was transformed into the instrumental necessity for oil. Not only was the 2005 agreement between the Khartoum government and the SPLA buttressed, but the killing in Darfur actually could be diminished in response not only to the instrumentality of this outcome, but also to the recognition that international agencies can be favorable to this Islamist government. Hence, in the future, it might be less willing to flout international opinion.

All of this indicates that, as in any medical or social pathology, early intervention is required to avoid a fatal outcome. Hitler in Germany and Vladimir Zhirinovsky in Russia experienced very different historical trajectories in part because of the contrasting reactions of international diplomacy in the two cases. During the 1990s, the rise of extreme Russian nationalism was greeted not with hostility and isolation, as in the case of Germany after World War I, but with financial and diplomatic efforts to shore up the emerging Russian democracy.

Even the extraordinarily virulent Nazi hatred of the Jews leading to their mass murder in Nazi-occupied Europe could be mitigated by instrumental necessity. The bizarre and obscene offer by the Nazis (including Hitler and Himmler) of 1 million mainly Hungarian Jewish lives for 10,000 trucks[30] is a perverse illustration of the transformation from the affective to the instrumental. During World War II, it was generally not recognized how dependent the German army was on horse-drawn transport. The need to manufacture tanks and fighter aircraft took precedence over the mundane but necessary transportation requirements that became crucial as the German army retreated on the Eastern front. Although this barter of trucks for human lives never came to pass, it does illustrate how even the most savage hostilities can be mitigated in the face of instrumental need.

Defeating urgency and the limits of democracy

Mortality and a precipitous fall ending the ephemeral gain suggest an urgent response frequently taking the form of anger and violence. After World War I, Hitler, for example, frequently referred to the "urgent problem of international

---

[28] Cockett 2010, 95.   [29] *Breaking News 24/7*, July 22, 2009.   [30] Hecht 1961.

Jewry." Urgency, however, as we know, can be self-defeating. Extreme responses typically are unsuccessful, as we saw in the historical trajectories of fascism, Nazism, communism, rampant militarism, and extreme nationalism. In contrast to the extremist autocracies, democracies that typically eschew urgency have shown remarkable success not only in persisting over time, but in prevailing over autocratic enemies in armed combat. And the democratic impulse seen so graphically in the June 2009 Iranian demonstrations against a presumed fraudulent election strongly suggests that democracy will someday prevail over radical Islamism in much of the Muslim world.

The workings of democratic governance contain checks and balances of various sorts that frequently do not allow the concentrated fury often associated with extremism. In a functioning democracy, it takes time to enact legislation and have it executed. Even if the executive branch somehow circumvents this legislative process, there often occur responses by the legislature that require executive attention. Within that time-consuming process may lay the seeds of cognitive reflection that can stop the headlong plunge into self-defeating extremist acts. And even if one democratic leader may fail in this regard, there always exists the option of removing that leader at the next election.

Yet, democracy is no panacea. We have the genocidal behavior by the Athenians at Melos as an example, and in attenuated fashion, the brutalities of the United States in Guantanamo, the "renditions," and Abu Ghraib after 9/11.

Upon their defeat at Mantinea in the Peloponnesian War, the Athenians clearly were experiencing an ephemeral gain. The earlier victory over Persia by the Greeks (culminating in 448 BCE) led to the liberation of the Ionian cities in Anatolia, formerly under Persian domination. They, along with other Athenian maritime allies, founded the Delian League that became the core of the Athenian Empire. From the subordination of the Ionians by Persia and the threat of the same to Athens (it was burned by the Persians in 480), the Delian League under Athenian leadership emerged as the most powerful victorious Hellenic alliance. But by 418, the massive defeat of Athens and its allies on land at Mantinea signaled the serious possibility of losing the Peloponnesian War among the Greek city-states themselves, begun in 431. Thucydides[31] tells us that this was "certainly the greatest battle that had taken place for a very long time among Hellenic states, and it was fought by the most renowned states in Hellas." To ensure its continued maritime supremacy, especially in light of the forthcoming Sicilian naval expedition, the mass murder of Melian males by Athenian forces and sale into slavery of the women and children ensued in 416,[32] Melos being the only sizable Aegean island not allied with Athens.

---

[31] 1954, 353.
[32] A more detailed examination of the mass violence in Melos is found in Midlarsky 2005b, 79–82.

Certainly, US behavior after 9/11 does not descend to the level of extremism analyzed in the preceding pages. Yet, brutalities not heretofore tolerated by previous American administrations were committed in Guantanamo, the "renditions" and Abu Ghraib. A limited ephemerality was experienced by the US government after 2001. Although not subordinate, the US nevertheless was engaged in an intense protracted conflict with the communist world. After World War II, advances of the communists in China and East-Central Europe, followed by a Third World gravitation toward the Soviet bloc were seen as major US losses, including of course the Vietnam debacle. And as a harbinger of future loss, the 1979 Iranian Islamic revolution occurred with its takeover of the US embassy, and lengthy retention of the American hostages.

Emerging victorious in 1991 with the dissolution of the USSR after its failure in Afghanistan, the stellar victory by the US and its allies in the Gulf War of that year reinforced this important ascendancy. But the elation of this post-Cold War period was vitiated by the meteoric rise of China. More important, the ignominious withdrawal of the US from Somalia in 1993 (*Black Hawk Down*) followed by the feckless US response to the 1994 Rwanda genocide (*A Problem from Hell*,[33] signaling the absence of US resolve in the face of blatant mass murder) began the entry into the domain of losses vis-à-vis radical Islamists, culminating in the extraordinarily successful terrorist acts of 9/11. Although technically inaccurate (the attacks took place during a Republican presidency less than 8 months old), the not infrequent Republican claim that the events of 9/11 occurred under Democratic auspices, while the earlier victories took place during Republican governance nevertheless has some merit.

This attenuated ephemeral gain was followed by the atrocious behavior of US agents of confinement, and an accelerating polarization of the American polity that even has some denying the US birth of its president, and intensely partisan disputes over issues like health care. Wishing the death, or at least incapacitation, of a Democratic proponent of health care reform by Senator Tom Coburn (R-Okla.)[34] prior to a close critical vote is an egregious illustration. As we have seen, increasing polarization is associated with an ephemeral gain, including worldview defense that is also a major consequence of mortality salience. Undoubtedly, additional factors like the machinations of party politics influenced this polarization process. Yet, the raw emotions displayed during the past decade and a half of American politics suggest that something beyond politics as usual was at work here.

---

[33] The title of Samantha Power's 2002 book. In *The Killing Trap* (Midlarsky 2005b, 391–2), I suggested a relationship between the withdrawal from Somalia and the US response to the Rwandan genocide, even preventing a strengthened United Nations presence in Rwanda, with the military component of the United Nations Assistance Mission for Rwanda already in that country prior to the onset of the genocide.

[34] Milbank 2009.

Hence, for all of the checks and balances within a contemporary representative democracy, largely absent in ancient Athens, care still must be taken to dampen the impulse of urgency in response to momentary loss. This is especially true when the loss occurs after hard-fought gains (e.g., victory over Soviet Communism), and a still earlier period of tumultuous conflict entailing major losses that yielded a debilitating uncertainty of its eventual outcome.

~

References

Aase, Tor ed. 2002. *Tournaments of Power: Honor and Revenge in the Contemporary World*. Burlington, VT: Ashgate.

Abel, Theodore. [1938] 1986. *Why Hitler Came into Power*. Cambridge, MA: Harvard University Press.

Abele, Andrea. 1985. "Thinking about Thinking: Casual, Evaluative, and Finalistic Cognitions about Social Situations." *European Journal of Social Psychology* **15** (July/September): 315–32.

Ajami, Fouad. 1998. *The Dream Palace of the Arabs: A Generation's Odyssey*. New York: Pantheon.

Albrecht-Carrié, René. 1958. *A Diplomatic History of Europe since the Congress of Vienna*. New York: Harper.

Almond, Gabriel A., Appleby, R. Scott, and Sivan, Emmanuel. 2003. *Strong Religion: The Rise of Fundamentalisms around the World*. Chicago: University of Chicago Press.

Aly, Götz. 1999. *"Final Solution": Nazi Population Policy and the Murder of the European Jews*, trans. Belinda Cooper and Allison Brown. London: Edward Arnold.

Andersen, Lars E. and Aagaard, Jan. 2005. *In the Name of God: The Afghan Connection and the US War against Terrorism. The Story of the Afghan Veterans as the Masterminds behind 9/11*, trans. Cindie Margaard. Odense: University Press of Southern Denmark.

Anderson, Benedict R. 1987. "How Did the Generals Die?" *Indonesia* **43** (April): 109–34.

  2006. *Imagined Communities: Reflections on the Origin and Spread of Nationalism*, rev. edn. London: Verso.

Anderson, G. Norman. 1999. *Sudan in Crisis: The Failure of Democracy*. Gainesville: University Press of Florida.

Anderson, Lisa. 1997. "Fulfilling Prophecies: State Policy and Islamist Radicalism." In *Political Islam: Revolution, Radicalism or Reforms?*, ed. John L. Esposito. Boulder, CO: Lynne Rienner Publishers, 17–31.

Andrew, Christopher M. and Mitrokhin, Vasili. 1999. *The Mitrokhin Archive: The KGB in Europe and the West*. London: Penguin.

Andrić, Ivo. [1959] 1995. *The Bridge on the Drina*, trans. Lovett F. Edwards. London: The Harvill Press.

377

Appiah, Kwame A. 2008. *Experiments in Ethics*. Cambridge, MA: Harvard University Press.

Appleby, R. Scott. 2000. *The Ambivalence of the Sacred: Religion, Violence, and Reconciliation*. Lanham, MD: Rowman and Littlefield.

Aristotle. 1991. *The Art of Rhetoric*, trans. John H. Freese. Cambridge, MA: Harvard University Press.

Art, David. 2006. *The Politics of the Nazi Past in Germany and Austria*. New York: Cambridge University Press.

Asada, Sadao. 2006. *From Mahan to Pearl Harbor: The Imperial Japanese Navy and the United States*. Annapolis, MD: Naval Institute Press.

Ascheim, Steven E. 1982. *Brothers and Strangers: The East European Jew in German and German Jewish Consciousness, 1800–1923*. Madison: University of Wisconsin Press.

Awan, Akil N. 2008. "Antecedents of Islamic Political Radicalism among Muslim Communities in Europe." *PS: Political Science and Politics* **41** (1): 13–17.

Axelrod, Robert. 1984. *The Evolution of Cooperation*. New York: Basic Books.

Ayub, Mohammed. 2005. *An Army, Its Role and Rule: A History of the Pakistan Army from Independence to Kargil, 1967–1999*. Pittsburgh, PA: RoseDog Books.

Baddeley, John F. 1908. *The Russian Conquest of the Caucasus*. London: Longmans, Green.

Baird, Jay. 1990. *To Die for Germany: Heroes in the Nazi Pantheon*. Bloomington: Indiana University Press.

Baker, Peter, and Glasser, Susan. 2005. *Kremlin Rising: Vladimir Putin's Russia and the End of Revolution*. New York: Scribner.

Balakian, Grigoris. 2009. *Armenian Golgotha: A Memoir of the Armenian Genocide, 1915–1919*, trans. Peter Balakian and Aris Sevag. New York: Knopf.

Balakian, Peter. 2003. *The Burning Tigris: The Armenian Genocide and America's Response*. New York: HarperCollins.

Bale, Tim. 2007. "Are Bans on Political Parties Bound to Turn out Badly? A Comparative Investigation of Three 'Intolerant' Democracies: Turkey, Spain and Belgium." *Comparative European Politics* **5** (2): 141–57.

Ball, Patrick, Kobrak, Paul and Spirer, Herbert F. 1999. *State Violence in Guatemala, 1960–1996: A Quantitative Reflection*. Washington, DC: American Association for the Advancement of Science.

Baron, Salo W. 1976. *The Russian Jew under Tsars and Soviets*. New York: Macmillan.

Bates, Robert H., de Figueiredo, Rui J. P. Jr., and Weingast, Barry R. 1998. "The Politics of Interpretation: Rationality, Culture, and Transition." *Politics and Society* **26** (2): 221–56.

Baudrillard, Jean. 2002. *The Spirit of Terrorism and Requiem for the Twin Towers*. London: Verso.

Bauman, Zygmunt. 1989. *Modernity and the Holocaust*. Ithaca, NY: Cornell University Press.

Baumeister, Roy F., Smart, Laura, and Boden, Joseph M. 1996. "Relation of Threatened Egotism to Violence and Aggression: The Dark Side of High Self-Esteem." *Psychological Review* **103** (January): 5–33.

Baumeister, Roy F., Bratlavsky, Ellen, Finenauer, Catrin, and Vohs, Kathleen D. 2001. "Bad is Stronger than Good." *Review of General Psychology* **5** (December): 323–70.

Beasley, William G. 2000. *The Rise of Modern Japan*. New York: St. Martin's Press.

Beckman, Jonathan. 2008. "Otherness Anguish." *Times Literary Supplement* **5471** (February 8): 20.

Ben-Ghiat, Ruth. 2001. *Fascist Modernities: Italy, 1922–1945*. Berkeley: University of California Press.

Bennigsen, Alexandre and Wimbush, S. Enders. 1986. *Muslims of the Soviet Empire: A Guide*. Bloomington: Indiana University Press.

Berdyaev, Nicolas. 1937. *The Origin of Russian Communism*. London: Geoffrey Bles.

Berezhkov, Valentin M. 1994. *At Stalin's Side: His Interpreter's Memoirs from the October Revolution to the Fall of the Dictator's Empire*, trans. Sergei V. Mikheyev. Secaucus, NJ: Carol Pub. Group.

Bergen, Peter L. 2001. *Holy War, Inc.: Inside the Secret World of Osama bin Laden*. New York: The Free Press.

Bergen, Peter and Cruickshank, Paul. 2008. "The Unraveling: Al Qaeda's Revolt against bin Laden." *The New Republic* (June 11): 16–21.

Bergesen, Albert J., ed. 2008. *The Sayyid Qutb Reader: Selected Writings on Politics, Religion, and Society*. New York: Routledge.

Berkowitz, Leonard. 2003. "Affect, Aggression, and Antisocial Behavior." In *Handbook of Affective Sciences*, ed. Richard J. Davidson, Klaus R. Scherer, and H. Hill Goldsmith. Oxford: Oxford University Press, 804–23.

Berlin, Isaiah. 1978. *Russian Thinkers*, ed. Henry Hardy and Aileen Kelly. New York: Viking.

Berman, Paul. 2003. *Terror and Liberalism*. New York: Norton.

Berman, Sheri. 2003. "Islamism, Revolution, and Civil Society." *Perspectives on Politics* **1** (June): 11–26.

bin Laden, Osama. 1996. *A Declaration of War against the Americans Occupying the Land of the Two Holy Places: A Message from Osama bin Muhammed bin Laden unto His Muslim Brethren All over the World Generally, and toward the Muslims of the Arabian Peninsula in Particular*. Reprinted in Gunaratna 2002, 28–9, 44, 46.

Bix, Herbert P. 2000. *Hirohito and the Making of Modern Japan*. New York: HarperCollins.

Blainey, Geoffrey. 1988. *The Causes of War*, 3rd edn. New York: Free Press.

Bodenhausen, Galen V., Sheppard, Lori A., and Kramer, Geoffrey P. 1994. "Negative Affect and Social Judgment: The Differential Impact of Anger and Sadness." *European Journal of Social Psychology* **24** (1): 45–62.

Bodenhausen, Galen V., Mussweiler, Thomas, Gabriel, Shira, and Moreno, Kristen N. 2001. "Affective Influences on Stereotyping and Intergroup Relations." In *Handbook of Affect and Social Cognition*, ed. Joseph P. Forgas. Mahwah, NJ: Erlbaum, 319–43.

Bose, Sarmila. 2010. *Dead Reckoning: Memories of the 1971 Bangladesh War*. New York: Columbia University Press.

Bosworth, R. J. B. 1998. *The Italian Dictatorship: Problems and Perspectives in the Interpretation of Mussolini and Fascism*. London: Arnold.

2002. *Mussolini*. London: Arnold.

Bowker, Mike. 2004. "Conflict in Chechnya." In *Russian Politics under Putin*, ed. Cameron Ross. Manchester, UK: Manchester University Press, 255–68.

Box-Steffensmeier, Janet M., Brady, Henry E., and Collier, David. 2008. *The Oxford Handbook of Political Methodology*. New York: Oxford University Press.

Boyer, Peter J. 2008. "The Color of Politics." *The New Yorker*, February 4, 38–51.

Brackman, Arnold C. 1969. *The Communist Collapse in Indonesia*. New York: Norton.

Braham, Randolph L. 1981. *The Politics of Genocide: The Holocaust in Hungary*. New York: Columbia University Press.

2000. *The Politics of Genocide: The Holocaust in Hungary*, condensed edn. Detroit, MI: Wayne State University Press.

Braithwaite, John. 1989. *Crime, Shame, and Reintegration*. New York: Cambridge University Press.

Braudel, Fernand. 1984. *The Perspective of the World*, vol. 3 of *Civilization and Capitalism, 15th–18th Century*, trans. Siân Reynolds. New York: Harper and Row.

Breaking News 24/7. 2009 (July 22). "International Arbitration Panel Awards Sudan Government Disputed Oil Field." http://blog.taragana.com/n/international-arbitration-panel-awards-sudan-government-disputed-oil-field-117013/

Brickman, Philip, Coates, Dan, and Janoff-Bulman, Ronnie. 1978. "Lottery Winners and Accident Victims: Is Happiness Relative?" *Journal of Personality and Social Psychology* **36** (August): 917–27.

Brockett, Charles D. 2005. *Political Movements and Violence in Central America*. New York: Cambridge University Press.

Brondino, Emanuele E., Brondino, N., Bertona, M., Re, S., and Geroldi, D. 2008. "Relationship between Platelet Serotonin Content and Rejections of Unfair Offers in the Ultimatum Game." *Neuroscience Letters* **437** (2): 158–61.

Brooker, Paul. 1991. *The Faces of Fraternalism: Nazi Germany, Fascist Italy, and Imperial Japan*. Oxford: Clarendon.

Brosnan, Sarah F. and de Waal, Frans B. 2003. "Monkeys Reject Unequal Pay." *Nature* **425**: 297.

Brown, L. Carl. 2000. *Religion and State: The Muslim Approach to Politics*. New York: Columbia University Press.

Browning, Christopher R. 1992. *Ordinary Men: Reserve Police Battalion 101 and the Final Solution in Poland*. New York: HarperCollins.

2004. *The Origins of the Final Solution: The Evolution of Nazi Jewish Policy, September 1939–March 1942*. Jerusalem: Yad Vashem, and Lincoln: University of Nebraska Press.

Brustein, William. 1988. "The Political Geography of Belgian Fascism: The Case of Rexism." *American Sociological Review* **53** (February): 69–80.

1991. "The 'Red Menace' and the Rise of Italian Fascism." *American Sociological Review* **56** (October): 652–64.

1996. *The Logic of Evil: The Social Origins of the Nazi Party, 1925–1933*. New Haven, CT: Yale University Press.

Burgat, François. 2003. *Face to Face with Political Islam*. New York: I. B. Tauris.

Burke, Jason. 2003. *Al-Qaeda: Casting a Shadow of Terror*. London: I. B. Tauris.

Burleigh, Michael. 2000. *The Third Reich: A New History*. New York: Hill and Wang.

2007. *Sacred Causes: The Clash of Religion and Politics, From the Great War to the War on Terror*. New York: HarperCollins.

Burr, J. Millard and Collins, Robert O. 2003. *Revolutionary Sudan: Hasan al-Turabi and the Islamist State, 1989–2000*. Leiden: Brill.

Burrin, Philippe. 1994. *Hitler and the Jews: The Genesis of the Holocaust*, trans. Patsy Southgate. London: Edward Arnold.

Buruma, Ian. 2006. "Weimar Faces." *The New York Review of Books* **53** (17, November 2): 14–17.

Bush, Kenneth D. 2003. *The Intra-Group Dimensions of Ethnic Conflict in Sri Lanka: Learning to Read between the Lines*. New York: Palgrave Macmillan.

Byrnes, Robert F. 1968. *Pobedonostsev: His Life and Thought*. Bloomington: Indiana University Press.

Calotychos, Vangelis. 2003. *Modern Greece: A Cultural Poetics*. Oxford: Berg.

Capoccia, Giovanni. 2005. *Defending Democracy: Reactions to Extremism in Interwar Europe*. Baltimore, MD: Johns Hopkins University Press.

Carmichael, Cathie. 2002. *Ethnic Cleansing in the Balkans: Nationalism and the Destruction of Tradition*. London: Routledge.

Carney, Timothy. 1989. "The Unexpected Victory." In *Cambodia 1975–1978: Rendezvous with Death*, ed. Karl D. Jackson. Princeton, NJ: Princeton University Press, 13–35.

Caron, Vicki. 1988. *Between France and Germany: The Jews of Alsace-Lorraine, 1871–1918*. Stanford, CA: Stanford University Press.

Chandler, David P. 1990. "A Revolution in Full Spate: Communist Party Policy in Democratic Kampuchea, December 1976." In *The Cambodian Agony*, ed. David A. Ablin and Marlowe Hood. New York: M. E. Sharpe, 165–79.

1999. *Brother Number One: A Political Biography of Pol Pot*. New York: Westview Press.

2000. *A History of Cambodia*, 3rd edn. Boulder, CO: Westview.

Chang, Jung and Halliday, Jon. 2005. *Mao: The Unknown Story*. New York: Knopf.

Chivers, C. J. 2006. "The School." *Esquire* **145** (June): 145–60.

Cigar, Norman L. 1995. *Genocide in Bosnia: The Policy of "Ethnic Cleansing."* College Station: Texas A&M University Press.

Clayton, Susan and Opotow, Susan. 2003. "Justice and Identity: Changing Perspectives on What is Fair." *Personality and Social Psychology Review* **7** (4): 298–310.

Clogg, Richard. 1992. *A Concise History of Greece*. Cambridge: Cambridge University Press.

Cockett, Richard. 2010. *Sudan: Darfur and the Failure of an African State*. New Haven, CT: Yale University Press.

Cohen, Florette, Solomon, Sheldon, Maxfield, Molly, Pyszczynski, Tom, and Greenberg, Jeff. 2004. "Fatal Attraction: The Effects of Mortality Salience on Evaluations of Charismatic, Task-Oriented, and Relationship-Oriented Leaders." *Psychological Science* **15** (12): 846–51.

Cohen, Florette, Ogilvie, Daniel M., Solomon, Sheldon, Greenberg, Jeff, and Pyszczynski, Tom. 2005. "American Roulette: The Effect of Reminders of Death on Support for George W. Bush in the 2004 Presidential Election." *Analyses of Social Issues and Public Policy* **5** (1): 177–87.

Cohen, Stephen P. 1984. *The Pakistan Army*. Berkeley: University of California Press.

    2004. *The Idea of Pakistan*. Washington, DC: Brookings Institution Press.

Conquest, Robert. 1970. *The Soviet Deportation of Nationalities*. New York: St. Martin's Press.

    1986. *The Harvest of Sorrow: Soviet Collectivization and the Terror Famine*. New York: Oxford University Press.

Conrad, Joseph. 1929. *Under Western Eyes*. Garden City, NY: Doubleday.

Constitution of the Russian Socialist Federative Soviet Republic [RSFSR] of 1918. *SU* [*Sobranie Uzakonenii* – collected laws and orders] 1917–1918, no. 51, item 582.

Couloumbis, Theodore A., Petropulos, John A., and Psomiades, Harry J. 1976. *Foreign Interference in Greek Politics: An Historical Perspective*. New York: Pella.

Crawford, Neta C. 2000. "The Passion of World Politics: Propositions on Emotion and Emotional Relationships." *International Security* **24** (4): 116–56.

Crockett, Molly J., Clark, Luke, Tabibnia, Golnaz, Lieberman, Matthew D., and Robbins, Trevor W. 2008. "Serotonin Modulates Behavioral Reactions to Unfairness." *Science* **320** (5884): 1739.

Croker, John W. 1835. "Robespierre." *Quarterly Review* (September): 299–430.

Crone, Patricia. 2004. *God's Rule: Government and Islam*. New York: Columbia University Press.

Crowley, James B. 1966. *Japan's Quest for Autonomy: National Security and Foreign Policy, 1930–1938*. Princeton, NJ: Princeton University Press.

Dadrian, Vahakn N. 1997. *The History of the Armenian Genocide: Ethnic Conflict from the Balkans to Anatolia to the Caucasus*. Providence, RI: Berghahn Books.

    1999. *Warrant for Genocide: Key Elements of Turko-Armenian Conflict*. New Brunswick, NJ: Transaction Publishers.

Darley, John M. and Pittman, Thane S. 2003. "The Psychology of Compensatory and Retributive Justice." *Personality and Social Psychology Review* **7** (4): 324–36.

Davies, James C. 1962. "Toward a Theory of Revolution." *American Sociological Review* **27** (February): 5–19.

Davies, Norman. 1982. *God's Playground: A History of Poland*. New York: Columbia University Press.

Davies, R. W. 2001. "Making Economic Policy." In *Behind the Façade of Stalin's Command Economy: Evidence from the Soviet State and Party Archives*, ed. Paul R. Gregory. Stanford, CA: Hoover Institution Press, 61–80.

de Silva, K. M. 1995. *Regional Powers and Small State Security: India and Sri Lanka, 1977–90.* Washington, DC: The Woodrow Wilson Center Press.

de Waal, Frans. 1997. *Bonobo: The Forgotten Ape.* Berkeley: University of California Press.

de Waal, Frans, Wright, Robert, Korsgaard, Christine M., Kitcher, Philip, and Singer, Peter. 2006. *Primates and Philosophers: How Morality Evolved.* Princeton, NJ: Princeton University Press.

Deák, István. 1965. "Hungary." In *The European Right: A Historical Profile,* ed. Hans Rogger and Eugen Weber. Berkeley: University of California Press, 364–407.

de la Boétie, Étienne and Bonnefon, Paul. [1553] 2007. *The Politics of Obedience and Étienne de la Boétie.* Montreal: Black Rose Books.

Deng, Francis M. 1995. *War of Visions: Conflict of Identities in the Sudan.* Washington, DC: Brookings.

DeSteno, David N., Dassgupta, Nilanjana, Bartlett, Monica Y., and Cajddric, Aida. 2004. "Prejudice from Thin Air: The Effect of Emotion on Automatic Intergroup Attitudes." *Psychological Science* **15** (5): 319–24.

DeSteno, David N., Petty, Richard E., Wegener, Duane. T., and Rucker, Derek D. 2000. "Beyond Valence in the Perception of Likelihood: The role of Emotion Specificity." *Journal of Personality and Social Psychology* **78** (3): 397–416.

Deutsch, Morton. 1985. *Distributive Justice: A Social-Psychological Perspective.* New Haven, CT: Yale University Press.

Deutscher, Isaac. 1960. *Stalin: A Political Biography.* New York: Vintage.

Devji, Faisal. 2005. *Landscapes of the Jihad.* Ithaca, NY: Cornell University Press.

DeVotta, Neil. 2004. *Blowback: Linguistic Nationalism, Institutional Decay, and Ethnic Conflict in Sri Lanka.* Stanford, CA: Stanford University Press.

Diamond, Larry and Gunther, Richard. 2001. *Political Parties and Democracy.* Baltimore, MD: Johns Hopkins University Press.

Dieckmann, Christoph. 2000. "The War and the Killing of the Lithuanian Jews." In *National Socialist Extermination Policies: Contemporary German Perspectives and Controversies,* ed. Ulrich Herbert. New York: Berghahn Books, 240–75.

Diehl, Paul F., ed. 1999. *The Road Map to War: Territorial Dimensions of International Conflict.* Nashville, TN: Vanderbilt University Press.

Dillon, E. J. 1895. "The Condition of Armenia." *The Contemporary Review* **68** (July/December): 153–89.

Doran, Charles F. 1980. "Modes, Mechanisms, and Turning Points: Perspectives on the Analysis of the Transformation of the International System." *International Political Science Review* **1** (1): 35–61.

Doran, Michael S. 2002. "Somebody Else's Civil War." *Foreign Affairs* **81** (1): 22–42.

Doris, John M. 2002. *Lack of Character: Personality and Moral Behavior.* Cambridge: Cambridge University Press.

Doyle, William. 2009. *Aristocracy and its Enemies in the Age of Revolution.* New York: Oxford University Press.

Drakeley, Steven. 2005. *The History of Indonesia.* Westport, CT: Greenwood Press.

Dubnov, Simon. 1973. *History of the Jews: From the Congress of Vienna to the Emergence of Hitler,* vol. V, trans. Moshe Spiegel. New York: Thomas Yoseloff.

Dunlop, John B. 1998. *Russia Confronts Chechnya: Roots of a Separatist Conflict.* Cambridge: Cambridge University Press.

Dzerzhinskii, Feliks. [1918] 1936. "A Policy of Terror." In *Intervention, Civil War, and Communism in Russia, April–December 1918: Documents and Materials*, ed. James Bunyan. Baltimore, MD: Johns Hopkins University Press, 227.

Easter, David. 2004. *Britain and the Confrontation with Indonesia, 1960–1966.* London: I. B. Tauris.

Eisenberg, Nancy. 2000. "Emotion, Regulation, and Moral Development." *Annual Review of Psychology* 51 (1): 665–97.

Eksteins, Modris. 2008. "Drowned in Eau de Vie." *London Review of Books* 30 (February 21): 23–4.

Elias, Norbert. 1996. *The Germans: Power Struggles and the Development of Habitus in the Nineteenth and Twentieth Centuries*, ed. Michael Schröter, trans. Eric Dunning and Stephen Mennell. Cambridge: Polity Press.

Elliott, Andrea. 2007. "Where Boys Grow Up to be Jihadis." *The New York Times Magazine* (November 25): 70–100.

Elliott, John H. 2009. *Spain, Europe & the Wider World: 1500–1800.* New Haven, CT: Yale University Press.

Elster, Jon. 2004. "Emotion and Action." In *Thinking About Feeling: Contemporary Philosophers on Emotions*, ed. Robert C. Solomon. Oxford: Oxford University Press, 151–62.

Enciclopedia Italiana di Scienze, Lettere ed Arti. 1992. [Redattore capo Giorgio Stabile]. Roma: Istituto della Enciclopedia italiana.

Enescu, C. 1991. "Semnificatia Alegerilor din Decemvrie 1937 in Evolutia Politicia a Neamului Romanesc." In *Renaşterea unei Democraţii: Alegerile din România de la 20 mai 1990*, ed. Petre Datculescu and Klaus Liepelt. Bucharest: IRSOP (Romanian Institute for Public Opinion), 159–76.

Enssle, Manfred J. 1980. *Stresemann's Territorial Revisionism: Germany, Belgium, and the Eupen-Malmédy Question, 1919–1929.* Wiesbaden: Steiner.

Epstein, Seymour. 1994. "Integration of the Cognitive and the Psychodynamic Unconscious." *American Psychologist* 49: 709–24.

Erickson, Edward J. 2001. *Ordered to Die: A History of the Ottoman Army in the First World War.* Westport, CT: Greenwood Press.

Esposito, John L. 2003. *Unholy War: Terror in the Name of Islam.* Oxford: Oxford University Press.

Evans, Richard J. 2004. *The Coming of the Third Reich.* New York: Penguin Books.

Fagin Jones, Stephanie and Midlarsky, Elizabeth. 2007. "Courageous Rescue during the Holocaust: Personal and Situational Correlates." *Journal of Positive Psychology* 2 (2): 136–47.

Fair, C. Christine. 2004. *Urban Battle Fields of South Asia: Lessons Learned from Sri Lanka, India, and Pakistan.* Santa Monica, CA: Rand.

Fearon, James D. and Laitin, David D. 1996. "Explaining Interethnic Cooperation." *American Political Science Review* 90 (4): 715–35.

Fehr, Ernst and Gachter, Simon. 2002. "Altruistic Punishment in Humans." *Nature* 415 (10, January): 134–40.

Feldman, Gerald. 1993. *The Great Disorder: Politics, Economics, and Society in the German Inflation, 1914–1924.* New York: Oxford University Press.

Feldman, Noah. 2008. "Why Shariah?: Millions of Muslims Think Shariah Means the Rule of Law. Could they be Right?" *The New York Times Magazine* (March 16): 46–51.

Fellner, Fritz. 1981. "Introduction: The Genesis of the Austrian Republic." In *Modern Austria*, ed. Kurt Steiner, Fritz Fellner, and Hubert Feichtlbauer. Palo Alto, CA: Society for the Promotion of Science and Scholarship, 1–20.

Ferguson, Niall. 2006. *The War of the World: Twentieth Century Conflict and the Descent of the West.* New York: Penguin.

Fest, Joachim. 1974. *Hitler.* New York: Harcourt Brace Jovanovich.

Figes, Orlando. 2007. *The Whisperers: Private Life in Stalin's Russia.* New York: Metropolitan Books.

Filkins, Dexter. 2008. "Right at the Edge." *The New York Times Magazine* (September 7): 52–116.

Fischer, Klaus P. 1998. *The History of an Obsession: German Judeophobia and the Holocaust.* New York: Continuum.

Flags of the World. 2007. "Serbian Orthodox Church (Serbia and Montenegro)." www.crwflags.com/fotw/flags/rel-soch.html

Florian, Victor and Mikulincer, Mario. 1998. "Symbolic Immortality and the Management of the Terror of Death: The Moderating Role of Attachment Style." *Journal of Personality and Social Psychology* **74** (3): 725–34.

Fox, Elaine, Griggs, Laura, and Mouchlianitis, Elias. 2007. "The Detection of Fear Relevant Stimuli: Are Guns Noticed as Quickly as Snakes?" *Emotion* **7** (4): 691–6.

Fricker, Miranda. 2007. *Epistemic Injustice: Power and the Ethics of Knowing.* New York: Oxford University Press.

Frijda, Nico H. 1986. *The Emotions.* Cambridge: Cambridge University Press.

1994. "The Lex Talionis: On Vengeance." In *Emotions: Essays on Emotion Theory*, ed. Stephanie H.M. Van Goozen, Nanne E. Van De Poll, Joseph A. Sergeant. Hillsdale, NJ: Lawrence Erlbaum, 263–89.

Gallant, Thomas W. 2001. *Modern Greece.* London: Hodder Arnold.

Gammer, Moshe. 2006. *The Lone Wolf and the Bear: Three Centuries of Chechen Defiance of Russian Rule.* Pittsburgh, PA: University of Pittsburgh Press.

Ganguly, Sumit and Hagerty, Devin T. 2005. *Fearful Symmetry: India-Pakistan Crises in the Shadow of Nuclear Weapons.* Seattle: University of Washington Press.

Gartzke, Erik. 2006. "Globalization, Economic Development, and Territorial Conflict." In *Territoriality and Conflict in an Era of Globalization*, ed. Miles Kahler and Barbara F. Walter. Cambridge: Cambridge University Press, 156–86.

Gellately, Robert, ed. 2004. *The Nuremberg Interviews, Conducted by Leon Goldensohn.* New York: Knopf.

2007. *Lenin, Stalin, and Hitler: The Age of Social Catastrophe.* New York: Knopf.

George, Alexander L. and Bennett, Andrew. 2005. *Case Studies and Theory Development in the Social Sciences.* Cambridge, MA: MIT Press.

Gergel, N. 1951. "The Pogroms in the Ukraine in 1918–1921." *YIVO Annual of Jewish Social Science* **6**: 237–52.

Gerges, Fawaz A. 2005. *The Far Enemy: Why Jihad Went Global*. New York: Cambridge University Press.

Gerlach, Christian. 2000. "The Wannsee Conference, the Fate of German Jews, and Hitler's Decision in Principle to Exterminate All European Jews." In *The Holocaust: Origins, Implementations, Aftermath*, ed. Omer Bartov. New York: Routledge, 108–61. Reprinted from *Journal of Modern History* **70** (December 1998): 759–812.

Gieysztor, Aleksander, Kieniewicz, Stefan, Rostworowski, Emanuel, Tazbir, Janusz, and Wereszycki, Henryk. 1979. *History of Poland*, 2nd edn. Warsaw: PWN-Polish Scientific Publishers.

Gilbert, Martin. 1989. *The Second World War: A Complete History*. New York: Henry Holt.

Glenny, Misha. 1996. *The Fall of Yugoslavia: The Third Balkan War*. New York: Penguin Books.

1999. *The Balkans: Nationalism, War, and the Great Powers 1804–1999*. New York: Penguin Books.

Goertz, Gary and Diehl, Paul F. 1992. *Territorial Changes and International Conflict*. London: Routledge.

Goldhagen, Daniel J. 1996. *Hitler's Willing Executioners: Ordinary Germans and the Holocaust*. New York: Knopf.

Goldstein, Ivo. 1999. *Croatia: A History*, trans. Nikolina Jovanović. London: Hurst.

Goltz, Thomas. 2003. *Chechnya Diary: A War Correspondent's Story of Surviving the War in Chechnya*. New York: St. Martin's Press.

Gorodetsky, Gabriel. 1999. *Grand Delusion: Stalin and the German Invasion of Russia*. New Haven, CT: Yale University Press.

Goscha, Christopher E. 2006. "Vietnam, the Third Indochina War and the Meltdown of Asian Internationalism." In *The Third Indochina War: Conflict between China, Vietnam and Cambodia, 1972–79*, ed. Odd Arne Westad and Sophie Quinn-Judge. London: Routledge, 152–86.

Graham, Jesse, Haidt, Jonathan, and Nosek, Brian A. 2009. "Liberals and Conservatives Rely on Different Sets of Moral Foundations." *Journal of Personality and Social Psychology* **96** (5): 1029–46.

Grass, Günter. 1999. *My Century*, trans. Michael Henry Heim. New York: Harcourt.
2007. "How I Spent the War: A Recruit in the Waffen S.S." *The New Yorker* (June 4): 68–81.

Gray, John. 2003. *Al Qaeda and What it Means to be Modern*. New York: The New Press.
2008. "A Rescuer of Religion." *New York Review of Books* **55** (15, October 9): 43–5.

Greenberg, Jeff, Pyszczynski, Tom, Solomon, Sheldon, Rosenblatt, Abram, Veeder, Michael, Kirkland, Shari, and Lyon, Deborah. 1990. "Evidence for Terror Management Theory II: The Effects of Mortality Salience on Reactions to

Those Who Threaten or Bolster the Cultural Worldview." *Journal of Personality and Social Psychology* **58** (2): 308–18.

Greene, Joshua D., Sommerville, R. Brian, Nystrom, Leigh E., Darley, John M., and Cohen, Jonathan D. 2001. "An fMRI Investigation of Emotional Engagement in Moral Judgment." *Science* **293** (5537): 2105–8.

Gregor, A. James. 1979. *Young Mussolini and the Intellectual Origins of Fascism.* Berkeley: University of California Press.

1999. *Phoenix: Fascism in Our Time.* New Brunswick, NJ: Transaction Publishers.

2005. *Mussolini's Intellectuals: Fascist Social and Political Thought.* Princeton, NJ: Princeton University Press.

2006. *The Search for Neofascism: The Use and Abuse of Social Science.* Cambridge and New York: Cambridge University Press.

Gries, Peter H. 2004. *China's New Nationalism: Pride, Politics, and Diplomacy.* Berkeley: University of California Press.

Griffin, Roger. 1991. *The Nature of Fascism.* New York: St. Martin's Press.

Gross, Jan T. 2001. *Neighbors: The Destruction of the Jewish Community in Jedwabne, Poland.* Princeton, NJ: Princeton University Press.

2006. *Fear: Anti-Semitism in Poland after Auschwitz.* New York: Random House.

Gunaratna, Rohan. 2002. *Inside Al Qaeda: Global Network of Terror.* New York: Columbia University Press.

Gürün, Kamuran. 1985. *The Armenian File.* New York: St. Martin's Press.

Habeck, Mary R. 2006. *Knowing the Enemy: Jihadist Ideology and the War on Terror.* New Haven, CT: Yale University Press.

Hafez, Mohammed M. 2004. "From Marginalization to Massacres: A Political Process Explanation of GIA Violence in Algeria." In *Islamic Activism: A Social Movement Theory Approach*, ed. Quintan Wiktorowicz. Bloomington: Indiana University Press, 37–60.

Haffner, Sebastian. 2002. *Defying Hitler: A Memoir*, trans. Oliver Pretzel. New York: Farrar, Straus, and Giroux.

Haidt, Jonathan. 2003. "The Moral Emotions." In *Handbook of Affective Sciences*, ed. Richard J. Davidson, Klaus R. Scherer, and H. Hill Goldsmith. Oxford: Oxford University Press, 852–70.

2006. *The Happiness Hypothesis: Finding Modern Truth in Ancient Wisdom.* New York: Perseus.

Haidt, Jonathan and Graham, Jesse. 2007. "When Morality Opposes Justice: Conservatives Have Moral Intuitions that Liberals May not Recognize." *Social Justice Research* **20** (1): 98–116.

Halder, Franz. 1988. *The Halder War Diary: 1939–1942*, ed. Charles Burdick and Hans Adolf Jacobsen. Novato, CA: Presidio.

Hamburg, G.M. 1984. *Politics of the Russian Nobility: 1881–1905.* New Brunswick, NJ: Rutgers University Press.

Hampson, Norman. 1974. *The Life and Opinions of Maximilian Robespierre.* London: Duckworth.

Haney, Craig, Banks, Curtis, and Zimbardo, Philip. 1973. "Interpersonal Dynamics in a Simulated Prison." *International Journal of Criminology and Penology* **1** (February 1): 69–97.

Haqqani, Husain. 2005. *Pakistan: Between Mosque and Military*. Washington, DC: Carnegie Endowment for International Peace.

Harmon-Jones, Eddie, Simon, Linda, Greenberg, Jeff, Pyszczynski, Tom, Solomon, Sheldon, and McGregor, Holly. 1997. "Terror Management Theory and Self-Esteem: Evidence that Increased Self-Esteem Reduces Mortality Salience Effects." *Journal of Personality and Social Psychology* **72** (1): 24–36.

Harrison, Mark. 2001. "Providing for Defense." In *Behind the Façade of Stalin's Command Economy: Evidence from the Soviet State and Party Archives*, ed. Paul R. Gregory. Stanford, CA: Hoover Institution Press, 81–110.

Hasan, Mushirul and Pernau, Margrit, eds. 2005. *Regionalizing Pan-Islamism: Documents on the Khilafat Movement*. New Delhi: Manohar.

Hatzfeld, Jean. 2005. *Machete Season: The Killers in Rwanda Speak*, trans. Linda Coverdale. New York: Farrar, Straus, and Giroux.

2006. *Life Laid Bare: The Survivors in Rwanda Speak*. New York: Other Press.

Hauser, Marc D. 2006. *Moral Minds: The Nature of Right and Wrong*. New York: Harper Perennial.

Hecht, Ben. 1961. *Perfidy*. New York: Messner.

Heifetz, Elias. 1921. *The Slaughter of the Jews in the Ukraine in 1919*. New York: Thomas Seltzer.

Heinen, Armin. 1986. *Die Legion "Erzengel Michael" in Rumänien–Soziale Bewegung und Politische Organisation*. Munich: R. Oldenbourg.

Herb, Guntram H. 1997. *Under the Map of Germany: Nationalism and Propaganda 1918–1945*. London: Routledge.

Herodotus. [1954] 2003. *The Histories*, trans. Aubrey de Sélincourt, rev. John Marincola. London: Penguin Books.

Herz, John H. 1957. "Rise and Demise of the Territorial State." *World Politics* **9** (July): 473–93.

Heschel, Abraham J. 1969. *Israel: An Echo of Eternity*. New York: Farrar, Straus, and Giroux.

Hickey, Michael. 1995. *Gallipoli*. London: John Murray.

Hilberg, Raul. 2003. *The Destruction of the European Jews*, 3rd edn. New Haven, CT: Yale University Press.

Hirschon, Renée. 2003. "The Consequences of the Lausanne Convention: An Overview." In *Crossing the Aegean: An Appraisal of the 1923 Compulsory Population Exchange Between Greece and Turkey*, ed. Renée Hirschon. Oxford: Berghahn Books, 13–20.

Hitler, Adolf. 1939. *Mein Kampf*. Boston: Houghton Mifflin.

Hobsbawm, Eric. 1994. *The Age of Extremes: A History of the World, 1914–1991*. New York: Pantheon Books.

Hodgson, Marshall G. 1974. *The Venture of Islam: Conscience and History in a World Civilization*. Chicago: University of Chicago Press.

Hoffmann, David. L. and Kotsonis, Yanni. 2000. *Russian Modernity: Politics, Knowledge, Practices*. Houndmills, UK: Macmillan.

Höhne, Heinz. 1970. *The Order of the Death's Head: The Story of Hitler's SS*, trans. Richard Barry. New York: Coward-McCann.

Horowitz, Donald L. 2000. *Ethnic Groups in Conflict*, 2nd edn. Berkeley: University of California Press.

Hughes, John. 1967. *Indonesian Upheaval*. New York: David McKay.

Humphreys, Leonard A. 1995. *The Way of the Heavenly Sword: The Japanese Army in the 1920s*. Stanford, CA: Stanford University Press.

Huntington, Samuel. 1968. *Political Order in Changing Societies*. New Haven, CT: Yale University Press.

Huth, Paul K. 1996. *Standing Your Ground: Territorial Disputes and International Conflict*. Ann Arbor: University of Michigan Press.

Huth, Paul K. and Allee, Todd L. 2002. *The Democratic Peace and Territorial Conflict in the Twentieth Century*. Cambridge: Cambridge University Press.

Ignazi, Piero. 2003. *Extreme Right Parties in Western Europe*. Oxford: Oxford University Press.

Ioanid, Radu. 2000. *The Holocaust in Romania: The Destruction of Jews and Gypsies under the Antonescu Regime, 1940–1944*. Chicago, IL: Ivan R. Dee.

Iordachi, Constantin. 2004. "Charisma, Religion, and Ideology: Romania's Interwar Legion of the Archangel Michael." In *Ideologies and National Identities: The Case of Twentieth-Century Southeastern Europe*, ed. John R. Lampe and Mark Mazower. Budapest: Central European University Press, 19–53.

Isenberg, Daniel J. 1986. "Group Polarization: A Critical Review and Meta-Analysis." *Journal of Personality and Social Psychology* 50 (6): 1141–51.

Jackson, Karl D., ed. 1989. *Cambodia 1975–1978: Rendezvous with Death*. Princeton, NJ: Princeton University Press.

Jackson, Sherman A. 2001. "Domestic Terrorism in the Islamic Legal Tradition." *The Muslim World* 91 (Fall): 293–310.

Jelavich, Barbara. 1983. *History of the Balkans*, vol. II. Cambridge: Cambridge University Press.

Jelavich, Charles and Jelavich, Barbara. 1977. *The Establishment of the Balkan National States, 1804–1920*. Seattle: University of Washington Press.

Job, Cvijeto. 1993. "Yugoslavia's Ethnic Furies." *Foreign Policy* 92 (Fall): 52–74.

2002. *Yugoslavia's Ruin: The Bloody Lessons of Nationalism, a Patriot's Warning*. Lanham, MD: Rowman & Littlefield.

Jones, Bruce D. 1999. "The Arusha Peace Process." In *The Path of a Genocide: The Rwanda Crisis from Uganda to Zaire*, eds. Howard Adelman and Astri Suhrke. New Brunswick, NJ: Transaction Publishers.

2001. *Peacemaking in Rwanda: The Dynamics of Failure*. Boulder, CO: Lynne Rienner.

Jones, James W. 2008. *Blood that Cries out from the Earth: The Psychology of Religious Terrorism*. New York: Oxford University Press.

Jones, Matthew. 2002. *Conflict and Confrontation in South East Asia, 1961–1965: Britain, the United States and the Creation of Malaysia*. Cambridge: Cambridge University Press.

Judah, Tim. 2000. *The Serbs: History, Myth and the Destruction of Yugoslavia*, 2nd edn. New Haven, CT: Yale University Press.

Juergensmeyer, Mark. 2000. *Terror in the Mind of God: The Global Rise of Religious Violence*. Berkeley: University of California Press.

Kahler, Miles and Walter, Barbara F., eds. 2006. *Territoriality and Conflict in an Era of Globalization*. Cambridge: Cambridge University Press.

Kahneman, Daniel and Tversky, Amos. 1979. "Prospect Theory: An Analysis of Decision under Risk." *Econometrica* 47 (2): 263–92.

eds. 2000. *Choices, Values, and Frames*. Cambridge: Cambridge University Press.

Kang, David C. 2007. *China Rising: Peace, Power, and Order in East Asia*. New York: Columbia University Press.

Kaplan, Robert D. 1993. *Balkan Ghosts: A Journey through History*. New York: St. Martin's Press.

Karpat, Kemal H. 1985. *Ottoman Population, 1830–1914: Demographic and Social Characteristics*. Madison: University of Wisconsin Press.

2001. *The Politicization of Islam: Reconstructing Identity, State, Faith, and Community in the Late Ottoman State*. New York: Oxford University Press.

Katz, Michael R. and Wagner, William G. 1989. "Introduction: Chernyshevsky, *What is to be Done?* and the Russian Intelligentsia." In Nikolai Chernyshevsky *What is to be Done?*, trans. Michael R. Katz. Ithaca, NY: Cornell University Press, 1–36.

Kaufman, Stuart J. 2001. *Modern Hatreds: The Symbolic Politics of Ethnic War*. New York: Cornell University Press.

2006. "Symbolic Politics or Rational Choice?: Testing Theories of Extreme Ethnic Violence." *International Security* 30 (4): 45–86.

Kekes, John. 1993. *The Morality of Pluralism*. Princeton, NJ: Princeton University Press.

2005. *The Roots of Evil*. Ithaca, NY: Cornell University Press.

Kellermann, Kelly. 1984. "The Negativity Effect and its Implications for Initial Interaction." *Communication Monographs* 51 (March): 37–55.

Kelman, Herbert C. 1973. "Violence without Moral Restraint: Reflection on the Dehumanization of Victims and Victimizers." *Journal of Social Issues* 29 (4): 25–61.

Keltner, Dacher, Ellsworth, Phoebe C., and Edwards, Kari. 1993. "Beyond Simple Pessimism: Effects of Sadness and Anger on Social Perception." *Journal of Personality and Social Psychology* 64 (5): 740–52.

Kenez, Peter. 1992. "Pogroms and White Ideology in the Russian Civil War." In *Pogroms: Anti Jewish Violence in Modern Russian History*, ed. John D. Klier and Shlomo Lambroza. Cambridge: Cambridge University Press, 293–313.

Keohane, Robert O. 1984. *After Hegemony: Cooperation and Discord in the World Political Economy*. Princeton, NJ: Princeton University Press.

Keohane, Robert O., Nye, Joseph S., and Hoffmann, Stanley, eds. 1993. *After the Cold War: International Institutions and State Strategies in Europe, 1989–1991*. Cambridge, MA: Harvard University Press.

Kepel, Gilles. 2002. *Jihad: The Trail of Political Islam*, trans. Anthony F. Roberts. Cambridge, MA: Belknap Press of Harvard University Press.

Kershaw, Ian. 1997. "'Working Towards the Führer': Reflections on the Nature of the Hitler Dictatorship." In *Stalinism and Nazism: Dictatorships in Comparison*, ed. Ian Kershaw and Moshe Lewin. Cambridge: Cambridge University Press, 88–106.

1998. *Hitler, 1889–1936: Hubris*. New York: Norton.

2000a. *Hitler, 1936–1945: Nemesis*. New York: Norton.

2000b. *The Nazi Dictatorship: Problems and Perspectives of Interpretation*. New York: Oxford University Press.

Kersten, Krystyna and Szapiro, Paweł. 1993. "The Contexts of the So-Called Jewish Question in Poland after World War II." In *From Shtetl to Socialism: Studies from Polin*, ed. Antony Polonsky. London: Littman Library of Jewish Civilization, 457–70.

Keynes, John M. 1920. *The Economic Consequences of the Peace*. New York: Harcourt, Brace and Howe.

Khan, M. Asghar. 2005. *We've Learnt Nothing from History–Pakistan: Politics and Military Power*. New York: Oxford University Press.

Kiernan, Ben. 1996. *The Pol Pot Regime: Race, Power, and Genocide in Cambodia under the Khmer Rouge, 1975–79*. New Haven, CT: Yale University Press.

King, Gary. 1997. *A Solution to the Ecological Inference Problem: Reconstructing Individual Behavior from Aggregate Data*. Princeton, NJ: Princeton University Press.

Kircheimer, Otto. 1966. "The Transformation of the Western European Party System." In *Political Parties and Political Development*, ed. Joseph La Palombara and Myron Weiner. Princeton: Princeton University Press, 177–210.

Kisriev, Enver. 2004. "Societal Conflict-Generating Factors in Daghestan." In *The Caspian Region, Volume II: The Caucasus*, ed. Moshe Gammer. London, Routledge, 107–21.

Knox, MacGregor. 1996. "Expansionist Zeal, Fighting Power, and Staying Power in the Italian and German Dictatorships." In *Fascist Italy and Nazi Germany: Comparisons and Contrasts*, ed. Richard Bessel. Cambridge: Cambridge University Press, 113–33.

Koliopoulos, John S. and Veremis, Thanos M. 2004. *Greece: The Modern Sequel from 1821 to the Present*. London: Hurst.

Komjathy, Anthony and Stockwell, Rebecca. 1980. *German Minorities and the Third Reich: Ethnic Germans of East Central Europe between the Wars*. New York: Holmes and Meier.

Kontogiorgi, Elisabeth. 2003. "Economic Consequences Following Refugee Settlement in Greek Macedonia, 1923–1932." In *Crossing the Aegean: An Appraisal of the 1923 Compulsory Population Exchange Between Greece and Turkey*, ed. Renée Hirschon. Oxford: Berghahn Books, 63–77.

Koonz, Claudia. 2003. *The Nazi Conscience*. Cambridge, MA: Harvard University Press.

Korzec, Paweł and Szurek, Jean-Charles. 1993. "Jews and Poles under Soviet Occupation (1939–1941): Conflicting Interests." In *From Shtetl to Socialism:*

Studies from Polin, ed. Antony Polonsky. London: Littman Library of Jewish Civilization, 385–406.

Krain, Matthew. 1997. "State-Sponsored Mass Murder: The Onset and Severity of Genocides and Politicides." *Journal of Conflict Resolution* **41** (3): 331–60.

2005. "International Intervention and the Severity of Genocides and Politicides." *International Studies Quarterly* **49** (3): 363–87.

Krystal, Arthur. 2007. "Age of Reason: Jacques Barzun at One Hundred." *The New Yorker* **83** (32, October 22): 94–103.

Kuromiya, Hiroaki. 2005. *Stalin*. Harlow, UK: Pearson.

2007. *The Voices of the Dead: Stalin's Great Terror in the 1930s*. New Haven, CT: Yale University Press.

Laffan, Michael F. 2003. *Islamic Neighborhood and Colonial Indonesia: The Umma below the Winds*. New York: Routledge.

Lake, David A. and O'Mahony, Angela. 2006. "Territory and War: State Size and Patterns of Interstate Conflict." In *Territoriality and Conflict in an Era of Globalization*, ed. Miles Kahler and Barbara F. Walter. Cambridge: Cambridge University Press, 133–55.

Lake, David A. and Rothchild, Donald S., eds. 1998. *The International Spread of Ethnic Conflict: Fear, Diffusion, and Escalation*. Princeton, NJ: Princeton University Press.

Lamoureux, Florence. 2003. *Indonesia: A Global Studies Handbook*. Santa Barbara, CA: ABC Clio.

Laqueur, Walter. 1996. *Fascism: Past, Present, Future*. New York: Oxford University Press.

Latsis [1918]. *Pravda*, December 25. In *Intervention, Civil War, and Communism in Russia, April–December 1918: Documents and Materials*, ed. James Bunyan. Baltimore, MD: Johns Hopkins University Press, 261.

Lawrence, Bruce, ed. 2005. *Messages to the World: The Statements of Osama Bin Laden*, trans. James Howarth. London: Verso.

Lear, Jonathan. 2006. *Radical Hope: Ethics in the Face of Cultural Devastation*. Cambridge, MA: Harvard University Press.

LeDoux, Joseph E., Romanski, L., and Xagoraris, A. 1989. "Indelibility of Subcortical Memories." *Journal of Cognitive Neuroscience* **1** (3): 238–43.

Lenin, Vladimir I. [1899] 1964. "Our Programme." In V. I. Lenin, *Collected Works*, 4th edn. Moscow: Foreign Languages Publishing House.

[1902] 1963. *What is to be Done?*, trans. S. V. and Patricia Utechin. Oxford: Clarendon Press.

[1918] 1967. "Report on the Review of the Programme and on Changing the Name of the Party." In V. I. Lenin, *Selected Works in Three Volumes*, vol. 2. Moscow: Foreign Languages Publishing House.

Leopold, John A. 1977. *Alfred Hugenberg: The Radical Nationalist Campaign against the Weimar Republic*. New Haven, CT: Yale University Press.

Lepenies, Wolf. 2006. *The Seduction of Culture in German History*. Princeton, NJ: Princeton University Press.

Levy, Jack S. 2000. "Loss Aversion, Framing Effects, and International Conflict: Perspectives from Prospect Theory." In M. Midlarsky 2000a, 193–221.

Lia, Brynjar. 1998. *The Society of the Muslim Brothers in Egypt: The Rise of an Islamic Mass Movement, 1928–1942*. Reading, UK: Ithaca Press.

Lifton, Robert J. 1968. *Revolutionary Immortality: Mao Tse-Tung and the Chinese Cultural Revolution*. New York: Random House.

Linz, Juan J. 1980. "Political Space and Fascism as a Late-Comer." In *Who Were the Fascists?: Social Roots of European Fascism*, ed. Stein U. Larsen, Bernt Hagtvet, and Jan P. Myklebust. Oslo: Universitetsforlaget, 153–89.

Loewenstein, George. 1996. "Out of Control: Visceral Influences on Behavior." *Organizational Behavior and Human Decision Processes* **65** (3): 272–92.

Loewenstein, George and Lerner, Jennifer S. 2003. "The Role of Affect in Decision Making." In *Handbook of Affective Sciences*, ed. Richard J. Davidson, Klause R. Scherer, and H. Hill Goldsmith. Oxford: Oxford University Press, 619–42.

Long, William J. and Brecke, Peter. 2003. *War and Reconciliation: Reason and Emotion in Conflict Resolution*. Cambridge, MA: MIT Press.

Loomis, Stanley. 1964. *Paris in the Terror: June 1793–July 1794*. Philadelphia, PA: Lippincott.

Luu, Phan, Collins, Paul, and Tucker, Don M. 2000. "Mood, Personality, and Self-Monitoring: Negative Affect and Emotionality in Relation to Frontal Lobe Mechanism of Error Monitoring." *Journal of Experimental Psychology: General* **129** (March): 43–60.

Lyons, Robert and Straus, Scott. 2006. *Intimate Enemy: Images and Voices of the Rwandan Genocide*. New York: Zone Books.

Lyttelton, Adrian. 1966. "Fascism in Italy: The Second Wave." *Journal of Contemporary History* **1** (1): 75–100.

1996. "The 'Crisis of Bourgeois Society' and the Origins of Fascism." In *Fascist Italy and Nazi Germany: Comparisons and Contrasts*, ed. Richard Bessel. Cambridge: Cambridge University Press, 12–22.

Macedo, Stephen and Ober, Josiah. 2006. "Introduction." In Frans de Waal, Robert Wright, Christine M. Korsgaard, Philip Kitcher, and Peter Singer. *Primates and Philosophers: How Morality Evolved*. Princeton, NJ: Princeton University Press, ix–xix.

Machiavelli, Niccolò. 1950. *The Prince and the Discourses*, trans. Luigi Ricci and Christian E. Detmold. New York: Random House.

Malia, Martin (alias "Z"). 1990. "To the Stalin Mausoleum." *Daedalus* **119** (1): 295–344.

1999. *Russia under Western Eyes: From the Bronze Horseman to the Lenin Mausoleum*. Cambridge, MA: Harvard University Press.

Mamdani, Mahmood. 2001. *When Victims Become Killers: Colonialism, Nativism, and the Genocide in Rwanda*. Princeton, NJ: Princeton University Press.

Mann, Michael. 2000. "Were the Perpetrators of Genocide 'Ordinary Men' or 'Real Nazis'? Results from Fifteen Hundred Biographies." *Holocaust and Genocide Studies* **14** (3): 331–66.

2004. *Fascists*. New York: Cambridge University Press.

2005. *The Dark Side of Democracy: Explaining Ethnic Cleansing*. New York: Cambridge University Press.

Mann, Thomas. [1918] 1983. *Reflections of a Nonpolitical Man*, trans. Walter D. Morris. New York: F. Ungar.

Marcus, George E., Neuman, Russell, and MacKuen, Michael. 2000. *Affective Intelligence and Political Judgment*. Chicago: University of Chicago Press.

Margalit, Avishai. 2002. *The Ethics of Memory*. Cambridge, MA: Harvard University Press.

Marrus, Michael R. and Paxton, Robert O. 1995. *Vichy France and the Jews*. Stanford, CA: Stanford University Press.

"Marx after Communism," *The Economist* (December 21, 2002): 17.

Mason, T. David. 2004. *Caught in the Crossfire: Revolutions, Repression, and the Rational Peasant*. Lanham, MD: Rowman & Littlefield.

Mastny, Vojtech. 1995/96. "A Palpable Deterioration." *Cold War International History Project Bulletin: The Cold War in Asia* (6–7, Winter): 22–3.

Matthäus, Jürgen. 2004. "Operation Barbarossa and the Onset of the Holocaust, June–December 1941." In *The Origins of the Final Solution: The Evolution of Nazi Jewish Policy, September 1939–March 1941*, by Christopher R. Browning. Jerusalem: Yad Vashem, and Lincoln: University of Nebraska Press, 244–308.

Matveeva, Anna. 2004. "Daghestan: Inter-Ethnic Tensions and Cross-Border Implications." In *The Caspian Region, Volume II: The Caucasus*, ed. Moshe Gammer. London, Routledge, 122–45.

Mavrogordatos George T. 1983 *Stillborn Republic: Social Coalitions and Party Strategies in Greece, 1922–1936*. Berkeley: University of California Press.

Mayaram, Shail. 2005. "Living Together: Ajmer as a Paradigm for the (South) Asian City." In *Living Together Separately: Cultural India in History and Politics*, ed. Mushirul Hasan and Asim Roy. New York: Oxford University Press, 145–71.

Mazour, Anatole G. 1962. *Russia: Tsarist and Communist*. Princeton, NJ: Van Nostrand.

Mazzetti, Mark. 2006. "Spy Agencies Say Iraq War Worsens Terrorism Threat." *The New York Times* (September 24): N1–8.

McCarthy, Barry W. 1999. "Marital Style and its Effects on Sexual Desire and Functioning." *Journal of Family Psychotherapy* **10** (3): 1–12.

McDermott, Kevin. 2006. *Stalin: Revolutionary in an Era of War*. New York: Palgrave.

McDermott, Rose. 2004. "The Feeling of Rationality: The Meaning of Neuroscientific Advances for Political Science." *Perspectives on Politics* **2** (4, December): 691–706.

McDermott, Terry. 2005. *Perfect Soldiers: The Hijackers, Who They Were, Why They Did It*. New York: HarperCollins.

McGreal, Chris. 2008. "War in Congo Kills 45,000 People Each Month." *The Guardian*. www.guardian.co.uk/world/2008/jan/23/congo.international

McNeill, William H. 1995. "Introduction." In Ivo Andrić, *The Bridge on the Drina*, trans. Lovett F. Edwards. London: Harvill Press, 1–6.

Mele, Alfred R. 2003. "Emotion and Desire in Self-Deception." In *Philosophy and the Emotions*, ed. Anthony Hatzimoysis. Cambridge: Cambridge University Press, 163–79.

Melson, Robert. 1992. *Revolution and Genocide: On the Origins of the Armenian Genocide and the Holocaust*. Chicago: University of Chicago Press.

Merkl, Peter H. 1975. *Political Violence under the Swastika: 581 Early Nazis*. Princeton, NJ: Princeton University Press.

Michlic, Joanna B. 2006. *Poland's Threatening Other: The Image of the Jew from 1880 to the Present*. Lincoln: University of Nebraska Press.

Midlarsky, Elizabeth and Midlarsky, Manus. 2004. "Echoes of Genocide: Trauma and Ethnic Identity among European Immigrants." *Humboldt Journal of Social Relations* **28** (2): 39–54.

Midlarsky, Elizabeth, Fagin Jones, Stephanie, and Corley, Robin. 2005. "Personality Correlates of Heroic Rescue during the Holocaust." *Journal of Personality* **73**: 907–34.

Midlarsky, Elizabeth, Fagin Jones, Stephanie, and Nemeroff, Robin. 2006. "Heroic Rescue during the Holocaust: Empirical and Methodological Perspectives." In *Strengthening Research Methodology: Psychological Measurement and Evaluation*, eds. R. Bootzin and P. McKnight. Washington, DC: American Psychological Association, 29–45.

Midlarsky, Manus I. 1984. "Political Stability of Two-Party and Multiparty Systems: Probabilistic Bases for the Comparison of Party Systems." *American Political Science Review* **78** (December): 929–51.

　　1998. "Democracy and Islam: Implications for Civilizational Conflict and the Democratic Peace." *International Studies Quarterly* **42** (September): 485–511.

　　1999. *The Evolution of Inequality: War, State Survival, and Democracy in Comparative Perspective*. Stanford, CA: Stanford University Press.

　　ed. 2000a. *Handbook of War Studies II*. Ann Arbor: University of Michigan Press.

　　2000b. "Identity and International Conflict." In M. Midlarsky 2000a, 25–58.

　　2002. "Realism and the Democratic Peace: The Primacy of State Security in New Democracies." In *Millennial Reflections on International Studies*, ed. Michael Brecher and Frank P. Harvey. Ann Arbor: University of Michigan Press, 107–30.

　　2005a. "The Demographics of Genocide: Refugees and Territorial Loss in the Mass Murder of European Jewry." *Journal of Peace Research (special issue on the demography of conflict and violence)* **42** (4): 375–91.

　　2005b. *The Killing Trap: Genocide in the Twentieth Century*. Cambridge: Cambridge University Press.

　　2009a. "Genocide Studies: Large N, Small N, and Policy Specificity." In *Handbook of War Studies III: The Intrastate Dimension*, ed. Manus I. Midlarsky. Ann Arbor: University of Michigan Press, 280–300.

2009b. "Territoriality and the Onset of Mass Violence: The Political Extremism of Joseph Stalin." *Journal of Genocide Research (special issue on Soviet mass violence)* **11** (2–3): 265–83.

Milbank, Dana. 2009. "An Ugly Finale for Health-Care Reform." *The Washington Post*, December 21. www.washingtonpost.com/wp-dyn/content/article/2009/12/20/AR2009122002872.html

Miltner, Wolfgang H. R., Braun, Christopher H., and Coles, Michael G. H. 1997. "Event Related Brain Potentials Following Incorrect Feedback in a Time-Estimation Task: Evidence for a 'Generic' Neural System for Error Detection." *Journal of Cognitive Neuroscience* **9** (November): 788–98.

Minault, Gail. 1982. *The Khilafat Movement: Religious Symbolism and Political Mobilization in India.* New York: Columbia University Press.

Mishal, Shaul and Sela, Avraham. 2000. *The Palestinian Hamas.* New York: Columbia University Press.

Mitchell, Richard P. 1969. *The Society of the Muslim Brothers.* London: Oxford University Press.

Mosse, George L. 1966a. "Introduction: The Genesis of Fascism." *Journal of Contemporary History* **1** (1): 14–26.

ed. 1966b. *Nazi Culture: Intellectual, Cultural, and Social Life in the Third Reich,* trans. Salvator Attanasio and others. New York: Grosset & Dunlap.

1986. "Two World Wars and the Myth of the War Experience." *Journal of Contemporary History* **21** (4): 491–513.

Most, Benjamin A. and Starr, Harvey. 1989. *Inquiry, Logic, and International Politics.* Columbia, SC: University of South Carolina Press.

Mosyakov, Dmitry. 2006. "The Khmer Rouge and the Vietnamese Communists: A History of Their Relations as Told in the Soviet Archives." In *Genocide in Cambodia and Rwanda: New Perspectives*, ed. Susan E. Cook. New Brunswick, NJ: Transaction Publishers, 41–71.

Mudde, Cas. 2007. *Populist Radical Right Parties in Europe.* Cambridge: Cambridge University Press.

Murray, Williamson and Millett, Allan R. 2000. *A War to be Won: Fighting the Second World War.* Cambridge, MA: Belknap Press of Harvard University Press.

Myers, David G. 1978. "Polarizing Effects of Social Comparison." *Journal of Experimental Social Psychology* **14** (6): 554–63.

Nagy-Talavera, Nicholas. 2001. *The Green Shirts and the Others: A History of Fascism in Hungary and Romania.* Iaşi: Center for Romanian Studies.

National Commission on Terrorist Attacks upon the United States. 2004. *The 9/11 Commission Report: Final Report of the National Commission on Terrorist Attacks upon the United States.* New York: Norton.

Nelson, Lori J., Moore, David L., Olivetti, Jennifer, and Scott, Tippony. 1997. "General and Personal Mortality Salience and Nationalistic Bias." *Personality and Social Psychology Bulletin* **23**: 884–92.

Newbury, Catharine. 1995. "Background to Genocide: Rwanda." *Issue: A Journal of Opinion* **23** (2): 12–17.

New York Times 2006 (February 20). "Bin Laden Reported to Vow to stay Free." A5.

Niemeijer, A. C. 1972. *The Khilafat Movement in India: 1919–1924.* The Hague: Martinus Nijhoff.

Nisbett, Richard E. and Cohen, Dov. 1996. *Culture of Honor: The Psychology of Violence in the South.* Boulder, CO: Westview Press.

Nolte, Ernst. 1966. *Three Faces of Fascism; Action Française, Italian Fascism, National Socialism,* trans. Leila Vennewitz. New York: Holt, Rinehart and Winston.

Nowak, Martin A., Page, Karen M., and Sigmund, Karl. 2000. "Fairness Versus Reason in the Ultimatum Game." *Science* **289** (5485): 1773–5.

Nussbaum, Martha C. and Sen, Amartya, eds. 1993. *The Quality of Life.* New York: Oxford University Press.

Ochsmann, R. and Mathy, M. 1994. *Depreciating of and Distancing from Foreigners: Effects of Mortality Salience.* Unpublished manuscript, University of Mainz.

Ochsner Kevin N. and Schacter, Daniel L. 2003. "Remembering Emotional Events: A Social Cognitive Neuroscience Approach." In *Handbook of Affective Sciences,* ed. Richard J. Davidson, Klaus R. Scherer, and H. Hill Goldsmith. Oxford: Oxford University Press, 643–60.

Ogg, Frederic A. 1913. *The Governments of Europe.* New York: Macmillan.

O'Neill, Barry. 1999. *Honor, Symbols, and War.* Ann Arbor: University of Michigan Press.

Opotow, Susan. 1995. "Hate, Conflict, and Moral Exclusion." In *The Psychology of Hate,* ed. Robert J. Sternberg. Washington, DC: American Psychological Association, 121–53.

Overy, Richard. 2004. *The Dictators: Hitler's Germany and Stalin's Russia.* New York: Norton.

Padfield, Peter. 1991. *Himmler: Reichsführer-SS.* New York: Henry Holt and Company.

Palmer, R. R. 1959–64. *The Age of the Democratic Revolution: A Political History of Europe and America, 1760–1800.* Princeton, NJ: Princeton University Press.

Pape, Robert A. 2003. "The Strategic Logic of Suicide Terrorism." *American Political Science Review* **97** (August 2003): 343–61.

2005. *Dying to Win: The Strategic Logic of Suicide Terrorism.* New York: Random House.

Paxton, Robert O. 2004. *The Anatomy of Fascism.* New York: Knopf.

Payne, Stanley G. 1995. *A History of Fascism, 1914–1945.* Madison: University of Wisconsin Press.

Peebles, Patrick. 2006. *The History of Sri Lanka.* Westport, CT: Greenwood.

Pelekanos, Adelle C. 2008. "Each Other, Ourselves." *The New York Academy of Sciences Magazine* (Winter): **19**.

Petersen, Roger D. 2002. *Understanding Ethnic War: Fear, Hatred, and Resentment in Twentieth-Century Eastern Europe.* Cambridge: Cambridge University Press.

Pinker, Steven. 2008. "The Moral Instinct." *The New York Times Magazine* (January 13): 32–58.

Pipes, Richard. 1990. *The Russian Revolution.* New York: Knopf.

2003. *The Degaev Affair: Terror and Treason in Tsarist Russia.* New Haven, CT: Yale University Press.

2005. *Russian Conservatism and its Critics: A Study in Political Culture*. New Haven, CT: Yale University Press.

Pobedonostsev, Konstantin P. [1898] 1965. *Reflections of a Russian Statesman*. Ann Arbor: University of Michigan Press.

Pók, Attila. 1997. "Germans, Hungarians, and the Destruction of Hungarian Jewry." In *Genocide and Rescue: The Holocaust in Hungary 1944*, ed. David Cesarini. Oxford: Berg, 147–58.

Politkovskaya, Anna. 2001. *A Dirty War: A Russian Reporter in Chechnya*, trans. John Crowfoot. London: Harvill.

Posen, Barry R. 1993. "The Security Dilemma and Ethnic Conflict." In *Ethnic Conflict and International Security*, ed. Michael E. Brown. Princeton, NJ: Princeton University Press, 102–24.

Pottier, John. 2002. *Re-imagining Rwanda: Conflict, Survival, and Disinformation in the Late Twentieth Century*. Cambridge: Cambridge University Press.

Power, Samantha. 2002. *A Problem from Hell: America and the Age of Genocide*. New York: Basic Books.

Prinz, Jesse J. 2007. *The Emotional Construction of Morals*. New York: Oxford University Press.

Prunier, Gérard. 1995. *The Rwanda Crisis: History of a Genocide*. New York: Columbia University Press.

Pyszczynski, Tom, Solomon, Sheldon, and Greenberg, Jeff. 2003. *In the Wake of 9/11: The Psychology of Terror*. Washington, DC: American Psychological Association.

Pyszczynski, Tom, Abdollahi, Abdolhossein, Solomon, Sheldon, Greenberg, Jeff, Cohen, Florette, and Weise, David. 2006. "Mortality Salience, Martyrdom, and Military Might: The Great Satan versus the Axis of Evil." *Personality and Social Psychology Bulletin* **32** (4): 525–37.

Quigley, Brian M. and Tedeschi, James T. 1996. "Mediating Effects of Blame Attributions on Feelings of Anger." *Personality and Social Psychology Bulletin* **22** (12): 1280–8.

Quinn, Kenneth M. 1989. "Explaining the Terror." In *Cambodia 1975–1978: Rendezvous with Death*, ed. Karl D. Jackson. Princeton, NJ: Princeton University Press, 215–40.

Qutb, Sayyid. 1953. *Social Justice in Islam*, trans. John B. Hardie. Washington, DC: American Council of Learned Societies.

Rabbitt, P. M. A. 1966. "Error Correction Time without External Error Signals." *Nature* **212** (October): 438.

Ramet, Sabrina P. 2006. *The Three Yugoslavias: State-Building and Legitimation, 1918–2005*. Washington, DC: Woodrow Wilson Center Press.

Randal, Jonathan. 2004. *Osama: The Making of a Terrorist*. New York: Vintage.

Randolph, Eleanor. 2005. "Ultimate Soviet Henchman Returns to his Pedestal." *New York Times* (November 20): wk 11.

Range, Friederike, Horn, Lisa, Virányi, Zsófia, and Huber, Ludwig. 2009. "The Absence of Reward Induces Inequity Aversion in Dogs." *Proceedings of the National Academy of Sciences* **106**: 340–5.

Rasler, Karen and Thompson, William R. 2009. "Inside? Outside? Comparing Sources of Influence on the Opportunity Space for Rebellion and Civil War." Paper presented at the 21st World Congress of Political Science, July 12–16, Santiago, Chile.

Rawls, John. 1971. *A Theory of Justice*. Cambridge, MA: Belknap Press of Harvard University Press.

  1999. *The Law of Peoples; with "The Idea of Public Reason Revisited."* Cambridge, MA: Harvard University Press.

  2001. *Justice as Fairness: A Restatement*, ed. Erin Kelly. Cambridge, MA: Harvard University Press.

Rawson, Don C. 1995. *Russian Rightists and the Revolution of 1905*. Cambridge: Cambridge University Press.

Redlawsk, David P., ed. 2006. *Feeling Politics: Emotion in Political Information Processing*. New York: Palgrave Macmillan.

Rees, E. A. 2001. "Leaders and their Institutions." In *Behind the Façade of Stalin's Command Economy: Evidence from the Soviet State and Party Archives*, ed. Paul R. Gregory. Stanford, CA: Hoover Institution Press, 35–60.

Remnick, David. 2008. "Comment: Boundary Issues." *The New Yorker*, August 25: 21–22.

Richardson, John M. Jr. 2004. "Violent Conflict and the First Half Decade of Open Economy Policies in Sri Lanka: A Revisionist View." In *Economy, Culture, and Civil War in Sri Lanka*, ed. Deborah Winslow and Michael D. Woost. Bloomington: Indiana University Press.

Rizvi, Hasan. 1974. *The Military and Politics in Pakistan*. Lahore: Progressive Publishers.

Robb, Peter. 2002. *A History of India*. New York: Palgrave.

Roberts, Henry L. 1969. *Rumania: Political Problems of an Agrarian Society*. Hamden, CT: Archon Books, 33–7.

Robinson, Rowena. 2005. *Tremors of Violence: Muslim Survivors of Ethnic Strife in Western India*. Thousand Oaks, CA: Sage.

Rogger, Hans. 1964a. "The Formation of the Russian Right, 1900–1906." In *California Slavic Studies*, vol. III, ed. Nicholas V. Riasanovsky and Gleb Struve. Berkeley: University of California Press, 66–94.

  1964b. "Was There a Russian Fascism? The Union of Russian People." *Journal of Modern History* **36** (December): 398–415.

  1965. "Russia." In *The European Right: A Historical Profile*, ed. Hans Rogger and Eugen Weber. Berkeley: University of California Press, 443–500.

Röhl, John C. G. 1994. *The Kaiser and His Court: Wilhelm II and the Government of Germany*, trans. Terence F. Cole. Cambridge: Cambridge University Press.

Rorty, Amélie O. 1998. "The Political Sources of Emotions: Greed and Anger." *Philosophical Studies* **89** (2–3): 143–59.

Rosenblatt, Abram, Greenberg, Jeff, Solomon, Sheldon, Pyszczynski, Tom, and Lyon, Deborah. 1989. "Evidence for Terror Management Theory: I. The Effects of Mortality Salience on Reactions to Those Who Violate or Uphold Cultural Values." *Journal of Personality and Social Psychology* **57** (4): 681–90.

Ross, Marc H. 1993. *The Culture of Conflict: Interpretations and Interests in Comparative Perspective*. New Haven, CT: Yale University Press.

　2001. "Psychocultural Interpretations and Dramas: Identity Dynamics in Ethnic Conflict." *Political Psychology* **22** (1, Spring): 157–78.

Rowe, David C., Jacobson, Kristen C., and Van den Oord, Edwin J. C. G. 1999. "Genetic and Environmental Influences on Vocabulary IQ: Parental Education Level as a Moderator." *Child Development* **70** (September): 1151–62.

Roy, Olivier. 2004. *Globalized Islam: The Search for a New Ummah*. New York: Columbia University Press.

Rozin, Paul, Haidt, Jonathan, and McCauley, Clark R. 2000. "Disgust." In *Handbook of Emotions*, 2nd edn., ed. Michael Lewis and Jeannette M. Haviland-Jones. New York: Guilford Press, 637–53.

Rozin, Paul, Lowery, Laura, Imada, Sumio, and Haidt, Jonathan. 1999. "The CAD Triad Hypothesis: A Mapping between Three Moral Emotions (Contempt, Anger, Disgust) and Three Moral Codes (Community, Autonomy, Divinity)." *Journal of Personality and Social Psychology* **76** (4): 574–86.

Rummel, Rudolph. 1997. *Power Kills: Democracy as a Method of Nonviolence*. New Brunswick, NJ: Transaction Publishers.

　1998. *Statistics of Democide: Genocide and Mass Murder since 1900*. Münster: Lit Verlag.

Rus, Ionas A. 1998. "The Electoral Patterns of the Romanian Right in the Interwar Years, I." *Arhivele Totalitarismului* **6** (21): 8–24.

　1999a. "The Electoral Patterns of the Romanian Right in the Interwar Years, II." *Arhivele Totalitarismului* **7** (22–23): 12–31.

　1999b. "The Electoral Patterns of the Romanian Right in the Interwar Years, III." *Arhivele Totalitarismului* **7** (24–25): 8–32.

Ryan, Curtis C. 2008. "Islamist Political Activism in Jordan: Moderation, Militancy, and Democracy." *The Middle East Review of International Affairs (MERIA)* **12** (2): 1–13.

Sache, Ivan. 2008. *Malmedy (Municipality, Province of Liège, Belgium)*. www.crwflags.com/FOTW/FLAGS/be-wlgmm.html

Sageman, Marc. 2004. *Understanding Terror Networks*. Philadelphia, PA: University of Pennsylvania Press.

Sajer, Guy. 1971. *The Forgotten Soldier*, trans. Lily Emmet. New York: Harper and Row.

Salehyan, Idean. 2009. *Rebels without Borders: Transnational Insurgencies in World Politics*. Ithaca, NY: Cornell University Press.

Samuels, Richard J. 2003. *Machiavelli's Children: Leaders and their Legacies in Italy and Japan*. Ithaca, NY: Cornell University Press.

Sanger, David E. 2009. "Obama's Worst Pakistan Nightmare." *The New York Times Magazine* (January 11): 32–7.

Sang-hun, Choe. 2008. "Desolate Dots in the Sea Stir Deep Emotions as South Korea Resists a Japanese Claim." *The New York Times* (August 31): N6, 16.

Sarfatti, Michele. 2006. *The Jews in Mussolini's Italy: From Equality to Persecution*. Madison: University of Wisconsin Press.

Sathasivam, Kanishkan. 2005. *Uneasy Neighbors: India, Pakistan and US Foreign Policy*. Burlington, VT: Ashgate.

Schacter, Daniel. 2001. *The Seven Sins of Memory: How the Mind Forgets and Remembers*. Boston, MA: Houghton Mifflin.

Schell, Orville. 2008. "China: Humiliation & the Olympics." *The New York Review of Books* 55 (13, August 14): 30–3.

Scheuer, Michael. 2005. *Imperial Hubris: Why the West Is Losing the War on Terror*. Washington, DC: Potomac Books.

Schimel, Jeff, Simon, Linda, Greenberg, Jeff, Pyszczynski, Tom, Solomon, Sheldon, Waxmonsky, Jeannette, and Arndt, Jamie. 1999. "Stereotypes and Terror Management: Evidence that Mortality Salience Enhances Stereotypic Thinking and Preferences." *Journal of Personality and Social Psychology* 77 (5): 905–26.

Schivelbusch, Wolfgang. 2003. *The Culture of Defeat: On National Trauma, Mourning, and Recovery*, trans. Jefferson Chase. New York: Metropolitan Books.

Schmitt, Carl. [1932] 1996. *The Concept of the Political*, trans. J. Harvey Lomax. Chicago: University of Chicago Press.

Schroeder, David A., Steel, Julie E., Woodell, Andria J., and Bembenek, Alicia F. 2003. "Justice Within Social Dilemmas." *Personality and Social Psychology Review* 7 (4): 374–87.

Scott, James C. 1998. *Seeing Like a State: How Certain Schemes to Improve the Human Condition Have Failed*. New Haven, CT: Yale University Press.

Scurr, Ruth. 2006. *Fatal Purity: Robespierre and the French Revolution*. New York: Metropolitan Books.

Secher, Reynald. 2003. *A French Genocide: The Vendée*, trans. George Holoch. Notre Dame, IN: University of Notre Dame Press.

Sell, Louis. 2002. *Slobodan Milosevic and the Destruction of Yugoslavia*. Durham, NC: Duke University Press.

Sen, Amartya. 2000. *Development as Freedom*. New York: Anchor Books.

Service, Robert. 2004. *Stalin: A Biography*. London: Macmillan.

Shane, Scott. 2009. "Rethinking What to Fear." *The New York Times Week in Review* (September 27): 1, 4.

Shaw, Stanford J. and Shaw, Ezel K. 1977. *History of the Ottoman Empire and Modern Turkey*, vol. II, *Reform, Revolution, and Republic: The Rise of Modern Turkey, 1808–1975*. New York: Cambridge University Press.

Shepard, William E. 2003. "Sayyid Qutb's Doctrine of Jahiliyya." *International Journal of Middle East Studies* 35 (4): 521–45.

Shillony, Ben-Ami. 1973. *Revolt in Japan: The Young Officers and the February 26, 1936 Incident*. Princeton, NJ: Princeton University Press.

Shils, Edward. 1961. "Georges Sorel: Introduction to the American Edition." In Georges Sorel: *Reflection on Violence*, trans. T. E. Hulme. London: Collier Books, 11–25.

Shweder, Richard A., Much, Nancy C., Mahapatra, Manamohan, and Park, Lawrence. 1997. "The 'Big Three' of Morality (Autonomy, Community, Divinity) and the 'Big Three' Explanations of Suffering." In *Morality and Health*, ed. Allan M. Brandt and Paul Rozin. New York: Routledge, 119–69.

Siddiqi, Abdul R. 2004. *East Pakistan the End Game: An Onlooker's Journal 1969–1971*. Karachi: Oxford University Press.

Sigmund, Karl, Hauert, Christoph, and Nowak, Martin A. 2001. "Reward and Punishment." *Proceedings of the National Academy of Sciences* **98** (19): 10757–62.

Sikand, Yoginder. 2004. *Muslims in India since 1947: Islamic Perspectives on Inter-Faith Relations*. London: Routledge Curzon.

Silber, Laura and Little, Allan. 1996. *Yugoslavia: Death of a Nation*. New York: TV Books (distributed by Penguin USA).

Silverman, Dan P. 1972. *Reluctant Union: Alsace-Lorraine and Imperial Germany, 1871–1918*. University Park: Pennsylvania State University Press.

Skitka, Linda J. 2003. "Of Different Minds: An Accessible Identity Model of Justice Reasoning." *Personality and Social Psychology Review* **7** (4): 286–97.

Skocpol, Theda. 1979. *States and Social Revolutions: A Comparative Analysis of France, Russia, and China*. New York: Cambridge University Press.

Smith, Adam. 1966 [1759]. *The Theory of Moral Sentiments*. New York: A. M. Kelley.

Smith, Bradley. 1971. *Heinrich Himmler: A Nazi in the Making, 1900–1926*. Stanford, CA: Hoover Institution Press.

Smith, Michael L. 1998. *Ionian Vision: Greece in Asia Minor, 1919–1922*. Ann Arbor: University of Michigan Press.

Smith, Sebastian. 1998. *Allah's Mountains: Politics and War in the Russian Caucasus*. London: I. B. Tauris.

Snyder, Jack and Ballentine, Karen. 1996. "Nationalism and the Marketplace of Ideas." *International Security* **21** (2): 5–40.

Snyder, Jack and Jervis, Robert. 1999. "Civil War and the Security Dilemma." In *Civil Wars, Insecurity, and Intervention*, ed. Barbara F. Walter and Jack Snyder. New York: Columbia University Press, 15–37.

Sorel, Georges. [1906] 1961. *Reflections on Violence*, trans. T. E. Hulme and J. Roth. New York: Collier Books.

Soucy, Robert J. 1966. "The Nature of Fascism in France." *Journal of Contemporary History* **1** (1): 27–55.

Sprinzak, Ehud. 2006. "The Process of Delegitimation: Towards a Linkage Theory of Political Terrorism." In *Terrorism: The Third or New Left Wave*, ed. David C. Rapoport. London: Taylor & Francis, 159–79.

Steefel, Lawrence D. 1932. *The Schleswig-Holstein Question*. Cambridge, MA: Harvard University Press.

Stein, Nancy, Trabasso, Tom and Liwag, Maria. 1993. "The Representation and Organization of Emotional Experience: Unfolding the Emotion Episode." In *Handbook of Emotions*, eds. Michael Lewis and Jeannette M. Haviland. New York: The Guilford Press, 279–300.

Steinberg, Jonathan. 1990. *All or Nothing: The Axis and the Holocaust, 1941–1943*. London: Routledge.

Steiner, George. 2008. "Acts of Constant Questioning." *Times Literary Supplement*, **5491** (June 27): 8–9.

Stern, Fritz. 1974. *The Politics of Cultural Despair: A Study in the Rise of the Germanic Ideology*. Berkeley: University of California Press.

Sternhell, Zeev, with Sznajder, Mario and Asheri, Maia. 1994. *The Birth of Fascist Ideology: From Cultural Rebellion to Political Revolution*, trans. David Maisel. Princeton, NJ: Princeton University Press.

Straus, Scott. 2006. *The Order of Genocide: Race, Power, and War in Rwanda*. Ithaca, NY: Cornell University Press.

Sutter, John O. 1966. "Two Faces of Konfrontasi: 'Crush Malaysia' and the Gestapu." *Asian Survey* **6** (10): 523–46.

Tabeau, Ewa and Bijak, Jakub. 2006. "War-Related Deaths in the 1992–1995 Armed Conflicts in Bosnia and Herzegovina: A Critique of Previous Estimates and Recent Results." In *The Demography of Armed Conflict*, eds. Helge Brunborg, Ewa Tabeau, and Henrik Urdal. Dordrecht: Springer, 217–44.

Tannenbaum, Edward R. 1969. "The Goals of Italian Fascism." *American Historical Review* **74** (4): 1183–204.

Tanner, Marcus. 2001. *Croatia: A Nation Forged in War*, 2nd edn. New Haven, CT: Yale University Press.

Tanner, Stephen. 2002. *Afghanistan: A Military History from Alexander the Great to the Fall of the Taliban*. New York: Da Capo Press.

Taylor, Charles. 1992. *The Ethics of Authenticity*. Cambridge, MA: Harvard University Press.

Taylor, Shelley E. 1991. "Asymmetrical Effects of Positive and Negative Events: The Mobilization-Minimization Hypothesis." *Psychological Bulletin* **110**: 67–85.

The Week: The Best of the US and International Media. 2009. 9 (404, March 20): 26.

Thompson, Mark. 2008. *The White War: Life and Death on the Italian Front, 1915–1919*. London: Faber and Faber.

Thompson, William R. 1986. "Polarity, the Long Cycle, and Global Power Warfare." *Journal of Conflict Resolution* **30** (4): 587–615.

Thucydides. 1954. *History of the Peloponnesian War*, trans. Rex Warner. Baltimore, MD: Penguin Books.

Tice, Dianne M., Bratslavsky, Ellen, and Baumeister, Roy F. 2001. "Emotional Distress Regulation Takes Precedence over Impulse Control: If You Feel Bad, Do It!" *Journal of Personality and Social Psychology* **80** (1): 53–67.

Tierney, John. 2008 "Deep Down, We Can't Fool Even Ourselves." *The New York Times* (July 1): F6.

Tir, Jaroslav. 2006. *Redrawing the Map to Promote Peace: Territorial Dispute Management via Territorial Change*. Lanham, MD: Lexington Books.

Tishkov, Valery. 2004. *Chechnya: Life in a War-Torn Society*. Berkeley: University of California Press.

Toft, Monica D. 2003. *The Geography of Ethnic Violence: Identity, Interests, and the Indivisibility of Territory*. Princeton, NJ: Princeton University Press.

Tolstoy, Leo. 2007. *War and Peace*, trans. Richard Pevear and Larissa Volokhonsky. New York: Knopf.

Toth, James. 2003. "Islamism in Southern Egypt: A Case Study of a Radical Religious Movement." *International Journal of Middle East Studies* **35** (4): 547–72.

Treharne, R. F. and Fullard, Harold. 1969. *Muir's Historical Atlas: Medieval and Modern*, 11th edn. London: G. Philip.

Trenin, Dmitri, Malashenko, Aleksei V., and Lieven, Anatol. 2004. *Russia's Restless Frontier: The Chechnya Factor in Post-Soviet Russia*. Washington, DC: Carnegie Endowment for International Peace.

Tripp, Charles. 2006. *Islam and the Moral Economy: The Challenge of Capitalism*. Cambridge: Cambridge University Press.

Trivers, Robert L. 1971. "The Evolution of Reciprocal Altruism." *The Quarterly Review of Biology* **46** (1): 35–57.

Tucker, Robert C. 1973. *Stalin as Revolutionary, 1879–1929: A Study in History and Personality*. New York: Norton.

ed. 1975. *The Lenin Anthology*. New York: W. W. Norton.

Valdesolo, Piercarlo and DeSteno, David. 2007. "Moral hypocrisy: Social groups and the Flexibility of Virtue." *Psychological Science* **18** (8): 689–90.

van den Bos, Kees. 2004. "An Existentialist Approach to the Social Psychology of Fairness: The Influence of Mortality and Uncertainty Salience on Reactions to Fair and Unfair Events." In *Handbook of Experimental Existential Psychology*, ed. Jeff Greenberg, Sander Leon Koole, Thomas A. Pyszczynski. New York: Guilford, 167–81.

Van der Kroef, Justus M. 1970/1971. "Interpretations of the 1965 Indonesian Coup: A Review of the Literature." *Pacific Affairs* **43** (4): 557–77.

1972. "Origins of the 1965 Coup in Indonesia: Probabilities and Alternatives." *Journal of Southeast Asian Studies* **3** (2): 277–98.

Varshney, Ashutosh. 2002. *Ethnic Conflict and Civic Life: Hindus and Muslims in India*. New Haven: Yale University Press.

Vasquez, John A. 1993. *The War Puzzle*. Cambridge: Cambridge University Press.

2000. "Reexamining the Steps to War: New Evidence and Theoretical Insights." In M. Midlarsky 2000a, 371–406.

Vasquez, John A. and Henehan, Marie T. 2001. "Territorial Disputes and the Probability of War, 1816–1992." *Journal of Peace Research* **38** (March): 123–38.

Veremis, Thanos. 2003. "1922: Political Continuations and Realignments in the Greek State." In *Crossing the Aegean: An Appraisal of the 1923 Compulsory Population Exchange between Greece and Turkey*, ed. Renée Hirschon. Oxford : Berghahn Books, 53–62.

Vickers, Adrian. 2005. *A History of Modern Indonesia*. Cambridge: Cambridge University Press.

Vital, David. 1999. *A People Apart: The Jews in Europe, 1789–1939*. Oxford: Oxford University Press.

von Treitschke, Heinrich. [1916] 1963. *Politics* ed. Hans Kohn. New York: Harcourt, Brace & World.

Walter, Barbara F. 2003. "Explaining the Intractability of Territorial Conflict." *International Studies Review* **5** (4): 137–53.

Wang, Zheng. 2008. "National Humiliation, History Education, and the Politics of Historical Memory: Patriotic Education Campaign in China." *International Studies Quarterly* **52** (4): 783–806.

Weber, Eugen. 1964. *Varieties of Fascism: Doctrines of Revolution in the Twentieth Century.* New York: Van Nostrand Reinhold.

1965a. "France." In *The European Right: A Historical Profile*, ed. Hans Rogger and Eugen Weber. Berkeley: University of California Press, 71–127.

1965b. "Romania." In *The European Right: A Historical Profile*, ed. Hans Rogger and Eugen Weber. Berkeley: University of California Press, 501–74.

1966. "The Men of the Archangel." *Journal of Contemporary History* **1** (1): 101–26.

Weinberg, Gerhard L. 2005. *Visions of Victory: The Hopes of Eight World War II Leaders.* New York: Cambridge University Press

Weingartner, Joseph J. 1979. *Crossroads of Death: The Story of the Malmédy Massacre and Trial.* Berkeley: University of California Press.

2000. *A Peculiar Crusade: Willis M. Everett and the Malmedy Massacre.* New York: New York University Press.

Weisman, Steven R. 2004. "Crisis in Sudan Resists Simple Solutions." *The New York Times* (August 8): N6.

Wellhofer, E. Spencer. 2003. "Democracy and Fascism: Class, Civil Society, and Rational Choice in Italy." *American Political Science Review* **97** (February): 91–106.

Welsh, Alexander. 2008. *What is Honor?: A Question of Moral Imperatives.* New Haven, CT: Yale University Press.

Westad, Odd Arne. 1994. "Prelude to Invasion: The Soviet Union and the Afghan Communists, 1978–1979." *International History Review* **16** (February): 49–69.

Westen, Drew. 2007. *The Political Brain: The Role of Emotion in Deciding the Fate of the Nation.* New York: Public Affairs.

Westen, Drew, Blagov, Pavel S., Harenski, Keith, Kilts, Clint, and Hamann, Stephan. 2006. "An fMRI Study of Motivated Reasoning: Partisan Political Reasoning in the U.S. Presidential Election." Atlanta, GA: Emory University, Psychology Department.

Westermarck, Edward. [1908] 1912. *The Origin and Development of the Moral Ideas*, vol. 1, 2nd edn. London: Macmillan.

Wiktorowicz, Quintan. 2005. *Radical Islam Rising: Muslim Extremism in the West.* Lanham, MD: Rowman and Littlefield.

Wilkinson, Alec. 2008. "Picturing Auschwitz." *The New Yorker* (March 17): 48–55.

Witte, Kim. 1992. "Putting the Fear Back into Fear Appeals: The Extended Parallel Process Model." *Communication Monographs* **59**: 329–49.

Wolfe, Bertram. 1984. *Three Who Made a Revolution: A Biographical History.* New York: Stein and Day.

Wood, James. 2007. "Moveable Types: How 'War and Peace' Works." *The New Yorker* (November 26): 158–66.

Woodward, Peter. 1996. *The Horn of Africa: State Politics and International Relations.* London: I. B. Tauris.

Woodward, Susan L. 1995. *Balkan Tragedy: Chaos and Dissolution after the Cold War.* Washington, DC: The Brooking Institution.

Wright, Lawrence. 2006. *The Looming Tower: Al-Qaeda and the Road to 9/11.* New York: Knopf.

2008. "The Rebellion Within: An Al Qaeda Mastermind Questions Terrorism." *The New Yorker* (June 2): 36–53.

Wright, Robert. 2000. *Nonzero: The Logic of Human Destiny.* New York: Pantheon.

Zile, Zigurds L., ed. 1992. *Ideas and Forces in Soviet Legal History: A Reader on the Soviet State and Law.* New York: Oxford University Press.

Zimbardo, Philip. 2008. *The Lucifer Effect: Understanding How Good People Turn Evil.* New York: Random House.

Zuccotti, Susan. 1993. *The Holocaust, the French and the Jews.* New York: Basic Books.

2000. *Under His Very Windows: The Vatican and the Holocaust in Italy.* New Haven, CT: Yale University Press.

INDEX

'*umma*, 190

9/11, 1, 156, 163, 170, 171, 335, 374, 375
  as al-Qaeda victory, 66
  and Pearl Harbor attack, 66

Abdullah, Sheikh Mohammed, 253
Abel, Theodore, 88
Abu Ghraib, 164, 374, 375
Action française, 20, 74, 94, 95, 113–14
Adrianople (Edirne), 273, 283
  as capital of the Ottoman Empire,
    273
  home of Bayezid mosque, 273
  home of Selimiye mosque, 273
Afghanistan, 268–9, 370
  and the Iranian Revolution, 268–9
Ahmed, Dirdeiry Mohamed, 373
Aidit, Dipa Nusantra, 261, 262
  and Sukarno, 263
Akhnur, Battle of, 255–6
Akselrod, Pavel, 127
al-Assad, Hafez, 79
al-Azm, Sadik, 150
  and humiliation and failure, 152
al-Banna, Hasan, 16–17, 147–8, 329,
    336
  and British occupation of Suez,
    151–2
  and Muslim Brotherhood, 152–6
Alexander II, Tsar, 117
Alexander III, Tsar, 11, 117
Algerian Islamic Salvation Front (FIS),
    164–5
Algerian Salafist Group for Preaching
    and Combat (GSPC), 186
al-Husayni, Hajj Amin

and German funding, 154
Ali, Mehmet, 272, 273
Ali Jinnah, Mohammed, 187
'Ali Nadwi, Sayyed Hasan, 190–1
Aligarh Muslim University (AMU), 189
al-Mahdi, Sadiq, 174
al-Muhajiroun, 170–5, 186, 188, 339
  and the Caliphate, 172
  and humiliation-shame, 321
  and Kashmir, 172
  ephemeral gain of, 172
  and Muslim identity crisis, 172–3
  pathways to extremism, 321
    and perceptions of injustice, 321
    and threat and fear of reversion,
      173, 321
al-Qaeda, 10, 15, 156, 161–5, 186, 361,
    364, 370
  and Afghan war against Soviets, 56
  and Arab nationality, 49
  and the Caliphate, 163
  and the ephemeral gain, 165–8
  and external intervention, 364
  first use of term, 162
  gain and loss, 169–70
  and humiliation, 320
  Muslim criticism of, 165
  pathways to extremism, 320–1
    and perceptions of injustice, 320
    and threat and fear of reversion, 321
Alsace-Lorraine, 74, 95, 284, 287–93
  ephemeral gain in, 289
Aly, Götz, 283
al-Zawahiri, Ayman, 148, 150, 163, 164,
    335, 361, 362, 365
Amichai, Yehuda, 360
Anatolia, 369, 371

407